The EY Exhibition

IMPRESSIONISTS IN LONDON

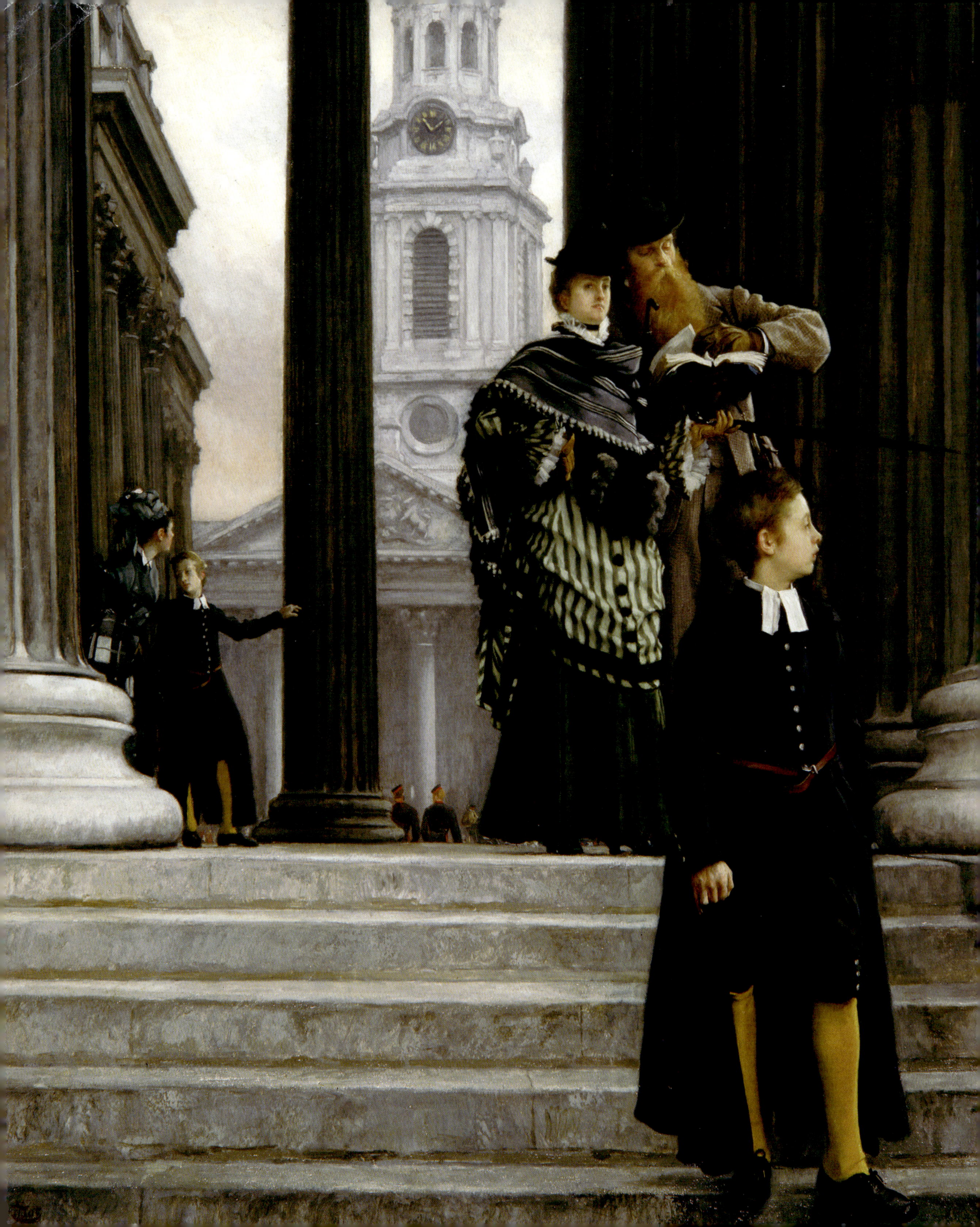

Edited by Caroline Corbeau-Parsons

The EY Exhibition

IMPRESSIONISTS IN LONDON

French Artists in Exile 1870–1904

First published 2017 by order of the Tate Trustees by Tate Publishing, a division of Tate Enterprises Ltd, Millbank, London SW1P 4RG
www.tate.org.uk/publishing

on the occasion of
The EY Exhibition
Impressionists in London
French Artists in Exile 1870–1904

Tate Britain, London
2 November 2017 – 7 May 2018
Petit Palais, Paris
20 June – 14 October 2018

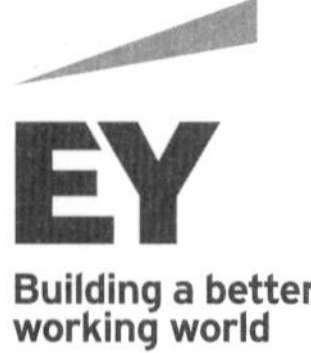

The EY Exhibition
Impressionists in London
French Artists in Exile 1870–1904
is part of The EY Tate Arts Partnership

A catalogue record for this book is available from the British Library

ISBN 978 1 84976 524 4 (hbk)
ISBN 978 1 84976 469 8 (pbk)

Distributed in the United States and Canada by
ABRAMS, New York

Library of Congress Control Number applied for

Designed by Adam Brown_01.02
Colour reproduction by
DL Imaging, London
Printed and bound in Belgium
by Die Keure

Texts by Cécilie Champy-Vinas, Isabelle Collet, Cyrille Sciama, Amélie Simier and Bertrand Tillier translated from the French by Christine Rolland

Front cover: Claude Monet, *Houses of Parliament* c.1900 (detail, see p.236)
p.2: James Tissot, *London Visitors* 1873 (detail, see p.108)
p.8: Claude Monet, *Hyde Park* 1871 (detail, see pp.200–1)
pp.10–11: Claude Monet, *The Thames below Westminster* 1871 (detail, see pp.66–7)
pp.20–1: Jean-Baptiste-Camille Corot, *The Dream: Paris Burning* 1870 (detail, see p.28)
pp.248–9: Alfred Sisley, *Molesey Weir, Hampton Court, Morning* 1874 (detail, see p.79)

Measurements of artworks are given in centimetres, height before width and depth

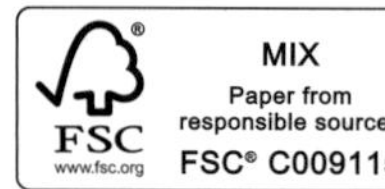

Contributors

Cécilie Champy-Vinas (CCV)
Isabelle Collet (IC)
Caroline Corbeau-Parsons (CCP)
Anne Robbins (AR)
Anna Gruetzner Robins (AGR)
Elizabeth Jacklin (EJ)
Carol Jacobi (CJ)
Krystyna Matyjaszkiewicz (KM)
Cyrille Sciama (CS)
Amélie Simier (ASi)
Alison Smith (ASm)
Bertrand Tillier (BT)
Philip Ward-Jackson (PWJ)

Contents

EY foreword

EY is delighted to support *The EY Exhibition: Impressionists in London*, a major show which traces the journey of artists who fled from France to Britain in the 1870s to escape the Franco-Prussian war. The extraordinary paintings highlight the influence they took from British art and culture and their profound contribution to the British art scene.

As part of The EY Tate Arts Partnership, and our long history of supporting the visual arts, we are proud to help make this ground-breaking exhibition possible. Continuing our commitment to building a better working world, we hope these works will offer you a new perspective on the impressionist movement and inspire new ways of thinking.

Michel Driessen
Partner Sponsor of the EY Arts Programme & Senior Partner TAS, UK & Ireland, EY

The EY Tate Arts Partnership

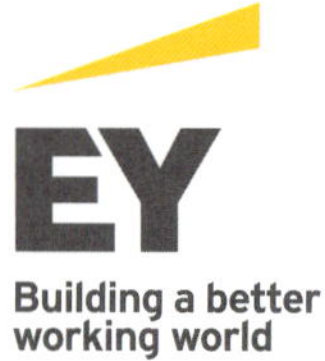

Foreword

In 1973, the Arts Council of Great Britain organised at the Hayward Gallery an exhibition entitled *Impressionists in London*, which formed part of 'Fanfare for Europe', a series of events to mark British entry into the European Economic Community. When Tate Britain and the Petit Palais decided four years ago to join forces to bring to fruition our own cross-channel project, the outcome of the EU Referendum was still ahead of us. Any resonances arising from the shared exhibition title and the current political context, therefore, are purely coincidental. The partnership between Tate Britain and the Petit Palais on this project, however, is not.

Our institutions are emblematic of London and Paris respectively. Founded in 1897 as the National Gallery of British Art, Tate Britain overlooks the Thames, a stone's throw away from the Houses of Parliament that so fascinated French artists, while the Petit Palais, built for the flamboyant 1900 Universal Exhibition, is the Museum of Fine Arts of Paris. *The EY Exhibition – Impressionists in London: French Artists in Exile 1870–1904* is a tale of these two cities, and of their connections throughout history. Taking the Franco-Prussian War and Paris Commune in 1870–1 as its starting point, it is the first exhibition on this scale to map the networks that French refugee artists either built up or relied upon while in Britain: networks of solidarity, patronage, and Franco-British artistic friendships. It tells the stories and trajectories of Charles-François Daubigny, Claude Monet, Camille Pissarro, James Tissot, Jean-Baptiste Carpeaux, Jules Dalou, Alfred Sisley, Edouard Lantéri, and others, all of whom were affected by the events in France. It also considers the fundamental role of Alphonse Legros, who had settled in London in 1863, as the pillar of this disparate community. The exhibition and publication seek to illuminate these artists' perceptions – as outsiders – of London and British culture, and to recognise the nature of their contribution to British art. The exhibition closes around the time of the Entente Cordiale, in 1904, at another high point in Franco-British history.

Relations between Tate Britain and Petit Palais while working on this ambitious project were more than cordial, and reflect a genuine enthusiasm for French and British art going hand in hand. At Tate Britain the exhibition finds its place in a lineage of cross-channel shows: *Constable to Delacroix: British Art and the French Romantics* in 2003, as well as *Turner, Whistler, Monet*, and *Degas, Sickert and Toulouse-Lautrec: London and Paris 1870–1910*, both in 2005. The Petit Palais celebrated the art of Richard Parkes Bonington in 1993, and the popular and critical success of *Oscar Wilde: Insolence Incarnate* in 2016–17 is still fresh in our memories.

We have been fortunate in that our enthusiasm for the project was echoed by museum colleagues and collectors, which resulted in outstanding loans. We are particularly grateful to the Musée d'Orsay, the National Gallery, London, the National Gallery of Art, Washington, and the Victoria and Albert Museum, London, without whose support and considerable generosity the exhibition would not have been possible. We are also indebted to Penelope Curtis for her input in the early stages of the project,

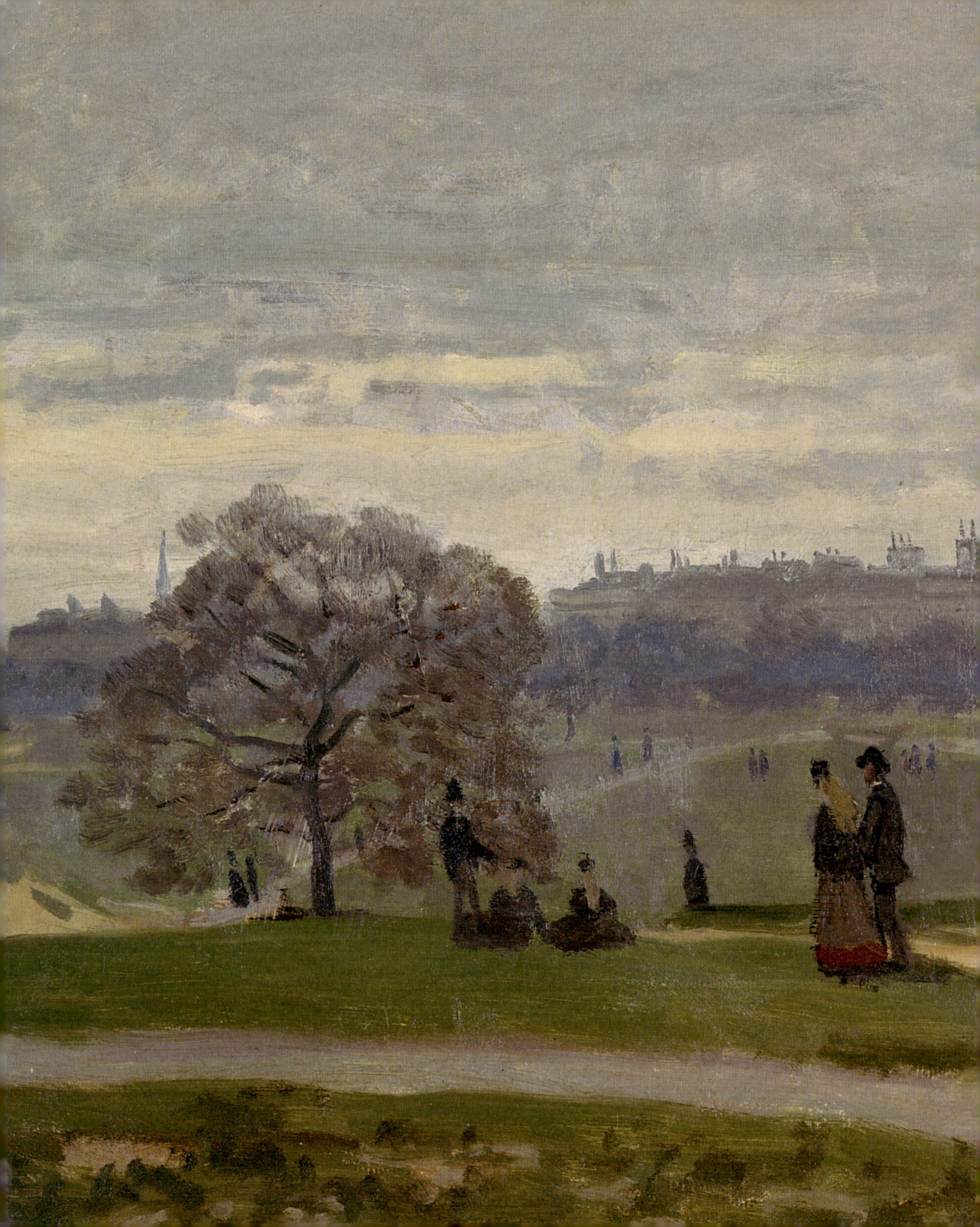

and for her continued support as a lender. Special thanks are also due to Lionel and Sandrine Pissarro, whose championing of the exhibition brought it to yet another level, and to Gretha Arwas, Andrew Brownsword, The Hon. Nicholas Howard, Professor Mark Kaufman, Wendy Makins, Michael and Jane Wilson, and other distinguished private collectors who wish to remain anonymous.

It is a pleasure to congratulate Caroline Corbeau-Parsons for her intelligent and rigorous curation of the exhibition, and also to thank her for the professionalism and commitment she has brought to its realisation. We are grateful to our colleagues for steering the project through each stage of its development. At Tate Britain, special thanks are due to Elizabeth Jacklin, who assisted Caroline in the curatorial team, to Gillian Buttimer, Sionaigh Durrant and Carolyn Kerr for their dedication to the project and invaluable expertise, and to Alison Smith and Carol Jacobi, who generously offered advice.

Isabelle Collet, Chief Curator of Modern Paintings, has expertly led the exhibition at the Petit Palais with the help of Agnès Faure and Fanny Hollman, while Amélie Simier, Director of the Musée Bourdelle, generously agreed to share her expertise on Dalou and joined forces with Caroline Corbeau-Parsons and Isabelle Collet to curate the sculptural component of the exhibition.

The catalogue has been overseen by Nicola Bion and copyedited by Colin Grant, with picture research by Emma O'Neill and production by Roanne Marner. We are grateful to them for their professionalism, to Adam Brown, who produced this handsome design, and to the distinguished scholars who contributed their varied insights to this publication.

At Tate Britain, the exhibition has been made possible by the provision of insurance through the Government Indemnity Scheme, for which we are grateful to HM Government and the Department for Digital, Culture, Media and Sport, and Arts Council England. We are also deeply grateful to EY, through the EY Tate Arts Partnership, for their sponsorship of the exhibition and continued support for our work at Tate. We would also like to recognise the support of our media partner the *Telegraph*.

Among those who have offered advice and assisted the project in various ways, we would like to thank: Kathleen Adler, Sébastien Allard, Evelyne Dorothée Allemand, Emanuela Angiuli, Mark Armstrong, Sandrine Balan, Chris Bastock, Katia Baudin, Marie-Claude Beaud, Claire Bernardi, Katie Blackford, Eric Blanchegorge, Marina Bocquillon-Ferretti, Antonia Boström, Ruth Brimacombe, Laurence des Cars, Vicky Carroll, Daphné Castano, Hugo Chapman, Catherine Chevillot, Margaret Christian, Keith Christiansen, Michael Clarke, Eleanor Clayton, Guy Cogeval, Philippe Cros, Nicholas Cullinan, Ana Debenedetti, Xavier Dectot, Markus Dekiert, Joao Carvalho Dias, Christiane Dole, Katherine Drake, Elise Dubreuil, Claire Durand-Ruel-Snollaerts, Lisa Edwards, Bruno Ely, Godfrey Evans, Mark Evans, Côme Fabre, Gabriele Finaldi, Polly Fleury, Hartwig Fisher, Frances Fowle, Bruno Gaudichon, Leon Gould, Matthew Green, Gloria Groom, Valérie Guillaume, Colin Harrison, Annette Haudiquet, Ruth Hibbard, Tristram Hunt, Amy Indyke, Nancy Ireson, David Fraser Jenkins, Victoria Jenkins, Jeremy Johnson, Elaine Kilmurray, Hope Kingsley, Perrine Le Blan, Brooke Lampley, David Liot, Nadine Loach, José de Los Lannos, Daniel Malingue, Joanna Martin, Jean-Luc Martinez, Dominique Marzotto, Lydia Meehan, Maïté Metz, Maxine Miller, Dominique Morel, Susan Morris, Guy Morrison, Mary Morton, Constanze Nogler, Maureen O'Brien, Darragh O'Donoghue, Léonée and Richard Ormond, Stéphane Paccoud, Edouard Papet, Amanda Partridge, Anne Pasternak, Tanya Paul, Charlotte Penton-Smith, Estelle Pietrzyk, Joëlle Pijaudier-Cabot, Elizabeth Prettejohn, Marcella Polednik, Earl Powell III, George Pissarro, Laura Pye, Sylvie Ramond, Christine Rew, Christopher Ridgway, Gordon Rintoul, Christopher Riopelle, Alicia Robinson, Florian Rodari, John Roles, James Rondeau, James Roundell, Laurent Salomé, Luisa Sampaio, Karen Serres, George Shackelford, the late Eric Shanes, John W. Smith, Sonia Solicari, Emmanuel and Laure Starcky, Susan Stein, MaryAnne Stevens, Robert Stoppenbach, Alexander Sturgis, Jennifer Thompson, Samuel Valette, Ernst Vegelin van Claerbergen, Sarah Vowles, Simon Wallis, Judith Weir, Nancy Whyte, Tim Wilcox and Barnaby Wright.

Alex Farquharson
Director, Tate Britain

Christophe Leribault
Director, Petit Palais

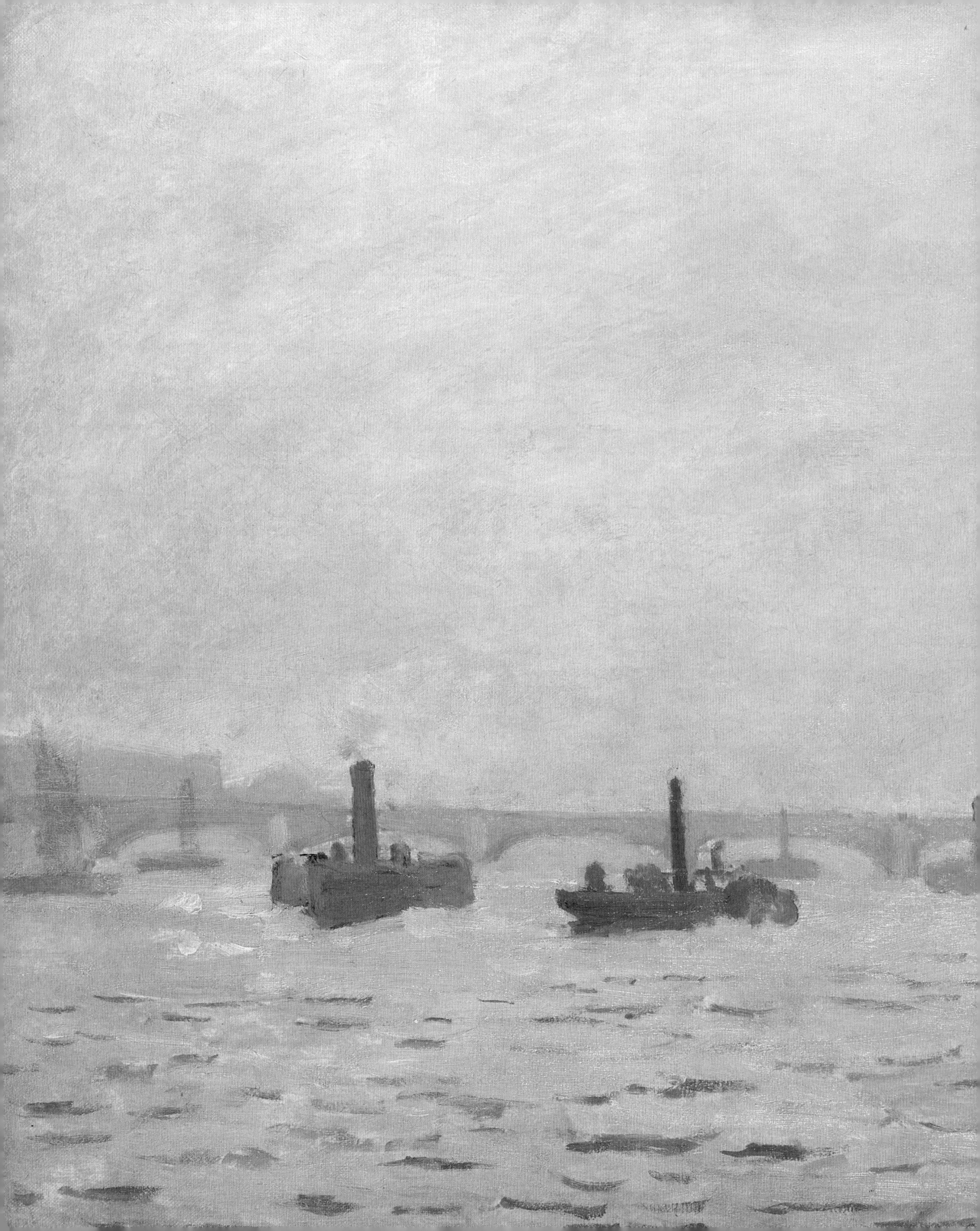

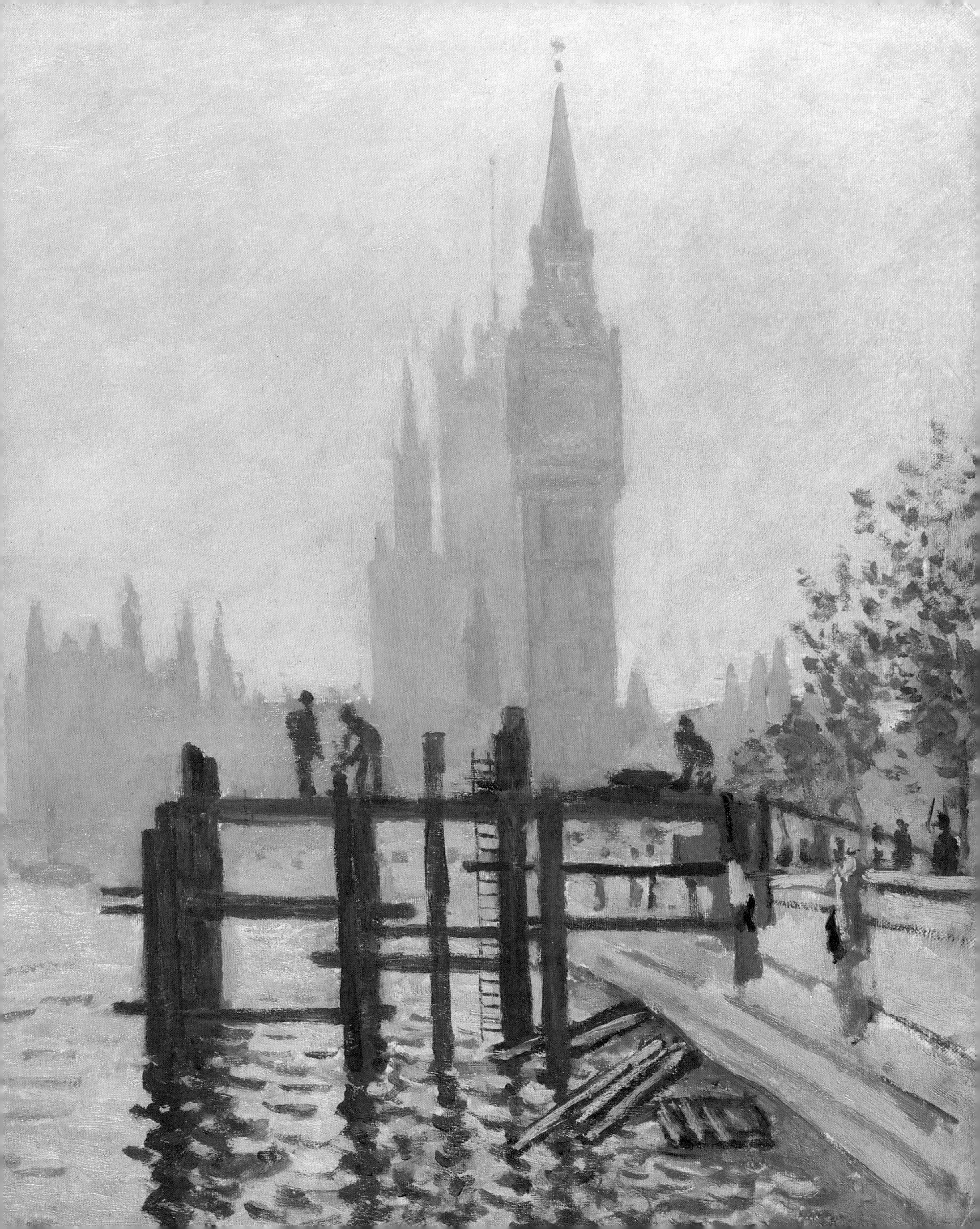

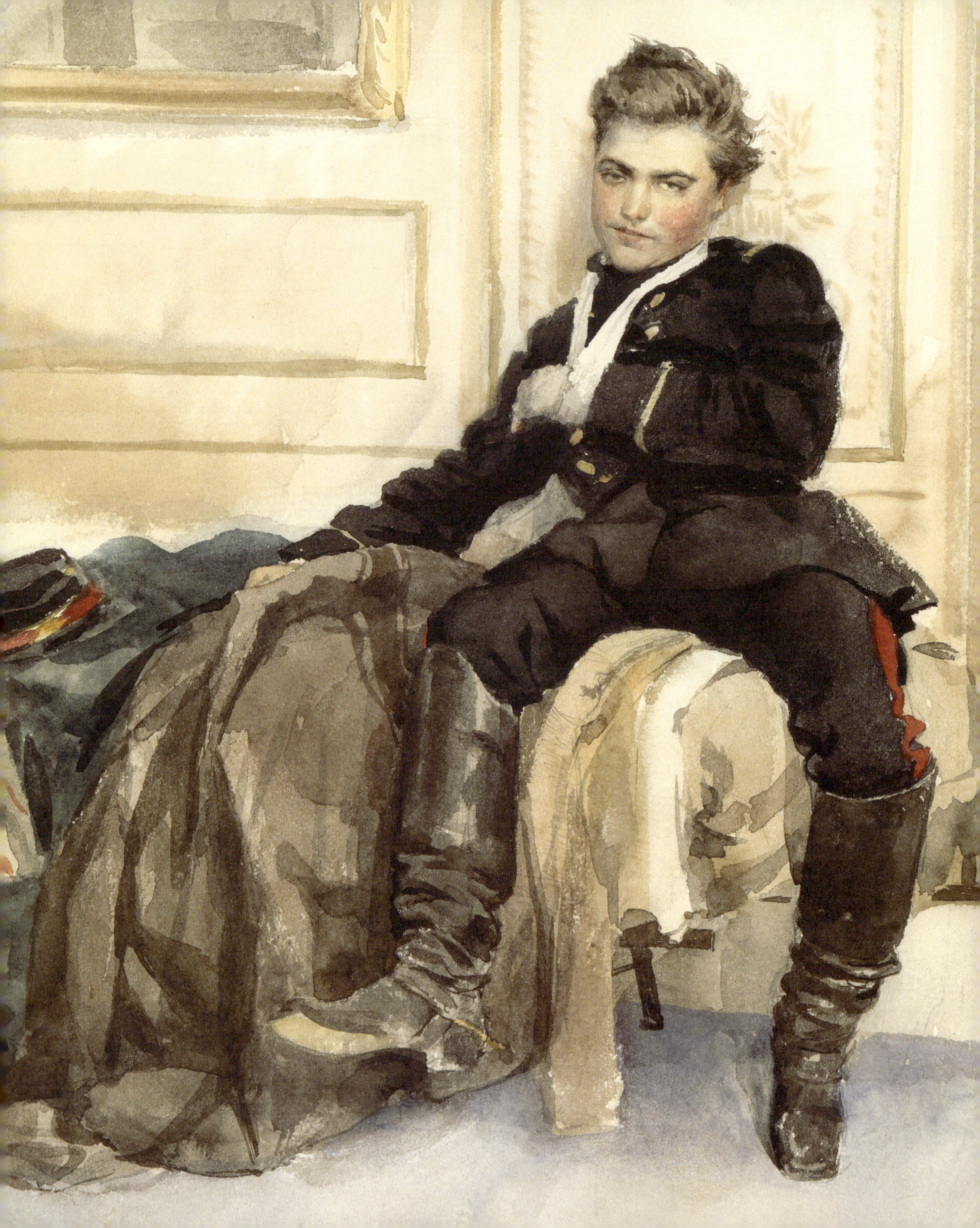

Caroline Corbeau-Parsons

Crossing the Channel

The escape to England is complete. Transatlantic liners make the journey to London. Two hundred passengers were left behind on the dock tonight. It is a sad sight.
Claude Monet, 1870[1]

When Monet wrote these words in September 1870, the Franco-Prussian War was still unfolding, and he was not yet among passengers seeking refuge in England. Two world wars later, this earlier conflict and the ensuing Paris Commune have faded from memory, but their consequences and the trauma they caused ran deep and had transformative effects on France and Europe.

Concerned with the growing power of Prussia and its German allies, an overconfident France had declared war on 19 July 1870. The Emperor Napoleon III was defeated at Sedan on 2 September and imprisoned at Wilhelmshöhe, before joining his wife Eugénie and their son in exile in Britain, where he would die. In less than seven weeks about 100,000 men were killed on either side. The Third Republic was proclaimed on 4 September, and the fight went on. The Prussians' Siege of Paris was made even harder for the French by an exceptionally cold winter: despite the use of air balloons to get supplies, and occasionally people, in and out of the capital, the threat of starvation was real, and Parisians had to resort to eating pets, rats and even animals from the zoo. On 28 January 1871 the temporary Government of National Defence agreed to an armistice for four weeks, until elections. Negotiations led to the humiliating Treaty of Frankfurt: Alsace and Lorraine were lost; the French had to suffer a Prussian victory march down the Champs-Elysées and pay a colossal war indemnity. Tested by months of privation and grief, many Parisians saw this acquiescence to the Prussians as an insult, and on 18 March 1871 the Paris Commune, or insurrection of the city against the government, started. Facing two enemies, the Prussians and the government army (or Versaillais), it was short-lived, ending on 28 May 1871, after what became known as Bloody Week. In the region of 20,000 people died, mostly through reprisal, and buildings and monuments went up in flames, leaving Paris scarred in many ways. A long period of repression, prosecution and censorship ensued. Some 3,300 Communards and their families fled to Britain,[2] joining the ranks of French refugees who had escaped the war in the months before, and a previous generation of political exiles who had opposed the Second Empire.

The crossing voyage was no mean feat: the painter François Bonvin, who had left Saint-Malo for Southampton, recorded in his diary: 'After sixteen hours of crossing and five hours of journey by railway, here I am in London, experiencing exceptional fog. Hell! It is not fun! I had been warned, but not sufficiently!'[3] Refugees on the whole were welcome in England, Communards included, to the irritation of a commentator, Montigny, who remained puzzled as to why 'ultraconservative newspapers and magazines' showed them 'the strangest partiality and the largest hospitality ... *The Times*, the *Pall Mall Gazette* – the organ of aristocratic clubs – really have no excuses.'[4] No regular entrance restrictions were in place in Britain at the time, and anyone,

James Tissot
The Wounded Soldier c.1870
(detail, see p.36)

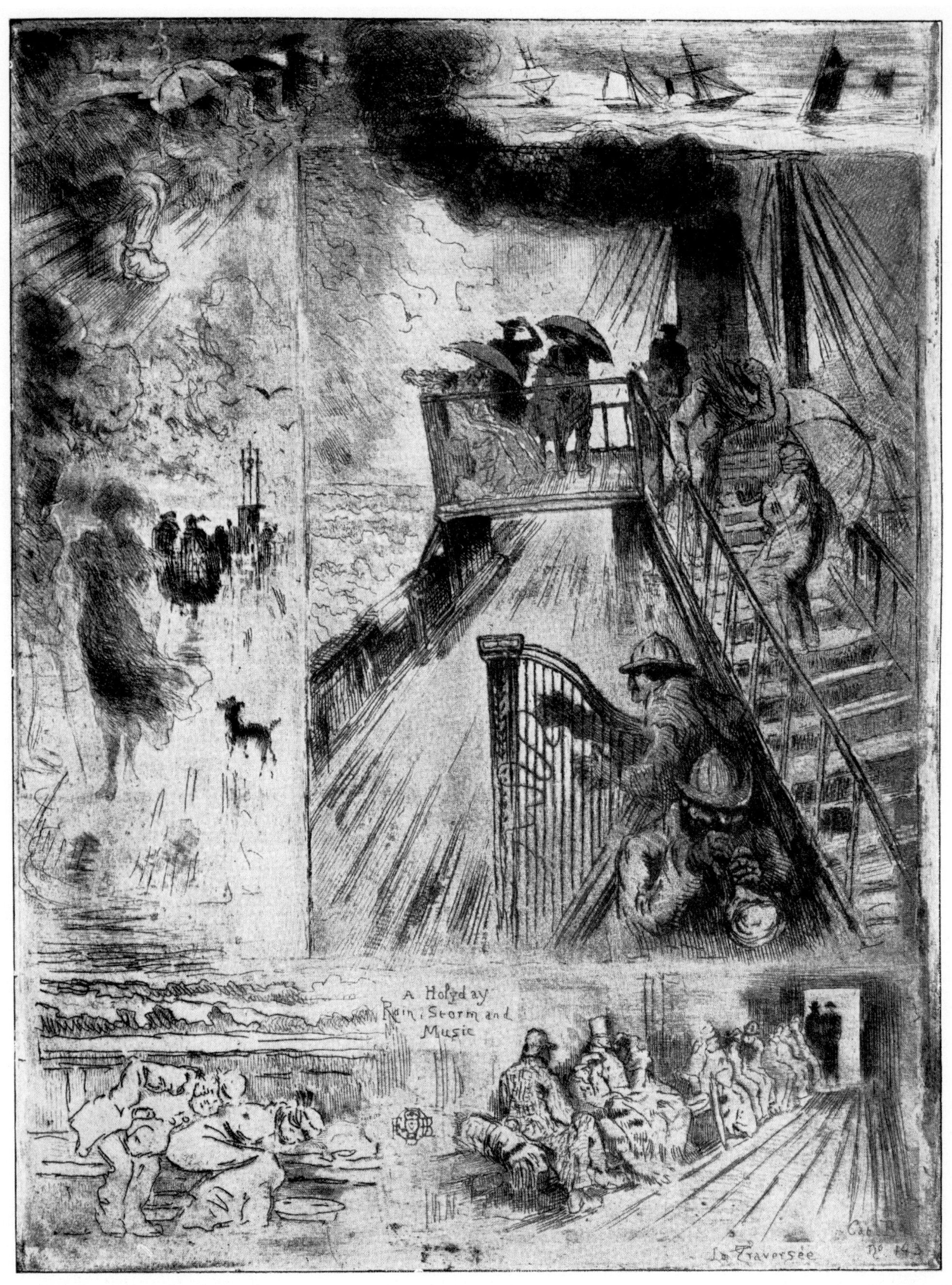

Félix Buhot
Crossing the Channel
The Magazine of Art, 1902

regardless of their nationality, could come and stay indefinitely. In accordance with a spirit of 'patriotic libertarianism in Victorian Britain's political culture',[5] political offences were excluded from extradition treaties.[6]

Impressions and sensations

It is forty-four years since the spectacular exhibition *The Impressionists in London* at the Hayward Gallery in 1973;[7] this book and the exhibition it accompanies do not share such a monographic approach. They chart the wider historic circumstances and story of French artists who took refuge in London and the networks that they developed or relied upon while working in Britain. They consider how, while transplanted to London, French artists interacted with their compatriots and British counterparts, as well as patrons and dealers. Central to this undertaking is the impact of this cultural encounter during such a traumatic and divisive time in French history, the contribution these artists made to British iconography and art education, and, reciprocally, the impact their cross-channel experiences had on French art.

Of different social origins and allegiances, both artistic and political, these painters and sculptors were brought together by history on British shores to form a disparate community. Monet escaped France to avoid conscription; Pissarro fled the Prussians, who requisitioned his house in Louveciennes and destroyed most of his artistic output, and some of Monet's too; James Tissot's motives are still unclear, but his post-war prospects were greater in Britain, a calculation the sculptor Edouard Lantéri also made in 1872; Carpeaux, a courtier, had hopes that the imperial family in exile would pursue their patronage abroad; and at the other end of the political spectrum, his pupil Jules Dalou was a convicted Communard. For all these differences, they formed a community nonetheless. The greater part of the show considers the main groups of artists, patrons and dealers that constituted this network, at the centre of which was the émigré artist Alphonse Legros, who had arrived in England in 1863, and the art dealer Paul Durand-Ruel. One strand of the exhibition is the outsider's perception of London and British society that transpired in the work of refugee artists. The last sections focus particularly on the main themes that caught their imagination and brought them together: the observation of social codes and the British class system through sports; the attraction to parks as venues of social interaction and freedom; the fascination for London crowds; and, above all, the Thames, its atmospheric effects, and the Palace of Westminster as symbols of Britain.

Some artists, such as Tissot and Lantéri, had a career in Britain. Others, including Claude Monet and Camille Pissarro, returned to France after a few months, only to come back to England on later occasions to revisit British motifs and 'rekindle earlier sensations' from their exile, in more propitious circumstances. Their London stories would have remained incomplete had we stopped the narrative in 1871. Starting with the meeting of Monet, Pissarro and Durand-Ruel during their exile at a 'miserable time' in their lives, the exhibition concludes with the Entente Cordiale (1904), at a high point in Anglo-French relations, with the evocation of Monet's highly successful show of thirty-seven *Views of the Thames* at Durand-Ruel's Paris gallery. As analysed in the last essay of the catalogue, following his sixtieth birthday, Monet had decided to revisit earlier motifs, including the Palace of Westminster and the Thames, 'to sum up … impressions and sensations of the past' in serialised form. We argue that Monet's ambition to capture the Thames's atmospheric effects was picked up from the time of his exile to be transformed in the early twentieth century. Pictures of the Houses of Parliament by de Nittis, Pissarro and Monet highlight how this key subject was used by artists to make stylistic statements and take their measure against fellow painters. Both André Derain and his dealer Ambroise Vollard saw Monet's *Views of the Thames*, which prompted Vollard to send the young artist to London. Derain himself explained that his London paintings were both a homage and a challenge to Monet, and a selection of these form a coda to the exhibition to cast light on this competitive spirit and the firm embedding of the Thames as a subject in French art.

Welcoming refugee artists

Britain did not turn its back on refugee artists. Jules Dalou was both flattered and surprised to enjoy aristocratic patronage through George Howard (pp.154–5) and, no doubt, the 1st Duke of Westminster (p.160). Such prestigious commissions culminated in 1877, when Queen Victoria asked him to make a private memorial to five of her grandchildren who died in infancy (Windsor Castle).[8] Not all exiled Communards were so successful, but the French artistic community in general received the support of no less than the Prime Minister, William Gladstone, who expressed his delight 'that our countrymen should have the opportunity of seeing and bearing testimony to how noble a development the art of painting and the art of sculpture have taken among those who are suffering so grievously in their public and national capacity'.[9] And they were supported by their British counterparts: Dante Gabriel Rossetti contributed money towards a fund set up by James Abbott McNeill Whistler's mother to support the widow of an exiled artist who had died in London,[10] and Alphonse Legros – of whom more later – contributed to the Société des Réfugiés de la Commune that provided Communards with advice, contacts, food and jobs.

The appeal of London as a thriving art market played a key part in attracting so many French artists, despite the language barrier, which was real.[11] Charles-François Daubigny, for instance, had already established links with England in 1866 in an attempt to make forays into the art scene. He exhibited at the Royal Academy, and so did Tissot, a keen anglophile, who contributed caricatures to *Vanity Fair* before moving to Britain in the aftermath of the Commune. *L'Illustration* boasted in September 1871: 'England, at the moment … strong enough not to be forced to expel our refugees, whoever they may be,

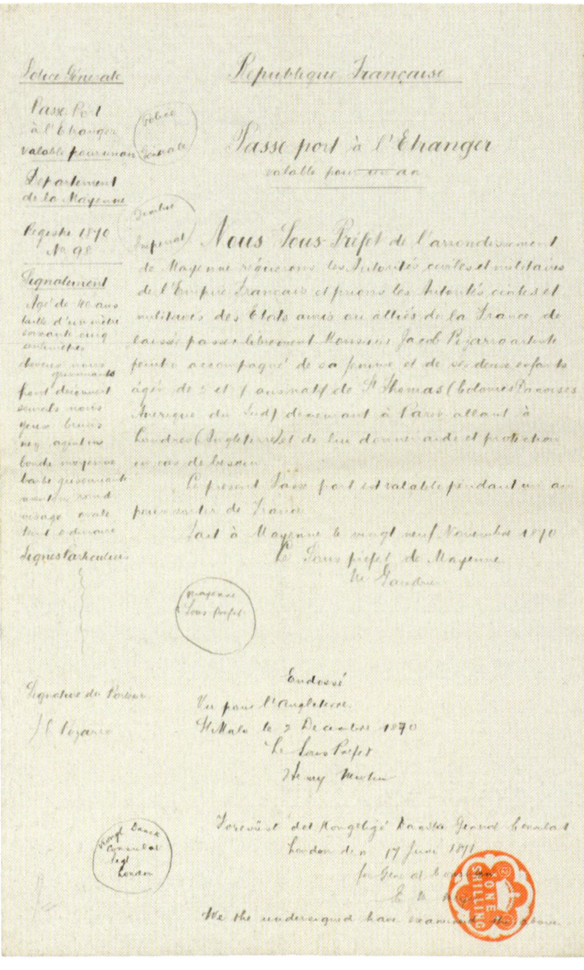
République Française
Passe port à l'Etranger

Camille Pissarro's passport
1870

The Pissarro Estate

welcomes with eagerness and vast hospitality our great artists of all kinds.'[12] Jean-Léon Gérôme had already been made an honorary member of the Royal Academy in 1869, and arrived in 1870,[13] the year he exhibited *Jerusalem* (Musée d'Orsay) and *The Execution of Marshal Ney* (Sheffield City Art Gallery) at the Academy Summer Exhibition. The following year, William Michael Rossetti identified Gérôme's *Cleopatra* 1866 (private collection) as the finest work on display in the same walls.[14] It belonged to Henry James Turner, also a patron of Tissot and Carpeaux (p.178). Despite Gérôme's success and his influence on the nude in Britain, his art as such did not evolve through contact with British culture, nor did he engage with landscape while in England. He is therefore only represented in the form of a bust by Carpeaux, with whom he associated in London. By the same criteria, artists such as Guillaume Régamey, Julien de La Rochenoire, Ferdinand Heilbuth, Jean-Charles Cazin and Eugène Isabey are not included in the exhibition. François Bonvin painted some very sensitive watercolours of London (p.17) and Gravesend, but being part of the Moreau-Nélaton bequest, these unfortunately cannot leave the Louvre. Bonvin otherwise mostly continued to paint the still lifes and Dutch-inspired interiors that occupied him in Paris. On the other hand, London views by the Italian painter Giuseppe de Nittis, who had settled in Paris before the Franco-Prussian war and, by his own admission, was French at heart, feature in the exhibition. Close to Edgar Degas and Edouard Manet, he was an exhibitor at the first impressionist show in 1874, and he became part of the network of his close friend Tissot in London. A type of economic migrant, de Nittis came annually to London, mostly to execute commissions for the wealthy colliery proprietor Kaye Knowles. His British pictures, painted with the detachment of an outsider who is also a keen observer – not unlike Tissot – brought much to the representation of London.

Alfred Sisley was another adoptive Frenchman in England: he was brought up in France by well-off British parents and spent most of his life there, while never gaining French citizenship. His home in Bougival was destroyed by occupying Prussian forces in the autumn of 1870, together with most of his works, and his family was ruined by the war. As a result, his life would be a constant financial struggle, with periods when he could not even afford to buy artist's materials. His sojourn in London between July and October 1874 was subsidised by the baritone Jean-Baptiste Faure. His situation can be linked to that of de Nittis or Lantéri, who did not have many options but to come to London, sporadically or permanently, to pursue their artistic careers in the aftermath of the conflict. No women artists feature in the exhibition: this is not to say that there were none, as the remarkable artist Marie Cazin came to England between 1871 and 1875. She exhibited at the Royal Academy in 1874 and 1878, but, like her husband, she mostly worked in ceramics during her stay, and was not in the habit of signing her landscapes, the subjects of which can be difficult to identify. Berthe Morisot visited the Isle of Wight in 1874, but on her honeymoon with Eugène Manet, so not as an economic migrant.

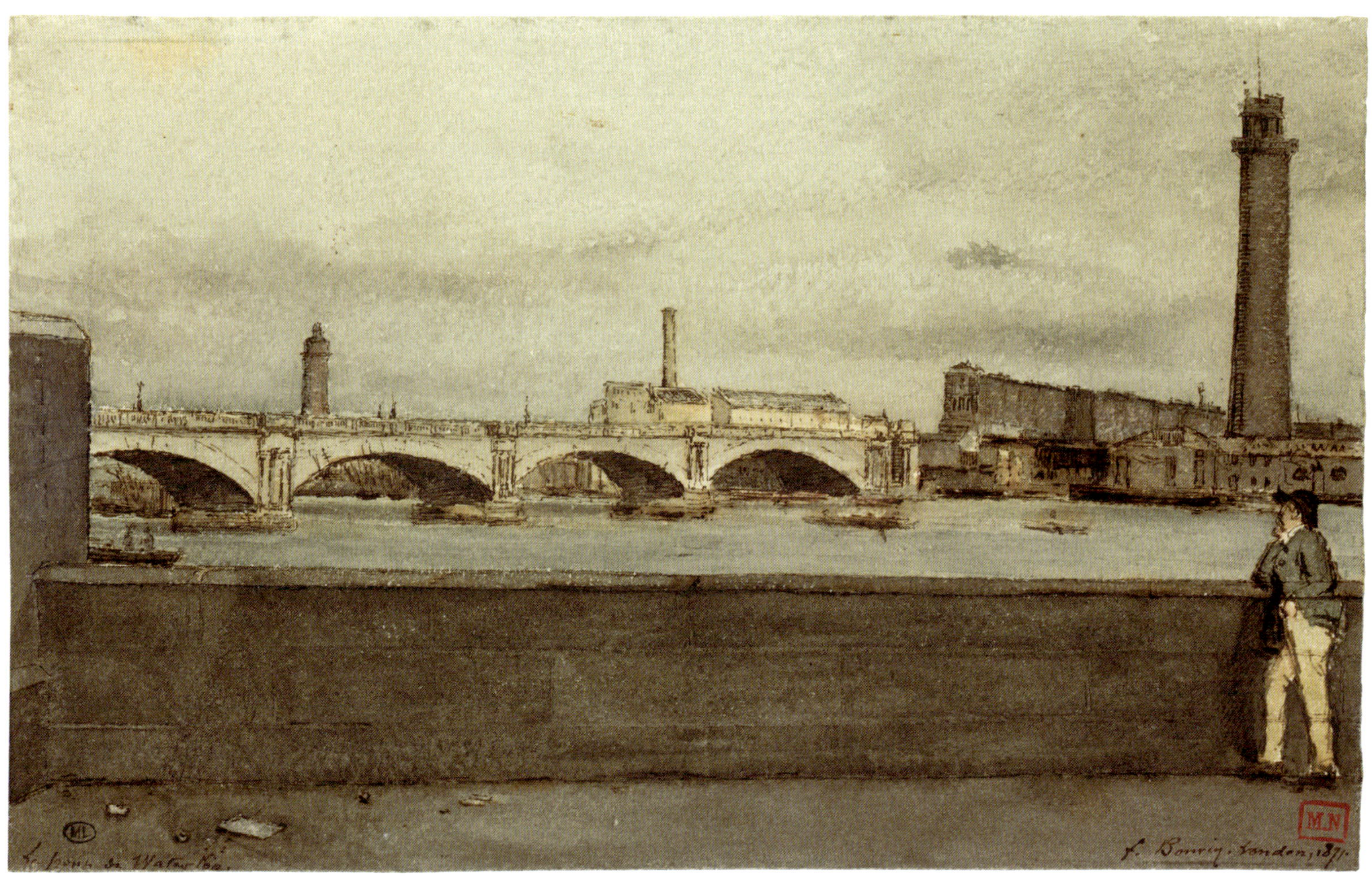

François Bonvin
(1817–87)
Waterloo Bridge, London
Watercolour on paper 15.5 × 21.2

Musée d'Orsay, Paris, deposited at the Musée du Louvre, Paris

Legros and Durand-Ruel at the heart of Anglo-French networks

Arguably, the support brought by the artist Alphonse Legros and the art dealer Paul Durand-Ruel to French émigré artists was unmatched. Legros, whose fame is not now on a par with many of his better-known contemporaries, is at the very heart of the exhibition. For French artists arriving in London, he was the first port of call and the keystone of their community. He had settled in Britain in 1863, encouraged by his then friend James Abbott McNeill Whistler, who persuaded him that his art would find a market that it had failed to win in France. As Anna Gruetzner Robins's essay highlights, he originally benefited from Whistler's support, but also from that of Dante Gabriel Rossetti, Edward Burne-Jones, George Frederic Watts and their patrons. He was perceived as a model of success by French artists, not least because of this extensive network. The diary of a member of Legros's household for 1874 shows that he associated with Communard artists, including Dalou – which is unsurprising, given their closeness – one of the Régamey brothers, probably Félix,[15] and François Jourde, who had been deported to Nouméa and escaped at the same time as the politician Henri Rochefort. Manet would make two unusual history paintings on the subject of their escape a few years later.[16] Jourde was received by Legros at the same time as Tissot and Heilbuth,[17] indicating that they too had sympathy for the cause of deportees and political exiles. Among frequent visitors to Legros's house were Lawrence Alma-Tadema, who lived in Paris until the outbreak of the Franco-Prussian war, Walter Crane and his wife, Burne-Jones, Constantine Ionides, and Sir Coutts Lindsay, who would found the Grosvenor Gallery.

Evidently, Legros had strong alliances in Britain, and as their most famous colleague in London, virtually all French artists came to him for help and advice. There is a sense that Legros replicated the assistance that he had himself warmly received from British artists when he arrived as an economic migrant. Bonvin, who visited Legros the day after he arrived, insightfully reported: 'Warm welcome and good news. Many French painters have found refuge here: Gérôme, Heilbuth, Régamey, Daubigny, La Rochenoire, Monet, [Jacques -Clément] Wagrez, the engraver Morand [Charles Maurand]'.[18] Tissot lost no time in seeing him after his arrival, while Pissarro and Monet had lunch with him and appear to have known him well.[19] How Guillaume Régamey and Dalou enjoyed both Legros's hospitality and commissions from his patrons is analysed in Anna Gruetzner Robins's essay. It was at the suggestion of Legros and Dalou that Joseph Edgar Boehm, another notoriously generous émigré artist, employed Edouard Lantéri in his studio. Legros was central in bringing the French artistic community together. Durand-Ruel, despite having his own network of dealers and clients in London,[20] could not dispense with the support of Legros, who was part of the 'imaginary committee' of the Society of French Artists set up by the art dealer in 1870.

Durand-Ruel was also a refugee, leaving Paris on 8 September 1870, 'determined to go to England and to send [his] pictures there',[21] in the hope that he would be able to continue to work, support his family and help his friends.[22] The safety of his stock and that of his clients – among them Jean-Baptiste Faure, his neighbour on Brompton Crescent in Knightsbridge – was certainly key to his self-enforced exile. Daubigny, like Bonvin, saw Durand-Ruel almost as soon as he arrived, and the sales and commissions that both artists secured from him kept them afloat during their exile. Cazin, Léon Lhermitte and others benefited from his support too. Business resumed almost as usual, albeit on foreign shores. At the first exhibition of the Society of French Artists, in December 1870, the reviewer of the *Art Journal* remarked: 'In looking round the room we stop at the works of certain men with a painful feeling, which finds expression in the low-voiced utterance, "Ay, he is in the Garde Mobile", and further on, "He too, and he"; the thoughts that succeed may be imagined.'[23] As Anne Robbins's essay stresses, Daubigny took both Monet and Pissarro under his wing and encouraged Durand-Ruel to support their work. The partnership would prove decisive: in Monet's words, 'It is thanks to [Daubigny] that I got in touch with Durand-Ruel, and on that day, my life was saved.'[24]

Edouard Lantéri and Alphonse Legros at the opening of the Alfred Stevens exhibition, 15 November 1911

Tate Archive

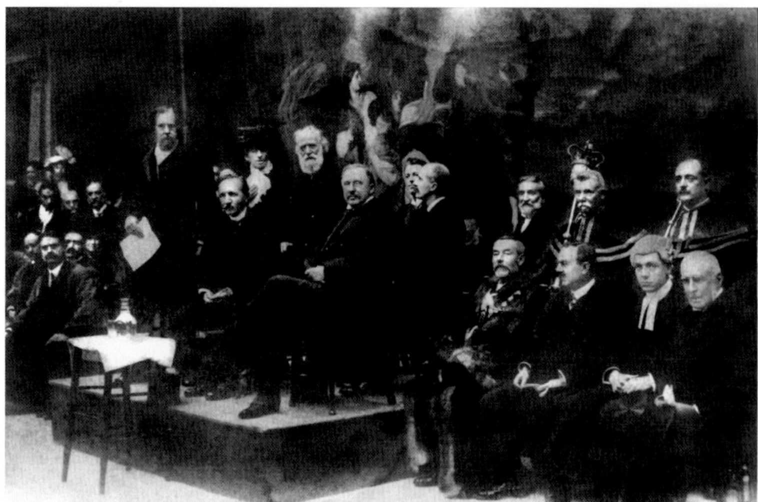

Interacting with British culture and art

Daubigny, Pissarro and Monet frequented the Café Royal, on Regent Street, not too far from the 'French ghetto' around Soho and Leicester Square. Museums and galleries appear to have been equally important places to socialise, along with restaurants such as Dieudonné hotel and restaurant, the Opéra Comique theatre on the Strand and Tavistock House (see p.184). Among them, too, was Dulwich Gallery, or 'Deuletche', as pronounced by Bonvin, who discovered this 'jewel of a museum' in May 1871, only to return in October and experience the 'same rapture as the first time'.[25] The visitors' book of the gallery for Friday 25 November 1870 shows that La Rochenoire, Monet and Legros, who would have been their guide, all went together. Pissarro, conveniently, lived in the neighbourhood.

The National Gallery was also a key destination for refugee artists. Carpeaux developed a fascination for Correggio, making a copy of *Venus with Mercury and Cupid* and filling in a small diary with sketches, notably of Rembrandt's *Woman Bathing in a Stream* (p.186). When it came to British art, Daubigny conceded that 'they [had] very good old masters',[26] and Pissarro famously told the English painter Wynford Dewhurst: 'The watercolours and paintings of Turner, the Constables and the Cromes, certainly had an influence on us. We admired Gainsborough, Lawrence, Reynolds, etc., but we were more struck by the landscapists, who were closer to our own researches into the open air, light and fugitive effects.'[27] Both Monet and Pissarro, however, later downplayed the importance of this foreign influence on impressionism.[28]

Modern British art, however, was not appreciated by most of the refugee artists, except for Tissot, who deeply admired John Everett Millais and Whistler, and Monet and Pissarro, who were 'strongly interested' by G.F. Watts and D.G. Rossetti.[29] That Monet was aware of Whistler's nocturnes, then in the making, remains speculative, as there is no evidence to date that they met in 1870–1. The background of *The Thames below Westminster* (pp.66–7), which is often presented as a visual clue that they did, appears more indebted to Daubigny than to the sweeping horizontal brushwork of *Nocturne: Blue and Silver – Chelsea* (pp.216–18). As for Pissarro, he bluntly reported that 'there [was] no art',[30] while Daubigny had some harsh words: 'How awful modern English painting is! They certainly have need of our influence … When they paint fruit or flowers, they appear to be made of glass or sugar. Landscapes seem to be made of chenille or seem to have been brushed in with hair. Figures are as rigid as iron.'[31] Dalou also made disparaging comments: he complained that the British public was deterred by nudes 'that were not treated in the manner of English soaps'.[32]

Legacy

Aside from the legacy of French artists on representations of London, examined in the last two essays of this book, there stands a less tangible one, that of the question of their influence, through style but also through teaching. The former deserves another exhibition in itself, but the origins of British impressionism are not limited solely to continental developments – and as Anne Robbins's essay highlights, the future impressionists' presence in Britain in 1870–1 did not make many waves. On the other hand, the impact of Tissot on artists such as William Quiller Orchardson, George Dunlop Leslie and Alfred Munnings is certainly discernible, and the critic Marion Harry Spielmann noted about New Sculpture, that it was 'to Carpeaux, no doubt, that the inspiration of the new trend was originally due'.[33] The inclusion in the exhibition of a bust by Carpeaux (p.185), once in the collection of Alfred Gilbert, suggests this much. As for influence through teaching, it is even more difficult to pinpoint. Amélie Simier, in her essay on the methods brought by Jules Dalou and Edouard Lantéri to Britain, delineates their impact on a generation of students. Legros and Lantéri in particular taught for twenty and thirty-seven years respectively. Both were naturalised as British, and Lantéri received special permission to continue teaching at the Royal College of Art beyond the normal age of retirement. Alfred Gilbert, Francis Derwent-Wood, Albert Toft, Charles Sargeant Jagger, to name but a few, all acknowledged their debt to him. Legros appears to have been more rigid as a teacher,[34] but despite reservations, William Rothenstein and Charles Wellington Furse, who would play an important part in British impressionism, praised his intransigence when it came to the purity of line.[35] He taught Rodin drypoint, introduced Watts to etching and taught printmaking to Edwin Edwards, William Strang, William Rothenstein and many others. He, Dalou and Lantéri probably inherited their desire to impart knowledge and savoir-faire from their unconventional and highly charismatic teacher Horace Lecoq de Boisbaudran. Lantéri recalled: 'The best teacher … to whom I owe so much, was M. Lecoq de Boisbaudran. His excellent lessons are still present in my mind.'[36]

In 1911 Legros made his last public appearance at the inauguration of the Alfred Stevens Memorial exhibition. The posthumous bust Lantéri made of Stevens (Tate) was unveiled on the occasion, and both men, with many former students in the audience, were given a standing ovation – a testimony to the transformation that they brought to British art education. Their nationality of origin at that stage seemed irrelevant, although Legros delighted in saying, in French, that now being British, he had 'won the battle of Waterloo'.[37]

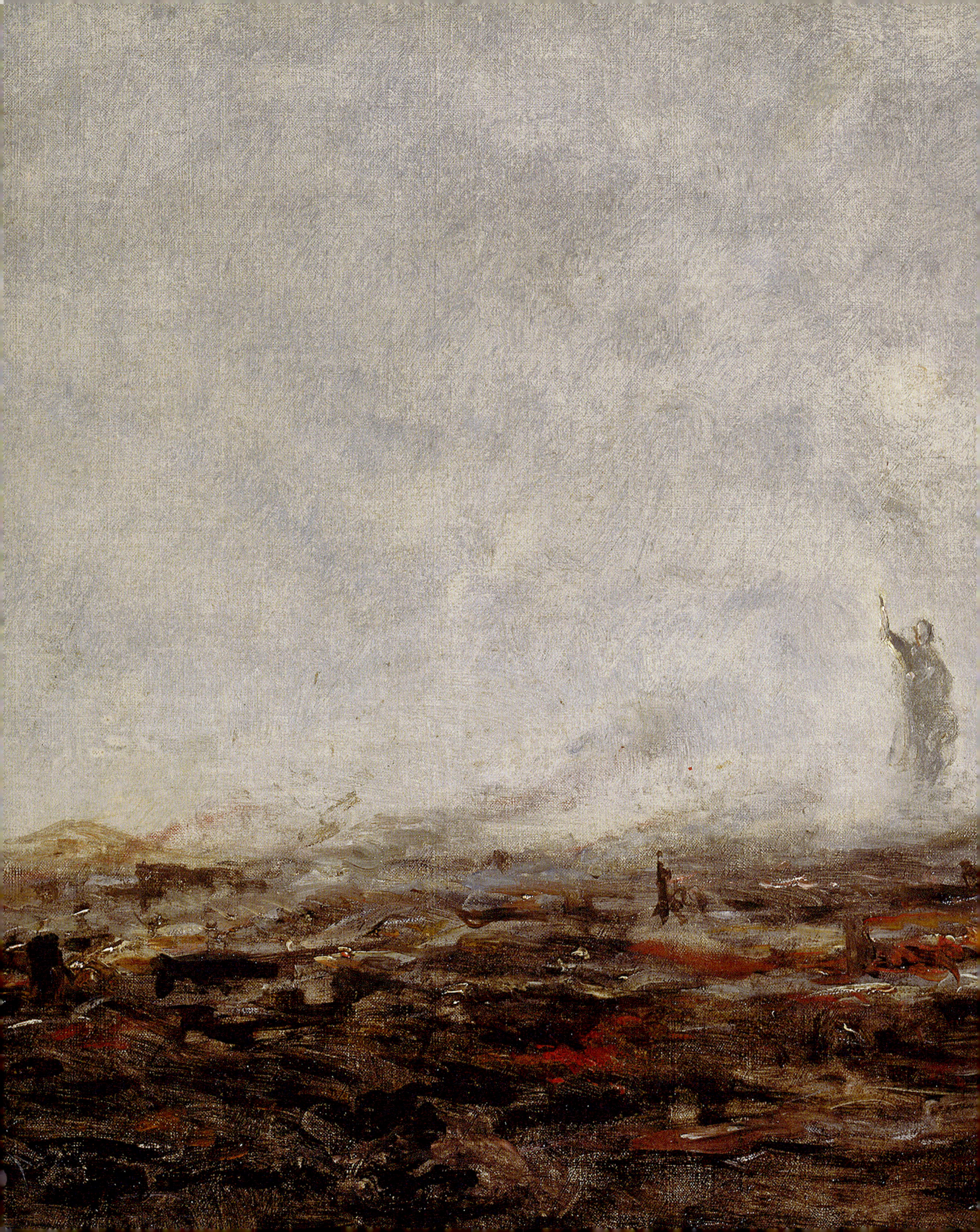

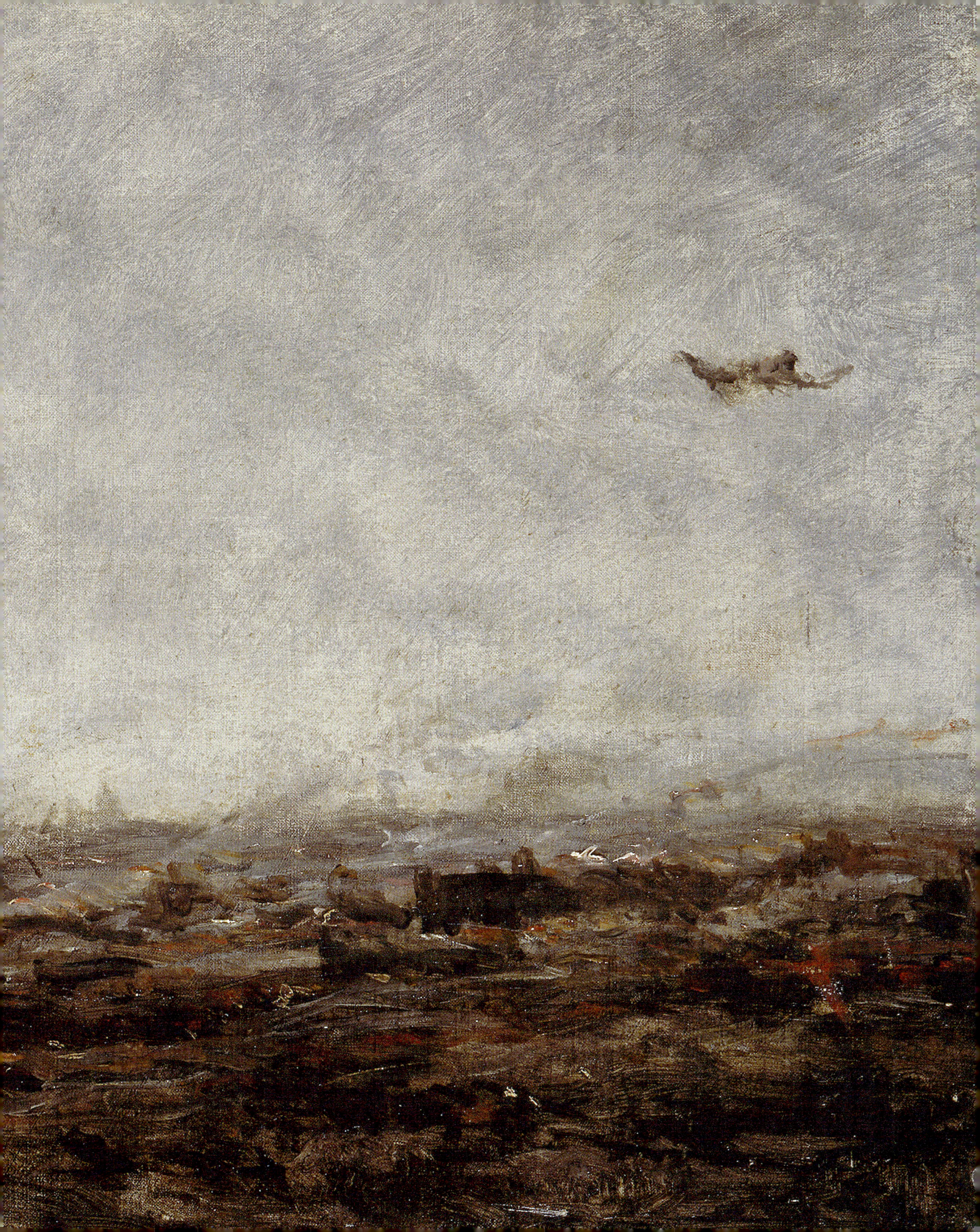

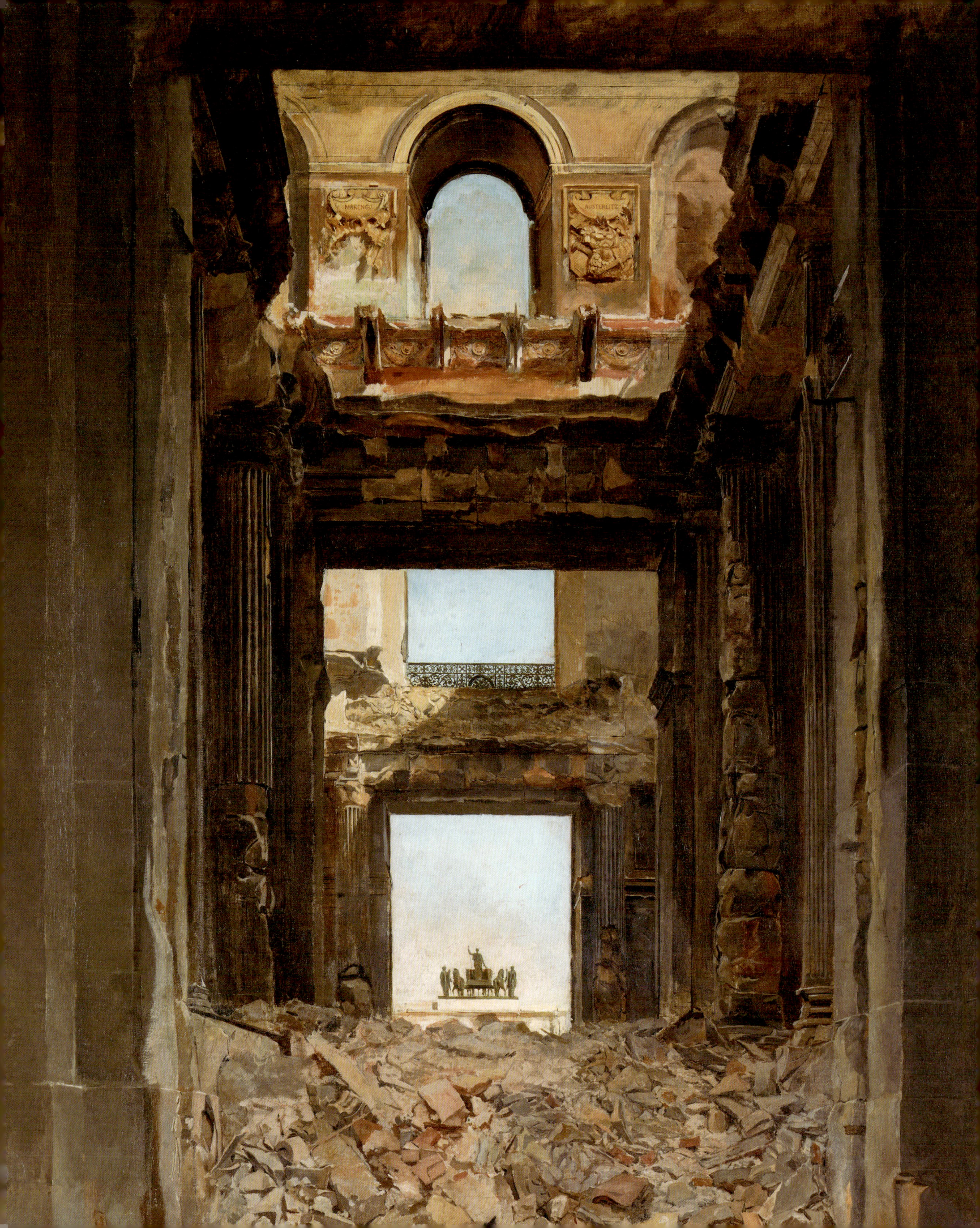
MARENGO
AUSTERLITZ

Bertrand Tillier

Painters Tested by the Terrible Year, 1870–1

After the defeat at Sedan, the collapse of the empire and the proclamation of a republic, a state of siege was declared in Paris on 19 September 1870, and the capital entered a long period of isolation and uncertainty. Henceforth, the encircled city, which one could only enter or leave with great difficulty, embodied much of what was at stake in this conflict both strategically and symbolically. Subject to the psychological pressure of a waiting war, which was soon aggravated by the rigours of an exceptional winter, food deprivation and enemy bombardment, Parisians found themselves cut off from the rest of the country and at the mercy of propaganda and disinformation that fed irrational fears, all sorts of fantasies and the most contradictory rumours. The armistice of 28 January 1871 encouraged the republicans and a radical fringe to denounce what they saw as a new, disguised capitulation. The legislative elections that followed on 8 February, hastily organised to create a National Assembly that would be responsible for negotiating definitive peace, became transformed into a referendum for or against the war, from which emerged an 'unobtainable chamber' ('chambre introuvable'), according to Victor Hugo, who was elected in Paris.

In contrast to the conservative provinces, Paris refused peace and progressively reinforced its autonomy, which on 18 March took a decidedly revolutionary turn with the proclamation of the Commune. Right up until it was crushed by troops from Versailles during the Bloody Week at the end of May 1871, this utopian government established itself as the 'Republic of Paris' complete with representatives who voted on political decisions and set up an administration that oversaw their application. Public opinion, won over by the power of national institutions entrusted to Adolphe Thiers and installed in Versailles, was used to undermine the Commune's work. The ensuing escalation of true violence – the execution of hostages, the Haxo Street massacre, the murder of the Dominicans of Arcueil, the fires during Bloody Week – succeeded in discrediting the Commune by promoting the spectre of a new Reign of Terror.

In Paris, closed in on itself and buffeted by the turmoil of events during the Terrible Year, political and social structures were subject to major upheavals, whose shockwaves affected artistic communities. Artists who had abandoned the city were by far the most numerous, to the extent that on 30 May 1871 Théodore Duret, Manet's friend, wrote to Pissarro: 'The horror and terror are still everywhere ... Paris is empty and will become even emptier ... Anyone would think there never were any painters and artists in Paris.'[1]

Fleeing Paris

Artists had indeed deserted the capital en masse. But this situation was not exclusively due to the Commune or its repression. It was more the result of successive waves of departures to the suburbs, provinces or abroad. After 19 July 1870, as soon as hostilities with Prussia began, Jean-François Millet left for his native hamlet of Gruchy, near Cherbourg, where he painted and drew a large number of bucolic landscapes free of

Jean Louis Ernest Meissonier
The Tuileries (May 1871)
(detail, see p.26)

any industrial references. In April 1871 he wrote to Alfred Sensier, who himself had taken refuge in Barbizon to flee the Commune:

> One would believe (if one wants to avoid certain modern events) oneself to be in old Brueghel's times.

And he further advised:

> Take … as much pleasure as you can in natural things; because there is always something solid there. I, for my part, strive to banish from my mind (but I cannot do it enough) all these horrors against which I can do nothing, in order to throw myself into work.[2]

As for Cézanne, he took refuge in L'Estaque, near Marseilles, where he lived almost in hiding until March 1871.

The declaration of a state of siege provoked a second wave of departures. In September 1870 Pissarro hurriedly left Louveciennes to join his friend the painter Ludovic Piette in the Mayenne, before reaching London, where he found Charles-François Daubigny, Julien de La Rochenoire and Claude Monet. Monet had spent the autumn in Trouville and had arrived in the British capital around the beginning of October, but he stayed until the end of the Commune and only returned to Paris after a stay in Holland. In the same circumstances, Eugène Boudin, who witnessed the massive embarkation of civilians for England at Le Havre, also decided to leave, but for Brussels, where he found a community of Parisian artists forced into exile by the events. Among them were Narcisse Diaz de la Peña, Carolus-Duran and Jean-François Raffaëlli, who would not regain the capital until sometime in summer 1871.

At the end of January 1871 a third wave of departures coincided with the armistice. Jean-Louis Ernest Meissonier shut himself away in his Poissy property where he was occupied with the conception of his monumental funereal painting, *Siege of Paris* 1870–84 (p.30). As for Manet, he joined his family in Oloron-Sainte-Marie in the Lower Pyrénées, before slowly going back up the Atlantic coast on a long tour. Degas, for his part, settled in Normandy at the home of his friends, the Valpinçons.

A last wave of departures from Paris followed the proclamation of the Commune in March 1871. Camille Corot, for instance, quit the capital on 1 April 1871 and remained throughout the Commune in the north of France: successively, in Arras with the painter Charles Desavary, in Douai with Alfred Robaut, and finally in Paluel, Oisy and Arleux until the end of July.

Stay and take action

Those who stayed in Paris during the siege and until the armistice often enrolled in the Mobile National Guard. They included Puvis de Chavannes, Eugène Carrière, Gustave Caillebotte, Gustave Doré, James Tissot, Georges Clairin, Léon Bonnat, Edouard Detaille, and Alphonse de Neuville. Manet, with the rank of lieutenant, was first a gunner in the artillery before being posted to the headquarters, where he served under Meissonier. Degas also joined the National Guard. Like Gustave Moreau, he was assigned to fortifications as a gunner under the command of one of his former school pals, Henri Rouart. More rarely, others were officers in the operating army or the reserves, such as Pierre-Georges Jeanniot, who participated in the Battle of Rezonville.[3]

The artists who remained in Paris also took an active part in the management of artistic institutions. As Gonzalo Sánchez has demonstrated,[4] the Federation of Artists founded on 13 April 1871 under the aegis of the communalist authorities and on one of Gustave Courbet's initiatives was, in principle and most of its actions, simply the continuation of the essentially republican Artistic Committee for the Preservation of National Museums created in September 1870. Their claims had a common ground: administration of artists' associations by the artists themselves, a ballot to appoint Salon juries, the formation of committees to award commissions and organise competitions, and so on. Moreover, most of the men concerned were the same, as for instance Courbet, who successively occupied the functions of 'president of the arts' at the heart of the commission and of the federation. His correspondence and public declarations prove that he confused the two, each being the result of a 'general assembly of artists', of which he had been elected president twice.[5]

The Federation of Artists was provided with an executive committee of forty-seven members.[6] The college of painters included, among others, François Bonvin, Corot, Courbet, Honoré Daumier, Eugène Feyen-Perrin, Amand Gautier, Jules Héreau, Eugène-Auguste Lançon, Eugène Leroux, Manet, Millet, Henri Oulevay and Ernest Pichio. Jules Dalou and Paul Moreau-Vauthier figured among the sculptors. Engravers were represented by Félix Bracquemond, Léopold Flameng and the caricaturist André Gill. But this list published in the *Journal officiel de la Commune* is not reliable, because certain individuals with known republican tendencies had been elected without their knowledge: Manet, Millet (he protested officially[7]), Bonvin, Daumier and Corot were in fact absent from Paris. Furthermore, six other elected artists rapidly resigned, among them Bracquemond, Flameng and Leroux. The last's letter of refusal is eloquent:

> 17 April 1871 – I have just, with great astonishment, read my name in the list of candidates for the Federative Commission of Artists in Paris. I refuse absolutely the honour that is thought to be done to me; I did not solicit it, I have never been present at any meetings of the federated artists. I have not expressed the ambition to take part in a selection panel and, in the present circumstances, even less so than ever. It is not when our colleagues are absent, when all the collectors are far from Paris, that artists can seriously consider freely drawing up their constitution or organising an exhibition.[8]

Courbet is one of the rare artists whose role went largely beyond arts administration and museum oversight. Member of the Central Committee of the Commune and the Commission of Public Instruction, and Mayor of the Sixth Arrondissement, he took an active part in legislative direction and official provisions for communalist bodies, despite Emile Zola's mocking remarks.[9]

These actions, along with the destruction of the Vendôme Column for which he was blamed, caused him to be arrested and condemned by the Third War Council.[10]

Acts of violence

If most artists went into exile, left Paris or, on the other hand, shut themselves away – as for instance Gustave Moreau, who became a recluse in his studio home on the rue de la Rochefoucauld with his mother, deaf to shooting and agitation, and Fantin-Latour, who retreated into a cellar with his father during the entire period of the Siege and Commune of Paris – it was because events could turn extremely violent.[11] At Malmaison and Chevilly (30 September 1870), twice at Bourget (28–30 October and 21 December), at Champigny (1–3 December), and Buzenval and Montretout (19–20 January 1871) the deadly sorties out of Paris attempted by French troops, who were demoralised by inaction and tried to get the siege lifted, ended in failure and heavy human losses that did not spare the artists' community. At the Battle of Champigny the painter Félix Ziem was hit by a bullet that broke his leg. Another painter, Georges Vibert, was injured at Malmaison, where the sculptor Joseph Cuvelier was also killed. The latter's death so affected Degas that he started quarrelling with Tissot when the latter mentioned it: Degas refused to look at a sketch of the corpse that Tissot shoved before his eyes, and reproached him violently: 'You would have done better to pick him up.'[12]

Frédéric Bazille's death at the age of twenty-eight, on 28 November 1870, at the Battle of Beaune-la-Rolande was felt very painfully by the future impressionists – especially Renoir – who displayed many of his paintings, among them *The Studio in Batignolles* 1870 (Musée d'Orsay), at the group's first exhibition in 1874, which the circumstances turned into a memorial. Above all, Henri Regnault's death on 19 January 1871 at Buzenval, where Clairin found his remains, caused immense emotion among the artists.[13] Born in 1843 and passing his *baccalauréat* in 1859, Regnault won the Grand Prix de Rome in 1866. In 1870 his *Salomé* had won a medal at the Salon, which earned him unanimous critical and public success. As a Prix de Rome holder, he had been exempted from military service, but just as he was preparing to settle in Tangiers, where he had acquired a studio, he returned to Paris to enlist at the end of August 1870. His funeral took place in the presence of Parisian high society, and his death was seen as a national catastrophe. Elevated to symbolic status, the young deceased artist became a hero with a briefly glittering life whose promising genius had been sacrificed for his country.

These experiences of combat, wounds and death were intensified for the artists who returned early or lived in Paris and were present at the outbreak of violence from the Versaillais repression of the Commune during Bloody Week. A letter from Auguste De Gas, Edgar Degas's father, addressed to his daughter Thérèse on 3 June 1871, describes the last week of May and mentions the painter's return to the capital:

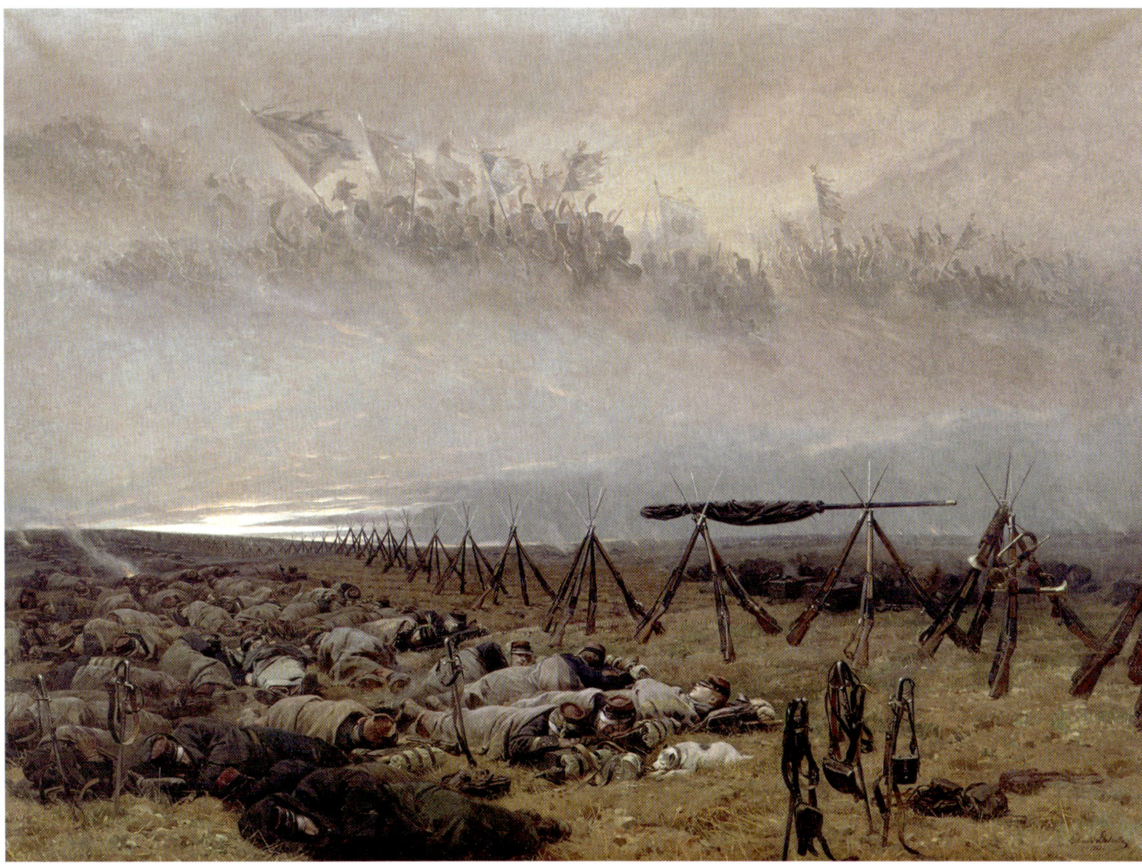

Edouard Detaille
1848–1912
The Dream 1888
Oil paint on canvas 300 × 400

Musée d'Orsay, Paris

> I fortunately escaped bullets and shells ... and it is not for lack of hearing them whistle around me ... I do not believe there has been such a war for the defending and taking of barricades after two days and two nights of unceasing fire, nor scenes such as those of the immense carpets for moving house, which you know can contain all a household's furniture and are now filled with corpses that are cleared away from the vicinity of the barricades to transport them to the closest places for burial. After the fighting came the shooting of all who had been captured carrying arms, new carpets full of corpses. Before these were collected, one had to climb over them in order to go down the street. And what a spectacle! Six days and six nights of incessant machine-gun volleys, shelling, shooting ... Edgar was at the Valpinçons in Mesnil-Hubert, he came back two days ago.[14]

Degas returned to Paris in this Bloody Week atmosphere, on 1 June, and found Manet. According to a letter from Madame Morisot to her daughter Berthe: 'Communards just when they are all being executed, Manet and Degas ... blame the energetic means of repression.'[15] Because their return to Paris was premature – as it was for many Parisians, most artists didn't return until the summer and even later – Manet and Degas had an exceptional take on the events. Manet's two lithographs *The Barricade* 1871 (p.49) and *Civil War* 1874 express the final violence of the repressed Commune, handled in much the same way as someone witnessing it would do a sketch on the spot.

Traumas

During the weeks following his return, several people close to Manet witnessed the kind of depression he had sunk into, making him irritable. About Courbet, who had tried to save his neck in front of the Third War Council, he even wrote: 'He behaved like a coward ... and is not worthy now of the least interest.'[16] Manet was not the only one. As Gustave Flaubert incidentally indicates in a letter to his niece Caroline on 22 August 1872: 'In Paris I learned that several people (including, among others, the painter Gustave Moreau) were affected by the same disease as I, that is to say *the inability to endure* crowds; it is apparently a common affliction following our disasters.'[17] This state of great fatigue, against which Moreau took thermal cures for several years, so affected his painting that he produced very few works in the years following the events of 1870–1, disappearing from the summits of the Salon until 1876.

Jean-Baptiste Carpeaux, whose health was very delicate, spent most of the siege at the Luxembourg Palace where his father-in-law General de Monfort was Military Governor of the Senate and his mother-in-law directed a first-aid station. He applied himself to drawing the troops' daily life – the enlistment of volunteers or the arrival of the wounded – with the intention of illustrating a work devoted to the Siege of Paris.[18] His painting, like those of Puvis de Chavannes and Gustave Doré, seemed to be plunged into mourning with its deadened palette, twilight hues and scenes of violence or destruction reinforcing the grammar of the Commune's apocalyptic imagination.[19]

Alphonse de Neuville
1836–85
The Last Cartridges 1873
Oil paint on canvas 110 × 165

Musée de la Maison de la Dernière Cartouche, Bazeilles

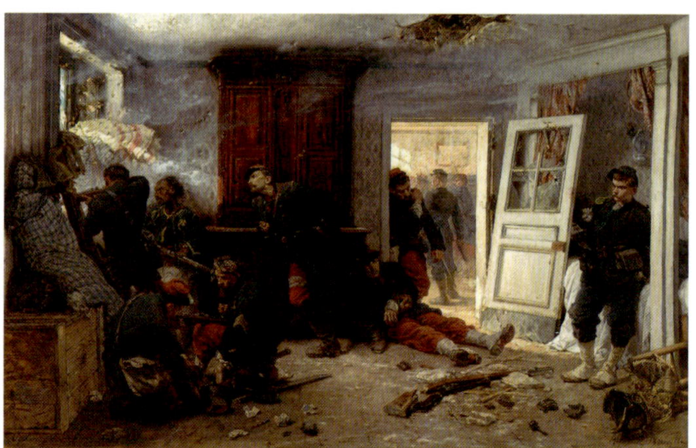

Jean Louis Ernest Meissonier
The Tuileries (May 1871) 1871–83
Oil paint on canvas 132 × 98

Musée national du Château de Compiègne

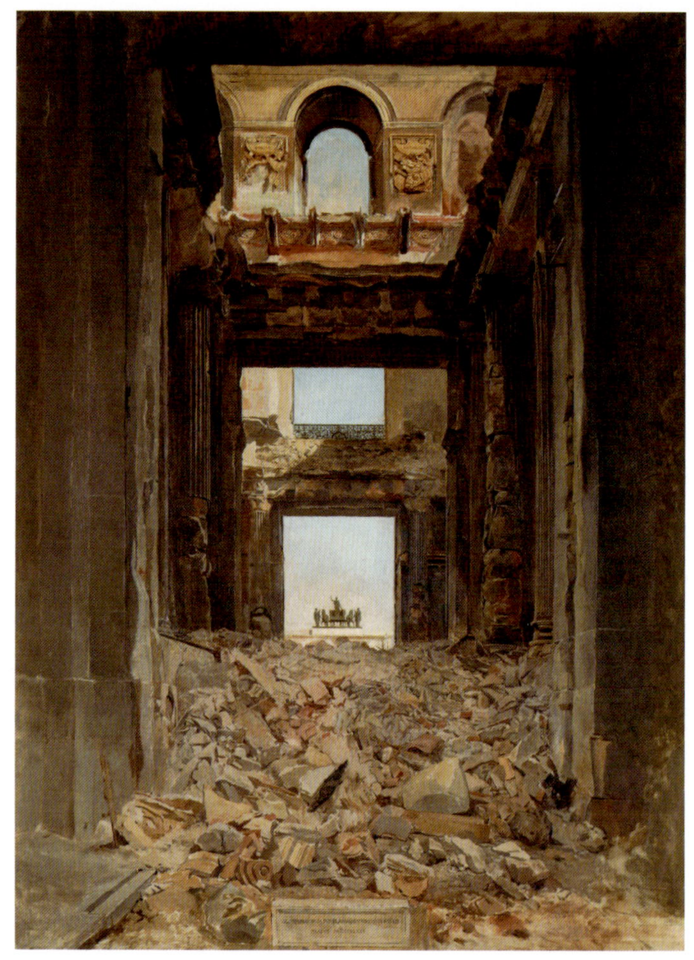

Conjuring defeat

From 1872 painters, often with the annual Salon in mind, began to devote their output to recent events. With ninety works dedicated to the War of 1870 and the Siege of Paris, the 1872 Salon championed the emergence of a pictorial practice that only began to decline towards the end of the 1880s. This type of heroic work was inaugurated by the *The Last Cartridges* 1873 (p.26), which was presented at the Salon by de Neuville in 1873, and shows the desperate resistance of a few soldiers holed up in a house besieged by the enemy on the evening before the surrender of Sedan.[20] It declined with Detaille's *Dream* 1888 (p.25) at the 1888 Salon, which evoked the bivouac of French troops on campaign dreaming of Napoleon's Grand Army surging forth victoriously through the clouds.[21]

These two paintings caused a sensation and were liberally promoted until just before the First World War.[22] They were emblematic of military painting of the Terrible Year, in that they sought to transmute defeat into a moral victory.[23] By compressing events, they brought the combat back into a particular space and time. This caused a reversal, as the critic Gustave Goetschy emphasised: 'Formerly the incident was relegated to a corner of the picture, and the battle occupied the place of honour right in the centre of the canvas; today, the roles have changed, the incident has taken the central place, and the battle is behind it.'[24] Presented as a fragment of the battle, the individual feat of arms progressively became the convention for depicting the events of 1870–1, with realism serving as a way of authenticating the heroic action.

The spectre of ruins

The 1872 Salon was also the first to initiate a custom and taste for burned-out Parisian ruins in a manner approaching contemporary photography, which made it possible to show the vandalism imputed to the Commune's destructive folly. The destruction of the Tuileries Palace, the Finance Ministry, the Palace of the Legion of Honour and the Court of Audit, the Palais-Royal, the Louvre, and the Hôtel de Ville had been planned, coordinated and methodically implemented during Bloody Week in order to open up a line of fire from east to west that was supposed to slow the advance of the Versaillais troops. This gave rise to lively debates between defenders of reconstruction (the Hôtel de Ville), advocates of their complete removal (the Tuileries) and supporters of their conservation, some of whom saw the ruins as an opportunity for a permanent public lesson on the dangers of insurrection, while others saw it as the place for an aesthetic experience. Edmond de Goncourt thus wrote in his *Journal* about his admiration for the Hôtel de Ville in ruins:

> The ruin is magnificent, splendid. In shades of pink, ash green, tinted like red-hot iron, sparkling with 'agatisation', the result of clay baked by petroleum, the ruin resembles that of an Italian palace coloured by several centuries of sun or better still the ruin of a magic palace bathed in an opera of gleams and electric reflections ... [This ruin] is a picturesque marvel, to be saved if the country was not condemned without appeal to the restorations of M. Viollet-le-Duc.[25]

In the regular, often virulent political debates about the ruins, their aesthetic quality was never a dominant question. The 'ruinist' views of Frans Moormans (p.48), Siebe Johannes ten Cate (p.50), Ernest Meissonier (p.30), Isidore Pils (p.44) and Charles-Joseph Beauverie (p.46), however, sought to communicate the strangeness of this spectral architecture of the Commune – superb when baked, to use the language and imagination of Joris-Karl Huysmans.[26] The artists were divided between moral condemnation of its source and the fascinating spectacle of its sudden collapse into an archaeological time zone. 'The flames, smoke, and combustion of chemical products intended to produce fire had imprinted on the rubble grey, orange-brown, russet, bronze and darkened tones of strange colourings that aged them and gave them the air of antique ruins,' remarked Théophile Gautier,[27] thus also explaining the vogue for illustrated works and photographic collections of ruins, where the picturesque continuously competed with dramatisation.[28]

The lesson of the ruins

The Commune's ruins, which thus lingered in both the Parisian landscape and its depictions, crystallised the idea of humanity wearing out and the fear of civilisation's decline, of which Meissonier's *The Tuileries (May 1871)* 1871–83 (p.26) was symptomatic and Corot's *Dream: Paris Burning* 1870 (p.28) had been seen as a phantasmagorical vision and a sort of premonition. During the night of 9 to 10 September 1870, while the Prussian troops marched on Paris, the painter dreamt that the enemy had entered the capital to set it on fire. The next day, 'on awakening, in a sketch feverishly thrown onto a canvas', according to his friend and biographer Alfred Robaut, Corot had translated his nightmare into a work that he kept in his studio until his death, like an intimate reliquary or a magic charm.[29] The work, in panoramic style, depicts the city enveloped in flames. The lower level is occupied by a dark shifting mass streaked with red lines, from which emerge a few smoking roofs and, on the right, the cupola of the Church of Sainte-Geneviève, dedicated to the patron saint of Paris. From this indistinct mass two colossal figures symbolising the warring nations stand out: on the right, the exterminating angel, who has just set the city on fire and flees through the air, and in the centre, the hieratic luminous figure brandishing a torch who represents France 'standing at the heart of the destroyed city, promising to repair everything'.[30] In many respects Corot's *Dream* summarises what the Terrible Year did to painting and to artists.

Jean-Baptiste-Camille Corot
1796–1875
The Dream: Paris Burning 1870
Oil paint on canvas 30.5 × 54.5

Musée Carnavalet – Histoire de Paris

This phantasmagorical painting by Corot is the pictorial synthesis of a nightmare that the painter had during the Franco-Prussian War. The night of 9–10 September 1870, while the Prussian troops were on their way to Paris, Corot dreamt that they were setting fire to the capital. He put this apocalyptic vision on canvas the following morning, at great speed. Corot's friend and biographer, Alfred Robaut, thus described the painting: 'Paris was on fire, as if submerged by an ocean of flames. The exterminating Angel, who had just accomplished his work, was flying away fast. But already France was appearing, standing at the heart of the destroyed city, promising to mend everything.'[1]

What was, from the start, a highly personal work took on even greater importance for Corot after the Commune set fire to many seats of power. The artist then came to see his dream as a type of premonition. As Bertrand Tillier has noted, the artist certainly saw *The Dream* as 'a sort of memorial of his most intimate traumas, confused with recent history'.[2] Corot kept the painting in his studio until he died, 'almost secretly'.[3] It remains one of the most vivid and unusual records of the impact that the events of 1870–1 had on artists who experienced them. CCP

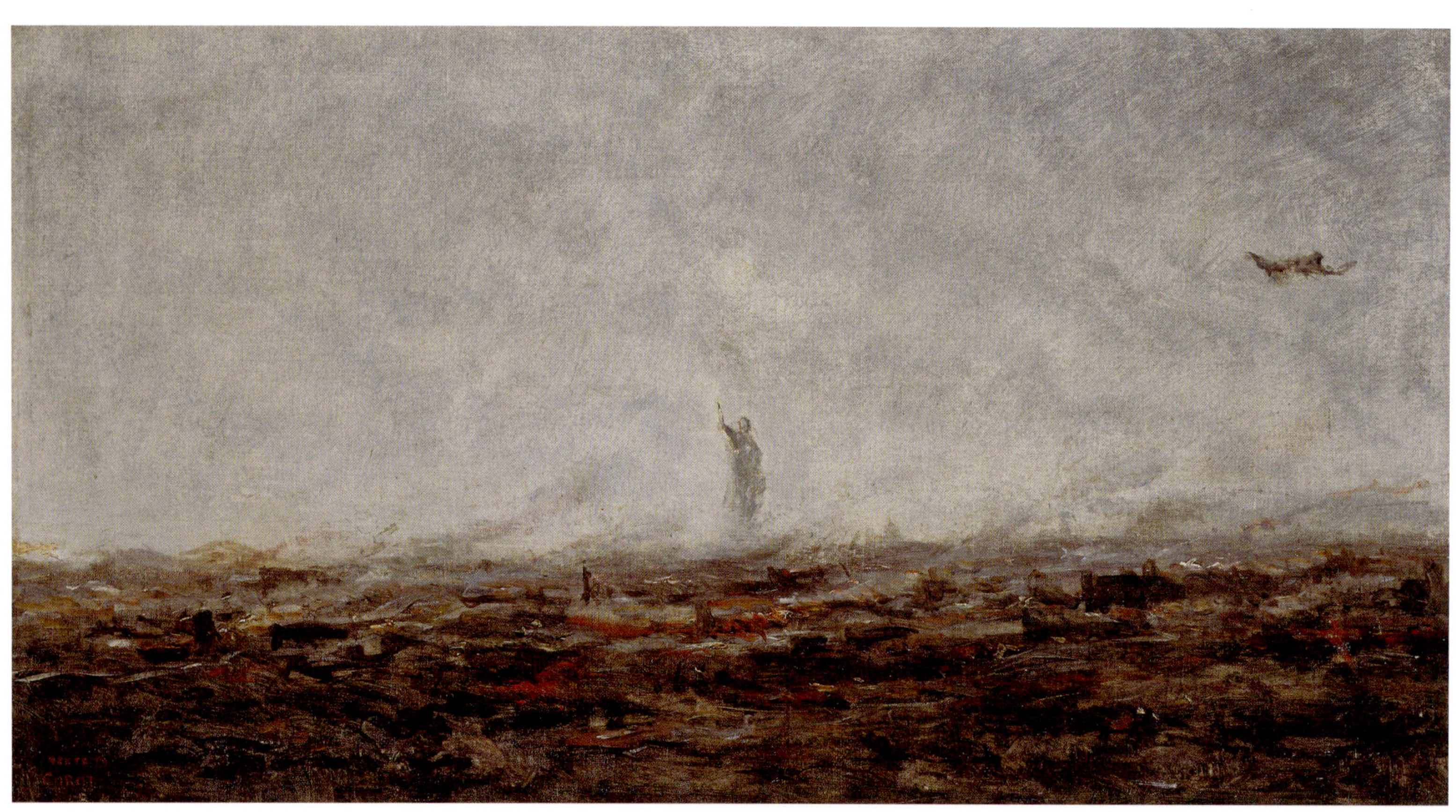

Gustave Doré
1832–1883
Sister of Charity Saving a Child, Episode in the Siege of Paris 1870–1
Oil paint on canvas 97 × 130

Musée d'art moderne André Malraux, Le Havre

During the war and the Siege of Paris Doré enlisted in the National Guard and remained, like Manet and Degas, in the capital. From July, having a foreboding of the inevitable outcome of war and witnessing many tragic events, he increased his production of sketches and quick documentary drawings. At almost forty years old, this prodigious draughtsman was tremendously successful and starting to establish a solid reputation in England as a religious painter. The events of 1870 awakened his ambition to win fame in history painting.

Whether painter or illustrator, Doré remained above all a wonderful storyteller whose compositions were genuine theatrical scenes. After the war this fervent patriot would paint large allegorical compositions fuelling the spirit of revenge that emerged from the loss of his native Alsace. Yet none of these works that appeared in the artist's posthumous sale would be acquired by the Third Republic's administration.

The *Episode in the Siege of Paris* was painted by Doré during the winter of 1870–1, as mentioned by Théophile Gautier, who saw the picture at the artist's studio, as did the Englishman Blanchard Jerrold, Doré's first biographer. The scene depicted takes place in rue Gay-Lussac, near the Val de Grâce. A convent had been built there for the Sisters of the Adoration during the Second Empire. The wall in front of which a young nun is running could be that of the monastery where she hopes to take refuge. The night is freezing cold. In the distance the sky continues to blaze because of a fire. During the siege the artillery installed by the Germans pounded the Left Bank and southern suburbs of Paris daily, causing many civilian casualties. The blood spattered on shrapnel-dotted snow recalls this incessant menace. The theatrical effect of the shadow projected onto the wall anticipates great moments of expressionist cinema.

The nun draped in black carrying a blanket-wrapped child forms a compact grouping. In his painting Doré, the mystic, inverts values. While a civic guard writhes on the ground and is powerless to protect the population, the nun, an anonymous heroine, leaves her contemplative life to rescue the weakest. Subsequently, Doré composed a sculpture from this moving subject. The original plaster was exhibited in the Salon of 1881 under the title *Christianisme* (Christianity; no.3824). IC

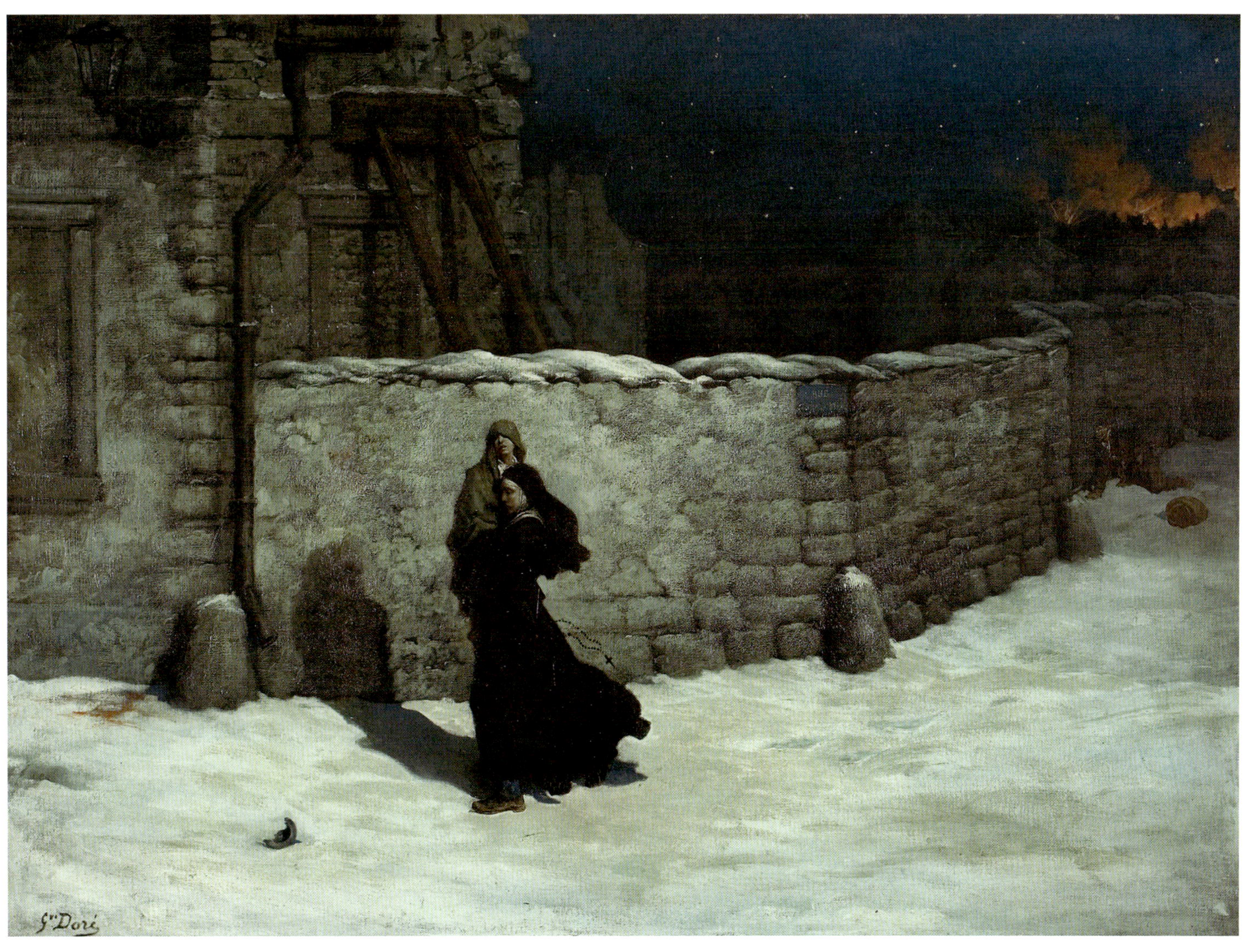

Jean Louis Ernest Meissonier
1815–1891
The Siege of Paris 1870–84
Oil paint on canvas 53.5 × 70.5

Musée d'Orsay, Paris. Bequeathed by Elisabeth Meissonier, the artist's widow, 1898

Meissonier was fifty-five years old when the Franco-Prussian War erupted. At the time, he was immensely popular with art collectors who acquired at premium prices his little genre paintings in which soldiers and costumed gentlemen evoke the pleasantness of a picturesque *ancien régime*. A fervent patriot, Meissonier remained in Paris during the siege by Prussian troops, and left his paintbrushes in order to serve as Lieutenant Colonel in the general staff of the National Guard. He was present at the catastrophic episode of the Second Battle of Buzenval on 19 January 1871, which was followed by the surrender of Paris. A witness to the first days of the Parisian insurrection, the artist displayed profound resentment against the Communards and, in particular, against Courbet, whom he helped exclude from the Salon.

The painting of the *Siege of Paris*, bequeathed by the artist's widow to the nation in 1898, is the result of a personal initiative reflecting an event experienced first-hand by Meissonier, who only very rarely tackled the history of his time. He worked on it during the year 1871, having returned to his large house in Poissy, which enemy officers had occupied during autumn 1870. Reworked and enlarged in 1884 for an exhibition at the Georges Petit Gallery, the work, based on a painful experience, remained partially unfinished. The patriotic agenda of the painting, which combines realism and allegory, is at first glance shown in the organisation of colours, favouring blue, white and red in keeping with the large tricolour flag placed in the centre. The imposing shrouded figure of the City of Paris clothed in a lion skin, symbol of courage, confronts Famine, an emaciated woman who flies through a stormy sky. The latter is accompanied by an eagle, emblem of a predatory Prussia. Victims writhe in the foreground strewn with the palm fronds of martyrdom, while on the knoll behind them, in a heroic symphony that brings together men of all ages and conditions, the combat against the assailants continues.

Certain figures were clearly identifiable for the artist's contemporaries, such as that of the talented young painter Henri Regnault, who died in combat at the age of twenty-seven and whom Meissonier depicts kneeling at the foot of the allegory of Paris, who is sheltering him in her lap. Among the ranks of the future impressionists, the painter Frédéric Bazille, who was close to Claude Monet, met the same destiny when, aged twenty-eight, he gave his life at Beaune-la-Rolande. Revolted by the human cost, for which he blamed not only the German attacker but also the incompetence of French officers and Napoleon III's pride, Meissonier delivered this particularly dark vision of events. IC

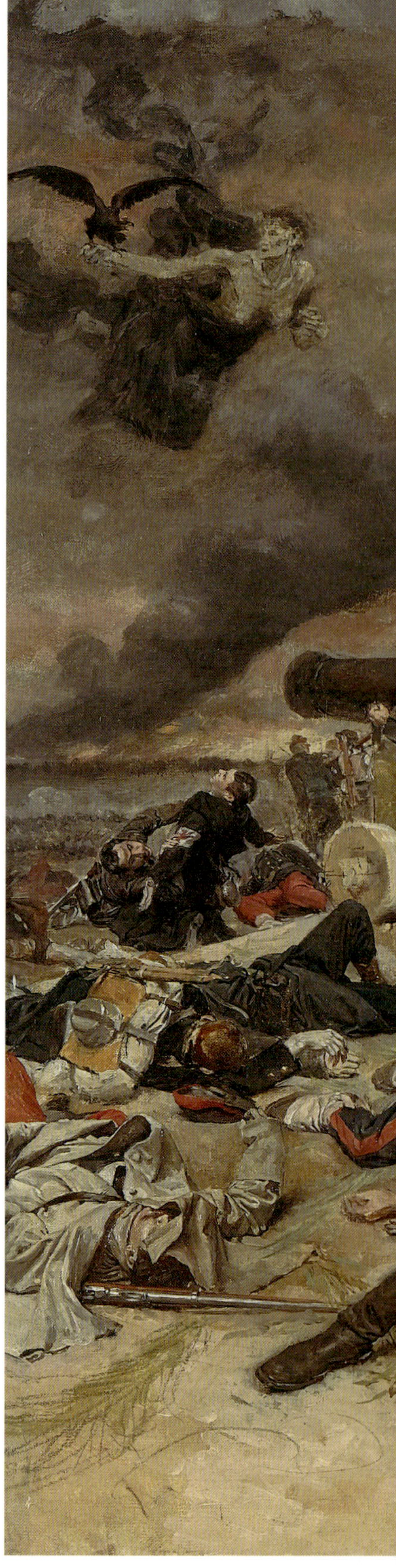

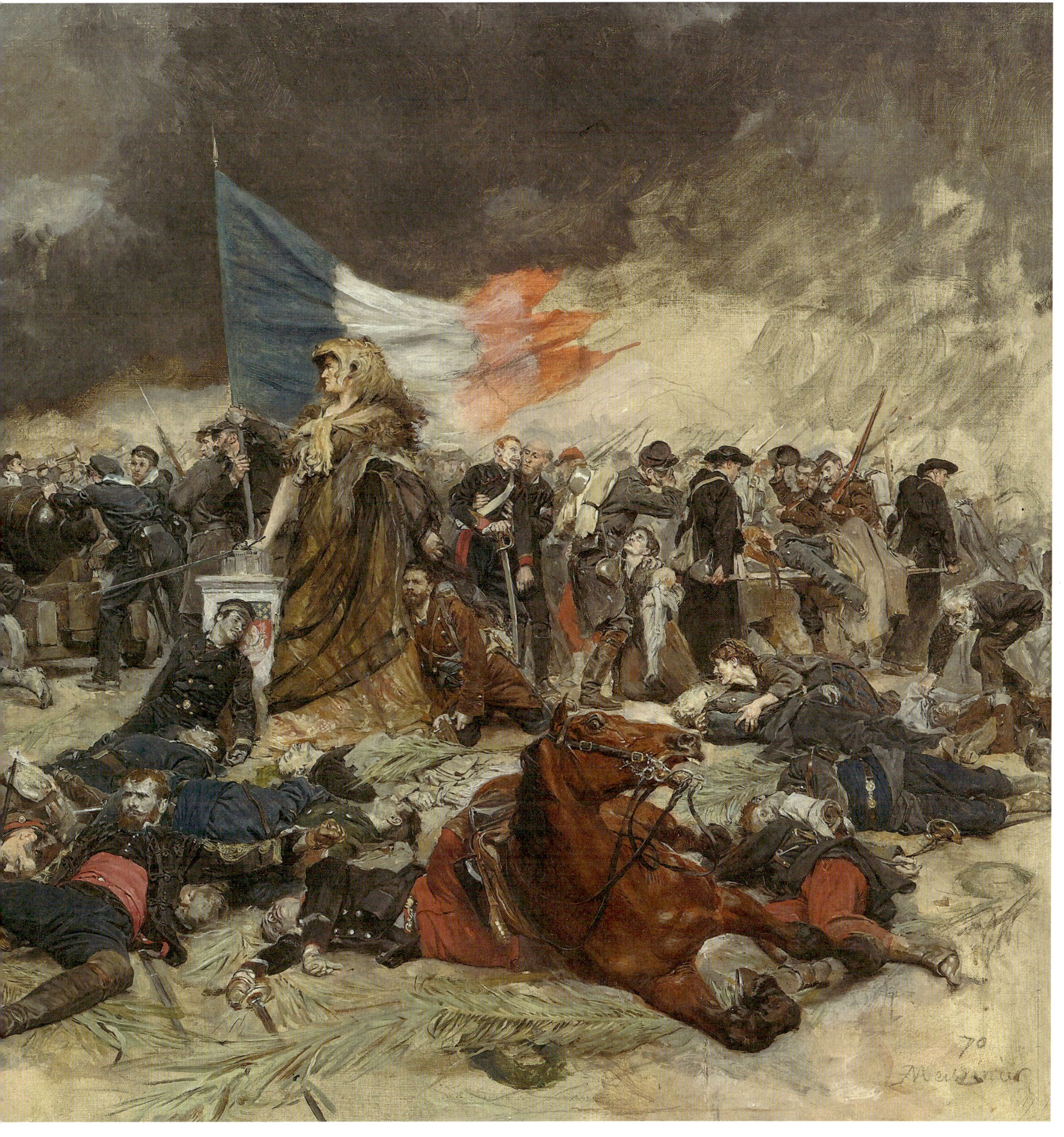

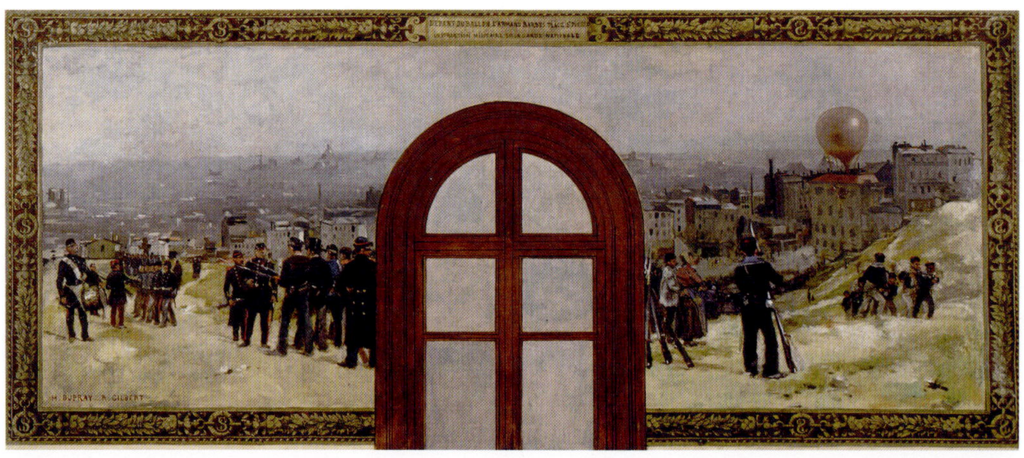

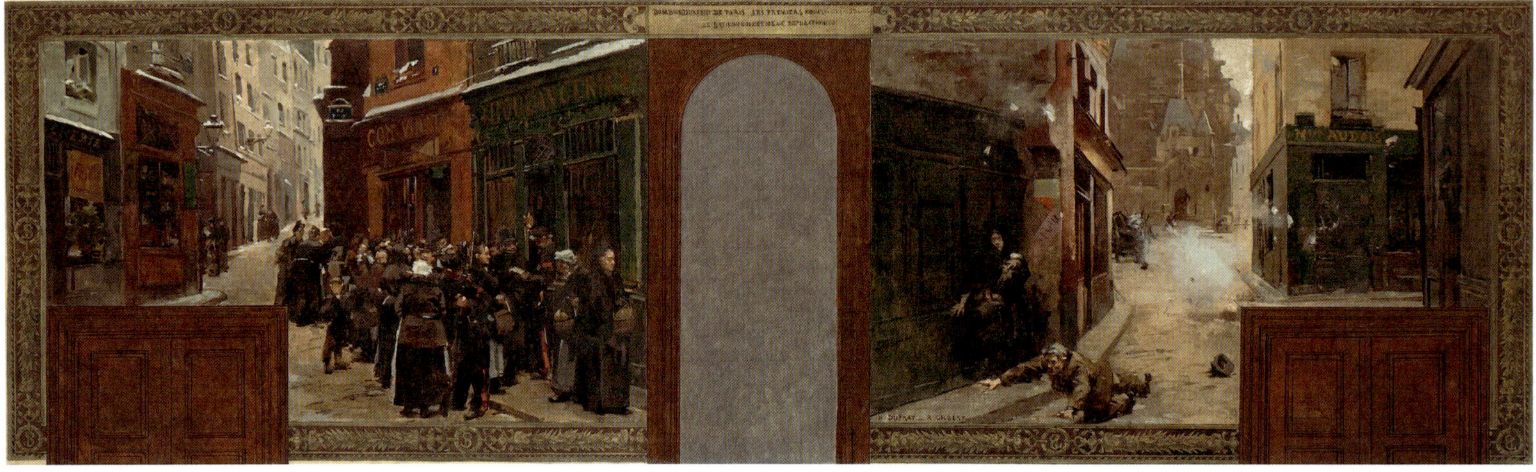

Henry Dupray
1841–1909 and
René Gilbert
1858–1914

Training the National Guard – The Departure of the Armand-Barbès Balloon, Place Saint-Pierre 1889
Sketch for the Prefect's Office in the Hôtel de Ville, Paris
Oil paint on canvas 49 × 109

Petit Palais, Musée des Beaux-Arts de la Ville de Paris

Rationing the Population – Bombardment of Paris 1889
Sketch for the Prefect's Office in the Hôtel de Ville, Paris
Oil paint on canvas 48.5 × 155

Petit Palais, Musée des Beaux-Arts de la Ville de Paris

Rebuilt after the fires of the Commune, the Hôtel de Ville was inaugurated on 13 July 1882. The salons on the first floor were intended as richly decorated reception spaces. The City of Paris was administrated by the Prefect of the Seine, who was appointed directly by the republican government. The rooms intended for this high representative of state were supposed to emphasise the importance of his executive power. The choice of commemorating the Siege of Paris almost twenty years later may seem paradoxical since it led to military defeat. The episodes depicted in the Hôtel de Ville would place more emphasis on the Parisians' determination to defend liberty, thus contrasting moral victory with a defeat that was felt to be undeserved.

The decoration in the Prefect's grand salon was supposed to follow a specific programme. Twenty painters participated in a selection competition that opened on 6 March 1889. The themes chosen called for a style that was more documentary than epic, so as to give a feeling of truth to the idealised memories of the Siege of Paris. The painters Dupray and Gilbert, working in collaboration, proposed a series of sketches that received a second prize, the commission finally going to the painter Adolphe Binet.

Henry Dupray, a native of the town of Sedan, specialised in large compositions with military subjects and worked occasionally as an assistant producing panoramas. He appeared among the artists who participated in *The Siege of Paris, 1870–1: Exhibition of Civil and Military Defence Episodes*, which opened at the Parisian gallery of Paul Durand-Ruel in November 1871. Dupray, whose studio was situated in Place Pigalle, had probably shared the daily life of the people of Montmartre during the Siege of Paris. His assistant René Gilbert brought to the project his skill as a portraitist and genre painter.

The sketches submitted to the judges accurately reproduced the layout of the walls intended for the artwork and took into account the position of the doors. One of the panels evokes an unusual event that took place on 7 October 1870 at Place Saint-Pierre in Montmartre. Léon Gambetta, Minister of the Interior, left besieged Paris by air in order to fly over the German lines, reach Tours and reorganise the defence. The balloon was symbolically named 'The Armand Barbès' in homage to a republican opponent of the July monarchy who died in exile a few months before the collapse of the Second Empire. Due to a lack of aeronauts in Paris, volunteer sailors and gymnasts were quickly recruited to be taught the rudiments of aeronautics. This detail did not escape the painters who depicted a group of sailors in training in the foreground on the right. In the decorative programme representations of military episodes and scenes of daily life were supposed to alternate. Dupray and Gilbert chose to show Parisians in a working-class neighbourhood in order to better portray the starving and bombarded city. These studies, which seem to have been done on the spot, describe without exaggeration, in the shadowy light of winter, the condition of the civil population during five long months of siege. IC

Jean-Baptiste Carpeaux
1827–1875
Sketchbook on the Siege of Paris during the Franco-Prussian War
1870–1
Drawings in chalk, pastel, pen and ink, sanguine, 76 pages, hardcover binding 11.7 × 15.3

Petit Palais, Musée des Beaux-Arts de la Ville de Paris

Throughout his life, starting with his formative years, Carpeaux utilised pocket-size sketchbooks with a preference for black chalk and charcoal, which made it possible to modulate the line and effects of depth. The rapidity of execution recreated movement, barely glimpsed scenes that sometimes became abstract motifs on paper. Used haphazardly vertically or horizontally, on single or double pages, the sketchbook of the Siege of Paris contains forty-five drawings.

Carpeaux was mainly interested in troop movements and especially fixed his gaze on cavaliers and foot soldiers. In particular, this admirer of Géricault loved to capture the movement of horses ridden by soldiers or pulling in harness (folios 55 and 62). Carpeaux sometimes even forgot military life and only saw the freely galloping mount (folio 72). Another animal, the sheep, also held his attention. Provisioning was one of the main preoccupations during the siege, which ended up starving the population, and Théophile Gautier, who left a very reliable account, reports immense herds of sheep gathered in the Bois de Boulogne to feed the capital. Gustave Doré did a striking drawing of them that is conserved in the Musée d'Orsay.[1] Carpeaux himself also drew the providential animal several times (folio 28, 34, 35, 44). Several scenes in a panoramic format make it possible to deduce city outskirts without being able to recognise precise topography. In their nervy and elliptical sketchiness, these drawings suggest, more than they describe, the inherent tensions of this state of siege that Carpeaux witnessed. IC

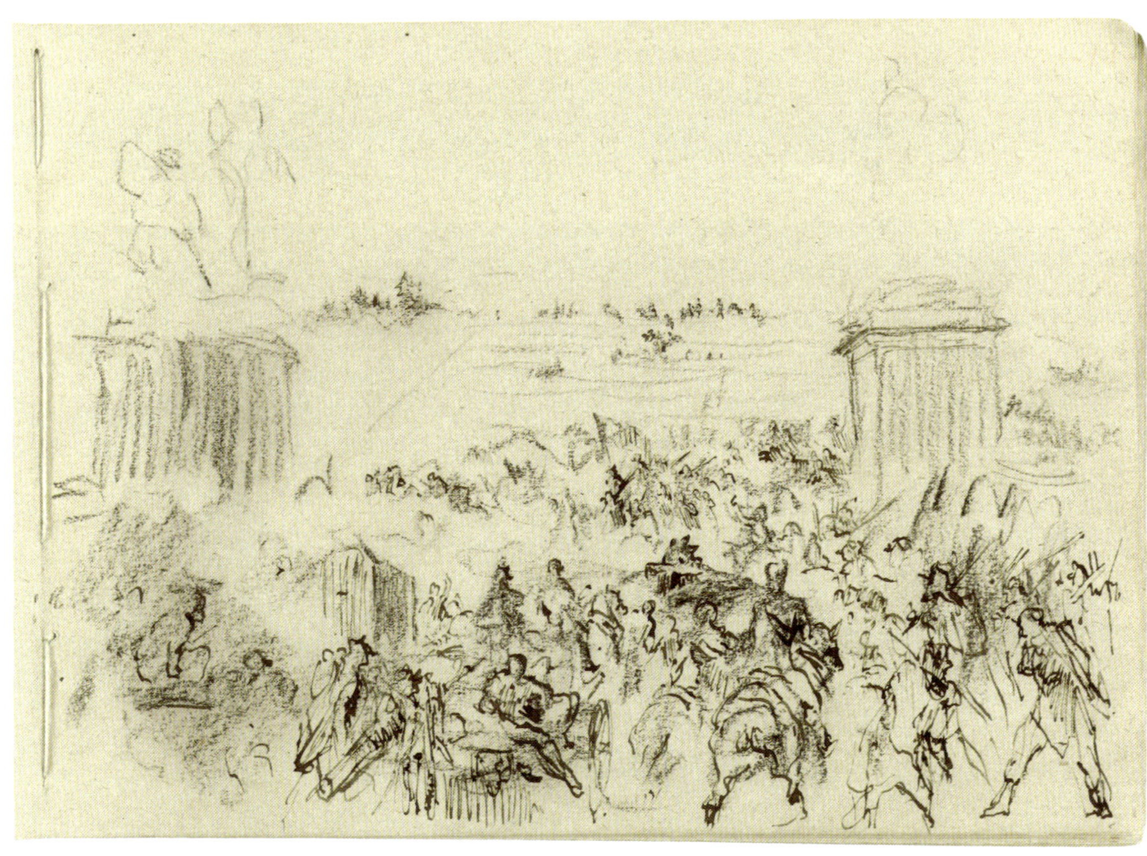

James Tissot
1836–1902
The Green Room of the Théâtre Français 1877
(Souvenir of the Siege of Paris) (1)
Etching on paper 38 × 27.6

Musée Carnavalet – Histoire de Paris

The Wounded Soldier c.1870 (2)
Watercolour on paper 35.5 × 25.2

Tate. Purchased 2016

Grand'garde 1878 (3)
Etching and drypoint on paper
45.5 × 29

Victoria and Albert Museum, London

A Cantinière of the National Guard
1870–1 (4)
Graphite on paper, 19.9 × 12.2

Malingue S.A., Paris

Thomas Gibson Bowles
1841–1922
The Defence of Paris; Narrated as it Was Seen, London 1871 (5)

Tate Library and Archive

Tissot's print series, the 'Souvenir of the Siege of Paris', recalls his time as both a soldier and witness during the Siege of Paris, when he served in the National Guard. While he made numerous on-the-spot sketches during the conflict itself, he waited until 1875 before beginning a series of six etchings to record his experiences. They made his own eyewitness account available to what he judged was an interested art-buying public.

The Green Room of the Théâtre Français is the only interior scene within Tissot's series. It depicts the sumptuously decorated Parisian theatre, the Comédie-Française, requisitioned as a military hospital. The etching shows an elegant room, flanked by portrait busts, in use as the unlikely home for two injured soldiers who are laid out in makeshift beds. There were reports that Tissot himself was injured during the conflict, and perhaps tellingly, he signed the print with his name across the cover of the empty bed in the foreground.[1] A number of Tissot's pencil sketches of wounded soldiers survive, suggesting he spent considerable time in the environs of the temporary hospital. Despite the use of the theatre's public foyers as a field hospital during the siege, a reduced programme of performances continued.[2]

The protagonist of Tissot's watercolour *The Wounded Soldier* is probably also shown within the environs of the Comédie-Française, as suggested by the panelled interior and the gilded mirror seen in the background. The injured soldier's uniform, to which Tissot, always taken with details of costume, pays typically close attention, is that of the Mobile National Guard. While the freshness of this watercolour might suggest it was made in situ at the Comédie-Française, it is also a highly resolved and carefully considered composition. Unlike the sketches that informed the etching of the theatre's interior, it did not result in a print. The watercolour remained in Tissot's possession until his death, perhaps kept as a private memento of the siege.

In *Grand'garde*, a second print from the Siege of Paris series, a determined soldier stands guard, a blanket wrapped around him as he battles against the wintry conditions. As Marshall has pointed out, many French soldiers froze to death during the siege, due to an abnormally cold winter.[3] The print is based in part on a sketch of the blanket-wrapped soldier made during the siege; this drawing had earlier been reproduced in print with the title *Out Post Duty*. In fact, seven of the drawings Tissot made recording his experiences during the siege were reproduced as illustrations to Thomas Gibson Bowles's book of 1871, *The Defence of Paris; Narrated as it Was Seen*. During the siege Bowles, a friend of Tissot's, was present in Paris as war correspondent for the *Morning Post*, something immortalised by one of the book's illustrations, in which he is depicted as 'a special correspondent' peering through a pair of binoculars. Tissot's illustrations were the perfect addition to a book lamenting the 'havoc and misery' Bowles had experienced in Paris,[4] as Tissot, too, was a genuine eyewitness to the conflict.

Tissot's drawing of a National Guard *cantinière* was also reproduced within Bowles's publication. The female *cantinières* accompanied the troops with provisions, their role something like 'nurse and sutler'; they also, however, took up arms on many occasions, playing an increasingly important role in the siege.[5] In his book Bowles described the 'smart little *cantinières*, in the nattiest of boots and "overalls"', who 'passed in and out of the ranks distributing the contents of their barrels'.[6] Despite the sometimes patronising attitude that they faced, many had considerable experience of battle and were among those who fought and were killed on both sides during the bloody defeat of the Paris Commune. Following the fall of the Commune, Tissot, a witness of much horror during both the siege and its grisly aftermath, left Paris for London. EJ

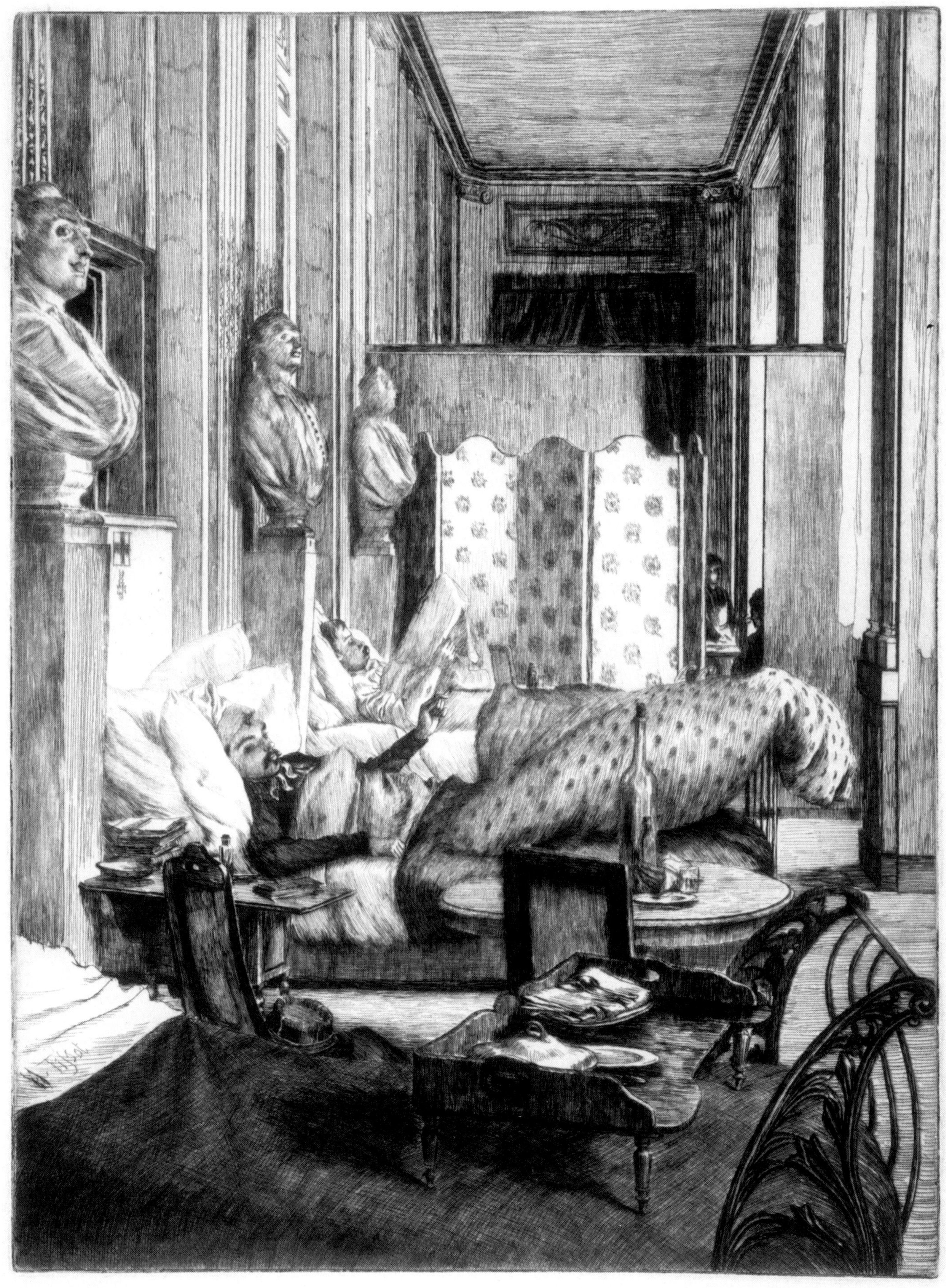

1

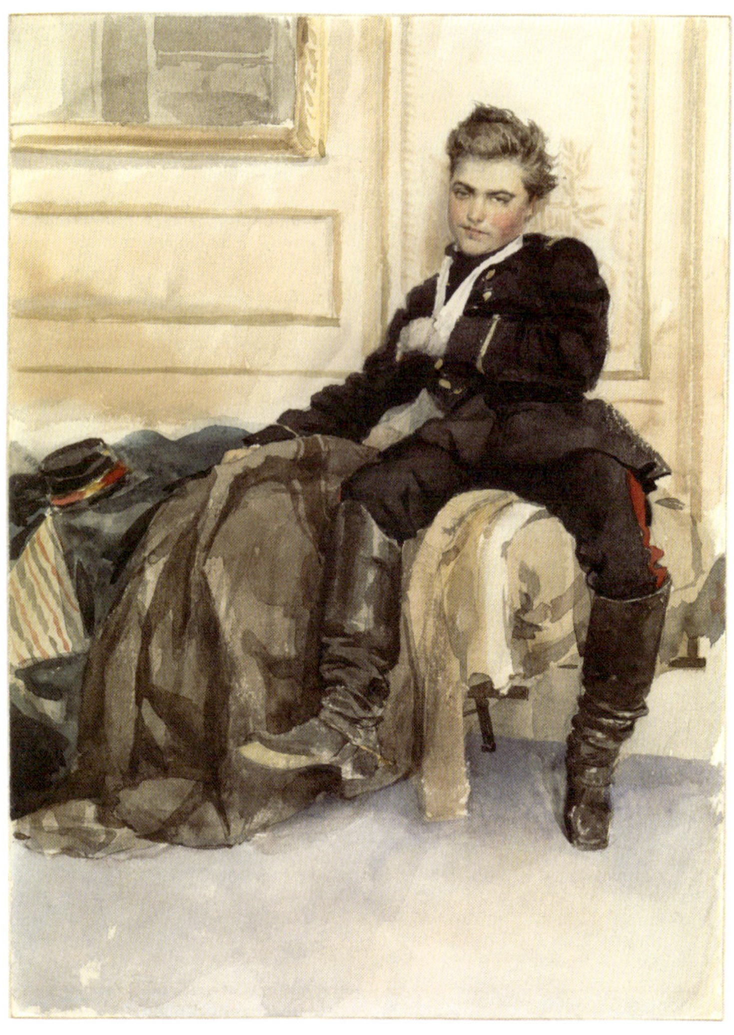

2

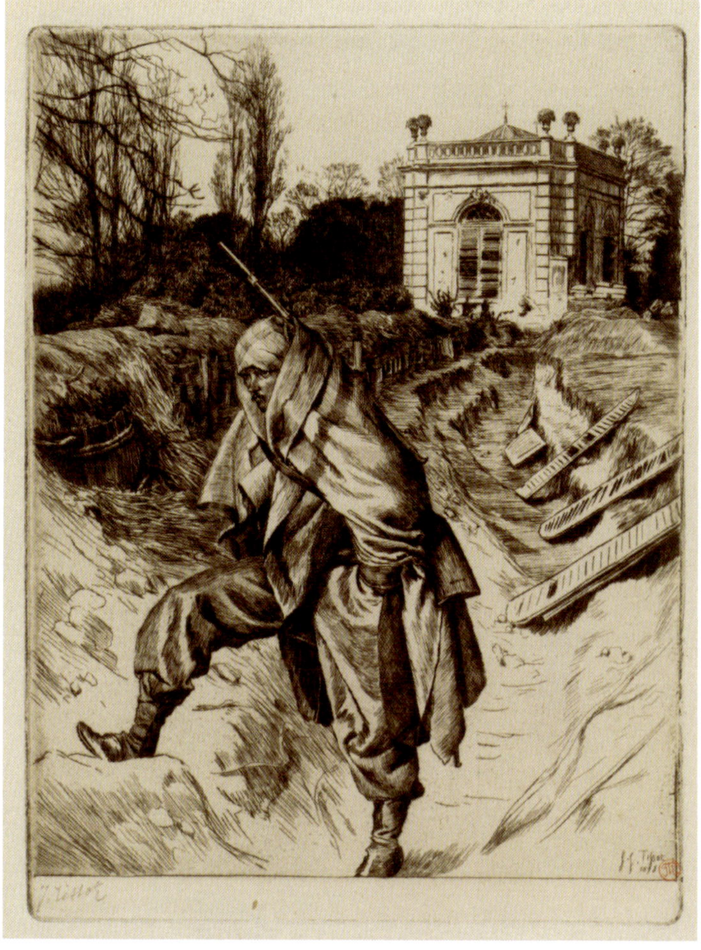

3

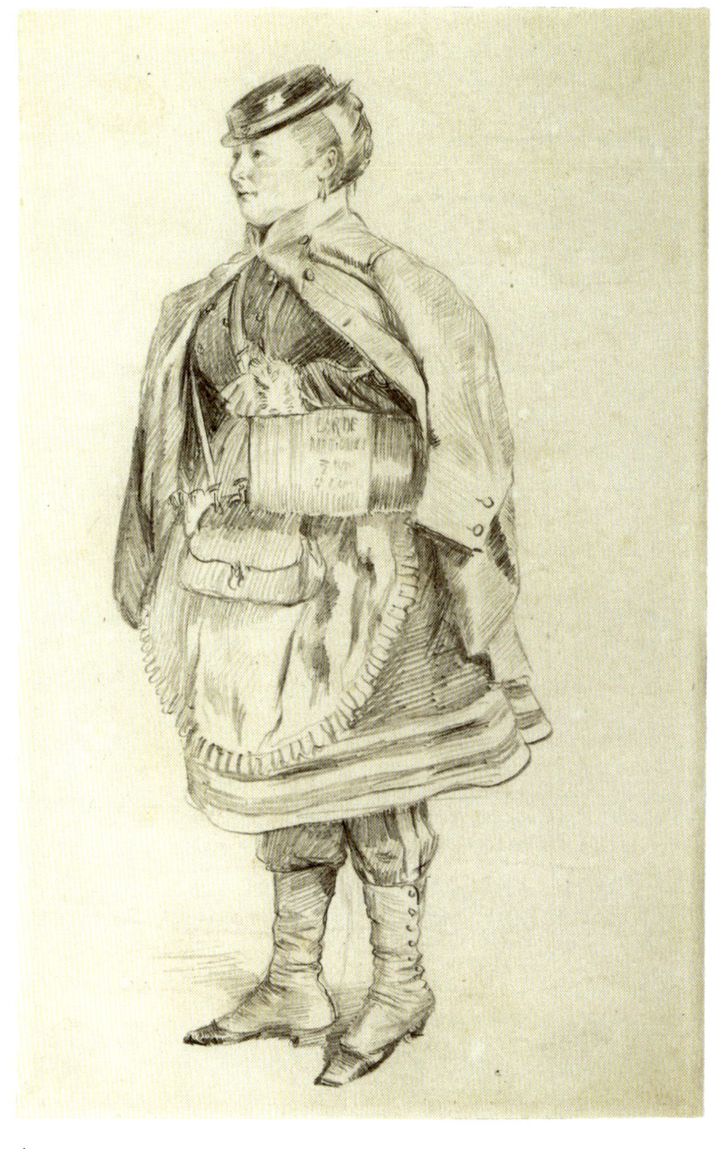

4

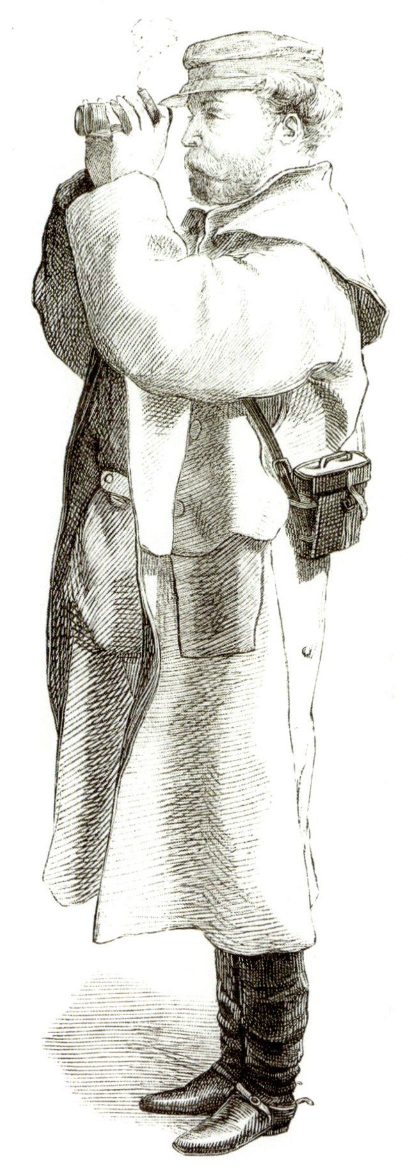

A SPECIAL CORRESPONDENT.

5

James Tissot
1836–1902
The Execution of Communards by French Government Forces at Fortifications in the Bois de Boulogne
29 May 1871
Watercolour on paper 28.3 × 19

Private collection

Thousands of Communards were killed during Bloody Week, the last days of the Paris Commune in May 1871. There are few visual records of the execution of the Communards by the French government forces, making this little-known watercolour and an accompanying sheet of notes by Tissot of great documentary as well as artistic importance. The events he witnessed may well have influenced his decision to leave Paris for London around this time.

The watercolour is based on a pencil sketch (Daniel Malingue S.A.) apparently made on the spot, in which thirteen dead bodies are shown laid out on the ground. The tall brick wall and, most disturbingly of all, a falling Communard only appear in the finished watercolour. The naturalistic depiction of the bricks, uneven in colour, and the green of the grass, scorched in some areas, serve to make the figures in the scene appear all the more shocking; what might have been an empty landscape scene is in fact littered with corpses and blood, the bodies of Tissot's countrymen.

Tissot's accompanying notes document the execution he saw, one of many such scenes in the city. The title translates as 'Notes taken during the execution of the National Guards who took part in the Commune on 29 May 1871'. Tissot's notes are fragmented and disjointed, the disorder of his writing surely reflecting the traumatic nature of the horrors he witnessed. He wrote of the Communards:

> You can see them from far away quickly going, each in turn, to the spot where they are killed. They fall like a rag doll and one can see the sergeant rushing to give the *coup de grâce*. Same ceremony the next day on other fortifications.[1]

Tissot's description does not shy away from the gory reality of these deaths. He added:

> There is very little blood on the spot where they were executed but lots of brains as a result of the *coup de grâce* in the ear.

There is a rough sketch of the fortifications on the back of Tissot's note, and the paper is signed: 'To Lady de Waldegrave [sic], with my highest consideration. James Tissot.' Lady Waldegrave was the owner of Strawberry Hill, which had been left to her by her second husband, George, 7th Earl Waldegrave, in 1844 – the note is stamped with the name of the house. In providing Lady Waldegrave with such uncensored descriptions, both written and visual, of the violence he had witnessed in Paris, Tissot was probably seeking to make the bloody events in Paris more widely known. Krystyna Matyjaszkiewicz has suggested that the watercolour and attached notes may have served as documentary evidence for Lady Waldegrave to share with her husband, the Liberal politician Chichester Parkinson-Fortescue, and his colleagues.[2] EJ

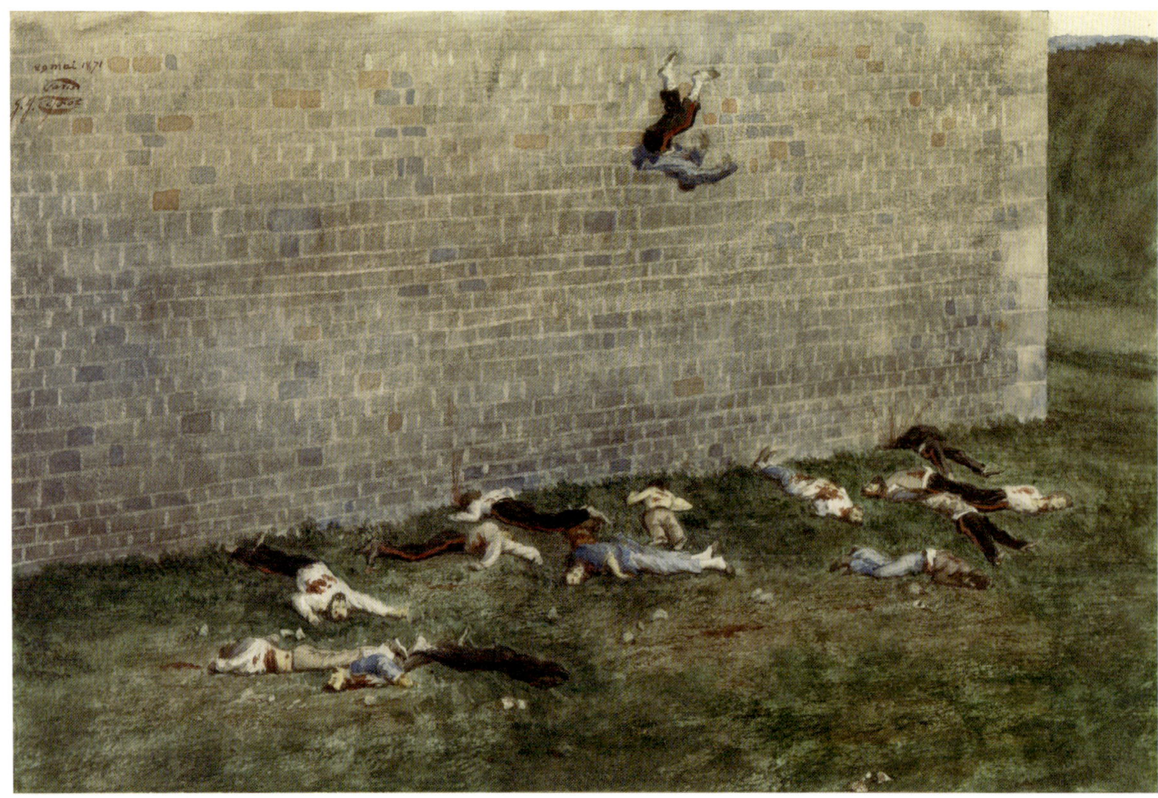

Anonymous artist
Untitled [Suresnes Bridge] c.1870 (1)
Albumen paper print 22 × 30

Alphonse Liébert
1826–1914
Châtillon, Redoubt on the Plateau, No.70 c.1871 (2)
Albumen paper print 17.5 × 25.2

Attributed to Charles Anthony Tune
1814–1887
Plate 179 [Vendôme Column] c.1871 (3)
Albumen paper print 17.2 × 22.1

Plate 176 [Marsan Pavilion, Louvre] c.1871 (4)
Albumen paper print 17.3 × 22.1

Charles Soulier
1840–1875
Paris in Ruins, May 1871 [The Ministry of Finance, Rue du Luxembourg] 1871 (5)
Albumen paper print 25.2 × 19.3

Paris in Ruins, May 1971 [Château d'Eau Fountain] 1871 (6)
Albumen paper print 19.3 × 25.1

Wilson Centre for Photography (all prints)

1

Photography was a favoured medium to record the destructions of the Franco-Prussian War and Paris Commune. On 3 July 1871 *Le Charivari* reported that an English merchant had purchased 50,000 photographs of the remains of the Column Vendôme for the London market.[1] This figure is rather difficult to reconcile with the number of prints now in circulation, but it has the merit of showing the importance given to photography capturing and disseminating images of the ruins of Paris and its surroundings at the time.

Châtillon and *Suresnes Bridge* both relate to the war and its impact on the outskirts of Paris. As a plateau, Châtillon, south-west of Paris, was a strategic place. French forces started to build a redoubt there when the conflict started. As well as being the location of two battles during the war, Châtillon was also the scene of combats between Communards and Versaillais. With its careful composition and single figure at the centre of a devastated landscape, Liébert's photograph is not so much about documentation than a meditation on war and aftermath. *Suresnes Bridge* offers another aesthetic view of ruins. The destruction of the suspended bridge that connected the Bois de Boulogne to Suresnes is not immediately apparent. The mirroring effect of the industrial landscape in the Seine creates a poetry that at first diverts attention away from the actual damage done to the bridge.

However traumatic and destructive the events of 1870–1 were, the ruins of Paris and its environs caused fascination, and the resurgence of an artistic tradition. As Théophile Gautier recounted in his *Tableaux de siège*: 'With a feeling which will be reproached, but which any artist would forgive because he surely will also have experienced it, we were struck, above all, by the beauty of these ruins.'[2] The Ministry of Finance, which Charles Soulier captured in his striking photograph (pp.42–3), was deemed more aesthetically pleasing as a ruin. In their *Guide through the Ruins: Paris and its Environs*, Ludovic Hans and J.J. Blanc remarked: 'The Ministry of Finances, which was never more than a mediocre monument, has become a superb ruin. Fire is a worker of genius. From this uniform, geometric, insolently regular mass, it has made a dynamic, decorative, interesting edifice.'[3] Soulier's superior, atmospheric composition of his *Château d'Eau Fountain*, on what is now known as the Place de la République, presents a rare subject within the 'repertoire' of views of the destruction.[4] Some specific sites, on the other hand, became prime choices for artists: not least the ruins of the Tuileries (pp.45–6), strongly associated with Napoleon III, and the Vendôme Column (see also p.44), which had been the first monument to be destroyed by the Commune at the hands of the Federation of Artists, of which Gustave Courbet was a leader. Photographs of both these sites, thought to be by Charles Tune, are typical of the representations of the ruins of the Commune in that they show the French capital in a state of desertion. Although this has partly to do with the time of exposure, which would have taken several seconds ('ghosts' are present in *Marsan Pavilion*), this was essentially an aesthetic choice, also adopted by other photographers of the ruins such as Franck (François-Marie-Alexandre Gobinet Franck de Villecholle) and J. Andrieu, as well as Alphonse Liébert. What became a convention in representing the destruction in Paris may well have been motivated by the restrictions implemented by the French authorities, and fear of repression. Indeed, an 1852 law requiring all commercial prints to be submitted to the Dépôt Légal was enforced, giving the state control over the type of images that were circulated. In addition to this, a decree enacted on 28 December 1871 banned images that 'disturbed the public peace', which did not apply to photographs of urban ruins. As Luxenberg has noted, 'the "disturbing outbursts" feared by the authorities must have been primarily anti-Communard, because no Commune sympathisers would have risked exposing their political stance at a time when criminal sentencing was often based on hearsay and suspicion'.[5]
CCP

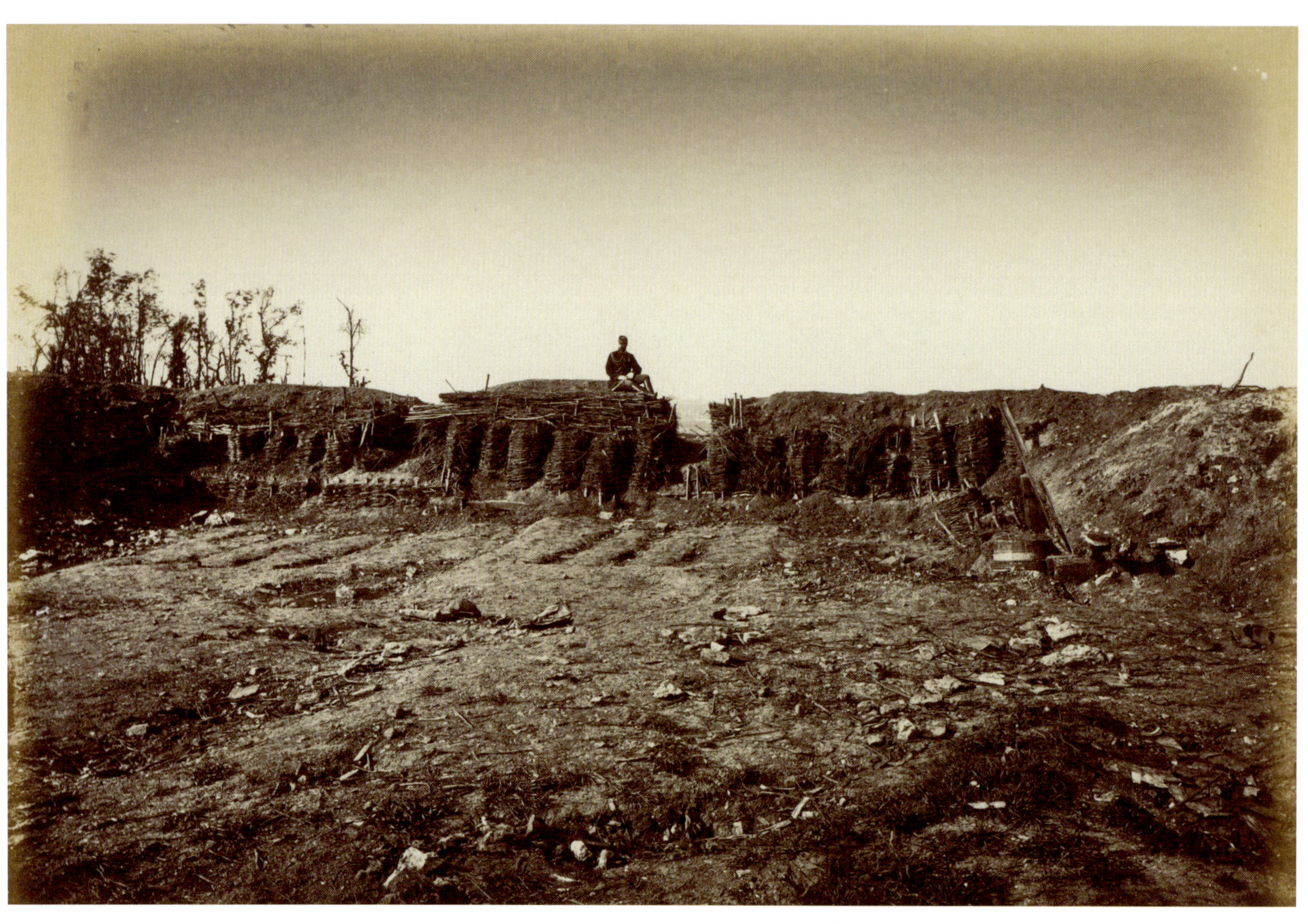

2

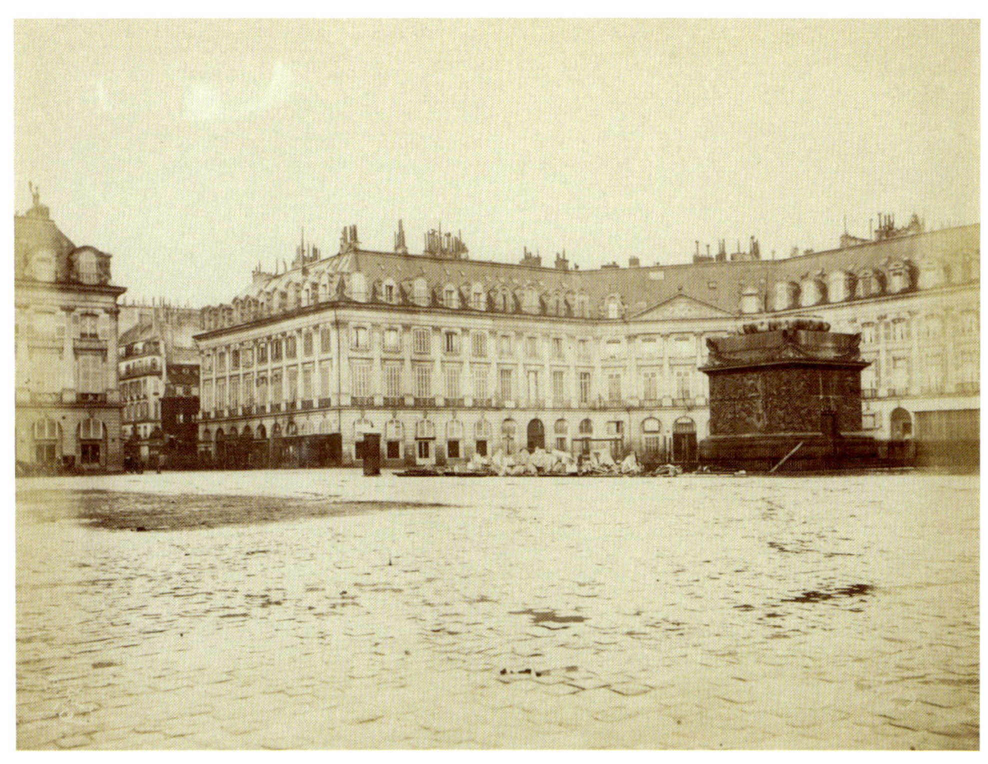

3

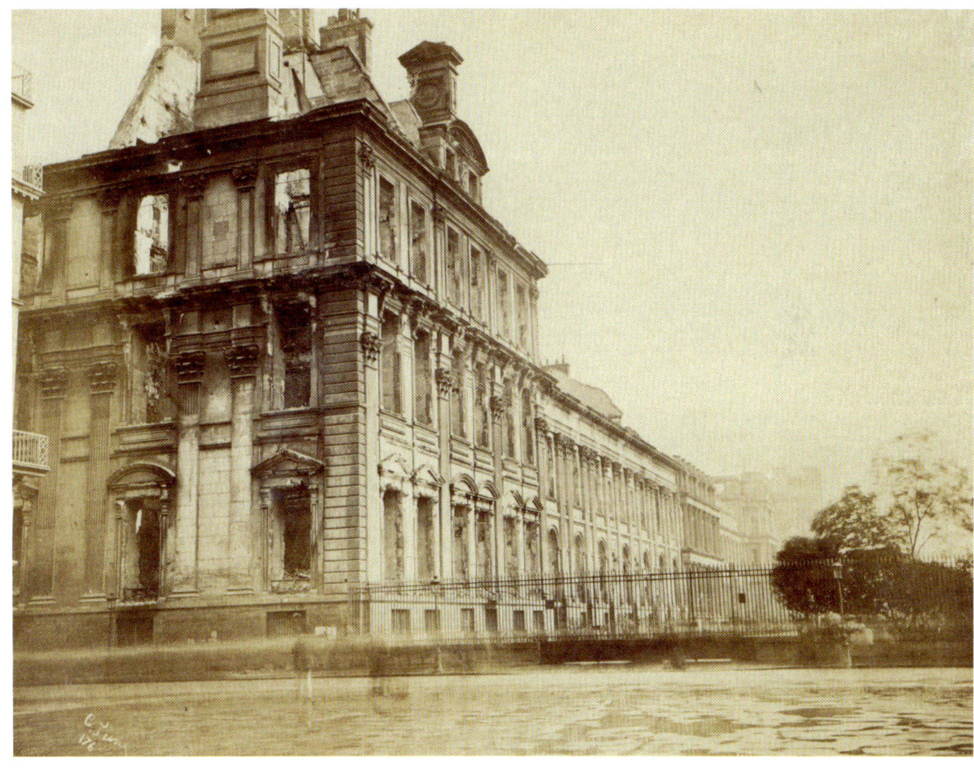

4

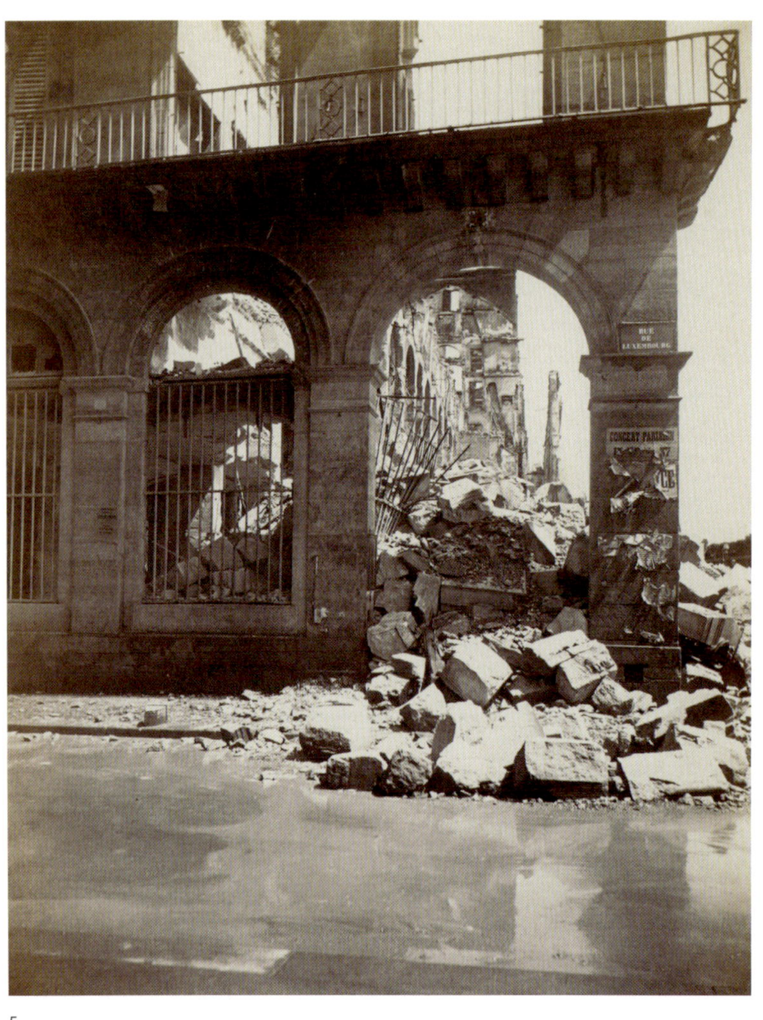

5

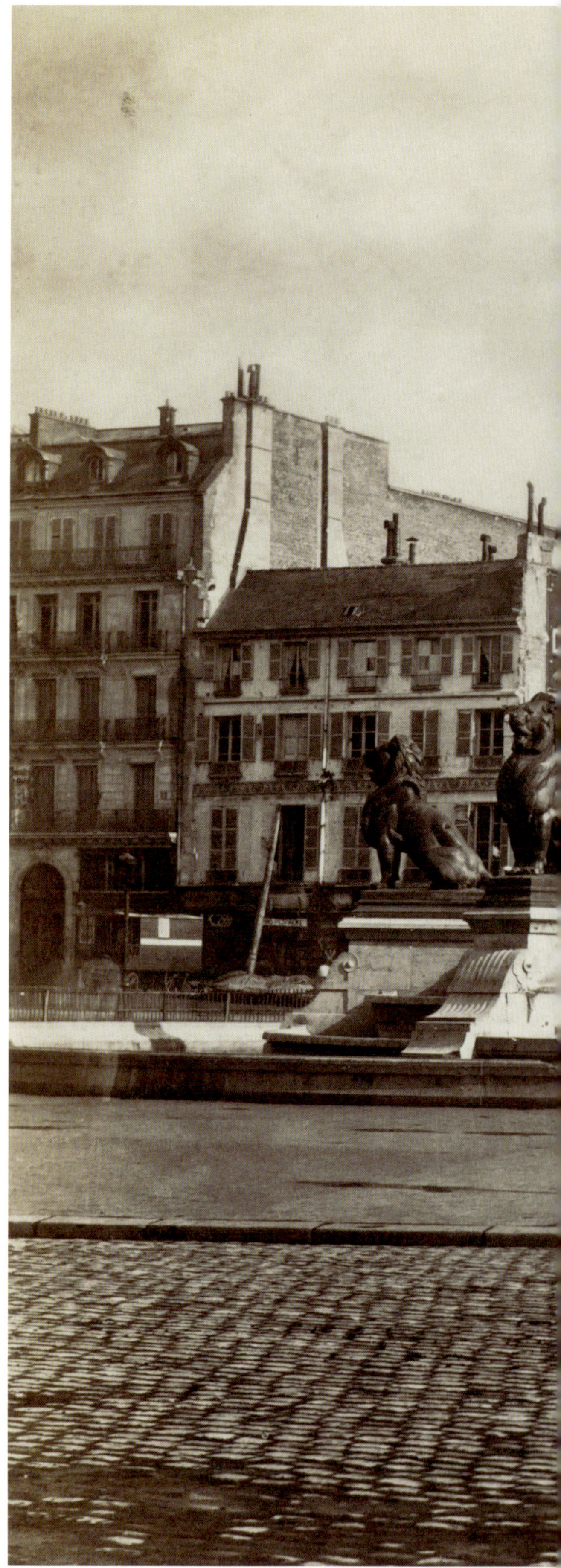

6

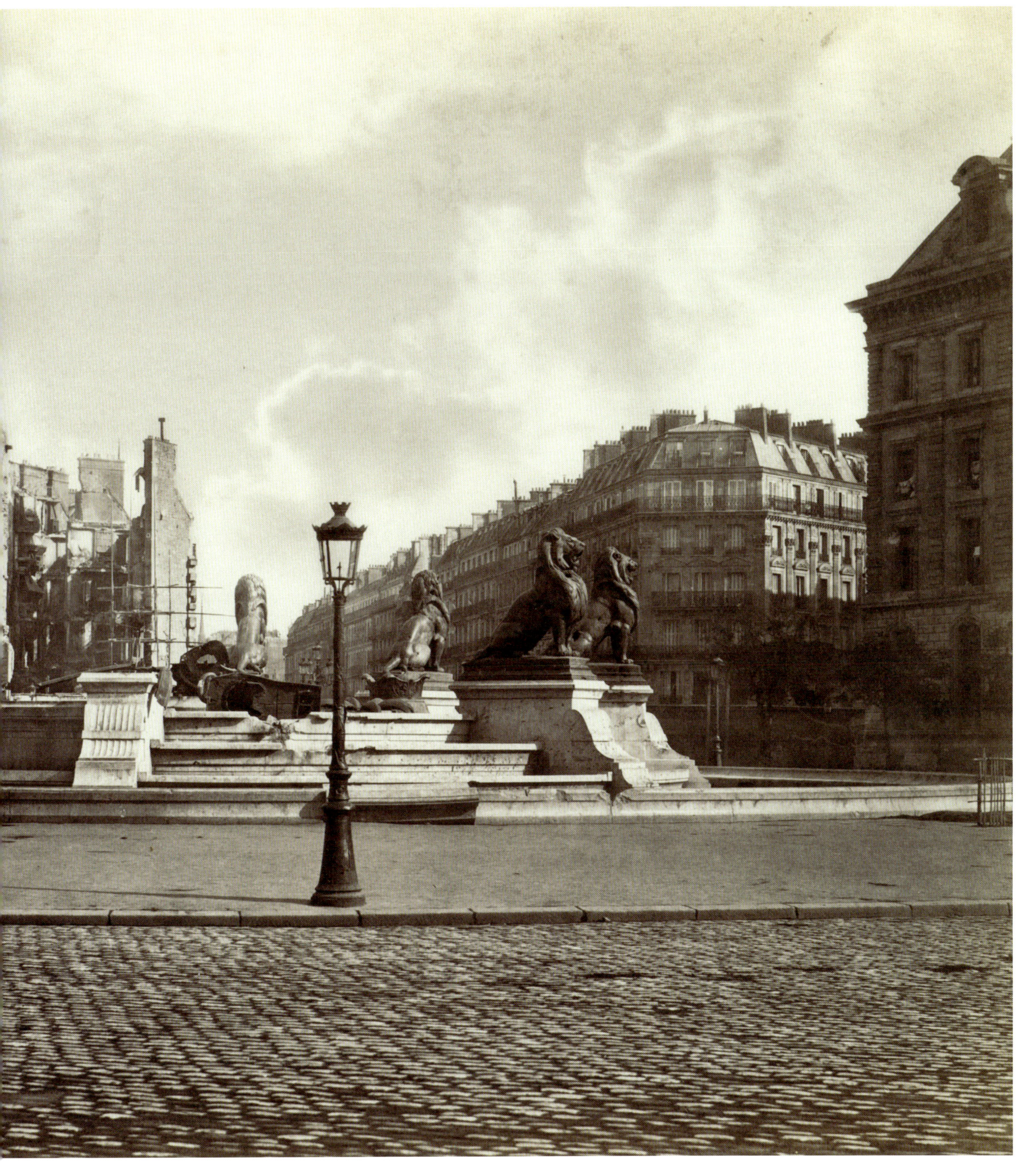

Isidore Pils
1813–1875
The Vendôme Column Toppled, 29 May 1871 1871
Graphite, watercolour and gouache on brown paper 32 × 51

Musée Carnavalet – Histoire de Paris

In taking care to date his drawing precisely to 29 May, that is less than two weeks after the demolition of the Vendôme Column by the insurgents, Pils situates himself at the heart of current events. At the end of Bloody Week the troops from Versailles came to put an end to the Commune of Paris. The spectacle of the pulverised monument erected to the glory of Napoleon I stands out as a metaphor of the chaos that has just overwhelmed the city. Photographs of Communards posing proudly in front of the stone debris while being acclaimed by the crowds were followed by those that exposed the vandalism caused by a futile insurrection.

Pils depicts the Place Vendôme deserted like a silent parenthesis between two episodes of a dramatic script which will make Courbet the expiatory victim of a return to order. On a pedestal, the republic's tricolour flag has replaced the reviled symbol of a new Caesar, the statue of Napoleon in a Roman toga. By placing the emperor's head outside the field of vision, Pils accentuates the disgrace. Even so, thc ruins of the levelled column still remain imposing. The idea of its reconstruction already seems to be under way. IC

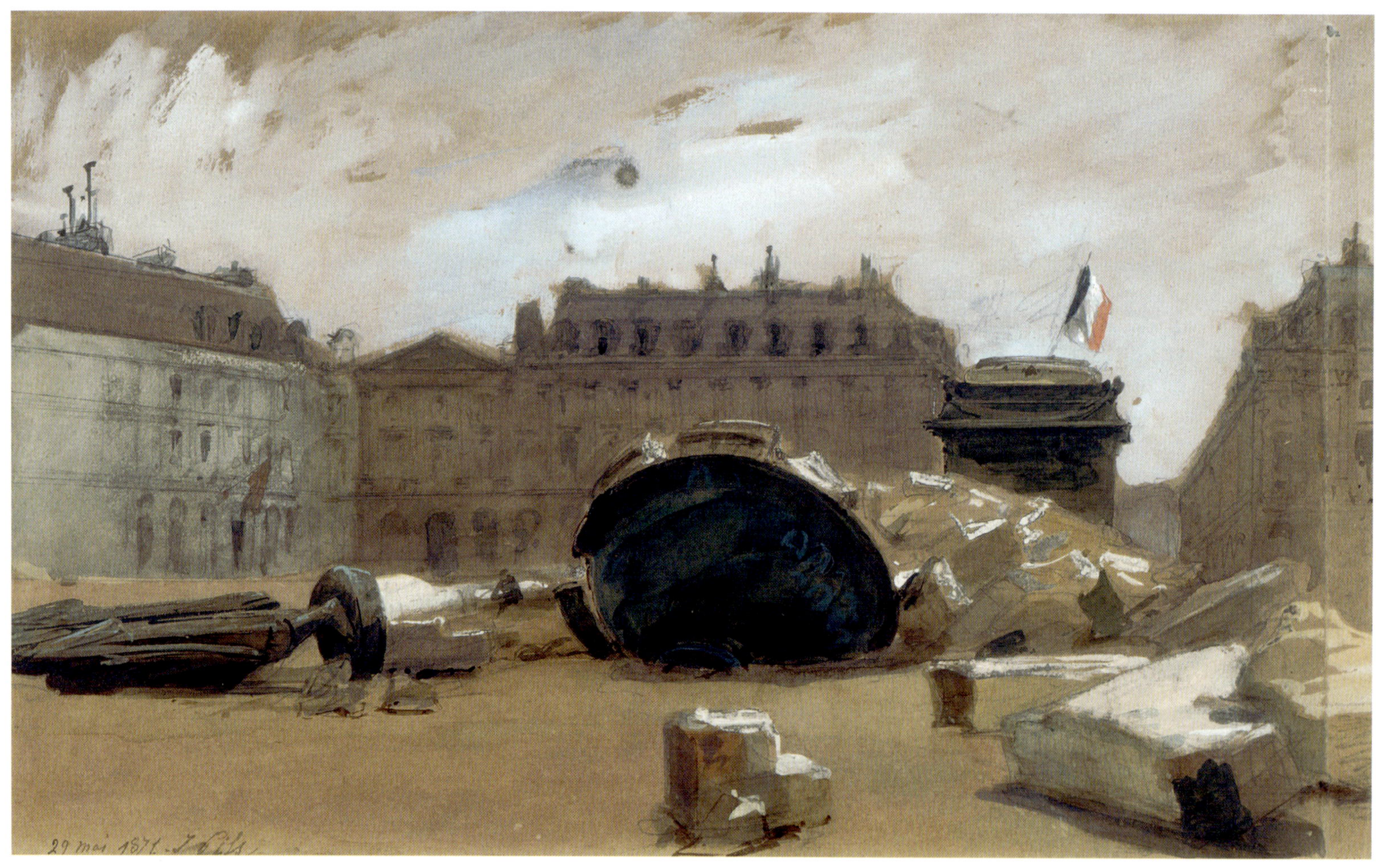

Isidore Pils
1813–1875
Ruins of the Tuileries 7 July 1871
Watercolour and gouache on paper
49.2 × 37

Musée Carnavalet – Histoire de Paris

Ruins of the Salon de Mars, Palais de Saint-Cloud 1871
Graphite, watercolour and gouache on paper 37.9 × 26.5

Musée Carnavalet – Histoire de Paris

Painting professor and member of the Academy of Fine Arts, Pils had led an honourable career during the Second Empire. Son of a soldier, the artist was familiar with the world of the military. He had followed the imperial army to Crimea and painted many scenes of troops during the siege of Paris. The reassuring presence of soldiers on guard in his diverse compositions that depict burned-out monuments adds a contemporary tone to the picturesque ruins, while giving the feeling that the situation is under control. The figures also served to emphasise the extent of the devastation sites, which would attract a flood of tourists after the events.

Of the various monuments that were burned down, the Palais des Tuileries was probably the one that was depicted the most. Spared from fire, the Arc du Carrousel, inaugurated in 1809, served as the entrance of honour to the palace courtyard. Its image in the background of the ruins kept alive the nostalgia for the glorious times of the Grand Army.

Built for Monsieur, Louis XIV's brother, the Palais de Saint-Cloud remained a major seat of dynastic power under the Second Empire. On 15 July 1870 war was declared during a council held by Napoleon III at the palace. From October the palace was occupied by the Prussians. It was set alight by a shell that the French fired from Mont Valérien during the Siege of Paris. The Prussians, who had no interest in defending a French edifice attacked by the French themselves, allowed the conflagration to spread. The building remained in ruins for twenty years before finally being razed in 1892.

Looking like a picturesque scene, Pils's watercolour conveys more profound feelings. The only fire that still burns in the Palais de Saint-Cloud is that of a simple bivouac. The irony of history is that ordinary soldiers settled into one of the most prestigious rooms of the grand apartments on the first floor, the Salon de Mars. Dedicated to the god of war, the room gave access to the ostentatious Gallery of Apollo. IC

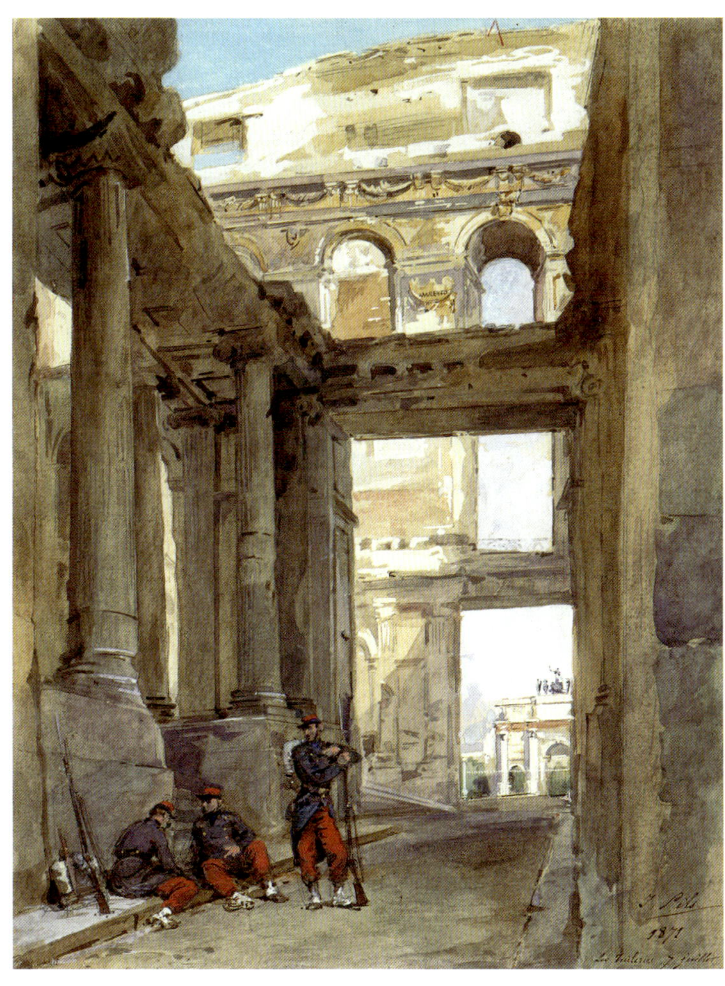

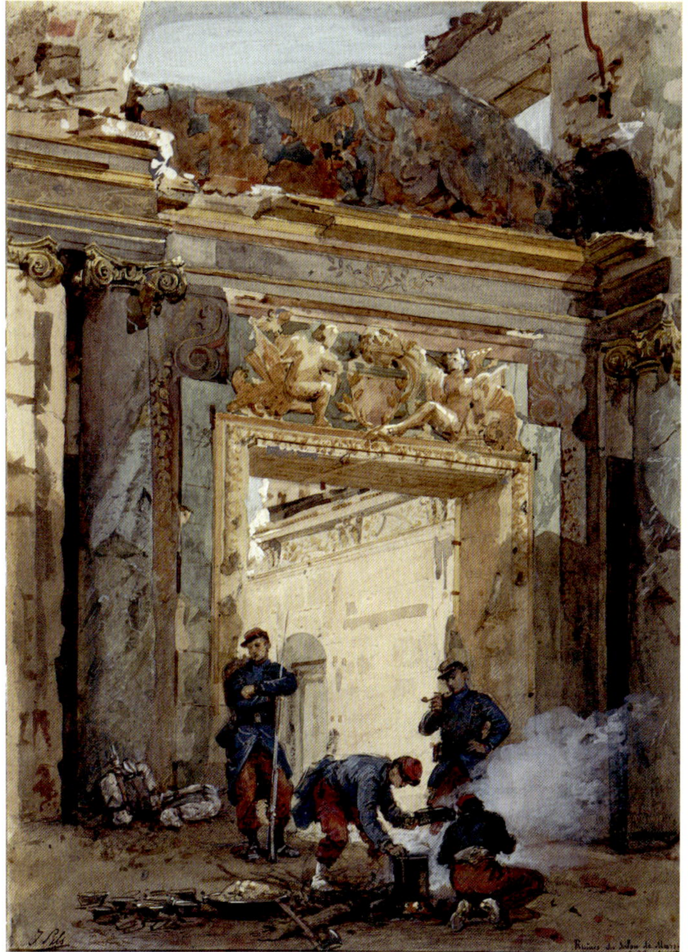

Charles-Joseph Beauverie
1839–1924
Ruins of the Hôtel de Ville: Stairway to the Prefect's Apartments June 1871
Pen and ink wash, white gouache highlights on paper 36.7 × 25

Musée Carnavalet – Histoire de Paris

Ruins of the Tuileries: View Taken from the Vestibule of the Grand Stairway June 1871
Pen and ink wash, white gouache highlights on paper 32.2 × 21

Musée Carnavalet – Histoire de Paris

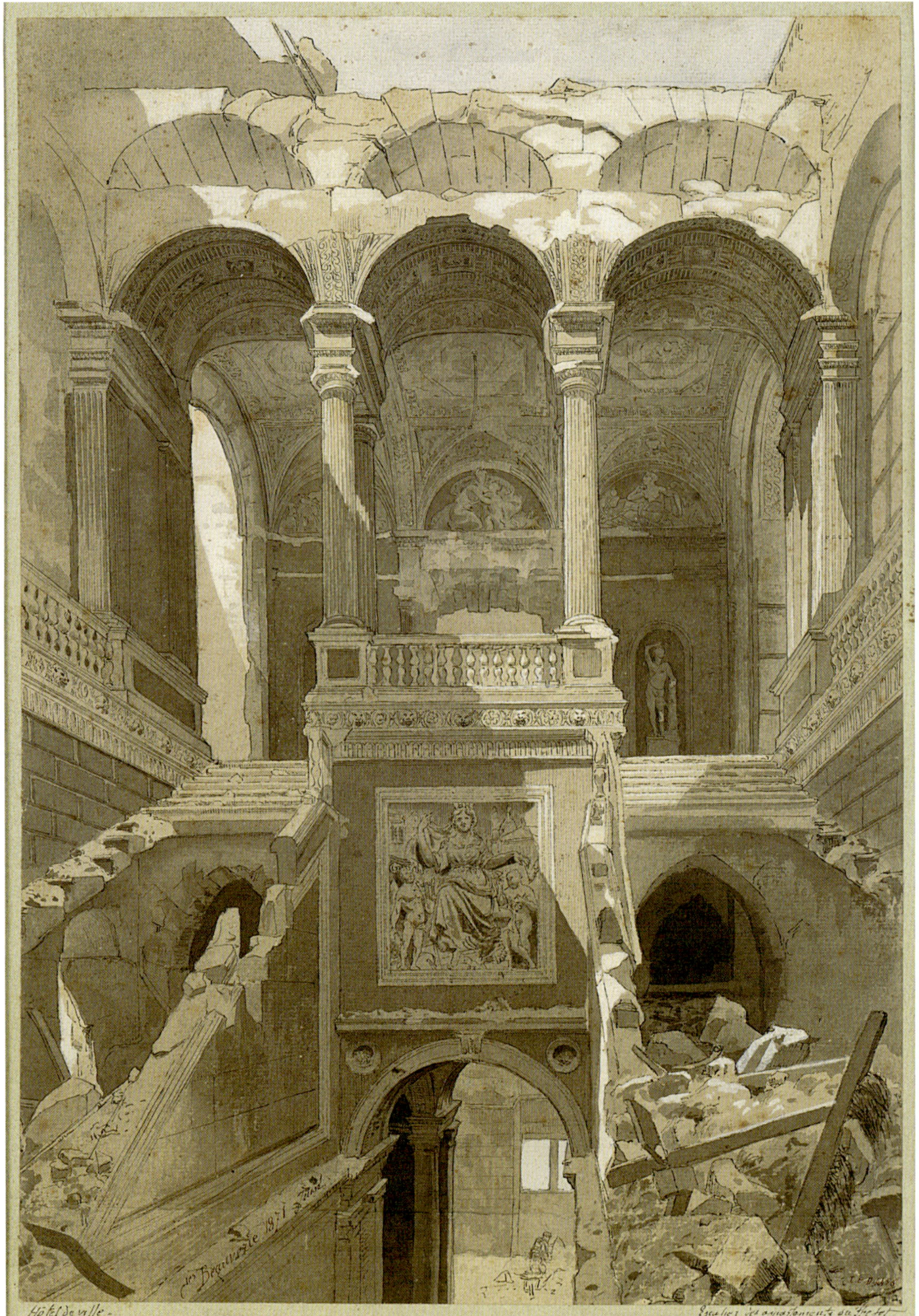

The suite of drawings that Charles-Joseph Beauverie carefully produced of sites consumed by fire during the Commune forms part of the post-romantic fascination for Parisian ruins that followed the Terrible Year. The frontal compositions seen from below emphasise the majesty of the places that seem to spring up as if from an ancient city. In its issue of 15 July 1871 *L'illustration, Journal Universel* published a view of the *Tuileries Chapel after the Fire* engraved in wood by Smeeton after an etching by Beauverie intended for *L'Illustration Nouvelle*, a review for collectors of original prints. In the columns of the bourgeois *Illustration*, views of the Tuileries in ruins accompanied a long text by Jules Claretie that compared the palace in the time of its imperial splendour with its remains after destruction by fire at the hands of the Communards. The language of Claretie's text describing the 'superb carcass' of the monument is in perfect harmony with Beauverie's drawings. The oxymoron could apply equally well to the ruins of the Hôtel de Ville, which burned on 24 May. After the roofs and floors had collapsed, all that was left of the grandeur of these seats of power was the strange beauty of their vulnerable stone skeletons.

The visual presentation of these relics with their powerful symbolic value made it possible to condemn the destruction while revealing the picturesque quality of modern ruins that tourists had plenty of time to contemplate: the reconstruction of the Hôtel de Ville of Paris only began in 1873, and the walls of the Tuileries were not razed until 1883. The drawing of the stairway to the prefect's apartment in the Hôtel de Ville was exhibited at the Salon de Lyon in 1874, and then in an etched version for the Salon des Artistes Français in Paris in 1875, showing that the subject was still appealing to collectors several years after the insurrection. IC

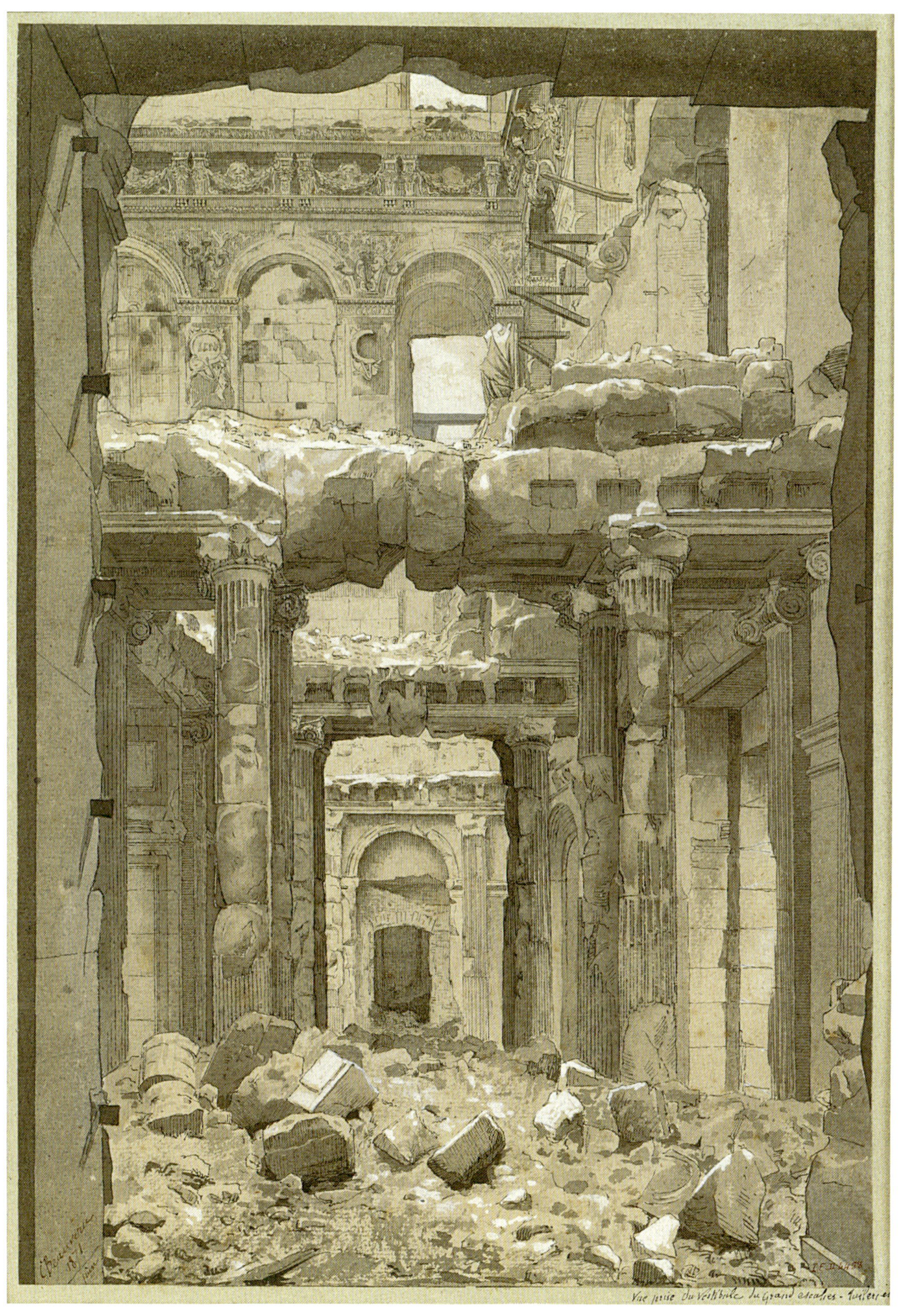

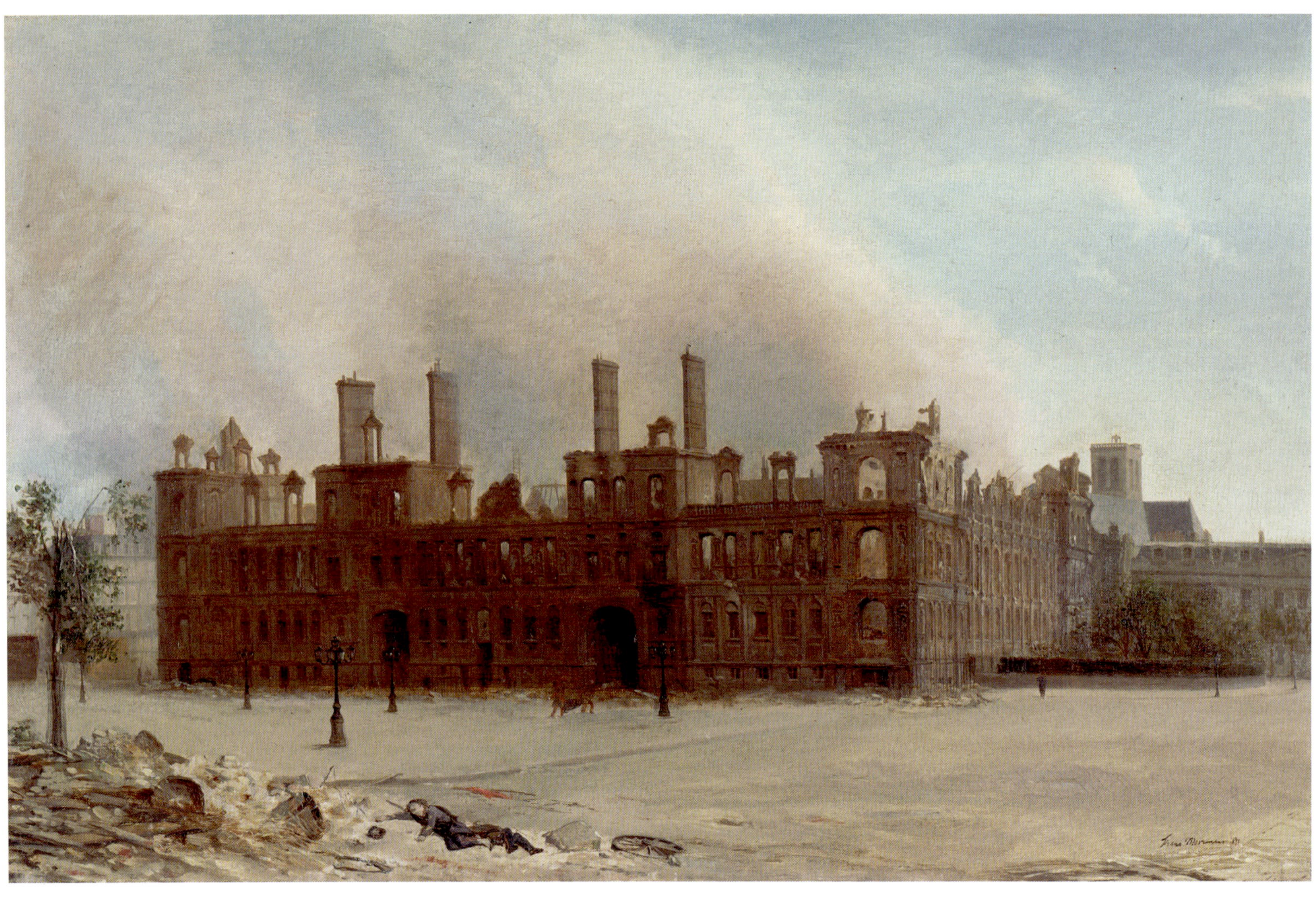

Frans Moormans
1832–1893
The Hôtel de Ville after the Fire of 1871 1871
Oil paint on canvas 55 × 82

Musée Carnavalet – Histoire de Paris

This painting by Dutch artist Frans Moormans shows the Paris Hôtel de Ville (City Hall) in smoke, in the aftermath of the fire started by the Communards on 24 May 1871. The building stood at the very heart of Paris, opposite the Ile de la Cité, and Moormans painted it from the Quai Pelletier (now Quai de l'Hôtel de Ville), looking south-east. Paintings of damaged architectural landmarks such as Moormans's are relatively rare, compared to the high number of photographs treating the same subjects. Whereas photographic prints tend to show deserted cityscapes (pp.39–44), this picture includes the bodies of two national guards on a pile of rubble in the foreground, and features a pool of blood nearby. To the left, a tree has been damaged by a shell. Further in the distance, walking past the remains of the Hôtel de Ville, two men carry a third corpse. Given the heavy human losses suffered during the Commune and ensuing reprisals, the likelihood is that the presence of these bodies in Moormans's painting makes for a more complete depiction of the scenes that were witnessed by Parisians.

The Renaissance palace itself, built between 1533 and 1628 after designs by Boccador, could not be salvaged after it burnt down. A new Hôtel de Ville was constructed on the site, replicating but also enlarging the original facade. It was completed in 1882. CCP

Edouard Manet
1832–1883
The Barricade c.1871
Lithograph on paper 46.2 × 32.5

The British Museum, London

Civil War 1871–3
Lithograph on paper 42.5 × 50.7

The British Museum, London
[not illustrated]

Edouard Manet was conscripted to be a member of the National Guard, and remained in Paris throughout the Prussian siege. His wartime correspondence reveals how trying this episode was for him and Parisians in general. Although he left the capital in February 1871, after the end of the siege, fellow artists enrolled his name as a member of the Federation of Artists of the Paris Commune. It appears that he did not return to the capital until after Bloody Week (21–28 May 1871), but Manet was deeply affected by the events and, according to Tabarant, even suffered a nervous breakdown.[1] Scenes of reprisal and repression were frequent after the Commune was crushed, and *The Barricade* and *Civil War* may have been inspired by Manet's witnessing of such scenes.[2] According to Théodore Duret, *Civil War* in particular was based on an on-the-spot drawing that Manet jotted down on paper at the corner of the rue de l'Arcade and Boulevard Malesherbes, where lay the lifeless body of a National Guard.[3]

Duret's account may or may not be reliable, but the fact that the lithograph is overtly inspired by Manet's *Dead Toreador* c.1864 (National Gallery of Art, Washington) is of primary importance in its genesis. *Civil War* is as indebted to that earlier painting as *The Barricade* is to the *Execution of Maximilian*, which Manet had been prevented from showing in Paris. Another level of mediation is added by Manet's referencing of Goya and his *Third of May 1808* (Museo Nacional del Prado, Madrid) and *Disasters of War* 1810–20 (plates 15 and 32) in particular. The lithograph of *The Barricade* is based on a drawing (1871, Szépművészeti Múzeum, Budapest) that made direct use, through a tracing, of the original composition of the *Execution of Maximilian*.[4] However, in this instance, the Mexican republicans forming the squad are replaced by French government troops targeting Communards. All these overt references to earlier works do not necessarily minimise the validity of Manet's contribution to representations of the events. As Juliet Wilson-Bareau has noted about the *Barricade*, 'it would appear that he deliberately turned to a source that represented, in a very similar context, a great expenditure of time and energy in order to express strong feelings in a "totally sincere" way'.[5]

In both *The Barricade* and *Civil War* the cobbles, or *pavés*, used to build barricades are omnipresent. In *Civil War* Manet signed his name and dated the lithograph on one such *pavé*, which had been emblematic of insurgency in Paris since 1830. *The Barricade* was never published in Manet's lifetime, but 100 lithographs of *Civil War* were printed by Lemercier in February 1874.[6] CCP

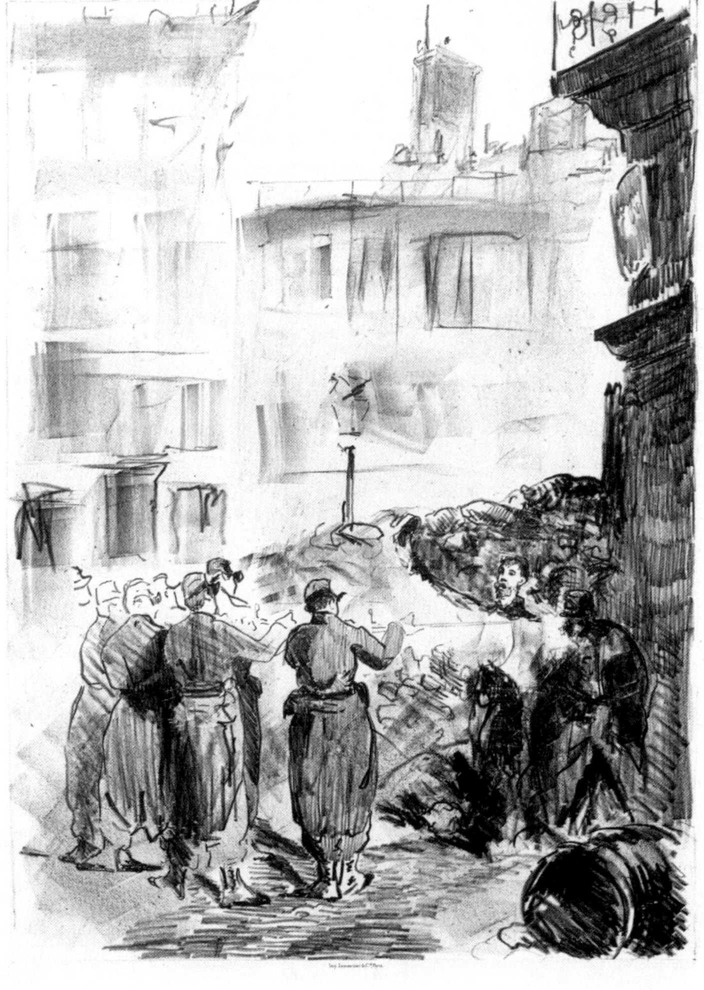

Siebe Johannes ten Cate
1858–1908
The Place du Carrousel and Ruins of the Tuileries 1883
Oil paint on canvas 83 × 165.5

Musée Carnavalet – Histoire de Paris

Dutch-born ten Cate spent most of his career in Paris. He painted this large view of what remained of the Tuileries Palace shortly before its ruins were levelled, or early on in the process, which started in February and was completed in September 1883. Built during the Renaissance, the palace had been the royal and imperial residence of most French rulers since Henri IV, until it was burnt down by the Commune as a symbol of power on 23 May 1871. Napoleon III and Eugénie had done considerable work on the Tuileries, which was also associated with the opulence of the Second Empire. *The Place du Carrousel and Ruins of the Tuileries* is a reminder that ruins were part of Parisians' daily lives, for almost twelve years in this instance, and nearly thirty in the case of the Court of Audit

The Tuileries Gardens, which stretch from the Louvre to the Place de la Concorde, give a sense of the scale of the former palace. Only the Flore and Marsan pavilions, which linked up the Tuileries to the Louvre, were restored and still stand, as does the triumphal arch erected between 1806 and 1808 to commemorate Napoleon I's victories. The arch is clearly visible here, off centre, to the right. Like Giuseppe de Nittis, who painted the ruins in his *Place des Pyramides* (p.228) and *Ruins of the Tuileries* 1882 (Musée du Louvre), ten Cate represented the Parisian population in all its variety, on a rainy day, going about their everyday business. CCP

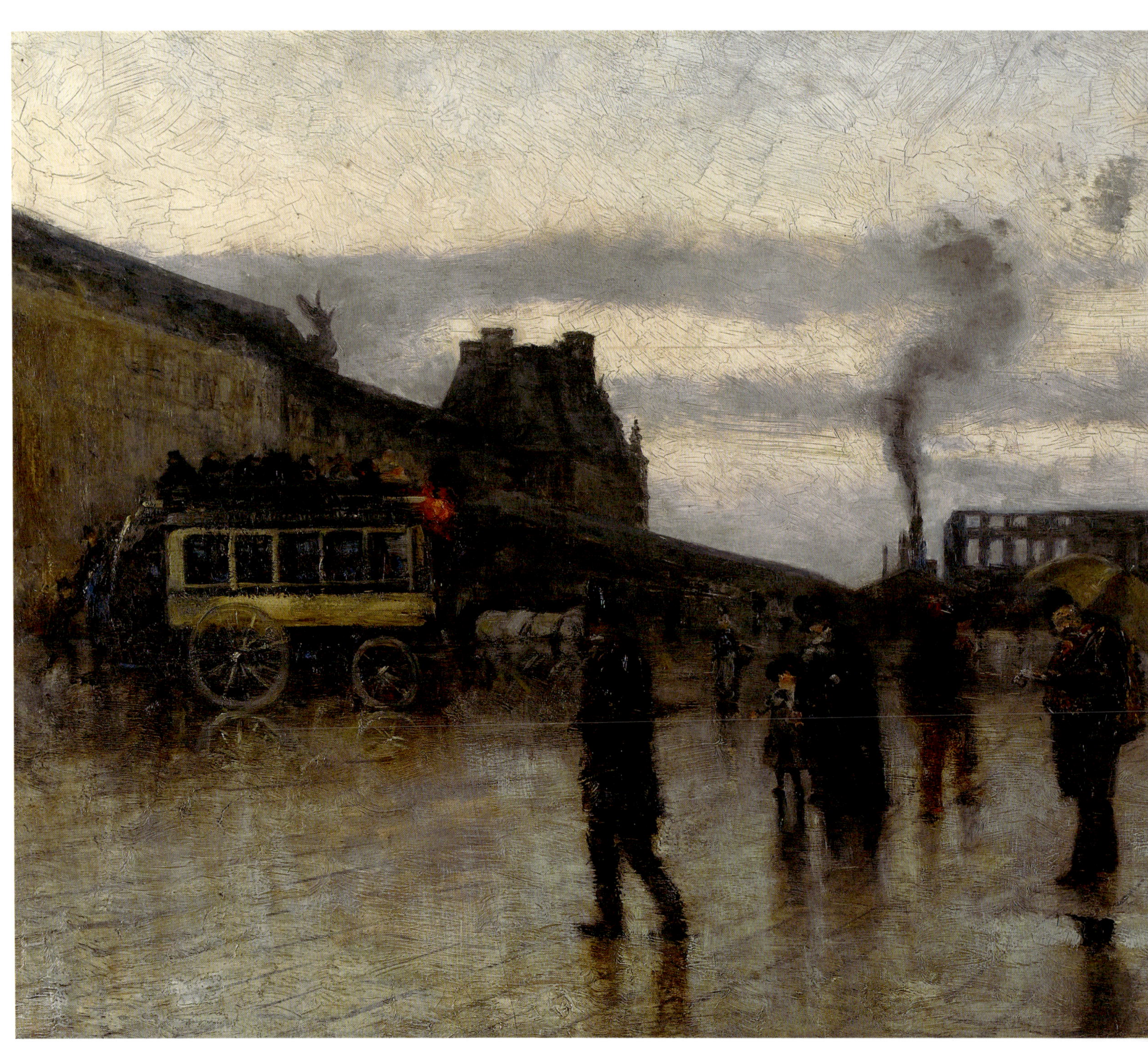

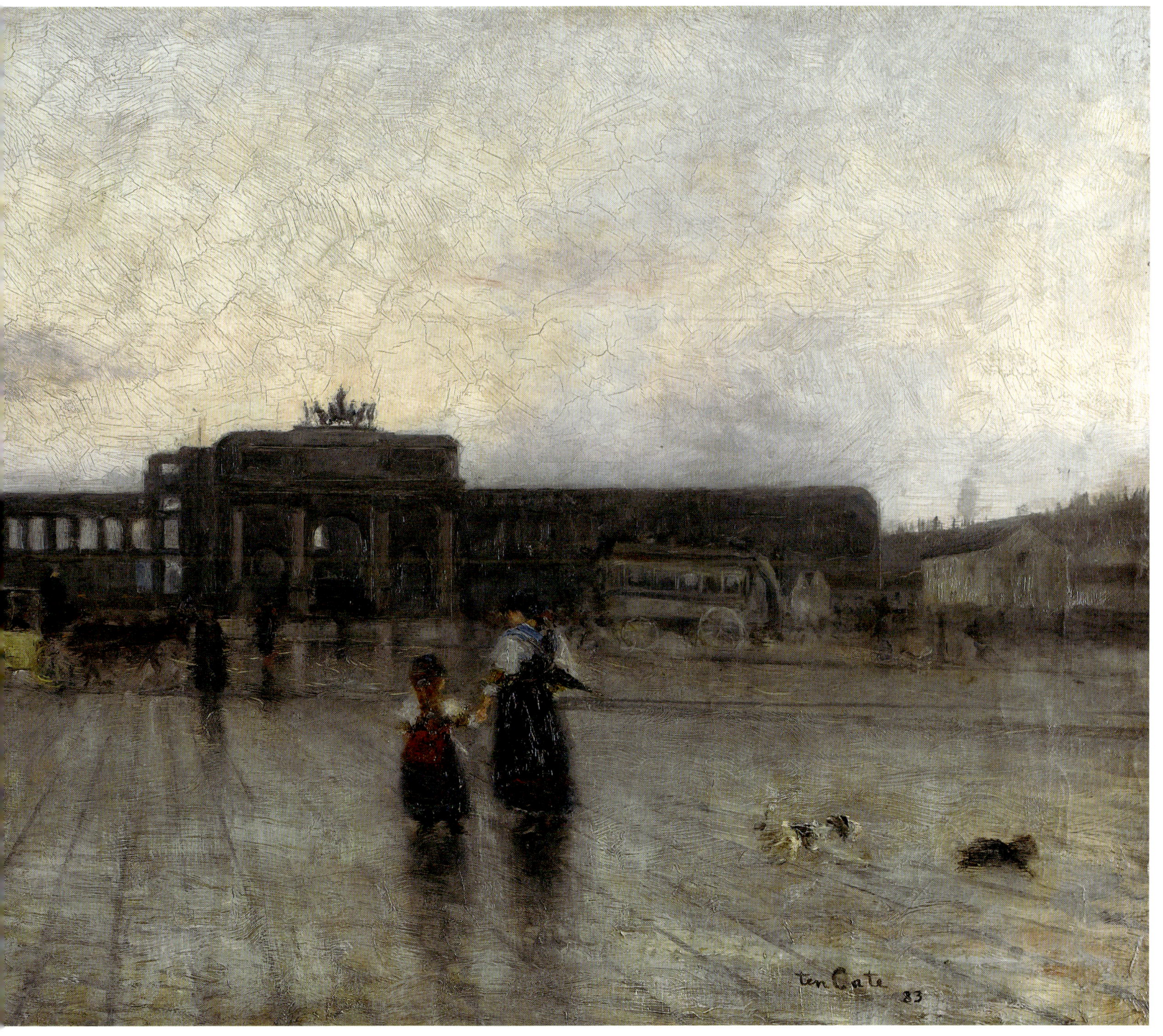
ten Cate
83

Gustave Doré
1832–1883
London Wharfs (1)
Wood engraving 30.7 × 18.6

Musée d'art moderne et contemporain de Strasbourg

The Docks of London (2)
Watercolour and gouache on paper
55.7 × 37.8

Musée d'art moderne et contemporain de Strasbourg

Over London – By Rail (3)
Wood engraving 19.8 × 24.7

Musée d'art moderne et contemporain de Strasbourg

Gustave Doré 1832–1883 and **William Blanchard Jerrold** 1826–1884
Westminster Stairs – Steamers Leaving, in *London: A Pilgrimage*, pub. Grant & Co., London 1872 (4)
42.5 × 32

Bibliothèque des Musées de Strasbourg

Gustave Doré made his first drawings for *London: A Pilgrimage* in 1869, forming an album to attract prospective publishers. This was later dismantled and most of the drawings were distributed to friends. Completion of the project was delayed until after the Franco-Prussian war, which Doré spent mostly in Paris (see p.29). He returned to London in the summer of 1871 to join his friend Blanchard Jerrold, who wrote the text of *London: A Pilgrimage*. They criss-crossed London extensively together, from the slums of Westminster and Whitechapel, where they were accompanied by a police superintendent in plain clothes, to upper-class events elsewhere.

Doré often worked from memory, as he loathed sketching in public. Jerrold recorded: 'I could seldom prevail upon him to make a sketch on the spot ... He made his old answer: "j'ai du collodion plein la tête!" ["My head is full of collodion"] But he was shy. The approach of a stranger made him shut up his book at once'.[1] The artist was accompanied by the draughtsman Emile Bourdelin, who provided some background architectural sketches.

Doré tended to work at the end of the day, after his travels through London, which inevitably translated into some inaccuracies that critics were quick to point out. Despite this artistic licence, he created a powerful vision of the largest city in the world, which chimed in French minds with the literary world of Dickens. Jerrold remarked that it was the work of 'a poet. The weird pictures of docks and rivers, and refuge, and slum in the darkness of the night, were those of the imaginative mind ... but they were real also.'[2] Doré often drew directly on wooden blocks, and achieved outstanding effects of light and darkness. His vision of London became a reference and caught the imagination of French artists who crossed the channel during the Franco-Prussian War, not least Tissot (see p.107) and Pissarro (see pp.222–3). CCP

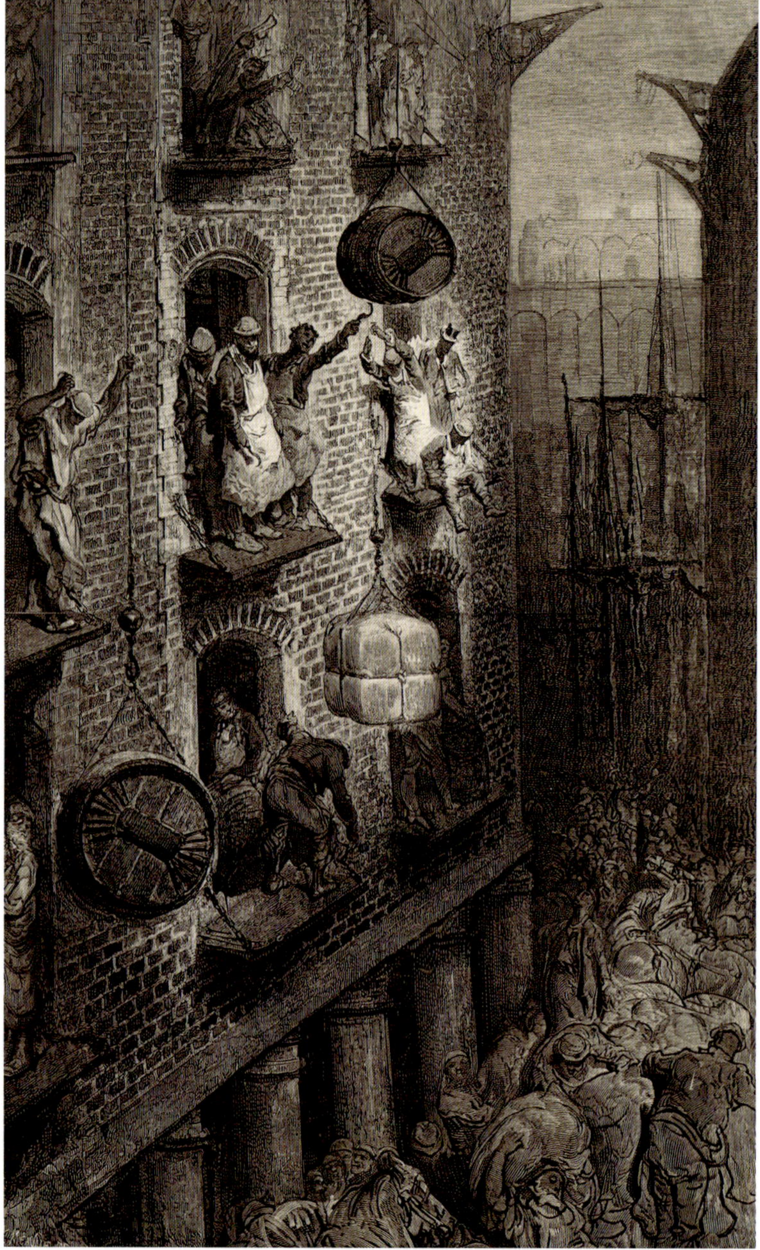

1

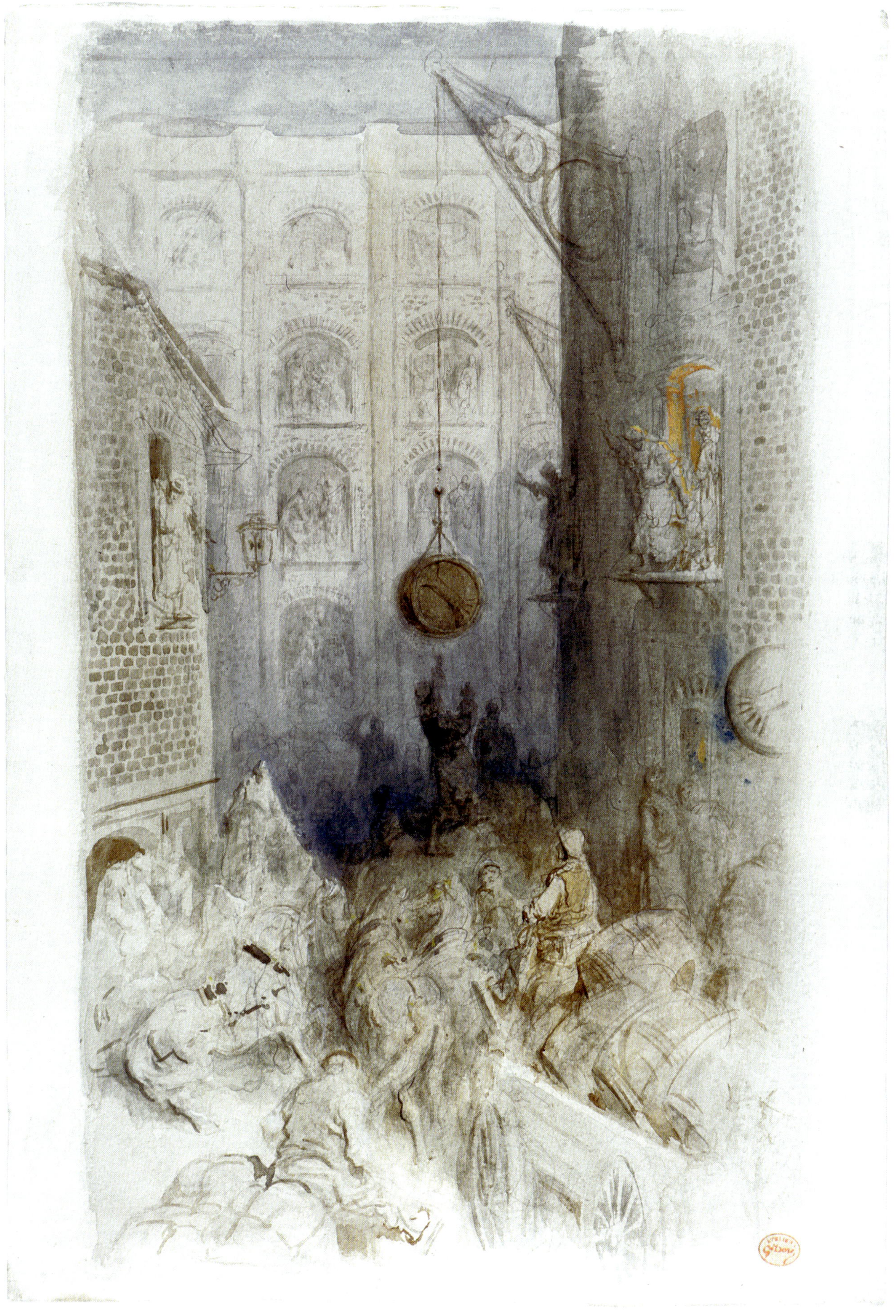

2

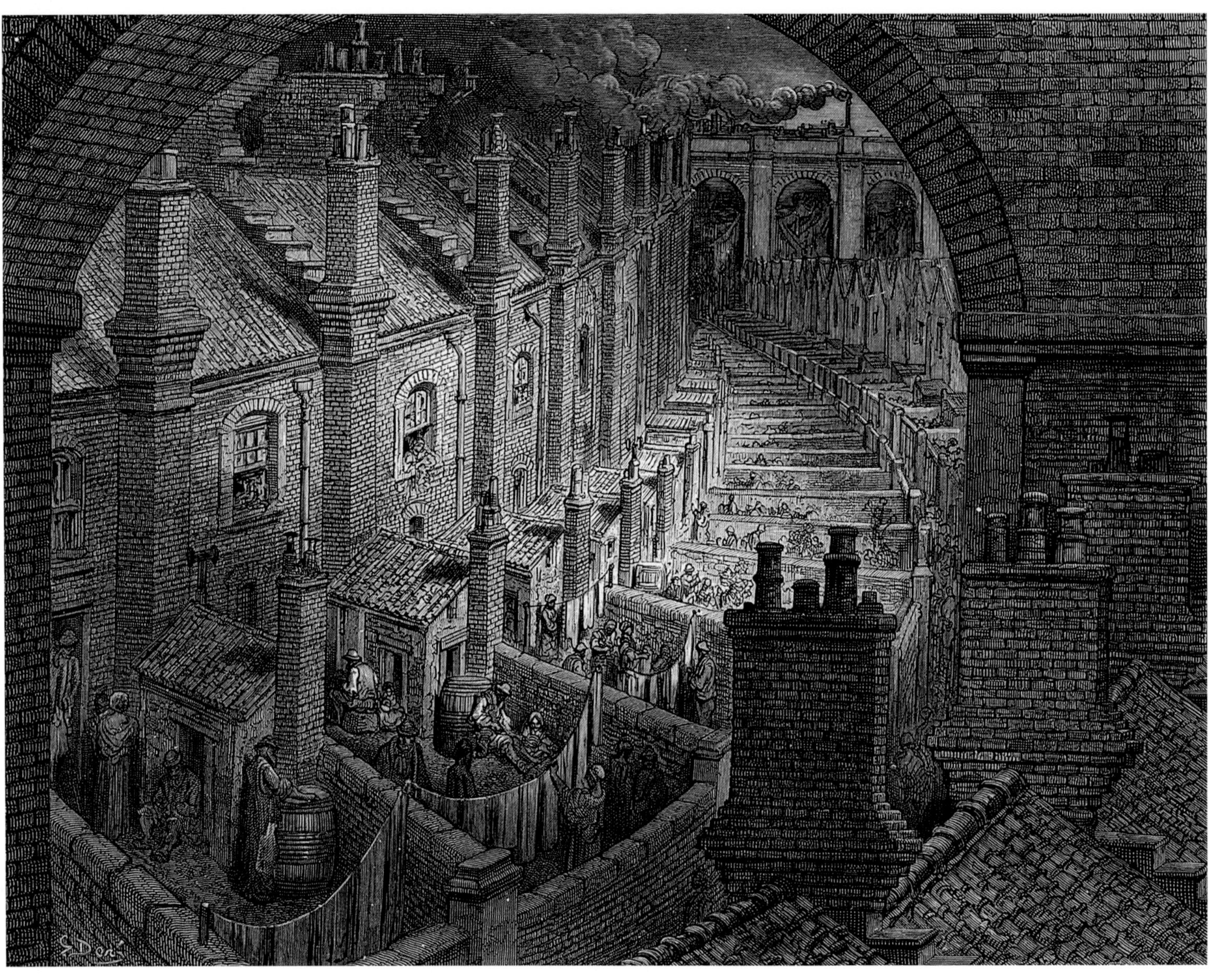

3

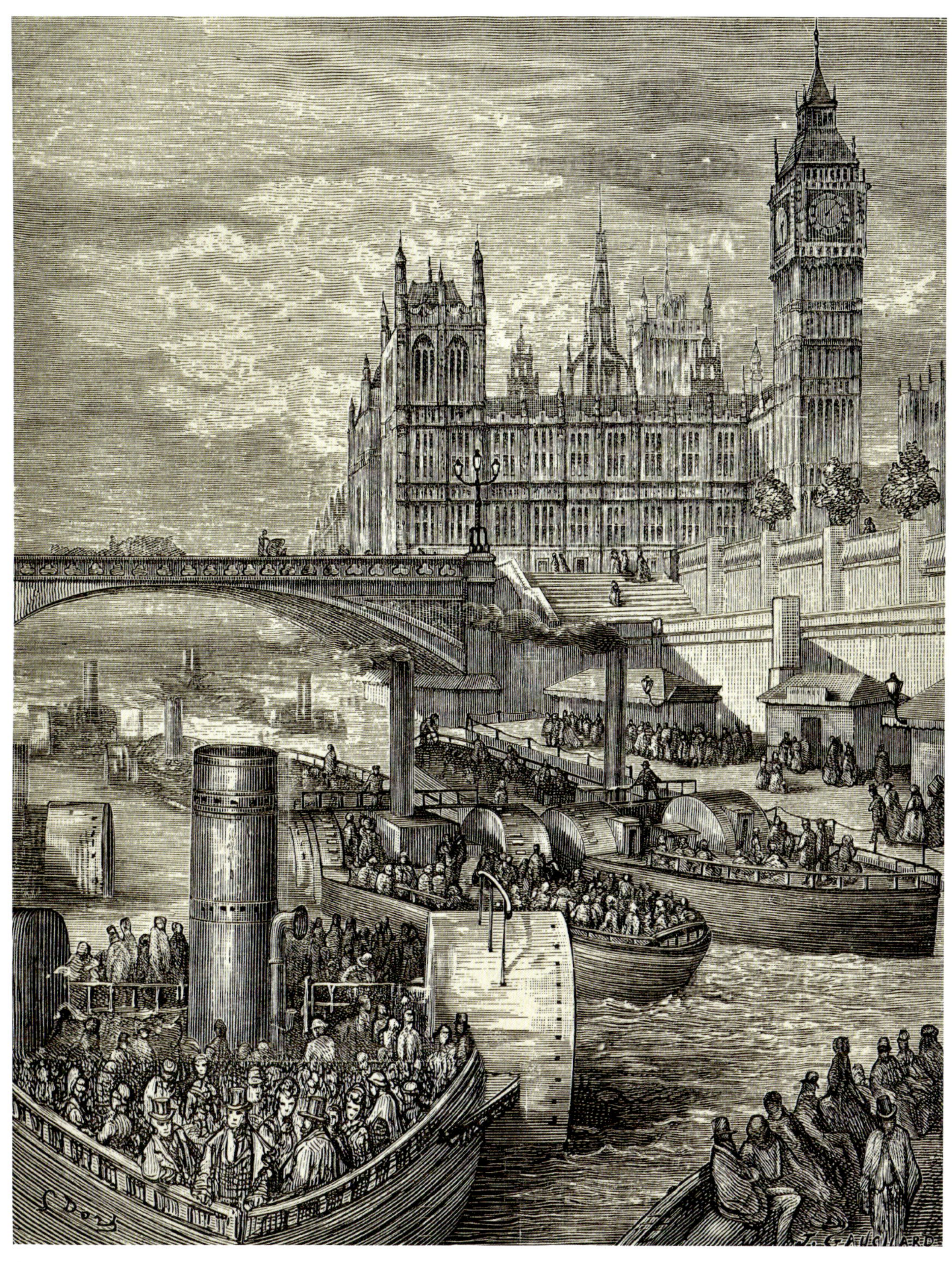

4

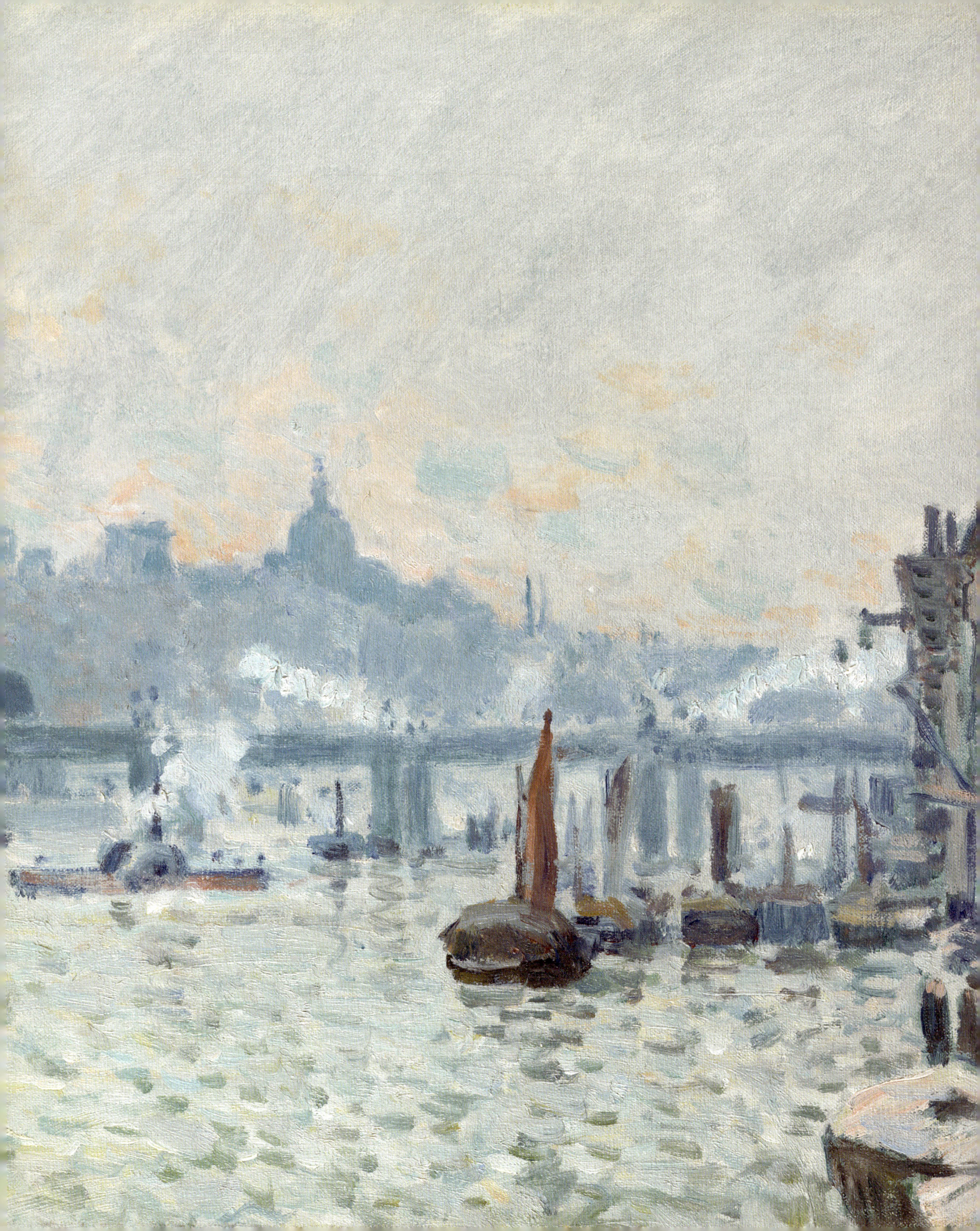

Anne Robbins

Monet, Pissarro and Fellow French Painters in London, 1870–1

Alfred Sisley
View of the Thames: Charing Cross Bridge 1874
(detail, see p.78)

Exiled from Paris by the war, French art has for the moment sought a home in England.
Times, 1870[1]

In the final months of his life, looking back on his career, Camille Pissarro recalled how 'in 1870 [he] found [himself] in London with Monet, and [they] met Daubigny and Bonvin'.[2] The last two were already well-established realist painters of landscape and genre subjects respectively; Claude Monet and Camille Pissarro painted fresh, plein-air scenes and pictures of modern life, struggling to earn a living while pursuing independent careers. The four of them arrived in London at different times in the autumn of 1870, settling in the city as war and insurrection were raging in France, encountering an important French artistic community relocated there for the same reasons. 'Many French artists have found refuge here',[3] noted François Bonvin, helpfully jotting down a list of names that included Charles-François Daubigny and Monet (see p.18). Their motivation for settling in London varied according to their personal circumstances; likewise their individual experiences of life in the city were to differ greatly. It is worth looking afresh at the impact of these few months spent in London on their morale and on the development of their artistic production, to try and assess how their future career was affected by the Franco-Prussian War and Paris Commune. Was it a turning point in their work? How did this period in Britain influence the evolution of their art? How far did it impact on the development of impressionism, whether through formal innovation and new subject matter elaborated in London, or through decisive encounters made there?

'I am in London by necessity', admitted Bonvin, having embarked at Saint-Malo for Southampton on 7 November 1870 – too old to be enrolled in the National Guard, but concerned about the progress of the German troops.[4] His preferred destination would have been picturesque Italy, or Belgium, more familiar to him and offering more business prospects, dealers and clients. These countries, however, shared borders with France and were not deemed as secure as England, which had a long tradition of being a safe haven for refugees in times of political turmoil. The artists considered in this essay were not political exiles, but fleeing on their own initiative, pushed by the danger of the war and the approaching Prussian army.[5]

This ever-growing threat provoked Daubigny's departure, in October 1870, from Villerville in Normandy where he was staying, anxious to get his family to safety.[6] Since the painter had already travelled to London on two occasions in 1865 and 1866, this destination must have seemed obvious. Daubigny's London address book for 1870–1, which included names of artists he had encountered during his previous London stays – such as James Abbott McNeill Whistler – gives a sense of the range of his contacts.[7] These may have facilitated Daubigny's involvement in a major exhibition in support of a cause no doubt close to his heart: a show mounted in aid of the Distressed Peasantry of France, to benefit his compatriots 'ruined by the Prussian invasion of their country'. The exhibition, aimed at raising awareness of (and funds for) the desolation brought by the Franco-Prussian conflict, opened on Pall Mall on 17 December 1870.[8] Daubigny was one of its contributors, alongside prominent French and British artists of the day – Jean-Léon Gérôme, Frederic Leighton (whom Daubigny had met in London in 1866), Lawrence Alma-Tadema – and also featured on the show's organising committee. In this capacity he may have encouraged Monet, freshly arrived in London, to send one of his pictures: indeed Monet showed a canvas he had just brought over from France, his recent *Breakwater at Trouville, Low Tide* (p.59), the first work by a soon-to-be-called impressionist artist to be included in an exhibition in Britain. Daubigny would certainly have supported this submission by a young painter he had already identified as showing much promise.[9]

In early September, from Le Havre, Monet had observed the incessant departures of huge boats across the Channel ferrying refugees to safety, often leaving hundreds behind (see p.13). A few weeks later he joined the exodus, setting foot on British soil presumably in mid-September or early October. Dire financial circumstances and the desire to escape conscription seem to have prompted his departure from Normandy, where he and his young wife, Camille, had just spent their honeymoon at Trouville (a view of which by Monet would be on show in Mayfair the following month).[10]

The politically engaged Pissarro – later to become an anarchist, but then still 'conservative'[11] – had actually considered conscription; his reasons for deciding to go to London, embarking from Saint-Malo on 2 December 1870, are harder to disentangle. Louveciennes had been invaded and his house there was occupied by the Prussian army; his main motivation was to create a new, safe home for his family, but he was also giving in to his mother's pleas not to enrol: 'I implore you not to put yourself at risk,' she pleaded, 'my dear son, do not be reckless.' She begged him to follow her to London instead, where she had settled in November, joining her English son-in-law (the widower of Pissarro's half-sister Emma, recently deceased) and her grandchildren.[12] Pissarro's other motive for leaving was his determination to marry his companion Julie Vellay, originally the Pissarro family's maid and by then, controversially, the mother of his own children. His upset mother had indicated she would only tolerate the marriage as long as it happened in London 'without [her] blessing and without anyone knowing'.[13] Pissarro finally realised his intention and the marriage took place at the Croydon Register Office on 14 June 1871.

Shunned by Pissarro's family, Julie felt miserable in London: 'You must be bored there, in this dreadful foggy weather ... [and without] being able to make [yourself] understood,' her sister commiserated.[14] Indeed the English language appeared unfathomable; 'this succession of curious noises could not be a language', Julie declared, and the couple's two young children felt just as homesick.[15] Pissarro, despite his mastery of English, experienced similar disenchantment and, in a letter to a friend, expressed his indefectible attachment to a largely idealised France: 'It is only when you are abroad that you realise how beautiful, grand and hospitable France is,' he wrote after six months in London, in June 1871, as the family was about to return home.[16]

Pissarro's nostalgia was no doubt triggered by the distance, and exacerbated patriotic feelings. In fact war remained at the forefront of his mind, and the news from Paris or Louveciennes was often disturbing: his house, in a sorry state, had been turned into a stable by Prussian soldiers, and virtually all his paintings were destroyed (a loss of twenty years' work, he lamented). While in London, Monet heard the news of the deaths of his father and of his friend Bazille, with whom he had shared a studio in Paris, tragically killed in the fighting on 28 November 1870.[17] Monet's wife Camille and their three-year-old son Jean had joined him in the autumn; his picture of her sitting on a chaise longue (pp.68–9), her expressionless face bathed in pale winter light, her boredom palpable, seems to epitomise the notion of *exilité*, a term coined by a Communard exiled in London – a deep feeling of ennui and inability, or unwillingness, to integrate.[18]

Bonvin and even Daubigny, for whom this stay in London was a return visit, appear to have experienced a same sense of cultural disorientation, as attested in their letters. Bonvin complained: 'After sixteen hours of crossing and five hours of journey by railway, here I am in London, experiencing exceptional fog. Hell! It is not fun! I had been warned, but not sufficiently!'[19] Daubigny bemoaned the fog, the weather, and the cost of living and accommodation, warning his friend the painter Julien de La Rochenoire, then also considering refuge in London:

> Weigh up carefully all the drawbacks that I stated. Avoid hotels as much as possible, and bring some food ... So far to stay in London is to despair. We have already spent 600 francs since our departure from Villerville ... I have to stop writing my letter to you to light a candle: it is 11 am. Say no more about the climate. Fog so thick one cannot see beyond two paces.[20]

For all of them, this ambivalent experience abroad triggered a renewed energy for resuming their art. Refuge in London allowed them to continue painting, something they would have struggled to achieve in the Paris turmoil. The city offered them the possibility of pursuing their work, providing them with a safe environment and with subjects reassuringly reminiscent of home – parks, river banks, semi-rural suburbs – yet part of a drastically different city fabric and bathed in a unique atmosphere.

Daubigny worked *en plein air*, focusing on the banks of the Thames, capturing their humid atmosphere in paintings close in composition to seascapes and riverside views he had painted in France on the banks of the Oise or in the harbour of Bordeaux (pp.64–5).[21] He also explored sites where he had already wandered in 1866 (pp.62–3), looking downstream, one day encountering Monet on a similar painting expedition. The artist had set up his easel on the river bank. Monet later remembered: 'By chance I met Daubigny who had shown interest in me in the past. At that time he was painting views of the Thames.'[22]

Monet was drawn to the modern city, its vibrant, industrial river banks and busy parks (pp.200–1), in the same way in which landscapes with newly built bridges had interested him before

Claude Monet
Camille Monet 1866
Oil paint on wood 81 × 55
The National Museum of Art of Romania, Bucharest

Claude Monet
Breakwater at Trouville, Low Tide 1870
Oil paint on canvas 54 × 65.7
Szépművészeti Múzeum, Budapest

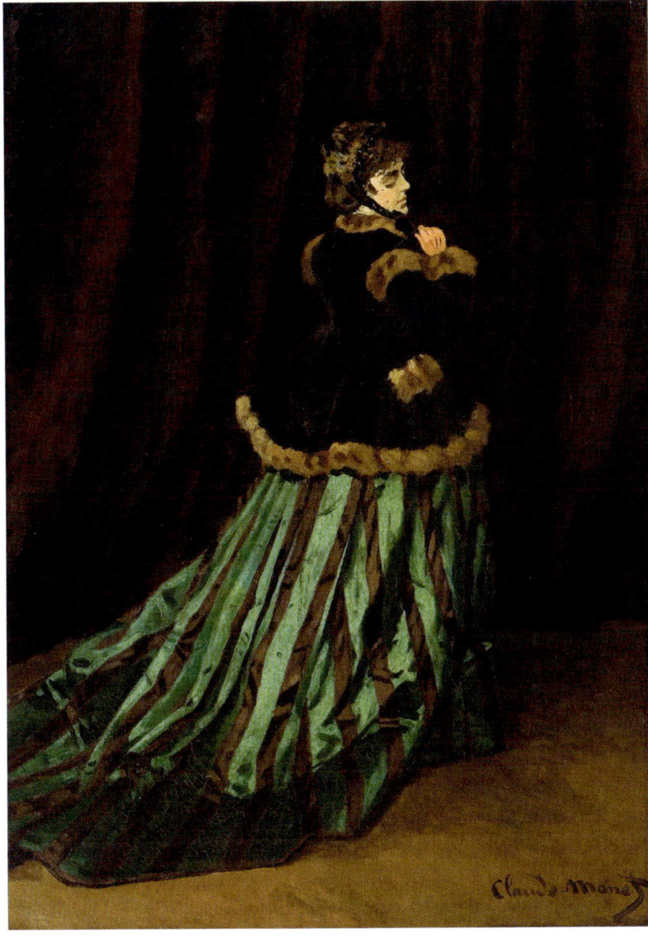

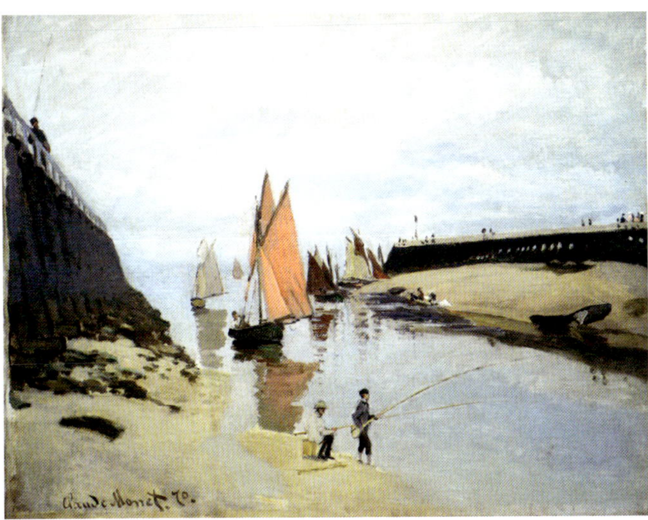

the war – or popular places of entertainment outside Paris and recent hotel buildings on the Normandy coast.[23] The six paintings by Monet executed during the eight months he spent in London in 1870–1 tell us about the artist's favourite painting spots in the city. He favoured the brand new Embankment (pp.66–7) and the Pool of London with the silhouettes of its boats (p.227), casting on it the same look with which he had depicted the tall, elegant masts in the port of Honfleur.[24] Likewise his painting *Meditation*, showing his wife, followed a mode of representation (in semi-profile, distant, looking afar) he had already experimented with in portraits of Camille in the mid-1860s (p.59).[25]

'Monet and I were very enthusiastic over the London landscapes,' Pissarro wrote. 'Monet worked in the parks, whilst I, living at Lower Norwood, at that time a charming suburb, studied the effects of fog, snow and springtime. We worked from Nature, and later on Monet painted in London some superb studies of mist.'[26] Having settled in the suburb (Upper Norwood), Pissarro explored his immediate surroundings, painting at least seventeen views of this particular area of South London, encountering on his walks and recording in two canvasses the huge, glittering glass structure of the Crystal Palace, installed there in 1854.[27] A rapid, nervous pencil sketch done by Daubigny in 1866 succeeds in evoking the building's gigantic scale (p.60), whereas Pissarro's painting shows it half-buried behind the road at the crest of Fox Hill (p.71). In another painting it is faced with a row of new suburban houses strangely matching its height, as if Pissarro had wanted to play down its vast size and startling modernity, integrating it into the semi-rural fabric of the neighbourhood (p.60).[28]

Like Monet, Pissarro incorporated into his paintings the distinctive architectural and topographical elements of London, but also captured its unique atmosphere, its special, transitory quality of light, conveyed with lively brushwork. Verlaine's poem 'London' admirably conjures up the sense of crisp, fresh air on a clear spring day that Pissarro captures in *The Avenue, Sydenham* (pp.74–5): 'Trees strong and rotund from frail lawns sprouting / Tender green, an air far from mists and gases grows fine / So much so they appear to be planted in pastoral country / Limpid sunshine feathery in the fine sky, though blue-ish / Hardly.'[29] As acute observers of their immediate environment, these artists laid emphasis on atmosphere rather than topography. Daubigny and Monet shrouded their cityscapes in the 'furious fog that resents the sun', as Jules Vallès, the famous French exile, put it.[30] Faced with a technical challenge to evoke light filtered through opaque clouds and smoke, they imbued their pictures with a singular mood.

Museum visits, which were part of the daily routine, gave the French artists taking refuge in London many opportunities to socialise. Networks of friendships or acquaintances soon emerged, or re-formed, in a city where exiles and refugees from France occupied specific areas, centred mostly around Soho, from Covent Garden to Oxford Street; there, chances of coming across compatriots were high. French refugee artists chose to settle in this part of town, in the Rathbone Hotel for Bonvin or Hôtel de l'Etoile for Daubigny, who later lived on Lisle Street near Leicester Square.[31] Monet's first address in London, 11 Arundel Street (now Coventry Street, off Shaftesbury Avenue), formed part of this enclave.[32] Both artists eventually moved to Kensington, yet still gathered in Soho's numerous cafés and restaurants, such as Maison Bertaux, founded that year on Greek Street by M. Bertaux, a Communard fleeing from Paris, or the Café Royal on Regent Street, established and run by a French wine merchant, and the meeting place of artists and writers. Three decades later, Monet remembered:

> Several Frenchmen gathered in the Café Royal and we didn't know how to earn any money. One day Daubigny asks me what I am doing. I tell him, some little landscapes in the park. He tells me, 'But how wonderful ... I am going to introduce you to a dealer.' He goes to find Durand, who had set up a shop in London to sell paintings during the war.[33]

The art dealer in question was Paul Durand-Ruel, who proved instrumental in consolidating and expanding these networks. Like the artists he soon started to support, he had relocated to London, arriving on 8 September 1870, in order 'to spare [his] wife and five little children the horrors of the siege that would soon begin'.[34] He also aimed to continue business, intent on using his existing contacts – there was a well-established network of galleries in London's Mayfair. Durand-Ruel ended up playing a pivotal role in promoting and exhibiting the work of these artists, for whom he created unhoped-for opportunities. A respected name on the Paris art scene, he had five years earlier taken over his father's gallery, which specialised in the romantic, realist schools and mid-nineteenth-century landscape; crucially Durand-Ruel was also a fellow French refugee.

Using paintings he had brought over from Paris for safe-keeping – more than 35 crates of pictures from the gallery stock, shipped in one consignment – the dealer immediately embarked on organising exhibitions, starting with a display in the gallery of his colleague Thomas McLean on Haymarket, but with the 'intention of establishing a gallery of note', as Daubigny reported.[35] On 10 December the dealer was ready to open in his own gallery, in rented premises on New Bond Street (the inopportunely named German Gallery), his first exhibition of the Society of French Artists, an imaginary, official-sounding committee of painters, under the aegis of which he decided to place his shows. As early as March 1871 he displayed a few works by the future impressionists, whom he had met a few weeks earlier, including Monet's *Breakwater at Trouville*, already recently exhibited in London, and probably Pissarro's *Fox Hill, Upper Norwood* (p.70).[36] Pissarro, on hearing of Durand-Ruel's presence in London, had dropped off one of his canvasses at his gallery; the dealer responded enthusiastically: 'The painting you have brought me is charming and I am sorry that I was not at the gallery to compliment you myself ... Your friend Monet asked me for your address. He didn't know you were in England.'[37]

Durand-Ruel was certainly not prey to exilic ennui, deploying extraordinary energy on countless fronts. As a member of the Organising Committee for the French section of the 1871

Charles-François Daubigny
Crystal Palace, London, July 1866
Charcoal and pencil on paper 32.4 × 50

Musée Bonnat-Helleu, Bayonne

Camille Pissarro
Crystal Palace 1871
Oil paint on canvas 47.2 × 73.5

The Art Institute of Chicago

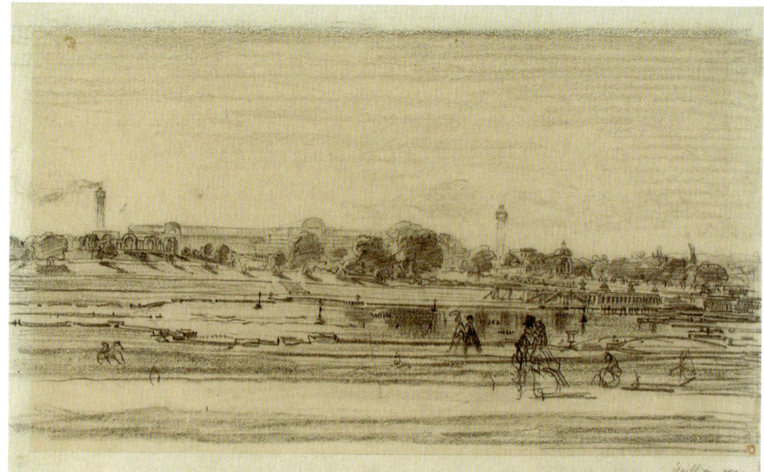

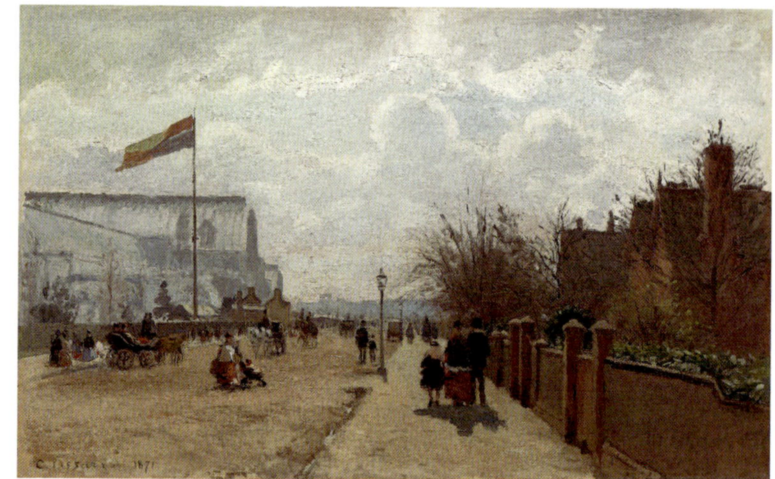

International Exhibition in South Kensington, he helped select pictures, sending paintings from the gallery stock and ensuring that the young, progressive school of landscape was represented: Pissarro with two snowscapes (possibly p.70) and Monet with a portrait of Camille (p.69). 'Days fly by so quickly that I never have time to do anything,' he wrote to Pissarro.[38]

Indeed, while subsidising 'his' artists who remained in France and often lived in harsh conditions in the war-ridden country (in exchange for recent pictures they sent to the London gallery), Durand-Ruel also backed French refugee painters as soon as they set foot in London.[39] Having already enjoyed the dealer's support at home, Bonvin benefited straight away from his generosity while in London, with immediate financial help (47 francs) and the sale of two paintings for 600 francs each, together with further commissions.[40] Keen to increase his stock, Durand-Ruel wasted no time in approaching another 'regular' artist of the gallery, Daubigny, placing an order with him for 'three paintings after [his] studies of Villerville'.[41] The painter may have had a decent grasp of London's business opportunities, from his previous visits, but he still welcomed the dealer's support.[42] Durand-Ruel's legendary 'discovery' of Monet and Pissarro in London during the war and his early purchases brought them much-needed economic relief. Long after, Monet expressed eternal gratitude for the dealer who 'for [them] was the saviour'.[43]

Despite these fruitful encounters, and Durand-Ruel's vigorous championing of these French artists' work in London, their paintings garnered little success among collectors and amateurs. The dealer only showed a handful of their pictures during the war itself, a number that was to increase in subsequent years. Durand-Ruel reminisced how these pictures 'went almost unnoticed by almost all the visitors to our galleries ... In London we sold very few.'[44] One rare such sale, of a Pissarro painting (*Road in Upper Norwood* 1871), was arranged directly between the artist and a young French cognac merchant established in Covent Garden, Jules Berthel, on 17 June 1871, a few days before Pissarro's disheartened return to France.[45] Pissarro bitterly noted:

> With regard to sales, I have had nothing, apart from Durand-Ruel who has bought two small paintings from me, my painting doesn't catch on, at all, it's the same story everywhere ... Here, one is only met with disdain, indifference, and even rudeness; one experiences the jealousy and most selfish defiance of colleagues – here, there is no art: everything is a business matter.'[46]

He long remembered his unsuccessful submission to the Royal Academy that spring: 'You know very well that the English have never appreciated anything that we did! – In 70 [actually 71] I had sent [paintings] to the Academy exhibition with Monet, and we were booted out.'[47] Monet summed up this feeling of rejection: 'England did not want any of our paintings. It was tough.'[48]

However, pioneer collectors had been alerted to the soon-to-be-called 'New Painting', not least Jean-Baptiste Faure, the illustrious baritone and longstanding client of the Durand-Ruel gallery, who had arrived in London in the autumn of 1870 to perform in the opera *Hamlet* in Covent Garden.[49] Friend and

Camille Pissarro
Road in Upper Norwood 1871
Oil paint on canvas 45.5 × 55.6

Neue Pinakothek, Munich

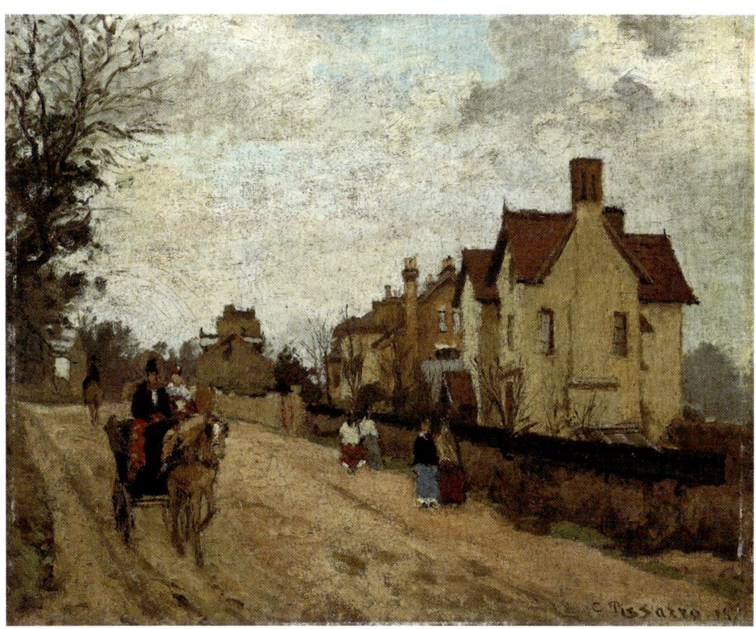

next-door neighbour of Durand-Ruel on Brompton Crescent, he was similarly pious, and a staunch patriot.[50] Faure was to make daring purchases of works by Pissarro and Monet. He also supported their friend Alfred Sisley, a painter of equally bold, fresh landscapes who likewise had been affected by the Franco-Prussian war, albeit in different ways. Despite his English ancestry, Sisley had not taken refuge in London, but war had caused the bankruptcy of his father's already ailing business, and his own ruin. Three years later, captivated by Sisley's fresh, crisp landscapes, Faure funded the painter's trip to London and acquired six of the pictures that he completed there. In the city Sisley turned to subjects similar to the ones his impressionist friends had painted during their stay: the bustling river near St Paul's with its sparkling surface, also reminiscent of Daubigny's views; the clear light of spring; and the stunning scenery of a London suburb, Molesey, animated by boat races and joyful bathers.

Whether their London stay in 1870–1 paved the way for the new style of painting developed by the impressionists, based on modern subjects and executed with a free handling skill, remains the subject of debate. Their London works are directly related formally and compositionally to the pictures they painted in the previous decade.[51] But isolation, *exilité* and homesickness encouraged them to work outside rather than in their cramped lodgings, seeking the company of fellow refugee painters and thus consolidating their commitment to plein-air painting, whatever the weather. The material conditions they found in London systematised this type of artistic practice, and reinforced the ties between artists who were soon to band together, resulting in the impressionist adventure, which had started 'on the streets of London, where the storm had driven [them]'.[52]

Charles-François Daubigny
1817–1878
The Thames at Erith 1866
Oil paint on panel 38 × 67

Musée du Louvre, bequeathed by Georges Thomy Thiéry, 1902

The Mouth of the Thames 1866
Oil paint on panel 27 × 45.5

Musée des Beaux-Arts de Lyon, bequeathed by Wuillermoz, 1875

According to James Abbott McNeill Whistler, Daubigny first visited Britain in 1865, in the company of the print publisher and art dealer Alfred Cadart.[1] The following year, Daubigny was invited by a group of British artists led by Frederic Leighton to come to London, and his *Moonrise*, despite being 'skied' (hung high), enjoyed considerable success at the Royal Academy exhibition. These trips and the fact that he exhibited his work in Britain show that Daubigny was willing to explore the potential of the London art market prior to his exile during the Franco-Prussian War, and that he was in a favourable position to benefit from it. Unlike the impressionists in the 1870s, his work and that of the Barbizon school in general found a market in Britain, which profited the art dealer Paul Durand-Ruel.

All of the eighteen recorded oil paintings that Daubigny executed in Britain (Hellebranth 746–63) are views of the Thames. The majority of them were based on drawings and sketches executed on the spot, and later worked up in his studio. *The Thames at Erith* was one of them. In the mid-nineteenth century Erith, with its pier and salt marshes, was a popular tourist destination, especially for day-trippers, who could arrive either by railway or pleasure boats. Unlike Francis Seymour Haden, who in 1865 etched the town with its elegant passers-by, Daubigny represented the decayed banks of the Thames, under a grey sky. His focus on the industrial side of London, combined with the sulfurous palette that he adopted to suit this choice of subject matter, contrasts with the bucolic aspect of his French landscapes.

A notable exception is *The Mouth of the Thames*, which represents the Thames estuary and was executed in a more high-keyed palette. Daubigny's broad, fluid brushwork was bound to appeal to the younger Claude Monet. As early as 1859, Monet had written to Eugène Boudin: 'Daubigny, the man I told you about, is a wonderful artist. It would be very unfortunate if you were not able to see his work.'[2] Théophile Gautier had criticised Daubigny for his 'impressionism' as early as 1867, and as one of the most progressive members of the Salon jury from 1868, Daubigny was a staunch supporter of the future impressionists, so much so that he resigned over the rejection of their works at the Salon of 1870. CCP

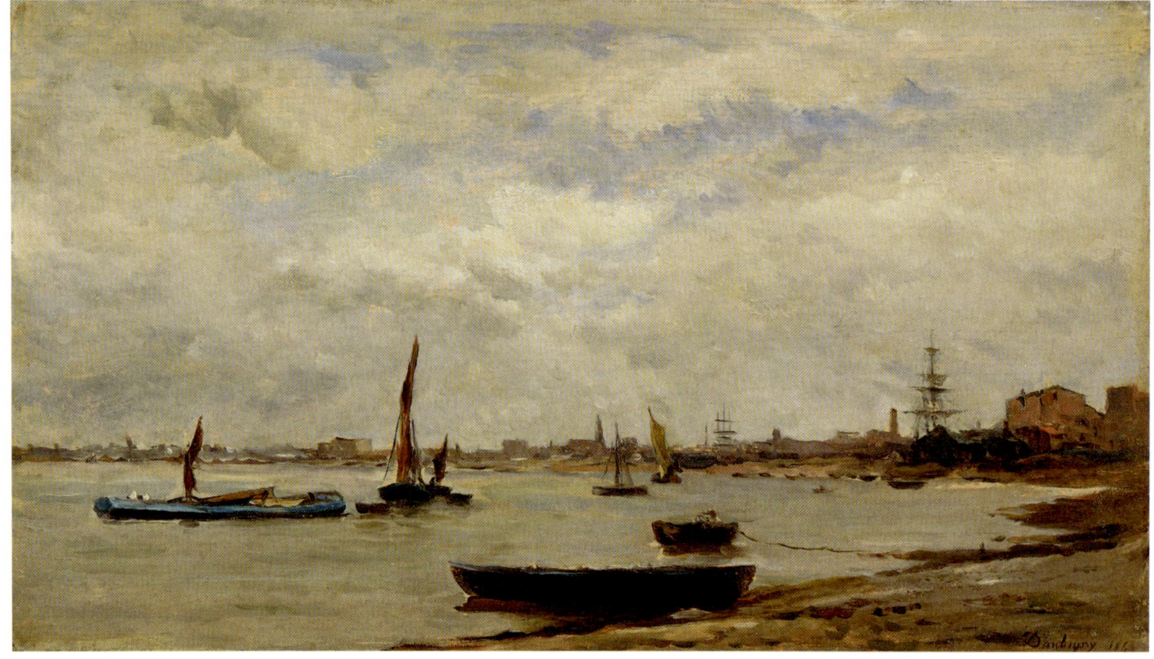

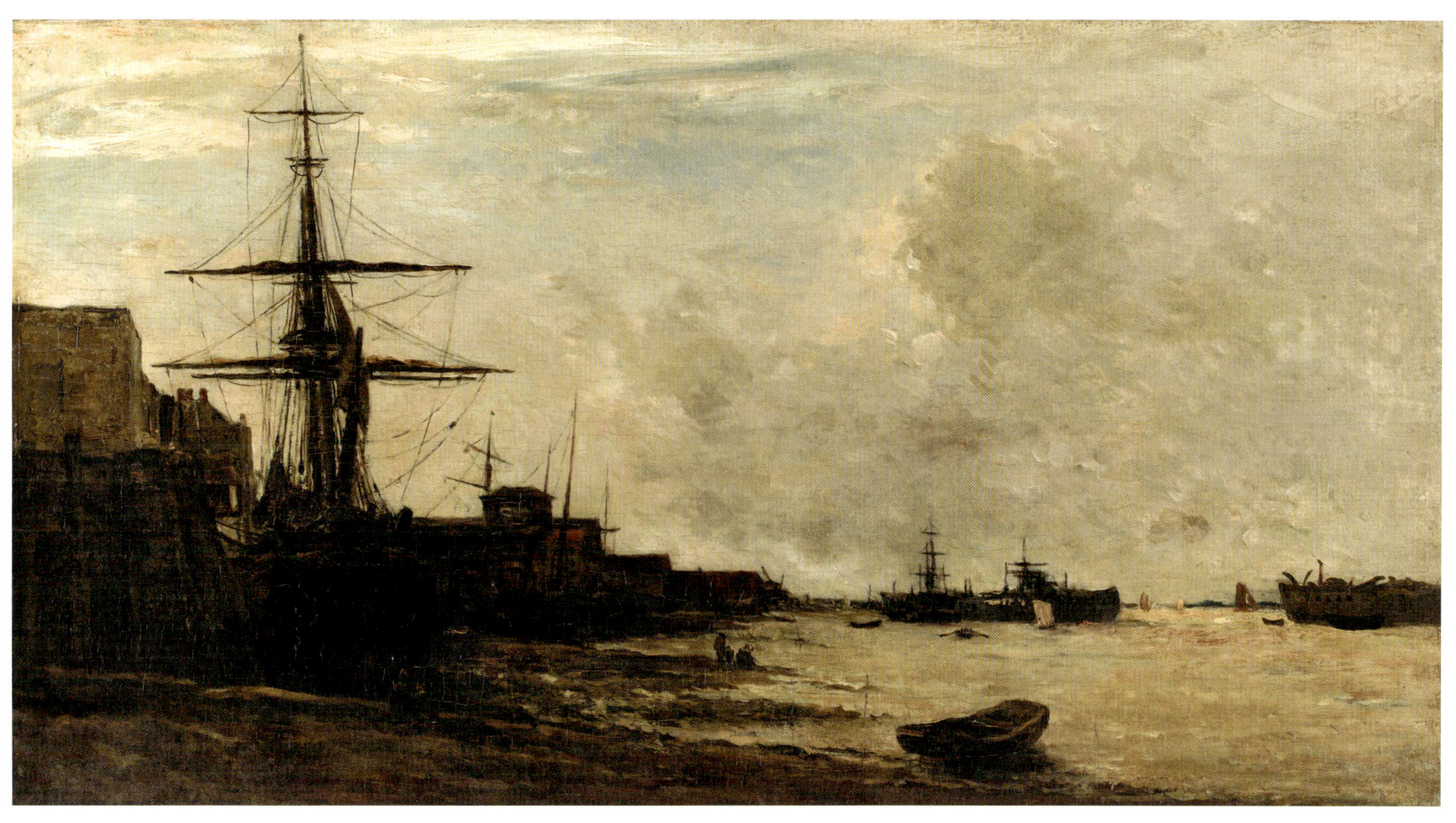

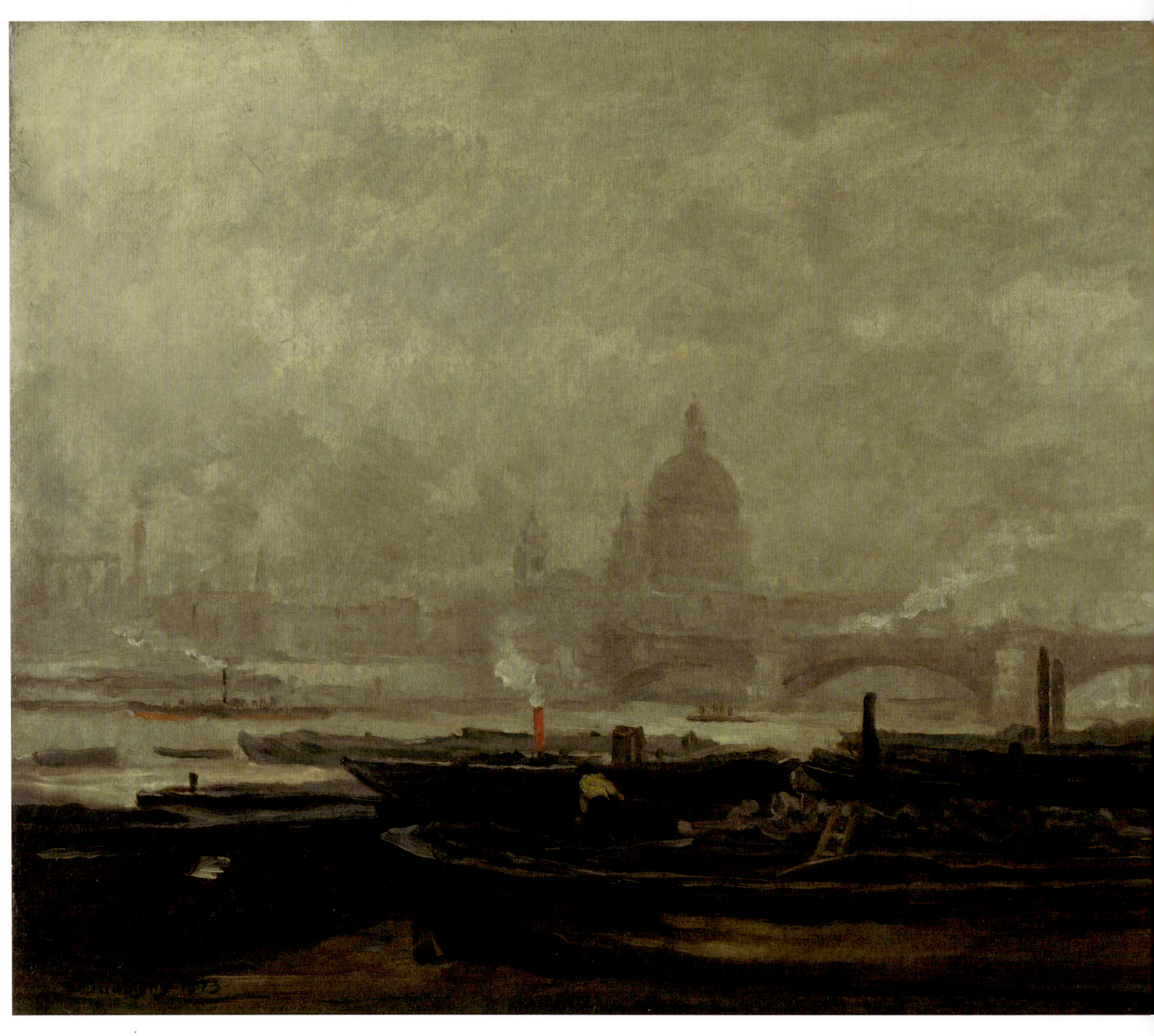

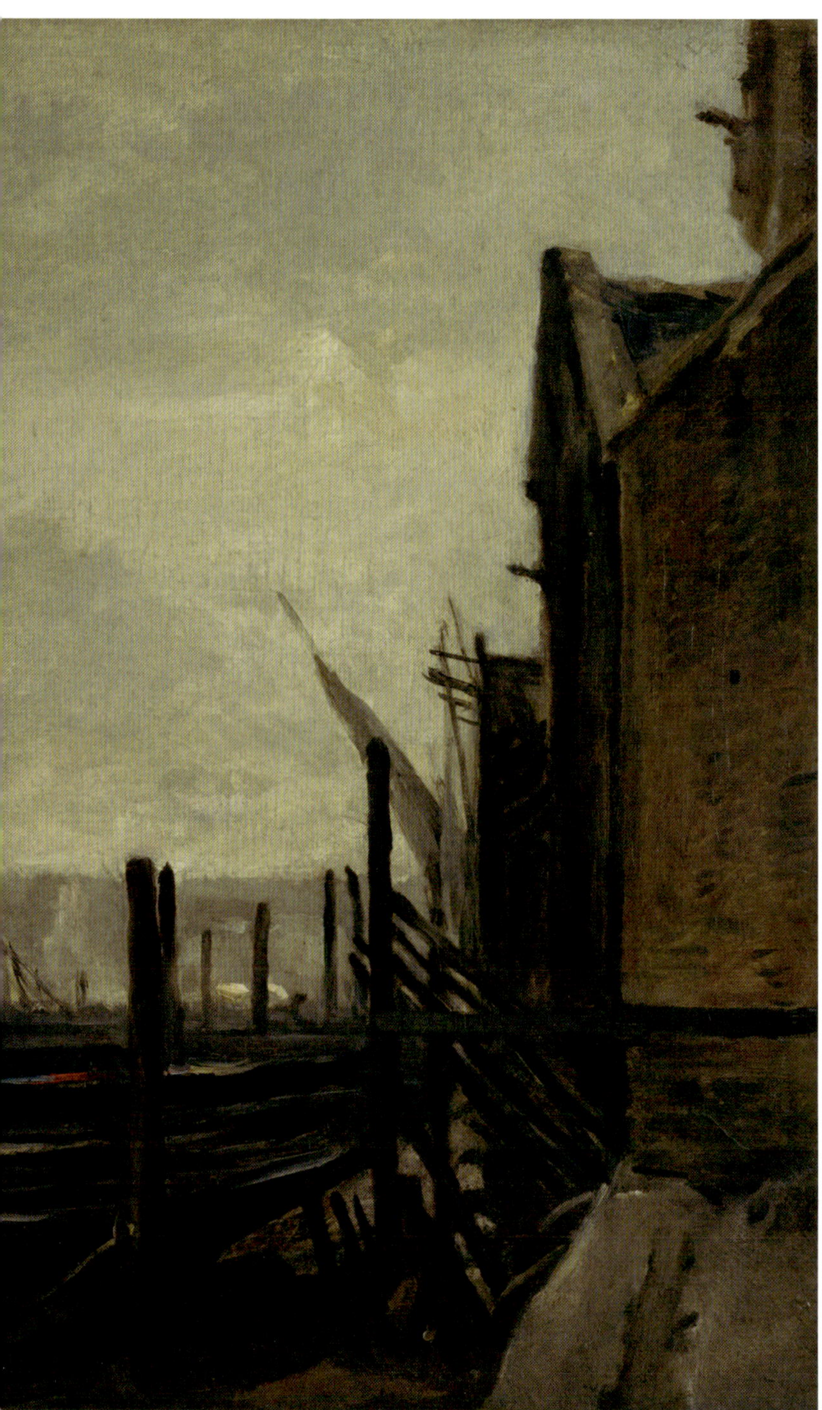

Charles-François Daubigny
1817–1878
St Paul's from the Surrey Side 1871–3
Oil paint on canvas 44.5 × 81

The National Gallery, London, presented by friends of Mr J.C.J. Drucker, 1912

Daubigny was in Villerville in Normandy when the Franco-Prussian War broke out. Bar his son Karl, who remained in Paris during the siege and served in the Mobile National Guard, Daubigny, his family – including his heavily pregnant daughter – and a servant all fled to Britain in early October 1870. The six of them first stayed at the Hôtel de l'étoile, which was popular with French refugees, before taking temporary lodgings in Lisle Street, near Leicester Square. In a letter to his friend the artist Julien de La Rochenoire, who later came to London,[1] Daubigny wrote: 'All the Englishmen who would be likely to acquire paintings have left. There is not much hope to earn anything at the moment.'[2] Five days later, on 20 October, his mood had lifted after moving to a 'very *chic*, small furnished house' in West London,[3] at 13 Cunning Place, West Kensington, and by 2 November, Paul Durand-Ruel had commissioned him to paint three pictures of Villerville.[4] A sign, perhaps, that Daubigny embraced the opportunities brought by his London exile and felt settled to a certain degree was that, unlike Camille Pissarro and Claude Monet, he gave his London address for the catalogue of the 1871 International Exhibition. Daubigny stayed until the end of May 1871, and during his seven-and-a-half month sojourn in London, it appears that he mostly worked on French subjects.

St Paul's from the Surrey Side is an exception of note. It shows the cathedral and Blackfriars Bridge from the South bank, with decaying wharves in the foreground. Some figures offloading sacks are difficult to make out, being painted with black, like the numerous surrounding barges. Apart from a few red and orange highlights dotted horizontally across the lower third of the composition, Daubigny's palette is dominated by the grey of the pervading smoke that shrouds St Paul's in the distance, and by dark hues. This subject is in stark contrast with the peaceful rural scenes or seascapes that Daubigny usually favoured. During his previous trip to London, Daubigny had not focused on central London as he did here and in his *Westminster* of 1866 (p.229). His encounter with Monet while the latter was painting by the Thames may have played a part in Daubigny's own choice of subject. With its focus on the effect of fog on an architectural landmark, *St Paul's from the Surrey Side* presents a number of similarities with *The Thames below Westminster* (pp.66–7). At the 1874 Exhibition of the Society of French Artists, Durand-Ruel hung *St Paul's from the Surrey Side* next to Sisley's *View of the Thames: Charing Cross Bridge* (p.78), which draws on Daubigny's painting.[5]
CCP

Claude Monet
1840–1926
The Thames below Westminster 1871
Oil paint on canvas 47 × 73

The National Gallery, London, bequest of Lord Astor of Hever, 1971

By choosing to paint the Palace of Westminster and the Embankment of the Thames, Monet adopted a resolutely modern subject. Following the fire that destroyed most of the old palace in 1834, the new one as a whole was not completed until 1870, the same year as the Victoria Embankment. In the middle ground, workers are depicted dismantling the scaffoldings that were assembled for the construction of the latter. The trees that were planted alongside the Embankment, painted by Monet the morning of a spring day, were still young, and George Vulliamy's now iconic dolphin lamps had not been installed yet. In the hazy distance the new Westminster Bridge had only been inaugurated in 1862, while across the river, far left, St Thomas's Hospital was still a building site. Monet would paint his celebrated canvases of the Houses of Parliament from its terrace at the turn of the twentieth century (pp.232–41).

In *The Thames below Westminster* Monet used a subtle palette of modulated blue and purple grey tones to depict the palace veiled in fog in the background. To convey the depth of the smoky sky but also its luminosity, he used a scumbling technique with long brush strokes contrasting with the broken ones that he adopted to paint reflections on the Thames. Parallels have been drawn between this painting and Whistler's first nocturnes,[1] then in the making, but despite having some shared contacts, there is still no evidence that Monet knew the American. Their methods diverged too: Monet did not veer away from the credo of plein-air painting, while Whistler often painted his nocturnes from memory; Monet's brush strokes were already broken and varied, whereas Whistler favoured long, horizontal liquid strokes. More striking are parallels between Daubigny's Thames paintings (pp.62–3) and *The Thames below Westminster* in their focus on the effect of fog on architecture and the presence of workers in the foreground.

The Thames below Westminster was one of the first canvases by Monet to be purchased by Durand-Ruel, in 1872. The art dealer exhibited it in London at the seventh exhibition of the Society of French Artists in November 1873 (no.114), but it was still unsold in 1877.[2] The famous baritone Jean-Baptiste Faure acquired it at Ernest Hoschedé's sale in 1878 for 250 francs and kept it until December 1906, when he sold it to Durand-Ruel for 10,000 francs. Three months later, Durand-Ruel sold it to Ernst Cassirer for 30,000 francs. This rapid rise in monetary value may have reflected the new appreciation of the painting as a precursor of Monet's Thames series, exhibited to great acclaim in 1904 at Durand-Ruel's gallery. CCP

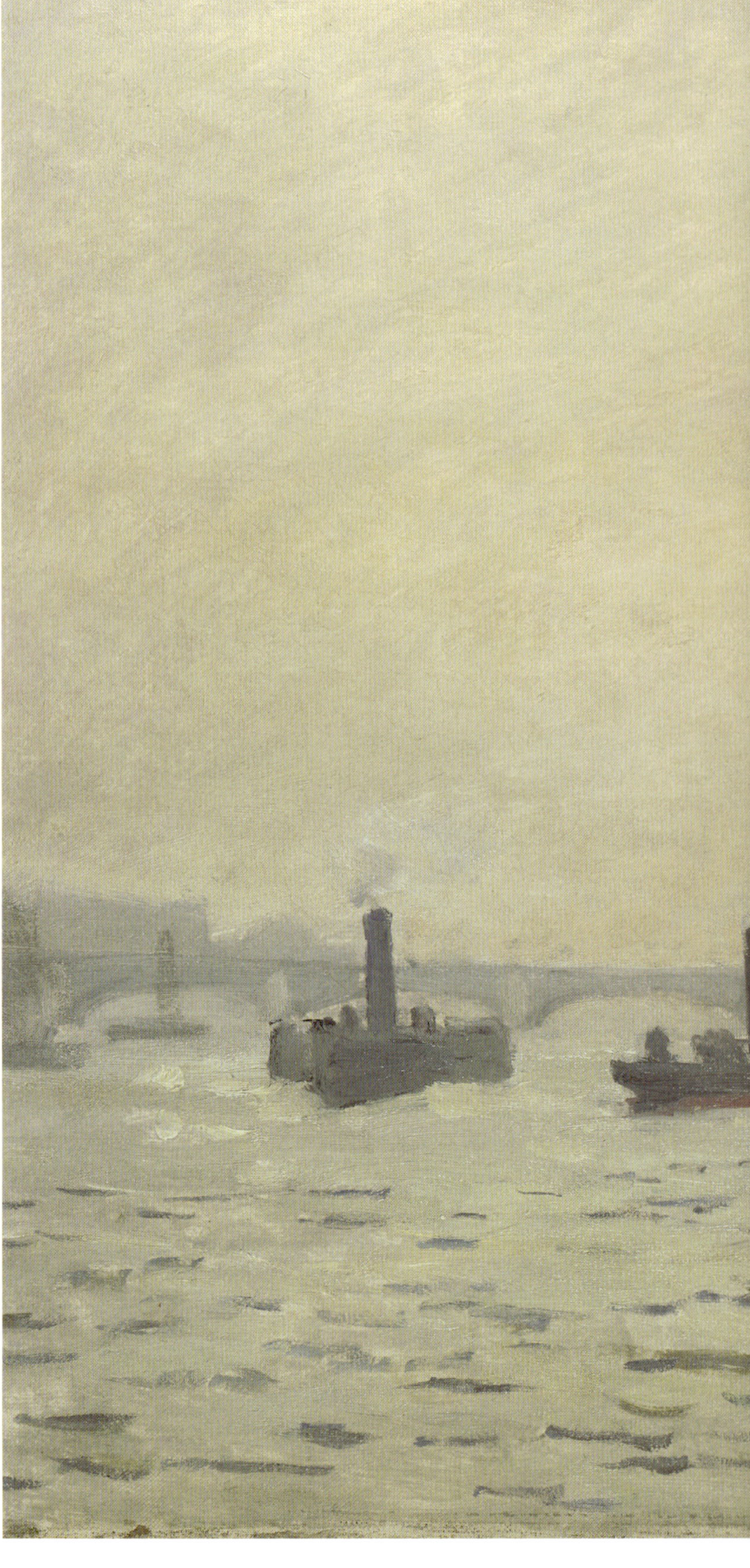

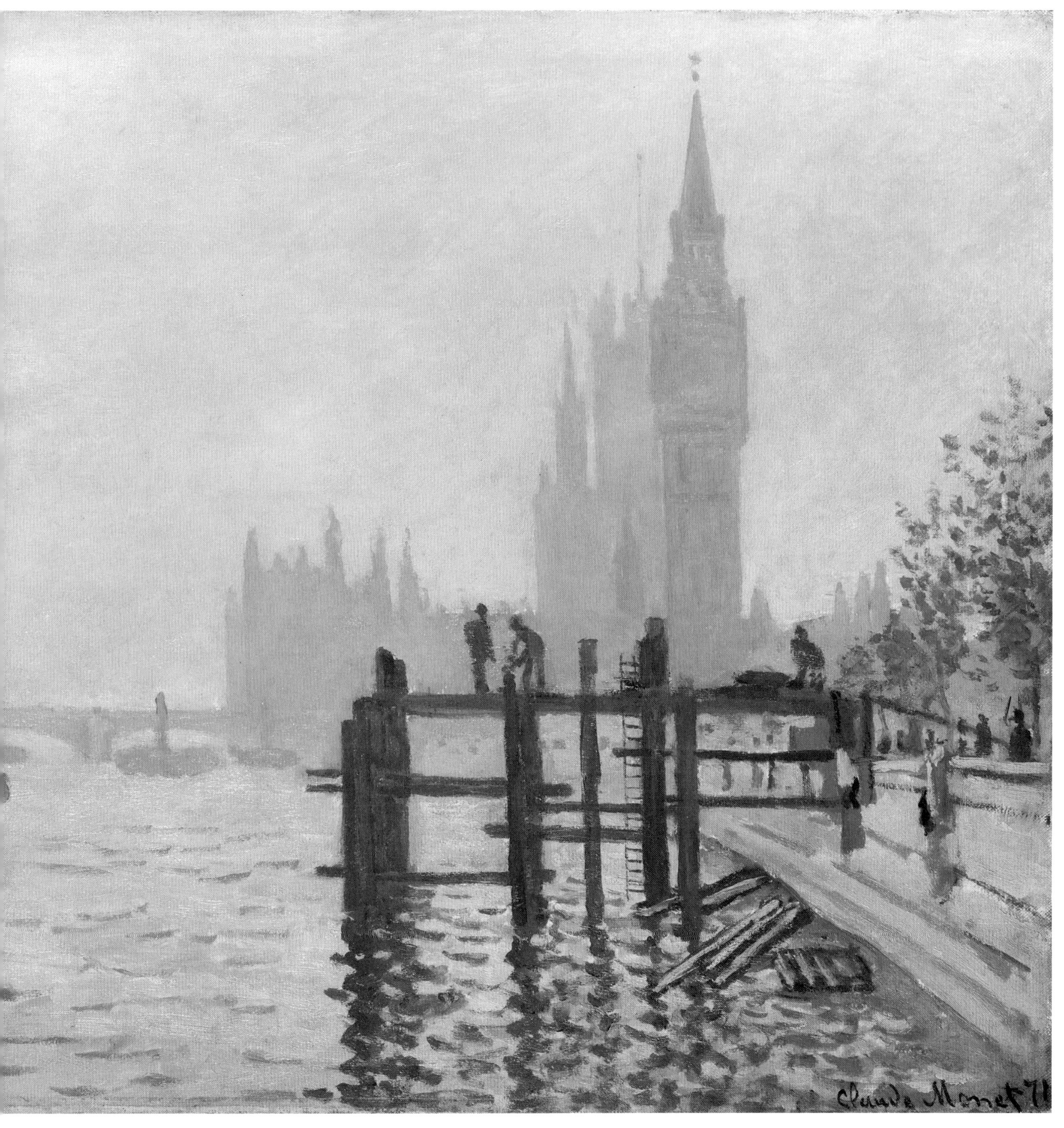
Claude Monet 71

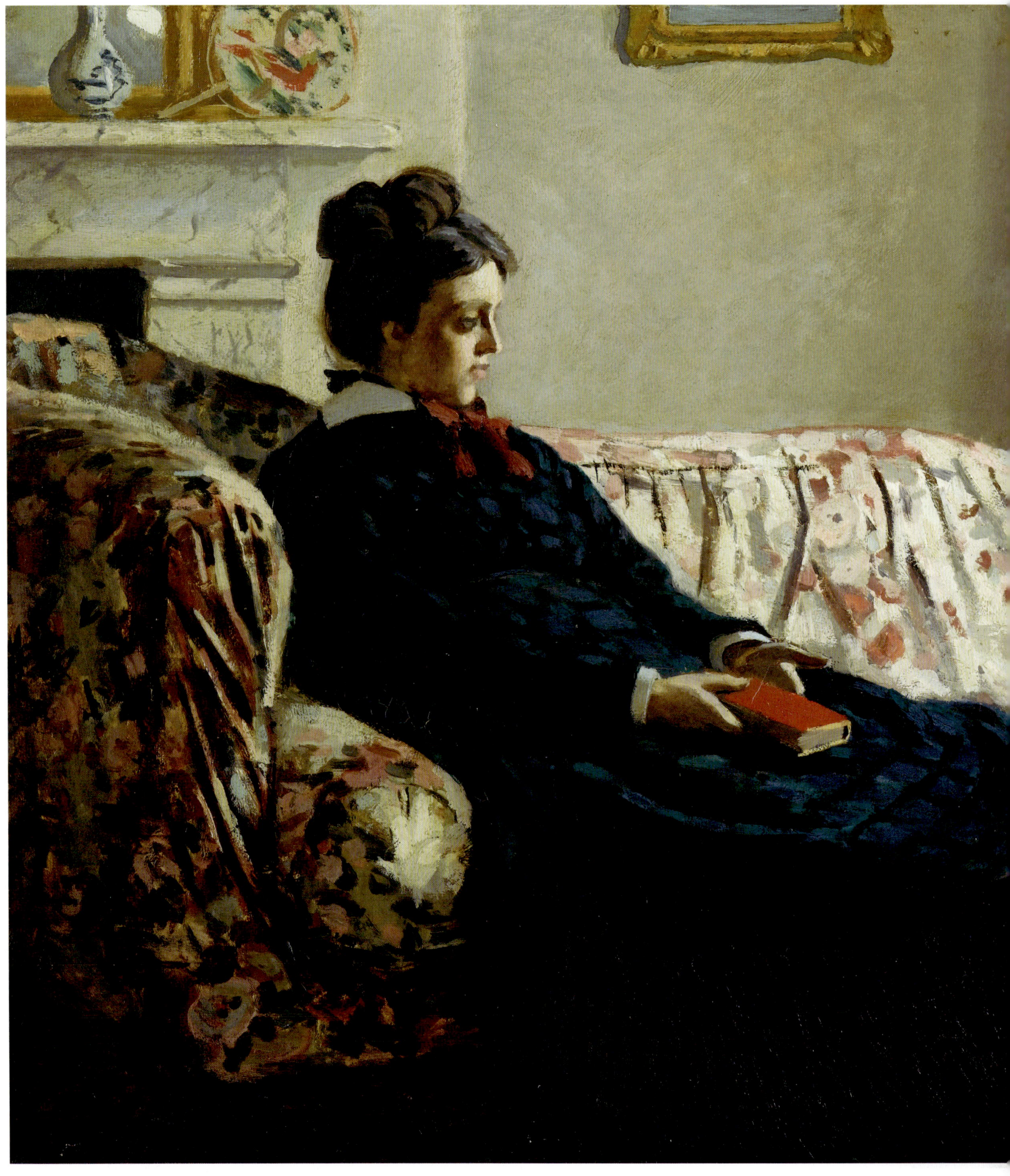

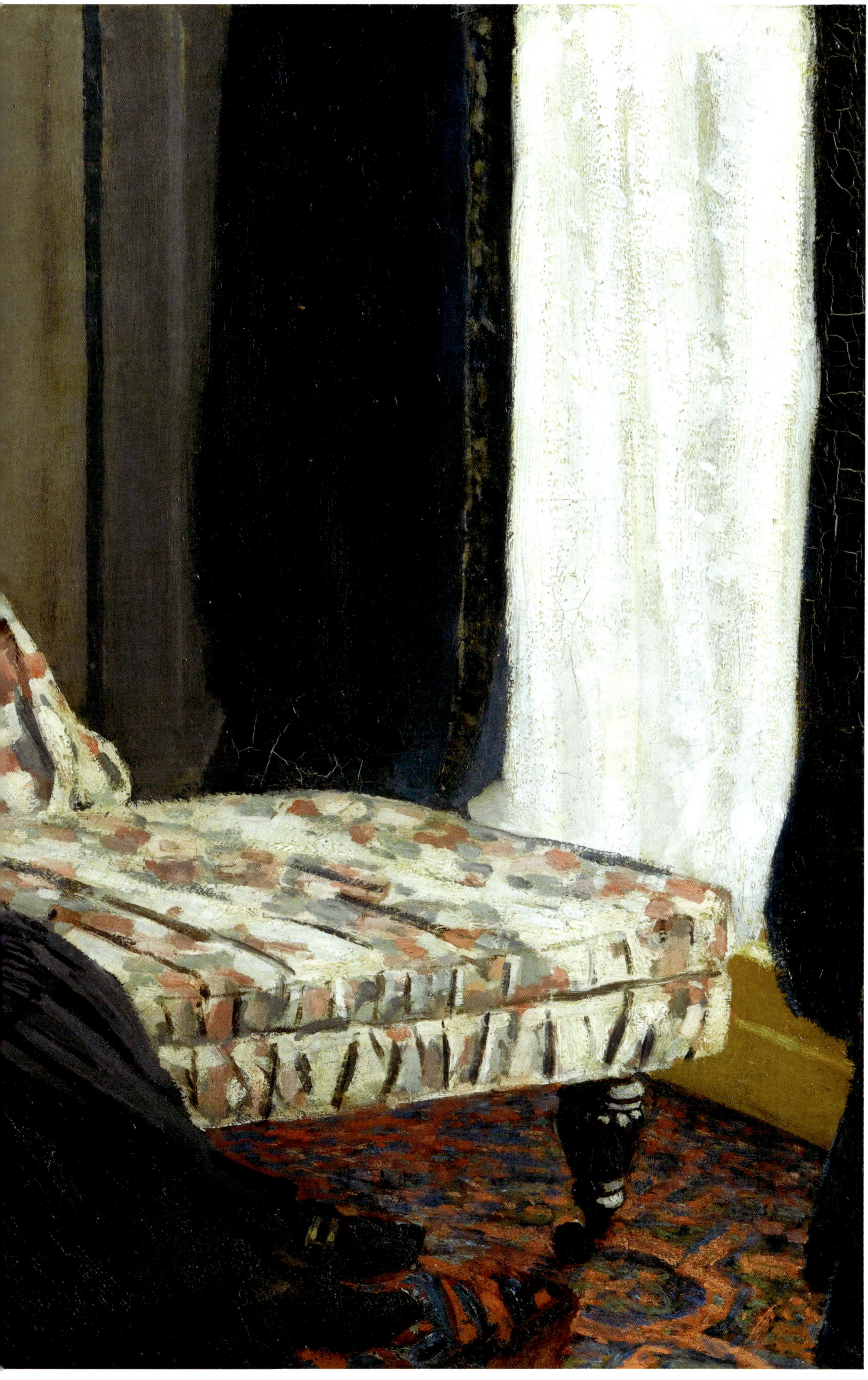

Claude Monet
1840–1926
Meditation (Madame Monet on the Sofa) c.1871
Oil paint on canvas 48.2 × 74.5

Musée d'Orsay, Paris. Bequeathed by M. and Mme Raymond Koechlin, 1931

The pensive woman in *Meditation* is Camille Doncieux, Monet's wife. They got married on 28 June 1870, only a few months before fleeing to London either in mid- to late September or very early October, so that Monet could avoid military conscription. Both Camille and their three-year-old son Jean followed Monet into exile, but whether they made the crossing with him or joined him later remains unclear. After a spell in temporary accommodation at 11 Arundel Street (now Coventry Street), near Piccadilly Circus, which he had left by 6 October, Monet moved to 1 Bath Place in Kensington. It is likely that Camille is represented in this new environment in this picture. The interior depicted by Monet is unmistakably British. The chintz-upholstered chaise longue, complete with floral motifs, and a Japanese fan and blue china on the mantelpiece, are typical of early aesthetic interiors. However, there is also a sense of sparsity in the decoration and a lack of cosiness, only accentuated by the crude London daylight that illuminates Camille's gloomy expression. She was originally portrayed with her hands clasped, the red book on her lap being a later addition. As John House noted, this alteration gave 'a suggestive dimension to the picture'[1] and may have justified the change of title from *Repose*, as it was known in 1871, to *Meditation*, while also appealing to the Victorian taste for literary subjects. From this point of view, the picture may indicate Monet's willingness and attempt to adapt to a British clientele.

Repose was exhibited in the French section of the International Exhibition in South Kensington (no.1273), of which Paul Durand-Ruel was one of the organisers. Of the three paintings Monet exhibited there, it was the only one to have been painted on British shores. Nevertheless, it did not find any English buyers. Nor did any of Monet's pictures during his nine month stay in 1870–1. CCP

Camille Pissarro
1830–1903
Fox Hill, Upper Norwood 1870
Oil paint on canvas 35.3 × 45.7

The National Gallery, London. Presented by Viscount and Viscountess Radcliffe, 1964

Camille Pissarro arrived in London at the beginning of December 1870, and remained in England until mid-June 1871. He originally settled with his partner Julie Vellay and their two children in Lower Norwood, but quickly moved to Upper Norwood, where this wintry scene was painted. Dated 1870, this was one of the first, if not *the* first, to have been painted by Pissarro in England. Although executed in the London suburbs, there is a rural quality to the landscape and the dwellings depicted by Pissarro. Crystal Palace, one of the great marvels of nineteenth-century architecture, could be seen from the top of Fox Hill, a view painted by Pissarro in *Crystal Palace, Upper Norwood* (p.71). The city attires of the man and two ladies seemingly engaging in conversation, however, give a clue about where the scene is set. If not for these and the red bricks, the painting is not dissimilar to some of Pissarro's Louveciennes landscapes of the previous year.

As Anne Robbins has suggested, *Fox Hill, Upper Norwood* may have been the painting exhibited by Paul Durand-Ruel in his New Bond Street gallery in March 1871 as *Winter Scenery* and/or *Upper Norwood*, shown in the French section of the International Exhibition in May 1871.[1] Unlike Daubigny and Monet, who crossed the channel with some of their paintings, Pissarro did not, which explains why the works that he exhibited in London were all British landscapes. CCP

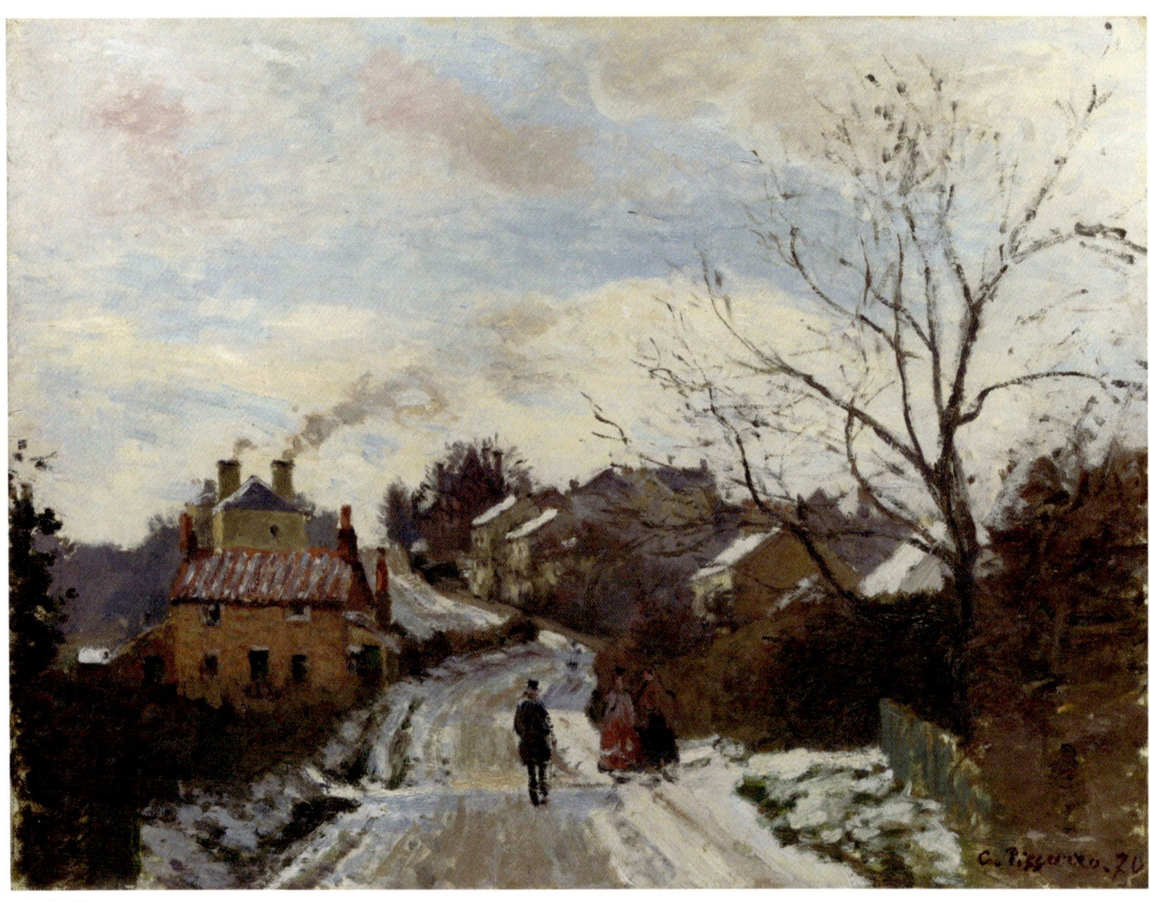

Camille Pissarro
1830–1903
Crystal Palace, Upper Norwood c.1871
Oil paint on canvas 40 × 50.8

Private collection

Pissarro painted Crystal Palace twice. Designed by Joseph Paxton, it was originally built in Hyde Park to house the Great Exhibition of 1851, and was transferred to Upper Norwood in 1854. The building itself, its attractions and varied programme of events drew in large crowds – in the region of two million visitors a year. As a result, the surrounding suburb became very fashionable and expanded rapidly.

In this painting the iron and glass structure of the palace is noticeable to the right mostly because of its 85-metre-high water towers. These were added to the building by Isambard Kingdom Brunel to replace Paxton's original ones when the palace was moved.

In *Crystal Palace, Upper Norwood*, even more so than in Pissarro's second view of the landmark (p.60), the building is not taking centre stage. Pissarro placed as much emphasis on the suburban pavilions and inhabitants as he did on what was popularly known as the 'people's palace', relegated to the background. He shifted emphasis from an international symbol of modernity to modern life itself. By comparison with *Fox Hill, Upper Norwood* (p.70), which shows a rural part of Norwood, this uphill view, only a stone's throw away, encapsulates life in London's new suburbs. CCP

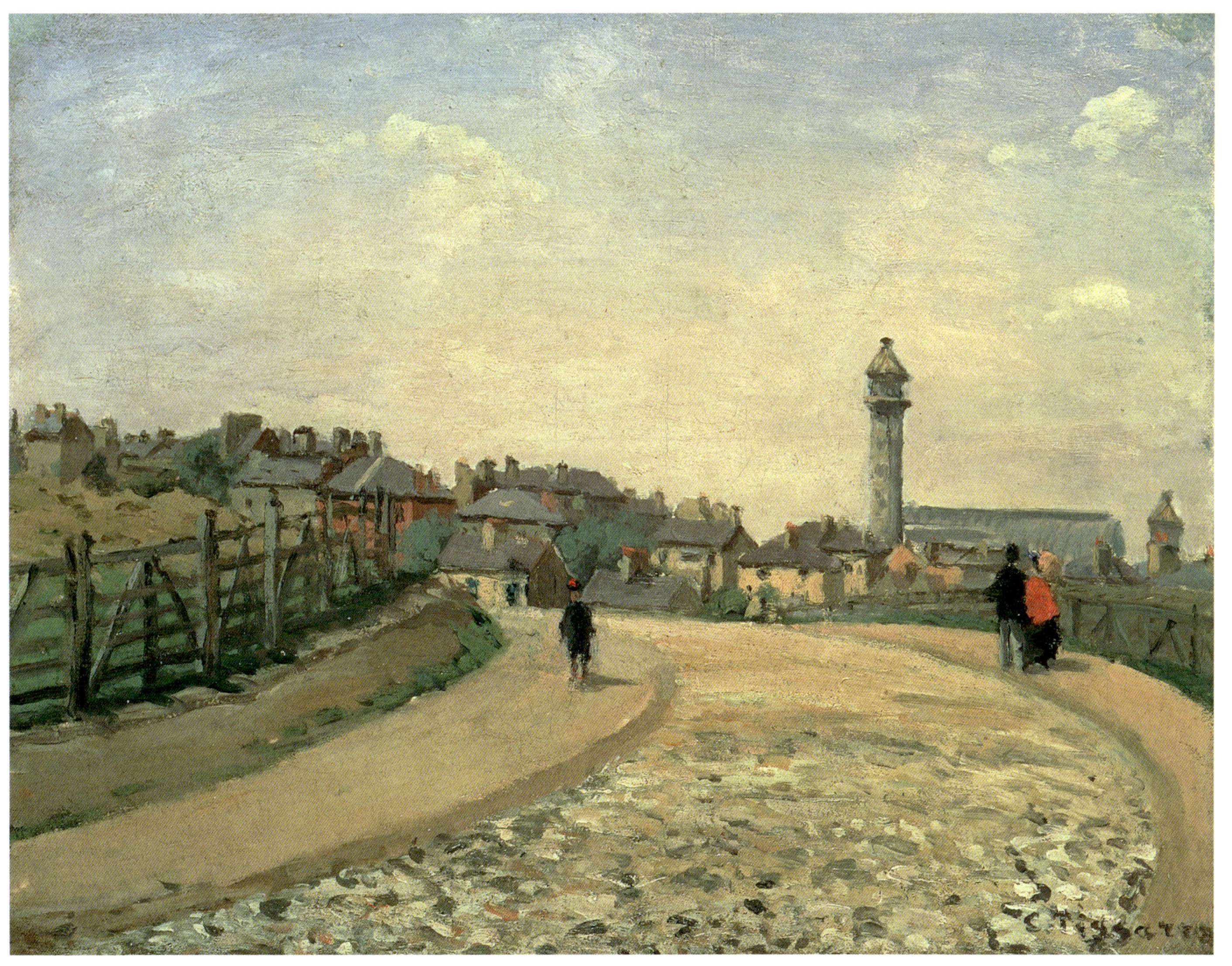

Camille Pissarro
1830–1903
Dulwich College c.1870
Oil paint on canvas 50 × 61

Fondation Bemberg

Dulwich College was not dated by Pissarro, but judging by the trees in the picture, it is likely that he painted it in the late autumn or early winter 1870, shortly after his arrival in Britain. Dulwich College was close to West Norwood, where Pissarro had settled, and as such was a building of prime interest in his neighbourhood. 'New College', as it was known, was designed by Charles Barry Jr.. Freely inspired by the northern Italian Gothic style, it was officially opened on 21 June 1870 by the Prince and Princess of Wales.

The black figures dotting the centre of the picture are certainly pupils in their black gowns. Pissarro's own nephew Alfred Isaacson would join their rank in September 1871. The warm tones of the building's red-brick facade with its terracotta ornaments accord harmoniously with the yellow leaves of the tree reflected in the Old Mill pond, and the golden light of the low sun. The free broken brushwork adopted by Pissarro to depict the pond is particularly impressionistic (even though he and his friends did not appropriate the term until the mid-1870s), and bolder than in his other London works of 1870–1. The picture is unsigned and bears his studio stamp with his initials: its broader treatment may therefore be explained by the fact that it was not quite finished by Pissarro's standards. CCP

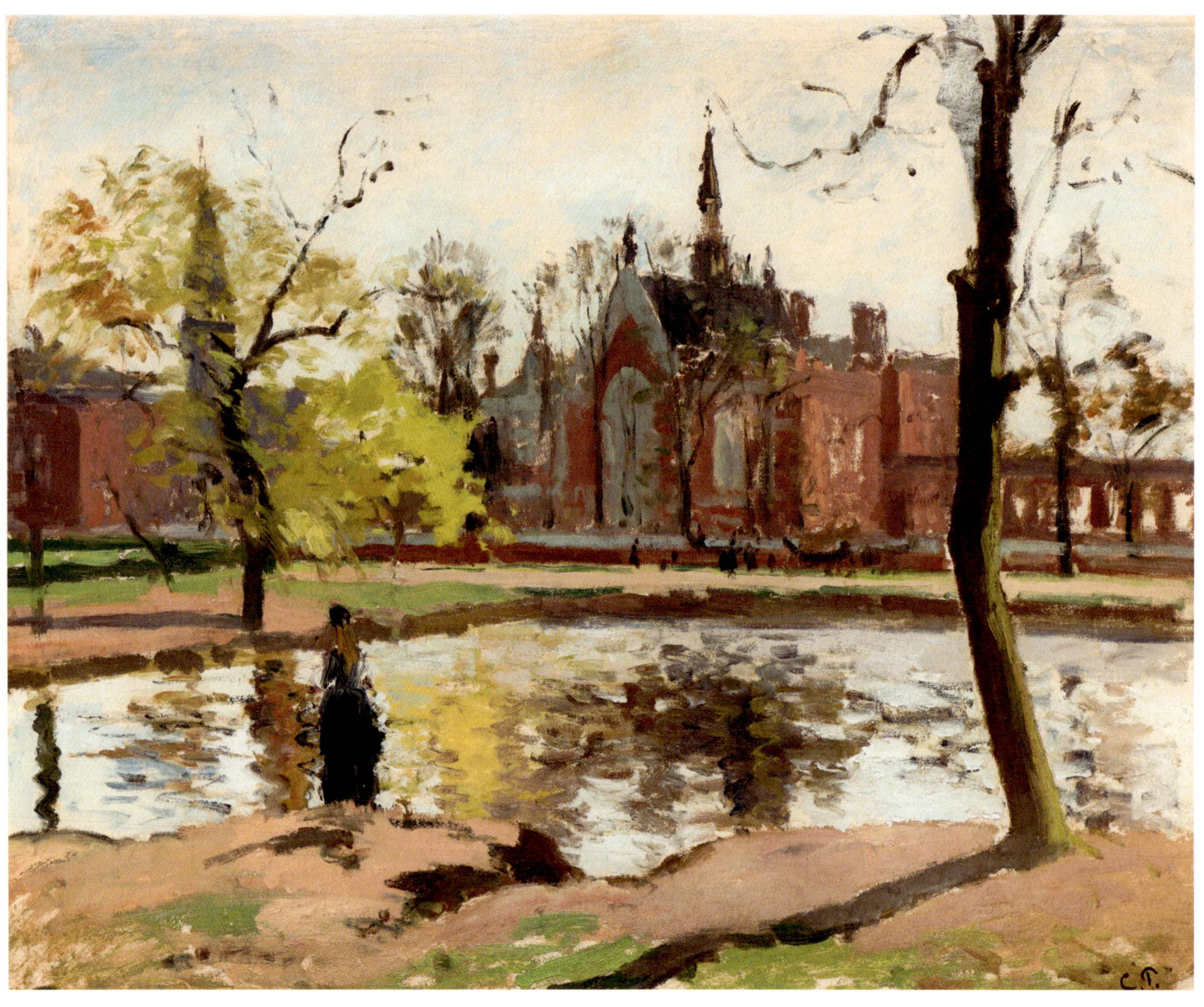

Camille Pissarro
1830–1903
All Saints' Church, Beulah Hill, Upper Norwood 1871
Gouache on paper, 18.2 × 22.8

Private collection

This gouache relates to an oil painting of Beulah Hill in the snow (1871; private collection), which includes more of the street in the right part of the composition, just like a watercolour of the same view kept at the Ashmolean Museum, Oxford. The remarkable luminosity that infuses the gouache radiates from the sun through a multitude of small cross-hatched brush strokes in varied pastel shades, almost mirrored by the treatment of the snowy road. It exemplifies at its best Pissarro's mastery of the medium. His primary concern with the diffusion of light in this work is also key to the warm glow of the related oil painting (private collection), and the animated treatment of the sky in both media would point to his recent contact with Turner's oeuvre. The composition of the gouache is firmly structured by the street lamp in the centre, and by the verticality of the tower and spire of All Saints' Church (added in 1841 to the original design of James Savage, built in 1827–9), echoed to the right by tall trees. Pissarro must have found this subject compelling: three drawings survive at the Ashmolean Museum, and an additional one is kept at the Metropolitan Museum of Art, New York. CCP

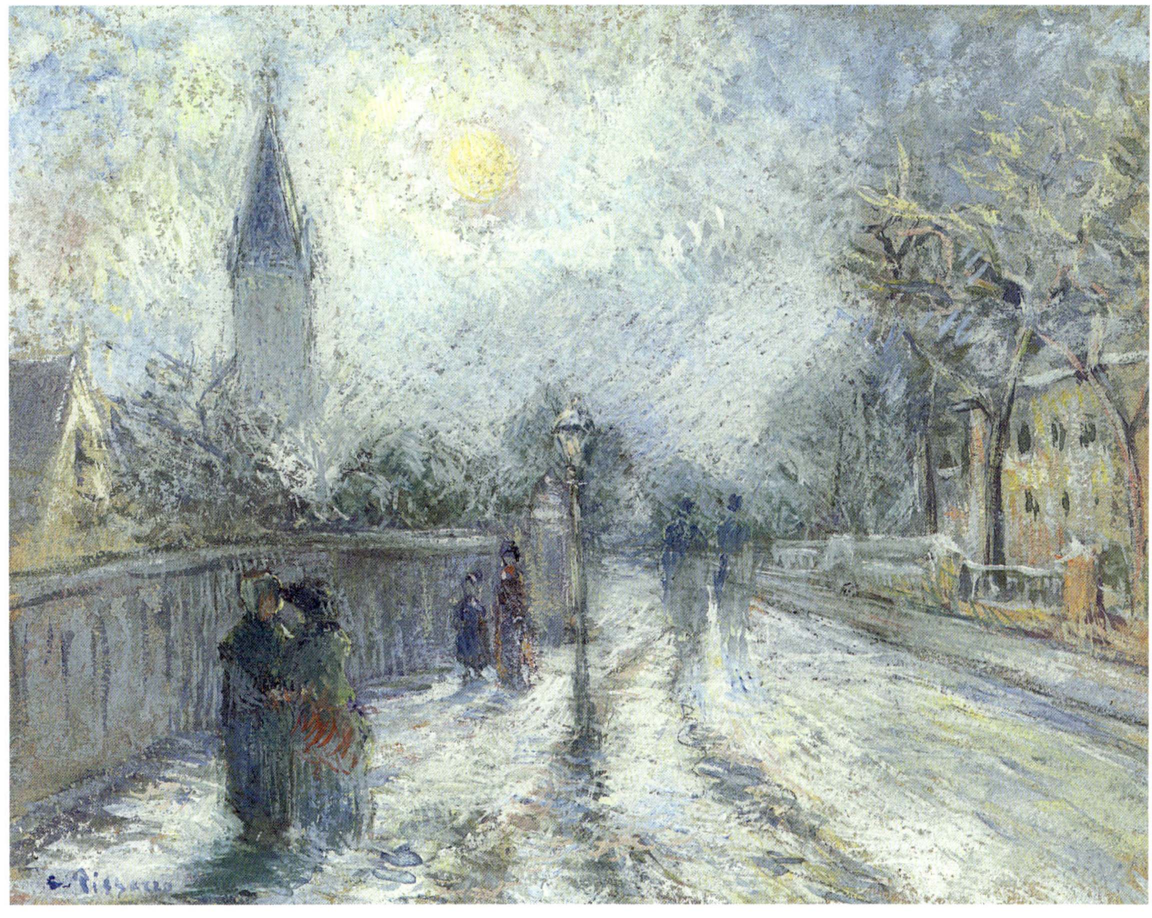

Camille Pissarro
1830–1903
The Avenue, Sydenham 1871
Oil paint on canvas 48 × 73

The National Gallery, London. Bought, 1984

On the horizon of this picture, where its vanishing lines meet, stands St Bartholomew Church in Sydenham, built by Lewis Vulliamy in the 1830s and remodelled by Edwin Nash. Alterations were close to completion when Pissarro painted this Victorian thoroughfare, which has little changed but is now known as Lawrie Avenue.

The Avenue, Sydenham is one of the largest paintings produced by Pissarro in London. The canvas is divided vertically by the road in a highly controlled composition, a principle favoured by Pissaro in the late 1860s and 1870s. The firm resulting structure is accentuated by the symmetry of two tall trees, either side of the avenue. The figures of passers-by, concentrated in the middle plane of the picture, were added later, with calligraphic brush strokes and a great economy of means. The wheels of the carriage, in particular, were executed with very little paint on top of a dry layer showing through.

Compared with paintings executed just before his exile, Pissarro adopted a higher-keyed palette, using bright shades of blue and green. The contrasting hues of the red brick house with the green roof to the left, echoed on the horizon by another similar house, provide strong highlights. Pissarro later wrote to his son Lucien about his time in Britain: 'I recall perfectly those multicoloured houses, and the desire I had at the time to interrupt my journey and make some interesting studies.'[1] *The Avenue, Sydenham* was the first painting to be purchased by Paul Durand-Ruel after their meeting in London. As well as marking the start of a lifetime partnership, it is also significant in that Durand-Ruel kept it in his own collection until his death. When Pissarro saw the picture again in 1899, he wrote to his niece: 'It is admirably well preserved and far superior to what I thought of this painting back then; there is a striving for unity in it that filled me with joy, it is almost what I am searching for today, minus the light and brilliance.'[2]
CCP

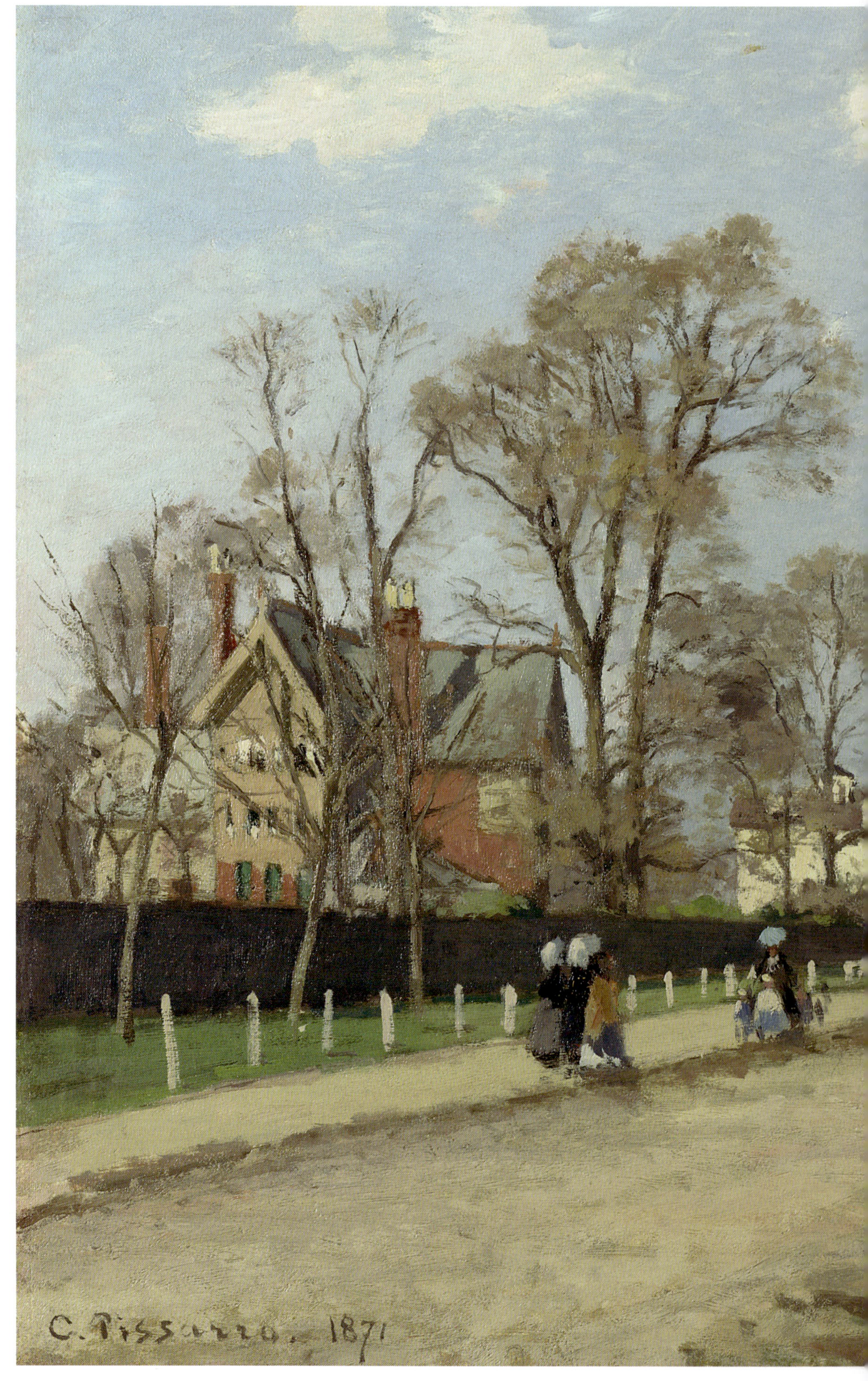

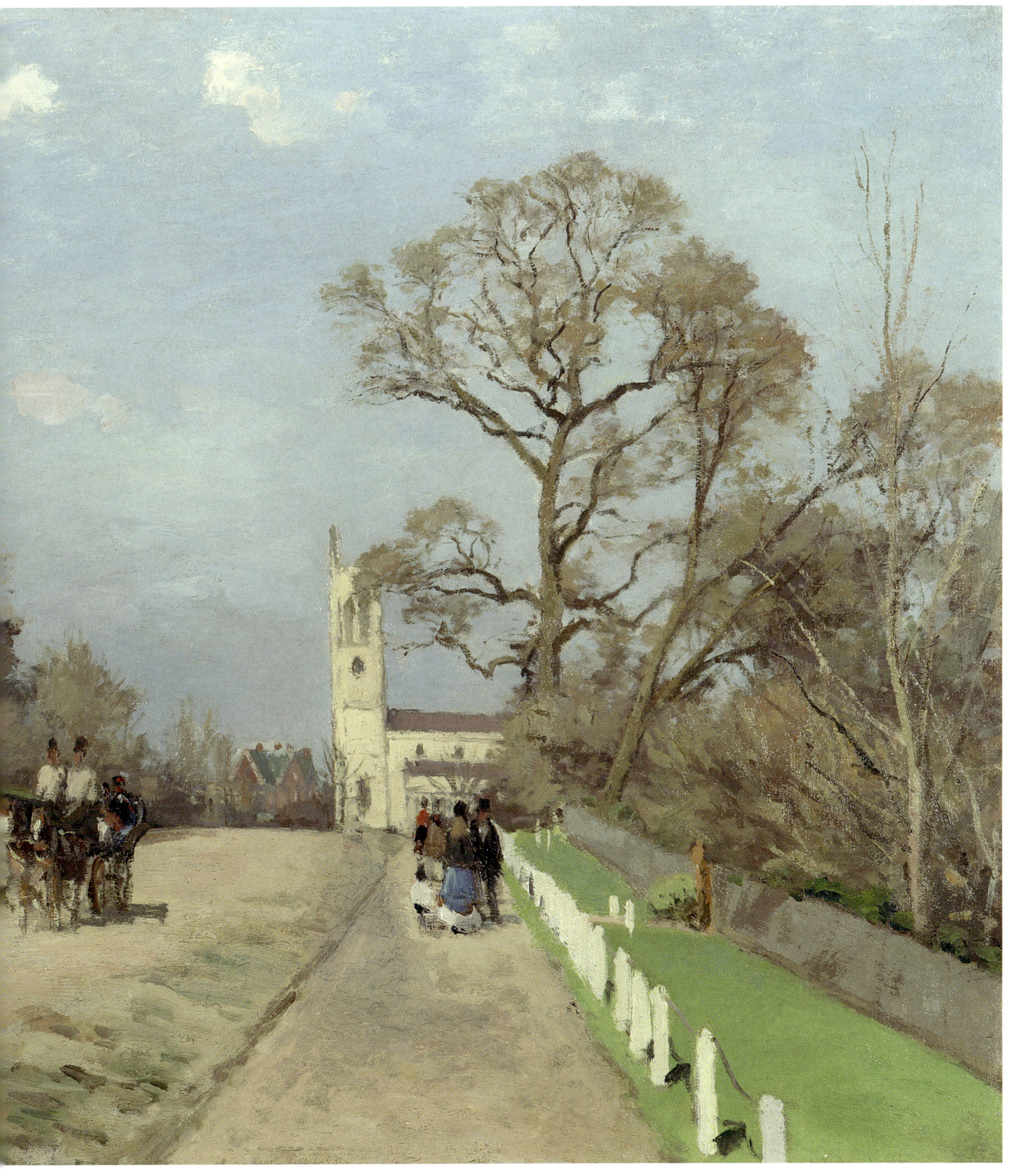

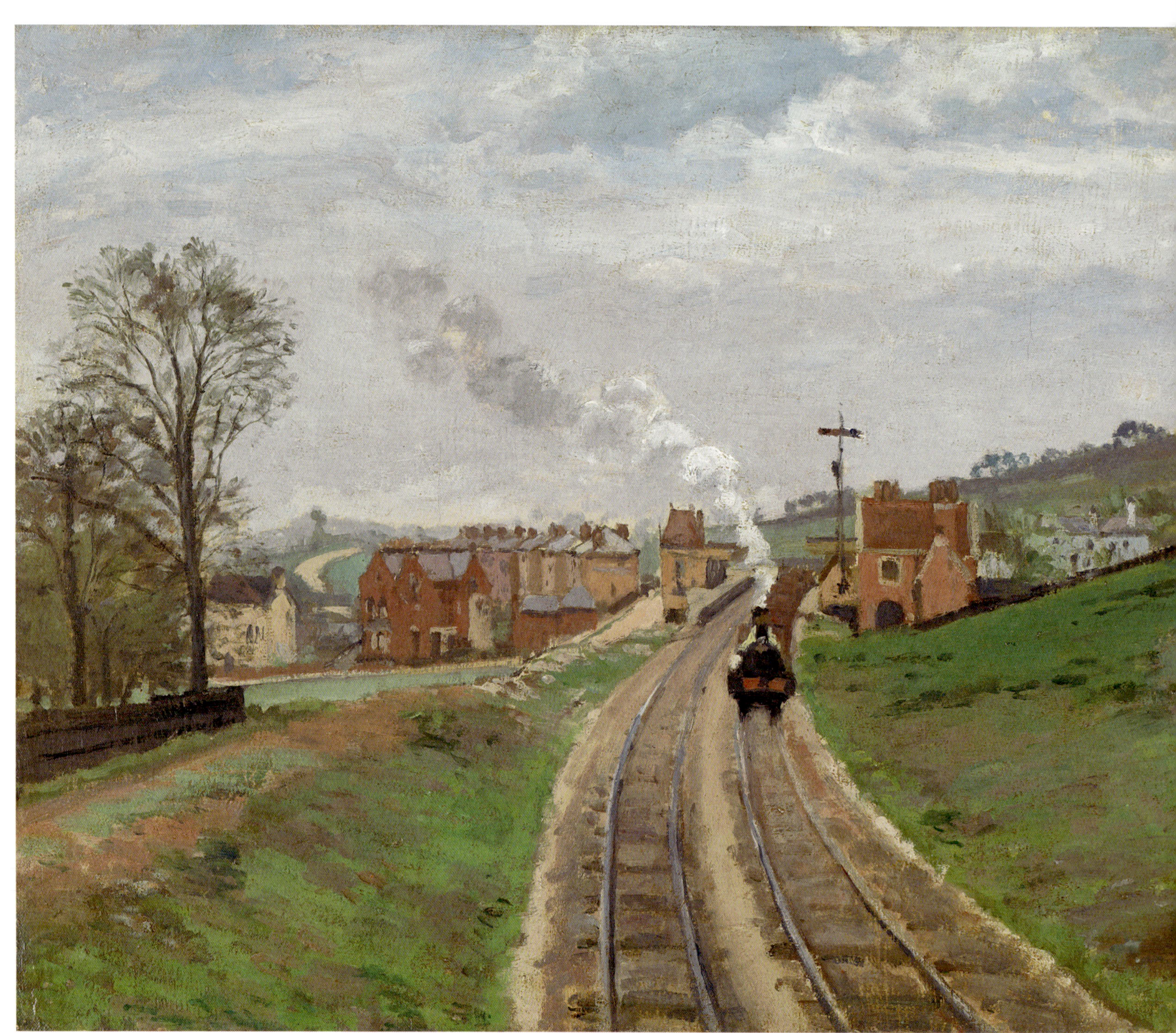

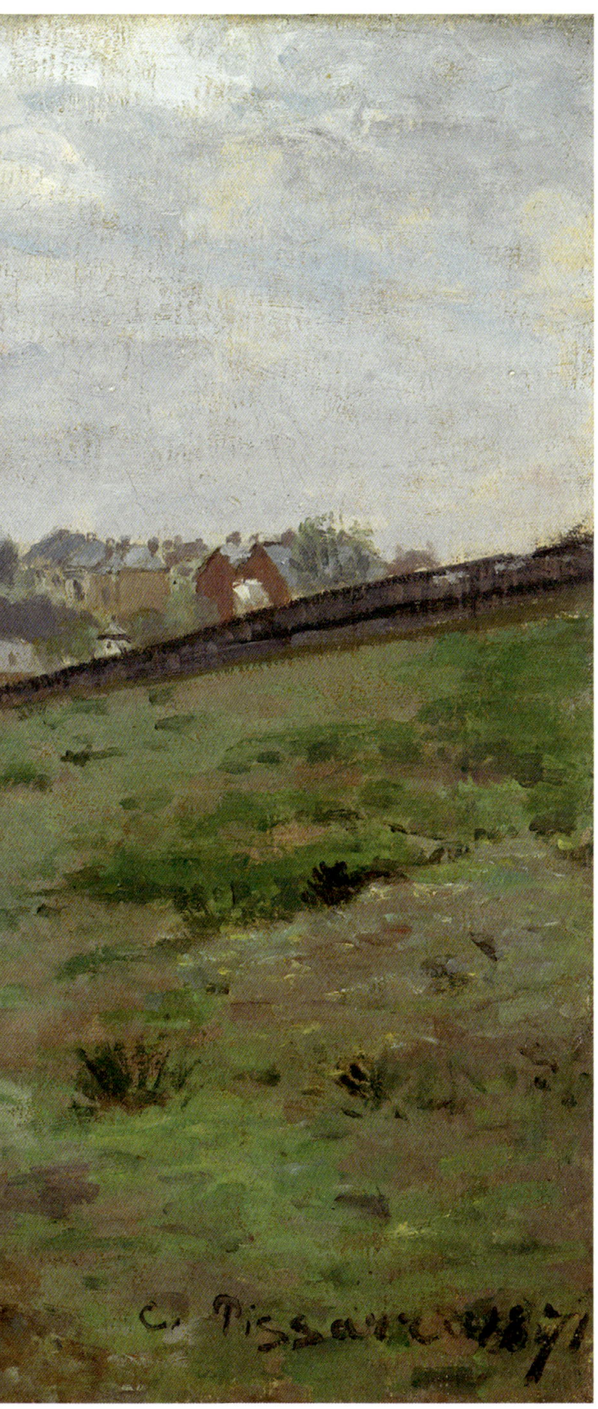

Camille Pissarro
1830–1903
Lordship Lane Station, Dulwich 1871
Oil paint on canvas 44.5 × 72.5

The Samuel Courtauld Trust, The Courtauld Gallery, London

Lordship Lane Station, Dulwich is one of Pissarro's best-known pictures of his London exile, possibly because of its quintessentially modern subject. Like his other English works of 1870–1, it demonstrates his interest in suburbs as a liminal space, urban yet still rural, and *Lordship Lane* firmly extols Pissarro's embrace of modernity and the expansion of suburbia as subject matter. The development of the railway in the late nineteenth century was instrumental in agglomerating Dulwich village and its neighbourhood to London, but East Dulwich was still only partly built up, as the dominant green slopes indicate.

Pissarro placed his easel on a footbridge overlooking the scene: a train departs slowly from the now defunct Lordship Lane station. The smoke puffing out of the locomotive reveals its feeble celerity. Pissarro's use of plunging perspective – a novelty for him – casts light on his recent discovery and appreciation of J.M.W. Turner, but also on the distance that he took from his art. Bar the subject and composition of *Lordship Lane* itself, Pissarro's picture greatly contrasts with *Rain, Steam and Speed* (1844; The National Gallery, London), with which it has been canonically compared. The frontal depiction of the train makes it look almost stationary in its peaceful environment. Pissarro's interest in his subject matter lies more in the normality of a familiar daily scene than in dazzling atmospheric effects and gestural brushwork. *Lordship Lane* is a picture of the ordinary. Apart from the blue showing through the clouds and the green of the meadow, Pissarro used a muted palette: numerous shades of earthy brown and grey emerge from the patchy grass. These and the cloudy sky impart the painting with slight melancholy.

Lordship Lane is highly significant in the history of those who would soon be known as impressionists, as being amongst the first of many occurrences of a train as prime focus within the composition. This motif would become strongly associated with their preoccupation with all aspects of modern life. In the context of Pissarro's exile, the departure of the train resonates with his own displacement. *Lordship Lane* was one of the last paintings that he executed before his return to France, at a time when he had repeatedly expressed his homesickness and his despondency at not finding a British clientele. The painting was purchased by a Frenchman living in London, Jules Berthel, alongside two or three other works by Pissarro.[1] Berthel was the manager of a cognac- and wine-producing company belonging to the father of the art critic Théodore Duret, who had urged Pissarro to go and meet this prospective buyer. This he did at least on two occasions during his stay in London.[2] CCP

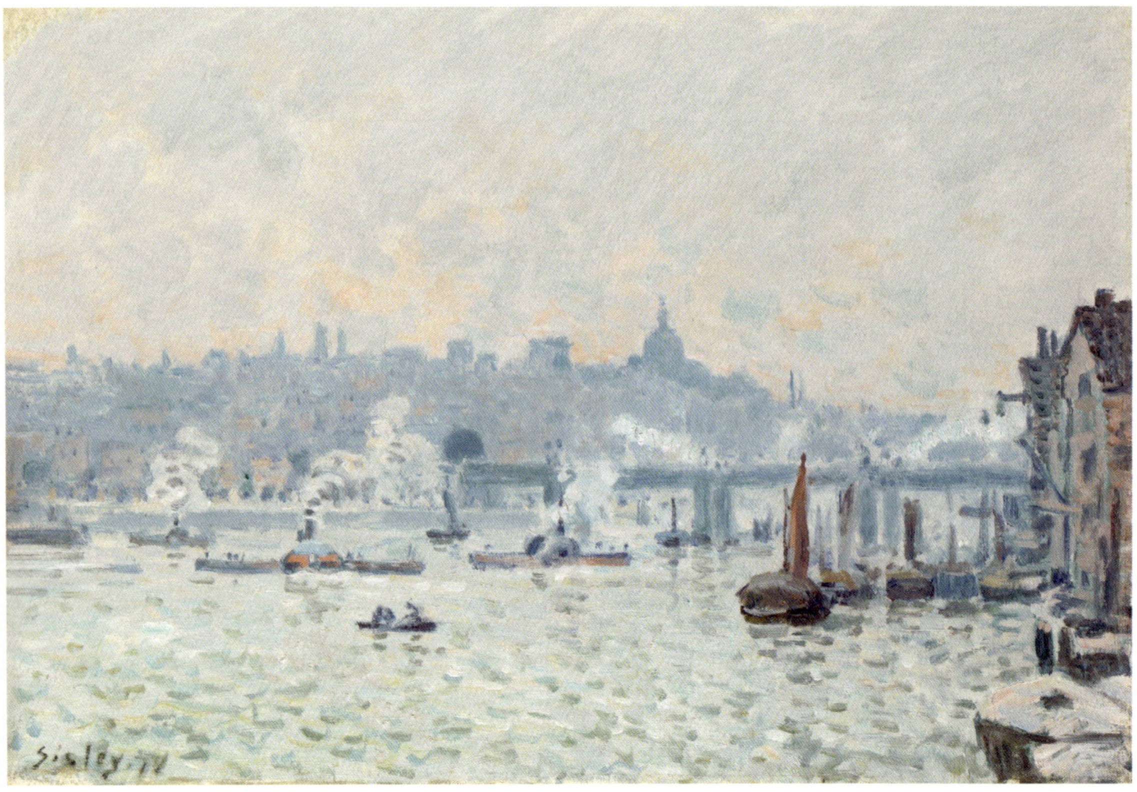

Alfred Sisley
1839–1899
View of the Thames: Charing Cross Bridge 1874
Oil paint on canvas 33 × 46

Andrew Brownsword Arts Foundation, on loan to the National Gallery, London

Although born in Paris, Sisley retained the English nationality of his parents. London was already familiar to him when he came to stay in June 1874. A merchant's son, he had already crossed the Channel seventeen years earlier, ostensibly to study commerce, though he had spent most of his four years being educated in London's museums. Back in Paris, he abandoned the business world in order to follow his vocation. He entered Gleyre's studio where he made friends with Bazille, Renoir and Monet. As young Sisley was relatively well off, he could be relaxed about sharing the bohemian lifestyle of his studio companions with whom he painted in the Paris area along the Seine. Having been scattered during the War of 1870 that had led to Bazille's death, the friends gathered to face the hazards of the art market together with an exhibition of the 'Anonymous Society of Painters, Sculptors, Printmakers'. Open from 15 April to 15 May 1874 in Nadar's photography studio, this first independent event marked the 'official' birth of impressionism.

In addition to his mastery of English, Sisley knew the art of English landscape painters well: Constable, Turner and Richard Parkes Bonington. Far from bringing Sisley's British nationality into view, Durand-Ruel had selected a few canvases for his collective exhibitions of the Society of French Artists.[1] The Parisian dealer used this name to introduce new French painting to the English people.[2] Henceforth Sisley, thirty-four years old, ruined by the war and father of two children, would face financial insecurity from which he would never have any respite. The trip to London funded by Jean-Baptiste Faure from July to October 1874 (see p.79) appeared serendipitous.

View of the Thames was probably begun as soon as he arrived. The canvas corresponds to a standard landscape format of French manufacture. It can be inferred that the artist, who had been anxious to get to work as quickly as possible, had taken care to bring it in his luggage. As Daubigny had done before him (p.62), he chose an unobstructed panoramic view. Paradoxically, of the fourteen canvases used during his stay in England, that of the centre of London is the smallest. Stationed on the south bank of the river near Westminster Bridge, the artist yields to the picturesque necessities of river traffic and, without worrying about topographical accuracy, places St Paul's dome on a hillside bristling with roofs.

Preceding Pissarro and Monet by a few years, he chose the modern Charing Cross Bridge, used by steam trains, to trace a horizontal line between the two shores. Here, the 'damp-looking dirty blackness' of the industrial city has metamorphosed into a haze of grey fog and blue vapours.[3] The brush dictates form, modifying the texture and orientation of the strokes to convey infinite variations in light. Since 1870 Sisley had been experimenting with this new way of painting, which overturned landscape traditions and sold so little.

The noise and discomfort of London could not suit this lover of the outdoors, so he soon left South Kensington in order to follow the Thames westwards. In this direction the outskirts quickly became residential and 'recreative',[4] whereas in the other direction, downstream from London, commercial and industrial activities were concentrated along the river from Westminster to the sea. IC

Alfred Sisley
1839–1899
Molesey Weir, Hampton Court, Morning 1874
Oil paint on canvas 51.1 × 68.8

Scottish National Gallery, Edinburgh

In the second half of the nineteenth century, with the extension of the railway and the opening of the great royal residence to the public, Hampton Court benefited from 'gentle' modernisation that made it an ideal destination for city dwellers. Sisley found lodging in one of the hotels near the train station, which allowed him, as at Louveciennes, Bougival and Marly-le-Roi, to stay closer to his subject. The locks at Molesey, whose renovation had made river navigation easier, were situated upstream not far from the Hampton Court estate. One could just follow the water to get there. Sisley came several times to paint from one side or the other of the weir.

On the canvas the composition is divided by the horizontal line of the dam with its bristling bicolour posts above the tumultuous foam of the rushing water. The overcast sky is painted monochromatically in grey half-tones in contrast to the intense greens of the foliage and the indigo water. With its wild energy, nature catches the eye immediately. Jerome K. Jerome was proud of the fact that this part of the river was far from urban complexes and so left 'the river-banks to woods and fields and water-works'.[1]

Molesey, however, was not Ville d'Avray, which the old master Corot had peopled with timeless nymphs. Sisley makes discreet indications apparent in his landscape that keep his viewpoint in the present. The calm expanse of the reservoir upriver of the dam is an invitation to swimming, as is suggested by the presence of the two bathers added later in the left corner of the picture.[2] Humorously, with a few touches of colour, Sisley paints a third man wearing a straw hat who is prosaically occupied with removing his socks before soaking his feet in the water. The town can be seen in the distance, with its bell tower and the dome of the Temple to Shakespeare situated in the gardens of Garrick's Villa; further to the right behind a screen of trees emerge the ochre walls of Tagg's Island Hotel.[3]

The work was one of the English paintings selected by Jean-Baptiste Faure, to whom Sisley had given the first choice of six pictures in exchange for having his travel costs covered. The famous baritone kept it all his life. It was exhibited in the first retrospective on the artist in Paris at the Galerie Georges Petit in March 1897. Sisley, who wanted to assemble the best from different periods and avoid all monotony, had solicited his most faithful patron for the occasion.
IC

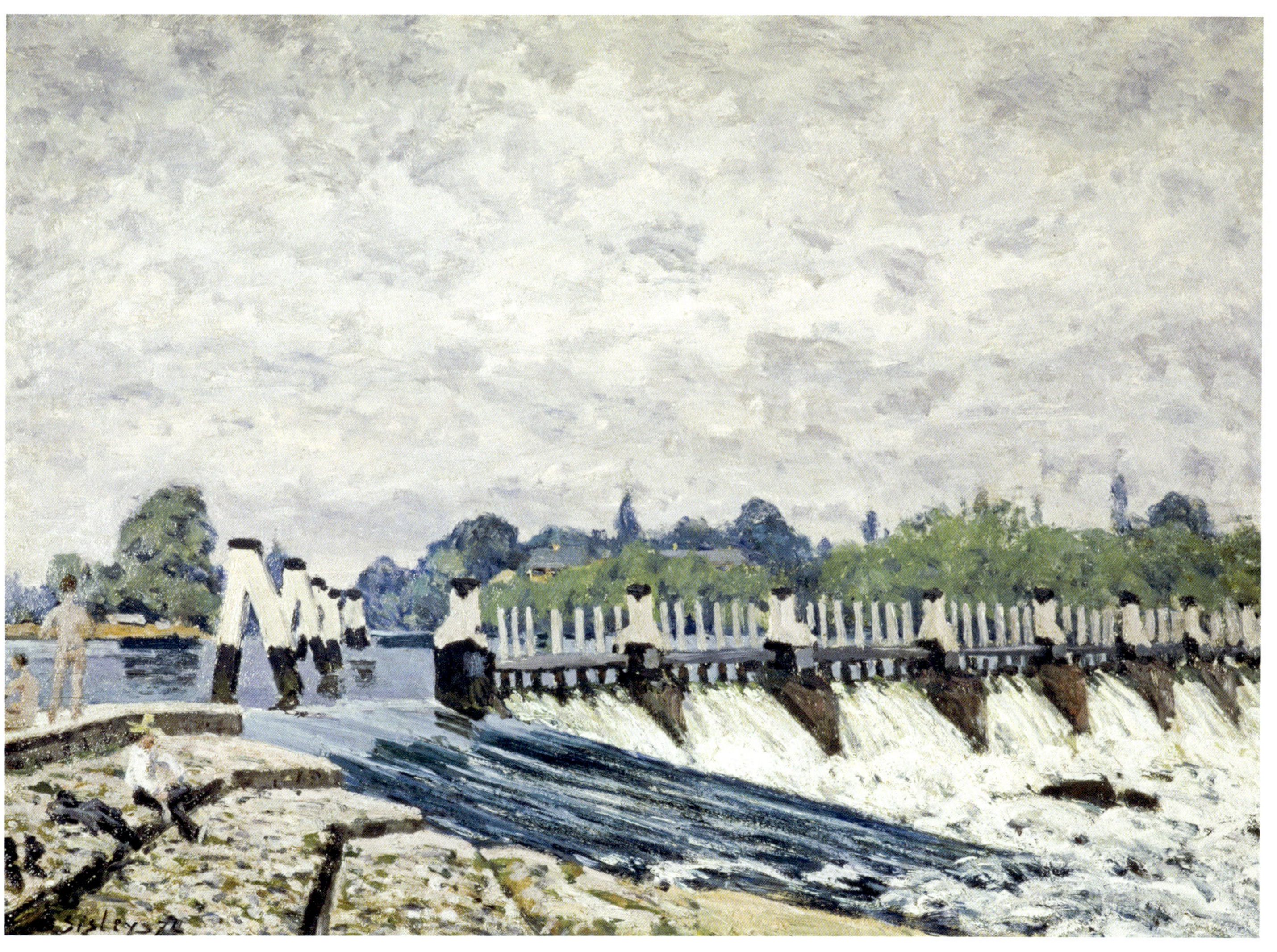

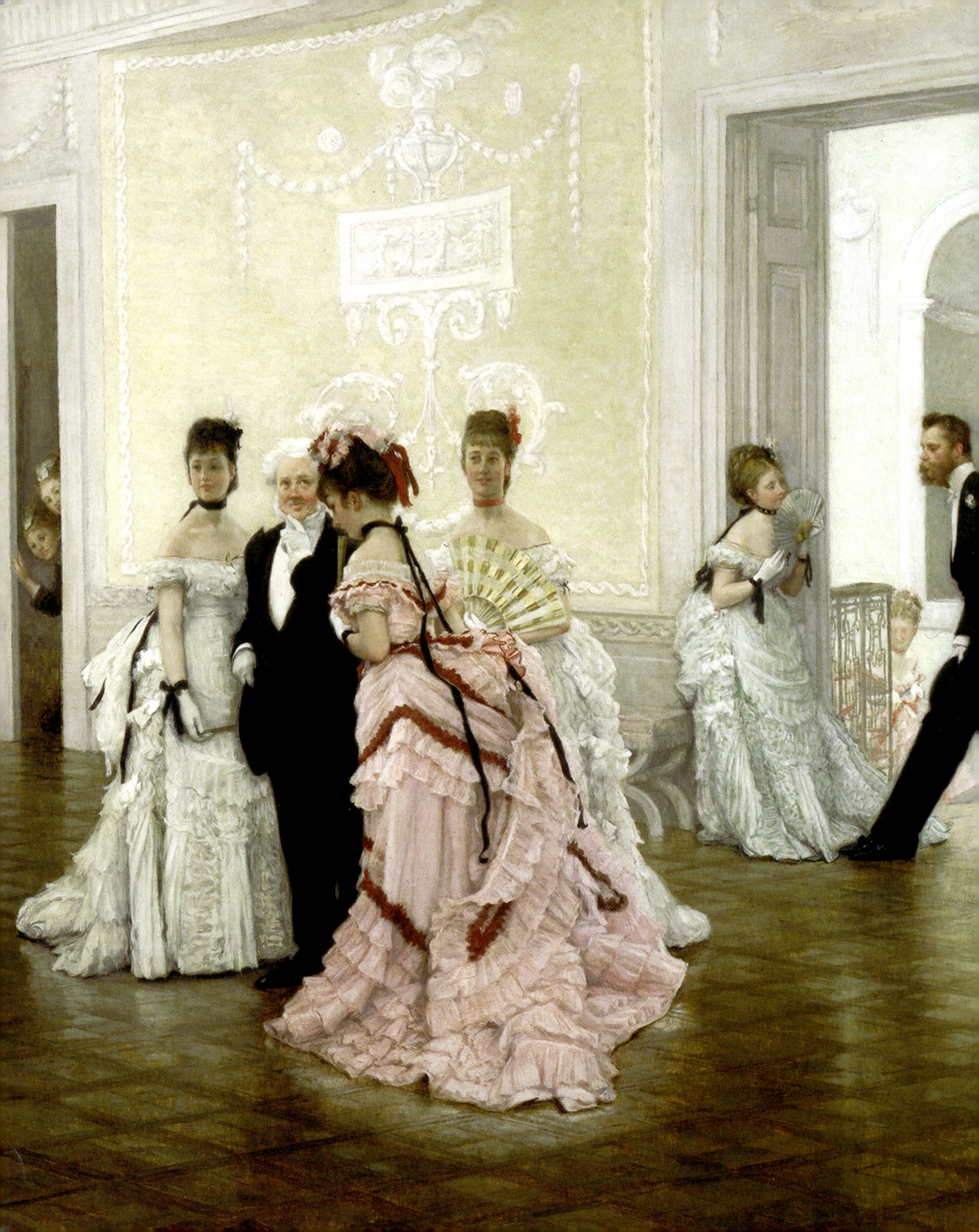

Cyrille Sciama

James Tissot, the Englishman

> Tall, strong, well balanced and with a solid appearance, James Tissot kept, perhaps unconsciously, a slightly British coldness when he found himself in the presence of someone he did not know. But he did not hesitate to lose his stiffness when the incognito was broken, and soon revealed himself in a benevolent light, captivating his visitor with the recital of his broad knowledge. [As] elegant in the way he dressed as he was fastidious in his choice of words, James Tissot appeared younger than he was. His facial features were regular; his eyes lit up an energetic face, borne out by his surprising activity. His nose was straight and thin, the expression of his intelligent appearance.[1]

Cold but benevolent, elegant but distant, James Tissot (Nantes, 1836–Chenecey-Buillon, 1902) appears elusive, a dandy who was difficult to figure out.[2] His correspondence is rare and documentation scattered. Part of his private life can only be discerned through his work. For his entire life the artist hesitated between France and England, between impressionism and Pre-Raphaelitism, between the outdoors and society life. A friend of Whistler, Degas and Manet, but also Paul Helleu, Giovanni Boldini and Henri Gervex, he incarnated a style, a certain French panache. Tissot enjoyed considerable success in his lifetime. He wished to be English in Paris and French in London, a paradox that renders him unclassifiable. His ironic gaze on British customs testifies to his French attachments, while his lifestyle identifies him as gentry.

From Paris to London

When Tissot arrived in London in June 1871, he was a well-known wealthy painter who was envied in France. In fact, his success was meteoric: after his studies in Nantes, he entered the Ecole des Beaux-Arts in Paris in 1857 in the studio of Hippolyte Flandrin. His parents, from a comfortable background, finally resigned themselves to letting him go.[3] The painter had a Catholic upbringing and would always remain very religious. He quickly exhibited his works in the Salon of French Artists without ever winning the Prix de Rome. All his life he would play the public against institutions, the art market against official art, critics against cliques. This 'complex being', as the Goncourts described him, began his career with medieval religious and literary subjects inspired by the Belgian Henri Leys.[4] His subjects demonstrated his interest for costumes and implicit narratives in which women were objects of covetous desire and incomprehension. As of 1855, he changed his traditional first name from 'Jacques-Joseph' to 'James' and dated his first signed painting (*Portrait of a Young Girl*, private collection). He became friends with James Abbott McNeill Whistler (whom he met at the Luxembourg Museum), Edgar Degas and Edouard Manet, and in 1864 built himself a mansion on the very chic Avenue de l'Impératrice.[5] Tissot was a society artist, a dandy. He presented himself as someone easily given to mockery, as can be seen in his *Self-Portrait* c.1865 (p.83).

Tissot introduced himself to the public with the insolence of a golden youth who could be caught instantaneously in a

James Tissot
Too Early 1873
(detail, see p.94)

photograph, as Degas would do a few years later (*Portait of James Tissot* 1867–8, Metropolitan Museum of Art, New York).[6] In this period he repeatedly made portraits influenced by Ingres in their treatment of figures, settings, costumes and psychology, as in the *Portrait of Mlle L. L.* 1864 (Musée d'Orsay, Paris) and *Eugène Coppens de Fontenay* 1867 (Philadelphia Museum of Fine Arts). He was already exploiting the style of the conversation piece borrowed from Thomas Gainsborough and Joshua Reynolds, with *The Marquis and Marchioness of Miramon and their Children* 1868 (Musée d'Orsay) and especially *The Circle of the Rue Royale* 1868 (Musée d'Orsay), one of the artist's masterpieces. At the same time, Tissot was collecting Japanese art: in 1864 he was even competing with Dante Gabriel Rossetti in Paris in acquiring objects from Mme Desoye.[7] This passion found its way into paintings such as *The Japanese Woman at her Bath* 1864 (Musée des Beaux-Arts, Dijon) and *Young Women Looking at Japanese Objects* 1869 (Cincinnati Art Museum). By the end of the 1860s, when the troubles broke out at the end of the Second Empire, Tissot was an established artist.

During the war with Prussia Tissot enlisted and defended the city of Paris. Along with Degas, he took part in the fighting and, on 21 October and 19 November 1870, demonstrated his bravery at Malmaison. He produced a drawing of it (Chatsworth) dedicated 'To Madame Millais affectionate souvenir James Tissot 19 June 1871' - proof of his arrival in London by June 1871, but also of his rapid integration into London's artistic circles. Relations with John Everett Millais had thus been established as early as 1871. Other drawings inspired by his experience of the Siege of Paris (*A Cantinière* 1870, pp.34–7) would be reused to illustrate *The Defence of Paris; Narrated as It Was Seen* (London 1871). Commissioned by his friend Thomas Bowles – correspondent of the *Morning Post* and editor of *Vanity Fair*, whom he had known since 1869 – this series reinforced his bonds with England where he had already exhibited his works at the Royal Academy in 1864.

It has been said that Tissot was a Communard, but that seems unlikely. Alfred de Lostalot explained in 1906 that in his opinion the artist's name had been confused with that of a genuine Communard, Pierre Tissot. Another source gives the first name of this Communard as Antoine.[8] James Tissot returned regularly to Paris, notably in 1879 when he produced several works showing his visits to the Louvre. He was not an outlaw. His sentiments were patriotic, but his fierce independence and individualism make an involvement with the Commune difficult to envisage. It was, moreover, his friend the painter Jacques-Emile Blanche who without any proof spread this rumour of Tissot being a partisan.[9] *Long Live the Republic!* 1870 (Baroda Museum, India), which dealt ironically with current events, shows that this theory is hardly plausible. Tissot did, however, create *A Party of Four*, shown at the Salon of 1870, where characters dressed as members of the revolutionary Directory give a republican toast.[10]

In fact, new documents shed light on Tissot's attitude during the fighting: a collection of seventy drawings made by him on site show that he was physically very close to the battle. He remained with the soldiers, as a stretcher bearer, and drew portraits of the fighters, which he reworked for *The Defence of Paris*. A quarrel broke out with Edgar Degas about a drawing that inspired Tissot's engraving *The First Person I Saw Who Had Been Killed*: Degas reproached him on 21 October 1870 for drawing their mutual friend, the sculptor Joseph Cuvelier, who died in the fighting at Malmaison.[11] Another document recounts testimony of the combat; notes addressed to Lady Waldegrave, on 19 May 1871, summarise the atrocity of the execution of Communards, of which he did a watercolour (p.38). Tissot saw the detachment pass on the Avenue de l'Impératrice, where his residence was situated. He made horrifying drawings of the subject, as in the *Execution of Two Communards by the Versaillais on 25 May 1871, Rue Saint Germain l'Auxerrois*.[12]

Various reasons can be given for Tissot's decision to leave for London: the civil war in France was hardly an encouragement to stay there, and he was an Anglophile who enjoyed European fame. His contacts with London merchants and his previous exhibitions at the Royal Academy made it possible for him to face the future confidently. In practical terms, Tissot used his networks and found contacts and connoisseurs, purchasers and friends ready to help him. He was initially welcomed by his friend Thomas Bowles at Palace Chambers, 88 St James Street.[13] Thanks to him, Tissot continued to illustrate *Vanity Fair* with caricatures and integrated rapidly into the artistic milieu. In March 1872 the artist moved to 73 Springfield Road (now destroyed) and then settled into his new house at 17 Grove End Road in 1873 (pp.96–7), in the nouveau-riche quarter of St John's Wood, a haven of greenery that would be his refuge. Alison Smith has written an illuminating article, putting into perspective the importance of England in Tissot's art.[14]

He spent eleven successful years in London (June 1871–November 1882), as is reported in 1874 by the Goncourt brothers, who describe the unfavourable impression the artist made on them during this period:

> Yesterday, Duplessis told me that Tissot, that plagiarising painter, had the greatest success in England. Did he not invent, this ingenious exploiter of English idiocy, a studio preceded by an antechamber where one could always find iced champagne at the disposition of visitors and, around his studio, a garden where one could see a servant in silk stockings occupied in brushing and polishing the leaves of the trees all day long?[15]

In fact, on 30 November 1871, Edgar Degas wrote a long letter to Tissot:

> Why in the devil have you not written me a word? I have been told you are earning a lot of money. So give me some figures. It could be that I'll go to London for a while with Achille in the coming days ... In the meantime, honour me with a few stories ... Give me some ideas of the way in which I, too, could gain some advantage in England ... Hello to Whistler, Legros.[16]

James Tissot
Self-Portrait c.1865
Oil paint on panel 49.8 × 30.2

The California Palace of Legion of Honour, San Francisco. Mildred Anne Williams collection

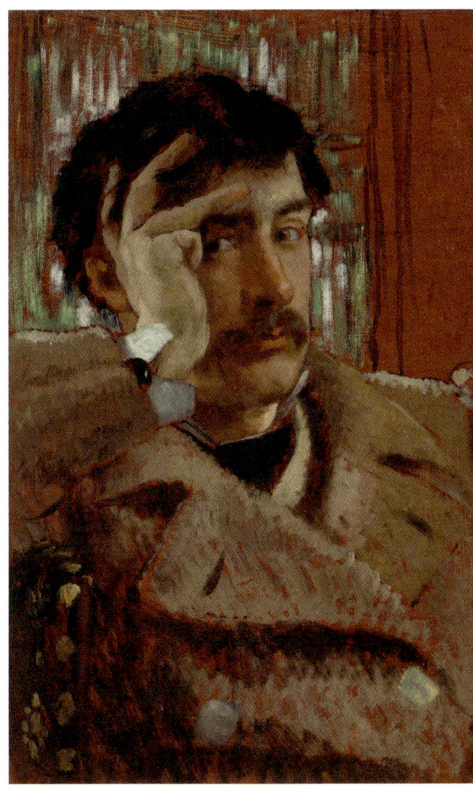

James Tissot c.1965
Photograph by Etienne Carjat

Musée d'Orsay, Paris

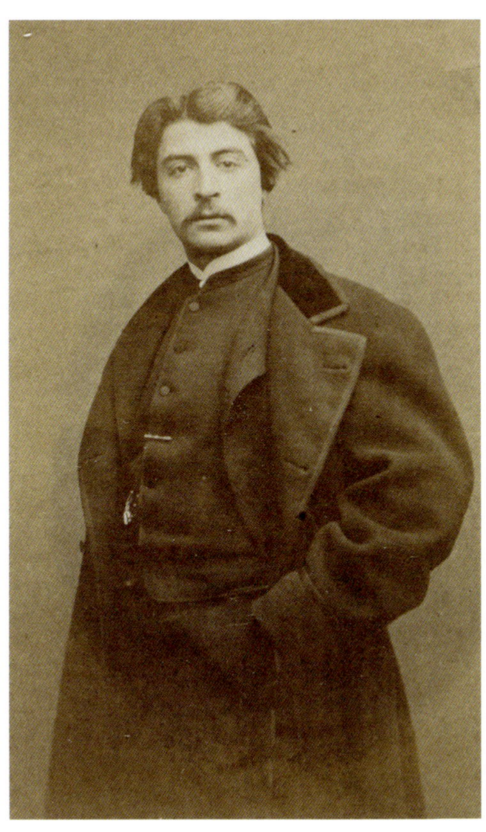

The allusion to Whistler and Legros suggests that Tissot had met them quickly. Another letter from Degas to Tissot dated 8 June (no doubt 1872; Musée des Beaux-Arts, Nantes) introduces him to Mr Mariott, Paul Durand-Ruel's agent in London, meaning that Tissot was known there. Thanks to Bowles, he received a commission for an important portrait, that of *Captain Frederick Burnaby* 1870 (pp.88–9), who had supported *Vanity Fair* in the beginning and was part of the Prince of Wales's entourage. Tissot's dealer at the time was Algernon Moses Marsden, whose portrait he painted in 1877 (private collection), but he also collaborated with Agnew's (see p.95). In addition, he did business with another important dealer, the Tooth Gallery, which bought several of his works, intermittently, up to 1885.[17]

In 1873 Tissot joined the Arts Club of Hanover Square, remaining a member until 1884. This smart cosmopolitan club brought together famous artists, including George du Maurier, Millais, Whistler and his brother-in-law Francis Seymour Haden, and Giuseppe de Nittis.[18] Tissot generously welcomed the last to his home and introduced him to the capital's artistic circles. De Nittis wrote to his wife Léontine in 1875: 'I saw Tissot at the [Arts] Club, he was very nice, very friendly.'[19] De Nittis, who was not picking up the English language and customs very well, must have seen this club as a refuge. It was either Tissot or Legros who presented him to their patron, the collector Kaye Knowles, whose financial support gave some freedom to this Italian who was French at heart. In 1876 de Nittis, after many unsuccessful attempts, settled in a house on 54 Wellington Road, just 300 metres from Grove End Road where Tissot resided. He lived, furthermore, in Tissot's house in Paris.[20] De Nittis made a portrait of Kathleen Newton, the muse whom Tissot encountered at the time – proof that the Italian shared his friend's private life. Tissot had in fact placed de Nittis in the door frame of his slightly humorous picture *Hush!* 1874 (p.95).

In 1886 Tissot made a series of enamel plaques on which he inscribed the names of his London friends: M. Jopling, G. du Maurier, Phil Morris, Sir J. Benedict, M. Montalba, F. Pils, W. Eglinton, Robert, N. Hemy, J.E. Millais, J. Whistler, Alma-Tadema, Seymour Haden, R. Macbeth.[21] As a collector, he helped his friends in London: he owned Manet's *Blue Venice* 1875 (Shelburne Museum, Shelburne, VT), which he hung in his residence in St John's Wood, but in 1873, to aid another painter who had previously sought refuge in England, he purchased a Pissarro that the Royal Academy had rejected.[22] Claire Durand-Ruel-Snollaerts has since identified it as *The Spillway at Pontoise* 1872 (Museum of Art, Cleveland). Tissot received Berthe Morisot, who witnessed his success with British clients. But the artist also knew not to compromise himself when his reputation was at stake, as in the 1878 trial where Whistler opposed Ruskin: he refused to testify for either, which is reminiscent of his lack of engagement with the impressionist cause, despite Degas's invitations and repeated requests from 1874. For Tissot knew how to find his market and adapt his subjects to his audience without compromising himself. He exhibited nonetheless at the Grosvenor Gallery from 1877 to 1879, which was less conventional than the Royal Academy and a hotbed of aestheticism.

English inspiration

Tissot's subjects evolved slowly. In London he began a series on the eighteenth century, dealing with amorous and complex subjects: *Bad News (The Parting)* 1871 (National Museum of Wales, Cardiff) and *Les Adieux (The Farewells)* 1871 (p.90) integrate characters in languorous atmospheres in which the woman seems to be the victim of her destiny. Thus *Les Adieux* corresponds in many respects to *A Huguenot* 1851–2 by John Everett Millais, in which a couple is entwined, but one senses the consequences will be unhappy and tragic. In *Les Adieux* Tissot plays with the Victorian interest in flower symbolism: the presence of ivy, a symbol of fidelity, leads one to suppose that the couple's patience will triumph in the end. Simultaneously, he received commissions for prestigious portraits. *Empress Eugénie and the Prince Imperial* 1874–5 (pp.92–3) is evidence both of his rank as a portraitist for the elite and of a certain nostalgia for the empire. The end of a world is rendered with melancholy, where the harmony of autumn hues also evokes the recently deceased Napoleon III. Tissot painted high-society women and their children, as in *Portrait of Catherine Smith Gill and Two of their Children* 1877 (Liverpool Museums), lingering over costume details and English customs in the period of Queen Victoria. The artist could also use the image of the woman as a timeless symbol of British grace, in which the sitter's identity made little difference: *Summer (A Portrait)* sums up all his talent as a colourist fascinated by feminine costumes (pp.110–11).

Tissot took advantage of his London sojourn to develop certain aspects of his technique. This is the period in which he developed a passion for etching. He frequented the etchers Francis Seymour Haden, Alphonse Legros and Frederick Goulding, who would become Tissot's most important printer in London until his death. As a businessman, Tissot made himself known in England and France through his prints. In 1876 he exhibited *On the Thames* (p.220) at the Royal Academy, and sent a print of the work to the Salon in Paris. In the same year he etched the *Portrait of Mrs B.* (p.87), and in 1880 he joined the Royal Society of Painter-Etchers. He organised the promotion of his etchings during an exhibition in London at the Dudley Gallery (*Exhibition of Modern Art*, 1882) and then in Paris.[23] His income became substantial as a result.[24] Tissot broadened his range of subjects: *The Rubens Hat* 1876 is evidence of his admiration for the old masters, it being a copy of the *The Straw Hat* 1622–5 by Rubens, acquired in 1872 by the National Gallery, London. He also etched more realistic themes, close to Whistler, such as *Ramsgate* 1876. Tissot gradually absorbed social subjects: *Trafalgar Tavern in Greenwich* 1878 (p.106) would seem to be a view of the end of a meal in an upmarket place, but a second version of the work presents street children under a stormy sky making unseemly gestures towards the spectator. Tissot's French outlook on social differences in England is seen in the gulf between the elites above the parapet and the popular classes on the quays of the Thames.

Tissot would later say to the Goncourts that he appreciated London because he was aware of 'the bitter fight for life' there,[25] a statement that indicates his sensitivity for the indigent. Understandably, Tissot was interested in the London river. He created a series about the Thames: *The Captain's Daughter* 1873 (Southampton City Art Gallery), *The Last Evening* 1873 (Guildhall Art Gallery), *Portsmouth Dockyard* 1877 (p.113), and *The Gallery of HMS Calcutta* c.1876 (p.112). In these, women are prey for the men. Tissot displays his mastery of rigging and the vaporous atmosphere along London shores. He dares to be irreverent: *On the Thames*, with two 'birds' accompanying a naval officer, was very badly received at the Royal Academy. He had to modify this work to make it respectable, when another version was presented at the Grosvenor Gallery (*Portsmouth Dockyard*). His series on ballroom dances, sometimes on ships, is virtuoso: *The Ball on Shipboard* c.1874 is a dizzying gallery of portraits (pp.196–7). In *Hush!* (p.95) and *Too Early* (p.94) Tissot's irony when faced with British social codes is manifested in the way in which he renders guests' faces almost as if they were caricatures. *The Gallery of HMS Calcutta* is also playful: the pun in French on 'Quel cul tu as!' (What an ass you have!) and the picture's title refers to the perspective on the young woman's posture. It also presents an example of Tissot's ironic point of view on Victorian social codes: the play of gazes between figures leaves one to guess the phrase or inappropriate remark uttered by the young sailor close to the young woman who protects herself with her fan. The second woman seems to step back in shock. By then Tissot had perfectly mastered the undercurrents of British conversation and was having fun sketching closely observed scenes on the spot.

A French lover

Tissot's portraits were to evolve during the 1870s, beginning with his encounter with Kathleen Newton in about 1876, which would profoundly change his life. Irish, with hieratic beauty, and tubercular, she was a divorced mother of two children: Violet and Cecil George. Tissot left the high-society circles of London artists to concentrate on his private amorous world. Kathleen Newton did not officially live with Tissot: she resided a few hundred metres from there, on Hill Road, in the company of her sister Mary Pauline Hervey. In reality, she actually did live with Tissot and only saw her children at tea time. Tissot's subjects at the time illustrate his private pleasures, such as croquet games (*Croquet* 1878, Art Gallery of Hamilton, Ontario), walks (*Lady with an Parasol* 1878–80, Musée Baron Martin, Gray), picnics (*In the Sunlight*, private collection), naps in the sun (*The Hammock* 1879, private collection), reading (*Reading in the Park* c.1881, p.103) and strolls along the Thames (*Autumn on the Thames* c.1875, private collection).[26]

These themes, which can be found at the same period in the works of his impressionist friends, are handled here in a very British atmosphere. The women's costumes conform to decorum, strolls are solitary and naps are not in the least erotic. The image

James Tissot
The Return of the Prodigal Son 1880
Oil paint on canvas 100 × 130

Musée des Beaux-Arts, Nantes

James Tissot
Lady with a Parasol 1878–80
Oil paint on canvas 142 × 54

Musée Baron-Martin, Gray, France

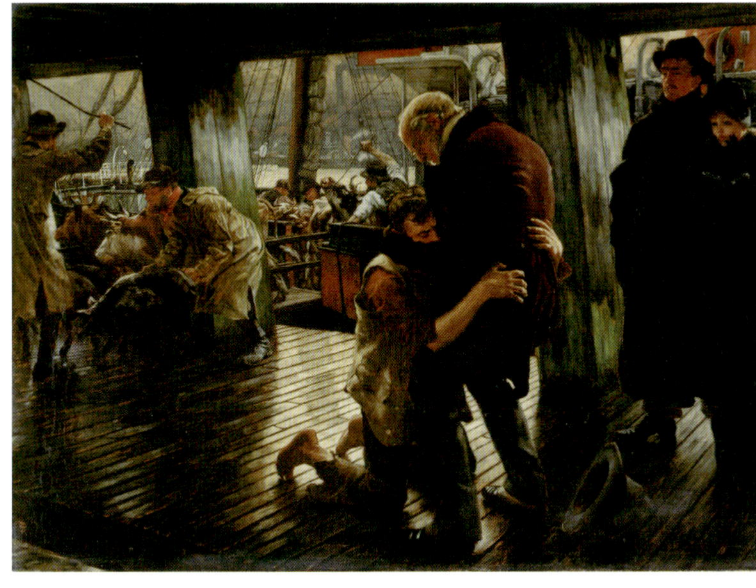

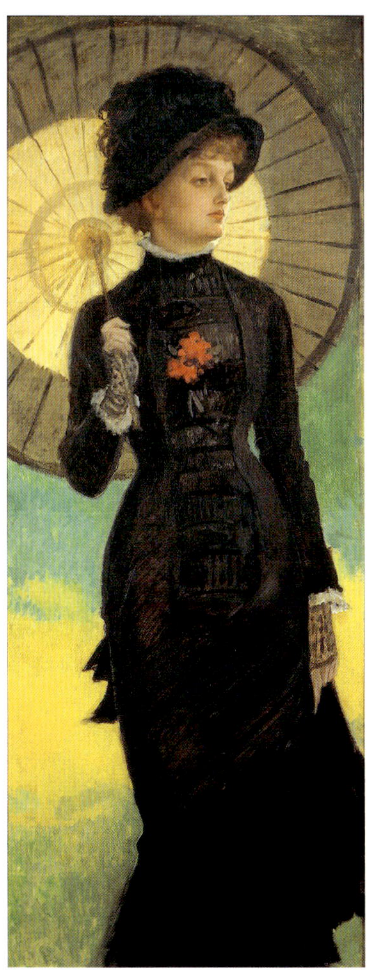

he gives to Kathleen Newton, ranging from muse to saint, from mother of two to amateur artist, mixes up, however, the idea of a conventional Victorian painter. He sets his feminine ideal in a protected bucolic setting, where the illness progresses and irremediably destroys the promise of a seized happiness. The feelings expressed in the pictures are those of a melancholic or anxious lover, as can be seen in *The Convalescent* 1875–6 (Sheffield Art Gallery) and *A Convalescent* 1880–2 (Musée Baron-Martin, Gray). He paints himself as the young woman's protector, both father and lover. As protector, he lavishes care on her, and at the same time paints her as an attractive self-confident woman (*Lady with a Parasol*). In this respect, his series illustrating *Renée Mauperin* by the Goncourt brothers is autobiographical. Composed of ten etchings, it tells the story of a young woman who follows her ideal to the end. At the time of Kathleen's death, which caused Tissot's return to France, Edmond de Goncourt described her as the 'English Mauperin'.[27] The threat of death, thwarted ambition, fear of scandal, and withdrawal into private life were as much subjects that inspired the artist. Five days after Kathleen's death on 9 November 1882, he returned to France during the night.[28]

A prodigal son

When Tissot was still in London, he began an original series, 'The Prodigal Son in Modern Life', which signalled a new direction in his career. In May 1882 an exhibition devoted to the artist opened at the Dudley Gallery, *J.J. Tissot: An Exhibition of Modern Art*, where the painter presented his new series. He turned to it again in March 1883, when the *Exhibition of the Works of M. J.-J. Tissot* opened, organised by the Union Centrale des Arts Décoratifs. The critics were full of praise.[29] The series is based on the Gospel according to St Luke and aims to be educational about the return of the young man who had been eager to discover the world. Having lost his fortune and his soul in vain pleasures, the son who had gone astray finds his father again on a wharf.

On returning to France, James Tissot attracted the attention of his Parisian friends in this way. In Paris he tried to resume his society portraits with a series of fifteen paintings on 'Women in Paris'. Exhibited at the Sedelmeyer Gallery in 1885, it was poorly received.[30] The artist then went through a mystical crisis, which he transcended by travelling to Palestine (1886) and then by conceiving a Bible, which would be an unexpected bestseller.

Between Victorian England and impressionist France, Tissot hesitated, evaded, yet pursued his career with complete independence. Uprooted, globetrotter, lover of landscapes and distant impressions, he sought to be the painter of lost loves and impossible stories. He spread a unique style in which the psychology of his beings was coupled with a troubling obsession with solitude. A Frenchman living in England, English in his habits in Paris, he undoubtedly reveals himself most in his painting. By turns imaginative, paternal and mystical, Tissot can be seen under close light for those who know how to decrypt him.

James Tissot
1836–1902
Napoleon III, Emperor of France ('Sovereigns No.1. "Le régime parlementaire."') 1869
Published in *Vanity Fair*, 4 Sept. 1869
Chromolithograph 34.2 × 21.4

National Portrait Gallery, London

Prior to both the Franco-Prussian War and his sojourn in England, Tissot began contributing caricatures to the English society publication *Vanity Fair*. His earliest, published under the pseudonym 'Coïdé, were for a series of European 'Sovereigns'. These are true satirical caricatures by comparison to the generally more portrait-like illustrations Tissot submitted to the magazine following his move to London in the early 1870s. Unlike those made for the 'Sovereigns' series, which utilised photographs and existing portraits to capture a (sometimes cruel) likeness, these later works were based on drawings made from life.[1]

In Tissot's 1869 depiction of Napoleon III, the emperor is shown as frail and unstable: he leans for support on the arm of Marianne, the symbol of the French Republic. The landmarks of Paris shown in the background of the composition appear threatened by a red sky. Within the pages of *Vanity Fair*, which was edited by Thomas Gibson Bowles, chromolithographs like this one were, like gossip, an important draw. Tissot took an interest in not only his designs but also the reproduction of them, drawing the outline on the lithographic stone himself and correcting the printed proofs.[2] Bowles commissioned sixteen caricatures from Tissot prior to the latter's move to London. When the artist left war-ravaged Paris in 1871, he initially found shelter with Bowles, who published a further forty-six of Tissot's caricatures in *Vanity Fair* following the Frenchman's arrival in London.[3]

A caricature like *Napoleon III* might appear to reflect an anti-imperial outlook but, as Marshall has argued, Tissot was apparently just as happy to caricature the prominent Republican Henri Rochefort for *Vanity Fair*.[4] Rather than providing him with an outlet for his political sympathies, *Vanity Fair* was a means of generating income for Tissot and, following his move to London, probably also a way of infiltrating high society to find patrons. In any case, any anti-monarchy feelings do not appear to have stood in Tissot's way when he came to make a group portrait of the Empress Eugénie and the imperial prince a few years later (pp.92–3). EJ

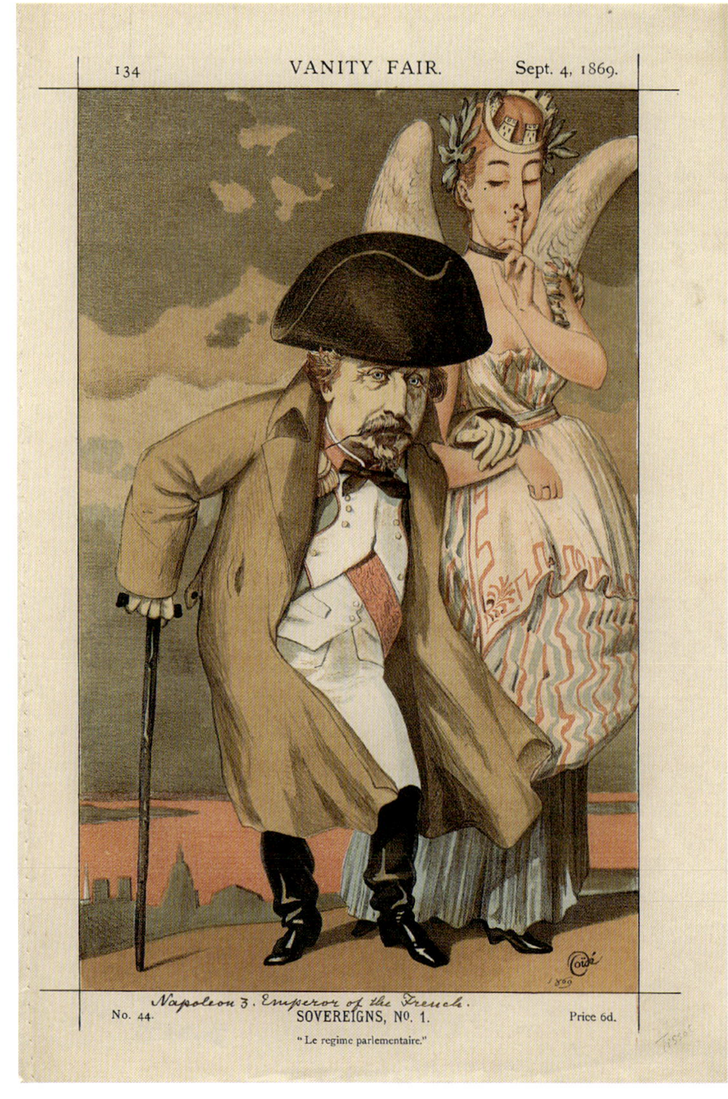

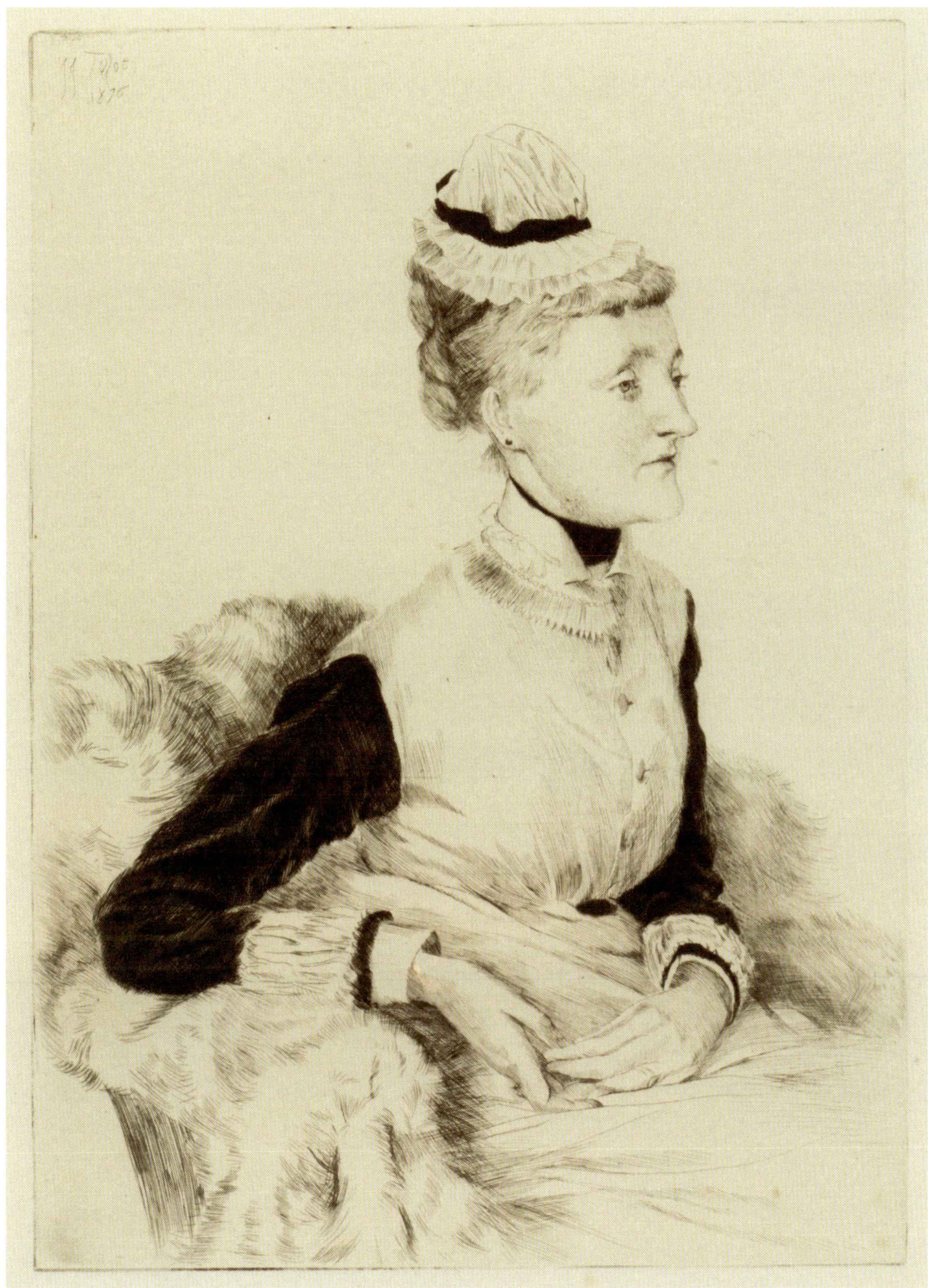

James Tissot
1836–1902
Portrait of Mrs B. 1876
Etching on paper 27.5 × 19.2

Victoria and Albert Museum, London

The 'Mrs B' of the title is Jessica Bowles, née Gordon, who had married Tissot's friend Thomas Gibson Bowles in December 1875. Tissot's etching was made the following year, when Jessie was twenty-four. Jessie's figure is elegant, if a little austere, the plain fabrics of her dress and morning cap effectively rendered in monochrome, the black of the sleeves and cap ribbon in stark contrast to the crisp white of her cap and bodice. Jessie Bowles suffered from poor health and died young at the age of thirty-five in 1887, having borne four children.

While this portrait was etched when Tissot had been living in London for some years, his acquaintance with Thomas Gibson Bowles had begun considerably earlier. He drew caricatures for *Vanity Fair*, Bowles's publication, from 1869 (see pp.34–7), and also encountered him while serving as a soldier during the Siege of Paris. It was with Bowles that the artist found a home on his arrival in London in 1871, staying with him at 88 St James's Street. In addition to offering Tissot a home and continuing work in the form of caricatures for *Vanity Fair*, Bowles helped his quest to establish a London career by introducing his friend to high-society patrons.

Tissot had first experimented with etching in 1860, but came back to the medium with seriousness when settled in London in the 1870s. Here, it is possible he was advised by Francis Seymour Haden or, more likely according to Krystyna Matyjaszkiewicz, by his fellow Frenchman Alphonse Legros.[1] EJ

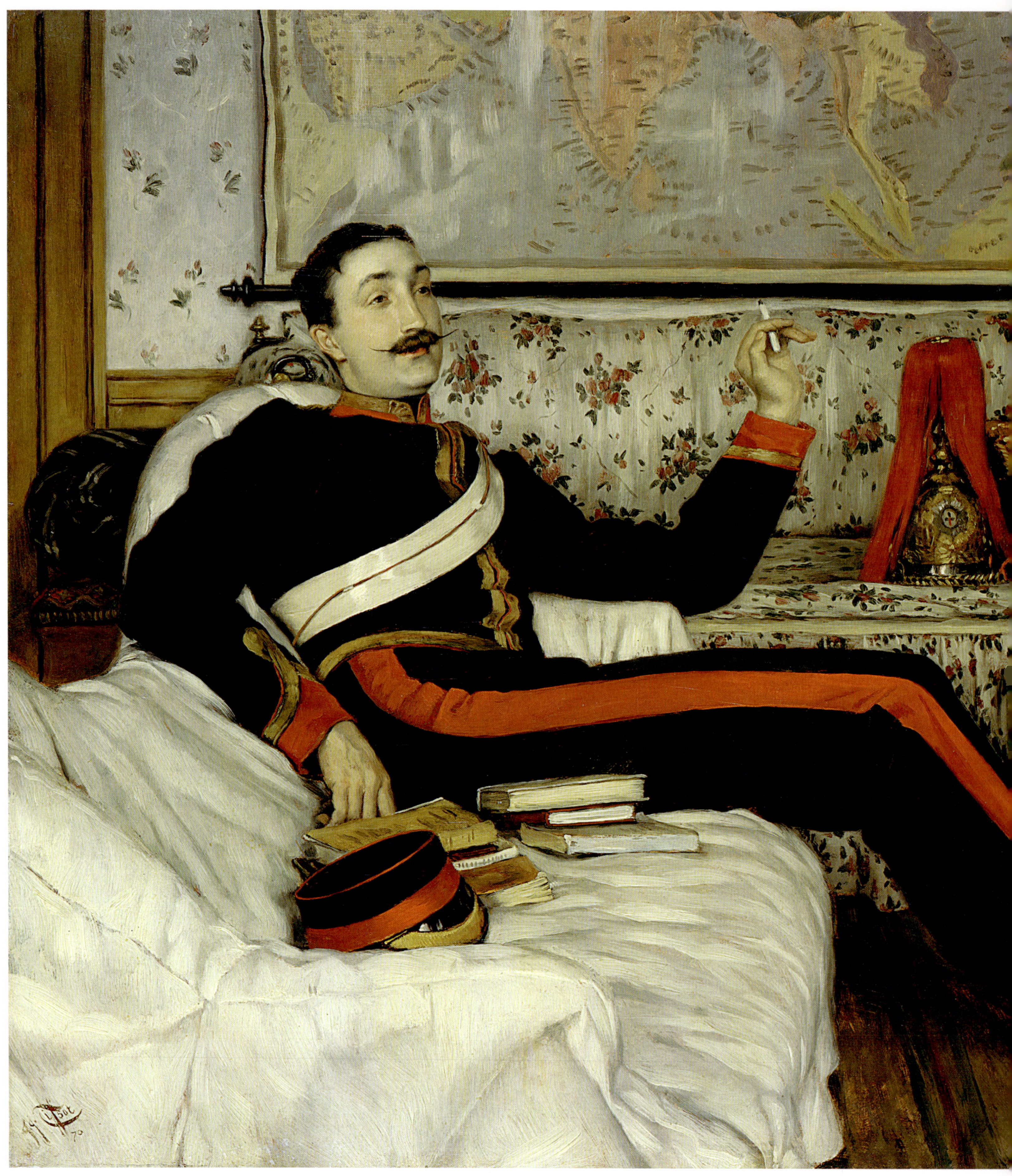

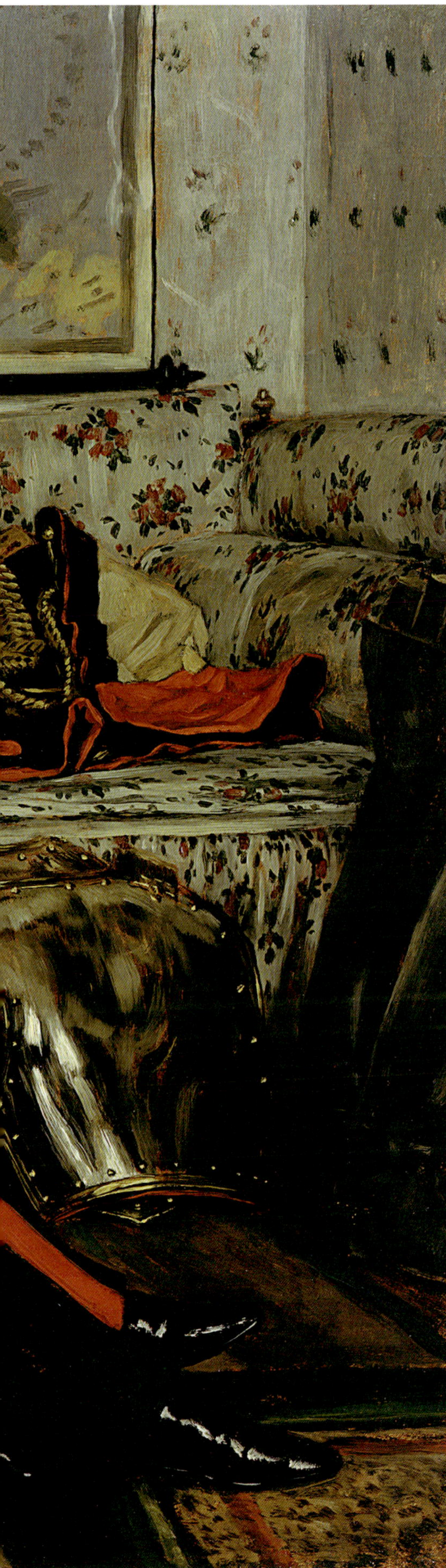

James Tissot
1836–1902
Captain Frederick Burnaby 1870
Oil paint on panel 50 × 61

National Portrait Gallery, London. Purchased. 1933

Tissot's first painting depicting an English subject was his portrait of the soldier, traveller and journalist Frederick Gustavus Burnaby. Renowned for his physical prowess and passion for ballooning, Burnaby was in his twenties when Tissot painted his portrait and had yet to attain fame for his exploits in Russian Asia and Africa. Burnaby had entered the Royal Horse Guards in 1859 and is accordingly presented as a captain in full dress uniform down to the plumed silver-gilt helmet on the sofa and the polished metal breastplate resting on the floor. What is thought to be an Arab burnous, or long cloak with hood, on the far left may refer to the sitter's recent travels in North Africa. Burnaby was later to serve in Egypt, meeting his death fighting hand-to-hand in the Battle of Abu Klea as part of the Gordon Relief Expedition to the Sudan.

In 1869 Tissot was commissioned to paint the portrait by Burnaby's friend, the journalist, Thomas Gibson Bowles (see p.83). The previous year Bowles had established the satirical journal *Vanity Fair*, with Burnaby providing some of the initial investment as well as suggesting its title (after Thackeray's novel of the same name). The portrait was probably started in London later that year and, typically for Tissot's work of the time, it is painted on panel in bright clear colour with an enamel-like finish. The location may be a room in Bowles's residence at 88 St James's Street, where the portrait most likely remained following Tissot's return to France.

Burnaby's informal pose dominates the picture, the sharp masculinity of his attire offset by the soft furnishings of the room, and the map focused on the Indian Ocean and Southeast Asia, an area dominated by the British via the recently opened Suez Canal, signalling a wider realm of adventure. The striking presentation of the figure underscores Tissot's fascination with military dress (as in *The Wounded Soldier*, pp.34–6), the white cross-belt and scarlet stripe of Burnaby's uniform echoing the border and rail of the chart. Tissot's fastidious attention to the trappings of Burnaby's uniform conveys something of the swagger ascribed to some British military personnel of the time in the minds of overseas observers. Exhibited in 1872 at the London International Exhibition under the title *Portrait of Captain…*, the portrait was generally received as conveying a type of British officer as much as an individual, one French critic describing the figure as 'well turned out and proper like a wax figurine'.[1] Posed as if about to exhale smoke from a cigarette in one hand and nonchalantly stretching out his long legs across the room, Burnaby is shown to be confident and relaxed as if engaged in conversation with his friend Bowles, whose shared literary and journalistic interests are indicated by the books at Burnaby's side. Tissot himself was to emulate such a suave model of a gentleman during his stay in London, his friend and fellow artist Louise Jopling later recalling: 'He was always well-groomed, and had nothing of artistic carelessness in his dress or demeanour.'[2] ASm

John Everett Millais
1829–1896
A Huguenot, on St Bartholomew's Day, Refusing to Shield himself from Danger by Wearing the Roman Catholic Badge 1851–2
Oil paint on canvas 92.7 × 62.2

The Makins Collection

James Tissot
1836–1902
Les Adieux (*The Farewells*) 1871
Oil paint on canvas 100.3 × 62.5

Bristol Museum & Art Gallery

Les Adieux was one of the first paintings Tissot produced after his move to London in June 1871, and it was one of the two pictures with which he made his debut at the Royal Academy the following year. Although, as an eighteenth-century costume piece, it is entirely in keeping with the kind of subject he was painting just prior to his departure from Paris, the wistful sentiment of the scene gestures towards an English taste for pathetic scenes involving distraught young lovers. This genre was exemplified by John Everett Millais's *Huguenot, on St Bartholomew's Day*, one of the pictures that had brought about a marked shift in the artist's reputation from being regarded as a radical outsider to being embraced by the British art establishment.

We know that Tissot's acquaintance with Millais developed soon after his arrival in London from a drawing of a soldier Tissot made during the Prussian siege, which he presented to Millais's wife Effie in June 1871 as an 'affectionate souvenir'.[1] The introduction may have been through Frances, Countess Waldegrave, the owner of Strawberry Hill, Horace Walpole's Gothic Revival villa at Twickenham, where she hosted visits from both Tissot and the Millais family. Tissot held Millais in great esteem as both a pioneer of poetic realism in art and as an astute businessman, the widespread popularity of *A Huguenot* having been established with the publication of Thomas Oldham Barlow's mezzotint in 1856.

Tissot's debt to Millais in *Les Adieux* is apparent in the foreground positioning of the couple, the deployment of a gate (instead of a wall) to indicate their impending separation, and in the use of period costume for picturesque effect. Significantly the revival of interest in eighteenth-century dress was being championed by Millais around the very time Tissot settled in London. The former's *Hearts Are Trumps* (Tate), exhibited at the same Royal Academy exhibition in 1872, had been

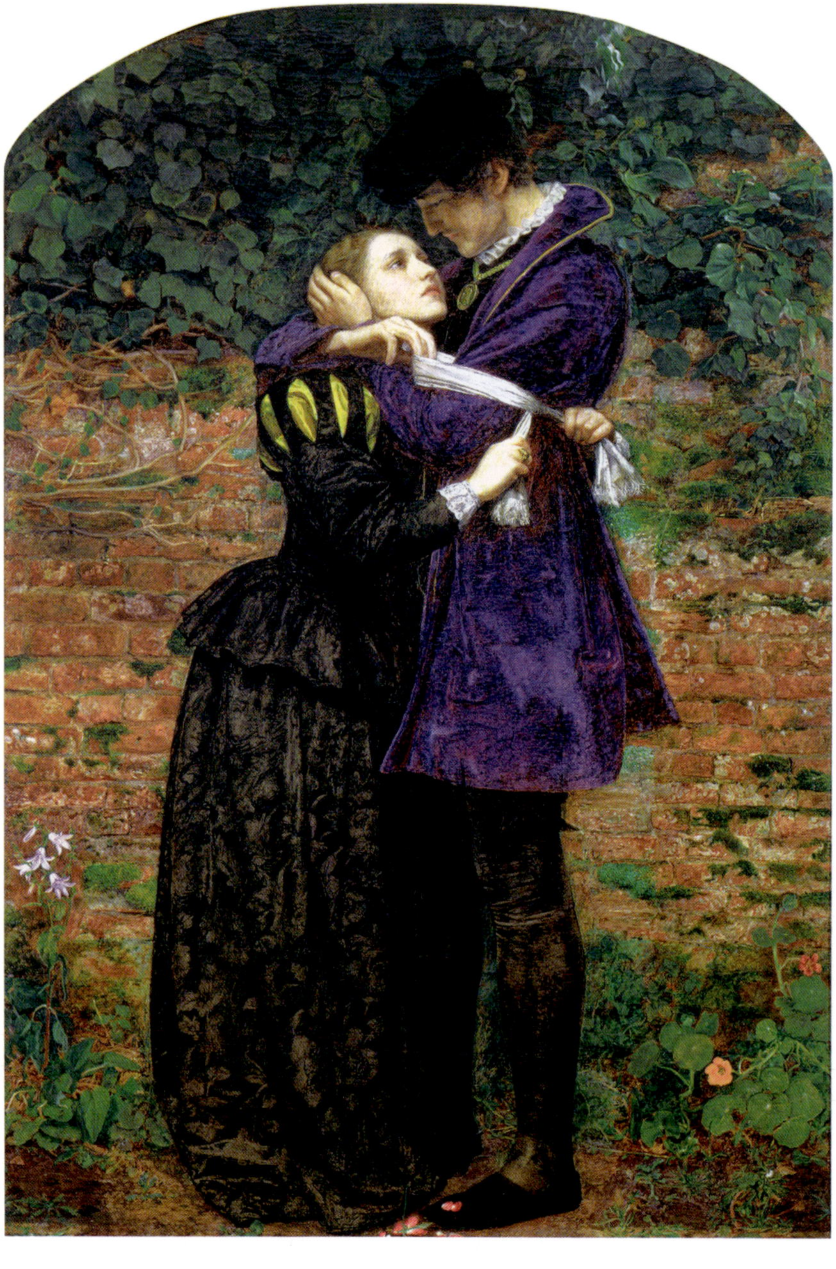

conceived as a riposte to Sir Joshua Reynolds's *The Ladies Waldegrave* 1780–1 (National Gallery of Scotland), a portrait both artists would have been familiar with from their visits to Strawberry Hill.[2] However, what Millais imparts in the way of a moral narrative in *A Huguenot* – the French Protestant's refusal to give in to his personal feelings by taking up the armband that would save him by falsely identifying him as a Catholic – is totally lacking in Tissot's picture. Here neither the title nor the composition itself provide any explanation as to why the couple should be parting on such awkward terms. The contrast between the desperate plea of the Catholic woman as she vainly attempts to tie the band around her lover's arm in *A Huguenot*, and the idle way Tissot's lady toys with her neck ribbon as she evades her amour's gaze in *Les Adieux*, is suggestive of both a less traumatic scene and a less specific story. Although the tragic overtones of Millais's picture – the slaughter of 3,000 Huguenots in Paris in 1572 and the enforced exile of others – would have resonated with Tissot (after all that he had witnessed during the Prussian siege and its bloody aftermath), he seems to have been intent on pursuing a more aesthetic mode of representation. Thus objects that point to a narrative of loss and parting – the scissors dangling from the woman's waist, the autumnal foliage in the distance and the withered leaves on the path – are countered by plants that in the language of flowers suggest a more propitious outcome. The ivy is traditionally symbolic of fidelity and marriage, and the holly of hope and passion. In this picture Tissot appears to have elided an English penchant for decoding pictures with the kind of neutralisation of meaning associated with French realists like Manet and the progressive English Aesthetic School. The latter included Millais himself who, in contrast to his earlier precise Pre-Raphaelite manner, was now advocating a more indeterminate, atmospheric style of painting.

Whether one would describe *Les Adieux* in terms of pastiche, homage or a synthesis of different stylistic elements, Tissot's gambit certainly paid off. John Ballin's steel engraving after the picture was published by Pilgeram and Lefèvre in 1873, and the success of this print encouraged Tissot to produce his own reproductive engravings so he could retain both the copyright and profit to himself. ASm

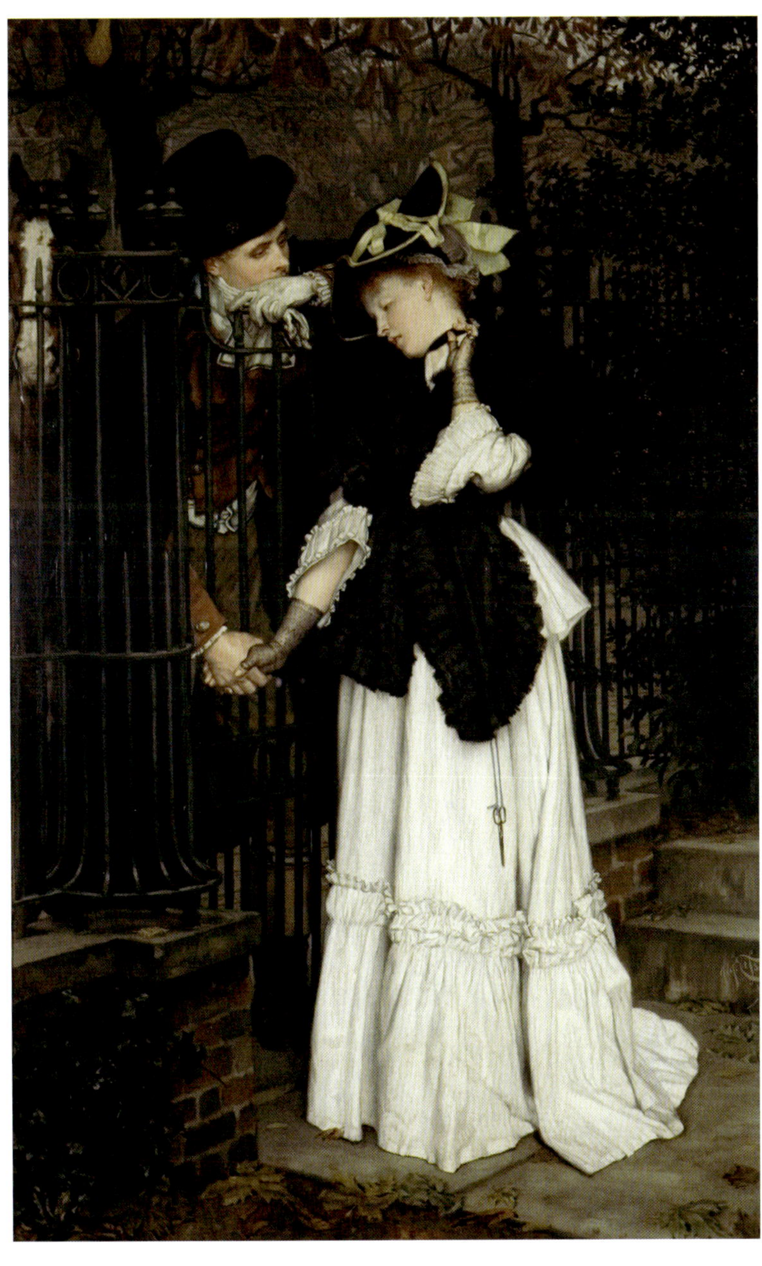

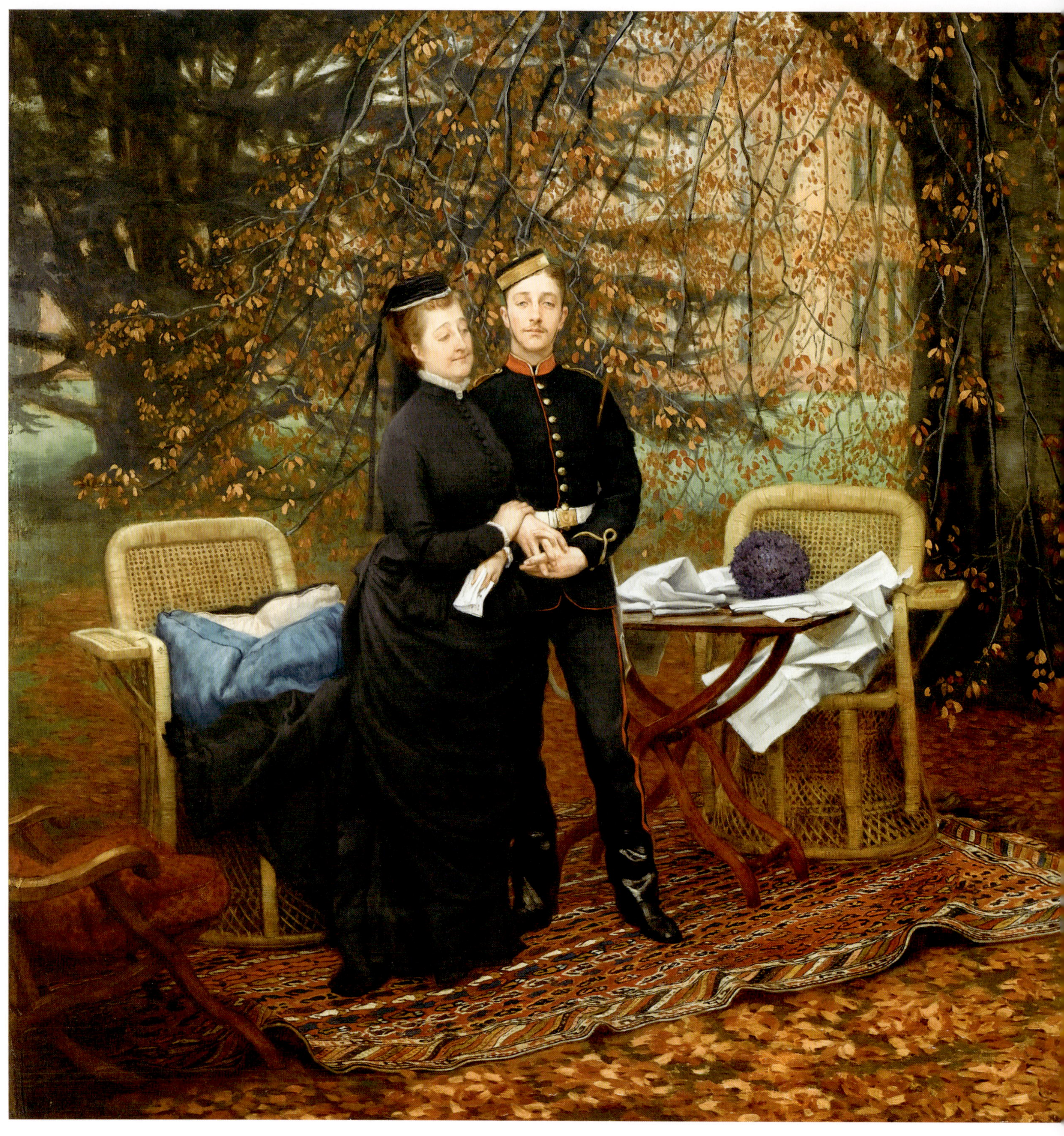

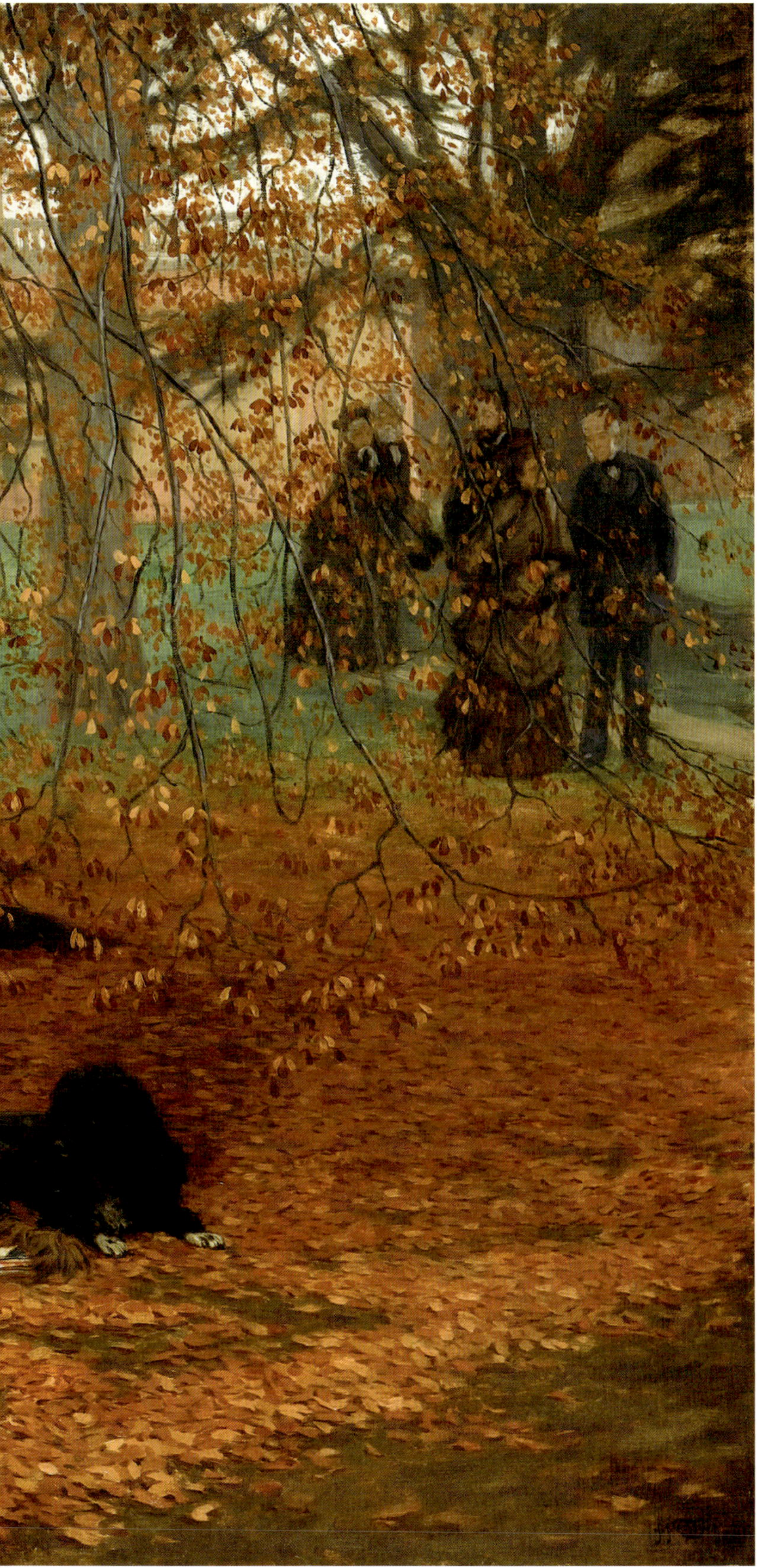

James Tissot
1836–1902
Empress Eugénie and the Prince Imperial in the Grounds of Camden Place, Chislehurst 1874–5
Oil paint on canvas 105 × 150

Musée national du Palais de Compiègne

Tissot's melancholy, poignant image of the exiled former Empress of France and her only son was painted for the 1875 Royal Academy exhibition. It was described by the *Observer*, *Graphic* and *Illustrated London News* among works to be sent in. Due to its size, Tissot asked the dealer Agnew to arrange collection from his house and delivery to the Academy, but the picture was rejected. Agnew billed the artist on 30 June for 'man's time and hire of horse and van' for journeys both ways. Two other paintings submitted by Tissot were accepted, including *Hush!* (p.95), but another two were rejected. This was a bitter blow to Tissot, whose increasing success in England had seemed unstoppable.

Having encountered difficulties with his unofficial royal portrayals in *The Ball on Shipboard* (pp.196–7) and lack of portraiture permissions for *Hush!*, Tissot was careful to obtain the empress's consent for his painting. She visited Tissot's studio in December 1874 to see the work in progress, and the French ambassador viewed the finished picture there in March. It is completely unlike standard royal portraits. Tissot's image of the modestly black-clad Eugénie and prince imperial is more than a portrait: he had been exploring radical new ways of presenting up-to-the-minute reportage, developing in oils the type of modern-life images published in black and white by the *Illustrated London News* and *Punch*. Clues point to deeper layers of meaning in the painting.

Eugénie wears full mourning for ex-Emperor Napoleon III, who had died in exile on 9 January 1873. Violets at the centre of the painting were the emblem of Bonapartism. Eugénie is looking away from the viewer and supported on the arm of her son, whose right hand she clutches. Louis Napoleon, wearing British Royal Artillery uniform, looks directly at us. His fingers are clasped to form the characteristic two-barred cross of Lorraine, symbolic of the territory lost to Germany in 1871. Its recovery was now a burden of expectation resting on his eighteen-year-old shoulders, as the Bonaparte heir to possible future power in France. Opposed to him was a Legitimist faction that wanted the return of monarchy, ousted by the French Revolution and Napoleon. Newspapers in October 1874, when the picture is set, were full of speculation following a visit by Edward, Prince of Wales, to the former French ambassador, the Duc de la Rochefoucauld-Bisaccia, leader of the Legitimists. Edward had earlier attended celebrations in Berlin of the French defeat at Sedan. British loyalties appeared not to be favouring the exiles. Louis Napoleon's precarious future is reflected in the furrowed rug on which he stands with his widowed mother, as on a raft in uncertain sea. Branches, almost bare of fallen leaves, separate them from distant figures of courtiers. The dog's presence recalls the famous sculpture commissioned by Napoleon III from Jean-Baptiste Carpeaux of the eight-year-old Louis with family dog Nero. Louis was killed in action during the Zulu wars in 1879. KM

James Tissot
1836–1902
Too Early 1873
Oil paint on canvas 71 × 102

Guildhall Art Gallery, City of London

In the early 1870s Tissot made his name at the Royal Academy with paintings of fashionable events. He had had success with such modern life scenes in Paris, but *Too Early* was the first of his more crowded, complex groups, recalling the scenes that were a popular success for English writers such as William Makepeace Thackeray and Anthony Trollope. It assembled thirteen figures in a drama in which the Academy audience could recognise, but also smile at, their contemporaries. Critics compared him especially with 'Jane Austen, the great painter of the humour of "polite society"',[1] but Tissot's scenes brought a French eye to English social mores, often with a hint of irony.

For the Victorian upper class, balls, parties and salons were ceremonies of social solidarity, through which it defined itself as prosperous, secure and entitled. There, wealth and taste were displayed, and marriages managed, ensuring the family's capital for future generations. *Too Early* reflects on the tensions new money and social mobility could cause. Countless etiquette books offered advice to the young and less experienced on the expectations of well-to-do society, but the picture shows a guest or guests who have apparently arrived at a ball prematurely. The critic of *The Builder* declared that Tissot had 'fairly out-Tissoted himself in character and expression'.[2] The attitude of the woman in pink, embarrassed by her faux pas, head bowed, closed fan held to her chin, contrasts with the lady of the house busy instructing the musicians. The central group is the object of glances from all around, including the musicians and two servants peeping irreverently through the far door, hinting at gossip to come.

Tissot may have been influenced by French and English fashion magazines and Charles Baudelaire's encouragement, in his famous essay 'The Painter of Modern Life' (1863), to find the poetry in the present: 'Beauty is made up of an eternal, invariable element ... and of a relative, circumstantial element ... the age, its fashions, its morals, its emotions.'[3] In the year that Tissot began *Too Early*, his friend Edouard Manet had painted a different kind of ball scene, *Masked Ball at the Opera* 1873 (Musée d'Orsay). *Too Early* shared its observation of the nuanced implications of clothing and gesture, and drama of black against the colour of modern costume, especially the stark intrusion of the evening suit. Tissot embedded his observations in the highly finished style of the Academy, however; the composition was novel but graceful, and the colour carefully harmonised. The painting won Tissot success. It was purchased by Charles Gassiot through the dealer Agnew's, before being shown at the Royal Academy Summer Exhibition and declared a great sensation by the critics. Fellow artists, such as Tissot's friend, Louise Jopling, recognised it as 'a new departure in art'.[4] CJ

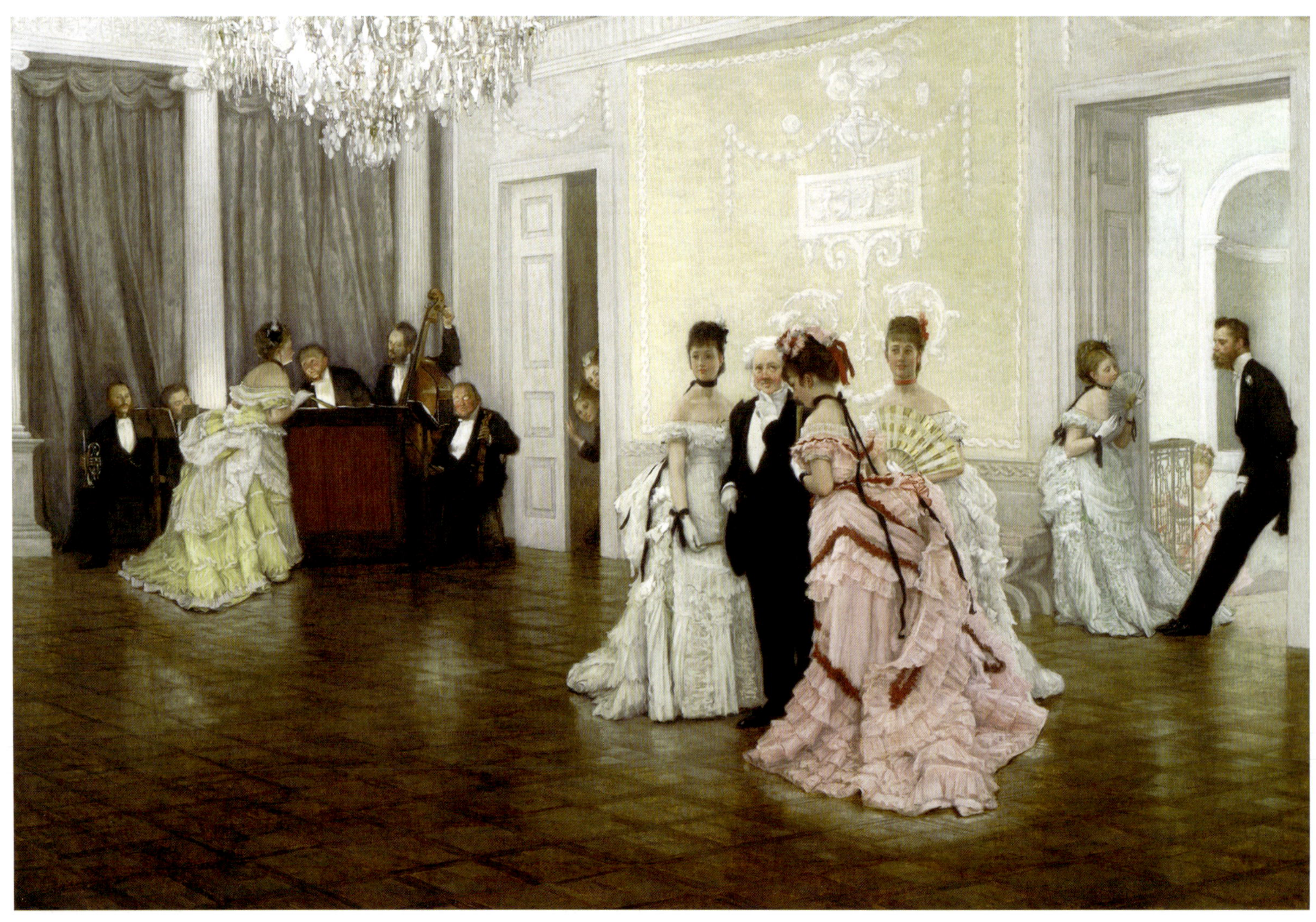

James Tissot
1836–1902
Hush! 1874
Oil paint on canvas 73.7 × 112.2

Manchester Art Gallery

The critical success of *Hush!*, in the tail of that of *Too Early*, was another assertion of Tissot's place as an artist of note in Britain. The picture was purchased by Agnew's in 1874 for the substantial sum of 1,200 guineas. According to tradition, *Hush!* refers to a musical soirée at the house of Octavius Coope, at which the famous violinist Wilhemine Neruda gave a performance.[1] The musician stands in a spacious circular room in the middle of Tissot's composition, and at the centre of a circle formed by the curved staircase and the sitting arrangement of the elegant guests gathered around her. A pianist, allegedly Tissot's friend Sir Julius Benedict, ruffles through his scores to find the right piece to accompany a concentrated Neruda, ready to start her recital. The audience, either bored or engrossed in the observation of fellow invitees, is not at this point very engaged with the imminent performance, and is about to be silenced.

The painting is significant in that it includes portraits of Tissot's own artistic circle, not least those of two fellow émigré artists Ferdinand Heilbuth and Giuseppe de Nittis, standing in the doorway. De Nittis was Tissot's close friend and a fellow member of the Arts Club of Hanover Square (see p.83). The singer Jules Diaz de Soria, with his beard, is sitting just behind the two Indian princes to the right. More conspicuous is the presence of Thomas Gibson Bowles, directly above the elderly man in the foreground. Bowles being the editor of *Vanity Fair* (see p.89), he represented the views of the happy few, and Tissot's emphasis of this connection was a reminder that he moved in the most distinguished circles. The artist did not get permission to take portraits at the performance as a matter of privacy,[2] hence, perhaps, his resorting to painting friends afterwards. *Hush!* was the talk of London, its viewers keen to identify guests, but also confused by the inclusion of some approximate likenesses or types. As noted by Krystyna Matyjaszkiewicz, this combination could explain why Agnew's failed to sell the painting until 1898.[3]

The low viewpoint chosen by Tissot, from the outer circle of the audience, is significant and representative of his own place in society. He adopted the standpoint of a detached observer, that of an outsider, like the two Indian princes, who were identified by contemporary critics as misfits, when, ironically, they are the only two people in the audience to pay attention to the performer. The comment of the *Illustrated London News* on the portrait but also on Tissot's ambivalent place in British society is enlightening in this respect: 'Many of the portraits will be recognised by persons "in society", and possibly with pleasure by the ill-natured; for if there is not a tendency to caricature, something smacking, as it were, of a Gallic sneer runs throughout. But polite people will, of course, be thankful to see themselves as a polished Frenchman sees them.'[4] CCP

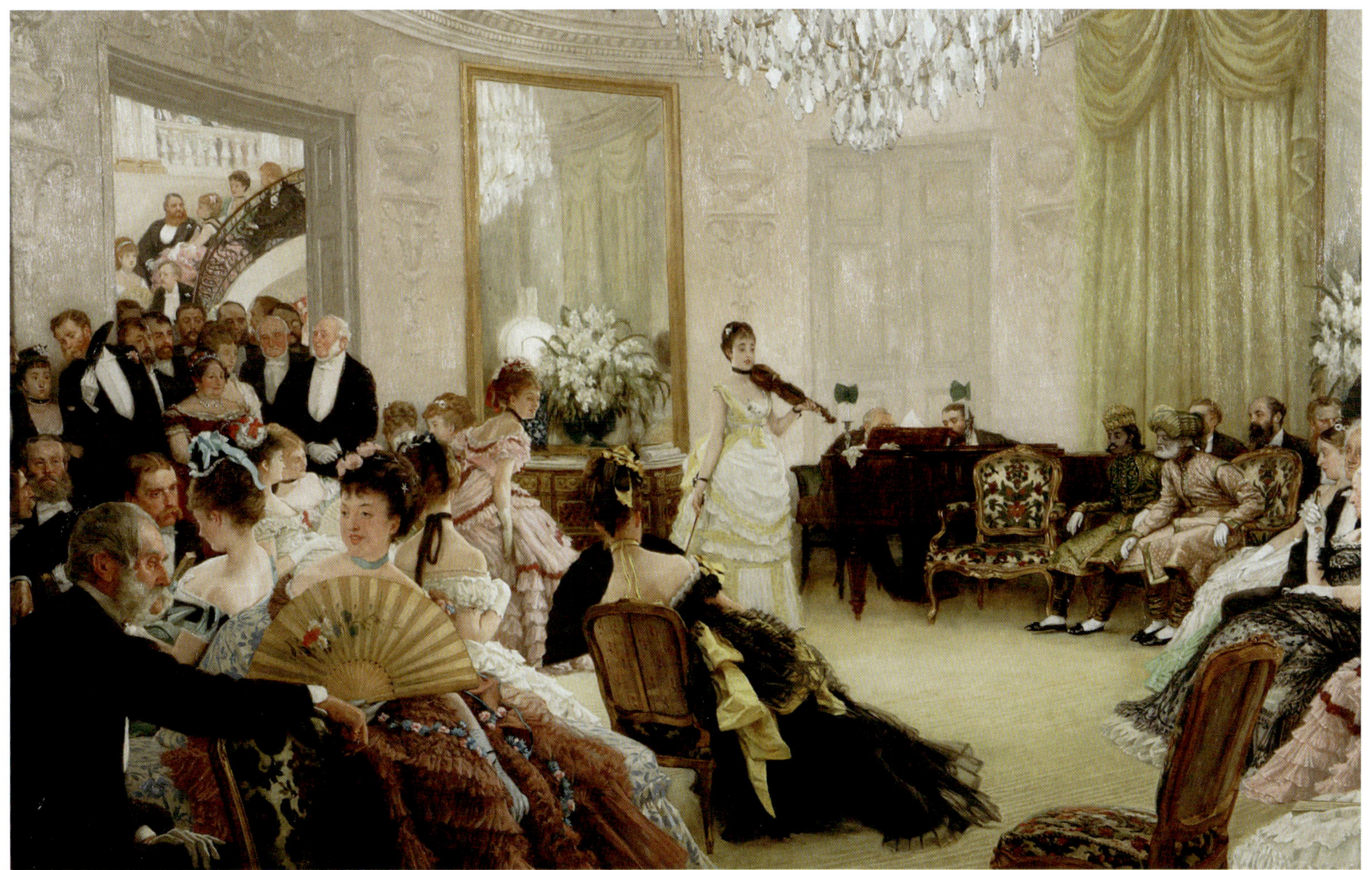

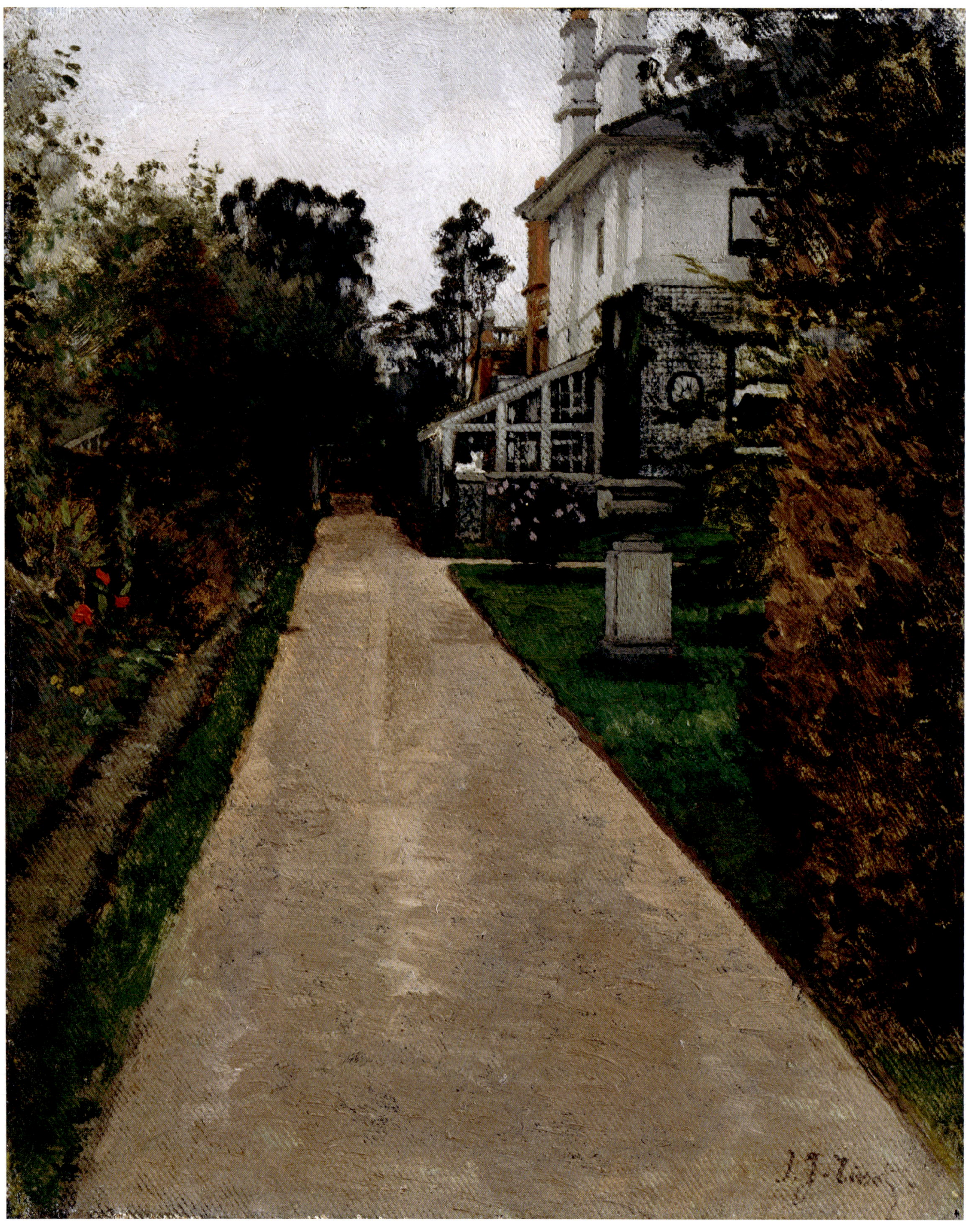

James Tissot
1836–1902
View of the Garden at 17 Grove End Road c.1874–1882
Oil paint on canvas 27 × 21

The Geffrye Museum of the Home, London

My Garden at St John's Wood 1878
Etching and drypoint on paper
18.7 × 11.5

Arwas Archives

In 1873, after just a couple of years in London, Tissot was able to purchase the house that would be his home until 1882. He chose a detached villa in the wealthy North London suburb of St John's Wood, an area said to be home to the nouveau riche. This house on Grove End Road would play an important role in his art, with both the sumptuous interior and carefully designed garden a source of inspiration for his canvases. He extended the house, adding a spacious conservatory, the setting for a number of his paintings, and inserting a bay window into his studio to assist the painting of nautical settings. For his French friends the house demonstrated Tissot's wealth and success on the other side of the channel; it was rumoured among them that the artist kept champagne on ice for potential guests.[1]

These depictions of the villa's garden, which he designed himself, are rare examples of Tissot treating a landscape subject without the addition of figures. We see the garden on its own terms, rather than as a setting for the ambiguities and intrigue characteristic of his more complex compositions. The distinctive cast-iron colonnade shown in the etching, copied from one in stone at the Parc Monceau in Paris, enclosed a large ornamental fishpond and features in a number of Tissot's paintings. In *Holyday* (pp.202–3), for example, the figures are shown in front of the pond, the background framed by the columns of the colonnade.

The next owner of the house, the painter Lawrence Alma-Tadema, remodelled it extensively, but kept many of the features of Tissot's lovingly designed garden. In the end the colonnade remained intact until the 1940s.[2] EJ

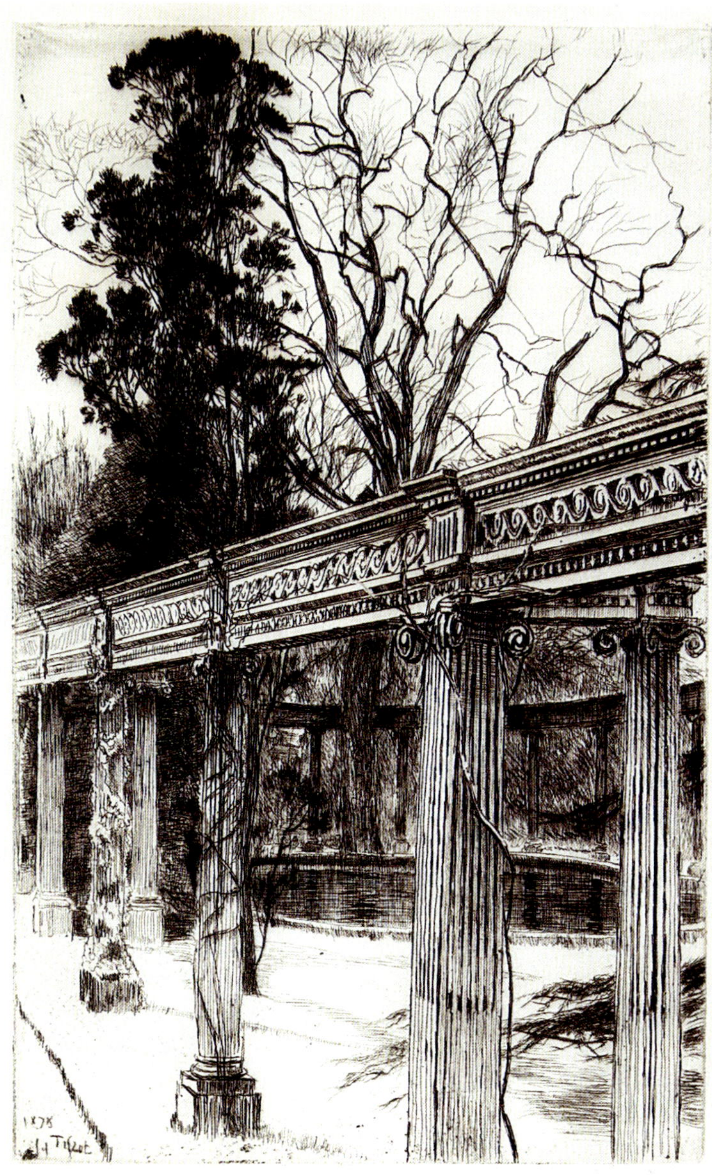

James Tissot
1836–1902
Woman in Outdoor Costume, Sleeping on a Couch c.1873
Chalk with watercolour and bodycolour on paper 22 × 28.8

Ashmolean Museum, University of Oxford. Purchased, 1951

The Japanese Scroll 1874
Oil paint on panel 38.7 × 57.2

Private collection
[not exhibited]

The subject of *Woman in Outdoor Costume, Sleeping on a Couch* appears to relate to *The Japanese Scroll* (1873; p.99), in which the same model reclines on the same striped sofa by the same green patterned cushion. In this watercolour, however, the overdress[1] that rests on her lap in the *Japanese Scroll* is wrapped around her, and details of her pleated skirt are only indicated in the watercolour. She is also wearing tan leather gloves here, and the central part of the sofa is covered by a shawl or throw. The theme of *Woman in Outdoor Costume* also relates to one of Tissot's drypoint prints, *La Dormeuse* (*The Sleeper*), and may intend to represent an exhausted model dressed in outdoor clothing who has fallen asleep – in this instance in a chilly sitting room. During his life at St John's Wood, Tissot turned to modern, intimate domestic subjects, even more so when his lover and model Kathleen Newton moved into his home at 17 Grove End Road sometime in 1877. When Newton became unwell with tuberculosis, images of rest and convalescence appeared in Tissot's work.

Tissot would have been aware of the long artistic tradition of images of women sleeping. The composition of *La Dormeuse* recalls one of Rembrandt's best-known ink drawings *A Young Woman Sleeping (Hendrickje Stoffels)* 1654, viewable in the Print Room of the British Museum. The subject was painted by William Powell Frith in his Royal Academy diploma work *The Sleeping Model* in 1853 (Royal Academy). *Woman in Outdoor Costume*, however, is a more modern image, its watercolour medium suggesting it may have been sketched quickly from life. It resembles the images of models caught unaware that Tissot's French associates were pursuing, particularly the intimate portraits of the impressionist painter Berthe Morisot, who visited Tissot in 1874. The same year Tissot had been able to visit Paris and catch up with friends such as Edgar Degas and Edouard Manet. *Woman in Outdoor Costume* shares the unusual cut-off, frontal viewpoint that these artists were using, framing the figure against the everyday setting of the upholstery of the sofa and a glimpse of a garden through a window. The outdoor hat and wrap appear more incongruous in the interior context, and the involuntary gesture of the hand over the face gives a sense of tender or voyeuristic observation. CJ & CCP

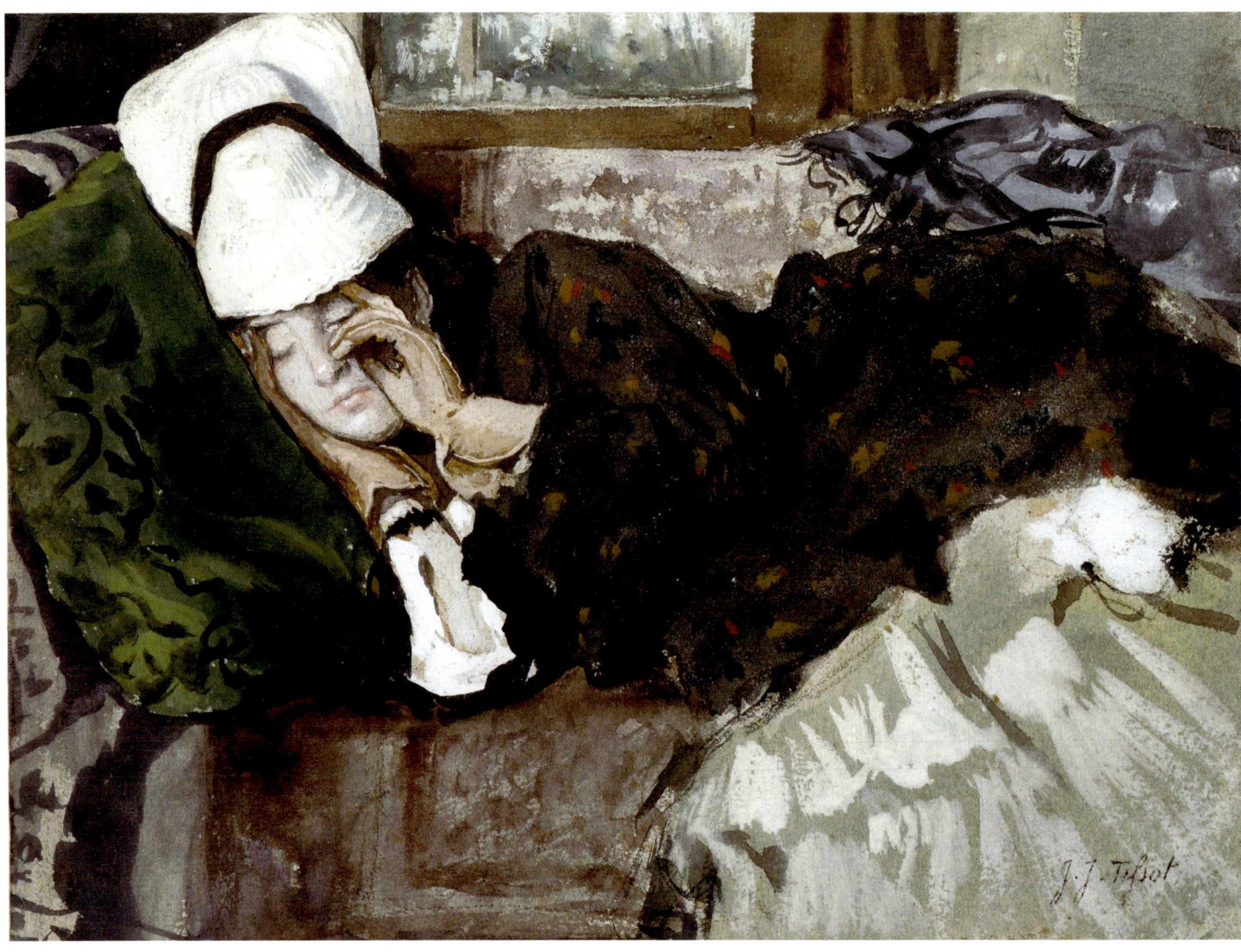

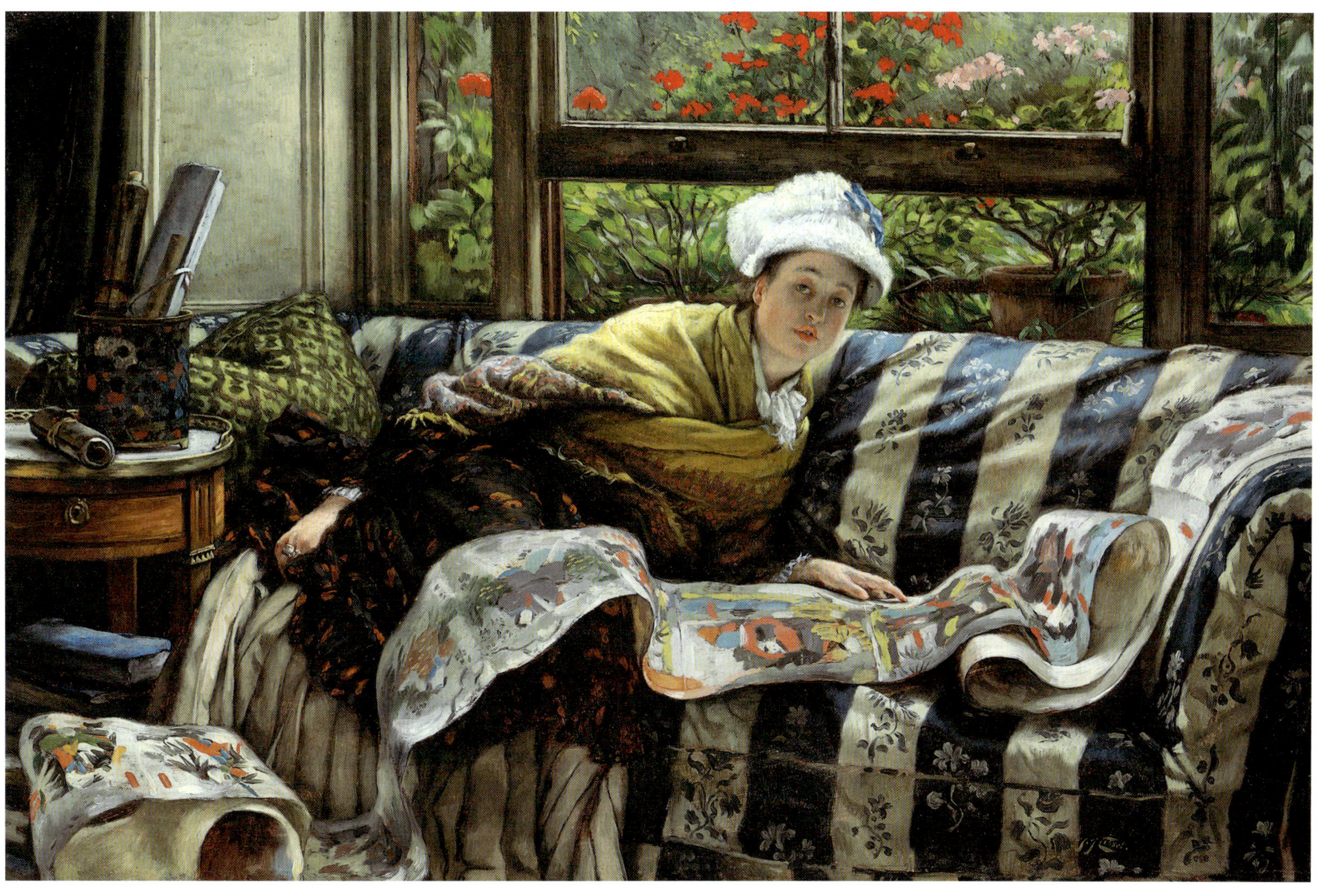

Anonymous
Kathleen Newton c.1881 (1)
Albumen print 21 × 14

Tate Archive

James Tissot
1836–1902
In Full Sunlight 1881 (2)
Etching and drypoint on paper
19 × 29.7

Arwas Archives

Anonymous
1879–82
Kathleen Newton (Rêverie)
c.1880–1 (3)
Photograph (modern print) 21 × 14

Tate Archive

James Tissot
1836–1902
Reading in the Park 1881 (4)
Oil paint on canvas 92 × 73

Musée des Beaux-Arts de Dijon

Tissot made his first London etchings in 1875. By the time he executed *In Full Sunlight* in 1881, printmaking had become a hugely important part of his practice, generating around 40 per cent of his artistic income.[1] His etchings, although made by his own, considerably skilled, hand, tend to reproduce his painted compositions quite exactingly. The painted version of *In Full Sunlight* (Metropolitan Museum of Art, New York) for example, varies only very slightly from the composition seen in the etching.

This print seems to exemplify some of the key characteristics of Tissot's London practice: his mistress and most important model, Kathleen Newton, is the key figure; his own carefully designed garden appears to be the setting; his interest in Japanese art and design is hinted at by the composition; and the print is an etched version of a subject that Tissot also painted. The work may borrow its French title, *En plein soleil*, from a print of 1858 by James Abbott McNeill Whistler, with whom Tissot was well acquainted. It has been suggested that Tissot's etching is a homage to Whistler's print, with parasols, female figures and perhaps the influence of Japanese aesthetics important in both compositions. However, Tissot's etching has a very different feel and includes a naturalistic background and additional figures. Kathleen's children Cecil and Violet both appear; the other figures may be her sister and niece. While it is probable that Whistler sketched the figure shown in his rather more spontaneous-looking etching from life, Tissot based his depiction of Kathleen Newton on a photograph (below). In the latter part of his London career Tissot instructed a studio assistant to take photographs for use in his paintings.[2] As Marshall has noted, the existence of a drawing by Tissot's friend Giuseppe de Nittis that appears to show Kathleen in identical costume and a similar pose suggests that the two artists may have been drawing and photographing her together at the same time.[3]

Reading in the Park is yet another depiction of Tissot's companion in his garden at St John's Wood. The picture is itself a reworking of *Quiet* c.1881 (private collection), which represented Kathleen Newton full-length with her niece Lilian Hervey and a dog. *Reading in the Park* focuses on Kathleen's intense gaze, which betrays tiredness, while her alabaster skin, much paler than in *Quiet*, is a reminder that Tissot's garden was certainly a setting of choice for intimate subjects, but also a place of confinement for his muse.

Kathleen Newton died from tuberculosis in 1882, the year after Tissot made these works. It would be

1

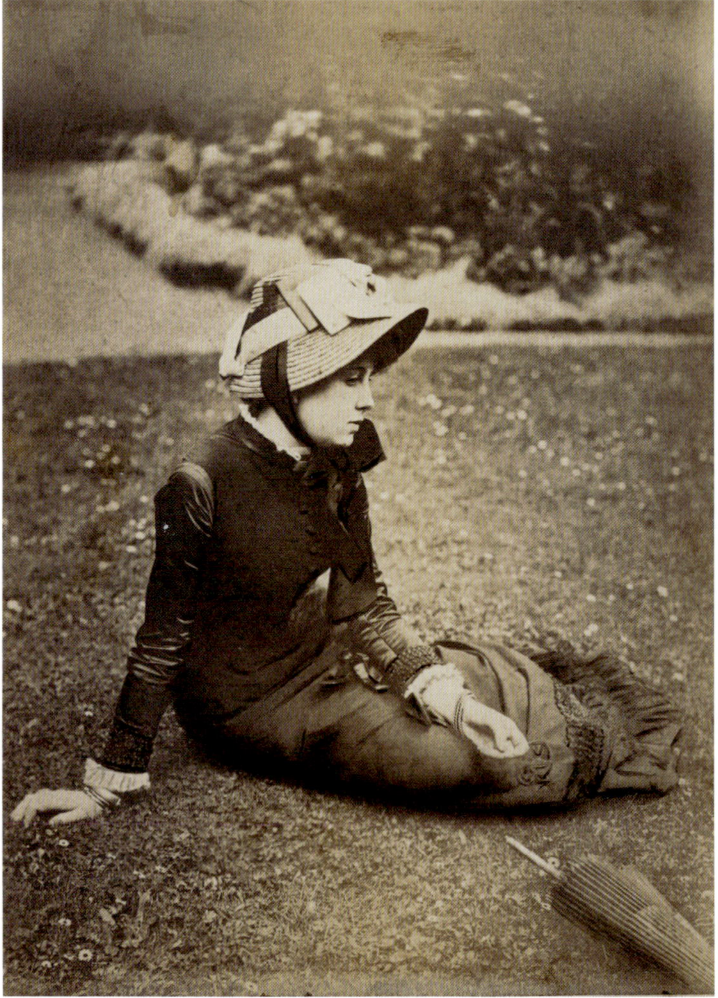

difficult to overstate her importance to his art during his London years. She was his most important muse and his partner during the period when he made many of his best-known paintings. After her death Tissot, by now forty-six years old, abandoned his London home and returned to Paris. EJ

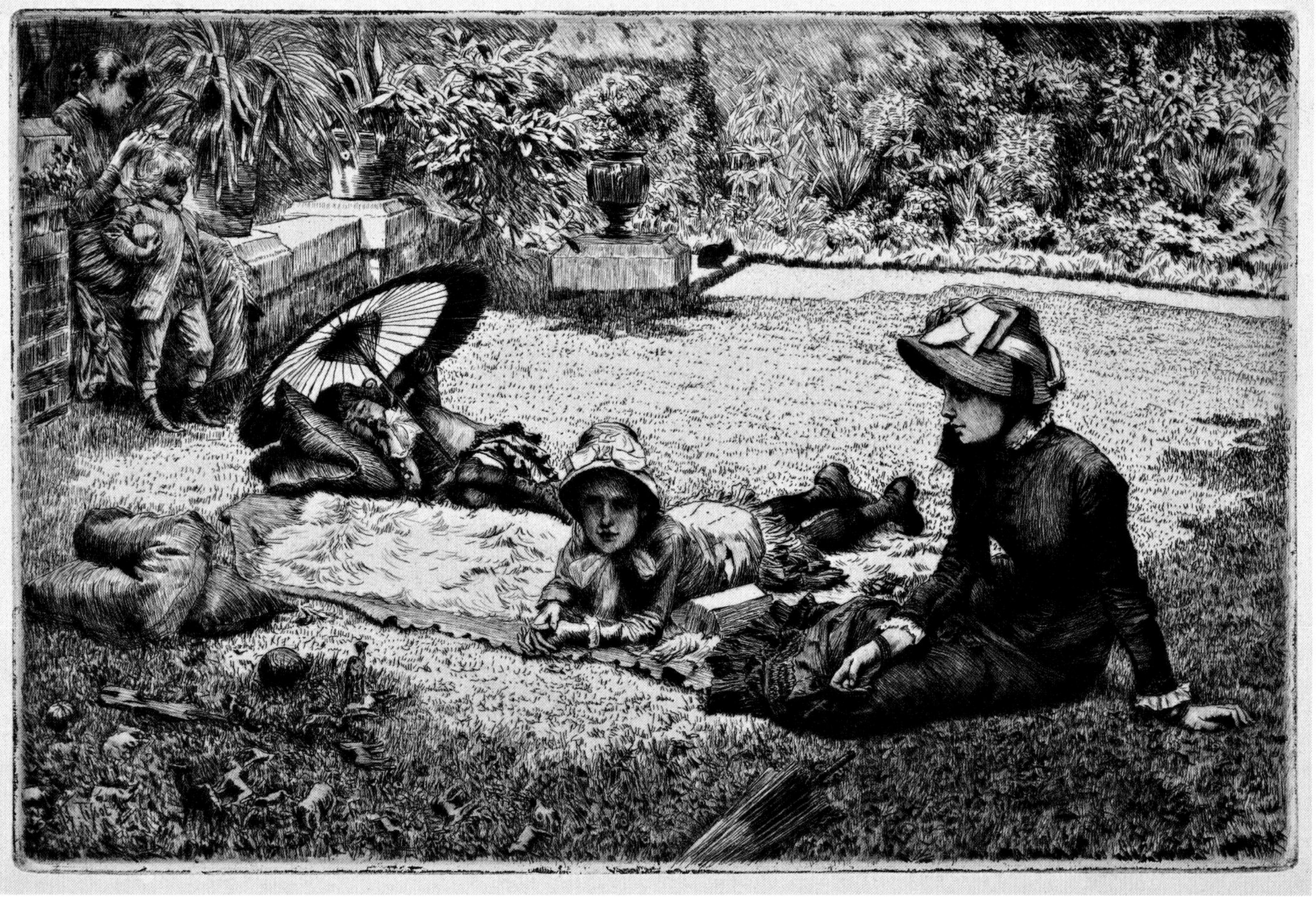

2

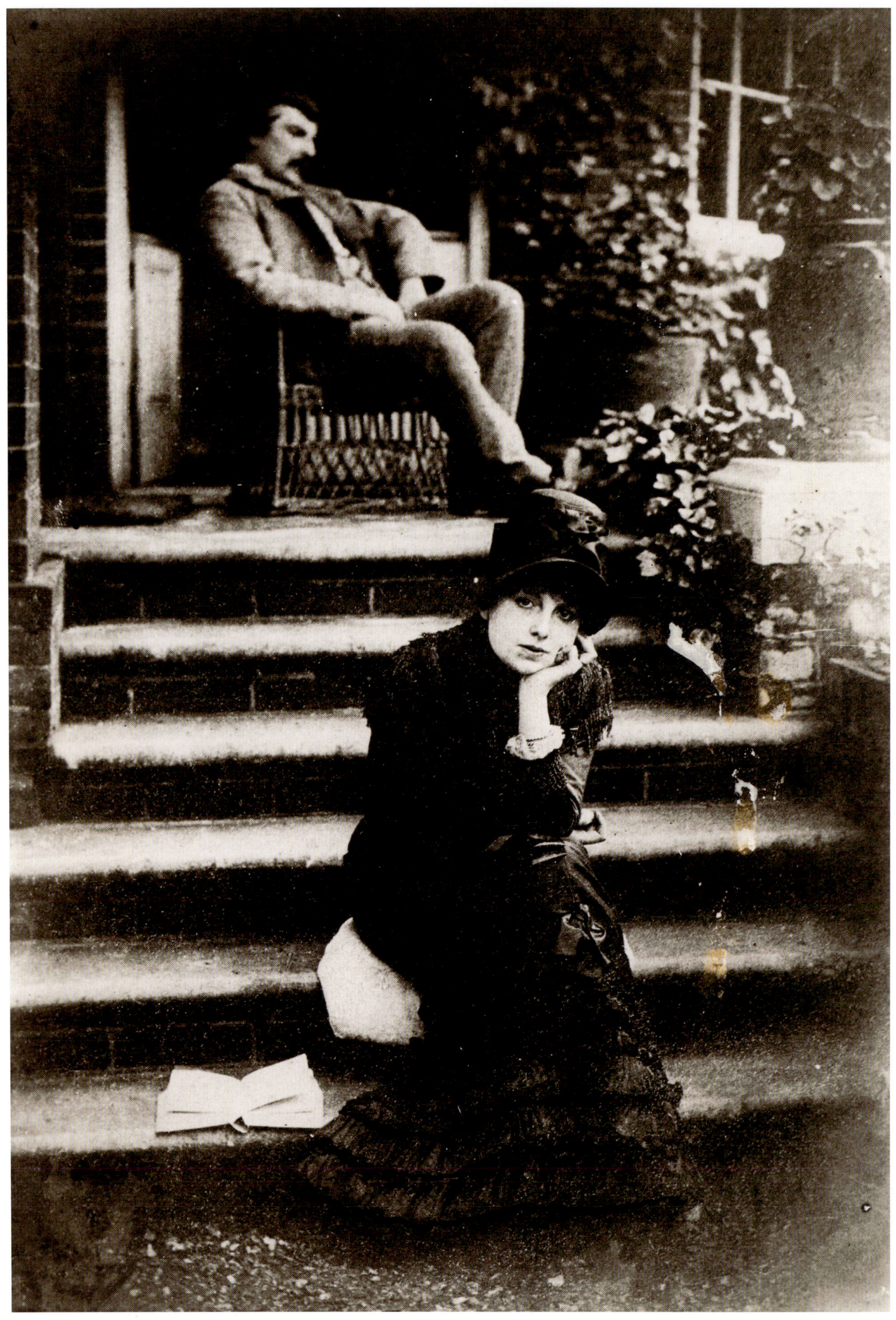

3

4

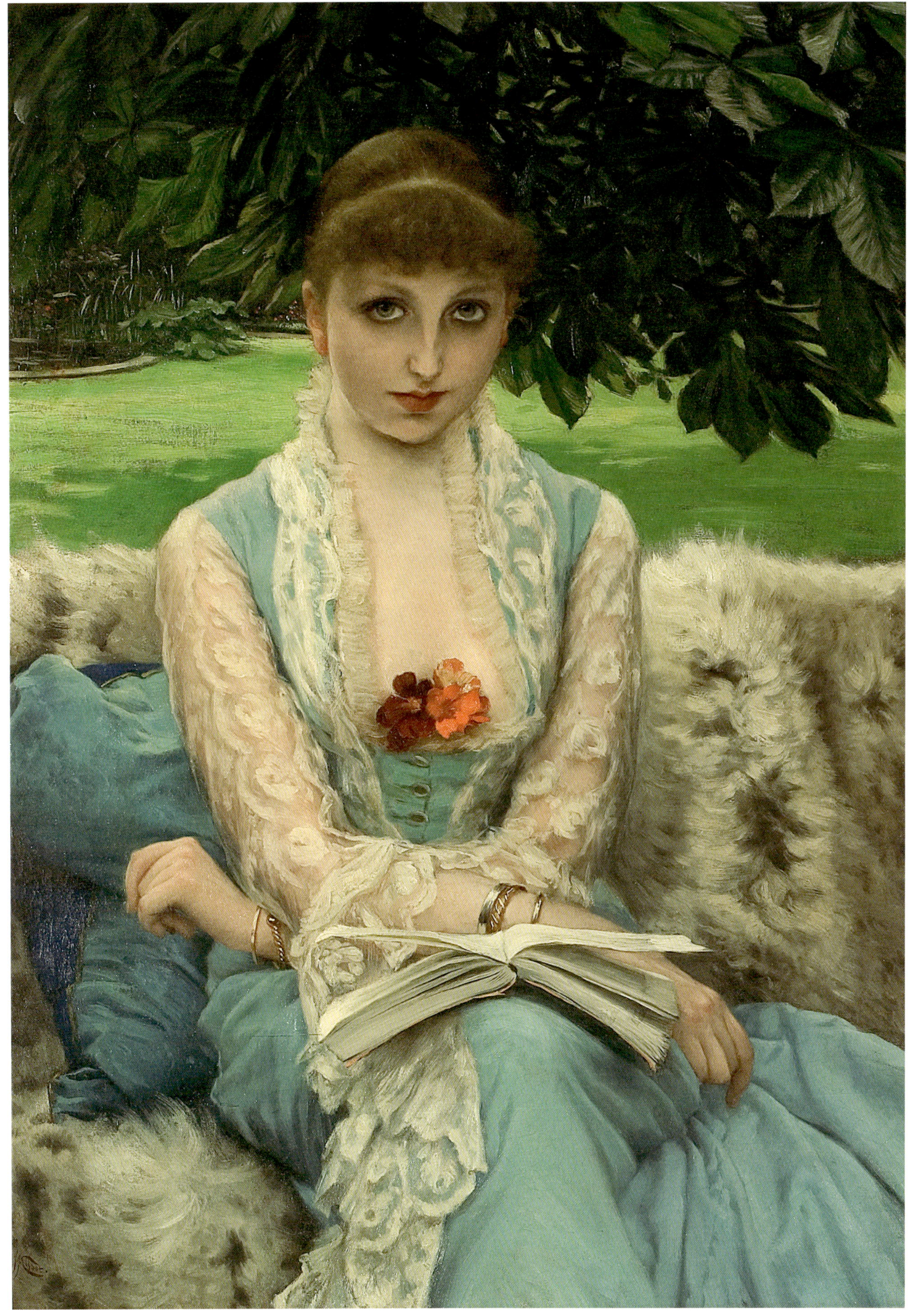

James Tissot
1836–1902
The Three Crows Inn 1877
Etching on paper 20.5 × 29.5

Arwas Archives

The Three Crows Inn treats the same subject as *Emigrants* (p.105), perhaps nodding towards the more socially conscious narrative paintings that were prominent during the Victorian era. The scene is set at Gravesend, at one of the main inns in which emigrants waited to board ship, actually called the *Three Daws*.[1] While the narrative itself remains typically ambiguous, the inhabitants of this composition are a far cry from the glamorous, fashionable figures seen in other nautical-themed works in Tissot's output, such as *The Gallery of HMS Calcutta* (p.112). Instead, they are dressed in much poorer attire and are clearly travelling, their luggage visible. As in *Emigrants*, the woman to the left is protecting a baby under her shawl. She is pensively looking at the horizon, either waiting for the ship to arrive or wondering what the future holds for her and her charge. The composition itself is a reworking of *The Captain's Daughter* 1873 (Southampton City Art Gallery), but it may also relate to an unlocated painting, *Leaving Old England (Gravesend)*.[2]

This impression bears the signature of Frederick Goulding, who printed editions of Tissot's plates in London. Goulding was a central figure in British etching at this time. He printed editions for the most important etchers of the day, including Whistler. He was also a good friend of Francis Seymour Haden's; Haden called Goulding 'the best printer of etchings in England, just now'.[3] Goulding assisted Alphonse Legros's teaching at the National Art Training School from 1876 to 1882, before taking over the classes there himself.[4] Tissot, too, became an important part of this circle. When Haden, perhaps the leading voice in British etching of the day, established the Society of Painter-Etchers in 1880, Tissot, along with Legros, formed part of the first committee. That same October, Tissot's prints were exhibited at the Fine Art Society's major exhibition of *Twelve Great Etchers*. Tissot's reputation as an etcher was such that his work was here seen alongside that of the prominent figures of Whistler and Haden. EJ

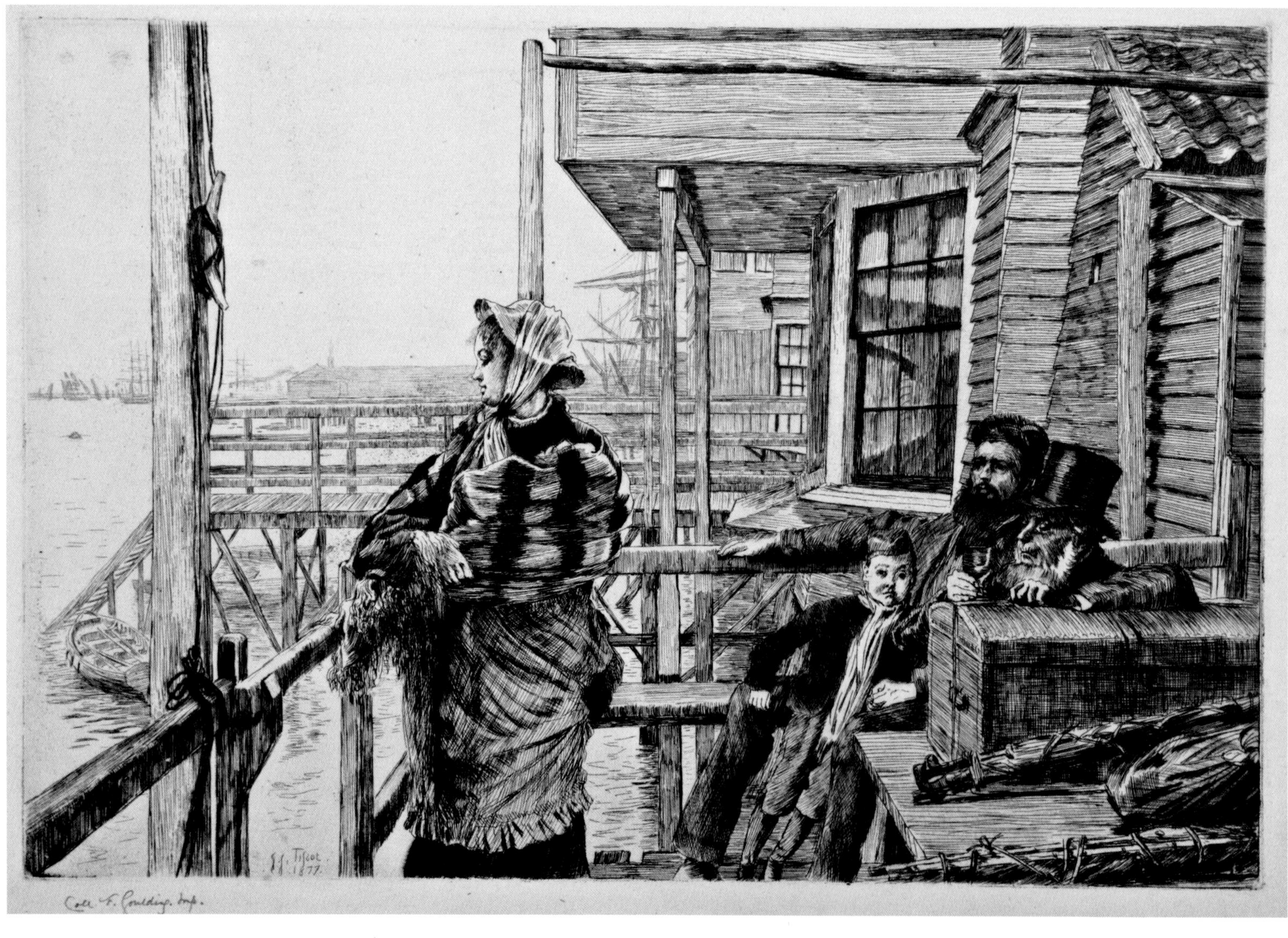

James Tissot
1836–1902
Emigrants 1880
Etching and drypoint on paper
34.5 × 16

Arwas Archives

The serious subject matter of *Emigrants* sets it apart from the majority of Tissot's London compositions. While many of his works are difficult to categorise, *Emigrants*, which Tissot based on a painting of the same name, sits relatively comfortably within the precedent set by Victorian narrative paintings like *The Last of England* 1855 (Birmingham Museums & Art Gallery), Ford Madox Brown's exploration of emigration. The subject was topical and presumably had a particular appeal for Tissot, who had left his own country to come to London in 1871, almost a decade before making this etching.

In *Emigrants* the mother and child at the centre of the narrative are about to step on board a ship; while a man stands by the steps ready to give them a helping hand, he is not obviously part of their family unit, implying that the woman and her child could be travelling alone. As Marshall has argued, Tissot's protagonists might have much to fear from the journey, the conditions on board potentially not only stormy but cramped and filthy too.[1] In such conditions the risk of disease was also very real. However, there is also perhaps cause for optimism, the woman's motivation presumably being a better life for herself and her child.

The busy background, an array of masts and ropes, creates the sense of a bustling seaport. The effect of the many criss-crossing black lines is enhanced with the use of drypoint, effective in creating a rich velvety black when printed. On one of the many ropes, in the upper left, sit two birds. Perhaps they reflect the woman's decision to begin a new life with her child as they take flight, but they could also allude to a freedom she does not have. EJ

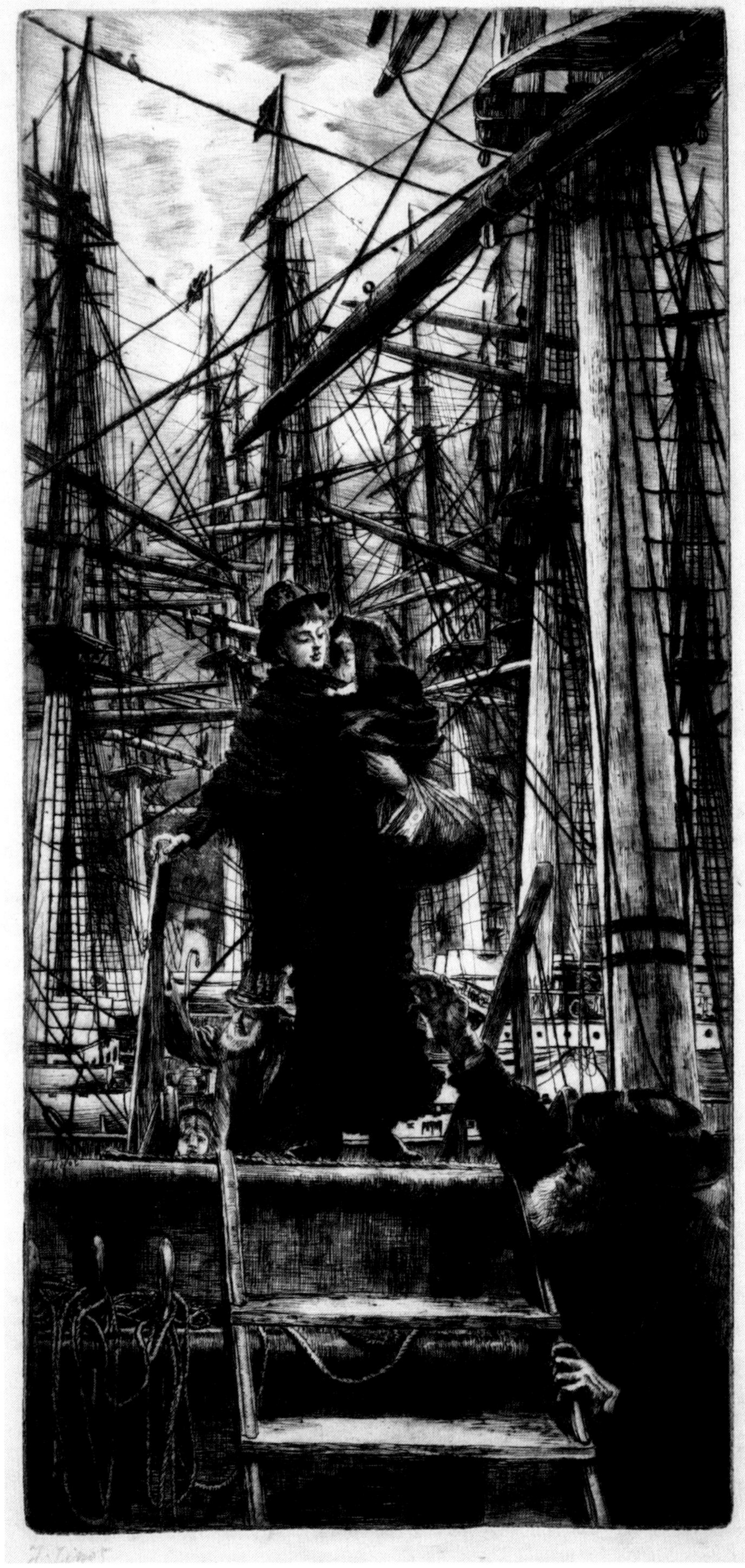

James Tissot
1836–1902
Sketch for the Terrace of the Trafalgar Tavern c.1878
Oil paint on panel
34.9 × 50.2

Collection of Ben Dollar, courtesy of Rafael Valls and Agnews
[not exhibited]

Trafalgar Tavern in Greenwich 1878
Etching and drypoint on paper
34.5 × 16

Arwas Archives

Tissot explored this subject both in paint and on paper. In the painted panel *The Terrace of the Trafalgar Tavern* (New Orleans Museum of Art) and its related preparatory sketch (below), Tissot chose a different vantage point: he painted from the balcony occupied by the men who are at the very centre of the print. Instead of replicating the horizontal composition that he adopted in paint – a format that emphasises the maritime heritage of Greenwich, and the Thames at high tide – Tissot made use of a vertical composition to highlight the contrast between the upper class on the balcony and those in need below. The three boys to the right were known as London 'mudlarks', the term referring to Londoners, usually children, who took advantage of the low tide to scavenge anything of value to survive.

Scenes with such social resonance are rare in Tissot's work, but he was not the first to have been shocked by the nature of the scene. In his preface to *London: A Pilgrimage* (p.52) Jerrold had already noted the presence of 'the Greenwich boys ... busy in the mud below [the Trafalgar Tavern], learning to be vagabond men by the help of the thoughtless divers flushed with wine, who were throwing pence to them'.[1] Later, in June 1874, Thomas Gibson Bowles witnessed a very similar scene to the one represented in his friend's etching, down to the very number of young boys depicted in it. Describing a group of diners after their 'whitebait supper', Bowles wrote: 'Beneath them are three naked little boys diving for coppers, which they, in the fullness of their generosity – or rather in the generosity of their fullness – throw out. Truly we are a brutal people, we English.'[2]

As fellow countrymen, Jerrold and Bowles probably found even more difficult to accept the attitude of these disdainful men, at the extreme opposite of the 'mudlarks' in the social spectrum, and in a position of power, with which come responsibilities. To make matters worse, the Trafalgar Tavern itself was emblematic of the British Empire, then at its height, and as such, it hosted the annual parliamentary fish dinner. Although the scene represented is damning for the diners, it is ambiguously etched in the dining room of the *Trafalgar Tavern*, from the chair of a guest about to order or be served, as suggested by the cutlery as yet untouched. CCP

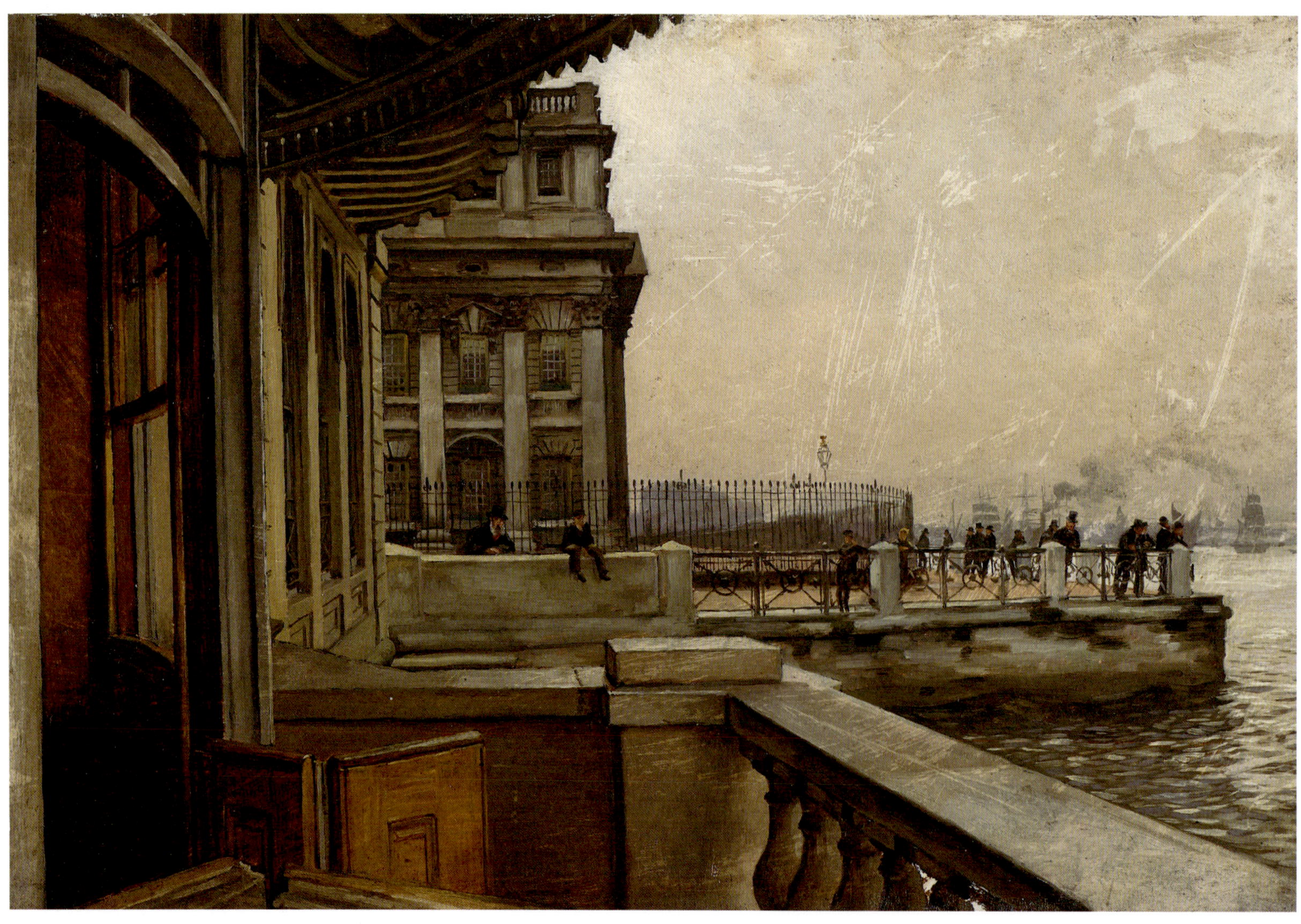

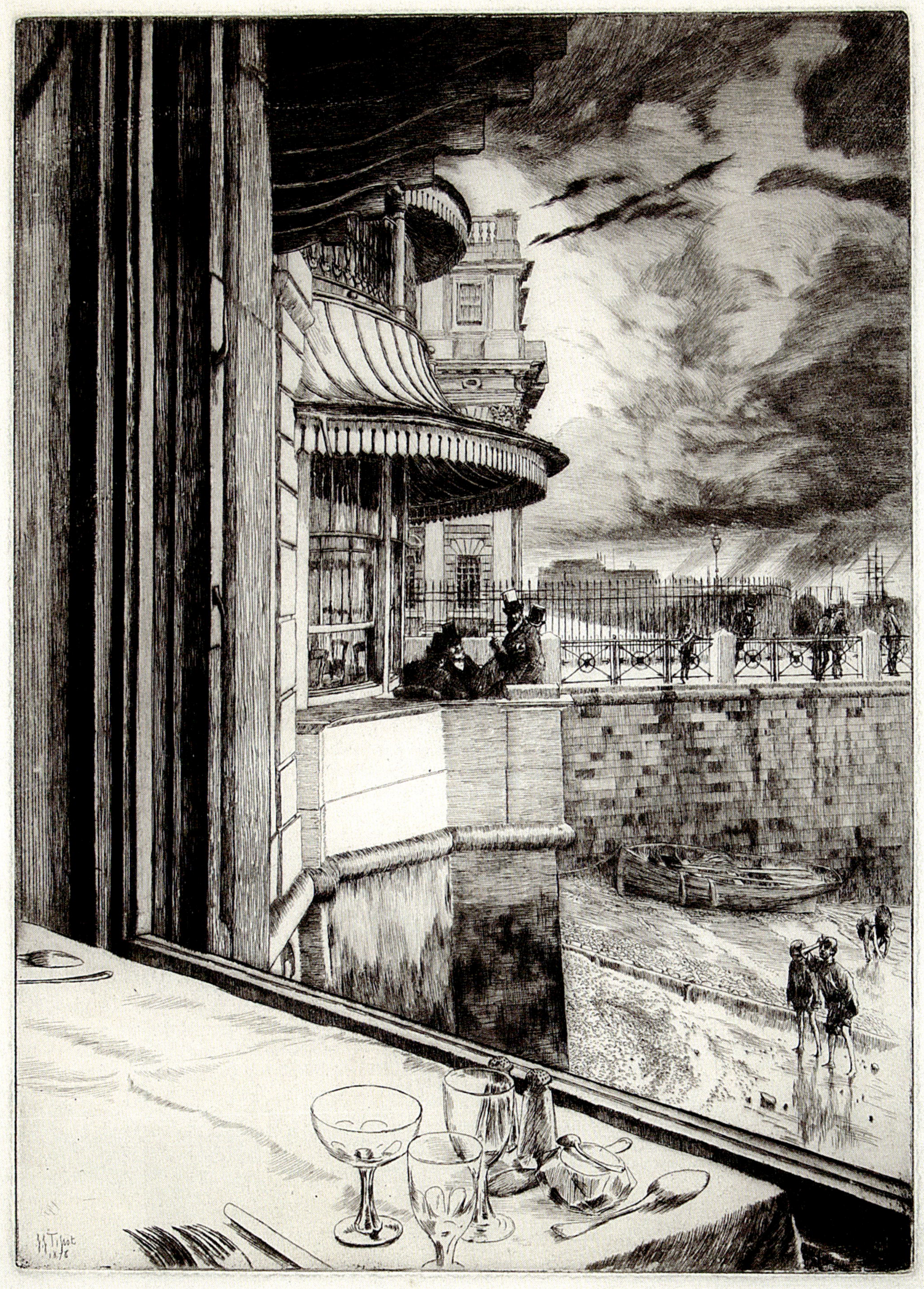

James Tissot
1836–1902
London Visitors
(originally *Country Cousins*) 1873
Oil paint on canvas 86.3 × 63.5

Milwaukee Art Museum, Layton Art Collection, Gift of Frederick Layton

One of the paintings by Tissot exhibited at the Royal Academy in 1874 was *London Visitors* (Toledo Museum of Art). Scholars have long thought that the Milwaukee version you see here was a smaller-size replica of the Academy picture, with variations made in response to newspaper criticism. However, the records of dealers Thomas Agnew & Sons Ltd (National Gallery archive) reveal that they received the finished painting from Tissot on 7 January 1874, several months before the Academy picture was completed, exhibited and reviewed.

Called at first *The Portico*, the Milwaukee painting was recorded and sold by Agnew with the title *Country Cousins*. This was a gently pejorative term for provincials – people who lived outside the London metropolis.

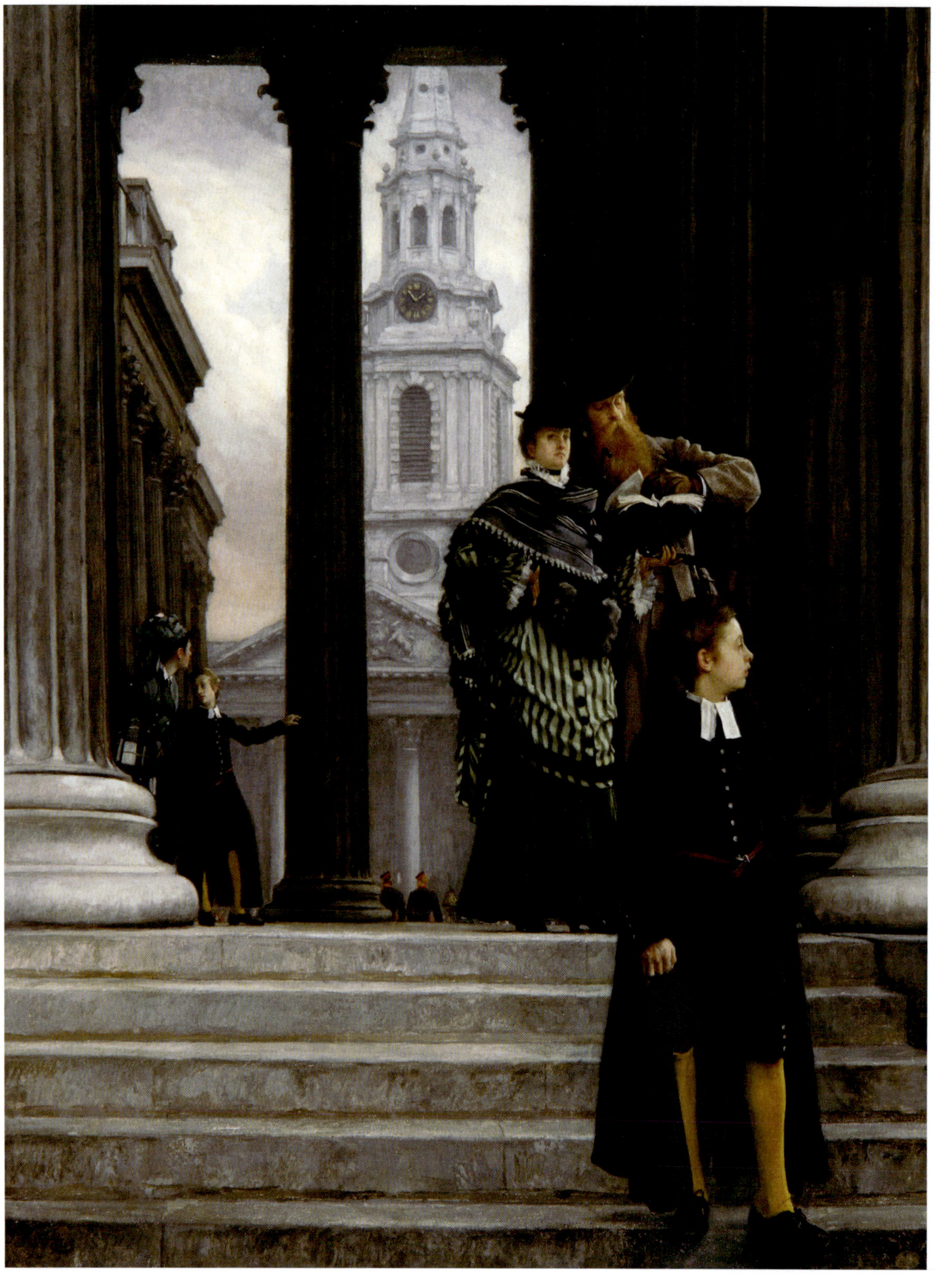

Tissot is presenting here a country couple, the man in tweeds and young woman in fashionable outfit, on a visit to the big city. Judging by the clock on the tower of St Martin-in-the-Fields Church, it is almost five to two. The tourists have visited the National Gallery and stand at the entrance portico, considering where to go next. While the bearded man consults, and perhaps reads from, a guidebook, his female companion points her umbrella in the direction of Trafalgar Square. She looks bored and indifferent, her eyes unfocused and thoughts clearly elsewhere. In front of them stands a 'Blue Coat School' boy in characteristic uniform of long dark-blue woollen coat, white clerical collar, red leather belt and yellow stockings. Another behind them points out landmarks or gives directions to a young woman in blue-grey dress. Pupils of the charity school Christ's Hospital, commonly called 'Blue Coat' boys, acted as volunteer guides at the National Gallery. Adding a note of colour in the distance are the red-banded caps of two soldiers, probably from St George's Barracks nearby. Beyond them are indications of busy carriage traffic in front of St Martin's.

The variant that Tissot painted for Royal Academy exhibition is almost twice the size and presents a number of differences. There are the same 'Blue Coat' schoolboys but no distant soldiers. The time, according to the clock on St Martin's, is ten thirty-five, barely half an hour after National Gallery opening; these *London Visitors* have clearly 'done' the gallery at speed. Although they are dressed the same as the *Country Cousins*, the young woman in striped dress is now looking directly at us. A discarded cigar on the gallery steps implies that a man has just descended and is the person with whom the woman has locked eyes. We, the viewers, are in the position of that man, and her pointing umbrella seems to propose a place of assignation in Trafalgar Square. Young ladies at this time were expected to look away modestly and not make direct eye contact. However, American women were noted for their directness and bold gaze. It is possible that Tissot's 'London visitors' in the Royal Academy picture are not 'country cousins' but ones 'from across the pond', that is Americans.
KM

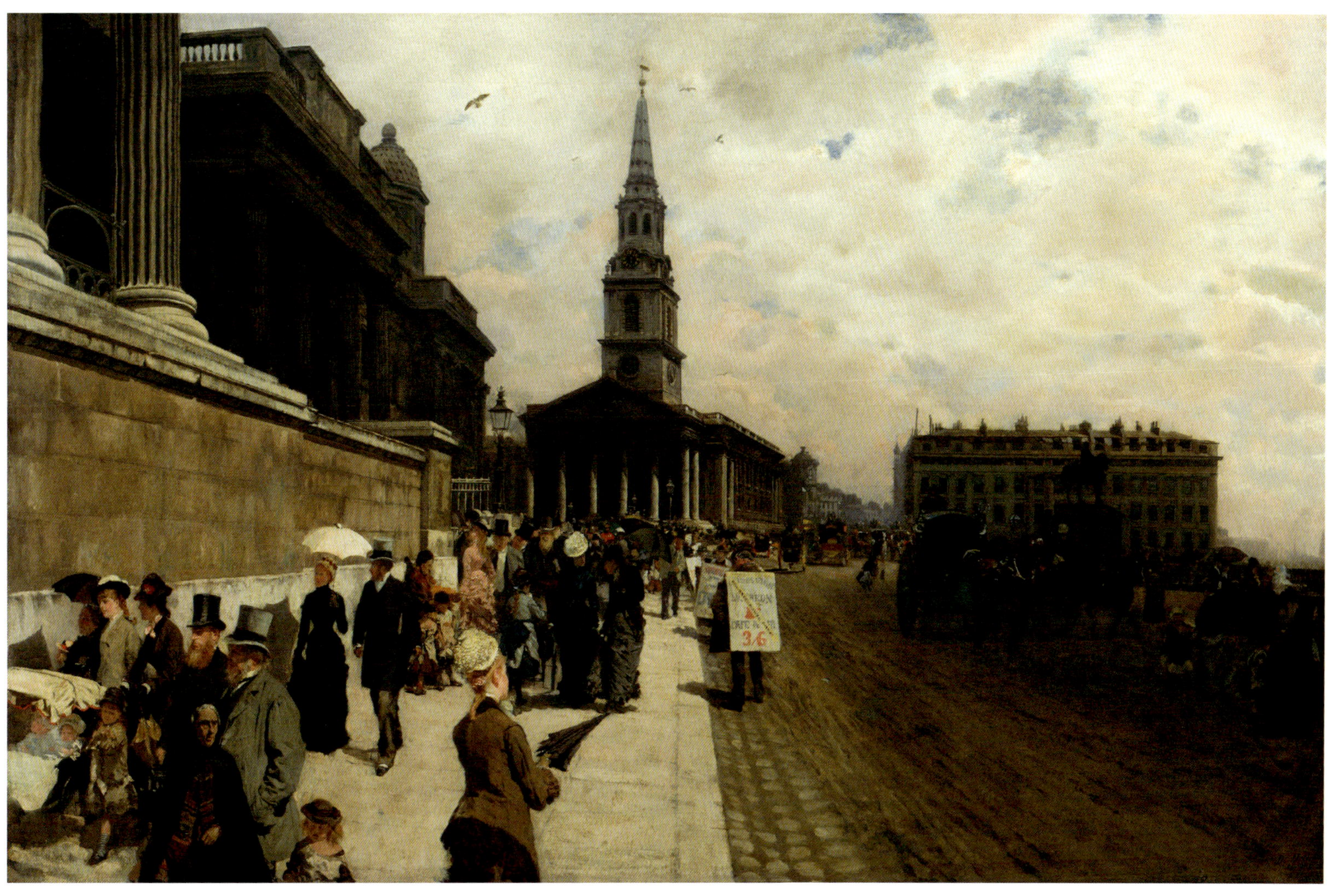

Giuseppe de Nittis
(1846–1884)
The National Gallery 1877
Oil paint on canvas 70 × 105

Petit Palais, Musée des Beaux-Arts de la Ville de Paris

Giuseppe de Nittis was Italian by birth, but settled in Paris in 1867 and claimed that 'France [was] the country that [he had] espoused'.[1] At the outbreak of the Franco-Prussian War, he and his French wife Léontine fled briefly to London, from where they headed for Giuseppe's home town, Barletta. They returned to Paris in September 1871. Like most French artists in the aftermath of the war and Paris Commune, de Nittis experienced financial difficulties, and felt trapped in a contract with Goupil, which required him to produce commercial subjects, paid cheaply.

Although the role of his Italian connections in London should not be downplayed,[2] the success of his friend James Tissot in the English capital was definitely the greatest inspiration and motivation for his yearly trips to London, the first of which took place in 1874. He set off for England the day before the opening of the *First Impressionist Exhibition* at Nadar's studio, at which he was an exhibitor.

In London Tissot was instrumental in gaining him entry to the select Arts Club. Their mutual acquaintance, the art dealer Algernon Moses Marsden provided an introduction to Kaye Knowles, their patron, who was later credited for putting an end to de Nittis's financial concerns: 'I came back from London after three months, my challenges overcome, and I was able to go back to my dear work.'[3] Knowles, a wealthy colliery proprietor from Lancashire, would in time own at least twelve views of London by de Nittis (see pp.208–11), including *The National Gallery*, which was painted when the artist was staying near Tissot at St John's Wood. A few years earlier, the French artist had set up his easel almost in the same spot as de Nittis to paint a couple of tourists outside the National Gallery in *London Visitors* (p.108). Both chose to represent one of the symbols of London and its culture from the point of view of outsiders, making of both pictures *mises en abyme* of their own condition as foreigners, be they satirical in Tissot's case.

De Nittis's approach, however, differs from that of his friend: while Tissot drew on the genre of the problem picture, he, on the other hand, privileged a time of the day when the pavement of the gallery was at its busiest to create a snapshot of the metropolis and its make-up. He recorded on canvas the movement of the modern city, people queuing to enter the gallery and passers-by of all ages and walks of life. Without ever being caricatural, de Nittis showed his grasp of the local colour of London through the introduction of types, not least a procession of sandwich-board men in the centre of the canvas. CCP

James Tissot
1836–1902
Summer (A Portrait) 1876
Oil paint on canvas 91.4 × 50.8

Tate. Purchased 1927

In 1877 Tissot ceased exhibiting at the Royal Academy and sent ten works, including *Summer*, to the newly opened Grosvenor Gallery. Another exhibit, *Winter* or *Mavourneen*, was referred to as *A Portrait* in the exhibition catalogue, and *Summer* mistakenly came to be known under this title, as recently elucidated by Krystyna Matyjaszkiewicz.[1] The Grosvenor Gallery was associated with the aesthetic circle of artists around Dante Gabriel Rossetti and James Abbott McNeill Whistler. The aesthetic movement advocated an art that appealed through its beauty rather than its story or moral. The luxurious fabrics and the narrow palette of blues and yellows employed in *Summer* invite the viewer to appreciate the painting as an aesthetic arrangement, especially the patterns on the curtains, Indian to the right, Japanese to the left, reminiscent of those used in Whistler's paintings. A letter written by Rossetti on a visit to Paris in 1864 gives a sense of the good-natured rivalry between the three artists even before Tissot arrived:

> I went to Japanese shop, I found that all the costumes were being snapped up by a French artist, Tissot, who it seems is doing three Japanese pictures, which the mistress of the shop described to me as the three wonders of the world, evidently in her opinion throwing Whistler into the shade. She told me, with a great deal of laughing, about Whistler's consternation at my collection of china.[2]

The suggestions of romance in *Summer* have more in common with a poem than a story. The hat, parasol and white muslin dress indicate holiday relaxations, and the dress was used in other paintings such as *July: Specimen of a Portrait* 1878 (Cleveland Museum of Art), sometimes called *Seaside*, and in *The Gallery of HMS Calcutta* (p.112). The yellow ribbons bring the sunny day beyond the window into the cool, shadowy interior. The blue and green curtains are parted in the foreground and a glass door is closed behind the woman's left shoulder and open to her right, but it is unclear whether she arrives or leaves. Tissot also made a drypoint after the painting called *Portrait of Miss L… or 'Il faut qu'une porte soit ouverte ou fermée' (A Door Must Be Open or Closed)*.[3] CJ

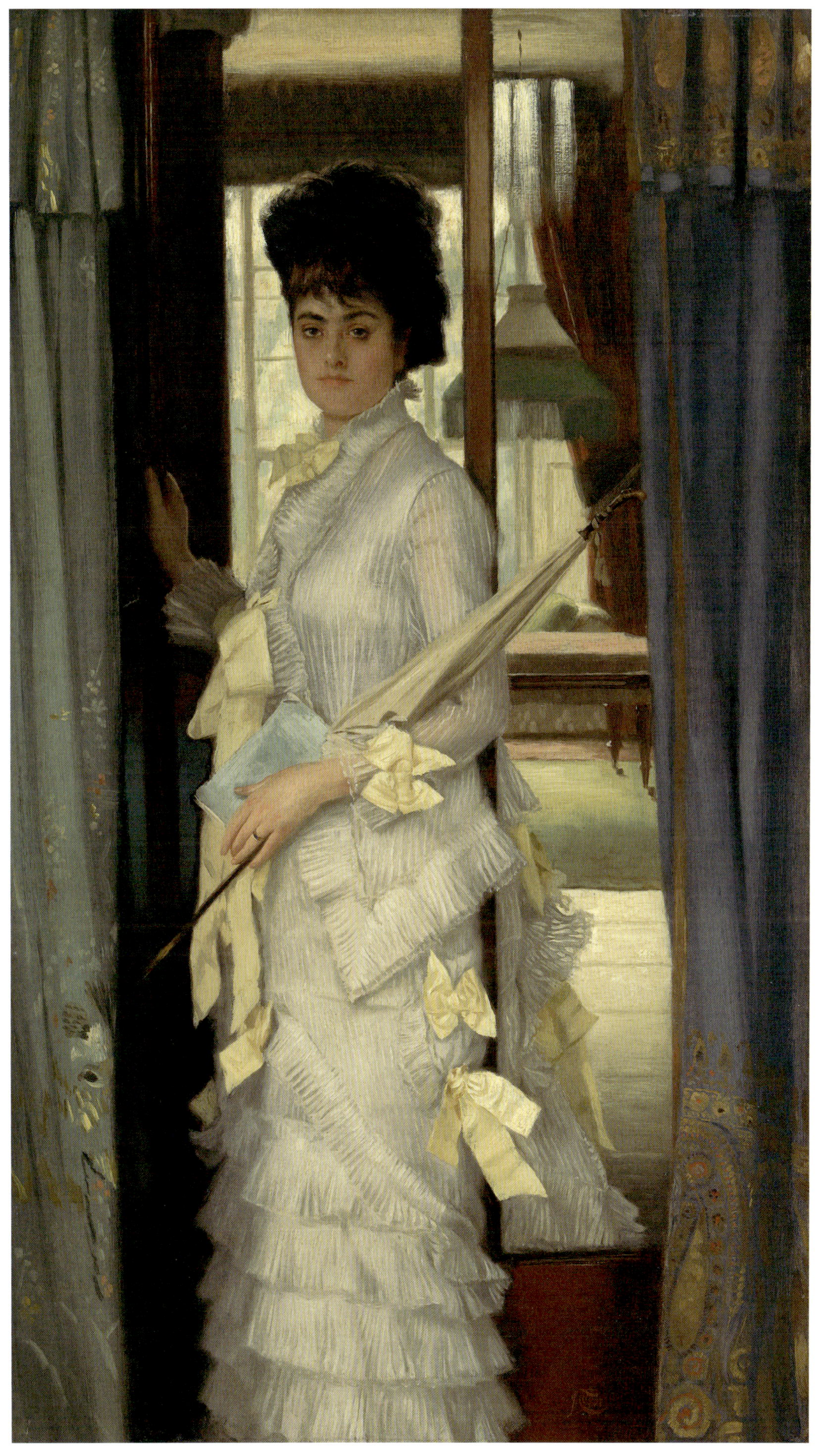

James Tissot
1836–1902
The Gallery of HMS Calcutta (Portsmouth) c.1876
Oil paint on canvas 68.6 × 91.8

Tate. Presented by Samuel Courtauld 1936

The deck of the HMS Calcutta, docked in a sooty Portsmouth, is here a setting for intrigue and ambiguity. Two finely dressed women stand in the foreground, their dresses almost like mirror images of each other's with the ribbons in complementary hues. A sailor has apparently just joined them, and the seemingly haughty lady in the foreground uses her fan as a barrier against her companions; her action may be due to annoyance or is perhaps more flirtatious. As Marshall has noted, the sailor wears a wedding ring, adding still further to the ambiguity of the narrative.[1] The picture attracted some criticism when exhibited at the Grosvenor Gallery in 1877, the writer Henry James calling its realism 'vulgar and banal' and commenting that a longer acquaintance with the foreground lady's 'stylish back and yellow ribbons' would be 'intolerably wearisome'.[2]

Tissot allowed the painting to be engraved for *The Graphic*, thus ensuring its dissemination to a broader public, but also reproduced it within an etching of his own for a more limited clientele. Marshall argues that this was characteristic of Tissot's desire to maximise both exposure and profits.[3] *The Graphic*'s reproduction was accompanied by the words: 'We look in vain for some clue to the story which these graceful forms and charming colours may be presumed to suggest ... especially as the title chosen does not help us one whit.'[4] The picture's title, however, *The Gallery of HMS Calcutta (Portsmouth)*, is sometimes interpreted as including a hidden meaning. Warner has suggested that the name of the ship, the 'Calcutta', and the picture's subject could be related, the word 'Calcutta' a playful reference to the French phrase 'Quel cul tu as', meaning 'What an ass you have'.[5] Whether or not this pun was intended, Matyjaszkiewicz believes the scene in fact relates to an actual ball on board the HMS Calcutta, which had retired into Portsmouth as an experimental gunnery ship.[6]

Whatever Tissot's intentions with regards to the word 'Calcutta' and the foreground lady's behind, the lead figure, with her distinctive white muslin dress, yellow ribbons and fan, certainly garnered attention. Tissot's evident interest in costume was longstanding: he was the son of a linen draper and his mother's company made and exported women's hats. He dressed the models in his paintings with the latest fashions, often reusing favoured items across different compositions. The white dress decorated with yellow seen in this picture reappears in *July: Specimen of a Portrait* 1878 (Cleveland Museum of Art), leading Marshall to suggest it was one of Tissot's carefully chosen studio props.[7]
EJ

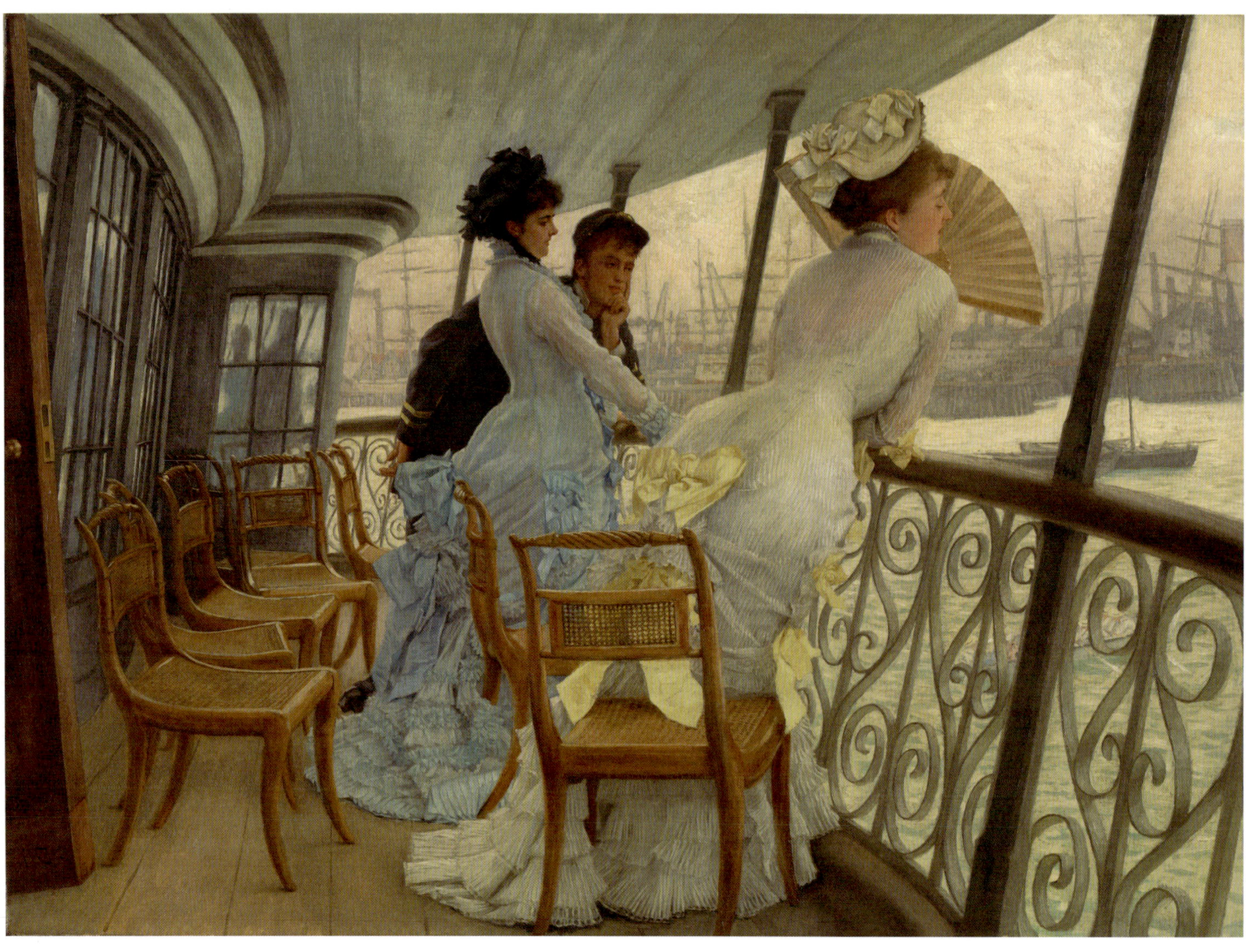

James Tissot
1836–1902
Portsmouth Dockyard c.1877
Oil paint on canvas 38.1 × 54.6

Tate. Bequeathed by Sir Hugh Walpole 1941

This canvas was first exhibited at the Grosvenor Gallery in 1877 under the current title, *Portsmouth Dockyard*. In the same year Tissot made an etching and drypoint of the composition, alternatively titled *How Happy Could I Be with Either*. As Wentworth has pointed out, this latter title is unusual within Tissot's oeuvre for its direct reference to the theme of comic romantic rivalry that finds its way into a number of his paintings of the 1870s: usually the artist allowed ambiguity to reign.[1] While the three figures in *The Gallery of HMS Calcutta (Portsmouth)* (p.112) might keep us guessing, the title given to Tissot's print of the present subject ensures the meaning of the composition is clearer. The Highland Sergeant, of the 42nd Royal Highlanders (or Black Watch), needs to choose between the two women on either side of him.[2] The lady on the left certainly appears more receptive to the sergeant's advances, her umbrella closed and out of his way, while the figure on the right has wrapped her shawl around herself protectively and remains framed by her cream parasol.

The painting reworks an earlier one by Tissot, the also ambiguously titled *On the Thames* c.1876 (p.220), which received both praise and considerable censure when first exhibited. In the present composition a Highland Sergeant has replaced the naval officer seen in *On the Thames*. And instead of conversing in a steamboat on the murky-looking Thames, the figures here sit more genteelly, within a rowing boat on the waters of Portsmouth Harbour. EJ

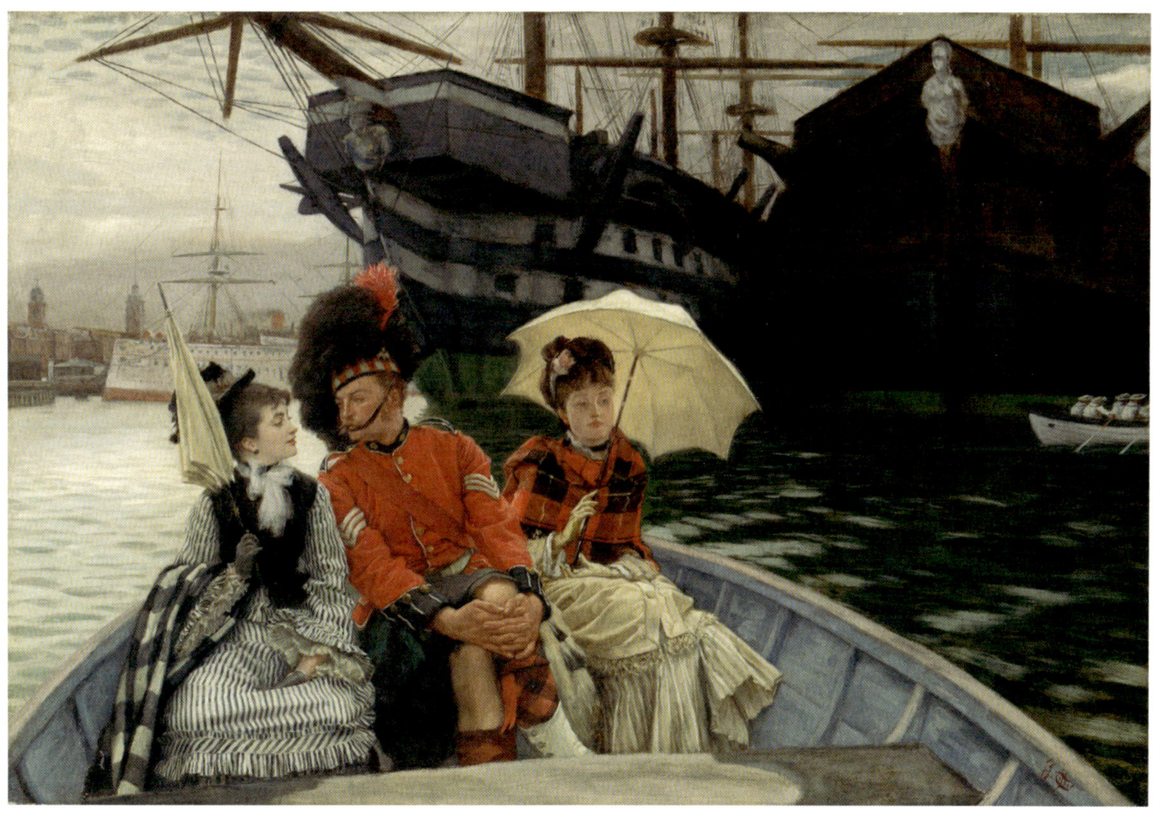

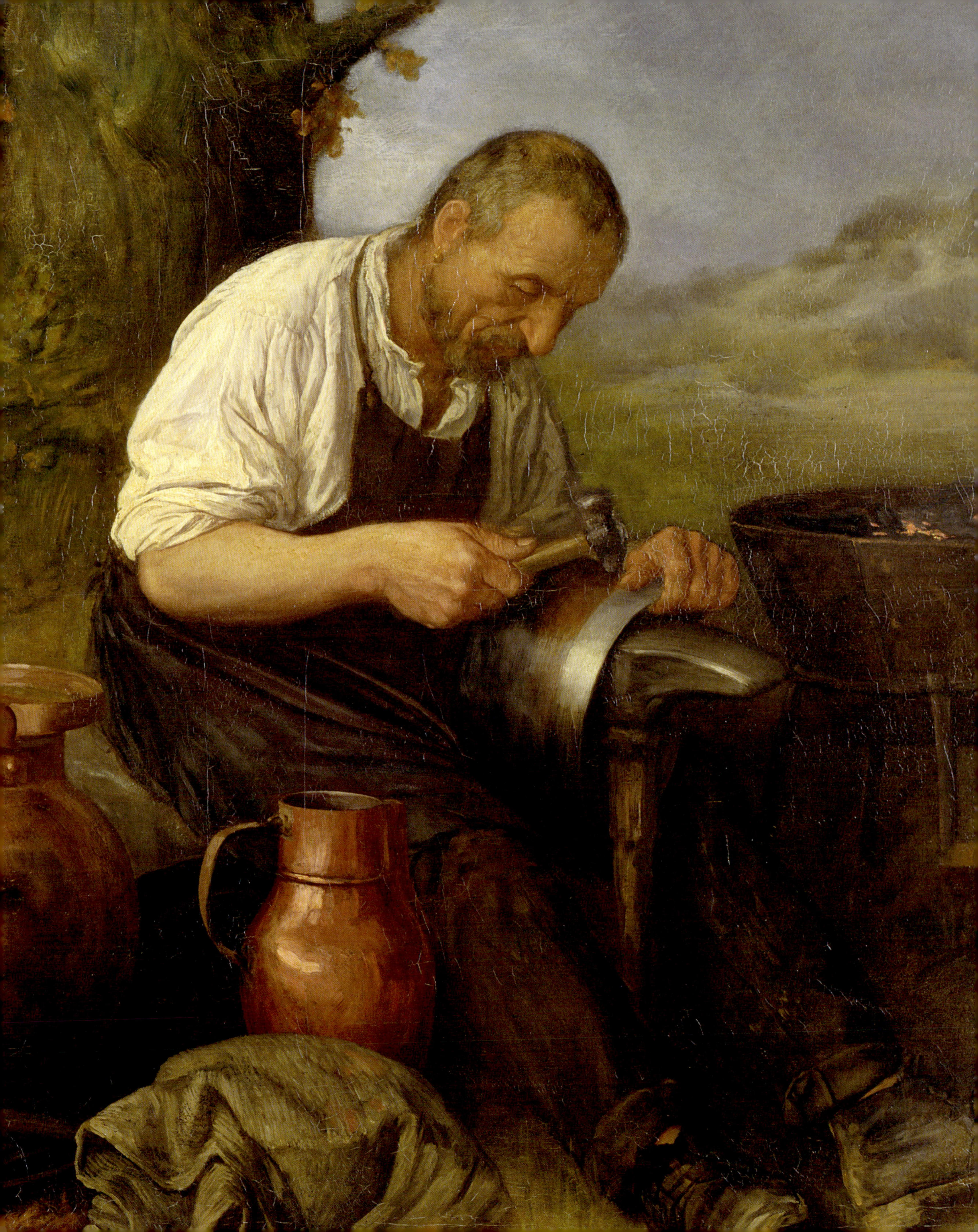

Anna Gruetzner Robins

Alphonse Legros: Migrant and Cultural Ambassador

Alphonse Legros
The Tinker 1874
(detail, see p.127)

London: world city

Alphonse Legros, who was born in Dijon in 1837, came to London in 1863, his second visit to the largest nineteenth-century city in the world. Although he would cross the channel many times over the years, he never returned to live in his native France. Previously, in 1861–2, he had stayed with the brother-in-law of James McNeill Whistler, the surgeon, printmaker and collector Francis Seymour Haden, who immediately acquired Legros's *L'Angélus* 1859 (p.117) and persuaded the British Museum and the South Kensington Museum (now the Victoria and Albert Museum), to buy his etchings. He visited the Francophile collectors, Edwin and Ruth Edwards, and marked the occasion with *The Drawing Room of Mr Edwin Edwards at Sunbury* 1861 (p.124), a depiction of Edwards with a flute beside his wife Ruth at the piano, Matthew White Ridley relaxing on the chaise longue, and Legros holding forth before them. Edwards had given up the bar to become a full-time painter and would take up etching after being taught by Legros, with the help of Ruth, who became a skilled printer.

Legros was one of the rising stars of the new 1860s generation of Paris-based realists who caught the eye of the critics Charles Baudelaire, Champfleury, Edmond Duranty and Zacharie Astruc. He was highly regarded as an original etcher and was one of the founders of the Société des Aquafortistes (1862), which promoted this neglected form of printmaking. He was enjoying the pleasures of a free-living bohemian with 'women, good food, wine, beer, new acquaintances' and nights spent at the Brasserie Andler, one of the haunts of Gustave Courbet with whom he got 'on very well'.[1] His work, however was not selling. He had reasons for returning to a foreign city that previously had been so welcoming to him. He was what we now call an economic migrant, and at first he had great financial success. The American-born Whistler, who first met Legros when he was living in Paris, used the promise of money to lure him to London, and 'in the space of three or four weeks' Legros 'made about eight thousand francs!!!'[2] This fat purse came from the cultivated Greek community in London, including members of the Ionides family who were passionate collectors.

Whistler wanted to be part of a transnational community that would include Henri Fantin-Latour, Legros and himself – the Société des Trois, as he named them – and also Dante Gabriel Rossetti. In autumn 1863, when Legros was living with him in Chelsea, he and his British and two French friends were planning 'to open an exhibition together'.[3] The following spring, Fantin-Latour invited Rossetti to pose together with himself, Legros, Whistler and many other leading figures of the French realist circle for his group portrait *Homage to Delacroix* 1864 (Musée d'Orsay), but Rossetti failed to make the sitting. He had little time for much recent French painting, although he did introduce Legros to some of his own most important patrons and was later hailed by Legros as his principal contact during his early years in London.

Legros was frequently to be found at Tudor House, Cheyne

Walk, where Rossetti held court to London's bohemia including the Francophile poet Algernon Swinburne. He was soon socialising with a wider Pre-Raphaelite and aesthetic group including Ford Madox Brown and Edward Burne-Jones. Moreover, he had the attention of the Pre-Raphaelite critic William Michael Rossetti (brother to Dante Gabriel) and of the champion of Degas and the Paris realists Edmond Duranty, both of whom praised his great work *Ex-Voto* (pp.120–1). Through his study of the old masters, Legros had developed considerable technical skill, which he used to express meaning in a pictorial way. Both critics recognised that the stark flattened forms of the praying women pushed against the picture surface and its deliberate primitive style were a visual expression of the women's religious belief.

Looking back at the exhibition season of 1864, Rossetti wrote that *Ex-Voto*, shown at the Royal Academy, was 'the greatest work contributed', awarding the 'Frenchman the honours of the British artistic year, 1864'.[4] In a summing up of the first seven years of the decade, Duranty, who saw the picture at the Salon of 1861, called it 'a remarkable painting' and praised Legros's ability to apply an 'interior impression', meaning his resolution of a pictorial means that would give 'the expression of the feeling of modern life'.[5]

Duranty was writing in 1867, the year he tried to persuade Legros to return to live in Paris. He probably knew that his relationship with Whistler had begun to sour in October 1864, the same month that William Michael Rossetti wrote his fulsome praise of *Ex-Voto*. Whistler's *Wapping*, a depiction of Legros and Joanna Hiffernan, Whistler's mistress, posing as a sailor and a prostitute in a rough public house in the East End of London, was also exhibited at the 1864 Royal Academy, and while Rossetti did not ignore it, he preferred *Ex-Voto*. The friendship eventually ended after Whistler physically attacked Legros, who subsequently publicly betrayed him, after which the two men never spoke again and Legros no longer saw the American or the Rossetti brothers socially, and also most of the Ionides family. Only Constantine Alexander Ionides continued with their friendship, bought his work and used him as an adviser on his growing collection.

The rupture with Whistler brought Legros closer to Edward Burne-Jones, who introduced him to George Howard, the future 9th Earl of Carlisle. Howard would become a friend and important patron and would bring Legros into contact with a new intellectual circle of collectors. *Edward Burne-Jones* (p.126) and *Le Repas des Pauvres* (p.128) are two of several pictures by Legros originally in Howard's collection.[6]

French visitors

Duranty stayed with Legros for two weeks in August 1866, and he may have encouraged others to contact him. Legros's address was in Charles-François Daubigny's address book. When proposing a trip to London together with Degas in July 1868, Manet explained that Legros would 'act as intermediary and Cicerone';[7] Legros introduced him to Edwin Edwards and was generally very hospitable.[8] Claude Monet looked up Legros when he came to London to escape the war. Legros took him and a friend of Manet, the painter Julien de La Rochenoire, to Dulwich Art Gallery in November 1870.[9] At some point early in 1871, after Monet learned that Camille Pissarro was also in London, the two had lunch with Legros. Pissarro would later tell his son Lucien

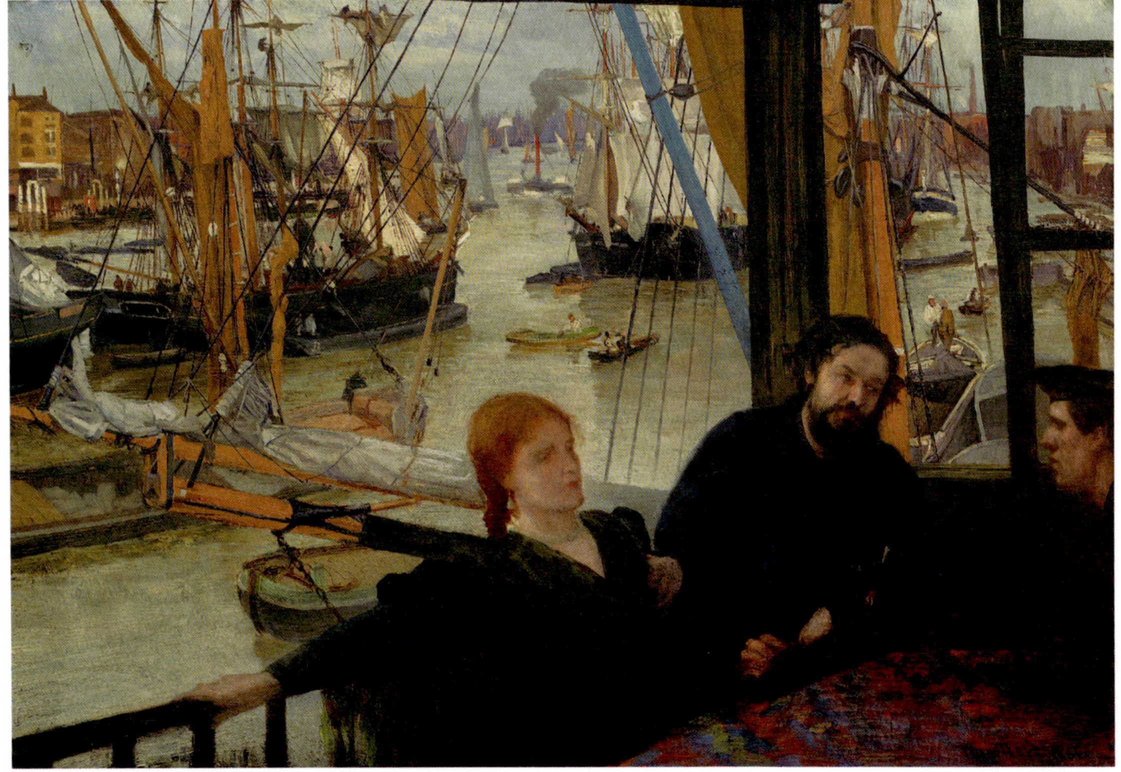

James Abbott McNeill Whistler
Wapping 1860–4
Oil paint on canvas 72 × 101.8

National Gallery of Art, Washington

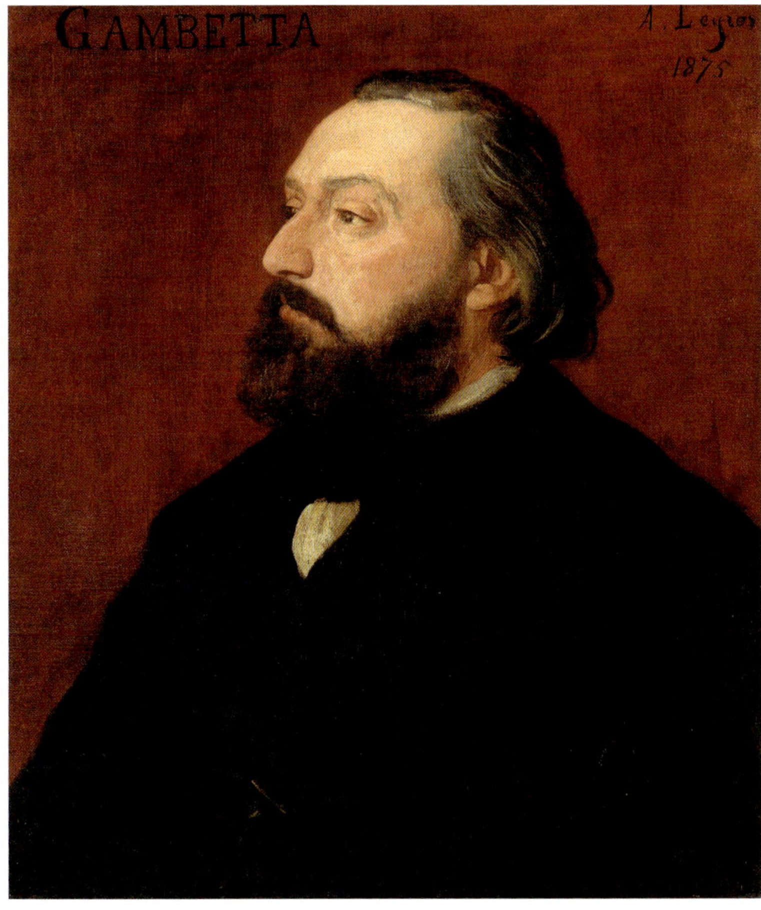

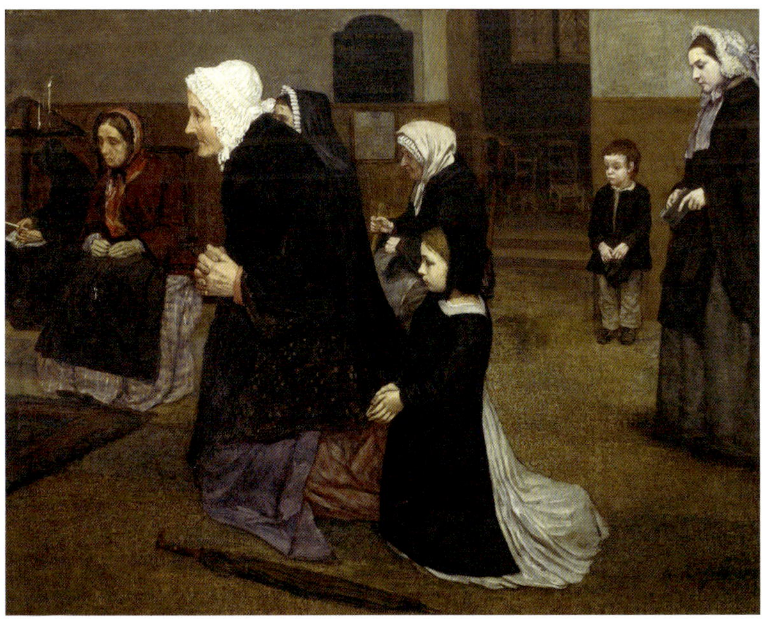

Alphonse Legros
Léon Gambetta 1875
Oil paint on canvas 66.5 × 54.2

Musée d'Orsay, Paris

Alphonse Legros
L'Angélus 1859
Oil paint on canvas 65.5 × 80.9

Private collection, USA

that he knew Legros 'quite well', suggesting that they must have met again.[10] François Bonvin, who in 1859 had lent his studio to Legros, Fantin-Latour, Guillaume Régamey and Whistler for a 'salon des réfusés' after their pictures were rejected by the Salon, left France in November 1870 and made plans to see Legros the day after he arrived, and again on 5 January 1871.[11] Legros offered his studio to Régamey, who had been a fellow student at the Ecole Gratuite de Dessin and who was in London in 1870–1.[12] He saw Marc-Louis Solon, another former student at the Petite Ecole, as it was known, who left France just before the Prussians besieged Paris and went on to have a successful career at the Minton factory in Stoke-on-Trent. After the fall of the Commune, Legros saw more students from the school, including Jean-Charles Cazin, the Communard Jules Dalou, who lived with Legros and his family for two months after fleeing France, and the two younger Régamey brothers, Félix and Frédéric (see p.130). Constantine Alexander Ionides was persuaded to buy three of Guillaume Régamey's oil paintings and became an important patron for Dalou; Howard was another who bought several sculptures (pp.152, 154–5). Legros talked to Cazin about opening a school together; instead the landscape painter found work at the Fulham Potteries where his Japonist designs were much admired. The correspondence of Fantin-Latour and the German-born artist Otto Scholderer, who left Paris for London, provides a revealing glimpse of a closely connected network of French artists that included Legros, Cazin and Félix Bracquemond, who appears in Fantin-Latour's *Homage to Delacroix* and who, together with Legros, had been a co-founder of the Société des Aquafortistes. Edwin Edwards staged an informal exhibition of Bracquemond's etchings at his home in August 1871.

Legros had given his public support to the victims of war, by donating a picture to the *Exhibition for the Benefit of the Distressed Peasantry of France*,[13] which took place in Pall Mall, first at the French Gallery and then at the gallery of the Society of British Artists in autumn 1870. He added 'a fine mournful snow-scene' when the exhibition moved to 168 Bond Street in February 1871, where the following month, the dealer Paul Durand-Ruel opened the first of the Society of French Artists exhibitions.[14] The landscape was probably *The Retreat* (Tate), which G.F. Watts subsequently acquired, a representation of the retreat of the French army during the Napoleonic wars, a subject that would have had a special resonance after the massive retreat of the French Army from the Prussians in autumn 1870.

Evidence suggests that Legros was politically sympathetic to the Republic and also the Commune. In 1875 Legros was in Paris after taking a commission for the portrait of Léon Gambetta, a hero of the Republic.[15] Gambetta was not popular in conservative circles in Britain but William Rossetti applauded the exhibition of 'the keen-brained and great-hearted Republican [...] patriot'[16] in Legros's small solo show in the upstairs gallery of the Society of French Artists in May 1875.[17]

Apparently Legros was close to the writer and political activist Jules Vallès, who got in touch with him shortly after arriving in London while on the run from arrest after the fall of the

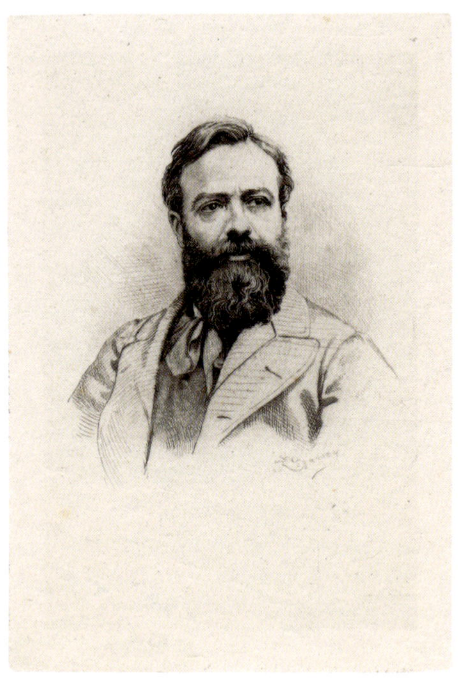

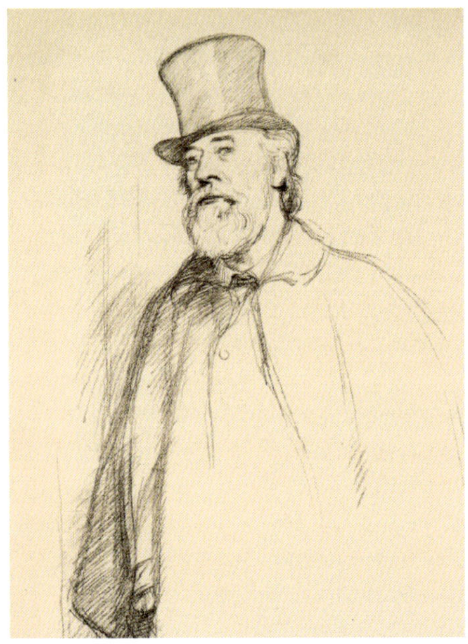

Frédéric Régamey
1849–1925
Alphonse Legros 1877
Etching on paper 15.1 × 10.1

National Portrait Gallery, London.
Purchased 1945

William Rothenstein
1872–1945
Portrait of Alphonse Legros
Lithograph on paper 37.7 × 25.4

Tate. Presented by Sir John Rothenstein through the Friends of the Tate 1981

Commune. At Vallès's funeral they shouted, 'Commune, Social Revolution, Anarchy', and it is tempting to think that Legros took an interest in this line of political thought. He etched the portrait of the Communard François Jourde, and his name appears on a list of contacts willing to help Communards in London drawn up by the Société des Réfugiés. This suggests that he must have helped the wider community of destitute and homeless Communards, as represented in a drawing by another Communard, Félix Régamey, whose brother also made a portrait of Legros (reproduced on this page).[18] It is likely, as Wilcox argues, that Legros was influenced by the radical socialist politics of Rosalind Howard, but the ideas of Vallès, Dalou (who was leftist and republican) and his other Communard friends must have been equally influential.[19] In its obituary of Vallès, the *Manchester Guardian* noted that he had 'a sincere sympathy with the suffering of the poor',[20] which might just as well describe the message of Legros's representations of French peasant life including *The Tinker* (p.127).[21] It equally compares to Dalou's sympathetic view of working people and also the pictures by Jean-François Millet he would have seen at the Society of French Artists. The work-worn tinker diligently repairing a metal pan, and its rough-hewn quality explain why some British critics stressed Legros's ties with rural French life: 'He has farmer cousins, and in his town breeding there is a rich dash of the peasant, a strong smack of the farmhouse and the fields.'[22] Not everyone could appreciate that the arrangement of the three rounded metal pots against the strong verticals of the three trunks, the careful placement of the dead leaves, and the simplified rounded silhouette of the tinker against the landscape, speak of a sophisticated visual intelligence.

This pictorial quality was applauded by Walter Pater in an essay, 'The School of Giorgione', his influential plea for art for art's sake where he praised Legros's etching *Le paysage aux meules* 1869 (New York Public Library).[23] The critic, Sidney Colvin, a close friend of George Howard, argued as early as 1870 that the subject of Legros's painting was of secondary importance, and that a 'set' of observed and remembered 'impressions' determined the 'pictorial' effect or, as he wrote, the 'look' of a picture and not its 'meaning'.[24] Here Colvin is repeating the influential ideas of Horace Lecoq de Boisbaudran who taught his students at the Petite Ecole to study the old masters and to work from memory. These two different interpretations explain why *The Tinker* found a place at the Royal Academy (1874), the Paris Salon (1875) and the Grosvenor Gallery (1877).

Legros continued to have his admirers in France, including Degas, who would have approved when Duranty mentioned Legros in his 1876 treatise 'The New Painting'.[25] Degas stayed in Paris throughout the troubles but came to London in autumn 1871 when he made several attempts to track Legros down, writing to him: 'I would very much like to chat with you about yourself and London.'[26] Three years later, Otto Scholderer informed Fantin-Latour: 'Legros is very close to Degas now, I am curious how long that will last.'[27] On another trip to London in August 1875, Degas must have persuaded Legros, with the help of

Alphonse Legros
Women Praying 1888
Oil paint on canvas 133.5 × 177

Tate. Presented by subscribers 1897

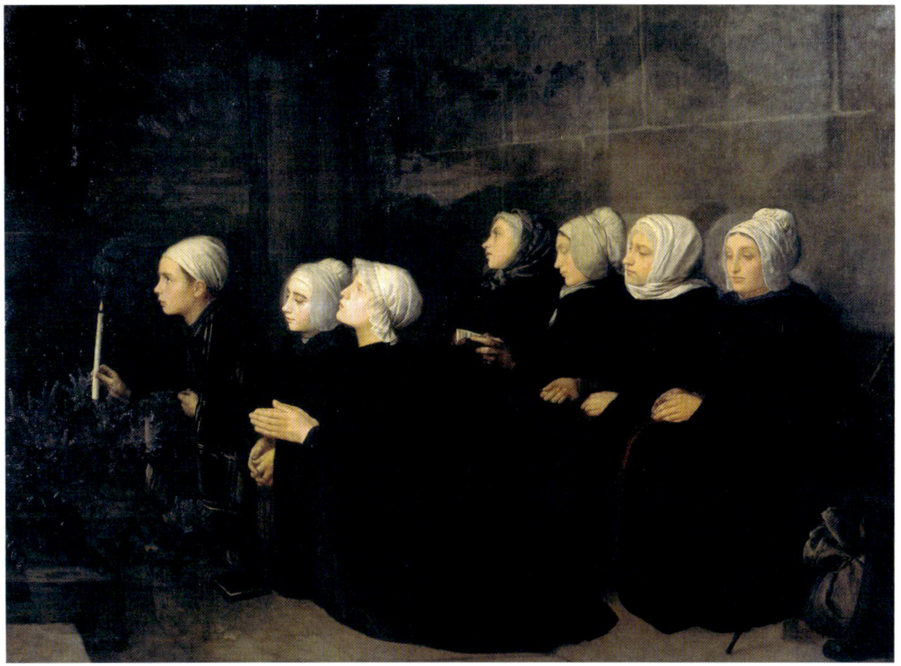

Durand-Ruel, to exhibit at the *Second Impressionist Exhibition.* In turn Legros advised Ionides to purchase Degas's *Ballet Scene from Meyerbeer's Opera 'Robert le Diable'* 1876 (Victoria and Albert Museum). It may be that Degas saw Legros again in London because he recorded his address at the Slade where Legros was appointed professor in 1876.[28] Their last meeting was probably in Paris in October 1897 when Legros made a portrait of Degas in silverpoint and touchingly Degas showed him and William Rothenstein a drawing, *Studies of Hands* (Musée du Louvre), by Legros hanging in his bedroom between two studies by Ingres.[29]

The professor

In some respects, Legros was an artist's artist who won the respect and admiration of a seemingly disparate group of artists and critics including Edward John Poynter (p.135). Their paths probably first crossed when Poynter, a member of the so-called 'Paris Gang' (the name he and his group of fellow artists took), was in Paris during the 1850s. He appointed Legros as Professor of Etching at South Kensington in 1875 and put up his name for the professorship at the Slade School of Art the following year, with the support of Burne-Jones, Howard and Watts.

Once at the Slade, where having no English, he taught by demonstration, Legros implemented the methods he learned at the Petite Ecole, including giving his students photographs of old master paintings to copy and sending them to museums. In 1879, after the amnesty, Dalou returned to France, but Legros decided that he would remain permanently in England, becoming a naturalised British citizen in 1880. He continued to reach out to French friends, including Auguste Rodin whom he first met at the Petite Ecole. They caught up after Dalou brought them together in Paris at the end of 1880 or the beginning of 1881. By summer 1881 Rodin had made his first visit to London staying through July and August, when Legros taught him to etch. On a return visit the following year, Legros painted his portrait, and in return Rodin sculpted a portrait bust of him. Legros also installed Rodin's *The Age of Bronze* 1877, over the entrance to the Slade. Rodin's rendezvous with Britain came to an abrupt end in 1886, when the Royal Academy rejected a sculpture. If Legros had not provided the young Rothenstein, a former pupil at the Slade, with a letter of introduction and later accompanied him to Paris where they saw Rodin in autumn 1897, it is unlikely that Rodin would have bothered with London again, but he was persuaded to exhibit at Rothenstein's newly established Carfax Gallery, and this time he took the London art world by storm.

Legros was not forgotten by others of the 1890s generation. The printmakers and painters Charles Ricketts and Charles Shannon welcomed him into their circle, introduced him to their dealer E.J. Van Wisselingh – who gave him an exhibition at the Dutch Gallery in 1897 – and helped to raise a subscription to buy *Women Praying* 1888 (see above), for the nation. The New Critics, including R.A.M. Stevenson, who wrote the preface for the Dutch Gallery catalogue, also supported him.[30] He, for one, appreciated Legros's ability to convey meaning through painterly technique, as his comments about *Auguste Rodin* reveal (p.139). He praised 'his power of modelling human forms', which revealed Rodin's 'veiled prophetic eye with its far-off gaze ... rugged energetic forehead ... large sensitive nose ... thought-worn cheeks ... vigorous tawny beard, and ... lank morbidly poetic hair'.[31] Legros's lasting contribution to this generation was his skill as a printmaker and his continuing respect for the art of the past, which, as Sickert observed, would call students back to 'the traditions of the masters' and send them 'to the National Gallery and the British Museum'.[32]

Alphonse Legros
1837–1911
Ex-Voto 1860
Oil paint on canvas 174 × 197

Musée des Beaux-Arts de Dijon

A manifesto of the realist movement that spread in Courbet's wake during the Second Empire, this *Ex-Voto* was greeted by Legros's friends as his first masterpiece. The artist had retained his taste for popular imagery and piety acquired during his apprenticeship with a house painter and producer of Epinal prints. This group of women praying in front of a crucifix planted beside a path could be understood as a nostalgic echo of traditions from his childhood in Burgundy. However, the origins of this picture, to which the artist added important modifications, were quite different. Legros had found his models in Paris while observing parishioners coming to pray at the Church of Saint-Médard, a parish near the rue Saint-Jacques that he frequented. Maurice Dreyfous, Dalou's biographer, considered Legros to be not a religious artist but 'the painter of a man or woman transformed by the emotion imparted by faith',[1] a description of an approach that was more moral than spiritual and characterised his entire oeuvre.

Initially Legros had depicted a funerary vigil around a coffin with the ambition that his picture would be noticed at the Salon. For that, he intended to paint an original modern subject in a large format like Courbet. According to the account of his friend Zacharie Astruc, Legros had shown the women praying in an interior. Then, fearing that the audience at the Salon would reject such a macabre subject, he suppressed the coffin by masking it in foliage and cutting off the left edge of the canvas to reduce its width by a third.

The compact group of women was kept in the second version, which won him a medal when exhibited at the Salon in 1861. For the enemies of naturalism who preferred Jules Breton's peasant idealism, the work recalled the aggressive ugliness of Courbet's *Burial at Ornans* (1849–50, Musée d'Orsay). Indeed, the realism of the faces, the authenticity of the hands with dirty fingernails, the choice of contemporary clothing for a genre scene ennobled by a large format could link *Ex-Voto* to the New Painting.

As a student of Lecoq de Boisbaudran in the 1850s, Legros had experimented with on-the-spot painting. He had drawn nudes posing *en plein air*, but without extending the practice to easel painting. Following the example of Courbet in *Burial at Ornans* and *Young Ladies by the Seine*, and soon of Manet in *Luncheon on the Grass* (*Déjeuner sur l'herbe*), the artist worked up his plein-air subjects in the studio. The concealment of the mortuary chamber by verdant scenery did not modify in the least the modelling of the figures who seem to be stuck onto a stage set. Legros favoured neutral shades with transparent half-tones through which clear detailed drawing could be seen.

Rather than choose a new work painted in England, Legros decided to exhibit this picture at the Royal Academy in 1864 to make his name. *Ex-Voto* did not fail to be noticed, William Michael Rossetti identifying it as 'the major work of the exhibition'.[2] IC

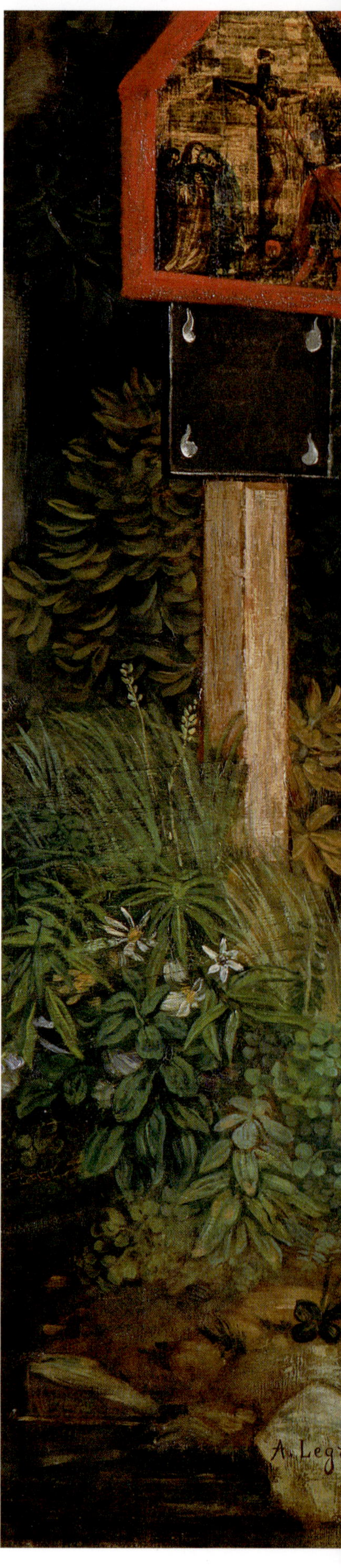

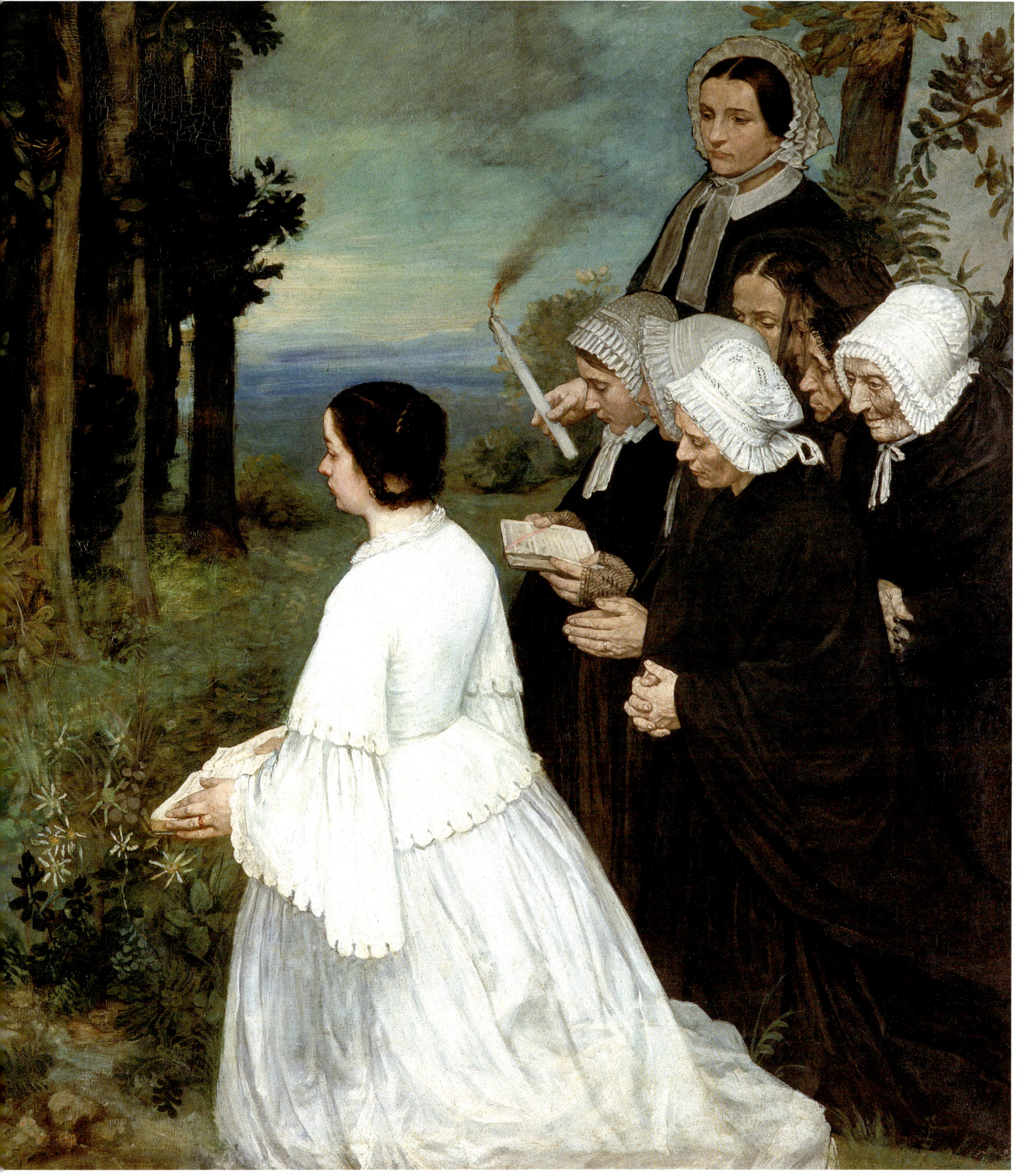

Alphonse Legros
1837–1911
A Lectern 1863–5
Oil paint on canvas 102 × 107

Petit Palais, Musée des Beaux-Arts de la Ville de Paris

This picture exhibited in the Salon of 1863 concluded Legros's French period. Painted during his days of hardship in Paris, it passed unnoticed, poorly served by a bad location above a door in a room filled with religious paintings. Legros's work had at least crossed the threshold of the Palace of Industry, unlike that of his friends Manet, Fantin-Latour, Whistler and Bonvin who had to content themselves with the Salon des Refusés, which opened on the fringe of the official Salon.

Returned unsold from the Salon, *A Lectern* was rolled up and transported to London, then remounted on a new Winsor and Newton stretcher. Legros was able to exhibit it in 1865 at the Royal Academy in reworked form. The musician who figured on the left of the composition in Paris was obscured by the large songbook and the rectangular shape of the canvas, cut down both at the top and at the bottom, was reduced to a square. Constantine Alexander Ionides acquired *A Lectern* and loaned it to the Salon of 1868 in Paris where it received a better welcome than in 1863. It appeared again in the posthumous exhibition devoted to Legros at the Tate Gallery, from June to September 1912, (no.120) as property of Mrs Dannreuther, heiress to Ionides.

The lectern, a pulpit that gave the painting its title, is almost invisible, as is the church choir where mass will take place. A secular community of three men accompanied by an altar boy is gathered around a large book of liturgical music. Emerging from a Caravaggesque chiaroscuro, the figures form a tight group. Legros's art as an etcher can be perceived in the mastery of variation in shades going from the brightest in the foreground to the darkest in the background. The faces are handled in a realistic manner, while the grouping of the figures takes on a certain archaic stiffness. The artist, who shared a great admiration for Spanish painting with Manet, relied here on the example of Francisco de Zurbarán, whose painting of *St Bonaventure's Body Lying in State* (1629) he could have studied in the Louvre, where it had been since 1858. The choirboy whose gaze seems to question the viewer forms an almost geometrical corner figure with the verticality of the candle echoing that of the cantoral staff held by the choir master. At the centre of the group, a priest, clothed in a choral cope closed with a large clasp, follows the score with his left hand.

At the time when the picture was painted, the Church of France was divided by two divergent ideological trends. The Gallicans defended liberal Catholicism upheld by the Faculty of Theology at the Sorbonne and the Seminary of Saint-Sulpice in Paris. They were opposed to the Ultramontanes, who supported the primacy of the pope in the Vatican. The attention that Legros gave to the canons' costumes and liturgical accessories leads one to assume that the artist knew the Catholic rituals of his time well. The band that the choir master wears around his neck had become a notable hallmark for the Gallicans. This choice could only attract the sympathy of an English Anglican audience, whose religious and social practices came close to those of the French Gallicans. IC

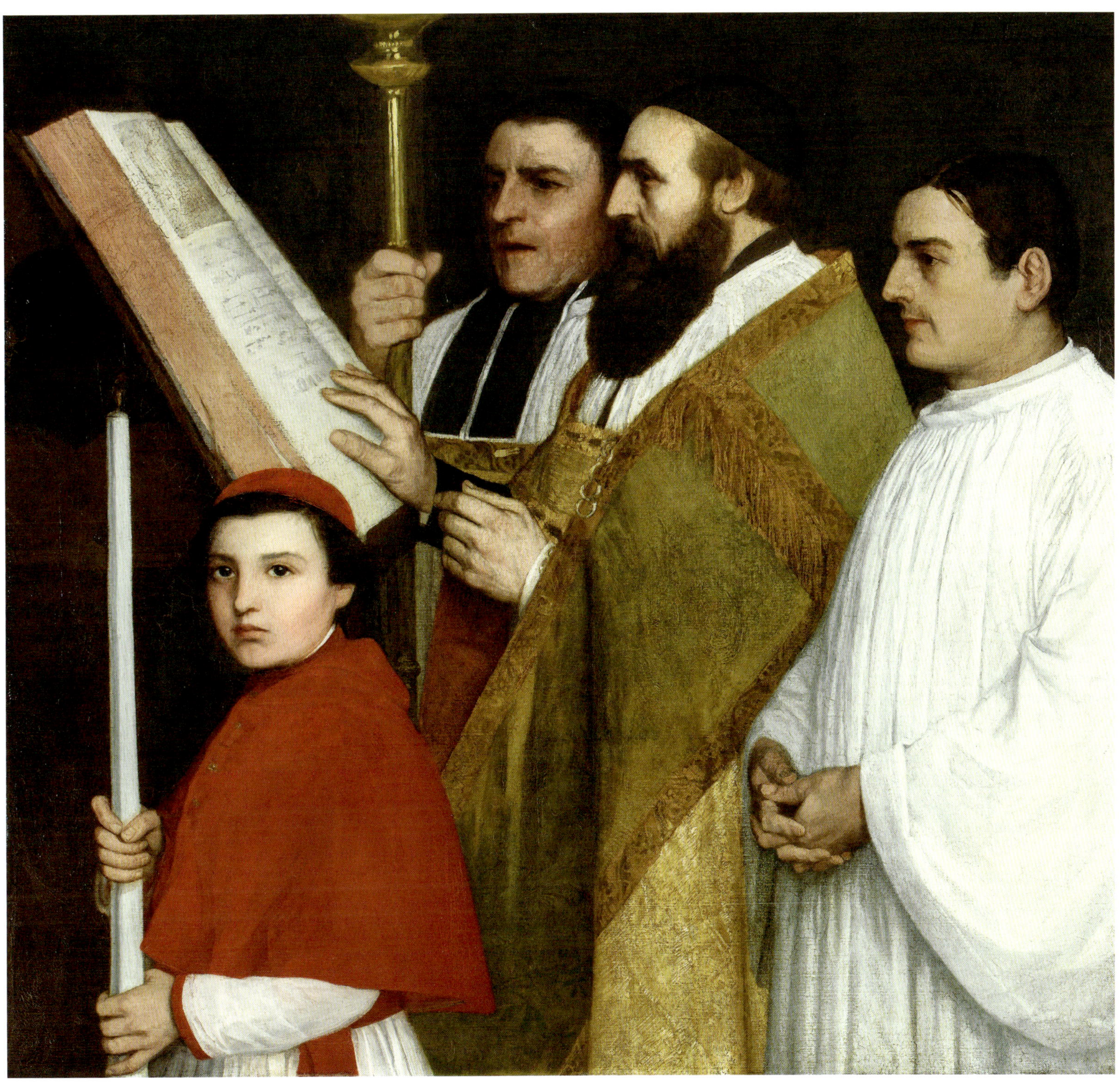

Alphonse Legros
1837–1911
The Drawing Room of Mr Edwin Edwards at Sunbury 1861
Drypoint on paper 16.3 × 23.8

Private collection

Henri Fantin-Latour
1836–1904
Mr and Mrs Edwin Edwards 1875
Oil paint on canvas 130.8 × 98.1

Tate. Presented by Mrs E. Edwards 1904

Despite the inscription on this painting, 'à / mon ami E. Edwards / Fantin', when Henri Fantin-Latour painted the lawyer-turned-artist Edwin Edwards and his formidable wife Ruth, their friendship was already giving way to a more business-like relationship. The Edwardses were ardent promoters of Fantin-Latour's works in Britain – especially of his still lifes of flowers – but in time they also discouraged some collectors by inflating the prices of his works.[1] The harsh and domineering expression of Ruth Edwards, in stark contrast with the softness that imbued Fantin-Latour's first portrait of her, in a white dress (1861–4, Petit Palais), may be an indication of the erosion of their friendship. His original intention, however, was to portray her standing by her husband's side, 'like a guardian angel', and to depict Edwards at work at his etching table.[2] The artist eventually represented Edwards studying a folio of prints, as a connoisseur, rather than as a printmaker, even though he enjoyed some success in that capacity. Legros had introduced Edwards to etching and he encouraged him to follow this artistic path. As for Ruth, she was a competent printer, and the couple had a press at Sunbury-on-Thames, where Legros's *Drawing Room of Ruth and Edwin Edwards* was printed.

Fantin-Latour was introduced to the Edwardses by the artist Matthew White Ridley in 1861,[3] the same year that Legros represented himself in Ridley's company at Sunbury, in the house of the Francophile and musical couple. Ruth was portrayed by Legros at the piano, and her husband playing the flute. Fantin-Latour spent a month at Sunbury with the Edwardses in the summer of 1861, and it is possible that he was in Ridley's and Legros's party when the latter did this intimate scene in drypoint. At the time Legros and Fantin-Latourwere still close. They had formed the 'Société de Trois' in 1859, their third acolyte being Whistler, but this friendship did not stand the test of time, and distance, in the case of Legros and Fantin-Latour. A spirit of emulation still animated them in the 1860s, however: in October 1864 Fantin-Latour produced *A Piece by Schumann*, an etching representing the Edwardses playing the piano and flute at Sunbury, which resonates with Legros's drypoint. CCP

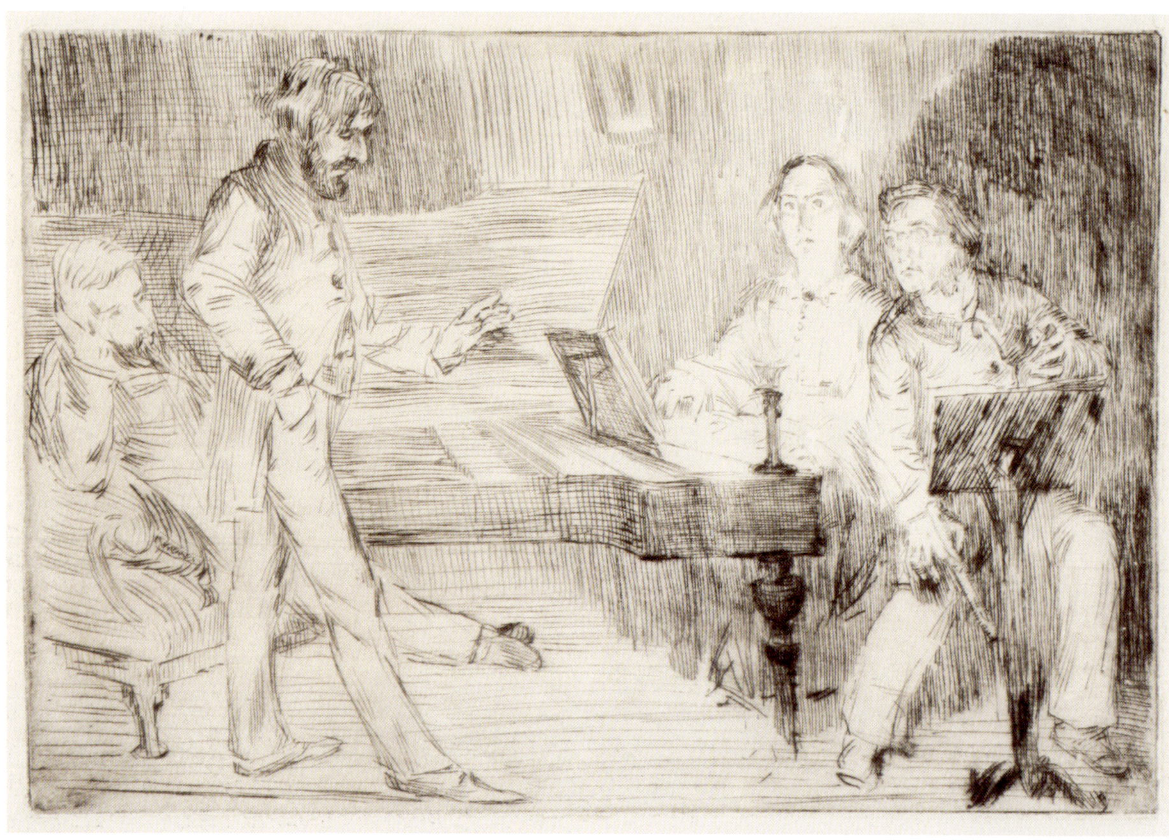

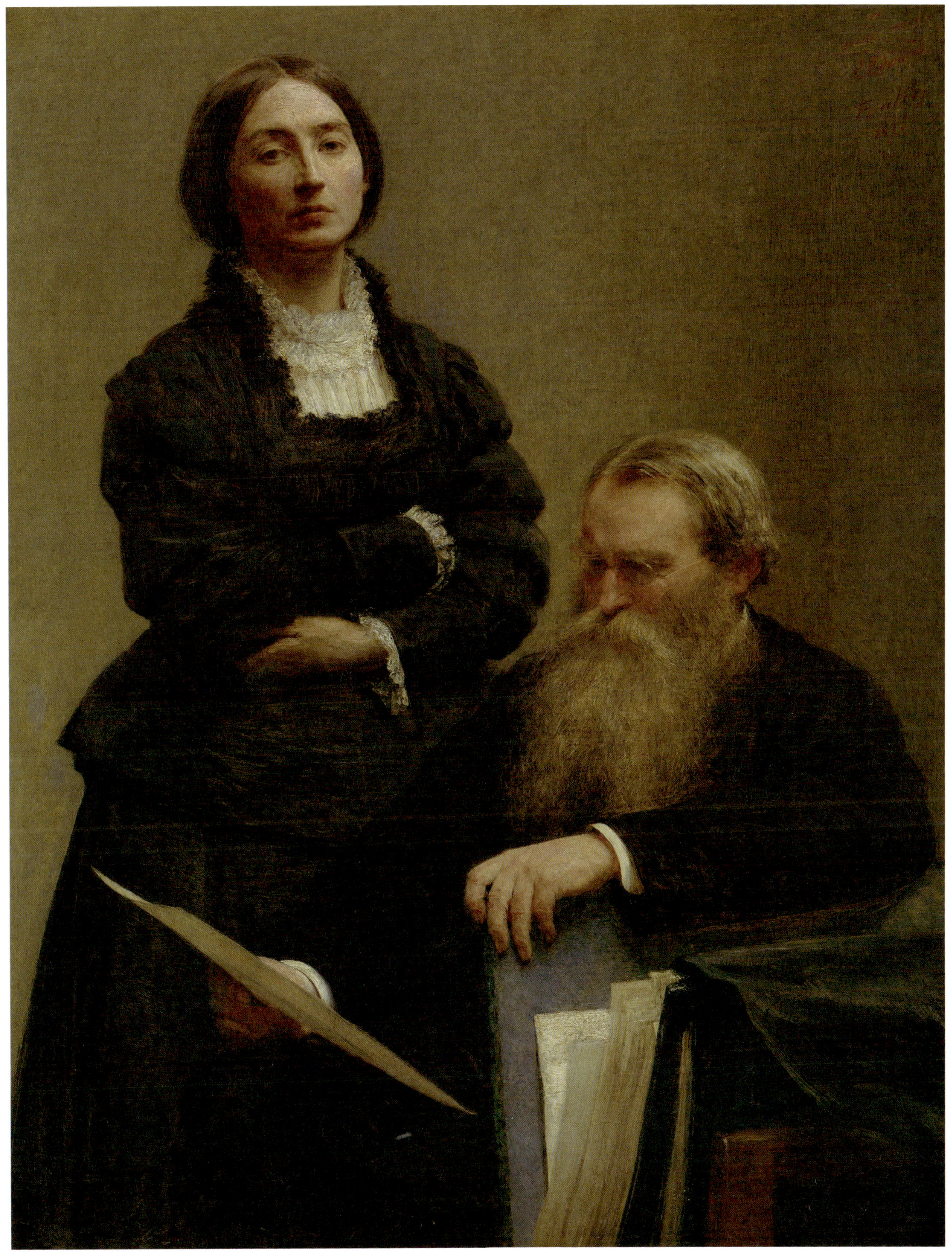

Alphonse Legros
1837–1911
Edward Burne-Jones 1868–9
Oil paint on panel 46 × 37.2

Aberdeen Art Gallery & Museum Collections. Presented in 1922 by Sir James Murray

The significance of this panel portrait of Burne-Jones in relation to Legros's circle of patrons and friends is twofold: it highlights how Legros was supported by the second generation of Pre-Raphaelites when he first settled in Britain, in 1863, as well as the way in which his key relationship with George Howard was formed. In turn, after the events of 1870–1, Legros's exiled friends benefited from these bonds, experiencing the same artistic solidarity that he had previously received on British soil.

When Legros first moved to London, he relied on his friendship with Whistler, but also with Dante Gabriel Rossetti, who became his agent in all but name. Rossetti secured Legros commissions from his own patrons and introduced him to friends who could further his interests. In the Frenchman's own words, Rossetti was then his 'best and most efficient friend'.[1] Through him, he became close to Edward Burne-Jones, who in 1867, at the time of the irremediable break with Whistler, sided with Legros, whereas Rossetti remained neutral. Burne-Jones's commitment may well have strengthened his bond with the French artist.

It was Burne-Jones who, on 16 November 1865, brought George Howard to Legros's studio. This proved to be a decisive meeting for the latter's career. The young aristocrat, who had decided to dedicate himself to art, had hitherto taken informal instruction from Burne-Jones, but Legros became his teacher the week that followed this introduction.[2] More importantly, perhaps, was the fact that Howard also became Legros's patron, commissioning this portrait of Burne-Jones. With its deep hues and Italianate landscape, it may reflect the sitter's, Legros's and indeed Howard's shared admiration for Venetian art. Its archaic aesthetic accords well with the sitter's red beard and intensity of expression, heightened in the portrait by the fact that the artist darkened Burne-Jones's characteristic limpid blue eyes. Legros's fascination for Italian art deepened after his first trip to Italy in 1872, which was funded – at least in part – by Howard. CCP

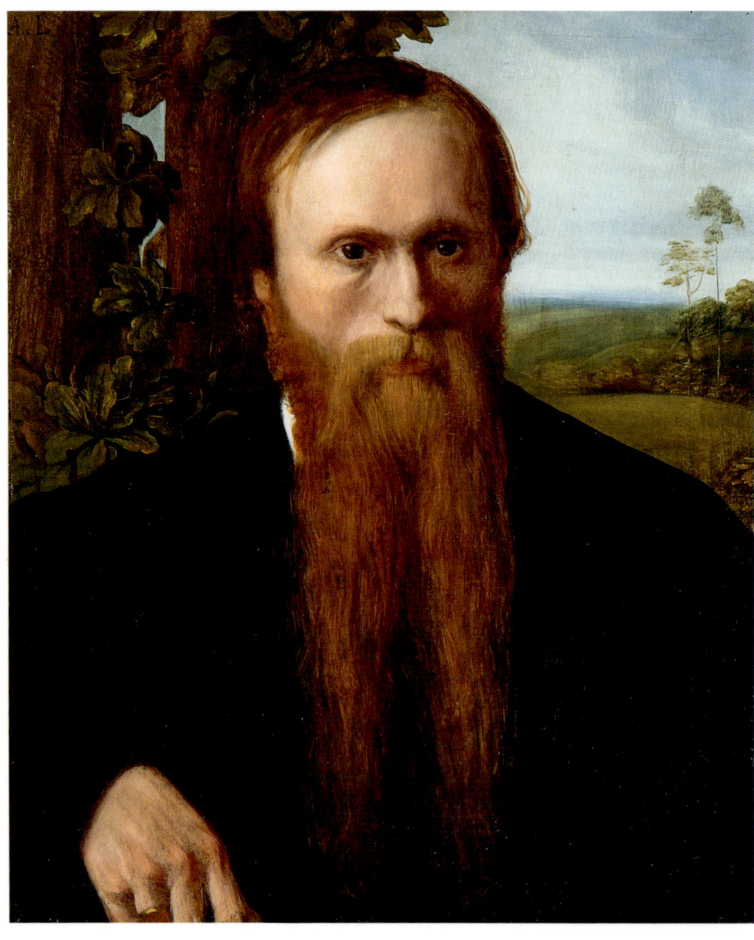

Alphonse Legros
1837–1911
The Tinker 1874
Oil paint on canvas 115 × 132.5

Victoria and Albert Museum, London. Bequeathed by Constantine Alexander Ionides

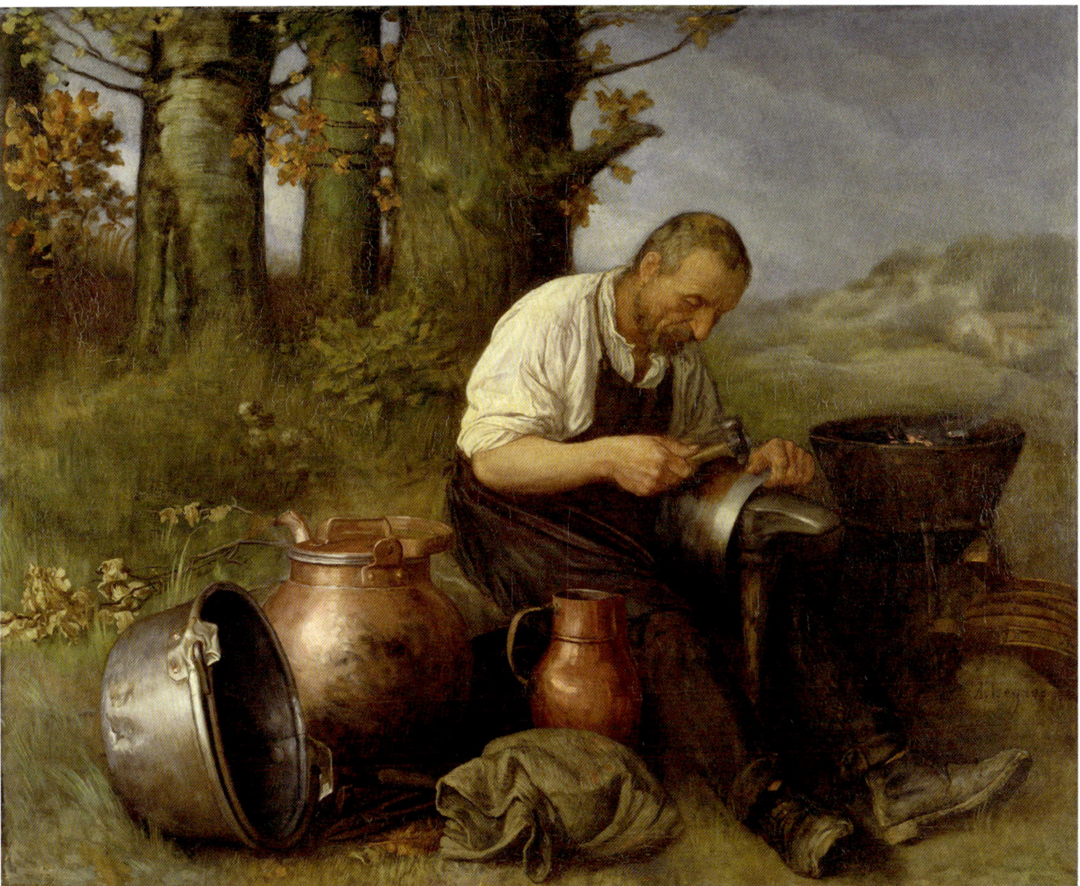

For the most part, Legros's characters belonged to the same modest respectable social class as this craftsman working on the ground at the foot of a tree. He is probably not a tinsmith or brasier, but a country tinker; that is, an itinerant workman of more modest condition whose job consisted of repairing (rather than making) tin kitchen utensils to prolong their use. Simply dressed in a white shirt that is protected by a long apron, he is depicted with a tool in one hand and paying attention to his actions.

This depiction of labour makes Legros one of the worthy successors of Jean-François Millet, a wide diffusion of whose work had been assured in London by Durand-Ruel since 1870. Legros could feel more than picturesque curiosity for the labouring classes, as he had worked from the age of eleven years old, was self-taught and ceaselessly questioned the masters of the past in order to progress patiently in the practice of his art. Nonetheless, his involvement was not that of the seething Courbet and his Communard friends.

Anchored in a readily identifiable social reality, the worker painted by Legros remains a timeless figure ennobled by his labour. Following the example of Jean-Siméon Chardin (1699–1799), the artist renders his subject unreal by giving close attention to the depiction of the cauldrons that are in the foreground of one of his most virtuoso still lifes. The painting was presented at the Royal Academy in 1874, and then in 1877 at the prestigious inaugural exhibition of the Grosvenor Gallery, where Legros sent nine pictures. Oscar Wilde, as a young man attempting to break into art criticism, remarked: 'A good bit of painting is of some metal pots in a picture called Le Chaudronnier.'

The work entered the collection of Constantine Alexander Ionides, one of Legros's main patrons in England. Descendant of a Greek family who had been settled in Istanbul until 1827, Ionides epitomised the successful entrepreneurial businessman in London's eldorado. Like his father before him, Constantine Alexander bought British painting eclectically, as well as that of northern schools and primitives. Legros encouraged him to become interested in French art and acquire works by Delacroix, Millet, Rousseau and even the very modern Degas. In the 1870s Ionides remained active in the stock market, but once his fortune was made, he retired in 1882 and moved his valuable art collection to his Brighton residence.

The Ionides collection, bequeathed in 1901 to the Victoria and Albert Museum to be used for education, provides unrivalled evidence of the evolution of taste in Victorian England. *The Tinker* is part of the 1,138 works in the legacy, as we are reminded by the gilt frame, on which are inscribed the names of both Legros and Ionides in honour of their long friendship. IC

Alphonse Legros
1837–1911
Le Repas des pauvres (*The Soup Kitchen*) 1877
Oil paint on canvas 113 × 142.9

Tate. Presented by Rosalind, Countess of Carlisle 1912

The placement of the figures in *Le Repas des pauvres* and the composition of the work are strongly reminiscent of Caravaggio's *Supper at Emmaus* (1601), which entered the collection of the National Gallery in 1839 as part of the Vernon collection and would have been very familiar to Legros. However, the dramatic tension heightened by the firm gesture and tight grouping of the figures in Caravaggio's painting greatly contrasts with the sense of total despondency of the three elderly men in Legros's picture. They are seated at a table in a soup kitchen and are waited upon by a standing young man. There is no interaction between them, and no eye contact either. Backs curved, looking down glumly and pensively while having a meagre meal, they inspire a pity that places the painting firmly in line with Victorian social realism. The subject of the painting itself is linked to Legros's illustration of Chapter III, 'La Soupe chez Misère', in an 1877 edition of *L'Histoire du Bonhomme Misère* (Bliss 174), published by Robert Guéraut. In the etching three old men are also gathered around a table, a younger figure (that of a woman in this instance), standing by. However, the verticality of the print and details in the background reveal substantial alterations in conception.

Legros exhibited *Le Repas des pauvres* at the Grosvenor Gallery in 1878 and at the Liverpool Autumn Exhibition the same year, with an asking price of £400, but it failed to sell, despite receiving fair reviews. His pupil and patron George Howard (see pp.154–5) bought the painting the following year for £125. CCP

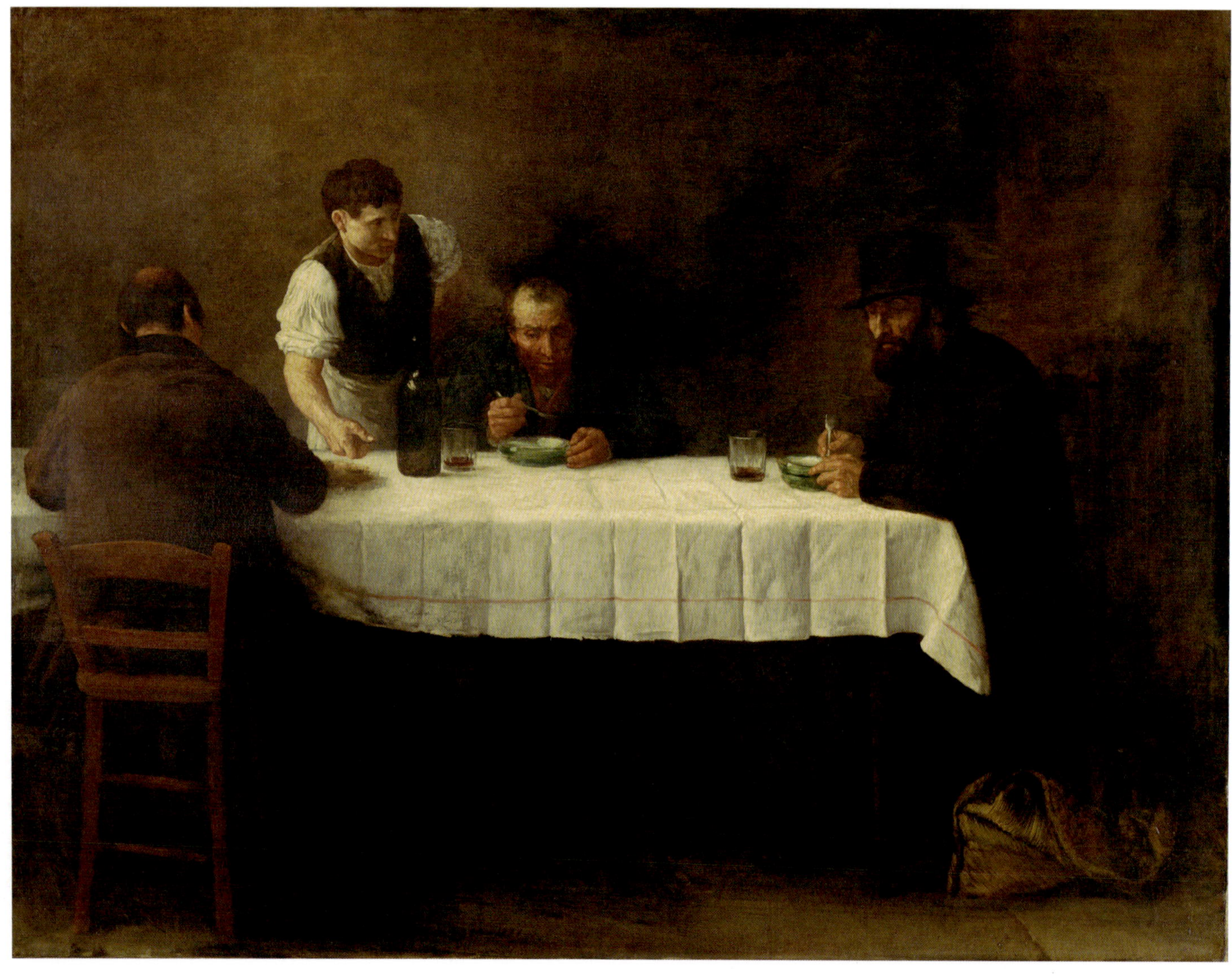

Alphonse Legros
1837–1911
Hilly Landscape 1876–7
Oil paint on canvas 76.2 × 50.2

Victoria and Albert Museum, London. Given by the artist

Alphonse Legros's *Hilly Landscape* shows a blustery vista looking across Hampstead Heath to Hampstead Church. The location was a favourite of John Constable, whose suburban views were admired by French artists in London. Two small Constable paintings, *Hampstead Heath, Branch Hill Pond* 1828 and *Hampstead Heath* 1820–30 (both Victoria and Albert Museum), were in the collection of the South Kensington Museum, close to the National Art Training School, where Legros taught until shortly before the work was made, when he took up the Professorship of the Slade School of Art. When Legros was studying in Paris, Constable's non-narrative landscapes, studied from nature, were important to the realist circle, where he was thought of as the 'father' of the French school.[1] At the Slade, Legros introduced the methods of French Barbizon and realist painters, departing from the established curriculum to take students out to paint *en plein air*. *Hilly Landscape* was a demonstration, created under timed conditions in front of a group, rejecting conventional landscape in favour of observed colours and atmospheric effects.[2] In 1877 Legros gave the landscape to the museum, along with two others, underlining its significance to the artist.

Legros's Parisian realism was modified in England by ideas being explored by his friend James Abbott McNeill Whistler, Dante Gabriel Rossetti and the aesthetic circle. In the 1860s they turned away from realism and advocated an art that was concerned with beauty and poetic effects. In 1877 Walter Pater published *The School of Giorgione*, a contemplation of the sensual qualities of Venetian Renaissance art, influencing aesthetic artists and Legros.[3] In a rare reference to the art of his own time, Pater illustrated his idea of the 'abstract language' with a Legros landscape. Although he refers to an etching, he could equally well be describing *Hilly Landscape*: 'Sometimes a momentary tint, or stormy light may invest a homely or all too familiar scene with a character which might have well been drawn from the deepest places of the imagination.'[4] The title of *Hilly Landscape* distances it from its precise topography and its vertical format associates it with classical landscapes such as Giorgione's *Tempest* 1508 (Gallerie dell'Accademia, Venice). The shape was associated with decorative views that ornamented panelling in houses, which, as a teenager, Legros had encountered when he trained with the decorative painter Maître Nicolardot. A set of such panels, *The Four Times of Day*, by the Barbizon master Jean-Baptiste-Camille Corot embellished the aesthetic London house of Frederic Leighton at this date. *Hilly Landscape* provides an intermediate stage between Legros's realist roots in Barbizon style and his return to Italian and French classical views such as *Stream and Hills* 1880 (Victoria and Albert Museum). CJ

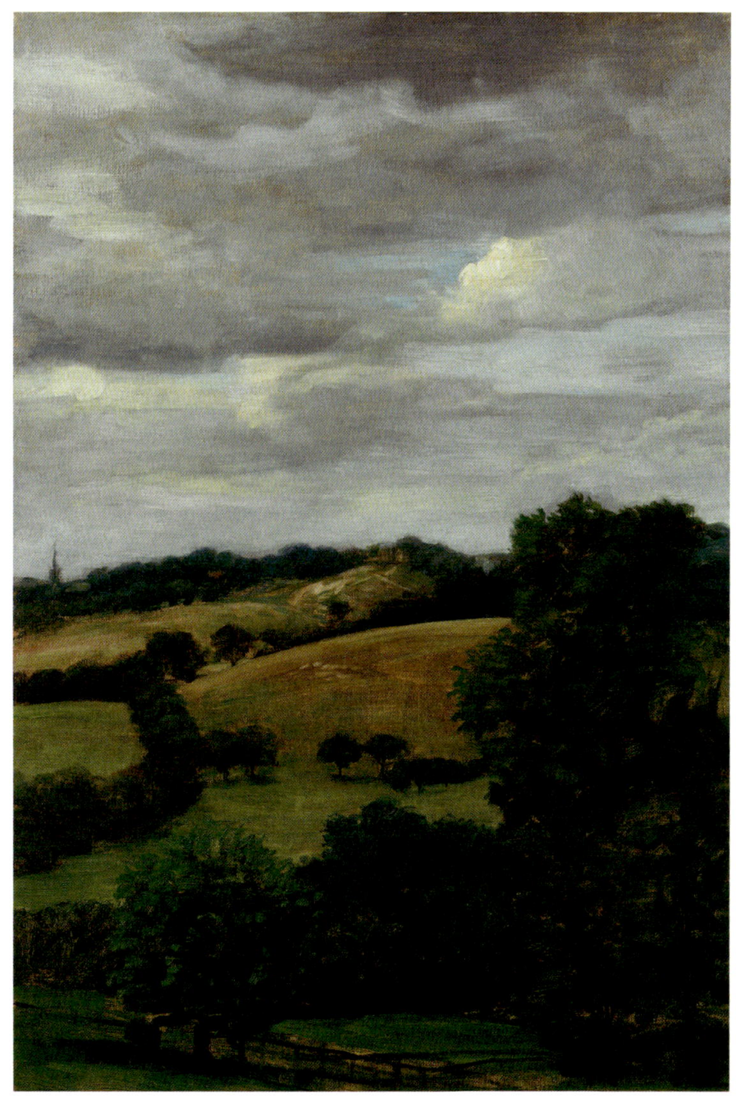

Alphonse Legros
1837–1911
Frédéric Régamey 1870s, before 1877
Drypoint on paper 23 × 16.4

The British Museum, London

Frédéric Régamey (1849–1925) was born to an artistic family, the youngest son of the draughtsman and lithographer Louis Régamey. His brothers were the painters Guillaume and Félix Régamey, the latter being a graphic artist of repute like Frédéric. All three brothers had been pupils of the inspiring teacher Lecoq de Boisbaudran, like Legros, who was in the same year as Guillaume at the Petite Ecole. And like Legros, their political allegiance was to the left. Félix in particular was involved in the Commune and had to live in London for several years as a political exile, where he became a contributor to the *Graphic* and *Harper's Weekly*. It was he who lent assistance to his friends the poets Paul Verlaine and Arthur Rimbaud when they came to London in 1872. He and his brothers were regular visitors to Tavistock House, which was frequented by Communards, but also by the French and Francophile community as a whole (see p.184). Although not a political exile like Félix, Guillaume also crossed the channel and was supported by Legros, who shared his studio with him and secured several purchases from his patron Constantine Ionides (now at the Victoria and Albert Museum) for him. Legros and Frédéric had in common that they played a part in the etching revival, on either side of the channel. Frédéric Régamey was with Richard Lesclide a founder of the weekly *Paris à l'eau-forte* (*Paris in Etching*; 1873–6), which in its first year published no less than 300 etchings, many of which were produced by Régamey himself. Key to the etching revival was a reassessment of Rembrandt, whose work was ardently promoted in *Paris à l'eau-forte*. The Dutch master's influence is also evident in some of Legros's etchings (see pp.131–3).

His rare drypoint portrait of Frédéric Régamey, then in his twenties, reveals sympathy for his subject. His youthful expression and eyes, although looking away from the viewer, suggest both seriousness and intensity, and his likeness demonstrates all of Legros's power of characterisation in this medium. The fine distinction between the treatment of the beard and shading on the neck is a tour de force in itself. Only one print of the first state, in the collection of the sitter himself, was produced. The present one belonged to A.-W. Thibaudeau, who owned two prints of the portrait. Régamey also etched a portrait of Legros, published in 1877 as a photogravure and used as the frontispiece of Poulet-Malassis and Thibaudeau's catalogue raisonné of Legros's etched works.[1] CCP

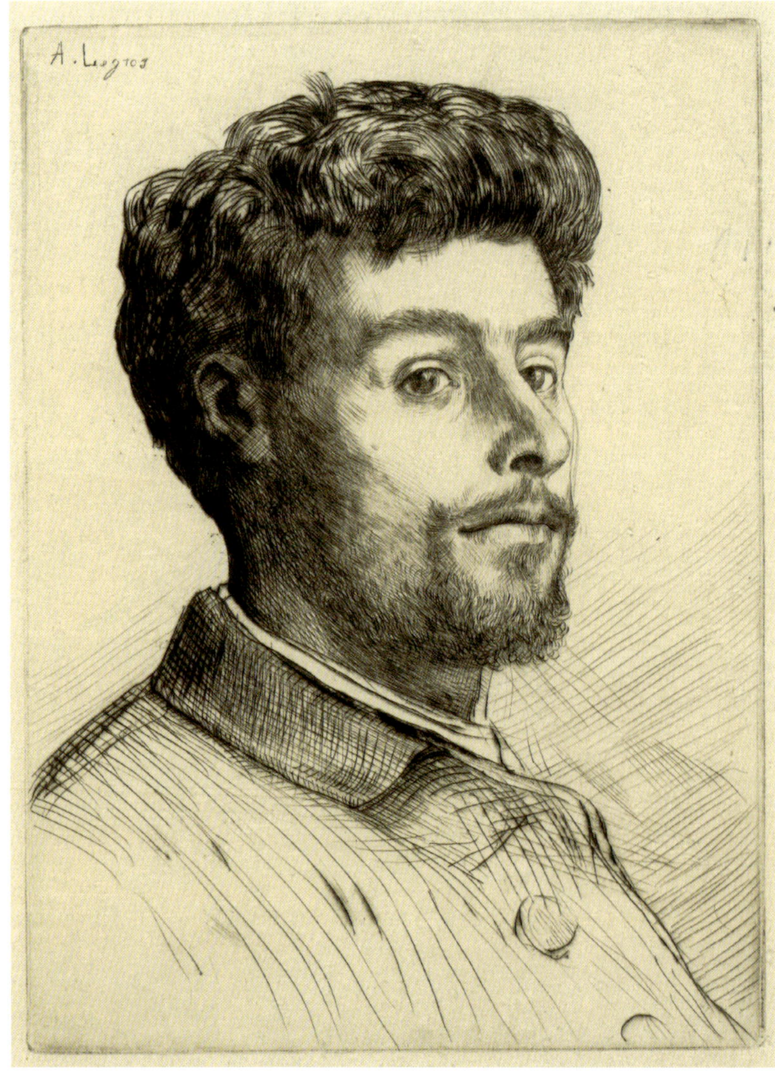

Alphonse Legros
1837–1911
Death of the Vagabond 1875?
Etching, aquatint and drypoint on paper 55.2 × 40

Musée des Beaux-Arts de Dijon

In *Death of the Vagabond*, a print described in 1876 as 'a perfect picture of squalid wretchedness',[1] the tree appears almost as close to death as the dying vagabond of the title, its trunk leaning dangerously and its branches bare. Legros admired Rembrandt's etchings, and it is possible that he knew of the hulking but barren trees included in the Dutch master's interpretations of another subject – that of St Jerome (*St Jerome beside a Pollard Willow*, Hollstein 244; *St Jerome Reading in an Italian Landscape*, Hollstein 275). While the tree features in earlier states of Legros's print, the main subject – the dying vagrant – was a later addition: earlier conceptions of the composition included alternative figures. As Wilcox has noted, something of Legros's method is revealed by a surviving preparatory study of the scene (The British Museum), onto which Legros pasted a sketch of the vagabond.[2] Making such a dramatic change to a composition does not seem uncharacteristic of Legros, who was no stranger to the radical reworking of an etching plate (see also p.134).

Legros exhibited an impression of the print at the Exhibition of Works in Black and White held at the Dudley Gallery in 1876.[3] A review of the exhibition for the *Pall Mall Gazette* singled out the work as 'remarkable', stating:

> Out of a few lines, not one of which is wastefully or insignificantly employed, the artist has composed a picture that lacks nothing in completeness or force of effect. The austerity and harshness of spirit which sometimes overpower the sense of beauty in M. Legros's art are here in perfect accord with the subject and give a certain savage grandeur to the result.[4]

Although the reviewer praised the print's simplicity, its effects perceived as the result of 'a few lines', it is a highly worked image, the tonal effects carefully created through use of etched lines, aquatint and the drypoint needle, and the print progressing through a number of states.

Wilcox has noted a macabre streak within Legros's etched oeuvre, which found form in his illustrations to Edgar Allan Poe, and in two etched series: *Death and the Woodcutter* and *The Triumph of Death*.[5] While only a small proportion of Legros's etchings are concerned with death, some of the most memorable, *Death of the Vagabond* in particular – a print, like *The Gust of Wind* (p.133), singled out for praise from very early on[6] – are ruminations on this theme. EJ

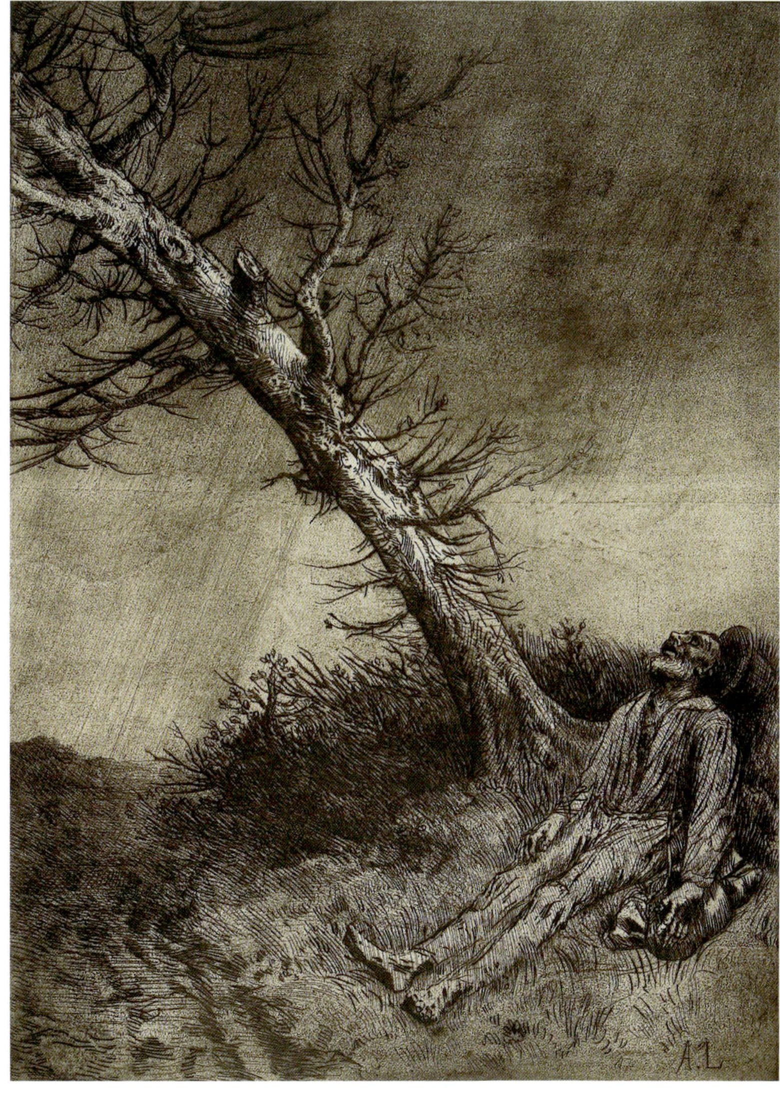

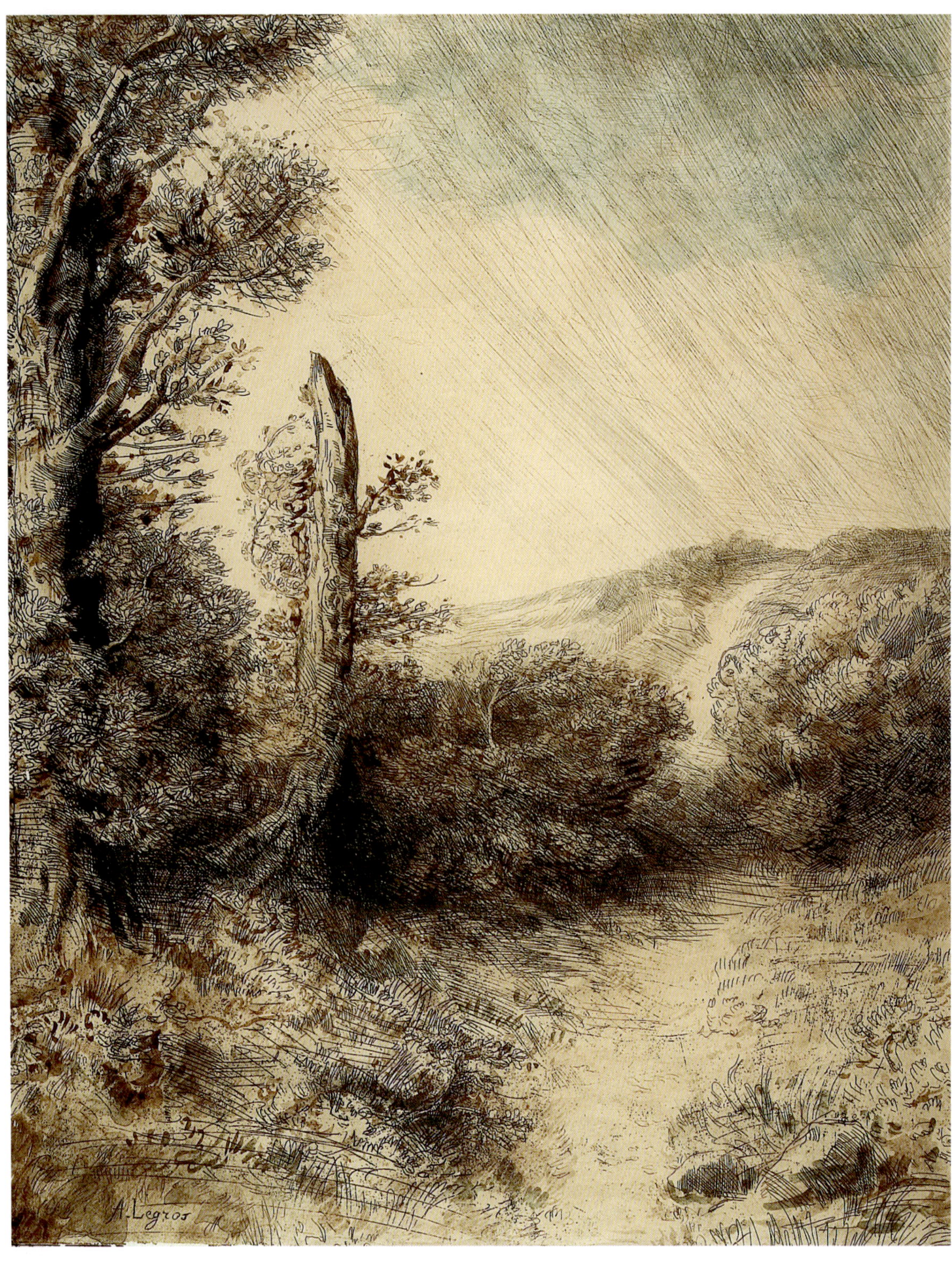
A. Legros

Alphonse Legros
1837–1911
The Gust of Wind exh. 1875
Etching on paper 57.4 × 44.5

Musée des Beaux-Arts de Dijon

The Gust of Wind exh. 1875
Etching on paper 56.9 × 46.6

The British Museum, London
[not illustrated]

By the Riverside, Morning Effect
1877–84
Etching, aquatint and drypoint
on paper 34.5 × 40.5

The British Museum, London

Prior to his arrival in London, Alphonse Legros, who produced several hundred etchings during his career, was associated with the revival of the technique in his native France, playing a role in the formation of the Société des Aquafortistes in 1862. Two of the most important artist-etchers working in London, Whistler, then a good friend of Legros's, and his brother-in-law Francis Seymour Haden, had also absorbed the influence of the etching scene in Paris, where much of the activity centred on the workshop of the master printer Auguste Delâtre.[1]

It was Whistler, who had settled in London in 1859, who persuaded Legros to try his luck in England, where the latter arrived in 1863. In London the Frenchman found both the teaching work and patronage to provide the income that had eluded him in Paris. He soon became an influential printmaker on this side of the channel too, his name associated with leading English etchers of the day such as Whistler, Haden and Tissot. He also made an impact on the teaching of printmaking, which he taught at both South Kensington and at the Slade School of Fine Art, and in 1880 he joined Tissot and others (but not Whistler, who had fallen out with both Legros and Haden by this time) as a committee member of the Society of Painter-Etchers, set up by Haden. *By the Riverside, Morning Effect* may correspond with the print entitled *By the Riverside* that Legros exhibited at the first annual exhibition of the Society of Painter-Etchers in 1881 (no.347 in the catalogue).[2]

The Gust of Wind is one of Legros's largest and best-known plates, celebrated both for its grand scale and the sense of movement achieved using the etching medium. Following its display at one of the Exhibitions of Works in Black and White held at the Dudley Gallery, Piccadilly, in 1875, the *Morning Post* singled out the etching for particular praise, before noting that 'the foreign works are, generally speaking, the best in the gallery'.[3] At the insistence of Degas, Legros also sent works to the *Second Impressionist Exhibition*, held at Durand-Ruel's gallery in Paris in 1876. All of his submissions were prints, *The Gust of Wind* among them.
EJ

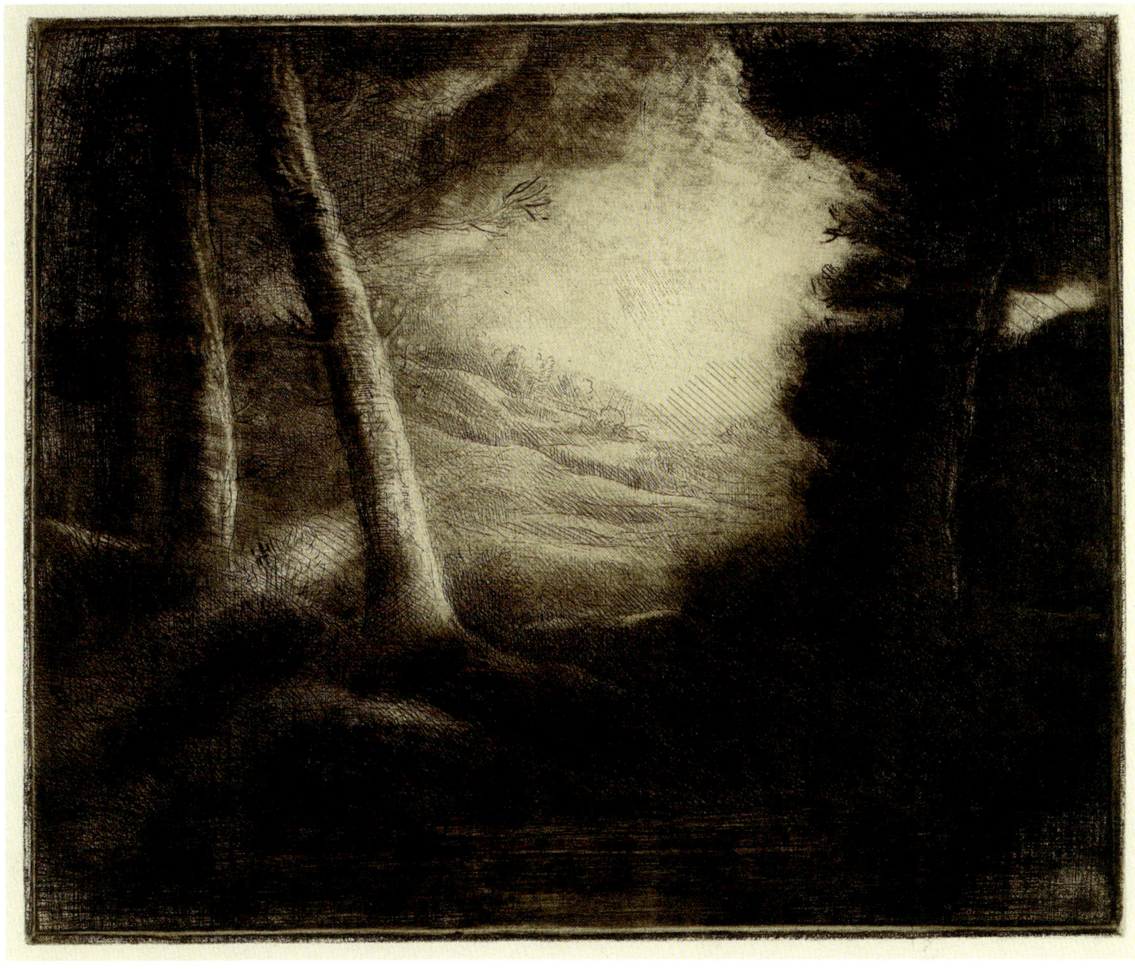

Alphonse Legros
1837–1911
A Storm 1887?
Drypoint on paper 17.9 × 25

The British Museum, London

A Storm 1887?
Drypoint on paper 17.9 × 24.5
Musée des Beaux-Arts de Dijon
[not illustrated]

A prolific and experimental etcher, Legros employed various techniques to achieve different landscape effects. In the present state of *A Storm*, the landscape has been transformed by driving rain, the earlier first state showing a calmer (albeit still stormy) scene. Legros created the sense of violent, stormy rain seen in the print through the use of drypoint; in this, the simplest intaglio technique of all, the printmaker uses a needle to scratch directly into the metal plate. A 'burr' of metal is created with the line, which when printed appears rich and velvety, at least in the earliest, best impressions.

The distinctive use of drypoint employed here suggests the influence of Rembrandt's prints. These were highly prized by many of the protagonists associated with the English etching revival, not least Francis Seymour Haden, who collected Rembrandt's etchings (incidentally, he also collected Legros's) and used drypoint in his own landscape etchings in a similar manner.[1] As Wilcox has noted, Legros's addition of drypoint to *A Storm* may well bring Rembrandt's *Three Trees* to mind.[2] But in the dramatic transformation of the plate, Rembrandt's *Three Crosses* also seems relevant: in the final states of this epic plate Rembrandt transformed the scene using dramatic diagonal drypoint lines. Legros often looked to the master printmakers of the past when interpreting his own subject matter. EJ

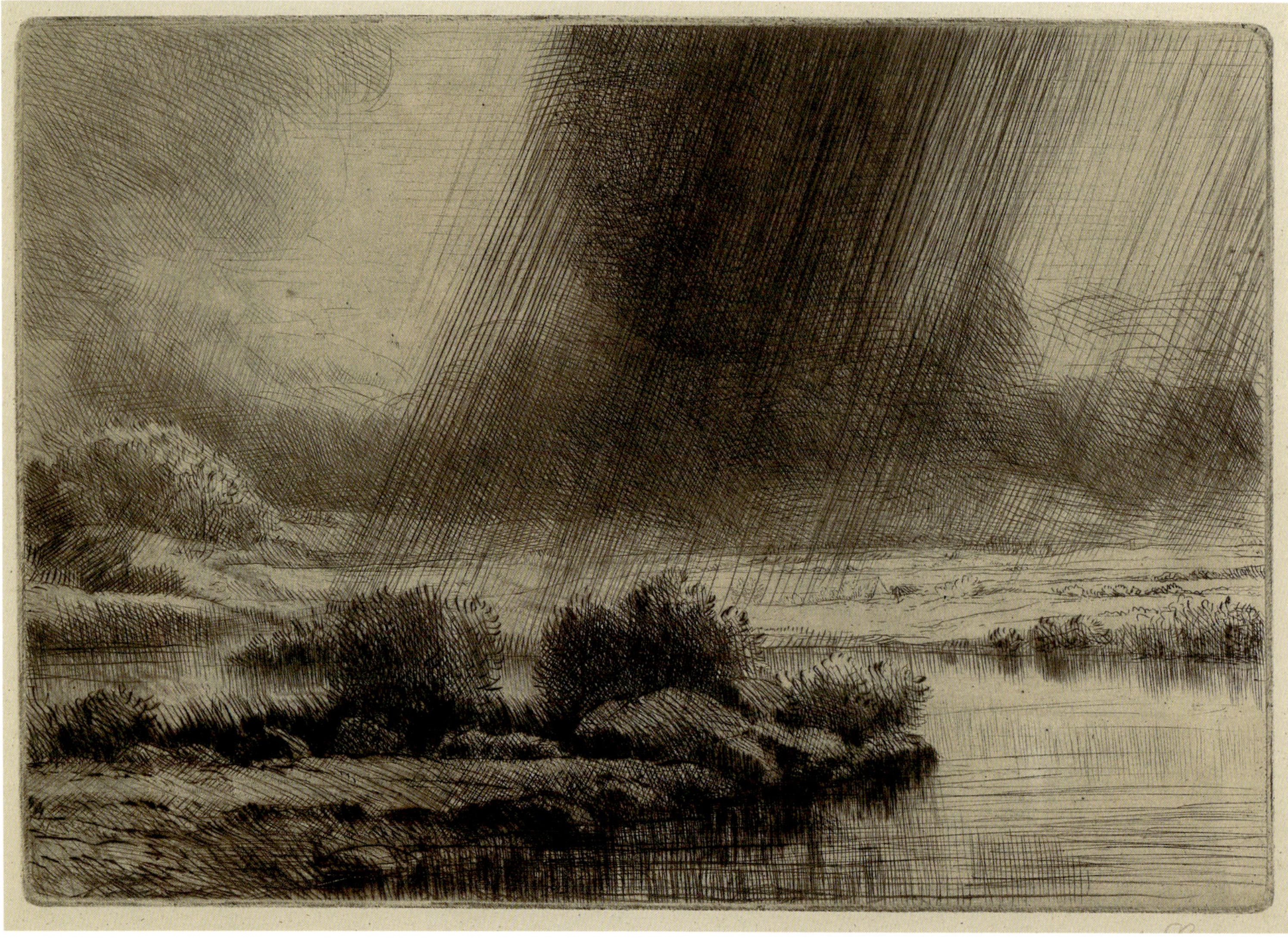

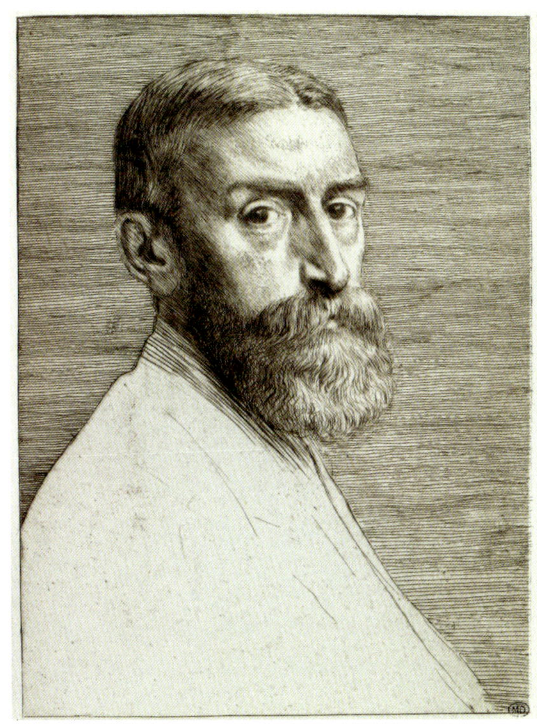

Alphonse Legros
1837–1911
Portrait of Edward Poynter 1876
Etching on paper 21.5 × 15.6

Musée des Beaux-Arts de Dijon

Although he grew up in England, Poynter was born in Paris and, like Legros, undertook artistic training in the French capital. He spent three years in the city from 1856, studying in the atelier of the Swiss painter and teacher Charles Gleyre, and at the Ecole des Beaux-Arts. He was one of the so-called 'Paris gang' of artists who met in Gleyre's studio; other members of note included George du Maurier, who in 1895 immortalised the group in what was in its day a hugely popular novel, *Trilby*, and James Abbott NcNeill Whistler, who was instrumental in persuading Legros to move to London in 1863.

Poynter's approach remained rooted in academic tradition, an outlook that shaped his time as Professor of the Slade School of Fine Art following his appointment in 1871. His choice of Legros as his successor at the Slade, an appointment also supported by Watts and Burne-Jones, ensured the continuance of this ethos. For Legros it also represented, at last, some financial security.[1]

Following his departure from the Slade, Poynter took up the post of director of the National Art Training School in South Kensington. Here he was quick to employ another Frenchman in Legros's circle, Jules Dalou, as head of modelling. Legros's etched portrait of Dalou (pp.150–1) is closely related to the present view of Poynter and it is probable that they were made as a pair, both prints being published in *The Portfolio* in 1877.[2]

Like so much of Legros's output, his portrait etchings seem to reflect the influence of the old masters he admired. The print scholar Arthur Hind wrote that in portraiture 'the revival of the noble simplicity of van Dyck's ideal is more the merit of Legros than any other'.[3] In the minimal attention paid to the sitters' clothes and the backgrounds, Legros's likenesses of Poynter and Dalou seem to aspire to the 'simplicity' characteristic of van Dyck's small but masterly etched oeuvre, with the faces of the sitters emphasised. While Dalou looks away from the artist, pensive, Poynter's gaze is direct. EJ

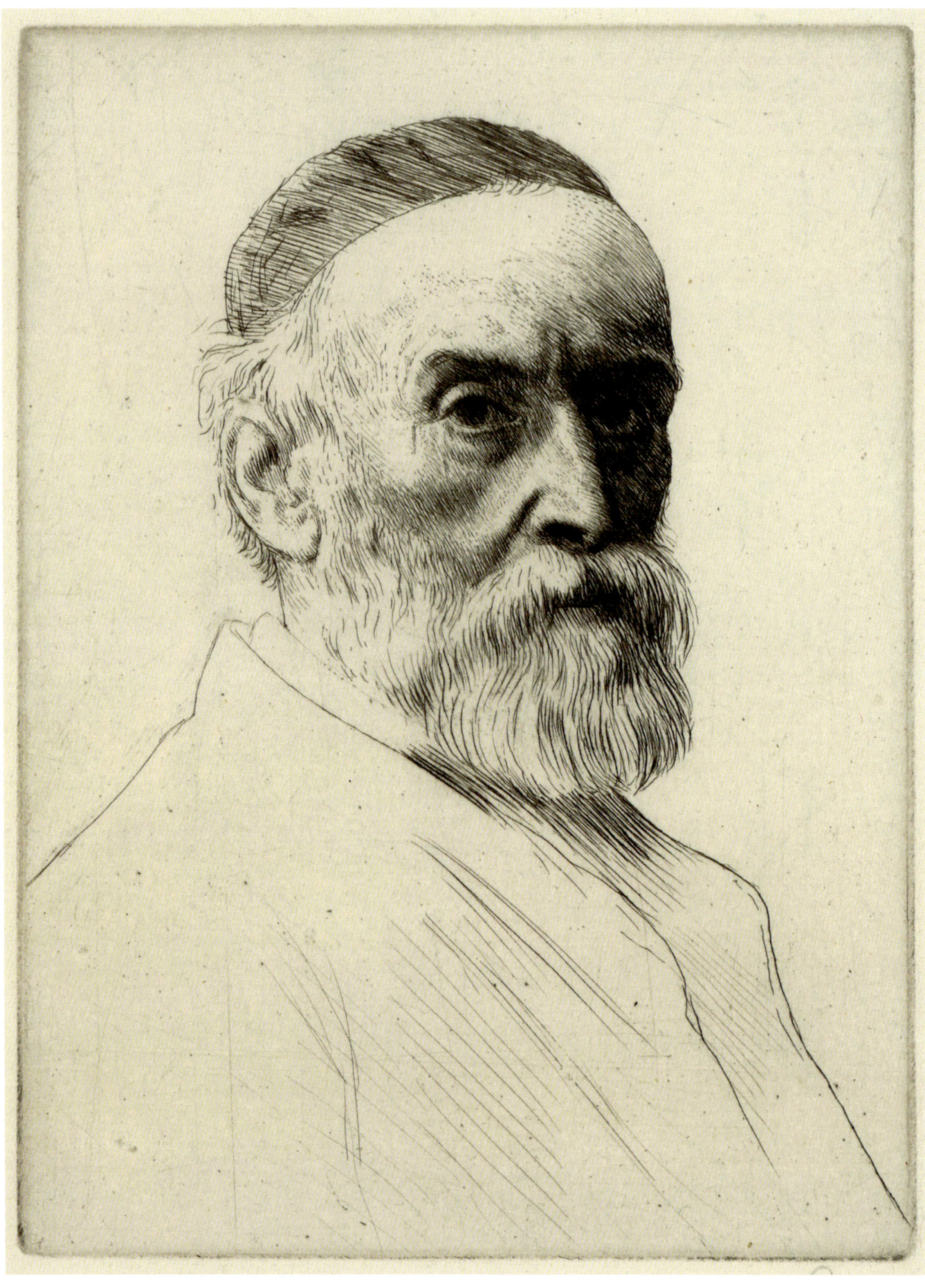

George Frederic Watts
1817–1904
Alphonse Legros c.1879
Etching on paper 12.8 × 9.9

National Portrait Gallery, London

Alphonse Legros
1837–1911
George Frederic Watts R.A. c.1879?
Etching and drypoint on paper
18.6 × 13.5

The British Museum, London

When Alphonse Legros settled in Britain, Whistler and Rossetti were not his only friends to play a part in securing commissions for him. The eminent painter George Frederic Watts also acted in favour of the young artist. In her reminiscences Watts's widow Mary stated how he urged his patron Charles Rickards to commission a painting from Legros, not without anxiety as to whether the émigré's 'grave simplicity' would be fully appreciated.[1] Reassured by Rickards, Watts went on to compare the Frenchman's work with 'the unconscious poetry of the bird's song, and not an elaborate effort, therefore so much more delightful, being perfectly natural – a most rare quality'.[2] The friendship between both artists endured, as these reciprocal portraits testify.

Watts's etching can be dated from about 1879, as per the inscription below the plate on this print: 'Portrait of Alphonse Legros / Etched by G.F. Watts RA about 1879 / Coll. F. Goulding. Imp.' Watts is known to have etched only one plate in his career, on which he made two portraits: that of Legros and the head of Mrs Frederick Myers just above (NPG D18062). That plate was cut down to produce the present proof. Given Legros's passion and skills for imparting knowledge and savoir-faire (Edwin Edwards and Auguste Rodin were among those he taught etching and drypoint), it is likely that Watts took up the medium on his encouragement. Although it appears that he did not renew the experience, this fluid portrait shows confidence, and is a fine likeness of Legros. It is undated, but the portrait of Watts by Legros was probably also executed in c.1879, judging by Watts's age and appearance, very similar to his self-portrait painted on that date (NPG 1406). CCP

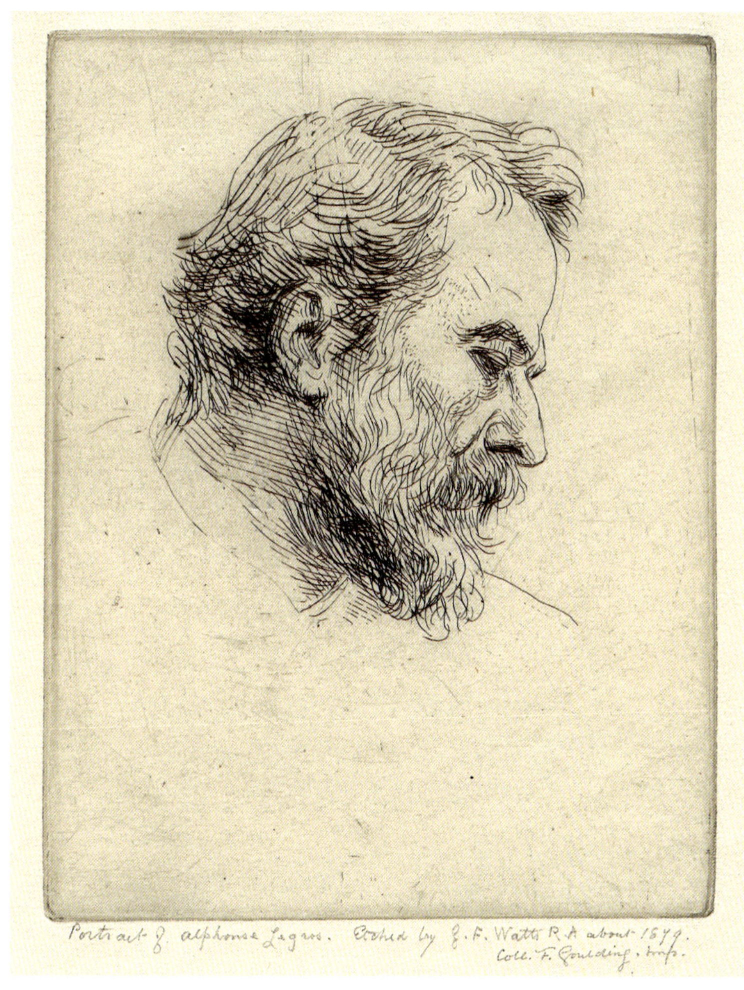

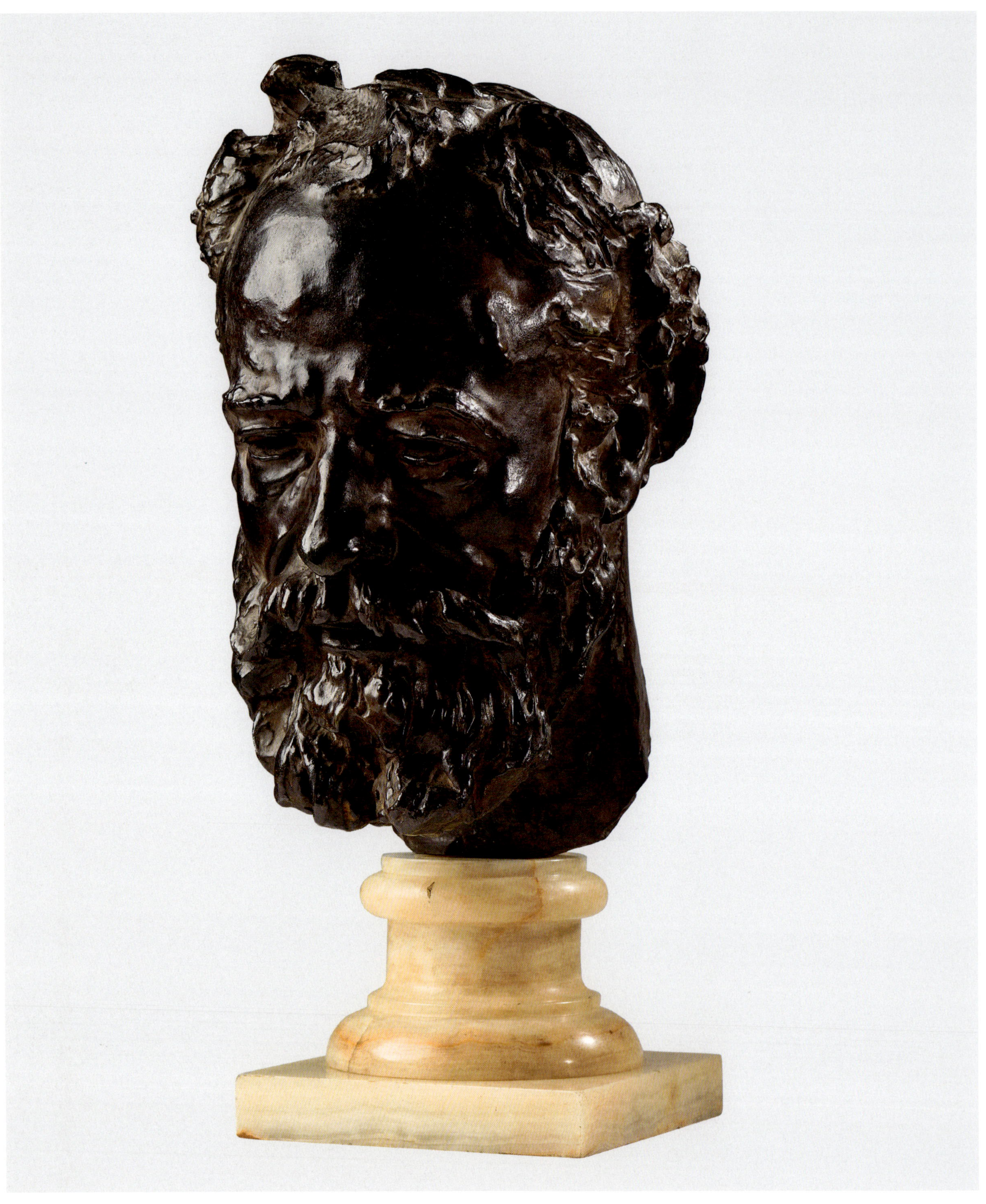

Auguste Rodin
1840–1917
Head of Alphonse Legros 1881–2
Bronze 41 × 27 × 25

Petit Palais, Musée des Beaux-Arts de la Ville de Paris

Alphonse Legros
1837–1911
Portrait of Auguste Rodin 1882
Oil paint on canvas 55 × 46

Musée Rodin, Paris

These two portraits are, once again, the fruit of exchange between artists, who were former students at the Petit Ecole and of Horace Lecoq de Boisbaudran. Alphonse Legros reconnected with Rodin during a trip to Paris in 1880; was it through the intermediary of Jules Dalou[1] or Jean-Charles Cazin, another co-disciple at the Petite Ecole and former exile in London?[2] While the career of Legros, aged forty-four, had finally blossomed and teaching had brought him material security, Rodin at the age of forty was still unknown in London. The sculptor, however, was starting to be noticed in Paris: in 1880 the nation purchased *The Age of Bronze* from him and commissioned a door for the future Musée des Arts Décoratifs.

Rodin in turn went to England during the summer of 1881. With Legros nearby, he began to do drypoint and etching, a technique that fed into his work as a decorator, as much for the Sèvres Manufacture as for that which would become *The Gates of Hell*. Through the painter, a new market and new networks opened up to him. He made his first contacts with the art critic who would support the spread of his work in Great Britain: William Ernest Henley, editor of the *Magazine of Art*. Thanks to Legros as well, from 1882 he was able to exhibit his works at the Royal Academy, Grosvenor Gallery and Dudley Gallery.[3]

That same summer of 1881, Rodin began a portrait of Legros, while Legros drew him in drypoint. Rodin finished his work during another stay in Paris by his sitter, and between mid-December 1881 and January 1882 Legros posed for Rodin in the studio of a former student, Gustave Natorp.[4]

As evidence of the enduring friendship of the two men, the *Head of Alphonse Legros*, with its lively and spirited workmanship, remains one of the best portraits from the 1880–5 period. 'I saw the bust you did of me. It's wonderful! It makes a big impact,' wrote an enchanted Legros on 6 May 1882.[5] Rodin quickly made several bronze versions,[6] including one for his sitter in 1882, which was dedicated 'To my friend A. Legros'.[7] Constantine Ionides, whom Legros introduced to Rodin in 1881, became one of the most important Rodin collectors in Great Britain. He acquired one of the bronzes exhibited at the Grosvenor Gallery in spring 1882. A series of casts would be made by the Alexis Rudier foundry, including two in 1910, the date when the nation acquired the example shown here.

The friendship that Legros felt for Rodin and his admiration for his work can be seen in his painted portrait of 1882. Rapidly painted in reserve in the middle of the canvas according to a formula favoured by the painter for painting demonstrations, it concentrates on rendering the sitter's personality. Auguste Rodin's majestic profile stands out against a neutral background, following a layout that Legros particularly liked for the composition of medals (see p.165). The choice of this profile was certainly not accidental, because in the same years, 1880–2, the two men were also connected through sculpture: Legros began modelling and introduced his teaching to the Slade School of Art education programme, which he directed.[8] Through his students who went to Paris, he regularly entrusted Rodin with finding a foundry in France for his works sculpted in London.

In 1900, while the reputation of Alphonse Legros dimmed, Rodin became celebrated in both France and Great Britain; notable events, including the gift by subscription of a *St John the Baptist* to South Kensington Museum in 1902 and the presidency of the International Society of Sculptors, Painters and Gravers in 1903, demonstrate the admiration in which he was held by young artists and a considerable network of collectors and critics. On Rodin's recommendation, a retrospective exhibition would finally be devoted to his loyal friend Legros at the Musée du Luxembourg in Paris in 1900. ASi

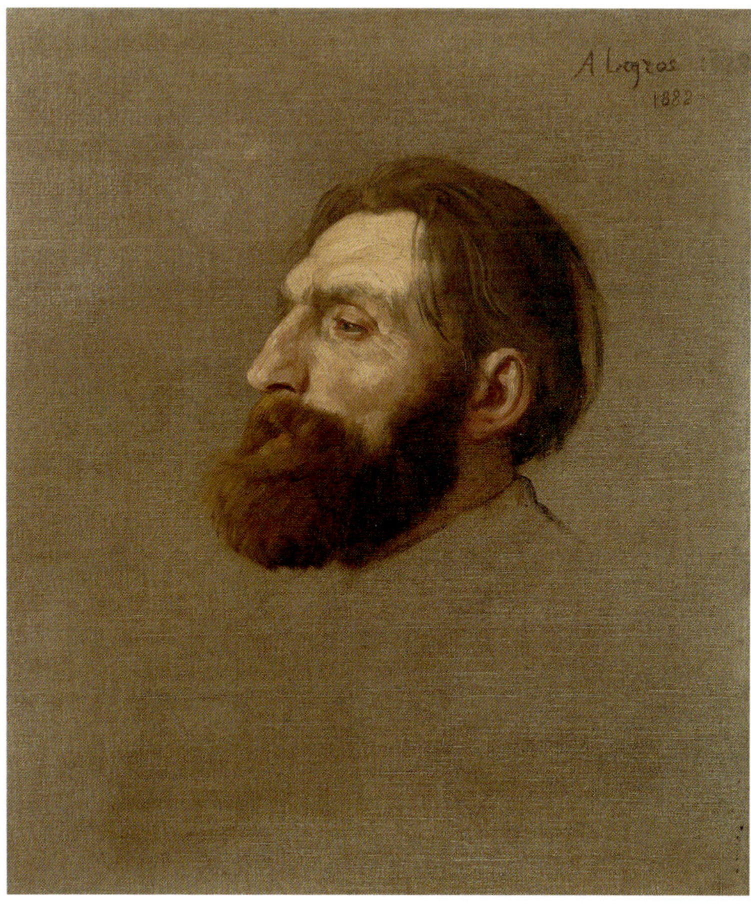

Auguste Rodin
1840–1917
Bust of Jules Dalou 1883
Bronze 52 × 43 × 24

Musée Rodin, Paris

Plaster 53 × 42.5 × 27

Musée Rodin, Paris, on long loan to the Petit Palais, Paris
[not illustrated]

At the beginning of the 1880s Auguste Rodin began to work on *The Gates of Hell*, which he kept secret in his studio although connoisseurs came to admire it.[1] Little by little, from his research on everything to do with Dante there emerged extraordinary drawings and modelled subjects that took on an independent life, such as *The Thinker* 1882 and *Paolo and Francesca* which became *The Kiss*. Simultaneously, following the advice of the journalist Edmond Bazire to do portraits to become better known, Auguste Rodin sculpted three admirable busts: those of the painter Jean-Paul Laurens and the sculptors Albert Carrier-Belleuse and Jules Dalou.

Returning from London in 1880 and determined to create a stir, Dalou brought back with him a project of grand sculpted compositions inspired by the baroque, for in the painting and sculpture of Louis XIV's reign he had found the sources for renewing a style that he wished to make clearly Republican. In June 1880 he received a commission from the City of Paris for his monumental group, *The Triumph of the Republic*, for the Place de la Nation. The audacious twisting composition had in fact persuaded the city councillors, some of whom were former comrades from the Commune. In 1881 the state commissioned a historic relief from him, *Mirabeau Answering Dreux-Brézé*, for the Deputies' Chamber. At the Salon of 1883, the first in which Dalou exhibited since his return, the large plaster reliefs that he presented were a triumph: *Mirabeau* and *Fraternity* (p.168), which would soon be purchased by the City of Paris, met with everyone's approval. He was decorated with the medal of honour and the Salon was dubbed, 'Dalou's Salon.'

Rodin thus made the portrait of a man whose career was in full swing, and he exhibited it in the Salon of 1884 with success. He modelled Dalou the artist with rare sensitivity and without any recourse to costume or attributes: Dalou's bust is nude, severe and cut off below the shoulders, *à l'antique*. His striking face, his flesh stretched over protruding bones, his high forehead and proud obstinate attitude would be described again and again by the press, and increasingly so when, over the years, critics would get to know the sitter better as a hard worker with poor health and an idealistic intransigent character. The beautiful quality of the cast reinforces that of the modelling. The original plaster exhibited in Paris, the closest to the clay sculpture produced during posing sessions, was dedicated by Rodin to Pierre Roche, one of Dalou's students and friends.

Rodin and Dalou were not very close friends, but they felt a bond when the latter returned from exile – and before rivalry separated them and before, for strategic reasons, critics close to Rodin accentuated this distance, which was reinforced by the strength of Dalou's character. This stunning bust shows that Rodin had an acute perception of Dalou's personality and demanding ideals; his realisation of it is masterly. ASi

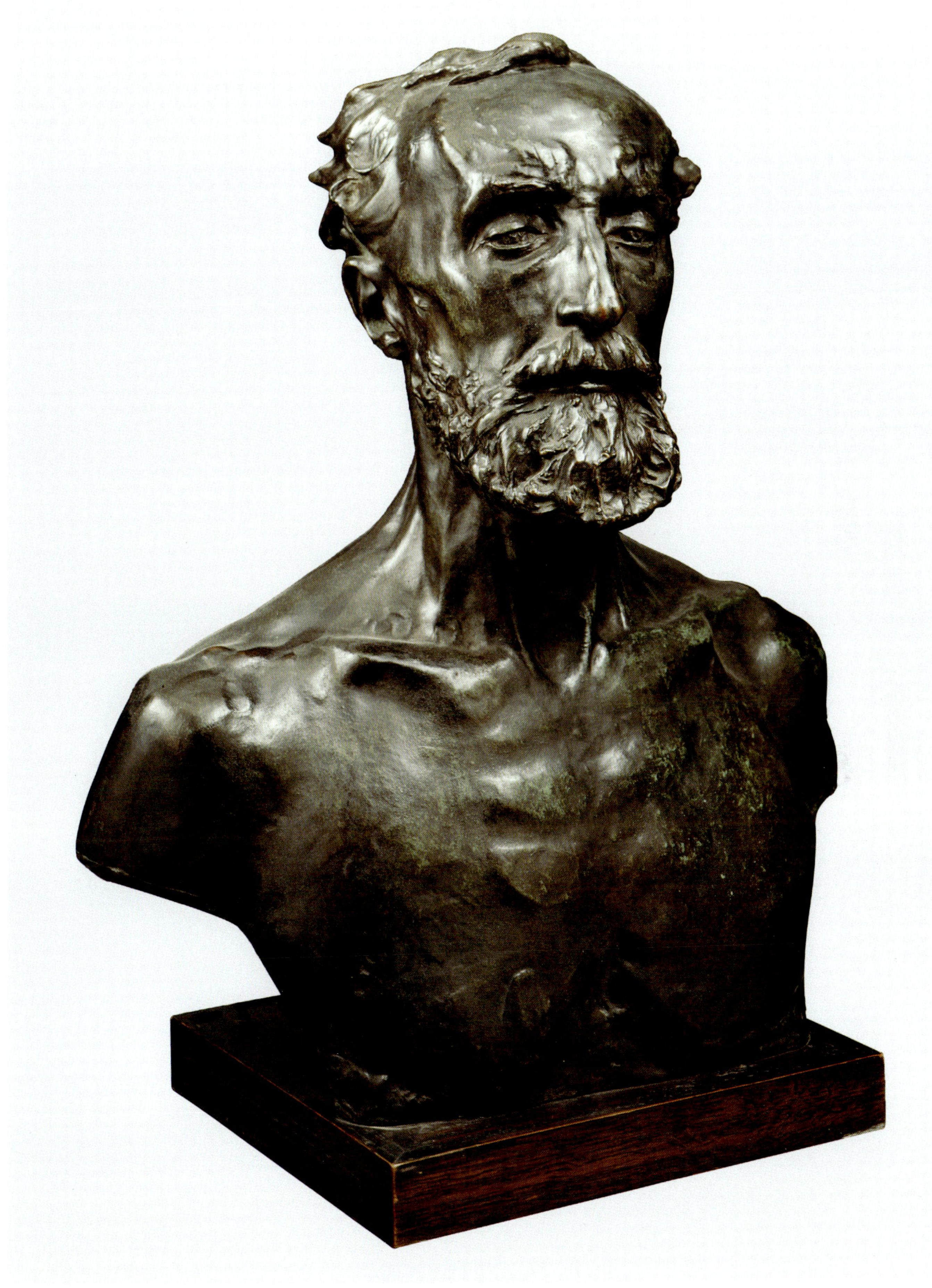

William Orpen
1878–1931
Group Associated with the New English Art Club c.1904
Pencil, black chalk (or charcoal), pen, ink and watercolour on paper
22.5 × 41.5

National Portrait Gallery, London

In 1904 the Irish painter William Orpen had recently graduated from the Slade School of Art and set up his own school with his fellow student Augustus John (1878–1961). He became well known as a portrait painter and *Group Associated with the New English Art Club* depicts nine artists who were leading British painting. The New English Art Club (NEAC), which embraced cross-channel artistic developments, was founded in 1886 as an alternative to the Royal Academy. The drawing places the French artist Alphonse Legros at the head of a genealogy of modern British art, accompanied by Rodin. Students from the Slade had organised a dinner in honour of the French sculptor in 1903, when his reputation in Britain was at its height. The two men lead younger artists, teachers and critics who represented French influence on British art through the Slade and the NEAC. In the nineteenth century French art had divided critics and public, reflecting a wider ambivalence between the two nations in the aftermath of the Napoleonic Wars, revolutions and imperial competition, but 1904 saw an Entente Cordiale agreement signed between Britain and France and a more general popularity of French styles. Orpen sets his characters on a breezy clifftop (overlooking the channel, perhaps), a reference to the famous challenges of plein-air painting in English weather, the wind tossing their hats into a pleasing rhythm above their heads. The prospect opens ahead into a promising vista, however.

Legros was Slade Professor of Fine Art from 1876 to 1892, succeeded by the painter Frederick Brown (1851–1941), seen fifth in the line in the drawing. Brown had trained in Paris at the Académie Julian and was influenced by James Abbott McNeill Whistler and Jules Bastien-Lepage. Just ahead of him is Henry Tonks (1862–1937), a doctor and painter who studied and taught under Brown and succeeded him as Slade Professor in 1918. Between the two pairs trudges the stout figure of the painter Philip Wilson Steer (1860–1942). Steer had been rejected by the Royal Academy of Art and studied in Paris where he was influenced by impressionism, especially Edouard Manet, Whistler and Walter Sickert. All three, Steer, Tonks and Brown, had been Orpen's teachers at the Slade. Steer, Whistler, Sickert and Brown were among the founding members of the NEAC, but some found the venture still not radical enough, and Whistler resigned. Sickert and Steer formed an impressionist group and staged *London Impressionists* in 1889. Orpen exhibited there from 1899.

Behind Tonks and Brown are younger Francophile members of the club. William Rothenstein (1872–1945) was taught by Legros and trained in Paris, and, following him, Orpen's fellow Slade student Augustus John (1878–1961), studied under Brown and Tonks and spent a lot of time in France. Charles Edward Conder (1868–1909), next, trained in Australia and Paris. The painter and critic Dugald Sutherland MacColl (1859–1948), another Slade student of Legros, brings up the rear. Brown, Steer, Tonks, John, Rothenstein, MacColl and Orpen frequently sat together on the NEAC selection jury and many of the group would become influential establishment figures. CJ

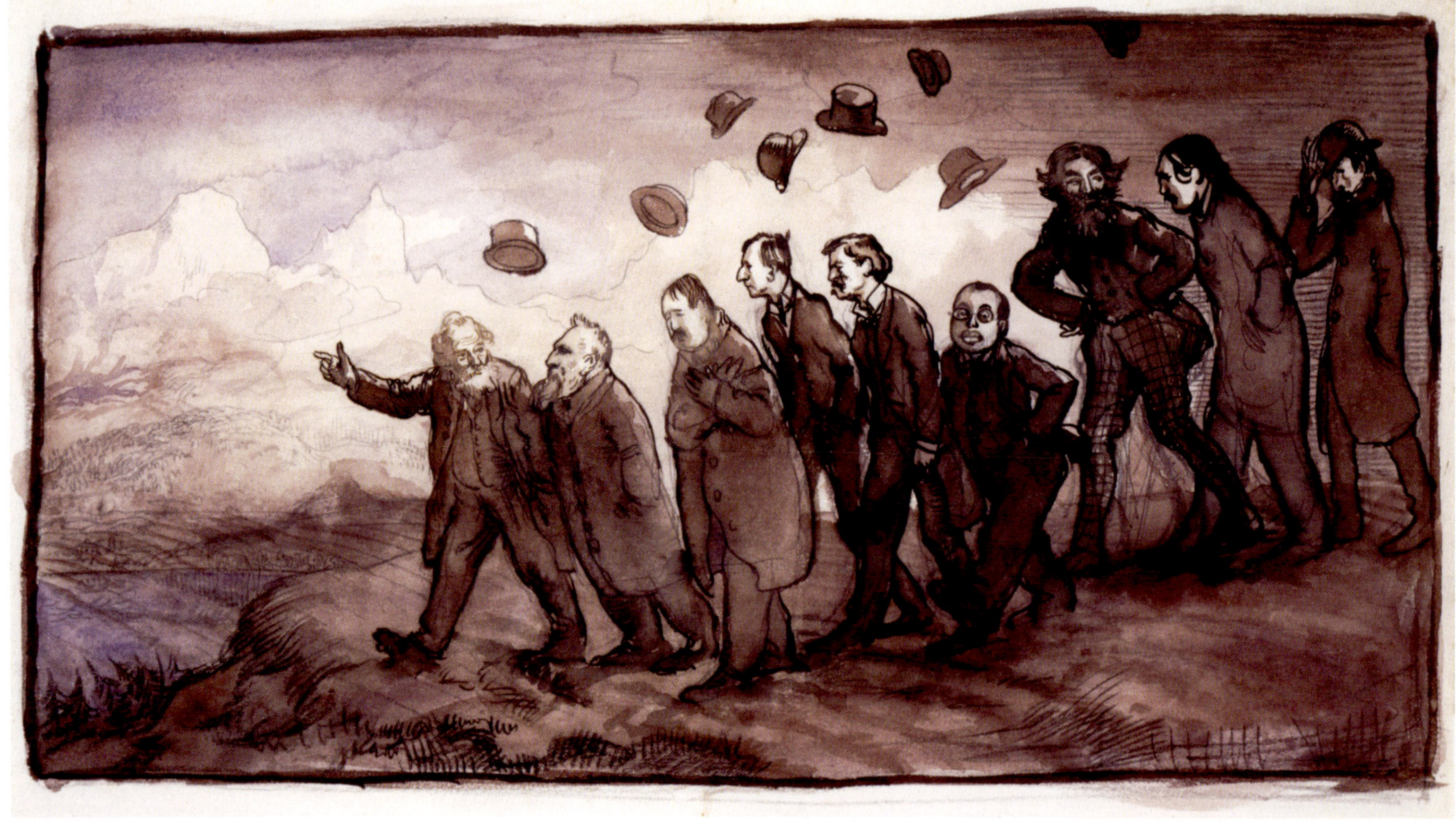

Alphonse Legros
1837–1911
Portrait of the Artist c.1890–1904
Etching and drypoint on paper
29.4 × 20.6

Musée des Beaux-Arts de Dijon

This self-portrait demonstrates Legros's tonal abilities as a printmaker, the heavily worked dark background effectively contrasting with the artist's pale beard and the highlighted areas of the face. His expression is serious, and the etching is one of a number in which Legros depicts himself looking away from the viewer. It was made during the latter part of his career, possibly following his departure from the Slade School of Art, where, as professor from 1876 until 1893, he had introduced etching to the syllabus. Although he apparently referred to his time at the Slade as twenty lost years,[1] his work as a teacher was clearly a very significant part of his life and career in England. He was, however, more productive as a printmaker in the years following his retirement from the Slade, finding additional time for his own practice once freed from the demands of teaching.[2]

This period of his life also saw recognition abroad, with a one-man show in Paris, at *L'Art Nouveau* gallery, and a retrospective at the Musée du Luxembourg in 1900. In 1904 Legros left the Hammersmith house he had lived in for the past two decades and moved to Watford, where he died in 1911. His death was marked by a large retrospective exhibition at the Tate Gallery, variants of which toured the English regions.
EJ

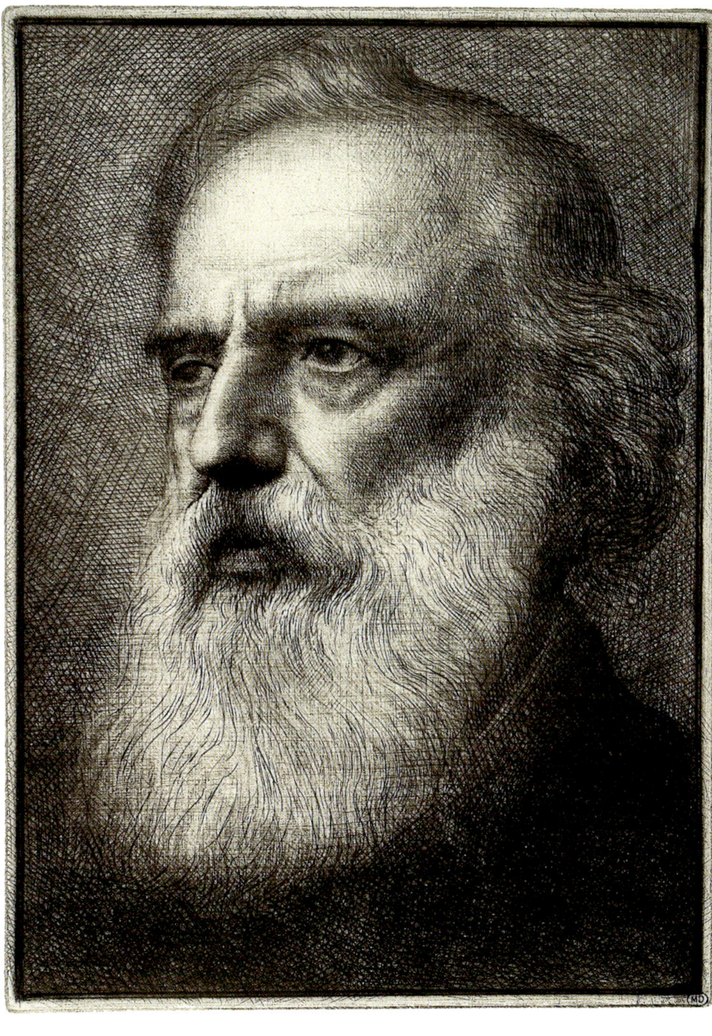

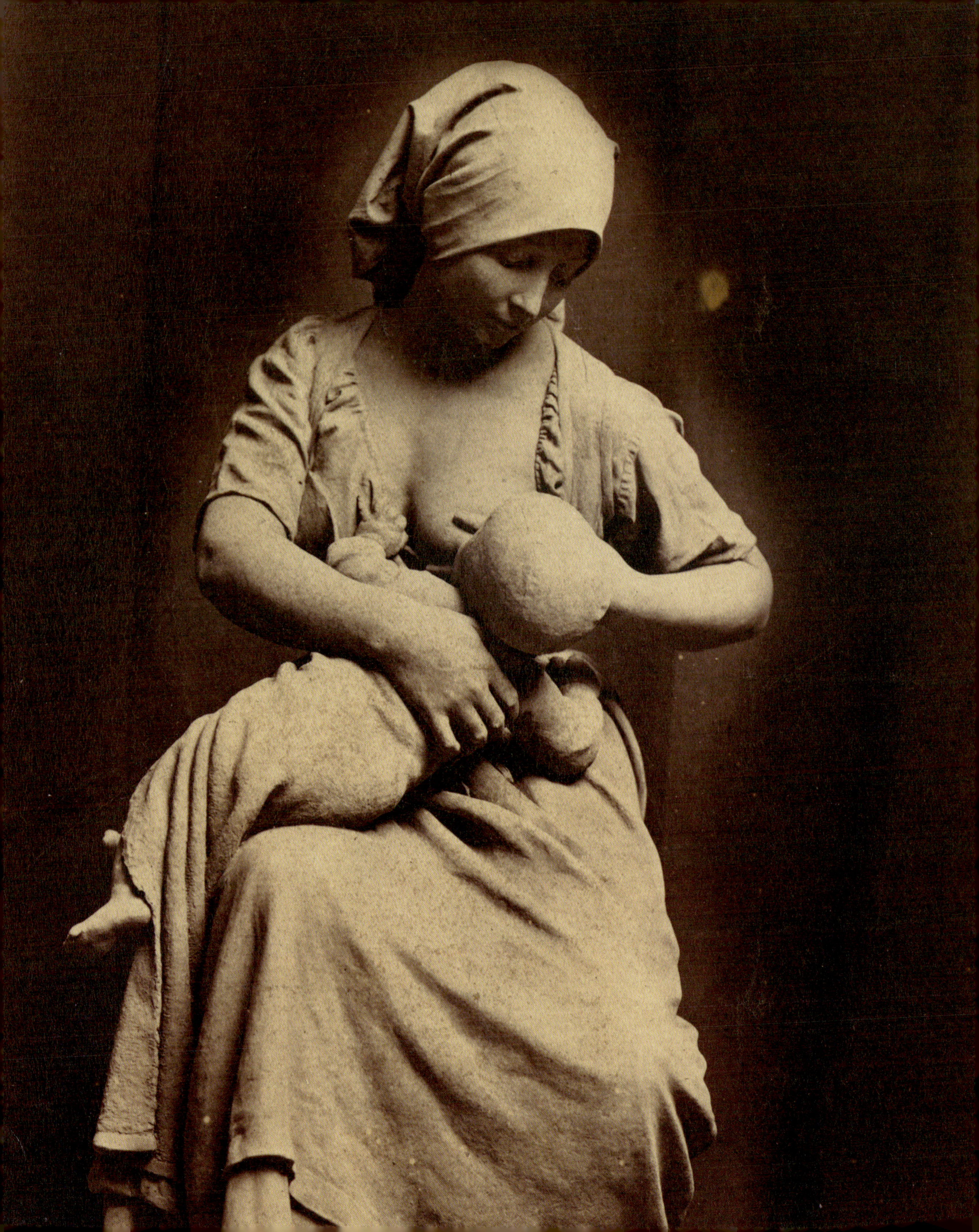

Amélie Simier

A French Demonstration: The Pivotal Roles of Jules Dalou and Edouard Lantéri in British Sculpture

Since the year 1875 or thereabouts a radical change has come over British sculpture ... To Carpeaux, no doubt, the inspiration of the new trend was originally due ... But it was to Monsieur Dalou that we chiefly owe the great renascence in England. (Marion Harry Spielmann, 1901[1])

There can be no doubt but that the revival of sculpture in England in recent times owes its inception and development to a systematic and intelligent training directed by one who has known how to lend the weight of his personality as a master as well as a teacher, and has thus been steadily creating an artistic moral influence worthy of the best tradition. To Edward Lanteri ... we are indebted for our school.
(Alfred Gilbert, Bruges, 1912[2])

In France it is not well known that the settlement of French artists in London in the 1860s and 1870s had a major impact on the teaching of the arts in Great Britain. Among the key figures, the singular trajectories of two sculptors stand out: Jules Dalou (1838–1902) and Edouard Lantéri (1848–1917).

Implicated in the Communard movement, the Parisian sculptor Jules Dalou fled to London in July 1871. Condemned in absentia on 1 May 1874, he remained in London until April 1880 and lived both off his talent as a sculptor and the lessons he gave to young artists. For all that, his English success did not hold him here; when pardoned, he chose to return to Paris. The end of his career was crowned with important public commissions, especially the *Triumph of the Republic*, Place de la Nation, in Paris. By this time he no longer taught but devoted himself entirely to his own work.

Edouard Lantéri, who was from Burgundy and became a British subject in 1901, is a forgotten sculptor both in France and Great Britain, despite interesting works kept in Auxerre and in London.[3] Through the intervention of Dalou, he arrived in England in October 1872 to be assistant to the sculptor Joseph Edgar Boehm, which he remained until the latter's death. He also taught generations of sculptors from 1874 until 1910. He left a collection of modelling manuals, the fruit of almost forty years of teaching, published between 1902 and 1911.[4]

First one, then the other of these two artists would bring the best of 'French style' instruction – the subject of lively debates in 1860s London – to British sculpture. The new practices, although challenged by some English artists, would prove to be providential for a generation of artists.

Art teaching in London and Paris, c.1870

In his introduction to the London International Exhibition catalogue in 1871, Sir Coutts Lindsay held British teaching methods responsible for the mediocrity of the arts in Great Britain.[5] The lag in sculpture was particularly noticeable, as Francis Turner Palgrave, an influential critic of the 1860s, noted: 'Our school [of sculpture] has fallen particularly low ... We have but one or two men of practiced skill and original gift.'[6] This

Jules Dalou
French Peasant Woman Nursing a Baby 1873
Albumen print

Private collection, Becker Estate

remark would become a leitmotif in the British press of the 1860s and 1870s.

In London in 1870, art teaching was mainly in the hands of the Royal Academy, a constituency of artists elected by their peers. At the heart of its schools, the academicians, reinforced by a series of invited professors, gave general training that was essentially theoretical. Practical instruction relied, as at the beginning of the century, on drawing from the antique, and the students received little supervision from their professors. In response to this conservatism, a new school of Fine Arts, the Felix Slade Faculty of Fine Arts, opened in 1871 at the core of University College. Edwin Field, one of its founders, had studied the Parisian system and tried to engage professors who had continental experience, such as Edward Poynter, who was director from 1871 to 1875 and placed drawing after nature at the heart of the curriculum, in accordance with the example set by French studios.[7] By 1875 the school had 220 students, and admission had to be limited. The same year, Alphonse Legros was named Professor of Engraving, replacing Poynter as head of the school when the latter was appointed to South Kensington.

Simultaneously, private studios such as Heatherley's opened, enterprises that responded to the need for a broader practice of drawing after nature. Most aspiring sculptors complemented their Royal Academy training with work for established artists. This was the case for two of Dalou's contemporaries: Hamo Thornycroft mainly trained under his father, who was a sculptor, and through contact with museums; Alfred Gilbert became Joseph Edgar Boehm's assistant in 1872,[8] the same year as Lantéri, who would be his professor at the National Art Training School in South Kensington.

Finally, since the beginning of the century, the most well-to-do artists would perfect their education in Parisian studios and come into contact with a Bohemian lifestyle unknown in London, which George du Maurier would recreate in his *roman-à-clef*, *Trilby* (1894). These artists, often painters, were enriched by their dual Franco-British experience and would use their influence to bring about teaching reforms, for which Legros, Dalou and Lantéri would be the main agents.

Workers in artistic crafts were trained in Government Schools of Design, which offered solid technical training and led to paid jobs. In West London, one of them was twinned with the Museum of Manufactures, the future South Kensington Museum promoted by Prince Albert. It would become the National Art Training School in 1853 and then the Royal College of Art in 1896. Poynter's arrival in 1875 and the hiring of French professors led to the gradual development of fine art instruction.

In South London the Lambeth School provided evening courses for workers; it was established near Doulton's Lambeth Pottery Works. John Charles Lewis Sparkes, who directed the school, urged Doulton to develop a line in ornamental ceramics, which was quite successful, and the factory recruited from the neighbouring school.[9] In the 1870s the well-trained Lambeth students won national competitions in modelling well ahead of the National Art Training School. In 1879 the Lambeth School merged with the City and Guilds of London Institute for the Advancement of Technical Education, becoming the South London Technical Art School.

In France, during the same period, public municipal drawing schools trained craftsmen and artists. Municipal fine arts schools and scholarships facilitated access to free upper education at the Ecole des Beaux-Arts (School of Fine Arts) in Paris. Famous artists, mainly academicians, taught both theory and practice there. To prepare their students for the competitions that punctuated this rigorous training, right up to the famous Prix de Rome, teachers at the Ecole des Beaux-Arts opened private paying studios. Very attentive, they imparted the techniques necessary for acquiring artistic method. Some, especially sculptors, took on students as assistants in their sculpture sites.

In France the boundaries between fine and applied arts were, then, less rigid than in England. Among the schools intended to train artisans and craftsmen in Paris, the Ecole Gratuite de Dessin (Free Drawing School), nicknamed the 'Petite Ecole' (Little School), stood out for its teaching in the applied arts as much as it did for entry into the Ecole des Beaux-Arts. With courses in drawing after engravings and reliefs, as well as from plants and living models, not to mention anatomy, modelling and sculpture courses, the school sought to turn young people into more than simple practitioners. Legros, Léon Lhermitte, Henri Fantin-Latour, Jean-Charles Cazin and Auguste Rodin were drawn from its ranks.[10] One of its teachers, Horace Lecoq de Boisbaudran, promoted an original technique of drawing from memory for which he published a method in 1847.[11] He developed each individual's personal vision, which he considered one of the tools of artistic invention, and he especially influenced the generation of Legros, one of his best students. That is where Dalou and then Lantéri were trained. Both were subsequently admitted to the Ecole des Beaux-Arts, but Dalou, an unsuccessful candidate in the Prix de Rome competition, would not have words hard enough to later condemn the Ecole des Beaux-Arts.[12] When invited in 1883, he refused to teach there.

The entire French system produced artists who seemed to British observers to be better equipped, but it was still the subject of lively debates in France. After the collapse of the empire and with the help of the newly founded Paris Commune, a Federation of Artists that included craftsmen and workers from the ranks of industry and the decorative arts was created on 13 April 1871 under the leadership of Gustave Courbet. The federation wished, through a democratic process, to deal with artistic questions that until then had been the preserve of the French state. Dalou's involvement in the Commune is also evidence of his preoccupation with questions of artistic instruction: on 21 April 1871 he was appointed to the subcommittee for the teaching of drawing, whose deliberations essentially concerned elementary artistic education. Anti-academic, they were in favour of an education in drawing and modelling that would start in the Parisian primary and professional schools, would be open to future craftsmen and artists and would rely on new methods and models provided by a body of professors chosen through competition.[13] However, the violent

Alfred Drury teaching modelling from life at the Goldsmith's Institute

The Worshipful company of Goldsmiths, London

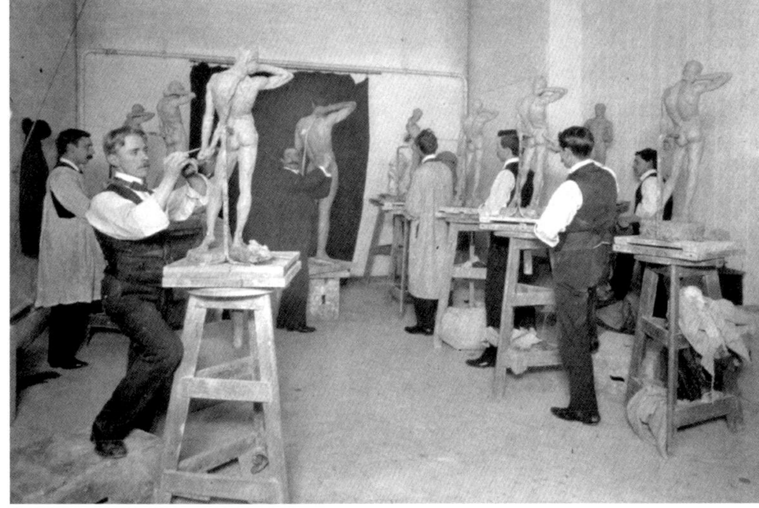

repression of the Commune put an end to this reform attempt.

When they arrived in London in 1871 and 1872, Dalou and Lantéri could have been considered by their hosts as exemplary products of a French education. It is not certain that Dalou thought it sensible to share his personal convictions about this approach with his peers and patrons, but there is no question that the positions he occupied fitted in with the pursuance of his political and artistic aims.

Dalou and Lantéri: masters of a generation of sculptors

Dalou and Lantéri essentially gave their British students technical and practical instruction, which was disseminated as much in their studios and at their sculpture sites as through the art schools. In the case of Dalou, it led to some scattered accounts from his students, whereas Lantéri left remarkable practical manuals for posterity. The latter accurately expressed his methods and convictions as a teacher, which were very close to those attributed to Dalou. Furthermore, the works Dalou exhibited between 1872 and 1879 would have an impact, difficult to discern but no less important, particularly on the generation of the 'New Sculpture',[14] a group of sculptors who were active from the 1870s to the 1890s and shared similar sensitivity to materials and depiction of the figure.

On his arrival in London in July 1871, Jules Dalou was warmly welcomed by his comrade Legros from the Petite Ecole, who found him lodging and a job, as well as introduced him to his network of patrons and artist friends. Thanks to them, Dalou was able to exhibit at the Royal Academy exhibition in spring 1872; his first English success, the sale of a terracotta statuette, *Palm Sunday in Boulogne* (p.152), made it possible for him to settle in the Chelsea area, noted for specialist workers, ordinary intellectual and artistic professions, and artists' studios near the ceramics manufacturers and the South Kensington educational and museum complex. In his studio at 217a Glebe Place, at the corner of the King's Road, Dalou took in paying students from 1873 until the end of his exile.

The studio as a teaching location

This was the case for Mary Fraser Tytler, future wife of the painter George Frederic Watts. She trained in Dresden and at the National Art Training School, and then in January 1873 was admitted to the Slade. She was said to have encountered Dalou during a modelling demonstration and was subsequently welcomed into his studio.[15] Her later achievement in training the local population at Compton in Surrey in architectural ceramics is evidence both of her persistence in pursuing modelling and of her use, like Dalou, of applied arts for social engagement. The presence of Henrietta Montalba and Randolph Caldecott in Dalou's studio in 1873–4 is also recorded. Caldecott was guided by Dalou, who willingly shared his techniques. The few reliefs conserved in the Victoria and Albert Museum demonstrate a facility for using clay to transform into three dimensions scenes that come straight out of his illustrations.[16]

An intriguing article in *The Academy* of 25 November 1876 mentions with approval the project of some young sculptors to establish a private studio according to the French system under the 'supervision of Mr. Dalou', who had apparently given his consent. The project, as far as we know, did not see the light of day, but the article, followed by another on Legros's success as an engraving professor, could have been written to encourage an official commitment to hire Dalou as a professor in one of the art schools.

Instruction at art schools

Several sources mention the influence of Dalou's interventions at the Slade. Even if the archives do not seem to conserve any trace of Dalou's presence there,[17] it is highly probable that he was invited to give modelling demonstrations either by Poynter, who was anxious to launch the young art school on new paths, or by his friend Legros, who taught there.

Evidence is more precise on the positions held by Dalou and then Lantéri at the National Art Training School. Fortified by his experience at the Slade, Poynter hired Dalou on 11 May 1877 as a supplementary teacher for the tenured professor F.M. Miller in order to renew methods of instruction in modelling.[18] Edouard Lantéri, Assistant Master of Modelling from 1874 to 1880, and officially recommended by Dalou, succeeded the latter on 20 February 1880,[19] first as Master of Modelling, then as Professor of Sculpture from 1890 to 1910.[20] Their students would have successful careers: in addition to Alfred Drury, Dalou's student to whom we will return, Spielmann names Albert Toft, Francis Derwent Wood and Conrad Dressler among Lantéri's students.[21] A remarkable effort at synthesis, the modelling manuals published by Lantéri at the turn of the twentieth century summarise the essential technical principles and practices that were taught to several generations of students.[22]

At the prompting of John Sparkes (who was both Headmaster of the National Art Training School and Superintendent of Studies of the South London Technical School of Art), Dalou was appointed Professor of Design and Modelling at the South London Technical Art School at the beginning of 1880. The training that the students received at this municipal school of applied arts in Lambeth was not much different from that which Dalou had received at the Petite Ecole. Paradoxically, if Dalou only taught for two or three months before returning to Paris, his stay nonetheless had a profound effect on his students, especially those who came out of long apprenticeships, such as Harry Bates, who felt liberated by 'the freedom of Dalou's method',[23] and Frederick Pomeroy. Acting on Dalou's advice, Bates would subsequently train with Rodin. Although the school was engaged primarily in training craftsmen, it gave birth to a generation of artists who used it as a stepping stone to enter the Royal Academy Schools, where they won all the competitions. 'The Lambeth Group' – Bates, Pomeroy, George Frampton, William Goscombe John, John and Henry Poole, Charles Allen and more – benefited from the extraordinary stimulus that resulted directly from Dalou's teaching or its impact.[24] The success of the French artists' students stirred up rival schools, and in the 1880s the Royal Academy Schools of Art would become more progressive under the leadership of the Royal Academy President, Sir Frederic Leighton.

Training at sculpture sites

Among Dalou's and Lantéri's students, a few fortunate ones were accepted as assistants or directed to a colleague's studio (Dalou sent his students to Rodin, but never to Frémiet, Mercié, Falguière or Puech, French academicians who were rival sculptors). In Dalou's case the best-documented example is Alfred Drury.[25] He studied at Oxford School of Art and then entered the National Art Training School in 1875. A talented student, he followed in the footsteps of Dalou, who was first his teacher and then his employer on Parisian sculpture sites from 1881 to 1885, at the time when Dalou was conceiving his monumental masterpieces. After Drury returned to Great Britain, Dalou took an interest in the career of his student, who worked initially as Boehm's assistant and then pursued a successful personal career in which he produced portraits, public monuments and architectural models. Although Drury's first works struggled to break away from his master's formal influence (*The Genius of Painting*, terracotta, 1886; Victoria and Albert Museum), those from 1895 to 1910 (*The Age of Innocence*, plaster, 1897; Victoria and Albert Museum) display attractive sculptural style and individual character. To be completely fair, it must be noted that Drury was also influenced by Alfred Stevens's work.[26] And finally Drury's position as a teacher at Goldsmiths' Institute in 1891 must surely indicate his continued liking for education.

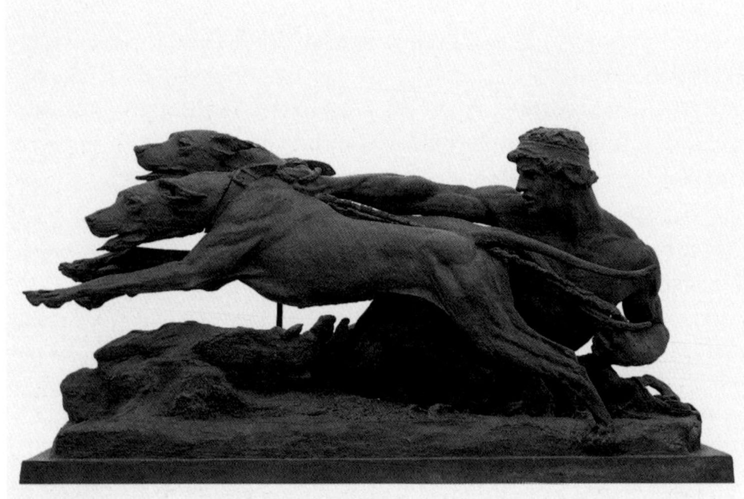

Harry Bates
Hounds in Leash 1888–9
Plaster patinated 116 × 220 × 108

Tate. Presented by Lord Wemyss 1899

A teaching method: the virtuoso demonstration

There are two ways to transmit knowledge: through speech or by setting an example. Dalou did not master English, as opposed to Lantéri, who did, but the two were virtuosos in modelling. Modelling 'demonstrations' were to make the French practice of teaching by example famous, especially at the National Art Training School.

Published witness accounts and a few rare objects (p.162) survive from the modelling sessions in which Dalou, and then Lantéri, demonstrate to their students the principles of constructing a figure in clay. In just an hour and a half they would create in clay on an armature the structure, planes and then details of a portrait from life. In 1902 Lantéri praised 'Dalou's marvellous rapidity of execution, and the telling and expressive touches so characteristic of him',[27] and I.G. McAllister would use the same words in relation to Lantéri.[28] No doubt one has to imagine the sessions as performances that attracted great numbers of aspiring sculptors and curious people; in 1888 Sparkes conceded to the committee investigating the decline in numbers of students at the National Art Training School: 'It is the glamour of a certain kind of teaching which attracts the students from here. In some cases the adoption of the French method had been an attraction.'[29]

The master's oeuvre: an example to follow?

Beyond the example-building method, the major impact of another public demonstration should not be neglected: the works that Dalou created and exhibited at the same time. His subjects taken from daily life, in his concern for a new contemporary realism, as well as his sensitive use of materials,

Edouard Lantéri
A Demonstration Bust
After 1 ¼ hours' work (a), and 4 hours' additional work (b)

From A. Lys Baldry, 'A Notable Sculptor: Alfred Drury ARA', The Studio, 1906, vol. xxxvii, p.84

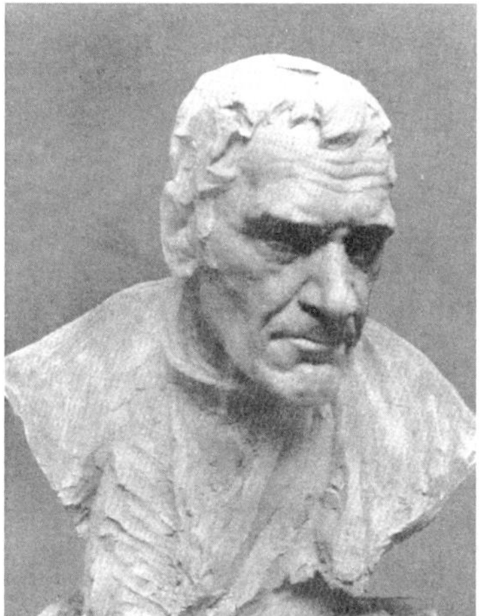

a

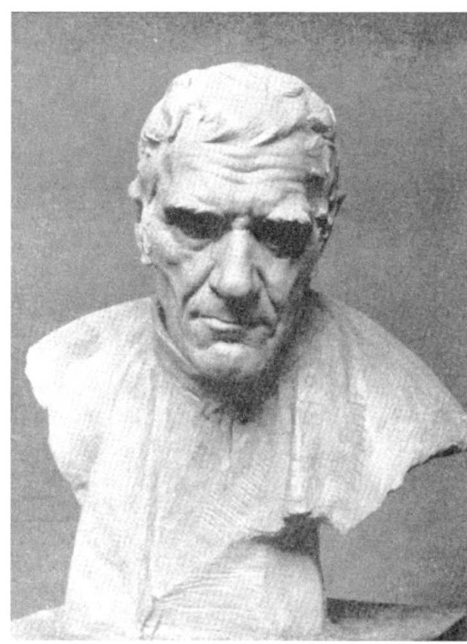

b

Alfred Gilbert
Icarus 1882–4
Bronze 49.5 × 21 × 15.9

Tate. Bequeathed by Frederick Harrison 1936

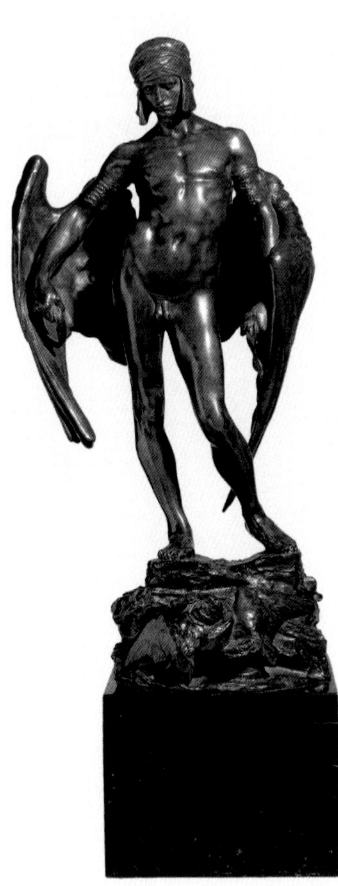

would distinguish him in the mid-1870s from his British peers. From *Palm Sunday in Boulogne* to *Woman from Boulogne Nursing a Baby* 1877 (National Gallery of Canada, Ottawa), the majority of his final works, even when large scale, are in terracotta. The art press welcomed the expressive touches of the modelled or carved clay surface, the skilfully rendered variations in texture, and the happy contrasts between finished and unfinished in the artists' busts.

A few years later this lesson in form would inspire the works of his New Sculpture followers: the fluidity of figures by Gilbert, Onslow Ford, Frampton and Pomeroy, which were elaborated first in clay but often translated into bronze, reflects, even indirectly, Dalou's very personal approach to clay with its plasticity and malleability. It would also combine with Leighton's, as in his *Athlete Wrestling with a Python* (p.163), exhibited in 1877 and a major stimulus for New Sculpture, and soon with Rodin's as well (*The Age of Bronze*, exhibited at the Salon of the Royal Academy in 1884). The quality of the cast, especially lost-wax casting, and of the chiselling made it possible for artists to maintain control of the desired final surface.

Teaching tailored to each student

Most of this tuition was not limited just to sculptural techniques, naturalist subjects or surface effects. Alfred Baldry wrote of Dalou: 'There was, as well, in his belief in the mission and purpose of sculpture, a firmness of conviction that was eminently satisfying to youthful aspirants who were seeking the right direction for the future expression of their own ideas.'[30] The teacher's authority and charisma were emphasised, as well as the fact that Dalou and Lantéri paid particular attention to their students' temperament, ideas, self-expression and individual qualities. Lantéri thus felt responsible for the career of his student Charles Sargeant Jagger.[31] Looking after the artist's individuality, as Lantéri's manuals repeatedly recommended, was also deeply embedded in the tradition of Lecoq de Boisbaudran's teaching.

The success of the instruction by the two sculptors whose careers we have examined relied mainly on a solid technique inherited from their French training. If today it is difficult to recognise the characteristics they have in common with their students, who only associated with them briefly during the course of a long and varied education, it is still possible to praise Dalou's and Lantéri's roles as trailblazers for a certain age group.[32] At the very beginning of the twentieth century, the sensitive, measured naturalism that Dalou helped introduce into British sculpture would be swept aside by the expressiveness of Rodin's works and, even more, by the sometimes radical choices of a new generation of British artists in full possession of their sculptural faculties.

Jules Dalou
1838–1902
Alphonse Legros c.1876 (1)
Painted plaster 51 h.

Victoria and Albert Museum, London
Gift of Mrs Knowles

Alphonse Legros
1837–1911
Portrait of M. J. Dalou, Sculptor
1876 (2)
Etching and drypoint on paper
25.2 × 16.5

Victoria and Albert Museum, London

Portrait of M. J. Dalou, Sculptor
1876
Etching and drypoint on paper
25.2 × 16.5

Private collection, France
[not illustrated]

Portrait of Jules Dalou c.1876 (3)
Graphite on paper 25.6 × 17

Private collection, Becker Estate

Charles B. Praetorius
1818–1900
Portrait of Jules Dalou after 1871 (4)
Albumen print 10.5 × 6
Private collection, Becker Estate

Jules Dalou mainly owed his warm welcome and means of subsistence, which facilitated his exile in London, to the painter Alphonse Legros, his old friend from the Petite Ecole in 1852–3. The latter is said to have sent Dalou his own passport when the sculptor had to flee Paris in haste.[1] He welcomed Dalou and his family whom he lodged as soon as they arrived in July 1871, and procured him work as a *praticien*, which was soon abandoned. As he had done for Guillaume Régamey and Jean-Charles Cazin, also former students at the Petite Ecole who had taken refuge in London at the same time, he introduced Dalou to his network of collectors – George Howard, Constantine Ionides, Sir Charles Dilke – who became Dalou's first clients. He was probably the one who acted as intermediary with their peers – Boehm, Leighton, Alma-Tadema, Poynter – this group of artists who had known the Parisian studios, who now held important positions in the London art world and ... who spoke French! Certainly it is due to Legros's benevolence that Dalou owes his first experiences and then his positions as a teacher.[2] There would be a few clashes between them, but nothing that would erase the memory of this strong friendship. Jules Dalou's inventory and post-mortem sale reflect how much space in his modest Parisian interior was occupied by his friend Legros's works.[3]

A measure of this friendship is that in 1876, each made a portrait of the other. The year is not insignificant: having been acting director in the place of Edward Poynter at the Slade School of Fine Arts since February 1876, Legros was officially appointed to the head of the school in July. Two versions are known of Dalou's portrait by Legros. The first portrait, a three-quarter view to the left (Bliss 40), of which the British Museum holds two states, is signed in the upper left. A series of states exist for the final more austere portrait in a three-quarter view to the right (Bliss 41) engraved in drypoint. An unpublished drawing preserved by Dalou is certainly preparatory to the second version; it is inverted in relation to the print. The definitive state, signed in the lower left, reprises the fairly spectacular arrangement adopted for other portraits of the same period by Legros, who was an excellent engraver: a detailed sculptural head with very dark hair and beard is perched on a triangular chest barely suggested by the white of the page in reserve and stands out from the background scratched with continuous horizontal stripes.[4]

Legros was proud enough of the result to offer two states in 1876 to the British Museum, which he passionately frequented. Dalou, who appreciated it, also kept two states (Becker estate). The sixth and last state was reproduced in May 1877 in the influential monthly, *The Portfolio*, published by the artist and critic Philip Gilbert Hamerton.[5] In the 1876 edition of his important work, *Etching and Etchers*, Hamerton had criticised the amateurism of Legros's technique as an etcher, all the while emphasising the general value of his contribution to the art of engraving on account of his 'strong mental gifts'.[6] From 1877 until Dalou's death, this portrait was the one most frequently chosen to depict the sculptor, along with the reproduction of Rodin's bust (pp.140–1).

The *head of Alphonse Legros* modelled by Dalou is all that remains of a bust portrait depicting the painter holding palette and brush. Dalou supposedly destroyed it, as he usually did when dissatisfied with his work. According to his biographer, the head, a terracotta fragment, was saved by his friend Edouard Lantéri.[7] A mould was then made from which Lantéri produced several copies in patinated plaster. One of them remains at the Slade – a just homage; in 1897 Lantéri gave another version to the Musée des Beaux-Arts in Dijon, Legros's native city. A third, shown here, was a gift from Mrs Guy Knowles to the National Gallery, London, in 1922. Since then, it has been transferred to the V&A collections.[8]

Finally, Dalou is the author of another portrait of Legros, a written portrait this time, drawn up in the same year. In *L'Art*, a Franco-British review published in French, Louis Decamps devoted several articles to the 'exhibition of works of art executed in black and white', which was held in the summer of 1876 at the Durand-Ruel Gallery, rue Le Pelletier in Paris. The first article, largely centred on etchings by Alphonse Legros, extensively cites a letter from an anonymous colleague, a Frenchman living in London, who recounts Legros's career and announces the appointment of his friend to the Slade.[9] The anonymity would be lifted later.[10] Dalou's text, filled with respect and admiration, is additional evidence of how close the two men were. ASi

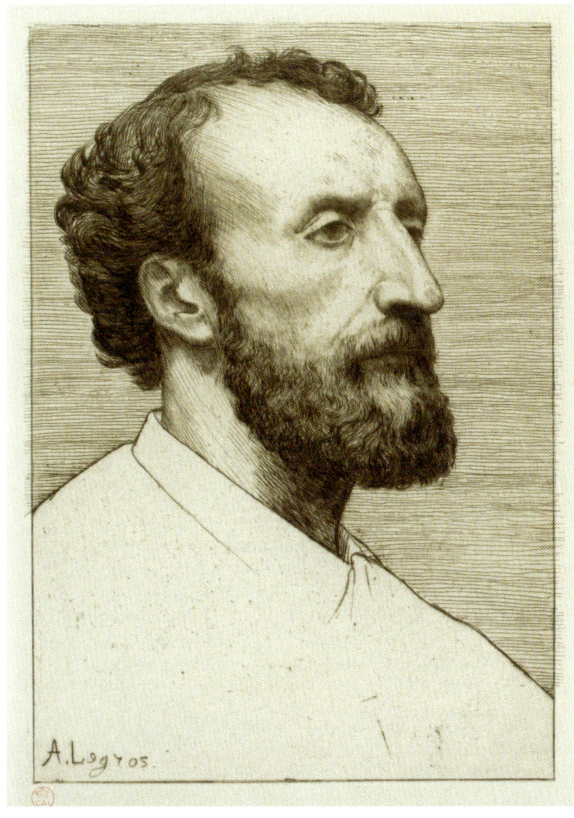

2

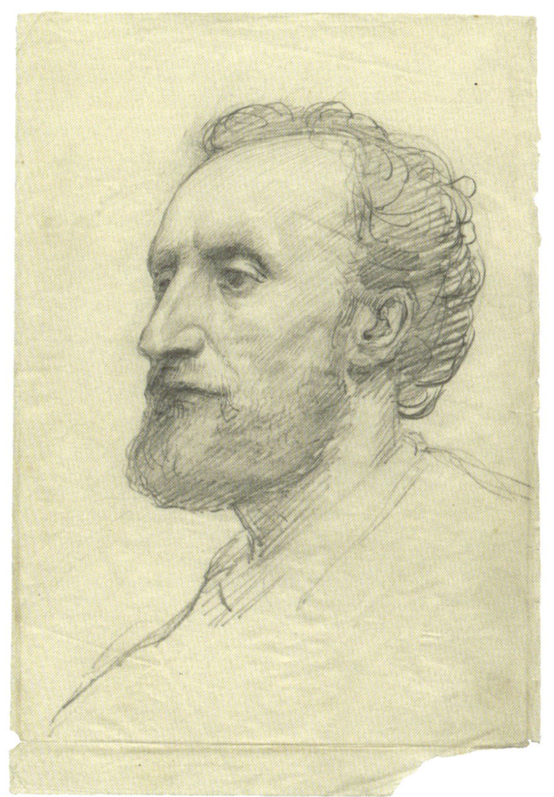

3

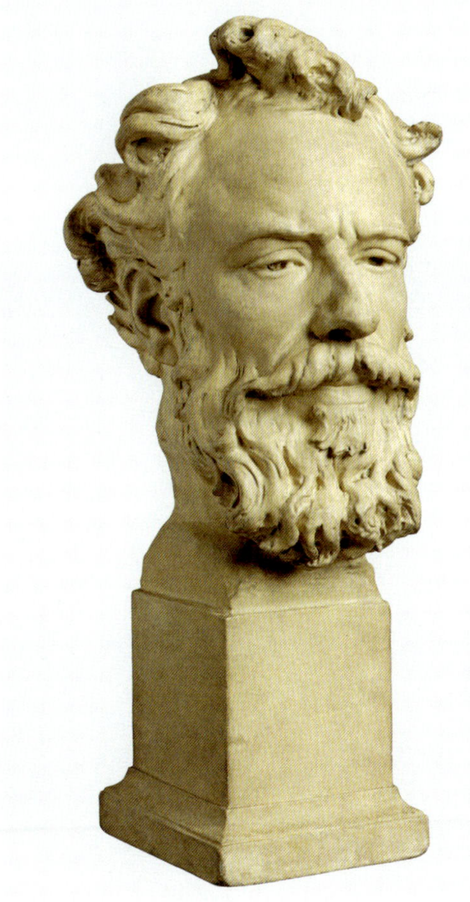

1

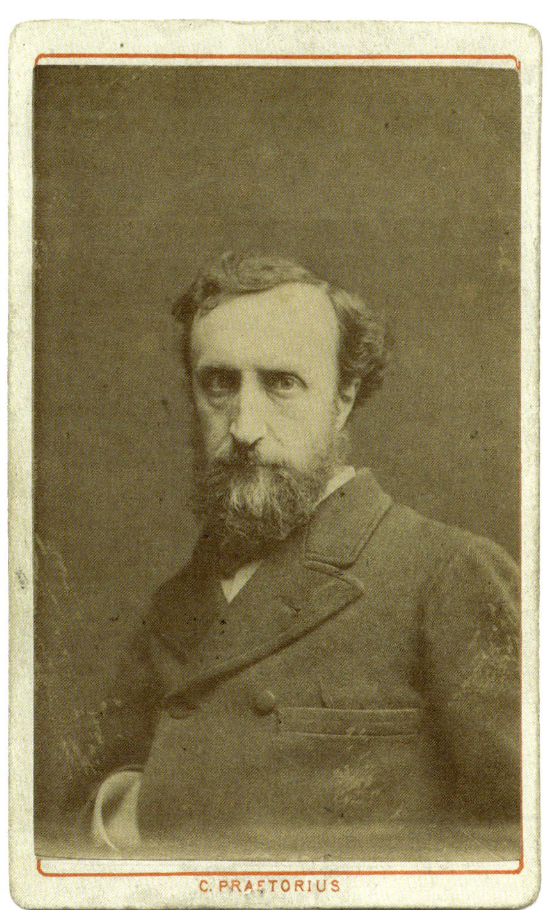

4

Jules Dalou
1838–1902
Palm Sunday in Boulogne,
or *Woman from Boulogne* 1872
Terracotta 65.5 × 21 × 21

The Castle Howard Collection

Draped in a cloak held by a double clasp, a young woman holds a missal in one hand. In the other is a sprig of boxwood that, in France, is taken to a Catholic church on Palm Sunday to be blessed in commemoration of the entry of Christ into Jerusalem. This scene of popular devotion is the first in a series of works by Dalou that met with much success in Great Britain and depicted peasant women praying, nursing babies or cradling children.

In some ways the sculpture is the descendant of romantic clay statuettes that the collector brought back from his travels: such is the case for the fisherwomen from the Pollet quarter in Dieppe fashioned by the Graillons in the 1850s and by Carpeaux in 1874. For the English, Boulogne, along with Dieppe, was one of the main ports for landing in France. Women's costumes in the region – such as the mantle (a large hooded cloak), headdresses and jewellery, especially the embossed silver clasp – as well as the religious practices of the sailors' wives, provided the artist with a picturesque repertoire. Alphonse Legros had made use of it in his painting since at least 1868,[1] and his trips back and forth to visit his mother in Boulogne in 1870 certainly fed his inspiration.

Yet, as in Legros's paintings, Dalou's young woman from Boulogne is endowed with a seriousness that is lacking in the picturesque figurines acquired while travelling. Its success was immediate. On 20 March 1872 George Howard, who had been brought to Dalou's studio by their mutual friend Legros, purchased the sculpture.[2] The same year, it was exhibited at the Royal Academy, and 'because women from Boulogne appealed to the public, he went to work making women from Boulogne'.

In the 1870s *Palm Sunday in Boulogne* was in fact the subject of a small set of reproductions in terracotta, of rougher construction, and were first acquired by the circle of artists who collected Dalou's work, such as Joseph Edgar Boehm and William Holman Hunt, as well as by a few collectors who were friends of the artist, such as J.H. Hutchinson.[4] This is the most documented case of terracotta reproductions, a practice that Dalou adopted exclusively for London (unlike Carpeaux or Carrier-Belleuse), probably because there he found the clay, qualified manpower, appropriate kilns and a clientele of collectors. ASi

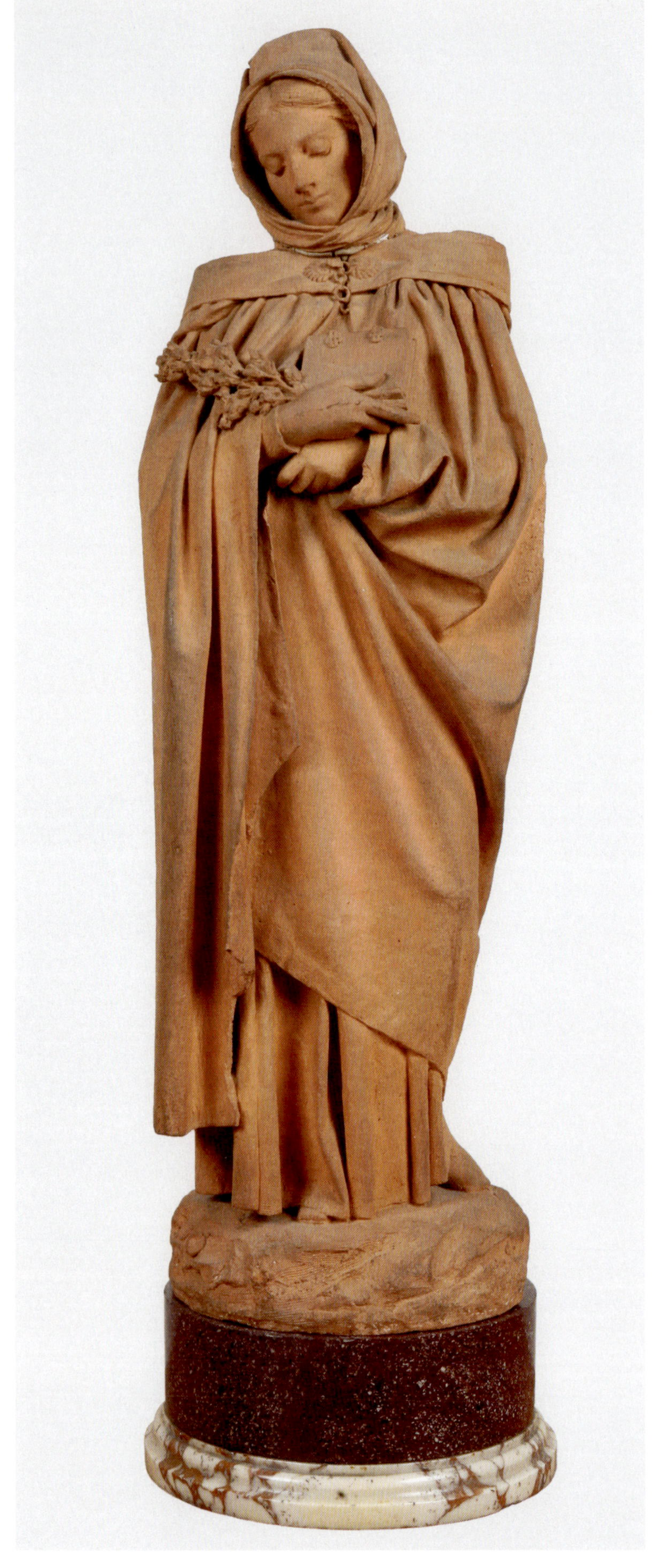

Jules Dalou
1838–1902
French Peasant Woman Nursing a Baby 1873
Terracotta 136.5 × 70 × 80

Victoria and Albert Museum, London

In spring 1873 Jules Dalou presented a spectacular terracotta to the Royal Academy, *French Peasant Woman Nursing a Baby*, a life-size free-standing sculpture depicting a robust young woman wearing a fichu, apron and wooden clogs. Seated on an upside-down wicker basket, she nurses an infant while gazing at it tenderly. The annual exhibition, conceived for painting, usually left little room for sculpture, but from the moment of his arrival, Dalou enjoyed preferential treatment.[1]

French Peasant Woman Nursing a Baby marked a turning point, as it was his first monumental terracotta. It is vividly shaped: the flesh is smooth, the fabric surfaces lively, and the peasant's wool dress contrasts with the infant's thick swaddling clothes. The execution in red clay is still experimental, and close inspection of the partially hollow sculpture reveals cracks that undoubtedly appeared during drying.[2] Four years later, the *Woman from Boulogne Nursing a Baby* 1877 (National Gallery of Canada, Ottawa), in a comparable format, also exhibited at the Royal Academy, displays perfect technical mastery. It seems that in the meantime Dalou had found the clay (finer and more elastic, less subject to shrinking), technique, assistants and kiln to be able to successfully carry out such work – a fact that is not very surprising, given the pre-eminence of terracotta industries, particularly ornamental ceramics, in Great Britain, especially London. The sculptural success of the *French Peasant Woman Nursing a Baby*, a modern, monumental *Virgin and Child*, is largely due to the idealised and timeless character that Dalou brought to the handling of an everyday subject.

The work was acquired on the spot for 300 guineas by Sir Coutts Lindsay of Balcarres, an amateur painter from a family of bankers. He financially supported *L'Art*, the review that followed Dalou's career closely. In 1877, with his wife Blanche, who was a watercolourist and rich heiress, Coutts Lindsay created the Grosvenor Gallery, a rival exhibition site to the Royal Academy. The work continued to be successful. Dalou made two slightly smaller replicas: one (Hermitage Museum, St Petersburg) was acquired by the future Tsar Alexander III during a visit to Dalou's studio in 1874, and the other (Victoria and Albert Museum) by James Staats Forbes, a collector of naturalist painters.[3] Lastly, in 1875 Linley Sambourne appropriated it for one of his caricatures in *Punch*: the peasant now represented the French republic trying to calm an infant capped with a Phrygian bonnet and brandishing a flag marked 'RED'.[4] ASi

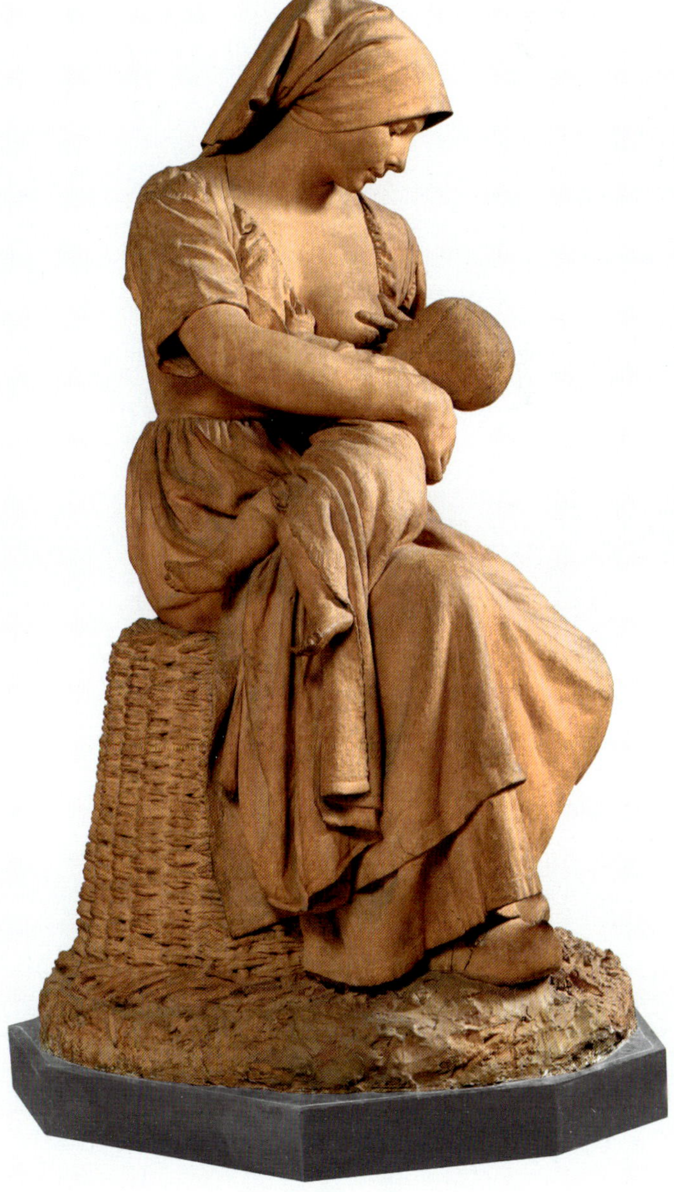

Jules Dalou
1838–1902
Rosalind Howard 1872
Bronze 52 × 40 × 44

The Castle Howard Collection

George Howard 1877
Terracotta 73 × 53 × 31

The Castle Howard Collection

In the 1870s, among British patrons of artists, the role of George Howard (1843–1911) merits attention. Descended from landed aristocracy, with properties in Cumberland and Yorkshire, he inherited the famous Castle Howard when he became the 9th Earl of Carlisle. A liberal Member of Parliament, he married a woman whose political engagement was stronger than his. He was a friend of the arts and artists, especially the Pre-Raphaelites, and he commissioned remarkable works. His house at 1 Palace Green in Kensington, London, built by Philip Webb, was completed in 1872. Its decoration was entrusted to William Morris and Edward Burne-Jones, who conceived of a *Cupid and Psyche* cycle for the dining room.[1] As a patron, Howard did not hesitate to buy works from artists in need and to support exhibitions that put them in the spotlight, and he would have a significant role in the creation of the Grosvenor Gallery. An artist himself, student of Burne-Jones, Nino Costa and then of Legros, he painted landscapes influenced by Italy, a favourite travel destination, and in 'Etruscan School' style, of which Leighton was another representative.

As both friend and collector, he frequented the select coterie of artists, of which Dalou – who was swiftly introduced to him by Legros – was a member: the Howard's residence was one of 'the richest houses and of the oldest nobility', in which the exile was proud to be received.[2]

On 20 March 1872 George Howard acquired *Palm Sunday* (p.152)[3]; the same year he commissioned a portrait of Rosalind Howard and their daughter Mary.[4] A short correspondence between Dalou and his patron is evidence of their friendly ties despite their social difference. Thanks to Howard, Dalou came into contact with other collectors from the same liberal aristocratic milieu.[5] In 1890 Dalou reminded Lord Carlisle again what he owed him, he whom 'ten years ago, you honoured with your friendship, you supported with your influence and who, having arrived in England in such sad condition, owes you a part of his favourable results and success'.[6]

George Howard's bust, exhibited at the Royal Academy in 1877, fits into the tradition of eighteenth-century artists' busts. Dalou depicted the aristocrat as a bohemian artist: a beret proudly jammed onto his hair and a hastily tied cravat enliven the respectable clothes. Clay, modelled with brio and sensitivity, is used as the final material. Contemporary critics only mentioned this bust – full of elegance – in passing, as they preferred to linger over Dalou's *Woman from Boulogne Nursing a Baby* 1877 (National Gallery of Canada, Ottawa) and especially Leighton's *Athlete Wrestling with a Python* (p.163). Only 'Talon Rouge', in *Vanity Fair*, stressed with reason, the influence of Dalou's teacher Carpeaux.[7]

The portrait of Rosalind Frances, the Honourable Mrs George Howard, is derived from *The Embroiderer*, Jules Dalou's Parisian success in the Salon of 1870: a seated woman is engaged in a daily activity, here that of reading, as is shown by the book on her lap and her pensive air. The terracotta seems to have been shown at the Royal Academy in 1873 at the same time as

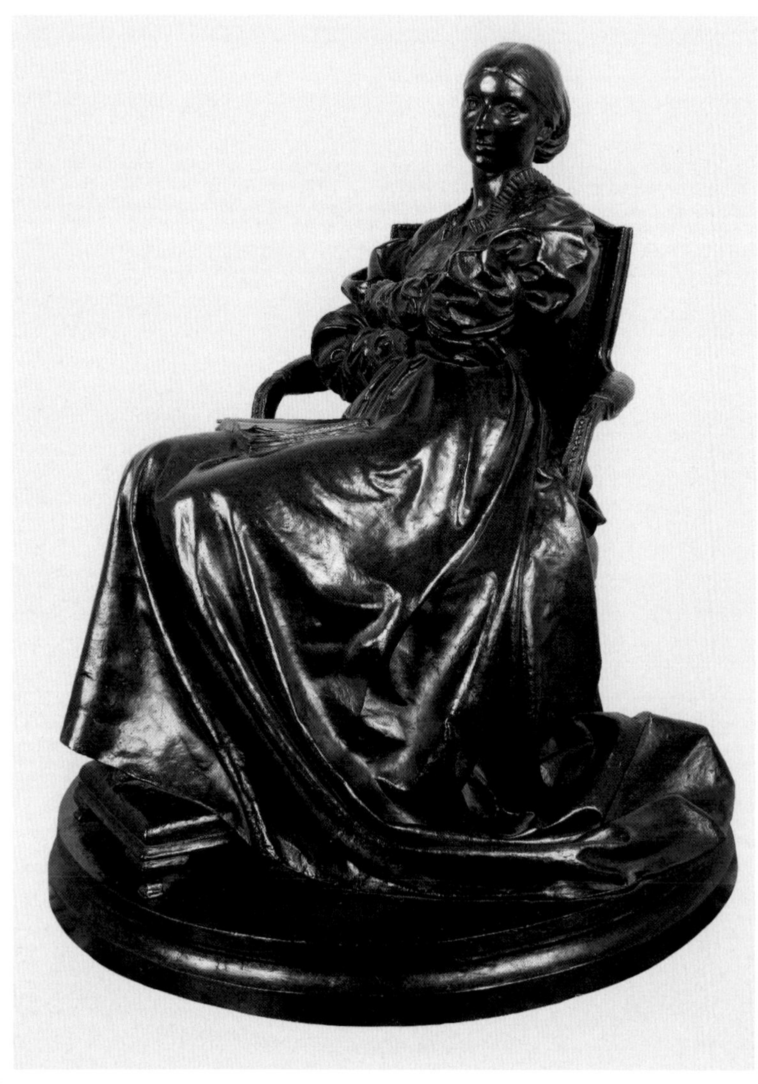

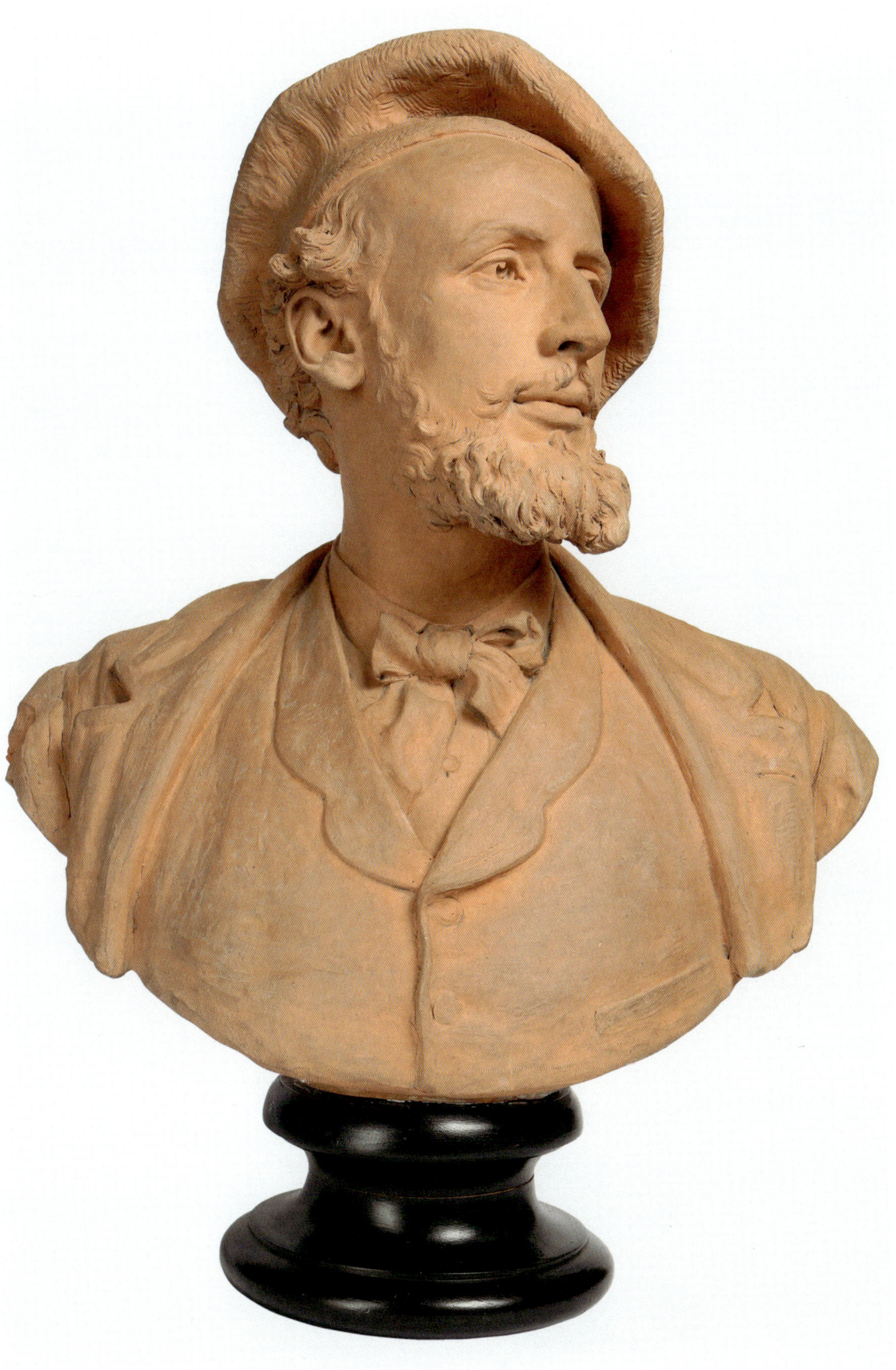

the charming clay portrait of their daughter Mary. The bronze exhibited here and conserved at Castle Howard bears the date of 1872 (probably that of the clay). The foundry owner to whom Dalou turned is not known;[8] perhaps it was cast later.

The political and social involvement of the headstrong Rosalind Howard, née Stanley, is well known.[9] Without a doubt, she shared the same ideals as the Dalous, including the moral value of work, and welcoming and protecting those in need, as well as equality between men and women. A woman reading was to be one of Dalou's favourite subjects in London. This portrait could be that of a reader of novels. But Rosalind, who managed the estate, and was an activist for women's rights, for those in the most humble conditions and against alcoholism, is depicted here as an intellectual and not in charming maternal scenes, a genre in which Dalou was a master. ASi

Lawrence Alma-Tadema
1836–1912
Jules Dalou, his Wife and Daughter
1876
Oil paint on canvas 61 × 30

Musée d'Orsay, Paris

Jules Dalou
1838–1902
Bust of Laura Theresa Epps, Lady Alma-Tadema 1875
Terracotta 69.1 × 49 × 26

Musée d'Orsay, Paris, gift of Anna and Lawrence Alma-Tadema, daughters of the painters, 1934

The painter Lawrence Alma-Tadema belonged to a circle of artists to whom Dalou was close during his exile in London. 'We were great friends, the three Dalous and the two Tademas,' wrote Tadema, when questioned by Léonce Bénédite in 1907, 'We liked each other very much, especially as artists.'[1] Dutch by birth, Alma-Tadema trained at the Antwerp Academy and under the painter Henri Leys. He was noticed in Paris at the Salon of 1864 by Ernest Gambart, a Belgian dealer established in London who exhibited three of his works in his French Gallery on Pall Mall in 1865. Gambart introduced him to the Pre-Raphaelite circle and to Legros with whom he became very close. Thus, when the Franco-Prussian War broke out, Tadema settled in London. In 1873 he was naturalised English, and in the same year was named an associate member of the Royal Academy. His first wife was French, and in 1934 Alma-Tadema's daughters, Laurence and Anna, in perfect French, offered a donation to the French nation of a bust of their stepmother, Laura Theresa Epps, the painter's second wife.[2] The couple's residence in the artistic area of St John's Wood also included a studio for Laura. A student of Ford Madox Brown, she exhibited at the Royal Academy and the Parisian Salon.

The bust of the very young woman is vividly modelled in pink clay characteristic of Dalou's busts during his English period, and according to a formula of a portrait on a black wood pedestal, which he preferred then. Her smooth youthful face is set off by the agitated handling of her undulating hair surmounted by an artful bun that Dalou used for his female sitters in the 1870s. The bust was exhibited at the Society of Artists in 1875.

As was often the case, Laura's bust and the lively portrait of the Dalou family by Alma-Tadema were the objects of a friendly exchange. The letter cited above reveals that 'Dalou had given me the terracotta bust in 1873, and had added the bust of my wife, also in terracotta ... in 1874. In 1876 I had the privilege of painting this friend, his wife, and child, and I always remember the pleasure that all of that was for us.' The pendant to Laura's bust, that of Lawrence, exhibited at the Royal Academy in 1874, was unfortunately 'smashed, alas! in a thousand pieces' in 1905, as Alma-Tadema reported to Bénédite.[3]

For his part, Lawrence Alma-Tadema chose to depict Jules Dalou, a cigarette in hand, close to his wife and daughter in a portrait full of tenderness. Obviously intended for the family circle, it is far removed from the large salon pictures rooted in archaeological study. Completed on 4 November 1876, the picture with its small intimate format also reflected the family's close bonds when exile separated them from

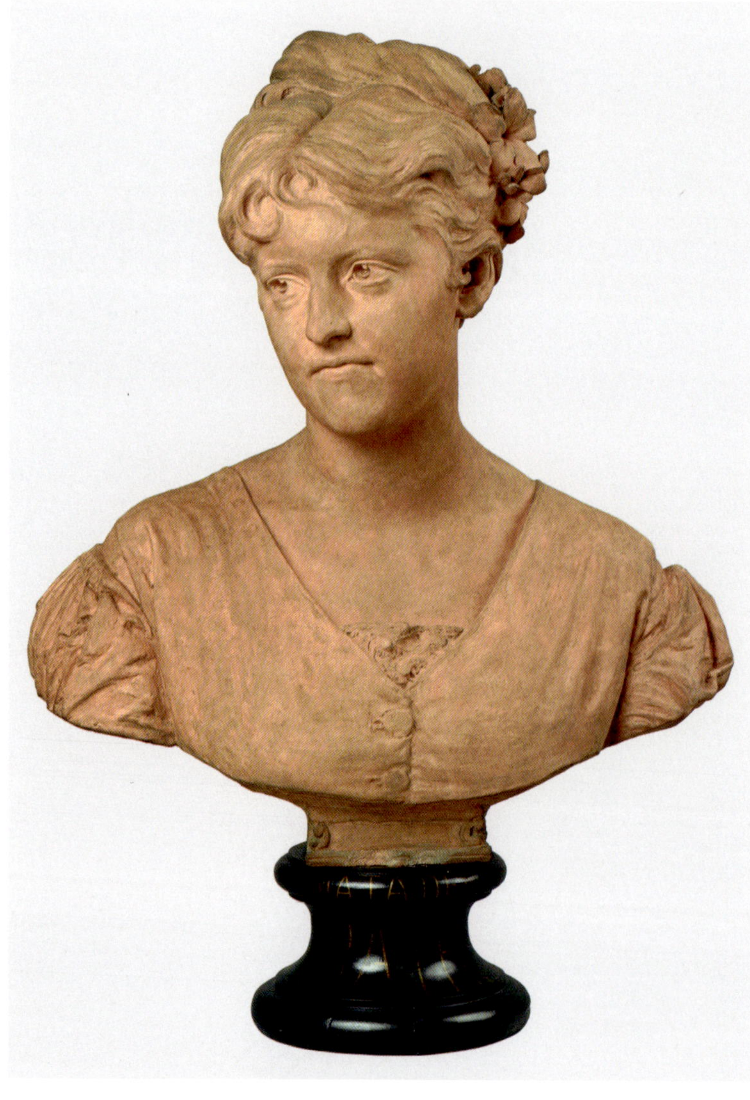

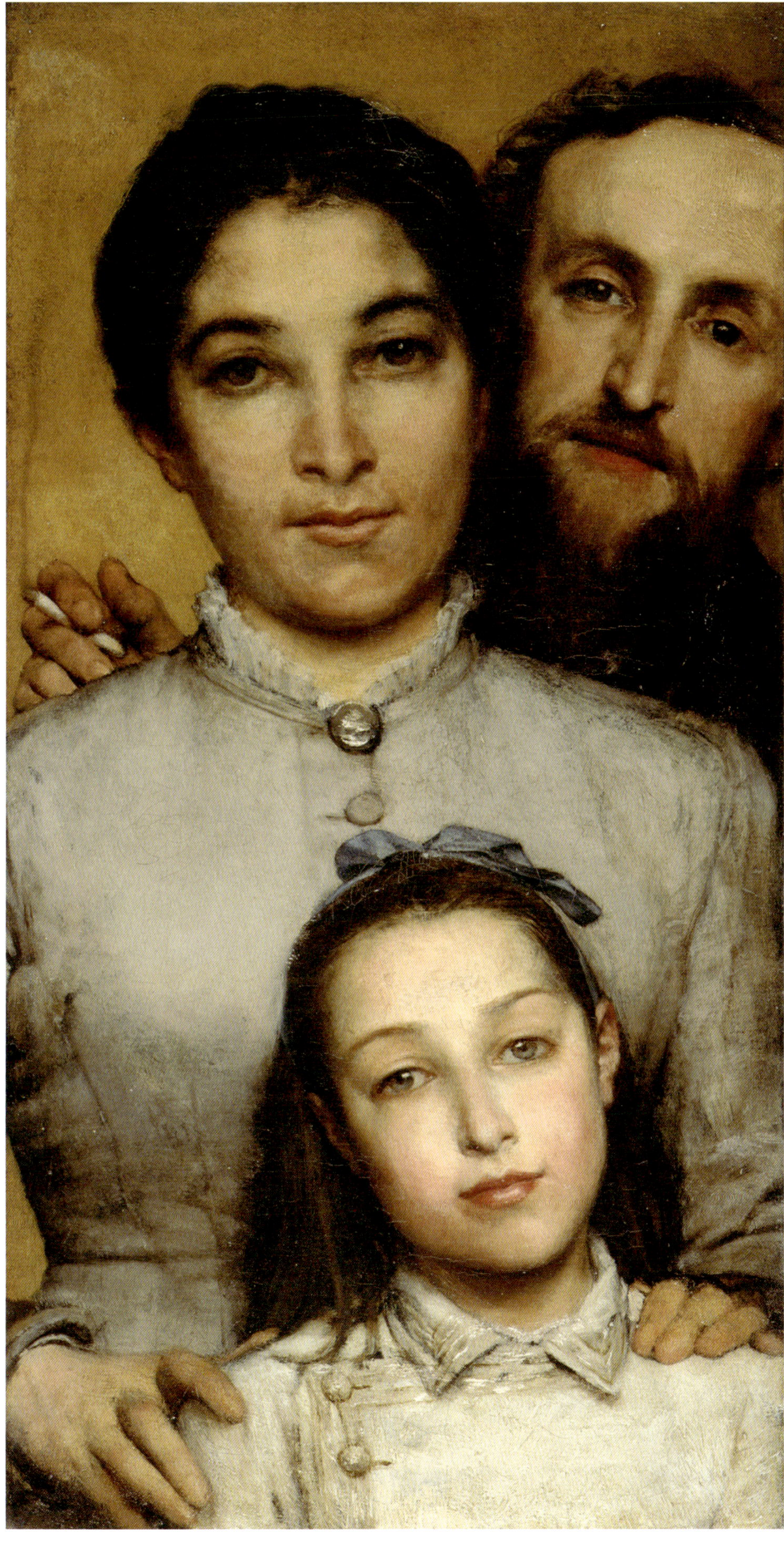

Parisian friends and neighbours. 'He was happy with my work and loaned it to my exhibition at the Grosvenor Gallery in 1883,' added Alma-Tadema.[4] The Dalou family treasured this portrait so much that, at the time of the sculptor's death, it hung in his wife's bedroom.

When acquiring this work for the French nation in 1906, Léonce Bénédite, then Director of the Musée du Luxembourg, paid explicit homage to Jules Dalou, while letting the first painting by Alma-Tadema enter a French public collection; he clearly hoped to benefit in the near future from a more important donation from the great British painter. In 1910 this happened with the *Roman Potter* (Musée d'Orsay), a fragment of a painting from 1884 that had been cut out and reworked by the artist, who offered it to the Musée du Luxembourg. ASi

Jules Dalou
1838–1902
Woman Reading in an Armchair (Mrs Dalou Reading) 1870s (1)
Pencil, pen and ink on paper
11.5 × 9

Private collection, Becker estate

English Sketchbook no.1 1874–7 (2)
Closed: 8 × 13 × 1

Private Collection, Becker estate

Woman Reading (Mrs Dalou Reading) 1877 (3)
Pencil, pen and ink, on a diary page
17.5 × 19

Private Collection, Becker estate

Woman Doing a Little Girl's Hair (Mrs Dalou and Georgette?) 1870s (4)
Pen and ink on paper 18.9 × 19.5

Private Collection, Becker estate

This group of drawn sketches, sometimes dashed onto loose leaves, sometimes in one of the little sketchbooks that never left Dalou's pocket, reveal the exile's domestic life in London. The sculptor brought them back to Paris (as opposed to many works created in London). After his death they were devotedly conserved by Dalou's *praticien* and friend Auguste Becker. Among them are young women reading, seated on upholstered furniture that seems typically British to French eyes – a chaise longue or wing chair similar to the one featured in *Meditation (Madame Monet on the Sofa)* (pp.68–9). Maurice Dreyfous, Dalou's friend and biographer, identified them as the portraits of Irma Dalou, née Vuillier, the sculptor's wife who, at the age of twenty-three, accompanied him into exile.

Irma was the ideal model, and the sculptor used these intimate sketches as a repertoire of forms. From them were produced a small group of statuettes that were much valued in London and then Paris, such as the *Woman Reading* purchased in 1877 by Constantine Ionides, one of the first collectors of Dalou's works.[1] When he returned to Paris in 1881, Dalou reused this composition in sandstone with a few variations. This was a perfect example of the 'little apartment statuettes', or 'little terracottas to keep the pot boiling',[2] as Dalou called them on a day when he was discouraged for he was only dreaming of ambitious works – that is, monumental ones.

The drawings implicitly reveal the solitary life of the companions of French refugee artist. The family lived enclosed in its own circle: Irma did the housework, looked after their daughter, whose health was frail, and took part in some evening parties with the Legros and de Nittis families, or at the Ionides's. If Dalou complained in his letters about having no close friends in London, what can one say about his wife who had left all of hers so as to follow him?

However, she was a strong woman. Dreyfous describes Irma, who came from a modest background, had been a seamstress before her marriage and liked reading, art, politics and discussions, as an ideal partner for the artist. She also guided his work and remarked in reference to a group of children entitled *Hide and Seek*: 'When one is strong enough to walk alone, one doesn't put on the shoes of Carrier-Belleuse.' And when Dalou was seeking inspiration for a 'bather' with eighteenth-century graces, she said, while 'pulling out a *Susannah* from a collection of Rembrandt images, "If I wanted to conceive of a Bather, this is what I would wish to look at."'[3] Throughout his life, Dalou would say she was his 'tutor'[4] as can be seen in a moving dedication on a photograph of his *French Peasant Woman* of 1873 (p.144): 'To the one who inspired this statue. J. Dalou. 1875.'[5] ASi

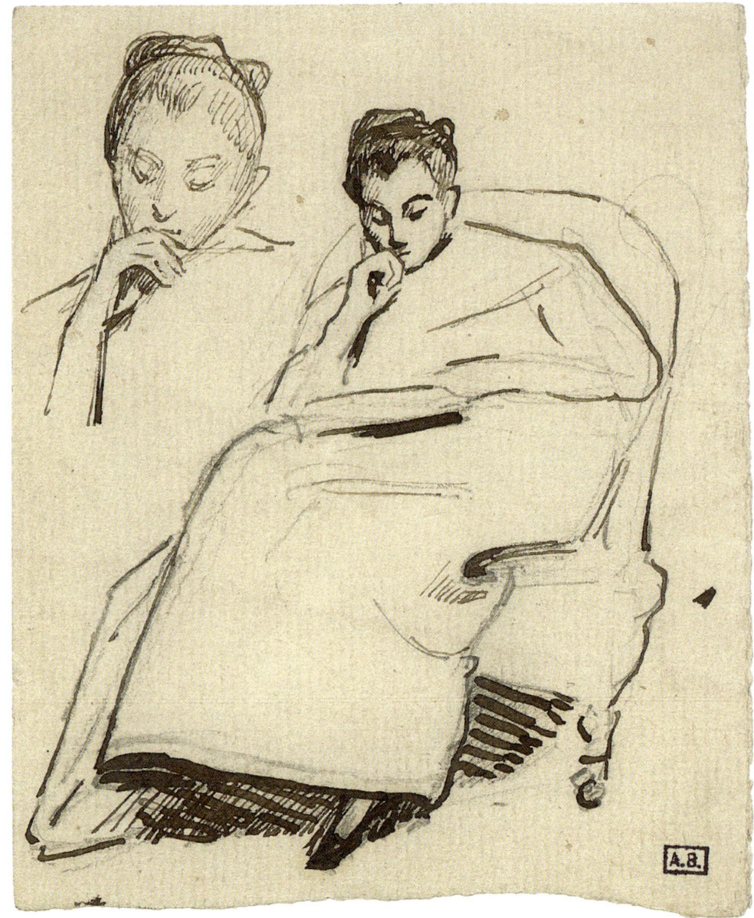

1

2

Juillet 1877
28. — Samedi. — Ste Anne. 209-156
Dimanche. — Ste Marthe. 210-155
Juillet 1877
30. — Lundi. — S. Abdon. 211-154
31. — Mardi. — S. Germain l'Aux. 212-153

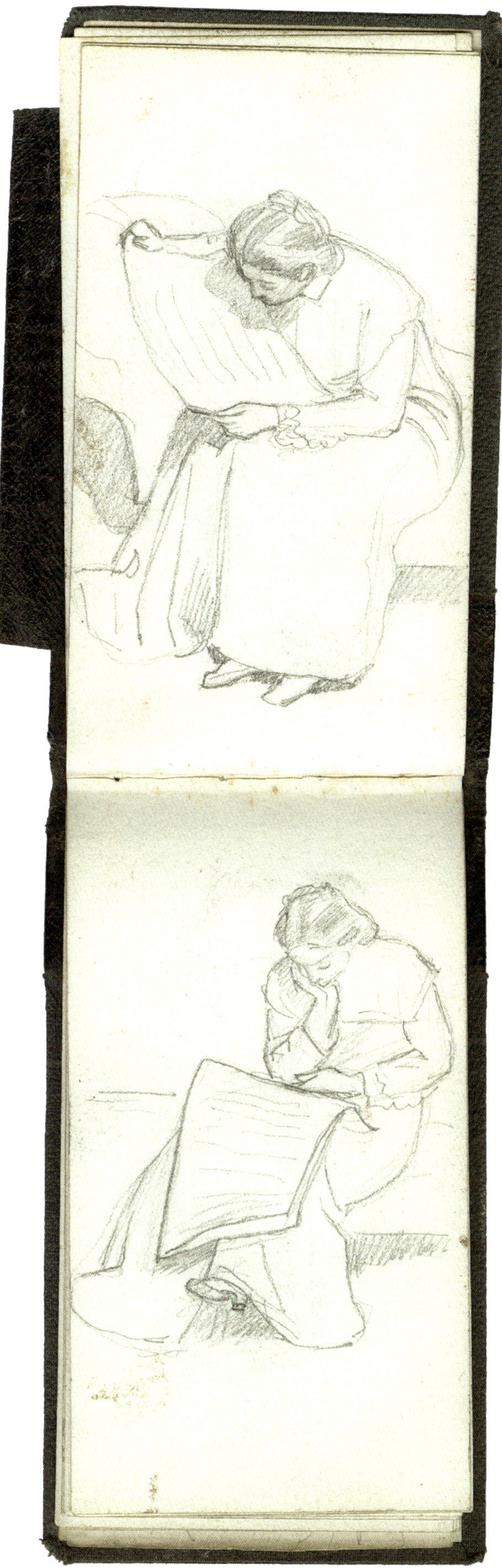

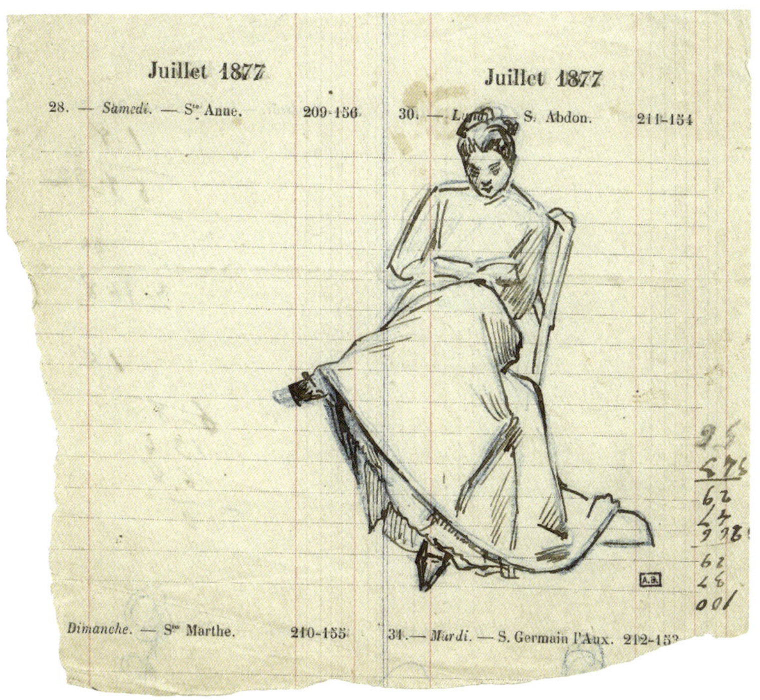

3

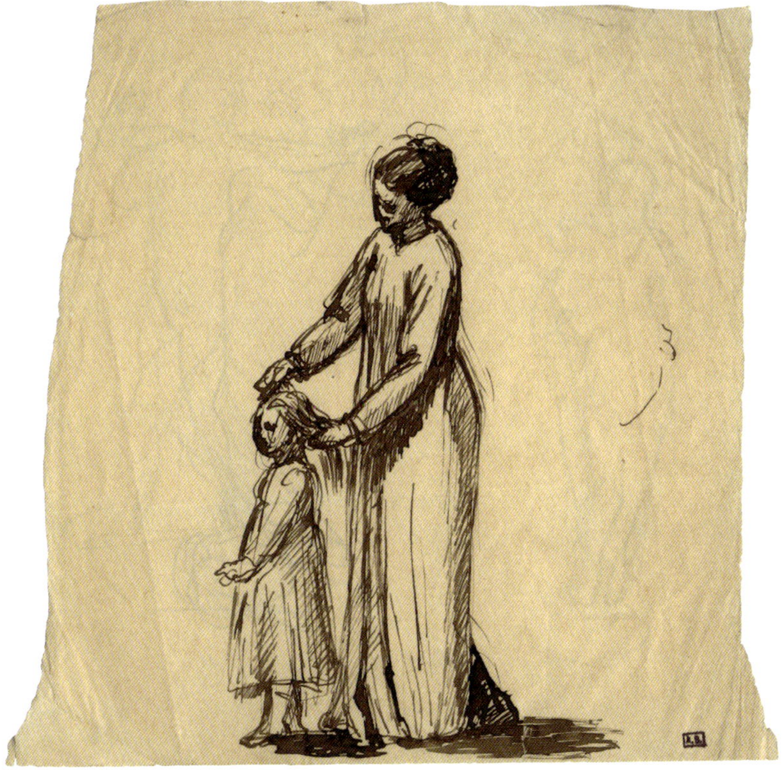

4

Jules Dalou
1838-1902
Hush-a-Bye, Baby, or *The Rocking Chair* 1875
Marble 116 × 105 × 64

Private collection

> Hush a bye baby on the tree top
> When the bough bends the cradle will rock

Every British person knows this nursery rhyme (though here slightly misquoted) engraved on the plinth of this charming group. In a sentimental scene that is well within Victorian taste in illustrations, a young mother croons her child to sleep. The young woman bears the features of Irma Dalou, the sculptor's wife; the baby's head is taken from a very sensitive life study that Dalou reused frequently, in particular for the monument to Queen Victoria's grandchildren.[1] Special care is given to details: the chair's upholstering is handled realistically, the striped velvet reproduced in marble contrasts well with the young mother's elegant dress.

Dalou exhibited the model for *Hush-a-Bye, Baby* in 1874 at the Royal Academy, at the same time as the busts of Frederic Leighton (untraced) and Lawrence Alma-Tadema (destroyed). A drawing dated the same year illustrates an article by John Dubouloz naming the patron who commissioned the marble as the 1st Duke of Westminster. Dubouloz's description indicates the work's key to success: 'One should not in the least seek a type of idealised woman ... The artist aims higher ... he has studied profoundly the blossoming of maternal feelings in an elite soul, and it is the incarnation of this saintly passion, motherly love, that he has taken as his mission to render in marble.'[2] Critics used the same terms in 1876 when Dalou exhibited the finished work in marble at the Royal Academy. The beauty, as well as the moral character of the subject, corresponded to the expectations of his British audience and Dalou was conscious of that. In 1879 he let slip a bitter comment: 'As long as I dealt with very sweet subjects here of gentle mothers and well-behaved infants, my hand was shaken affectionately.'[3] Periodicals especially gave visibility to this widely reproduced work.[4]

The aristocrats who collected Dalou's works came from a small circle of Whigs – Francophiles, travellers, collectors of foreign works. Hugh Lupus Grosvenor, the 1st Duke of Westminster and heir to large parts of Mayfair and Belgravia, played a key role in it.[5] Like George Howard (pp.154–5), who no doubt had introduced him to Dalou, he became interested in the works of the French sculptor very early. The 1st Duke was sensitive to the modern trend of intimate domestic naturalism conveyed by the artist, and *Hush-a-Bye, Baby* became part of a remarkable collection of contemporary sculpture. ASi

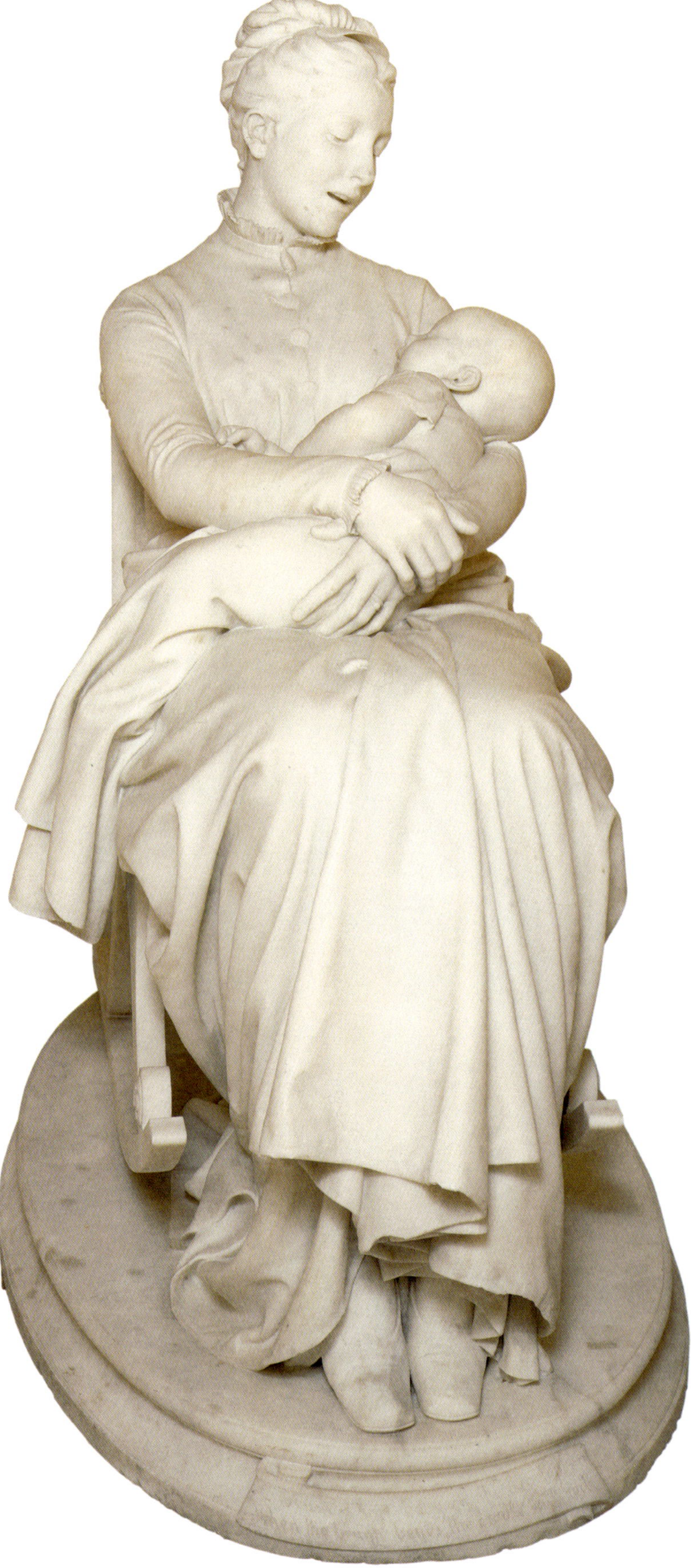

Jules Dalou
Arthur St Clair Anstruther Thomson
1877
Marble 114 × 40 × 38

National Museum of Scotland, Edinburgh

Young Arthur St Clair Anstruther Thomson was the seventh child of John Anstruther Thomson of Charleton and Carntyne,[1] a career soldier and Scottish landowner. A common passion for horses brought together Colonel Anstruther Thomson, a well-known master of fox hounds, and Joseph Edgar Boehm, a sculptor and gentleman whose brilliant career partially relied on equestrian statuettes of British high society. Boehm did a portrait of the colonel and his oldest son, and also gave lessons to one of his daughters.[2]

When he wished to commission a portrait of his youngest son, one can well imagine that Anstruther Thomson turned to Dalou, a remarkable observer of childhood, at the suggestion of their mutual friend Boehm. The precise circumstances of the commission are unknown. However, the sculptor's generosity towards his exiled colleague is unquestionable: hence in the same years, Boehm would act as Dalou's intermediary with one of his other clients, Thomas Baring, 1st Earl of Northbrook, for a marble group, *Hide and Seek* (untraced).[3] The French sculptor stayed in Scotland in 1877,[4] probably to observe his sitter and see the final position intended for the projected statue.

Little Arthur is portrayed standing, life-size, at the age of five, in white marble. The choice to represent the child nude, in a fashion inspired by ancient art, rather than in contemporary dress, is quite atypical of Dalou's British period, but apparently responds to a request by the patron to offer a pendant to an existing marble portrait of his wife, Caroline Maria Hamilton Gray, as a child. In it Maria was represented as Psyche, the lover of Eros, pensive and holding in one hand a butterfly, symbol of the soul, and in the other a drapery *à l'antique* veiling the lower part of her body.[5] It is an austere and rather stiff work by the Scottish neoclassical sculptor Lawrence MacDonald made in Rome in 1839.

Thirty-eight years later, Arthur, Maria's youngest son, is depicted as being as beautiful as a young god – perhaps an Eros. A commissioned portrait, the work is nonetheless conceived with remarkable sensitivity, which entirely revitalises the neoclassical formula by endowing it with movement that is full of life. The heroic ideal nudity of Arthur's body retains traces of childhood roundness. With his feet planted on a platform decorated with ripples and his hair flying in the wind like a conqueror, the little boy holds some shells in the folds of the drapery protecting his modesty; could this be a discreet allusion to the banks of the Firth of Forth, near the family residence of Charleton in the County of Fife?[6] ASi

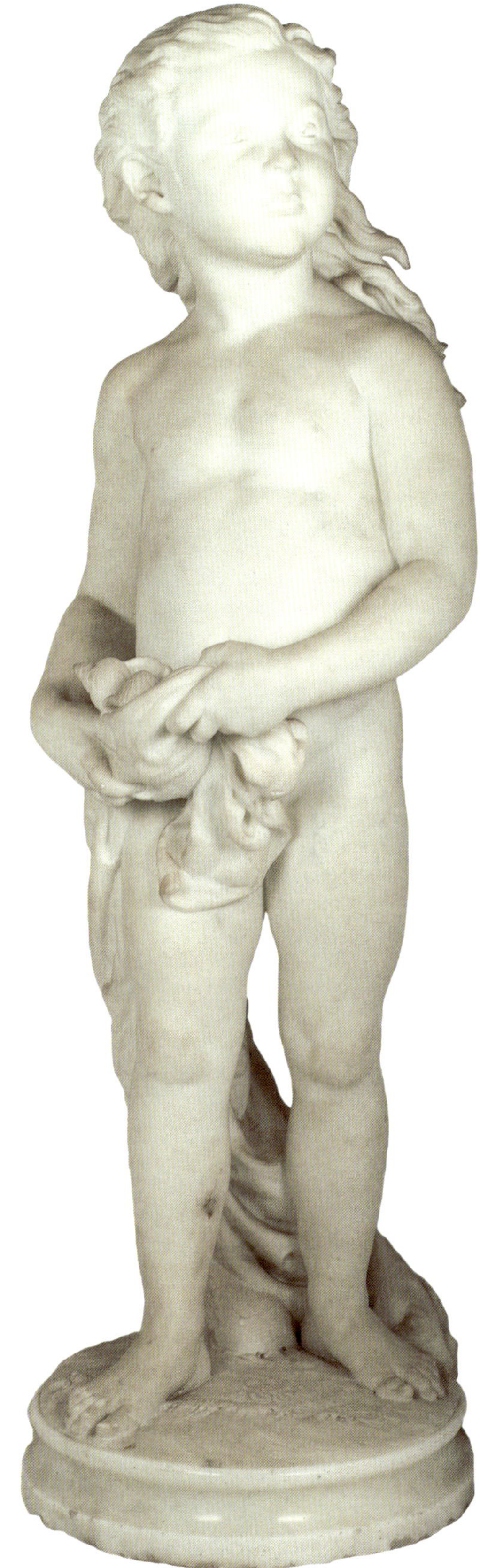

Jules Dalou
1838–1902
Bust of a Young Man 1877
Plaster 70 × 44 × 32

Private collection

Quite atypical among catalogued works by Jules Dalou, this bust is the result of a training exercise. It is said that it was modelled in clay by Professor Dalou in front of his students in 1877 (an inscription on the bronze example in Warsaw mentions the date 1876); once the modelling demonstration was finished, the clay, which was still fresh, should have been put back in the tub, but Alfred Drury, one of his students who was the closest to him (see p.148) supposedly preserved it by taking a mould on the spot; this original version would result from a mould made directly on the clay.[1]

A bronze cast was made of this bust in 1918: originally destined for the famous Kojiro Matsukata collection, it has been in the collection of the Warsaw Museum since 1971, having come from the Polish Embassy in London. A later bronze cast is in private hands. Also in 1918 a fragment of the bust, the head (William Morris Gallery, Walthamstow), was cast for the painter and engraver Frank Brangwyn, Alfred Drury's friend and Matsukata's adviser on his purchases.

The process of modelling, probably after a live model, was like a public performance. Dalou communicated with his hands, thus without speaking, as he produced a rapid sketch. This way of teaching bears the hallmark of Carpeaux's virtuoso lessons.[2] Dalou actually trained under him between 1850 and 1852 when Carpeaux was Assistant Master of Modelling at the Petite Ecole, and then entered his studio.

French artists active in Britain seemed to have been fond of this exercise, whose bravura made their reputations. Much evidence survives concerning similar sessions in drawing, painting and etching given by Alphonse Legros from 1876. A real performer, Legros did not hesitate to demonstrate his talents at the Slade, as well as at Liverpool and Cambridge. Seemingly, he asked Dalou to do the same, and his biographer recounts that Dalou punctuated his demonstrations with the magic phrase: 'You do so!'[3] An engraving by John Park, a student of Legros, survives in the British Museum and represents a study after a model by J. Dalou,[4] without question a bust modelled during similar exercises.

This bust is not a finished work. It was elaborated in one session, and one can barely distinguish Dalou's particular handling. However, as a study, it constitutes remarkable evidence of a specific mode of teaching whose purpose was above all to liberate the student's abilities. Alfred Drury, Dalou's student and then his assistant in Paris, carefully kept this relic from his youth, and was able to benefit from the master's instruction to become one of Britain's renowned sculptors of the early twentieth century. ASi

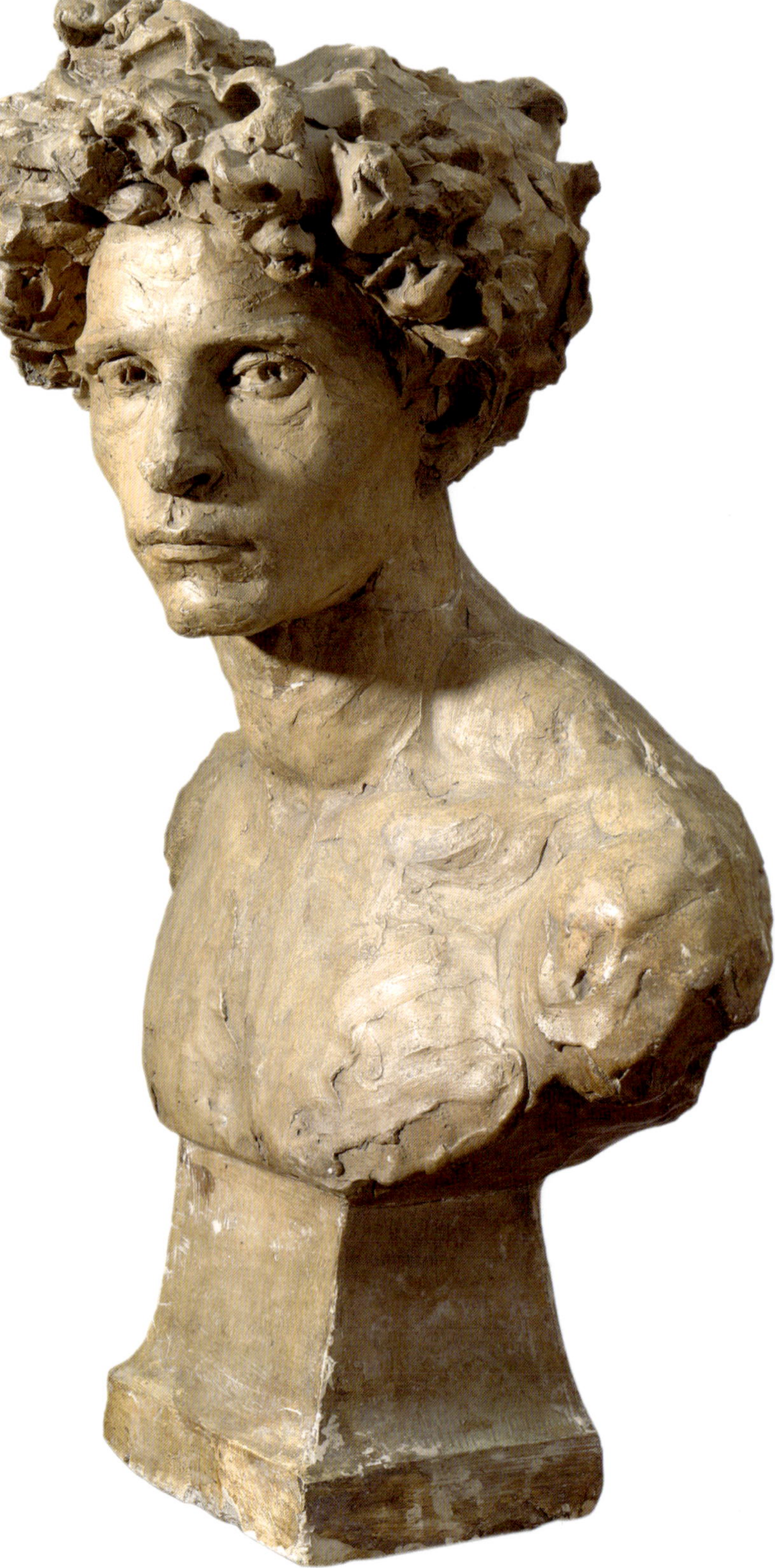

Sir Frederic Leighton
1830–1896
Sketch for '*An Athlete Wrestling with a Python*' c.1874
Plaster 25.1 × 15.6 × 13

Tate. Presented by Prof. Alphonse Legros 1897

The very first sculpture completed by Frederic Leighton, who was already an established painter, *An Athlete Wrestling with a Python* is a landmark in the history of British sculpture.[1] This sketch derives from a three-dimensional figurine that Leighton created to compose his most complex paintings, in this case *Daphnephoria* 1874–6 (Lady Lever Art Gallery, Liverpool). At the suggestion of Jules Dalou[2] or of Alphonse Legros,[3] the remarkable figural group was enlarged. The sculptor Thomas Brock supported the painter technically in order to produce this life-size sculpture. Studies from living models completed academic memories of one of the most famous statues from antiquity, the Belvedere *Laocoön*. Nonetheless, Leighton takes a radically different approach to this free-standing sculpture: the muscular body stretched to extremes demonstrates perfect anatomical mastery; differentiated treatment of the young man's flesh and the beast's scales reinforces the feeling of apprehension; the moment chosen – that of a fight to the death without knowing the result – prompts the viewer's terror; the complex construction of the scene plays on the serpent's coils to force one to look at the work from all sides. This tour de force proves Leighton's perfect understanding of what was at stake in sculpture, which he pushes to the extreme in tension, disequilibrium and rendering of the surface. Nothing could be better adapted to the fluidity of bronze.

Leighton exhibited this provocative manifesto at the Royal Academy in 1877, the same year that Dalou exhibited his *Woman from Boulogne Nursing a Baby*. Critical success was immediate, his peers' enthusiasm also. Dalou wrote to him: 'What good does it do to spend one's whole life scratching a piece of clay, when next door, all of a sudden, a masterpiece bursts from a hand to whom sculpture has until then been totally foreign?' And Boehm: 'It is superb. I think it is the best statue of modern days.'[4] The work was immediately purchased for the nation. The following year, Leighton would be appointed President of the Royal Academy and receive a gold medal for the statue at the Universal Exposition in Paris. The work would have a major impact on the generation of sculptors of 1875–80, and Leighton's interest in sculpture remained strong: he would make sure that young sculptors would be well represented at the Royal Academy.

The sketch presented here, a first idea for the famous work, is a studio work destined to delight connoisseurs. A plaster proof taken from the original clay, it retains the seam marks of the piece mould from which it was drawn. Several examples of this sketch circulated among Leighton's artistic circle. This one was a gift by Alphonse Legros to the Tate in 1897. ASi

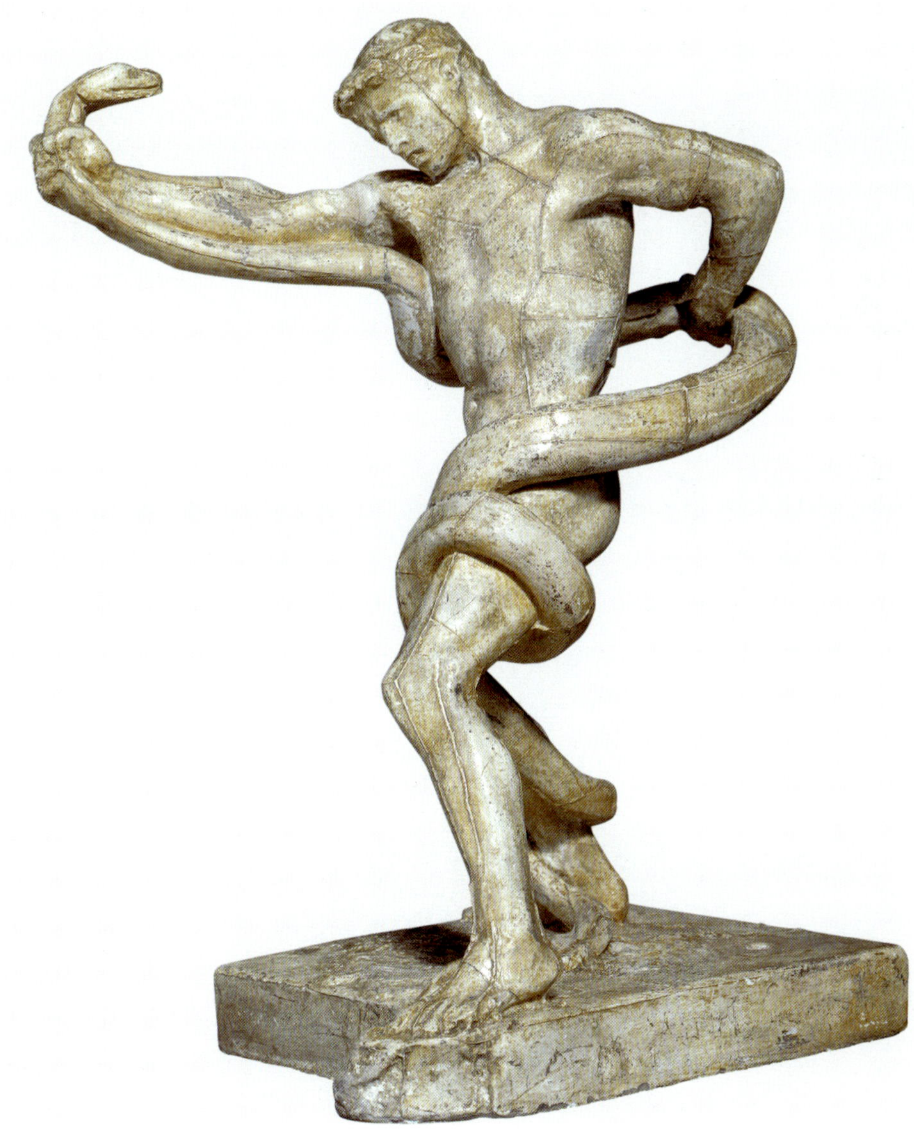

Jules Dalou
1838–1902
Italian Peasant 1889–98
Patinated plaster 43 × 28 × 23

Petit Palais, Musée des Beaux-Arts de la Ville de Paris

Within a few years of each other, on each side of the Channel, two sculptors who knew each other well – Edouard Lantéri living in London and Jules Dalou back in Paris – modelled worked-up portrait studies, clearly related, and said to be of peasants. The strong features of Dalou's *Italian Peasant* are comparable to those of Lantéri's *Head of a Peasant* (see pp.166–7).

The study from a live model posing for an artist belongs to the long process of a sculptor's work at the time. To conceive his dream of a monument to the glory of workers, which would never come to fruition, Dalou modelled a series of sketches to find the right gesture, and then he made repeated detailed studies – of heads, hands, implements, of nude then clothed figures, drawn and modelled, in relief and in the round.[1] The *Italian Peasant* belongs to a series of portrait types that were listed by name in the inventory of the contents of the sculptor's studio: *Breton Peasant*, *Lorrain Cart-Driver*, *Peasant Head*, *Bust of a Peasant Wearing a Smock*, etc. As Dalou never again left the Parisian area after his return from London, his models, whose identity is unknown, generally came and posed in the studio.

The title clearly indicates that it is one of the Italian models, as numerous in Paris as in London, who sat for him. The models were often originally from the poorest regions of Italy. Very different from the Italian youths with their smooth features so prized by Leighton and the Pre-Raphaelite painters, they were appreciated for the sculptural aspect of their faces and bodies marked by a hard life.

A full-length detailed study, *Large Peasant* 1897–1902 (original plaster, Petit Palais) – its title says everything – reuses this bust. Displaying a type rather than an individual, it has the same lowered furrowed face and hands covered with protruding veins. However, as previously in the *Peasant Woman Nursing a Baby* of 1873 (p.153), Dalou does not go any further with the realism of the depiction. Like Millet, he displays in this idealised, life-size figure the nobility of labour – that of the sculptor, someone who works with his hands, as do manual labourers and peasants, with whom he felt a distinct kinship. ASi

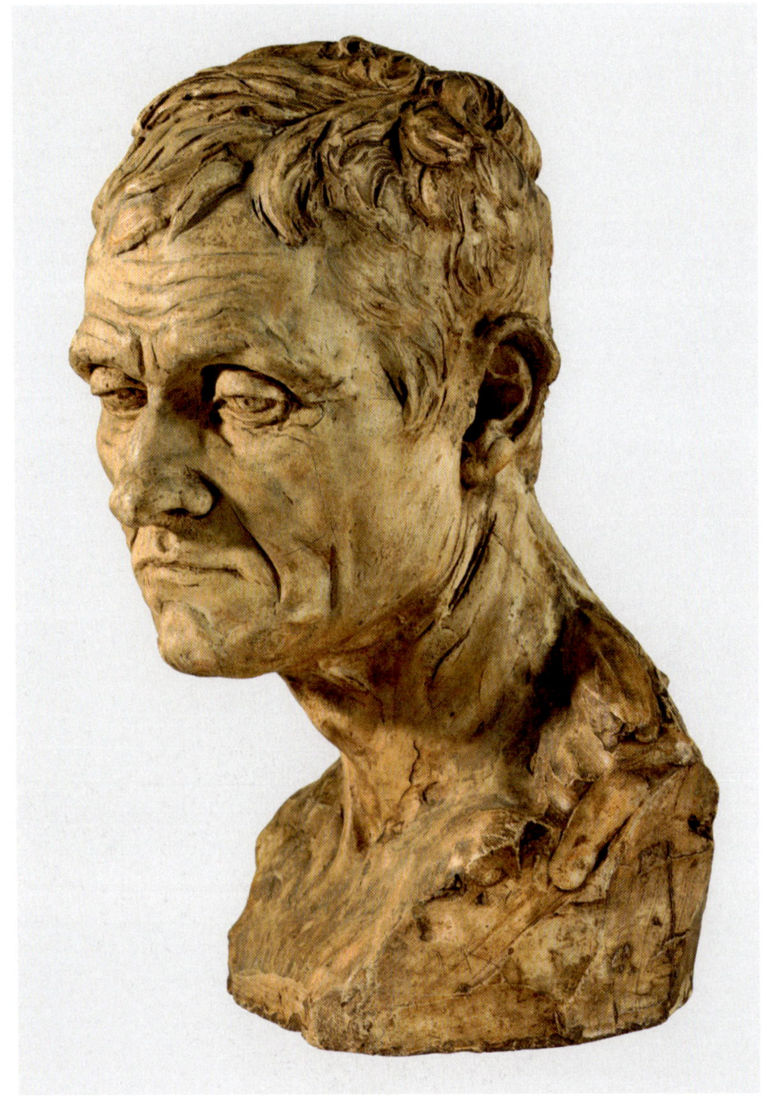

Alphonse Legros
1837–1911
Alfred Lord Tennyson c.1881
Bronze one-sided portrait medal
diam. 12

Victoria and Albert Museum, London

Legros came to modelling relatively late in his career, in his mid-forties. He was nevertheless quick to master this discipline and took charge of the modelling class at the Slade from 1883, or possibly even from the date of its inception at the school, in 1881. He designed this medal of the poet Alfred Tennyson in 1881 and had it cast in bronze in France, as was his custom.[1] This example in particular was donated just after Legros's death to the Tate Gallery by Constantine Ionides, who also owned the preparatory pencil drawing for the portrait (Victoria and Albert Museum, CA1 1128). As noted by Philip Attwood, Legros decided not to adorn the Poet Laureate with his customary laurel wreath – featured in the original drawing – 'to avoid weakening the vigour of the portrait'.[2]

Legros exhibited this medal alongside one of Charles Darwin in 1882, both at the Thibaudeau gallery and at the Royal Academy Summer Exhibition (no.1604), where they received great praise. *The Academy* reported that in these medals Legros 'has seized with great force the noble lines of their faces and the grand structure of their skulls' in 'adopting the style of the Italians of the Renaissance'.[3] The typography of the medal reveals Legros's weakness in that field, but alongside his friend Lantéri, he was credited for the renaissance of the medal in Britain in the 1880s.[4]

Even though Tennyson lived in Freshwater on the Isle of Wight, he was part of the Holland Park circle, like Legros, Constantine Ionides, George Howard, Edward Burne-Jones and George Frederic Watts, who also had a house there. One can speculate that Watts, as a loyal supporter of Legros and an intimate friend of Tennyson, was the link between artist and sitter, although there does not appear to be a record of how they met either in literature on Tennyson or Legros.[5] The latter also made a lithograph of the poet sporting a hat, in 1891. CCP

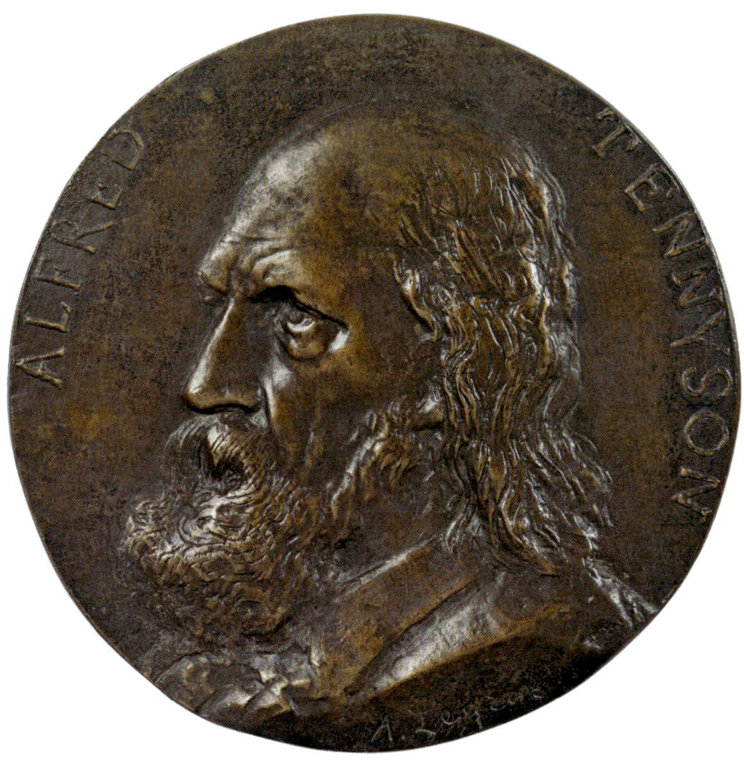

Edouard Lantéri
Proserpinae Cultor
1890
Bronze medal diam. 9.5

The British Museum, London

Sir Edgar Boehm
1891
Bronze medal diam. 11.8
(cast by Moore at Thames Ditton)

The British Museum, London

Modelling: A Guide for Teachers and Students

Pub. Chapman and Hall, London, 1902
Private collection
[not illustrated]

Head of a Peasant c.1901
Bronze 53.3 × 49.5 × 34.2

Tate. Presented by the artist's pupils 1902

Edouard Lantéri fought during the first battle of Châtillon in September 1870 and did not arrive on British soil until October 1872. In the aftermath of the war and Commune, work as a sculptor was scarce in Paris, and he had to take up cabinet making to survive. He did not come to Britain as a political exile, but simply to avoid poverty, and to resume his artistic career. He was encouraged to cross the channel by Jules Dalou, who supported him in all the ways that he could, thus emulating and extending the assistance that Legros had offered him the previous year. Dalou recommended Lantéri to the émigré sculptor Joseph Edgar Boehm, who hired him as his studio assistant, a position he kept until Boehm's death in 1890. As Mark Stocker noted, 'Boehm supported [Carpeaux and Dalou] in the face of artistic "racism", having suffered from this himself from chauvinistic and jealous critics',[1] and this generosity extended to Lantéri. In parallel to this, Lantéri succeeded Dalou as Master of Modelling at the National Art Training School in 1880,[2] an appointment referred to as the 'Dalou-Boehm' job by the critic Edmund Gosse.[3] It appears that, through Dalou, Lantéri immediately joined the inner circle of Legros, also a Burgundian. Like him, he would have a formative influence on several generations of British artists.

Perhaps even more so than Legros, Lantéri dedicated his life to teaching at the expense of his own artistic career. His method, *Modelling: A Guide for Teachers and Students*, is still in use today. Lantéri studied under the sculptors Aimé Millet, François-Joseph Duret, Eugène Guillaume and Pierre-Jules Cavelier, but he identified the teachings of Lecoq de Boisbaudran and their reliance on memory as decisive in his training. Lantéri's total devotion to his students is emphasised again and again in contemporary literature on him. As well as mentoring Alfred Gilbert (see p.169) Albert Toft, Francis Derwent-Wood and Charles S. Jagger were also dedicated pupils of Lantéri. One of his greatest legacies remains the method presented in his *Modelling* book.

Lantéri's *Head of a Peasant* is not a portrait as such. It was executed from life in front of his students as a demonstration bust in about four hours. It retains the quality and immediacy of his powerful modelling skills. *The Magazine of Art* recorded the prodigious rapidity at which he created this bust, publishing a photograph of the clay after an hour and a half of work and another one, presenting few further developments, after four hours (see p.149); the bust is also reproduced in his method. This testament to his practice highlights that his prodigious skills relied on a very thorough study and knowledge of the human anatomy. Marion Harry Spielmann identified *Head of a Peasant* as one of Lantéri's superior works, and – the term is not fortuitous – as 'one of [his] finest performances'.[4] Spielmann also referred to Lantéri's unsurpassed, 'extreme dexterity in the use of the

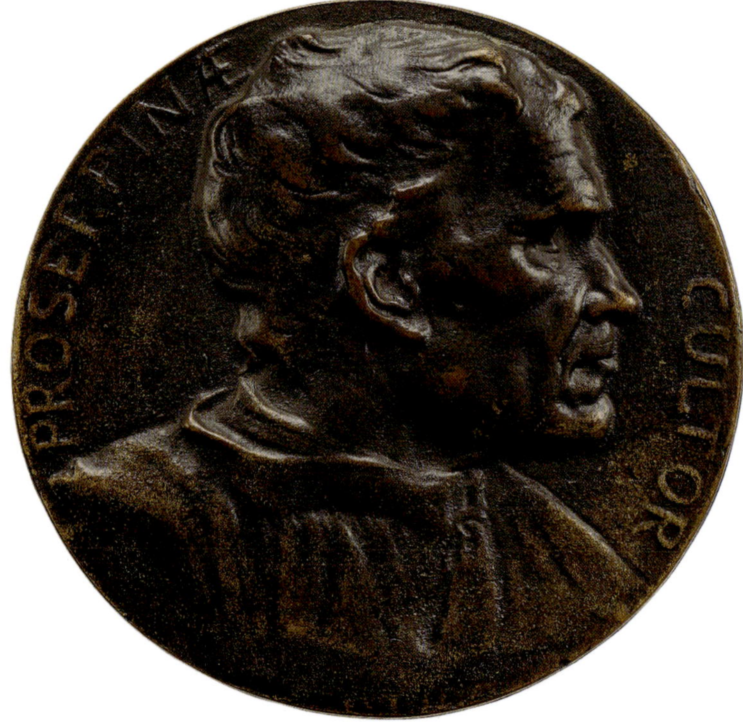

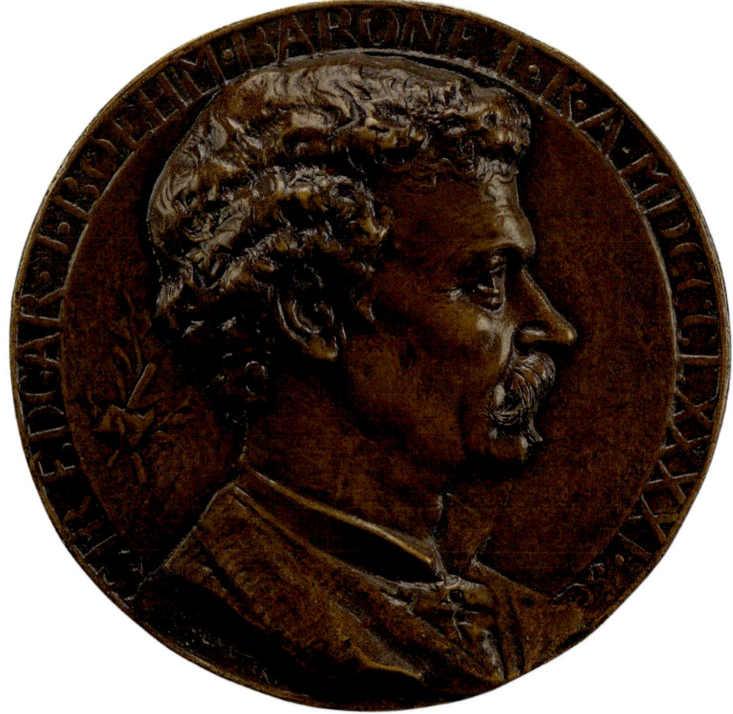

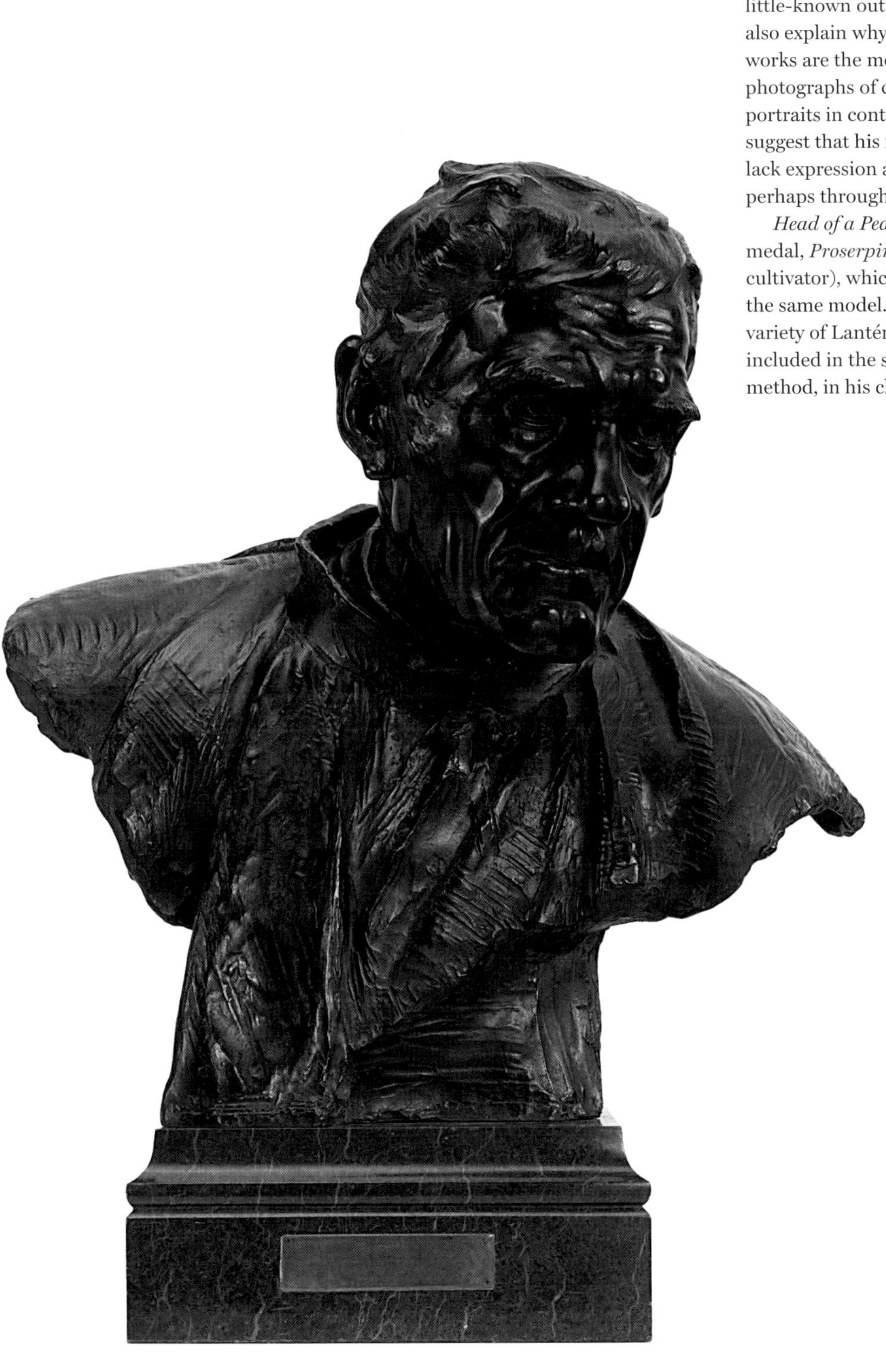

the clay',[5] hinting at the fact that he was a virtuoso rather than an artist of true genius. The bust was exhibited in plaster at the Royal Academy in 1901, and shortly after, Alphonse Legros gifted a bronze cast of it (untraced) to the Musée du Luxembourg in Paris. The present one was donated to the Tate Gallery by Lantéri's pupils in 1902. Marion Spielmann pointed out that the sculptor's perfectionism led him to destroy many of his works, which could also account for his relatively little-known output. This trait could also explain why his spontaneous works are the most accomplished: photographs of commissioned bust portraits in contemporary articles suggest that his more finished works lack expression and movement, perhaps through being overworked.

Head of a Peasant relates to a medal, *Proserpinae Cultor* (land cultivator), which visibly represents the same model. It highlights the variety of Lantéri's skills and is also included in the second volume of his method, in his chapter on medals.[6] Following introductory observations on Renaissance medals, each step of the creation of *Proserpinae Cultor* was photographed and reproduced in the method, from producing the wax model to making a plaster cast. Lantéri started working as a medallist in 1888, a few years later than his friend Legros and perhaps encouraged by him. It would appear that working on the same subjects both in the round and in relief became a regular practice for Lantéri,[7] who also did an 'animated statuette bust' of Boehm.[8] His medal was modelled from life, in high relief, shortly before Boehm's death in December 1890. Boehm's jacket, collar and hair particularly stand out, while his moustache and protruding veins on his temple and neck demonstrate a great degree of detailing. To the left, Lantéri added a mallet as a symbol of Boehm's art, as well as laurels to underline his successful career. The medal was cast in bronze by James Moore at the Thames Ditton foundry in 1891.[9]
CCP

Jules Dalou
1838–1902
Fraternity c.1878–9
Terracotta 51 × 34 × 10

Petit Palais, Musée des Beaux-Arts de la Ville de Paris

On 17 January 1882 Jules Dalou wrote to Joseph Boehm, his friend and English colleague:

> I hope to exhibit this year, the first time in Paris since 1870, it is a big deal for me because I have no doubt that the critics won't spare me ... The object is a large bas-relief of about 15 feet high and 9 feet wide, a republican subject, in fashion here and in my feelings, I want to leave it as a surprise for you as you must come.[1]

The sculptor's master stroke, this relief is a vibrant homage to the republic and its ideals of fraternity. It was exhibited at the same time as a horizontal relief, *Mirabeau Answering Dreux-Brézé*, and won its creator the Medal of Honour at the Salon of 1883.[2] Almost 4.4 metres high, the original plaster of *Fraternity*, acquired by the City of Paris, is today in the town hall of the 10th arrondissement, and the *Mirabeau* in bronze was commissioned by the state in 1881 for the Deputies' Chamber, which shows how far the exile had come since his return to Paris.

This lively sketch, one tenth of the final scale, swiftly manages to establish the composition of a complex relief. Edouard Lantéri described this step in his modelling manual as a 'rough sketch of composition' or 'general effect of composition'.[3] The relief is immediately organised on two levels: one is terrestrial, the other celestial, as in Rubens's altarpieces that Dalou had admired in Antwerp in 1875. In the lower level the composition fans out around a high relief of two men embracing, based on a motif by Pierre Puget (1620–1694), the sculptor from Marseilles who, along with Carpeaux, was another great role model for Dalou. The whole piece is sensitively modelled in light pink clay characteristic of his years in London.

'I also hope to make you see that I have not wasted my time and that I did not become a total cretin in England,' Dalou wrote to his close friend, the actor Ernest Cornaglia, in 1879.[4] The note is harsh about the English works, but without question, this sketch proves that exile allowed Dalou, while far from French competition, to develop a very personal style and to make new statements in sculpture. ASi

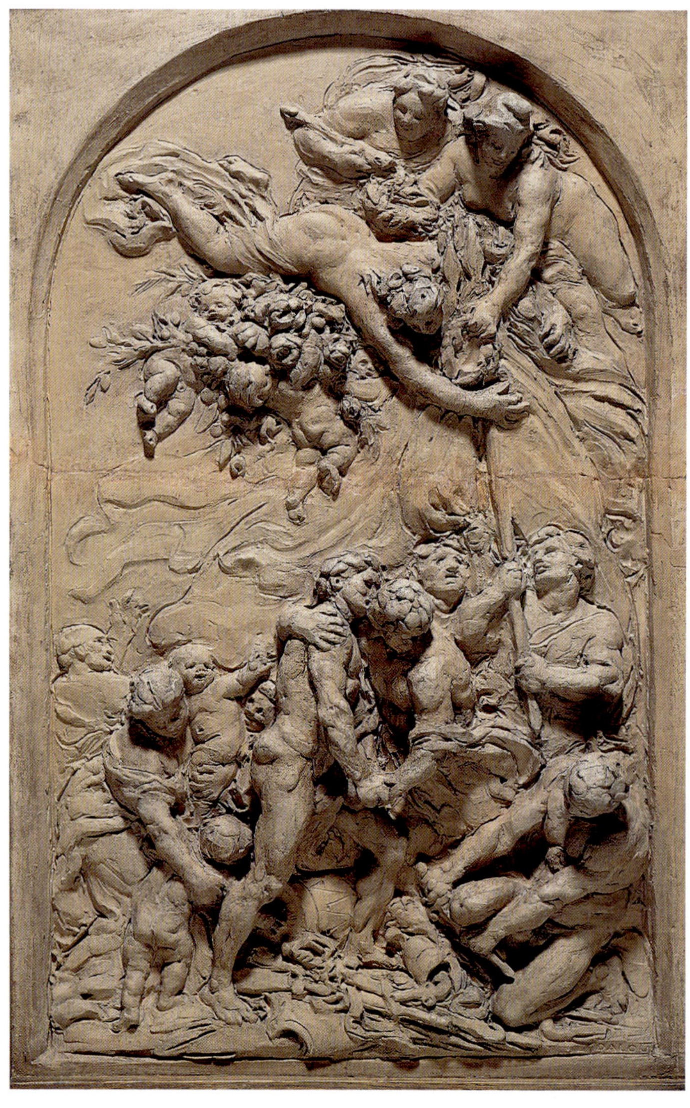

Alfred Gilbert
1854–1934
George Frederic Watts, O.M., R.A.
1888–9
Bronze 58.4 × 58.4 × 36.8

Tate. Presented by Mrs Watts by the wish of the late George Frederic Watts 1904

Eighteen sittings were necessary for Gilbert to make this bust of the artist G.F. Watts. Commissioned by Watts's wife Mary, the bust was begun in August 1888 at the painter's own studio at Little Holland House, and his enigmatic charisma meant that Gilbert found it challenging to achieve a good characterisation. The numerous sittings may also be due to the fact that he enjoyed Watts's company. The bust was exhibited in plaster at the Royal Academy in 1889,[1] where it was widely acclaimed and singled out in reviews for its expert modelling. The *Pall Mall Gazette* reported: 'The bust is in its pose and likeness as true to life as it is unconventional in treatment. The handling is remarkable for its breadth and facility.'[2] As Mary recorded in her reminiscences, 'Sir Frederic Leighton gave it high praise ... I remember his passing his hands over the planes of the cheek-bone and then to the planes of the coat, saying "It could not be better", and Signor [Watts] agreed with him ... and they congratulated each other on the disappearance of the bathing-towel from the shoulders of a modern bust.'[3] The bust was cast in bronze in the winter of 1889, and Gilbert categorically refused payment.

For all its vigour and expressiveness, this relatively early bust is not indicative of Gilbert's more animated mature style. Richard Dorment described it as 'a highly competent exercise in the Boehm style of portraiture'.[4] While Gilbert's time in Boehm's studio was surely formative, he himself acknowledged his greater debt to Edouard Lantéri, Boehm's first assistant and Gilbert's much loved teacher at the National Art Training School. His mentoring of Gilbert was highlighted by an examiner to the National Art Competition in 1882: 'A gold medal was awarded [to Gilbert] for a study of the figure from life of the South Kensington School, where the teaching of modelling is generally regarded as being of the highest character, a feature undoubtedly witnessed in Gilbert's piece.'[5] While his bust of Watts is indicative of Lantéri's impact on Gilbert's own development, it is not derivative as such. As Gilbert put it in an homage to his former master: 'Fate decreed that this man of infinite sensibility, subtle imagination and inflexible will ... should sink all to benefit others by teaching them how to express themselves.'[6] CCP

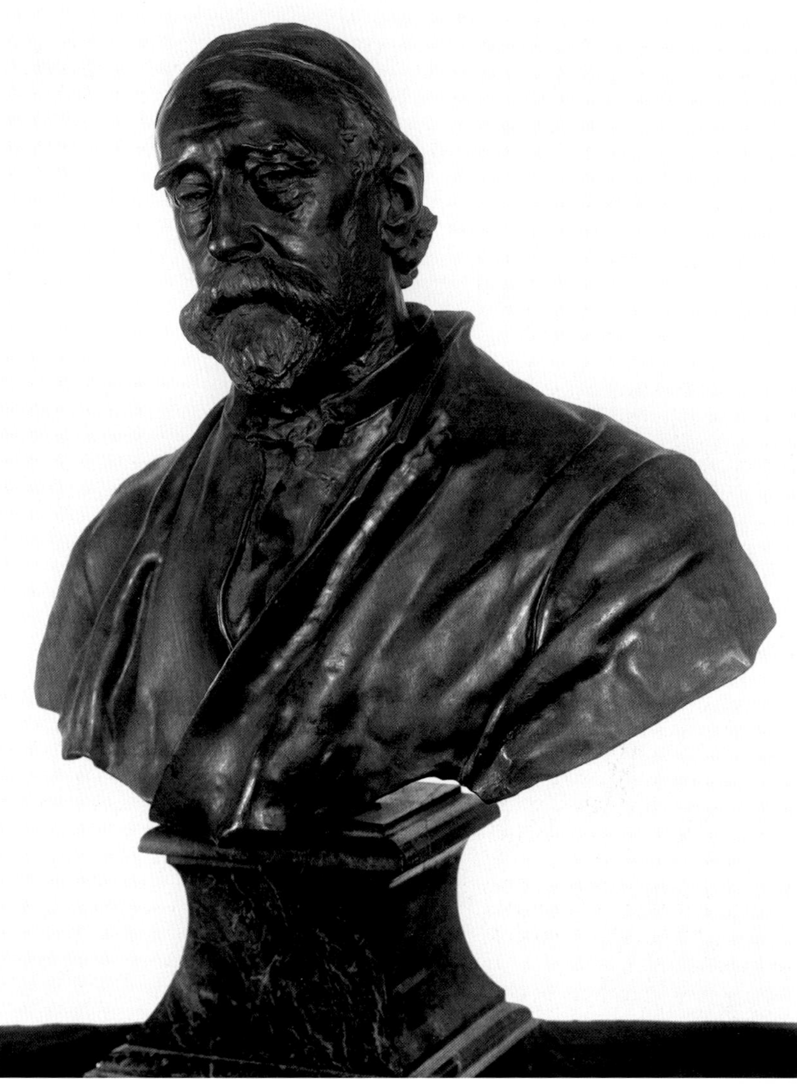

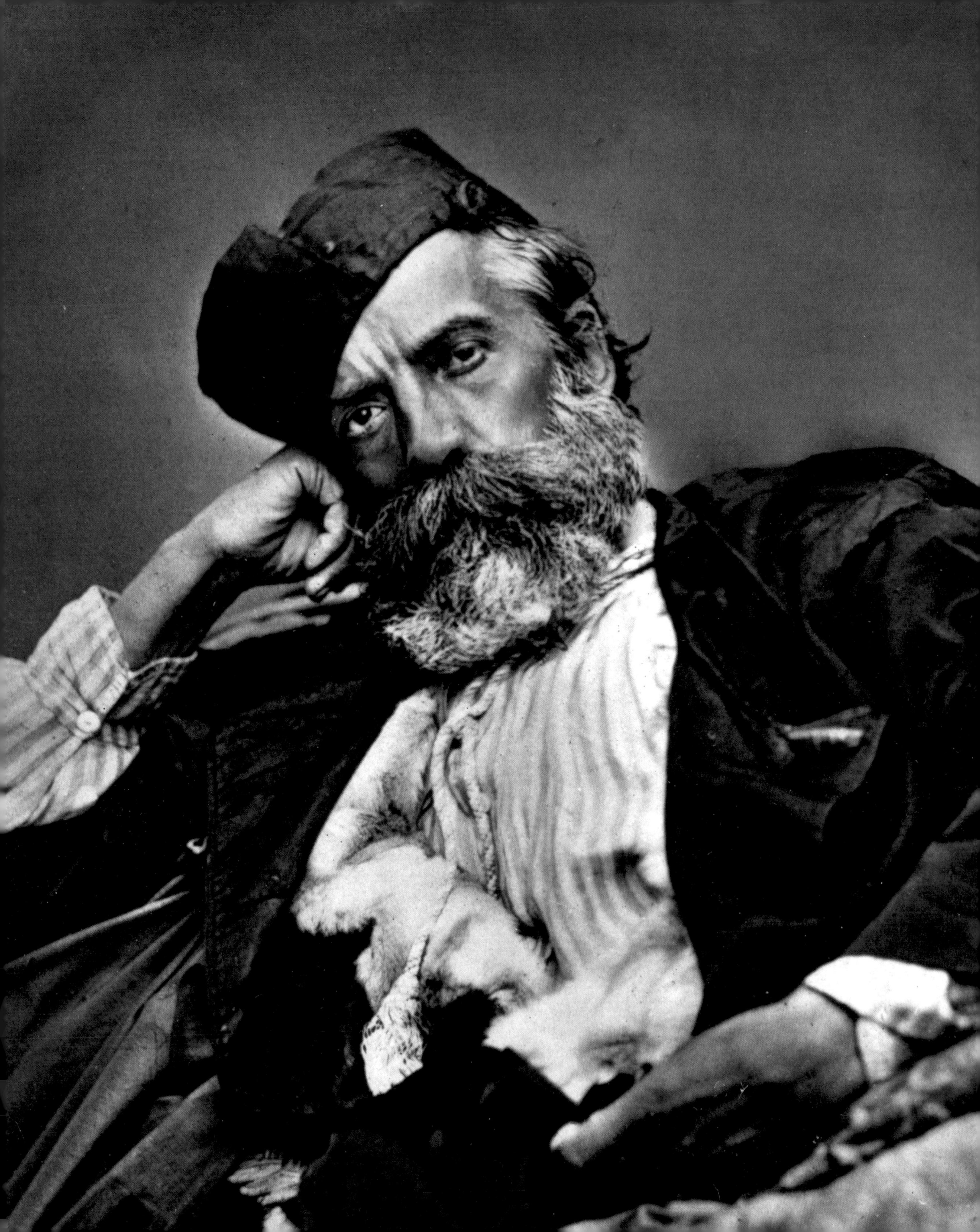

Philip Ward-Jackson

Jean-Baptiste Carpeaux in the Footsteps of his Idols

Portrait of Jean-Baptiste Carpeaux (detail, see p.172)

It can hardly be said of Jean-Baptiste Carpeaux (1827–75), as it definitely can of his pupil, Jules Dalou, that he established for himself a place in the English art world. He came to London in 1871, not, like Dalou, as a proscribed Communard but simply to escape the hardships of Paris under siege. He came also as a loyal courtier of the disgraced Napoleon III, whose period of rule, known as the Second Empire, had been brought to an end by the defeat of the French army by the Prussians at the Battle of Sedan in the previous year. At first Carpeaux's intention was to stay in London and carve out a new career for himself, but after the better part of one year this resolution faltered. For the next two years he would return sporadically to England, exhibiting regularly at the Royal Academy, initiating new work and finding new commissions, but, with failing health and a disintegrating marriage, there was a decreasing likelihood of any new critical recognition in England getting the better of his homing instinct. In March 1874 he crossed the channel for one last time, to accompany a selection of mainly retrospective and reproductive works to a sale at the auctioneers, Christie, Manson & Woods, and to see a half-size terracotta version of his *La danse* installed at the Royal Academy.[1] Two months later he would write from France to Dalou, regretting and apologising for never having paid him a visit in London, informing him that the doctors had given up on him and that his days were now definitely numbered. He was to die of prostate cancer on 12 October 1875.[2]

Shades of Watteau and Gericault

A prognosis based on historical examples meant that for Carpeaux there was every probability that the appeal of England would turn to its opposite. This had happened, as he would have known, to two of his artistic heroes from earlier times, Antoine Watteau and Théodore Géricault. What is more the details concerning the visits to London of both these artists towards the end of their short lives had been retailed in biographical studies written shortly before Carpeaux followed in their footsteps, by authors in his own social circle. The imaginative essay on Watteau by the brothers Edmond and Jules de Goncourt, accompanied by a recently rediscovered biographical summary delivered by the Comte de Caylus before the Académie Royale in 1748, was first published in *Portraits intimes du XVIIIe siècle* in 1857.[3] At that time Carpeaux had not become acquainted with the Goncourts. Their first dramatic encounter took place in March 1865, in the home of another writer on art, Philippe Burty.[4] In the meantime, in 1860, Carpeaux had proposed to the Mayor of Valenciennes to raise a memorial to Watteau in the city where both he and the painter had been born. Caylus's discourse, presented for the first time by the Goncourts, told how Watteau, deluded by the advice of certain friends into believing that a visit to London would be advantageous to him, had been well received there in 1719, and had tried to cash in on his popularity, only to find that the fog and coal fumes were deleterious to his already damaged lungs.[5] Géricault's London experience was recounted vividly, with much new documentation by Charles Clément in his

Portrait of Jean-Baptiste Carpeaux
c.1865–70
Photograph

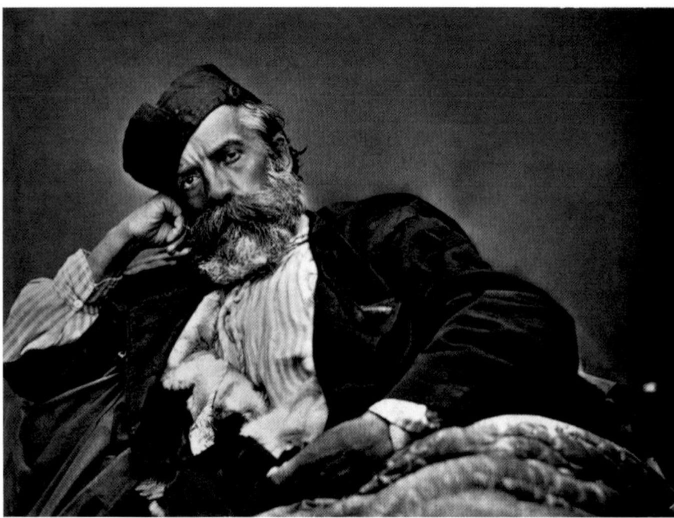

biography of the painter, which came out in book form in 1868. Géricault had travelled to London with his *Raft of the Medusa* in 1820, but stayed for two years. During this visit he told his friend Dedreux-Dorcy: 'I have given up Greek buskins and the Holy Scriptures and shut myself in the stables.'[6] A number of his London paintings and lithographs were of equine subjects. The downside was that he developed bad sciatica after a boat ride on the Thames and returned to France a sick man.

For Carpeaux, Géricault and the sculptor François Rude were the two luminaries of nineteenth-century France, whose legacy had been blanked out by the academic establishment. In his first year in London we find him following the painter's lead. One early biographer, Edouard-Désiré Fromentin, claims that Carpeaux had 'almost taken up residence in the splendid stables' of the shady financier, Hippolyte Lefèvre.[7] Numerous drawings from 1871 testify to a short-lived craze for racehorses and the amazons of Rotten Row. Whereas the equine world of Géricault was predominantly masculine, Carpeaux's tended more to the feminine. His access to Lefèvre's stables was procured through the businessman's young wife, who had commissioned from Carpeaux a portrait of herself, now in the Musée d'Orsay. The more ambitious end he had in view was to sculpt a Lady Godiva riding naked into Coventry, but the disgrace of Lefèvre over fraudulent share deals seems to have brought an end to this project. Fromentin indicates the direction in which Carpeaux seemed to be moving: 'Géricault's horses are forgotten; he manages to describe in his drawings the character of the English equestrian breed: rich, opulent, a little vain in its pride.'[8]

There was certainly little attempt by Carpeaux to live down the scandalous reputation, which, because of the publicity surrounding *Génie de la danse*, had preceded him to England. It was a reputation that, strange though it may seem to us now, he shared with Watteau. Though this may have encouraged identification with Watteau, it may also have discouraged anything resembling pastiche. Some entries in the journal of the Goncourt brothers imply that the *fête galante* was already in the 1860s a currency degraded by second-rate treatment and association with people or places of ill repute.[9] Certainly, when a second monument to Watteau was proposed for the church where he had been buried, at Nogent-sur-Marne, local *dévots* objected to so libertine an artist being commemorated on hallowed ground. The sculptor of the monument, which was finally erected outside the church, was Louis Auvray, Carpeaux's first artistic mentor.[10] The one beautiful drawing by Watteau that Carpeaux owned shows a young man in the act of embracing a woman. As a life study, the object of the attentions of this young man is a mere blank space, but the lustful look on the man's face, had they seen it, would probably have confirmed the Nogent worthies' feelings about the painter.[11]

Carpeaux in rococo mode

Napoleon III arrived in England shortly after Carpeaux, living in exile with his family at Camden Place, Chislehurst, until his

Jean-Baptiste Carpeaux
Woman on Horseback, Hyde Park
c.1871
Crayon on paper

Musée des Beaux Arts, Valenciennes

Jean-Baptiste Carpeaux
Monument to Antoine Watteau
1860–79
Bronze

Place Carpeaux, Valenciennes

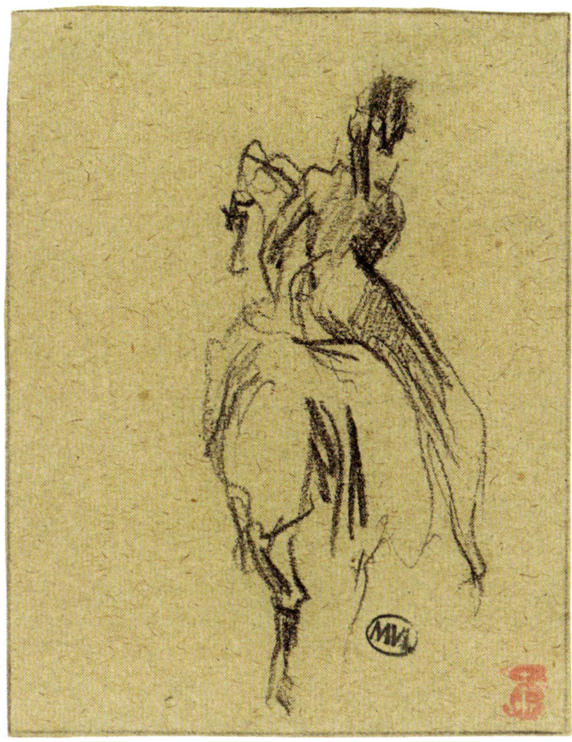

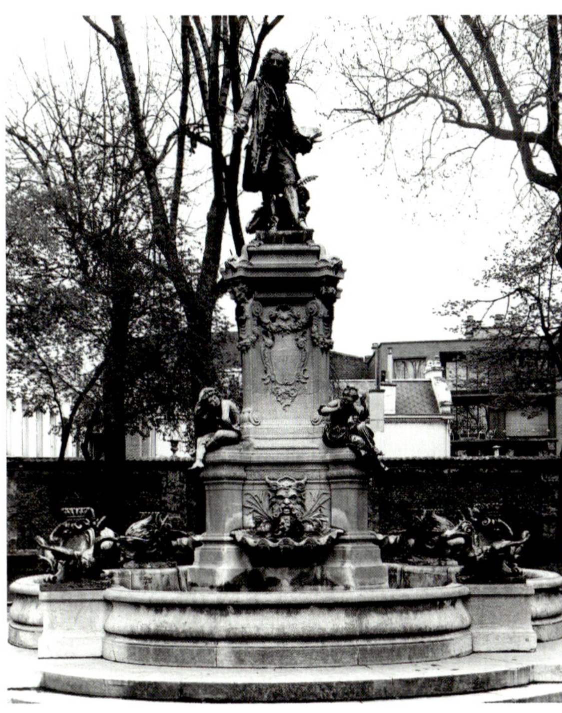

death in 1873. The sculptor's primary mission, encouraged by the Empress Eugénie and by the prince imperial, whose sculpture tutor he had been, was to make a final record of Napoleon III, first alive, in a portrait bust, and then dead, lying in state. A project for a tomb effigy advanced no further than a clay sketch, now in the Municipal Museum, Bucharest. These activities have contributed to the impression that Carpeaux's personal debacle echoed the emperor's military and political one, and this has resulted in his English works being treated, if anything, as an insignificant coda. One of the few commentators to attempt an explanation of this has been Edward Morris. In his compendious *French Art in Nineteenth Century Britain*, he argued that, while Carpeaux in his earlier work and particularly in the *Ugolino* had carried the 'expressive power and energy' of the romantic sculptors through the mid-century to Rodin at its end, the works that he produced in England, such as *Flora* (pp.180–1) and *Daphnis and Chloe* (p.182), 'represented the more decorative, erotic and Rococo aspect of his art'.[12] This was slightly to imply that these works were an escapist commercial diversion. Such a reading may have dictated the Royal Academy jury's decision to reject a pretty, but somewhat insignificant figure, entitled *La Frileuse*, which Carpeaux presented for exhibition in 1871, though they were happy to admit a selection of earlier works for the show.[13]

The use of the term 'Rococo' by Morris is clearly rather casual. The word was not commonly used until, in the 1880s, the architecture and furniture of the Louis XV period received more official recognition as the quintessential expression of the French spirit. Carpeaux himself would make an important contribution to this accommodation with the style, in his design for the plinth of his Valenciennes *Watteau*, but such works as the *Flora* and *Daphnis and Chloe* might more loosely be described as carrying on the French late-baroque tradition. The case of the *Daphnis and Chloe* was complicated by its commission by Lord Ashburton as a pendant to a standing *Cupid and Psyche* from a model by Canova. But Carpeaux particularised his group, giving his Daphnis a distinctive adolescent anatomy, while his Chloe is inspired by the Venus in Correggio's *Education of Cupid*, which the sculptor copied in the National Gallery. If these works by Carpeaux have anything in common with Watteau, it is their evocation of an Arcadian world, though a classical one in their case. Fromentin tells us that he was working simultaneously on representations of Eve, at various stages in her temptation and fall. In the background to these parallel pursuits were increasing doubts about his wife's fidelity, all contributing to the impassioned debate he was having around this time with Alexandre Dumas *fils* on the relative freedom from guilt of the antique world.[14]

English critics questioned whether Carpeaux and Dalou were not straying excessively into the domain of painting. Their work was seen as pictorial or picturesque. Where Carpeaux was concerned, they would not have been aware of just how prominently painting did in fact figure in his creative thinking. Throughout his career he had pursued a sideline in oils,

Jean-Baptiste Carpeaux
The Dance 1873–4
Terracotta 224 × 135

Ny Carlsberg Glypthotek, Copenhagen

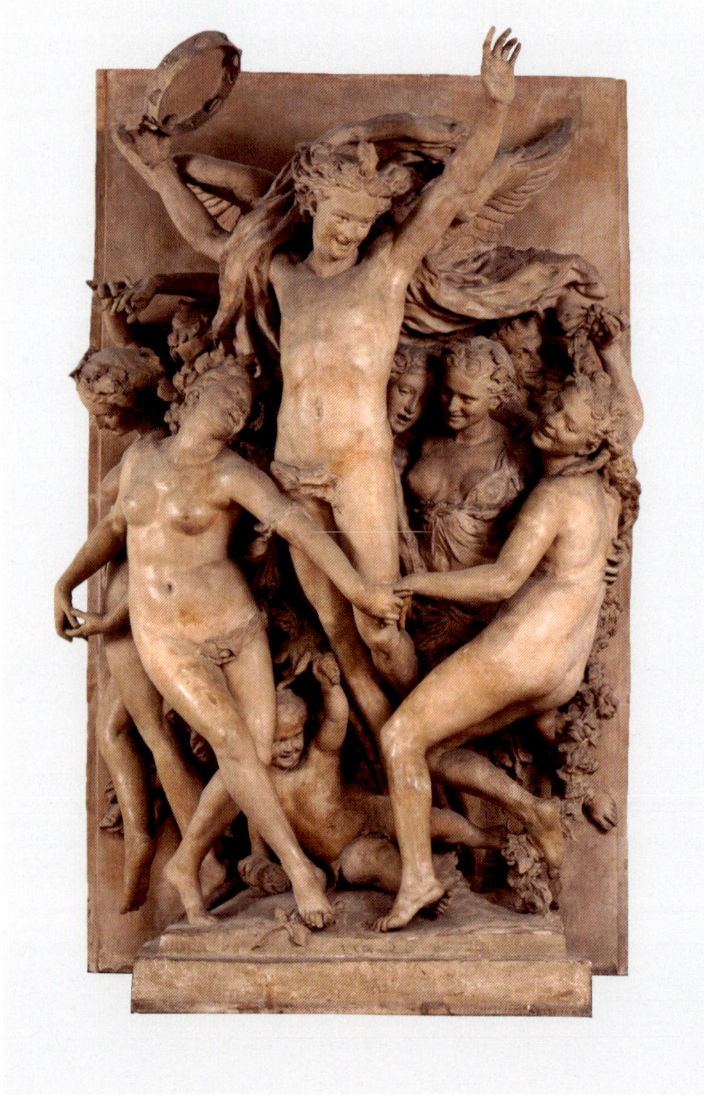

occasionally as a copyist of admired historical works, though more often as a portraitist and recorder of contemporary events.[15] It is easy to imagine that the fates of Watteau and Géricault would have discouraged too close an identification with them, but Carpeaux's sojourn in the British capital helped him to a new appreciation of Correggio and Rembrandt, both painters concerned with the way the human figure is revealed by light. Carpeaux's *Flora*, which was also the subject of a quite finished oil painting, must have presented itself to him as a lesson in chiaroscuro effect, the figure bent over on itself, creating its own light tunnel. It is a reworking of a theme already explored in the *Neapolitan Girl with a Shell* and the *Triumph of Flora* on the Louvre's Pavillon de Flore, but with the body, in a front view, receding far more dramatically. This was a style of sculpture in which an instantaneous effect, worked out in preliminary clay sketches, was retained in the final work. Nothing could have been further from the British expectations of sculpture, that it should possess graceful and easily legible outlines and an overall stability.

The subjects that Carpeaux chose to realise for his English patrons remained in the realm of the poetic and ideal. He did not, like Dalou, tap into a national predilection this side of the channel for sentimental modern genre. Once back in France, he did find, in his *Winkle Gatherer*, a home-grown equivalent of his earlier Neapolitan subjects. He had spotted this fisher-girl on the beach between Dieppe and Puys in 1874, and in modelling her from the life in the studio he took his rather belated first step into modern genre. *Flora*, when exhibited in marble at the Royal Academy in 1873, was entitled *Spring, Spring, Gentle Spring*, and when sold in 1903 from the collection of Carpeaux's patron, the paint and varnish manufacturer Henry James Turner, it was given as *Le Printemps*.[16] Even as Flora there is nothing remotely august about it. With its playful smile, reminiscent of the earlier *Neapolitan Girl*, it would have fitted quite happily into Turner's collection, consisting largely of genre paintings, whose subjects were variously oriental, historical and modern. Equally, the pair of busts that Carpeaux executed of Turner and his wife look very much as though they have walked out of one of James Tissot's pictures of contemporary London social life, such is their sense of fashionable modernity.

A critical honeymoon turns sour

In the case of *Daphnis and Chloe*, while it was intended initially to take its place in Lord Ashburton's predominantly neoclassical sculpture collection, Carpeaux admitted to Alexandre Dumas *fils* that his inspiration had been the sight of two young lovers exchanging confidences on a train.[17] This humdrum source was perhaps sniffed out by a critic for the *Leeds Mercury*, who complained that the expressions of the two figures were deficient in 'elevation of sentiment'.[18] The Goncourts had recognised in Carpeaux a personal propensity to respond to the life around him, very much like their own response to the modern world in their novels and journals. This meant that, for him, the ideal

Jean-Baptiste Carpeaux
Sketch for an Effigy of Napoleon III
Terracotta 11 × 40 × 6.5

The Bucharest Municipality Museum

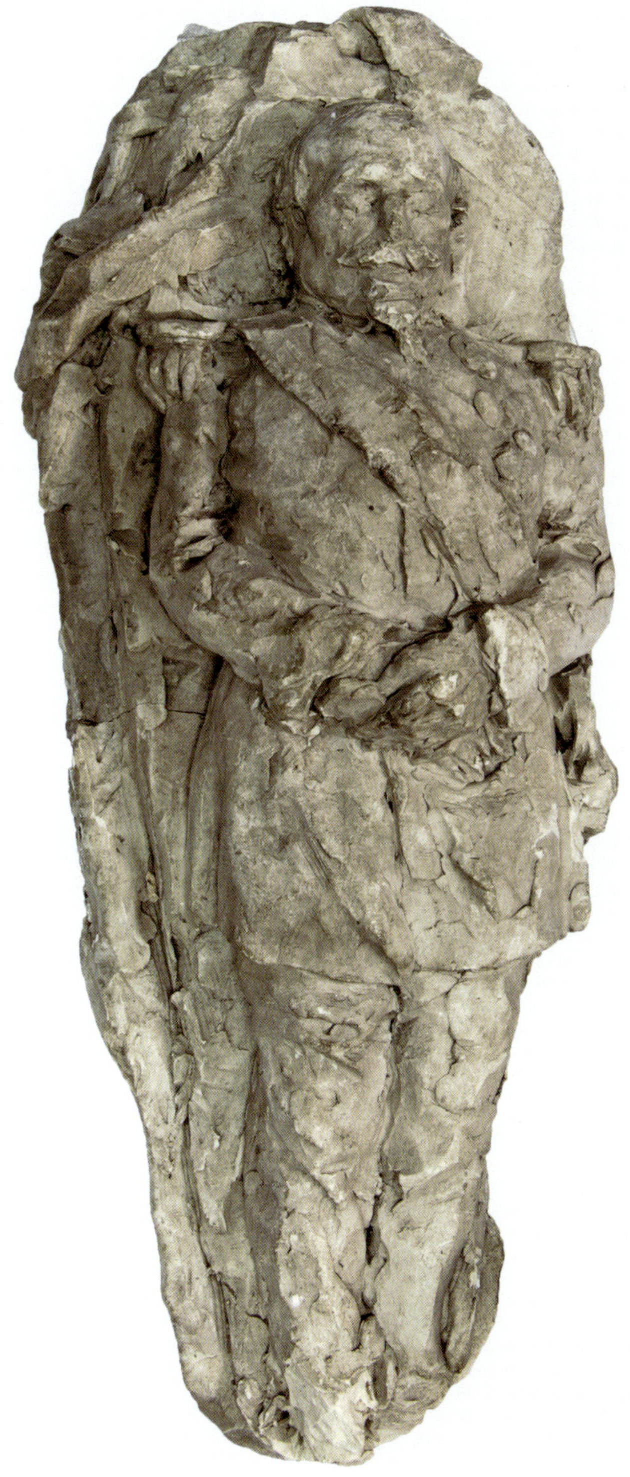

was never a static and timeless thing. Carpeaux, they said, was 'capable of sketching on a bus – something which that talentless imbecile the academic Cabanel feels justified in poking fun at'.[19] In a letter to his friend Bruno Chérier, the sculptor identified drama and despair as the essential ingredients of modernity, and the Goncourts sensed this, describing his aesthetic as 'fiévreuse', or febrile.[20] This heightened neurasthenic condition had a sort of godfather in Watteau, whom they saw as practising art as 'the pastime and distraction of a mind that suffers'.[21] For them it was an indispensable characteristic of the modern artist, a view that was to become something of a platitude among later 'decadent' writers.

There is a good likelihood that the Goncourts made such feelings known to Carpeaux, but, like Watteau before him, he showed his more practical side in battling against the odds to do business in England. It remains astonishing just how much of his oeuvre Carpeaux contrived, in a short space of time, to place before the British public. Having perceived that the establishment of a terracotta workshop would enable him better to compete with his rival Albert-Ernest Carrier-Belleuse in the sale of reproductive busts and statuettes, he proceeded to set one up at Auteuil. This workshop also enabled him to present the half-size version of *La danse* at the Royal Academy in 1874, a considerable feat, requiring the firing of the work in several sections. The revelation that his works must have represented can be judged from the response of the British press of the time. The arrival of a wave of French artists in London in 1871 brought greater publicity than had attended a similar phenomenon around 1848. The *Art Journal*, which had previously taken a rather censorious view of *La danse*, welcomed Carpeaux with the words 'we honour a great artist in works which we gladly welcome in our English Academy'. This promise of a critical honeymoon was not unfulfilled in the following years. In 1874, for example, the critic for *The Examiner*, with great magnanimity, acknowledged that *La danse* successfully challenged all accepted notions of sculptural propriety.[22] In the London art world Carpeaux found a champion in the Hungarian-born sculptor, Joseph Edgar Boehm, whose art had been to a great extent formed in the Paris of the early Second Empire.[23] And yet, as time went by, his technical brilliance was seen as regrettably offset by lack of idealism, poetic sentiment and purity of feeling, the censoriousness reaching a climax in the *Art Journal*'s tight-lipped obituary, which ended with the claim that Carpeaux 'should have lived longer in order to have realised a reputation for unequivocal goodness'.[24] It was almost certainly such comments in the press that persuaded Jules Dalou to renounce his gentle domestic genre subjects and in 1879 exhibit a *Bacchanal* of tremendously shameless sensuality, as a gesture of solidarity with his erstwhile master and friend.[25]

Jean-Baptiste Carpeaux
1827–1875
Self-Portrait 1874
Oil paint on canvas 40 × 32.2

Petit Palais, Musée des Beaux-Arts de la Ville de Paris

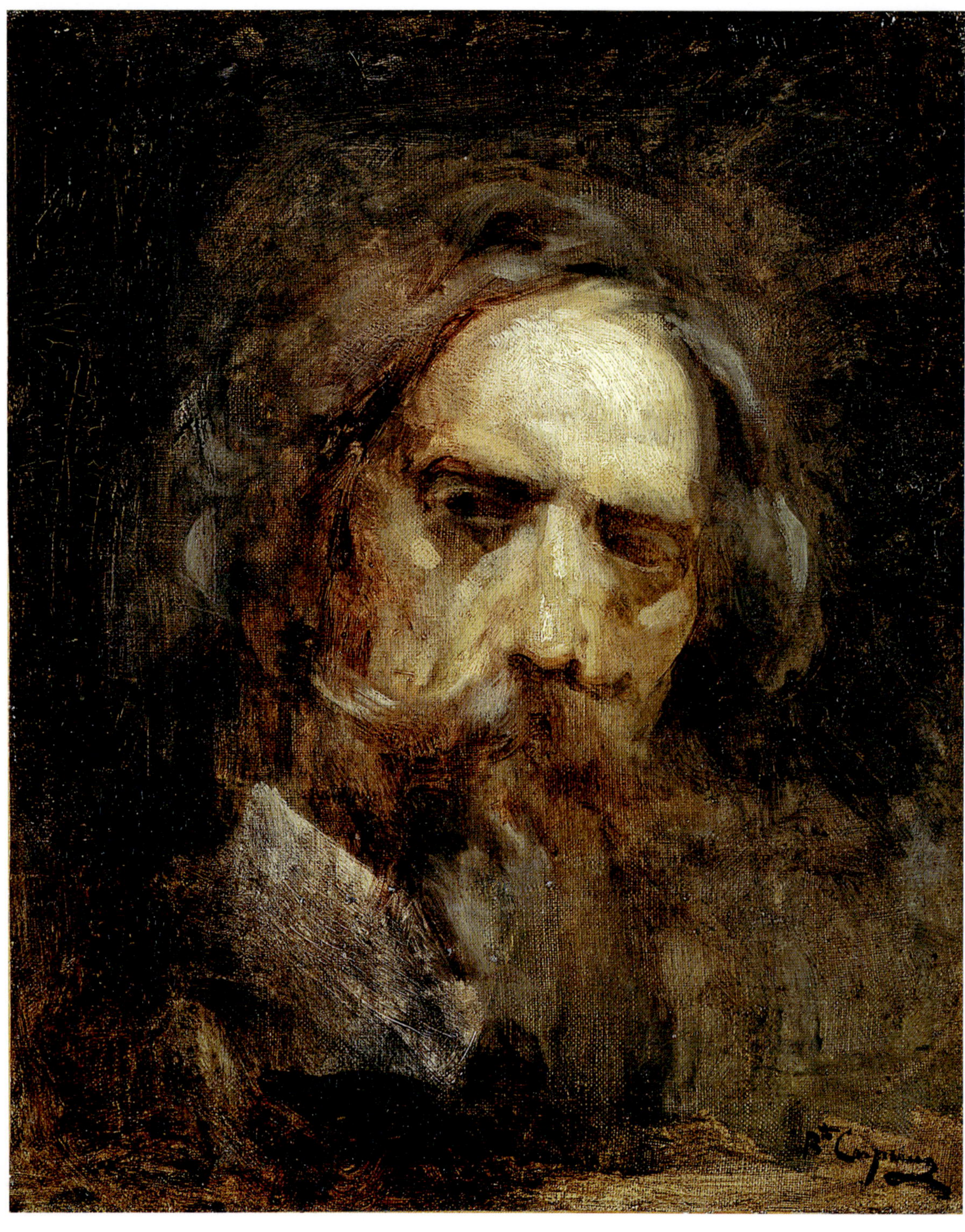

Jean-Baptiste Carpeaux
1827–1875
Brother and Sister, Two Orphans of the Siege 1871–2
Oil paint on canvas 170 × 100

Musée des Beaux-Arts Eugène Leroy, Tourcoing

The sculptor Jean-Baptiste Carpeaux spent the months of the Siege of Paris in his house in Auteuil and then, when the bombardment intensified, at the Palais du Luxembourg with his father-in-law General Montfort, and his wife and very young son Charles, born on 23 April. A self-taught painter, Carpeaux worked on his subjects without preparation and in an unrestrained manner as he let emotions of the moment surge forth. On the doorstep of a dwelling in ruins, a young girl holds her baby brother, whose nudity symbolises the vulnerability of a secular baby Jesus. As he did it on several occasions, Carpeaux treated his subject both in sculpture (Musée des Beaux-Arts de Valenciennes) and in painting (exhibited during the artist's lifetime at Durand-Ruel's gallery). Alphonse de Rothschild bought the picture at the Carpeaux studio sale organised in 1894 and immediately donated it to the Tourcoing museum.

An actual portrait of children taken in by Carpeaux, according to a late account by his daughter, or more likely a reminiscence of pictures of beggars from the Spanish Golden Age, the genesis of this work remains somewhat mysterious. Its format and dramatic intensity are exceptional. The distressed expressions are in stark contrast to the smooth beauty of the young faces and add a heroic dimension to these life-size innocent victims. This painting of childhood refers in antithesis to the figure of the imperial prince sculpted by Carpeaux during the glorious hours of the Second Empire. As a reminder of that standing portrait of the young prince posed next to his dog Nero, Carpeaux puts a symbolic figure of a faithful dog next to these two fleeing orphans. The same grace in these faces with their blond curly hair conveys opposite feelings: the glorification of the dynastic heir is succeeded by the bitter acknowledgement of a civilisation's decline. IC

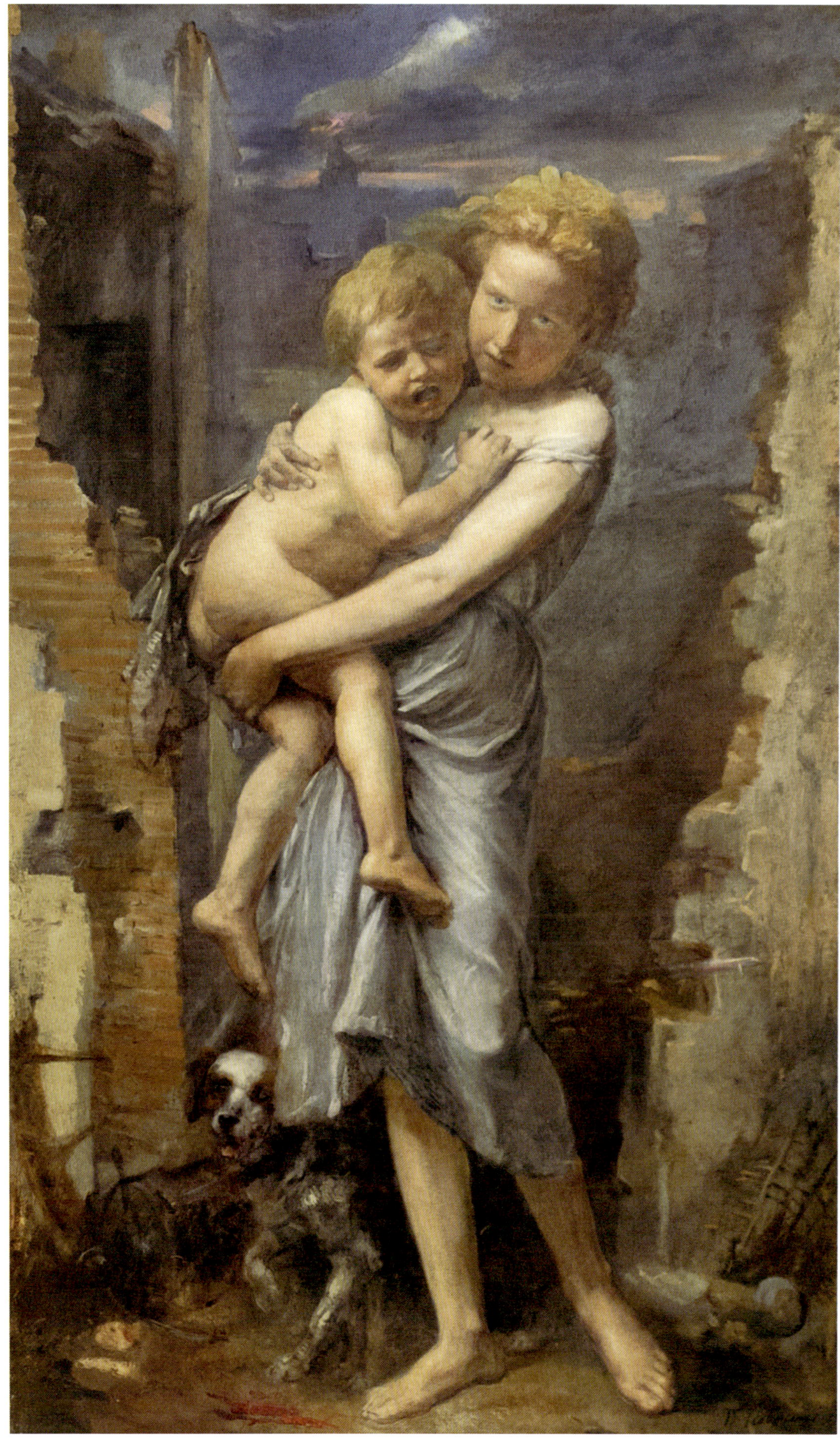

Jean-Baptiste Carpeaux
1827–1875
Henry James Turner 1873
Marble 63 × 57 × 31.5

Victoria and Albert Museum, London
Given by Miss Jessica Turner to the Tate Gallery and transferred to the V&A.

Mrs Henry James Turner 1871
Marble 80 × 60 × 37.5

Victoria and Albert Museum, London
Given by Miss Jessica Turner to the Tate Gallery and transferred to the V&A.

Henry James Turner inherited the fortune of his father, Charles Turner, wealthy owner of a painting and varnish business, which his son was able to diversify and make prosper. In 1859 he married Louisa Westall, who bore him seven children. A music lover and art collector, Henry James Turner owned a large painting collection that included several works by the painter Jean-Léon Gérôme, Carpeaux's friend who had also been exiled in London since 1870 (see p.16), and by James Tissot, who, like Turner, lived in St John's Wood. It was probably through the intermediary of Gérôme that Carpeaux came to know Henry James Turner, who, along with Lord Ashburton, would be one of his most important patrons in England. In addition to his own bust, Turner commissioned from the sculptor a portrait of his wife and a marble version of *Flora* crouching (pp.180–1).

The first commission was that of the bust of Louisa Turner: from a letter dated 1945 from their daughter Jessica Turner, the commission can be dated to the period of the Commune, that is between March and May 1871. Carpeaux completed the plaster version the same year; the latter is conserved in the Ny Carlsberg Glyptotek, Copenhagen, and still carries the long broken earrings that have disappeared from the marble. Seduced by the young woman's beauty, Carpeaux made two versions of the bust, one a *portrait d'apparat*, or formal portrait, presented here, and the other more intimate. The plaster model for the intimate version is in the Musée d'Orsay, Paris, whereas the marble is at the Musée de Valenciennes. The narrow contours of the 'intimate' bust focuses attention on the young woman's face and her regular beauty seems to have fascinated the sculptor. The formal portrait, on the other hand, emphasises the sumptuousness of Mrs Turner's costume, which consists of a ballgown with a plunging neckline. Here, Carpeaux reinterprets formulae inherited from eighteenth-century portraitists: the young woman, presented in a three-quarter view, turns her gaze away from the spectator and seems to be surprised in mid-conversation. Drapery with complicated folds is wrapped around her bust and confers a majestic character to the ensemble, which fully justifies the term *portrait d'apparat*. The young woman's beauty is brought out by the sophistication of her hairstyle, while the abundance of decorative accessories, flowers and jewels is a reminder of her wealth and sanctions the social rise of the Turners as rich bourgeoisie who have adopted an aristocratic lifestyle.

The commission for the bust of Henry James Turner probably took place between March and May 1871, during the same period as that for the bust of Mrs Turner; the original plaster of the bust must have been finished by 1871. It appeared in the sale of the Carpeaux studio on 30 May 1913 in the Manzi Gallery (lot 57), but its current location is unknown. On the other hand, Carpeaux only finished the marble in 1873, during his urgent

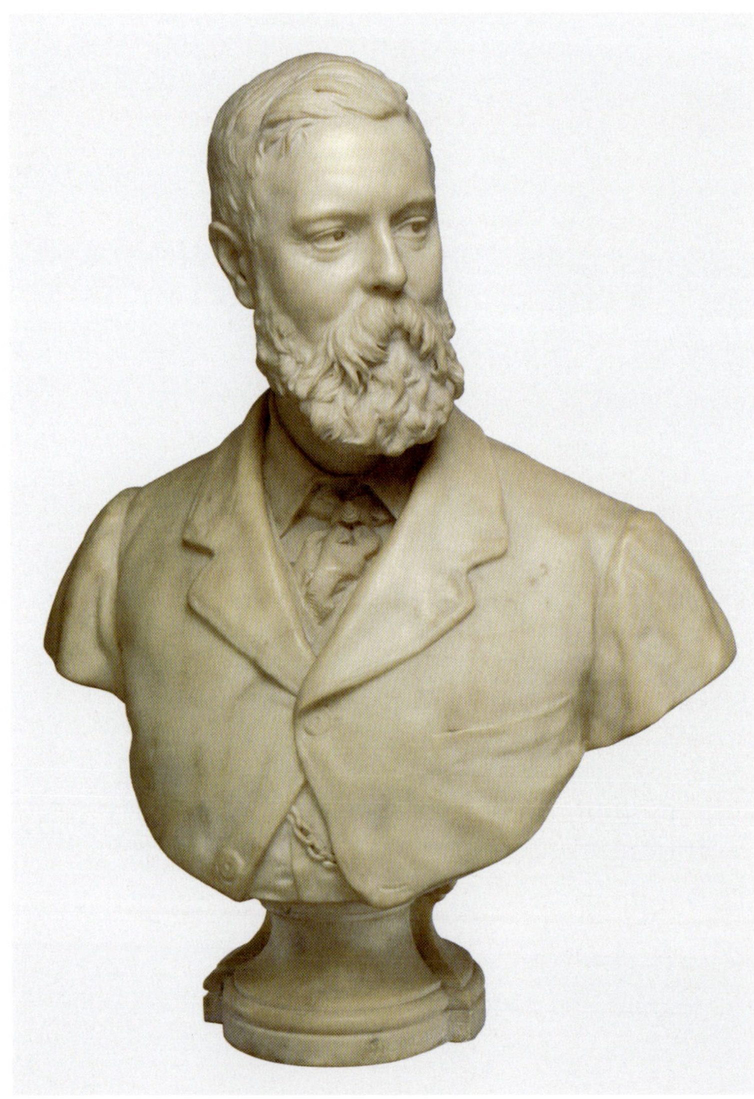

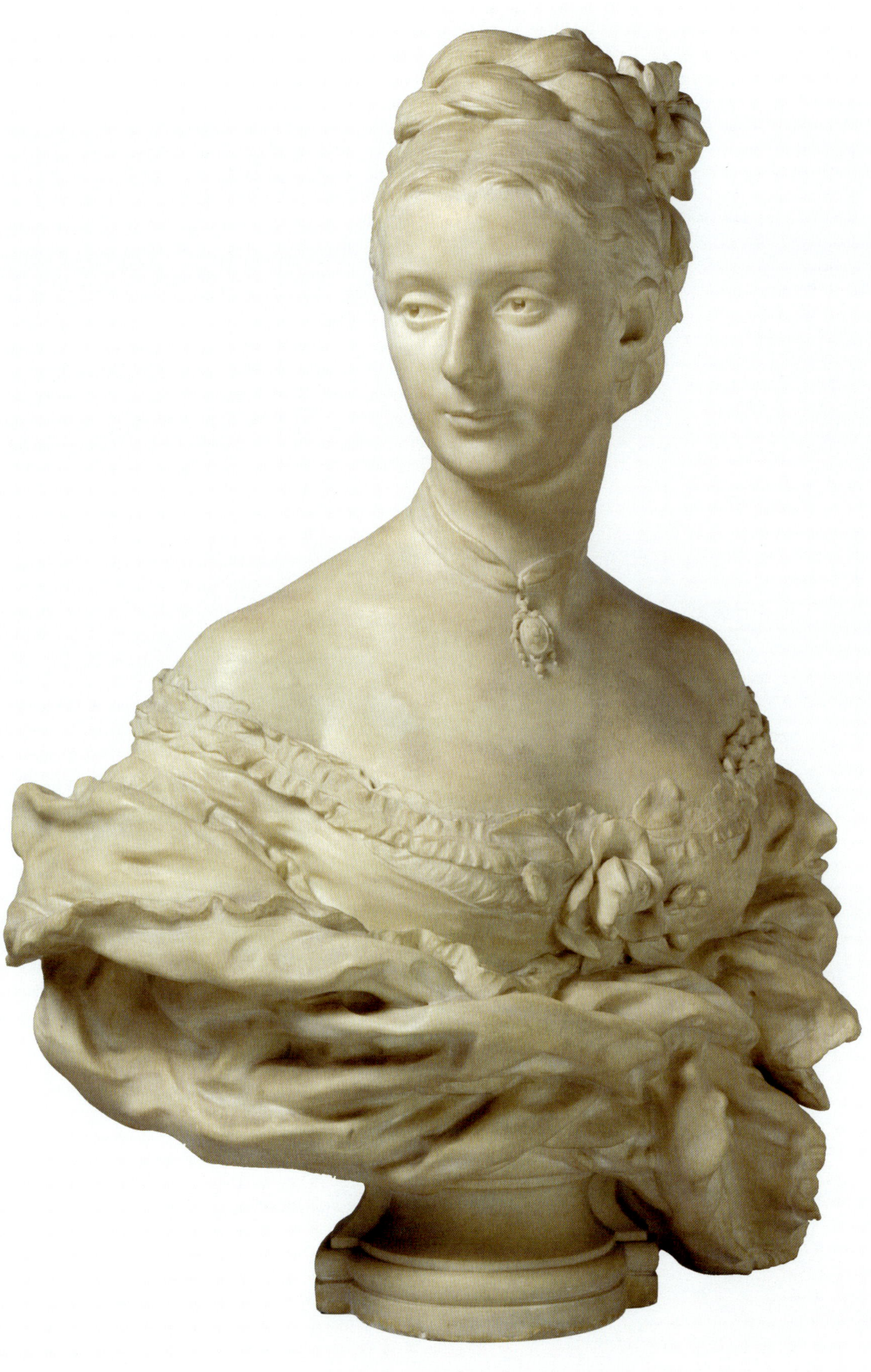

unplanned stay in England to attend Napoleon III's funeral (see p.188). In a letter dated 9 April 1873 Carpeaux sketched the silhouettes of the busts of the Turner couple and also indicated their dimensions:[1] the marbles, then, must already have been in process. The portrait of Henry James Turner exudes ease and respectability. He is depicted in a three-quarter view with hair and beard carefully combed. The sculptor has depicted the details of his costume very realistically: the negligently buttoned jacket reveals shirt collar and cravat. Carpeaux thus demonstrates that sculpture was perfectly appropriate for depicting both modern costume and the success of the industrial bourgeoisie.

The bust of Henry James Turner remained in the sitter's family before being given to the Tate Gallery in 1945, along with the bust of Mrs Turner, and was then transferred to the Victoria and Albert Museum in 1984. CCV

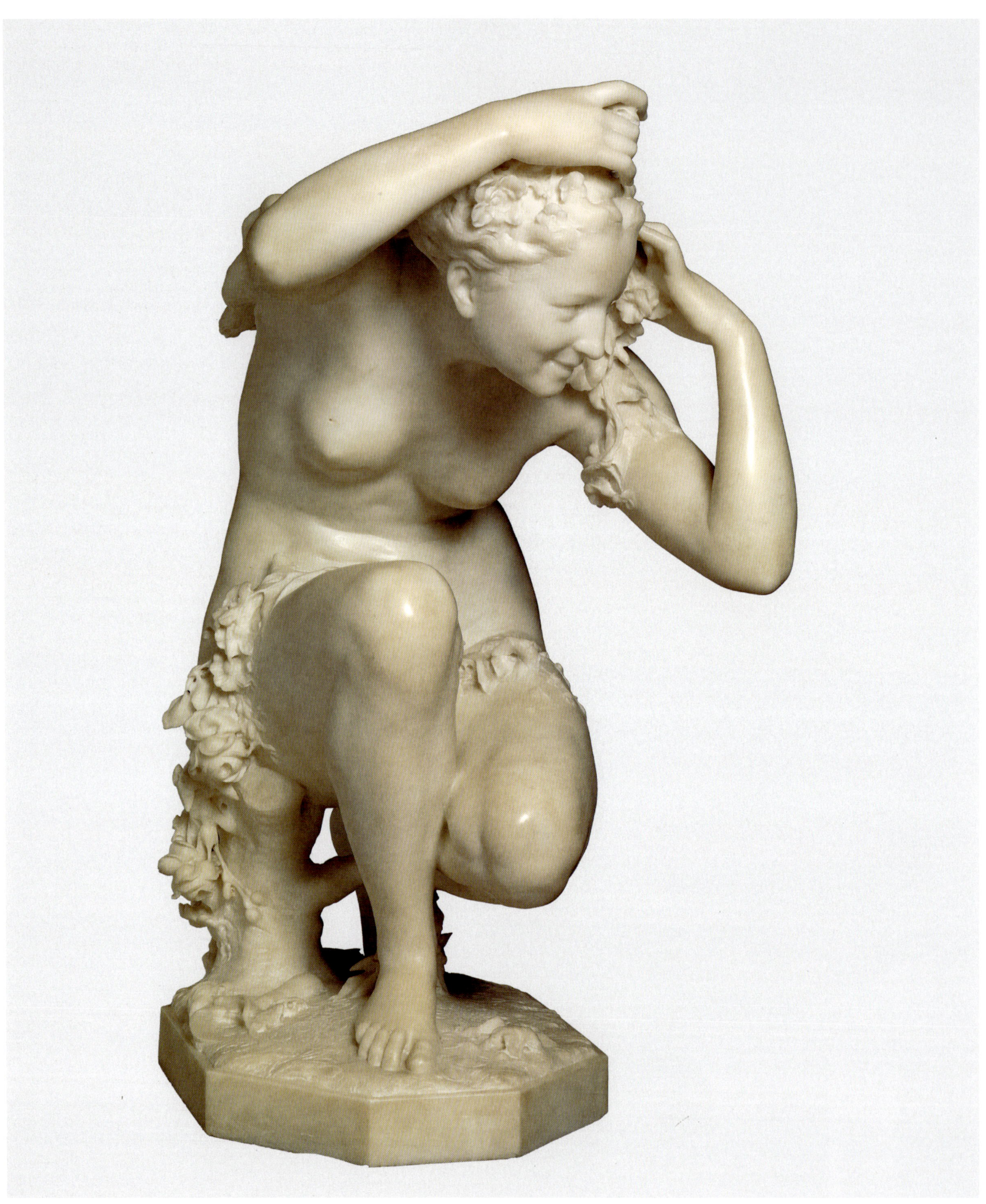

Jean-Baptiste Carpeaux
1827–1875
Flora 1873
Marble 97 × 65 × 60

Museu Calouste Gulbenkian-Founders Collection, Lisbon

Flora was commissioned by the wealthy industrialist Henry James Turner, one of the principal patrons of Carpeaux in London of whom the artist also produced a portrait (p.178). Carpeaux executed *Flora* in the studio he occupied at 28 Edward Street in London, and he presented the marble at the Royal Academy in 1873 under the title of *Spring, Spring, Gentle Spring*. The theme of springtime refers to Flora, the ancient goddess of flowers and gardens. Carpeaux had already handled the subject for the decoration of the facade of the Pavilion of Flora, which connected the Louvre with the Tuileries and was reconstructed under Napoleon III by the architect Hector Lefuel. Commissioned in 1863, the *Triumph of Flora* relief was, with *The Dance*, intended for the Paris Opera, and was one of Carpeaux's most famous monumental works. The sculptor depicted Flora in the form of a young woman with generous curves, kneeling to distribute armloads of flowers to little putti. Although Carpeaux partially used the pose from the Hellenistic *Crouching Aphrodite*, he was able to revitalise the ancient model by finding inspiration in life around him. Flora's face with its characteristic smile would thus reproduce the features of Anna Foucart, the elder daughter of one of Carpeaux's friends, Jean-Baptiste Foucart, who was a lawyer in Valenciennes.

The success achieved by the *Triumph of Flora* encouraged Carpeaux to reinterpret the main figure in order to create an independent work. The sculptor thus produced a painting of *Crouching Flora* (Musée des Beaux-Arts, Valenciennes), whose ample flesh recalls northern painting masters, and whose pose is closely related to the marble *Flora* sculpted in 1873. He made a bust as well, whose face was borrowed from *Flora* and to which he gave the title *Spring* 1866–70 (original plaster in Ny Carlsberg Glyptotek, Copenhagen). The marble made in 1873 for Henry James Turner reuses the pose of the *Neapolitan Fisherboy* 1858 (Musée du Louvre), a masterpiece executed in Rome during the sculptor's stay at the Villa Medici. He shows a slender laughing young girl who is busy decorating her hair with a wreath of flowers. The flowers, a reminder of the goddess's mythological attributes, opportunely veil the statue's private parts: her grace outshines the sensuality, and Carpeaux, undoubtedly to satisfy his patron's taste, has carefully effaced any reference to Rubens, obvious in the *Triumph of Flora* relief but probably too audacious for the British bourgeoisie in the Victorian era. The life-size marble remained in the collection of Henry James Turner until 1903. It then was put on the art market and acquired by the businessman Calouste Gulbenkian. The small version of *Flora* crouching particularly lent itself to reproduction and so was broadly distributed in both bronze and terracotta. CCV

Jean-Baptiste Carpeaux
1827–1875
Daphnis and Chloe 1873
Plaster 72 × 35 × 21.5

Petit Palais Musée des Beaux-Arts de la Ville de Paris. Gift of Louise Clément-Carpeaux in 1938

The *Daphnis and Chloe* group was commissioned by Alexander Baring, 4th Baron of Ashburton, a famous art collector. Lord Ashburton wished to acquire a pendant for a standing *Cupid and Psyche* by Antonio Canova, which was one of the sculptures decorating the gallery of his London residence, Bath House in Piccadilly. As he had many paintings by Jean-Léon Gérôme in his collections, Lord Ashburton probably turned to Carpeaux on the painter's recommendation. The subject, represented many times in sculpture as in painting, was inspired by the ancient pastoral by Longus, who narrated the amorous initiation of two young shepherds, Daphnis and Chloe, on the Ile of Lesbos. Carpeaux's sculpture complemented Canova's, which also staged two young lovers emerging from adolescence. The French sculptor perfectly adapted this iconography, which was 'dragged everywhere', to borrow the expression used by his daughter Louise Clément-Carpeaux. Carpeaux was inspired by the composition adopted by Canova, in which Cupid, entirely nude, leans tenderly on the shoulder of Psyche, who, in return, offers him a butterfly, symbol of the soul. Both Canova's and Carpeaux's young lovers hold each other side by side in chaste nudity evocative of Golden Age innocence. Carpeaux, however, modified the pose of the young man, who, instead of leaning on the young girl's shoulder, seems to wish to murmur a secret in her ear while she smiles the famous Carpeaux smile. The sculptor nonetheless succeeded in giving the mythological couple some humanity, in so far as Daphnis's tender pose was prosaically inspired by a couple of lovers he glimpsed on a train. On 19 November 1874 he wrote to Alexander Dumas: 'It was while returning from your place that I saw a young couple in a train compartment who were exchanging sweet secrets in each other's ear and formed a very interesting group; as soon as I arrived home, I took clay and in less than twenty minutes, the work was mounted.'[1]

Two works, a clay model kept in Valenciennes and a painting, *The Confidence*, which belongs to the Petit Palais, are evidence of the first composition imagined 'on the spot' by the artist. The genesis of the work was thus relatively rapid. The initial date of the commission is not known with certainty, but the completion dates for the two intermediary models, March 1873 for the small one and August 1873 for the large one, are given in the sculptor's correspondence. The models were executed in Paris, but Carpeaux made several trips to London to present them to his patron who was extremely satisfied, even though he demanded that draperies and foliage be added to modestly veil the figures' nudity. The marble (Sterling and Francine Clark Art Museum, Williamstown), for which Carpeaux was paid 25,000 francs, was completed in 1874, when Carpeaux, broken by illness, debts and family quarrels, was coming to the end of his career. The Petit Palais plaster is an early cast, given to the museum in 1938 by the sculptor's daughter, and is probably derived from an intermediary model executed in 1873. CCV

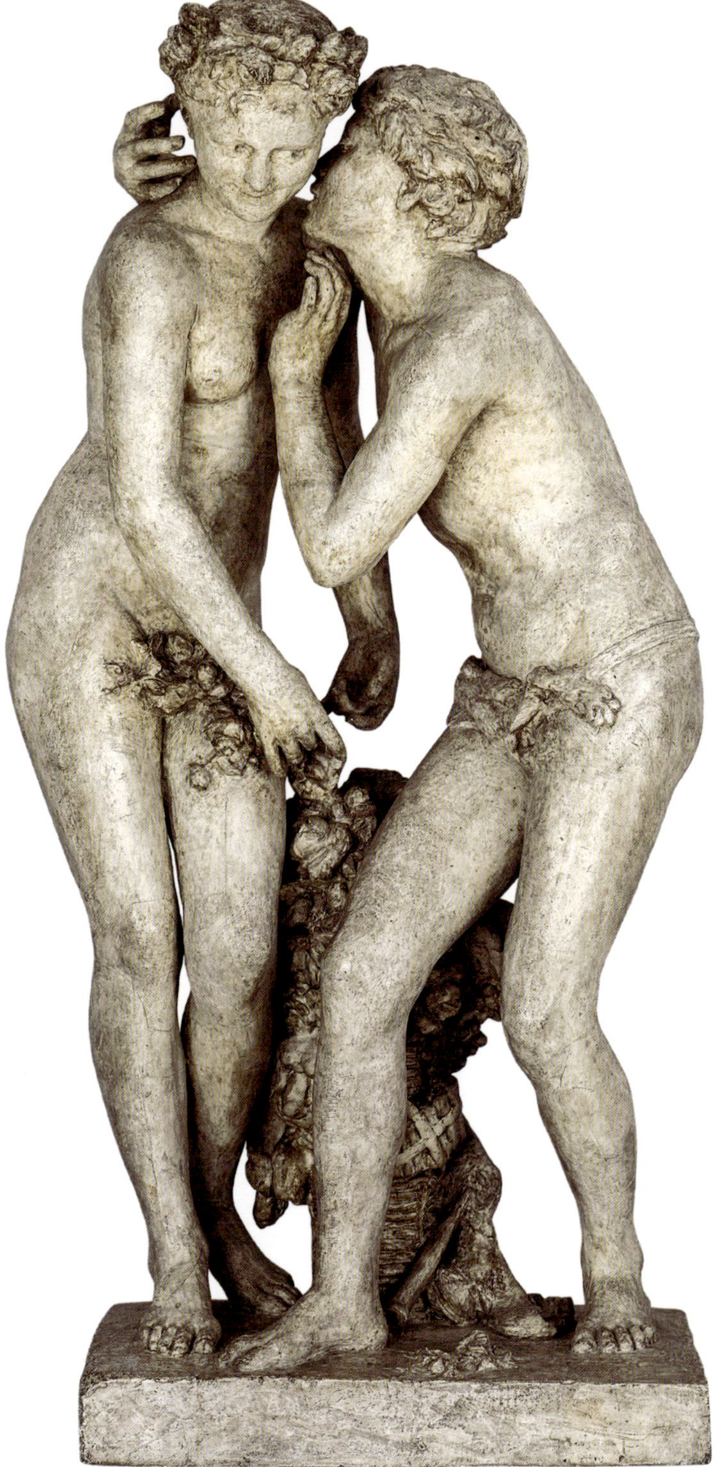

Jean-Baptiste Carpeaux
1827–1875
Jean-Léon Gérôme 1871
Plaster 61 × 26 × 24

Petit Palais Musée des Beaux-Arts de la Ville de Paris. Gift of the sculptor Hector Lemaire in 1907

In London, where he had taken refuge since spring 1871, Jean-Baptiste Carpeaux found several compatriots who were also in exile in the English capital. Among them was the painter Jean-Léon Gérôme. Gérôme had been settled in London since September 1870 and thus had escaped the horrors of the Siege of Paris. The painter, famous for his history paintings and orientalist scenes, enjoyed a solid reputation in England where he had been named an honorary member of the Royal Academy in 1869. Carpeaux admired him greatly: at loose ends on arriving in London, the sculptor offered to make a bust of the painter. In return, Gérôme was meant to paint Carpeaux's portrait, but the sculptor died before the painter had a chance to keep his promise. Gérôme's bust was modelled in a few sessions, between Carpeaux's arrival in London in March 1871 and the opening on 19 June of the French section of the International Exhibition, where the plaster model was exhibited. The painter was very happy with his sculpted portrait. In a letter addressed to Edouard-Désiré Fromentin dated 25 August 1878, Gérôme mentioned it with admiration: 'This bust was quickly made, one could almost say in one fell swoop, which is why it is characterised by a high degree of those qualities that distinguish works of the spirit, that is to say, life itself.'[1]

One bronze version of Gérôme's bust was exhibited in France in the Salon of 1872 where critics nicknamed it 'the beheaded talker' (*le décapité parlant*). This appellation referred to the irregular contour adopted by Carpeaux that stopped sharply at the base of the neck: rather than a bust, it really was a head, 'nothing but a head', but 'a masterpiece', as emphasised by Ernest Chesneau, one of the sculptor's first biographers. By choosing to cut the shoulders and chest narrowly so that it was impossible to depict costume, the sculptor deliberately placed the work outside the range of formal and commissioned portraits. Instead, he was getting closer to the 'tête d'expression' and emphasised the painter's face, whose likeness he knew how to convey perfectly. The painter's features, such as they are known to us through other portraits, especially a photograph by Félix Nadar, are perfectly recognisable. The sculptor faithfully reproduced the sitter's hairstyle and fine moustache, as well as the lofty, slightly haughty bearing of his head. Turning to a technique borrowed from eighteenth-century masters, Carpeaux depicted his sitter as if he were looking away in a three-quarter view and thus accentuated the illusion of movement and impression of a living being. As soon as it was created, the work was a success. The bust was widely reproduced mainly in plaster editions. The Petit Palais version is an early cast in which the marks left by the seams of the mould are clearly visible. CCV

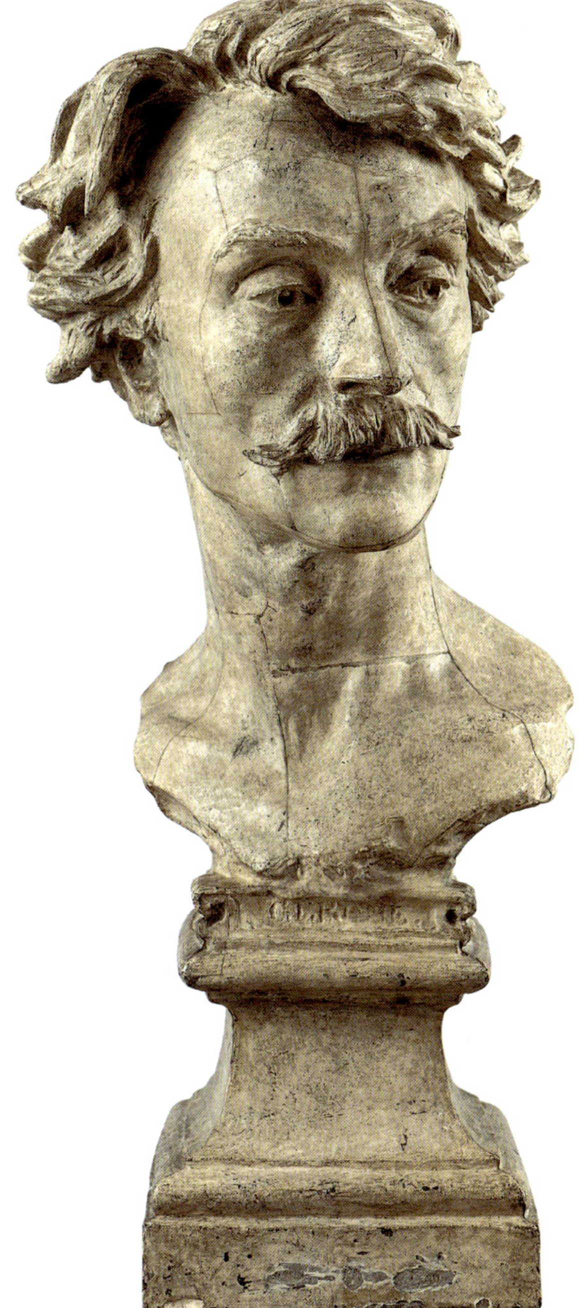

Jean-Baptiste Carpeaux
1827–1875
Bust of Charles Gounod 1873 (1)
Plaster 73 × 50 × 44

The Royal Society of Musicians of Great Britain

Charles Gounod Playing the Organ 1873 (2)
Charcoal and chalk on paper 30 × 20

Private collection
[not exhibited]

Georgina Weldon as Gallia 1872 (3)
Charcoal and chalk on paper 16 × 16

Private collection
[not exhibited]

Bust of Charles Gounod 1873
Plaster 70 × 48 × 44

Petit Palais Musée des Beaux-Arts de la Ville de Paris
[not illustrated]

Visitors' Book, Tavistock House 1871–1913
Mixed media on paper 28 × 21

Victoria and Albert Museum, London
[not illustrated]

Charles Gounod, one of the most famous French composers of the Second Empire, went into exile in England from September 1870. In June 1871 he left the conjugal residence to move into Tavistock House, Charles Dickens's former dwelling, where the eccentric singer Georgina Weldon and her husband William Henry Weldon lived. Georgina organised evening parties, concerts and various social and charitable events. Tavistock House soon became a gathering place in London for the French, including Communards, who were in transit or in exile. Drawings and signatures by the Régamey brothers punctuate the guest book, in which figure the names of Jules Vallès, Camille and Albert Barrère, and even Thomas Gibson Bowles (see p.87). The Carpeaux family is mentioned several times in Georgina Weldon's diary, occasionally in condescending terms. At Tavistock House Carpeaux met Charles Gounod and a sincere friendship soon formed between the sculptor and the musician. In the biography of her father, Louise Clément-Carpeaux recalls the agreeable times spent there, Gounod accompanying Madame Carpeaux singing, while Carpeaux was sculpting in clay or drawing.

Georgina's diary indicates that the bust was rapidly modelled between February and March 1873. A marble version, whose location is currently unknown, was presented to the Royal Academy in April 1873. Several terracotta examples of the bust were subsequently produced mainly for people close to the composer. The version belonging to the Royal Society of Musicians comes from the collection of the sculptor Alfred Gilbert, who had purchased it himself at the posthumous sale of Boehm's studio in 1891. Charles Gounod was extremely satisfied with his portrait, which he recollected thus in 1876: 'The twelve to fourteen sessions during which I posed helped me appreciate how much passion Carpeaux had for the great art to which he devoted his too short existence. As he was in his works, so he revealed himself in his conversation, ardent, impetuous, emotional and persevering; one felt the heat and swiftness of his design.'[1]

Carpeaux's *Charles Gounod* belongs to a remarkable group of artists' portraits, from Charles Garnier to Jean-Léon Gérôme. Carpeaux achieved a perfect likeness, 'more alive than life', to borrow the expression employed by the sculptor's friend, the writer Alexander Dumas *fils*. The sitter's physical characteristics, which Georgina Weldon described as 'fat and podgy', are immediately recognisable: Carpeaux faithfully transcribes in clay the model's plumpness, his beard and abundant moustache, as well as his elegant three-piece, slightly frayed suit. Aside from Gounod, Carpeaux also planned to do a portrait of his patroness, Georgina Weldon. Thus in her diary on 11 March 1873 the singer noted that Carpeaux intended to depict her as an allegory of song, a subject that, according to her, had never been treated in sculpture. The project never got off the ground, but Carpeaux produced several drawings of the singer performing *Gallia*, a patriotic and appropriate work composed by Gounod in 1871 in response to the French defeat.[2]
CCV

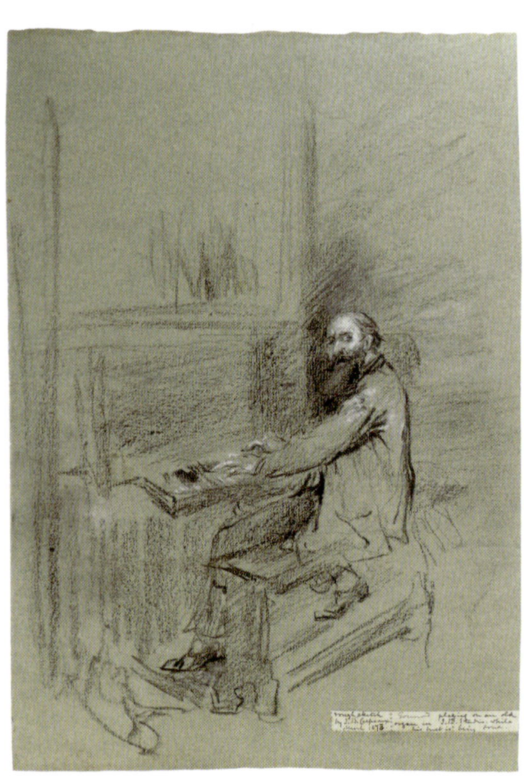

2

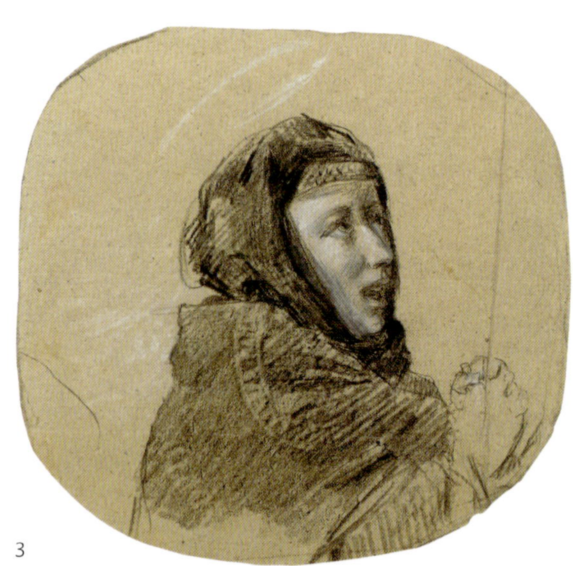

3

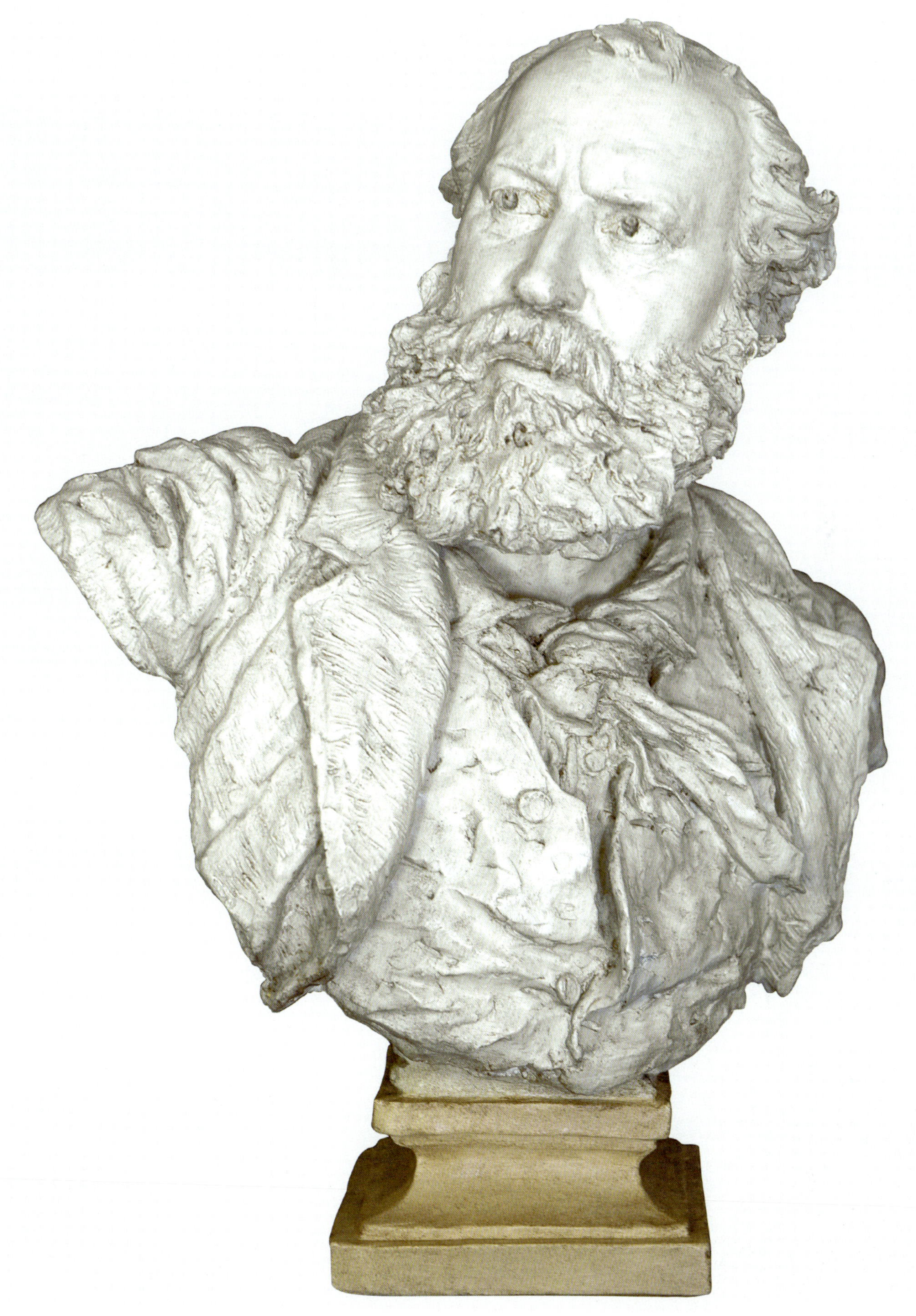

1

Jean-Baptiste Carpeaux
1827–1875
Venus, with Mercury and Cupid, after Correggio 1871–3
Oil paint on canvas 145 × 90

Petit Palais Musée des Beaux-Arts de la Ville de Paris

Notes and sketches in Blackwood's Small Pocket Book and Diary, London, 1871
Mixed media, 90 pages, portfolio binding in brown Morocco leather
10.7 × 7.5

Petit Palais Musée des Beaux-Arts de la Ville de Paris

In London, as in Italy or Paris, Carpeaux did a number of studies and copies that preserved the memory of compositions he had admired in museums. In the National Gallery two paintings by Correggio held his attention: *The Madonna of the Basket* c.1524, of which he painted a free interpretation of the central part (1871–3, Musée des Beaux-Arts de Valenciennes), and *Venus, with Mercury and Cupid (The School of Love)* c.1525, of which he did a full monochrome copy. Recently married and father of young Charles, born on 23 April 1870, Carpeaux displayed a sensitivity to both profane and sacred depictions of maternal figures and very young children. The sculptor's gaze examines these two illustrious masterpieces while privileging the way in which figures are modelled through subtle plays of light. The contrapposto of the sensual Venus as painted by Correggio inspired Carpeaux's *Chloé* intended for Lord Ashburton's sculpture group (p.182).

It is not known precisely when these copies were executed during the sculptor's sojourns in London, the first of which began in March 1871. They were to remain in his Parisian studio until the Carpeaux sale organised in 1894. A precious clue, nonetheless, indicates that *Venus, with Mercury and Cupid* was made in London: the verso of the canvas bears the stamp of the House of Lechertier Barbe, a colour merchant and artists' supplier who had been located at 60 Regent Street since 1844. This store, founded by a French family in the West End near the French quarter, was also used by Monet during his stays in London at the turn of the century. Carpeaux probably drew his models while visiting museums, before working on the canvas from memory at home. A drawing of the *Madonna of the Basket* conserved in the Musée de Valenciennes (1871–3, CD 1217) supports this idea.

On some pages of a diary that he had purchased at Euston Road on his arrival in London, Carpeaux fixed in a few pencil strokes the outline of works selected during his visits. He thus probably spent considerable time at the National Gallery, especially in front of Rembrandt's *A Woman Bathing*, which was the subject of a more finished stump drawing in the diary (folio 56). Exile in London gave the artist, who lacked commissions, leisure time to visit with his family the London Zoo at the north of Regent's Park. An entire menagerie invades the notebook, with birds of prey, felines and bears appearing on pages dated from May to July 1871 (folios 39, 40, 41, 46, 49, 50, 51, 52). A little toy terrier adopted during his English sojourn is also featured on two of the diary's sheets (folios 53 and 54). IC

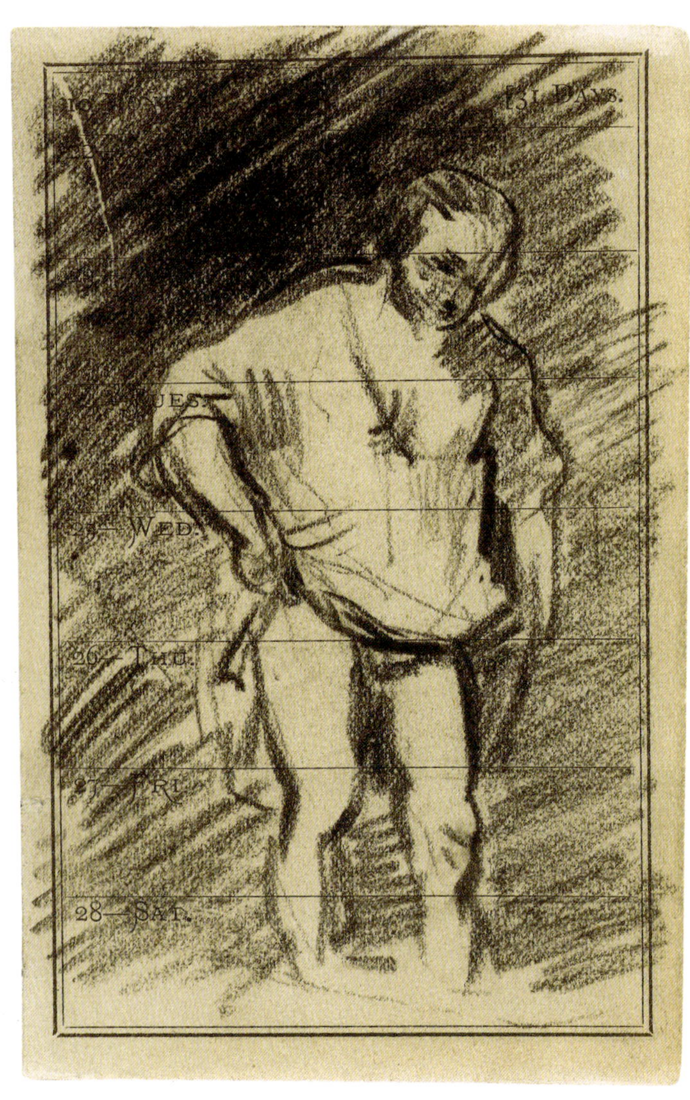

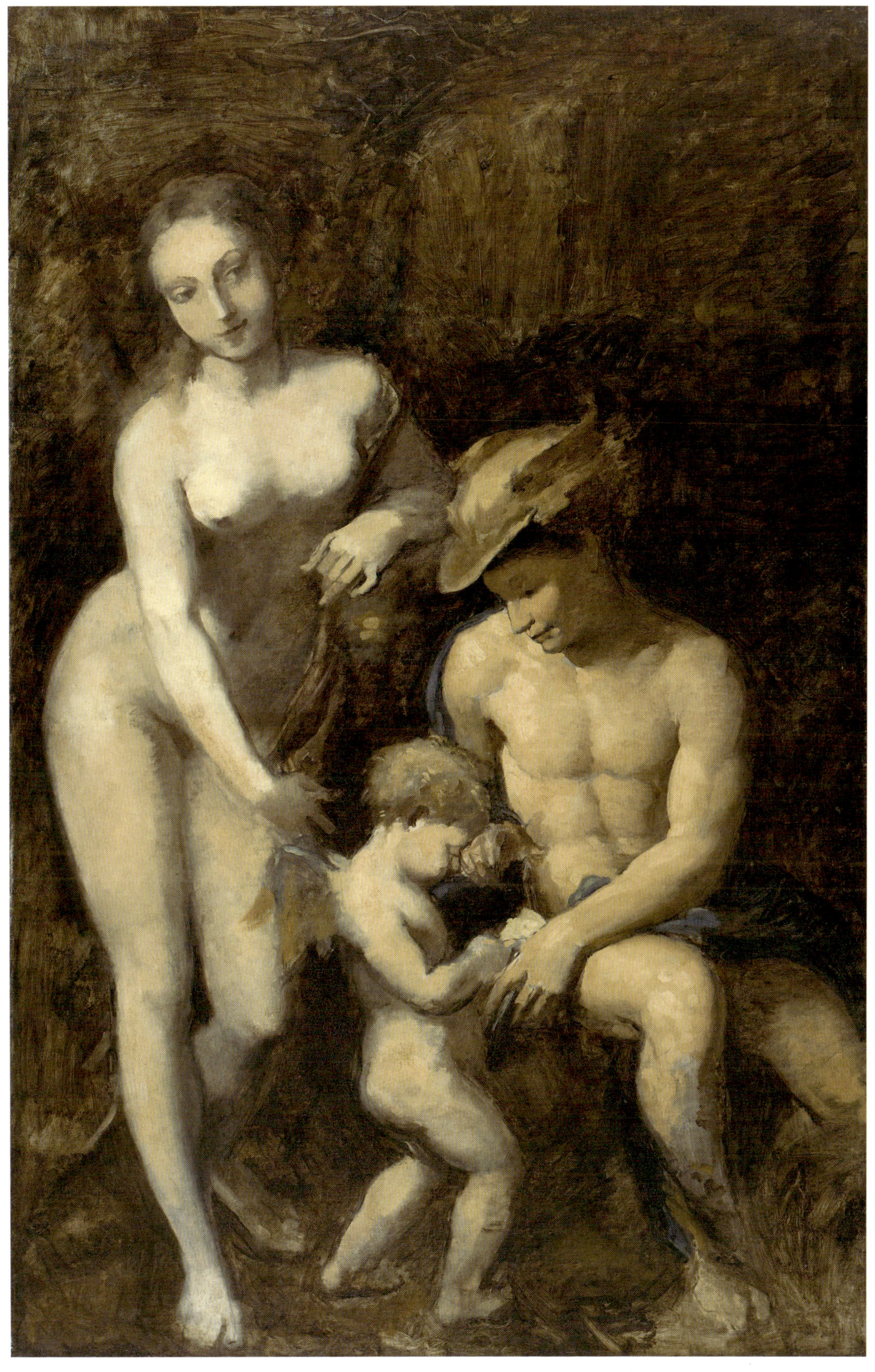

Jean-Baptiste Carpeaux
1827–1875
Napoléon III 1874 (1)
Marble 60 × 36.5 × 27

Victoria and Albert Museum, London

Funerary Service for Napoleon III at Chislehurst: The Chapel of Rest 1873 (2)
Black chalk heightened with white on paper
24.3 × 29.9

Musée d'Orsay, Paris, deposited at the Musée National du Château de Versailles

The Emperor Napoleon III in his Coffin on 13 January 1873 in St Mary's Church in Chislehurst 1873 (3)
Black chalk heightened with white on paper 55 × 34.1

Musée d'Orsay, Paris, deposited at the Musée National du Château de Versailles

Paradoxically, Carpeaux, the sculptor of the 'imperial festival' never produced a portrait of Napoleon III during the empire. He did not begin his bust until 1872, when the deposed emperor was living in exile at Camden Place at Chislehurst, south-east of London, where he had taken refuge with the imperial family in March 1871, after his captivity in Germany. According to Louise Clément-Carpeaux, the bust would have been commissioned in 1871, during one of the visits the sculptor made to the imperial family, to whom he demonstrated constant affection during their exile. The sittings nonetheless were interrupted by Carpeaux's return to France in 1872. When Napoleon III died on 9 January 1873, Carpeaux was called in haste to the bedside of the deceased, for the empress wished to have 'one last portrait' according to tradition. A death mask was commissioned from the *formatore* (mould-maker) Domenico Brucciani, but Carpeaux hardly used it, as he preferred to repeat the studies that he drew of the emperor on his deathbed. The sculptor was obviously very moved by the death of the deposed sovereign, whose benevolence on his behalf had never flagged. In the company of his wife, Carpeaux attended the exiled sovereign's funeral services, which took place on 15 January 1873 in St Mary's Church in Chislehurst.

Between 9 and 15 January Carpeaux was intensely active, as is evidenced by several drawings that are now part of the Musée d'Orsay's collections – they first belonged to the imperial prince and then to Empress Eugénie, who restored them to Amélie Carpeaux after the imperial prince's tragic death in 1879. A particularly striking drawing shows Napoleon III in his coffin, as the visitors could have seen him during the exhibition of his body in the hall at Camden Place, which had been transformed into a chapel of rest on 13 January 1873. Carpeaux scrupulously respects reality and depicts the late emperor attired in his major-general's uniform with his crossed hands holding a crucifix, while the grand sash of the Legion of Honour conspicuously covers his chest. He used the slope of the platform on which the coffin rested to reinforce the uneasiness triggered by the body's rigidity. A second drawing is not so concerned with the emperor's remains, but rather the ceremony of exhibiting the body in Camden Place hall. Carpeaux depicts the hall draped in black, while a white cross stands out above the raised coffin with, below, a highly visible escutcheon bearing the imperial 'N'. A crowd of dignitaries surround the platform in an atmosphere of somewhat suffocating reverence. Carpeaux's poignant drawings perfectly convey the collective emotion that reigned during those days of mourning when several thousand of the faithful came to render a last homage to the prematurely deceased emperor.

Napoleon III's bust is more solemn and perhaps less spontaneous, but for all that, is no less a portrait of great psychological acuity. The plaster model was finished on 13 January, and according to Louise Clément-Carpeaux, the empress and the prince attended some working

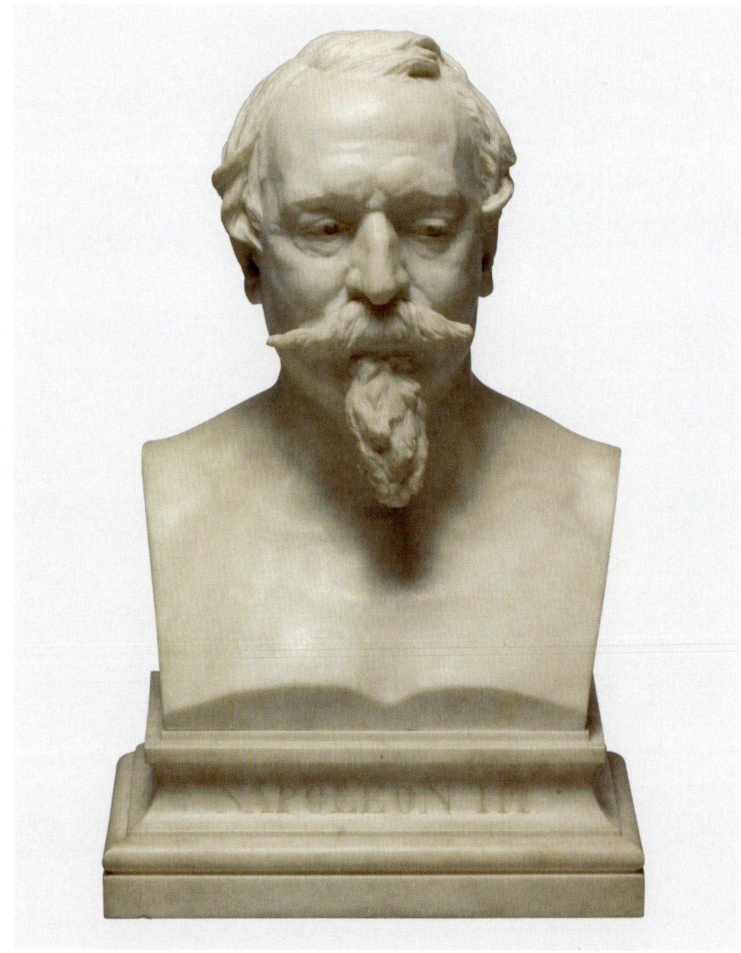

1

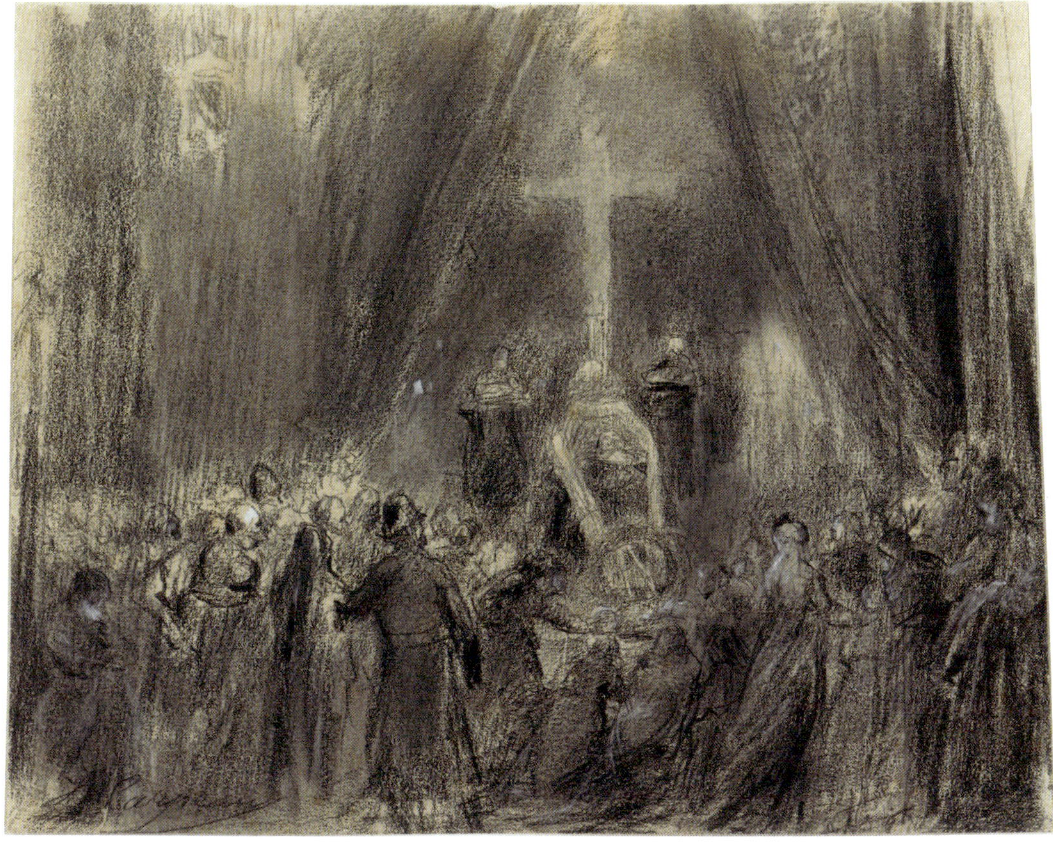

2

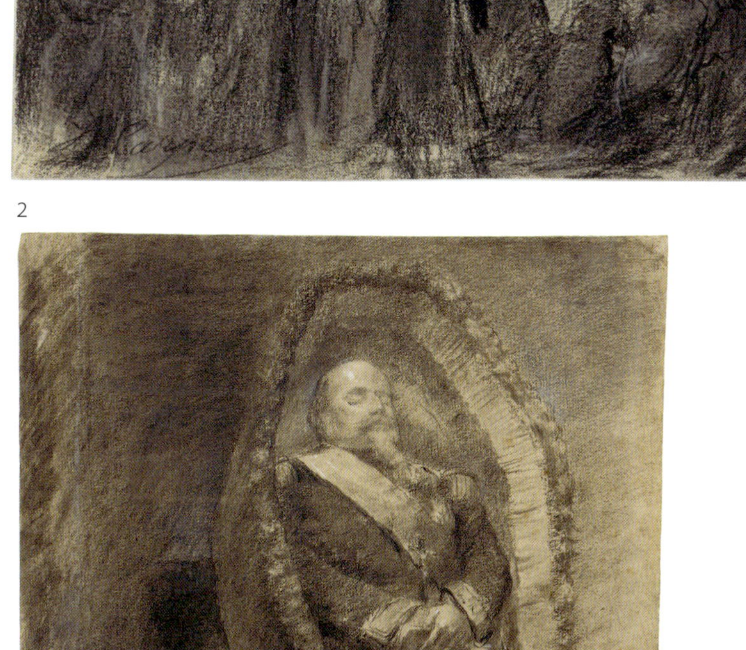

3

sessions where they advised the sculptor to reinforce 'the expression of gazing into the distance' and the 'bitterness in the lips', in order to give more suggestion of the deposed sovereign's distress. The Hermes bust formula, which was relatively uncommon for Carpeaux, allows attention to be concentrated on the monarch's face. Carpeaux, although a privileged witness of the empire's ostentatious displays, in no way depicts a glorious emperor, but rather a man tested by adversity. He does not seek to soften the features, which reveal traces of age and suffering.

The bust was not originally intended for wide distribution. Two marble examples were produced, one for Empress Eugénie – now conserved in the Metropolitan Museum of New York – and the other for Count Paul Demidoff and thereafter in the collection of the Victoria and Albert Museum. Nonetheless, the Carpeaux studio produced some duplicates in terracotta and plaster that were intended for the last supporters of the imperial family. CCV

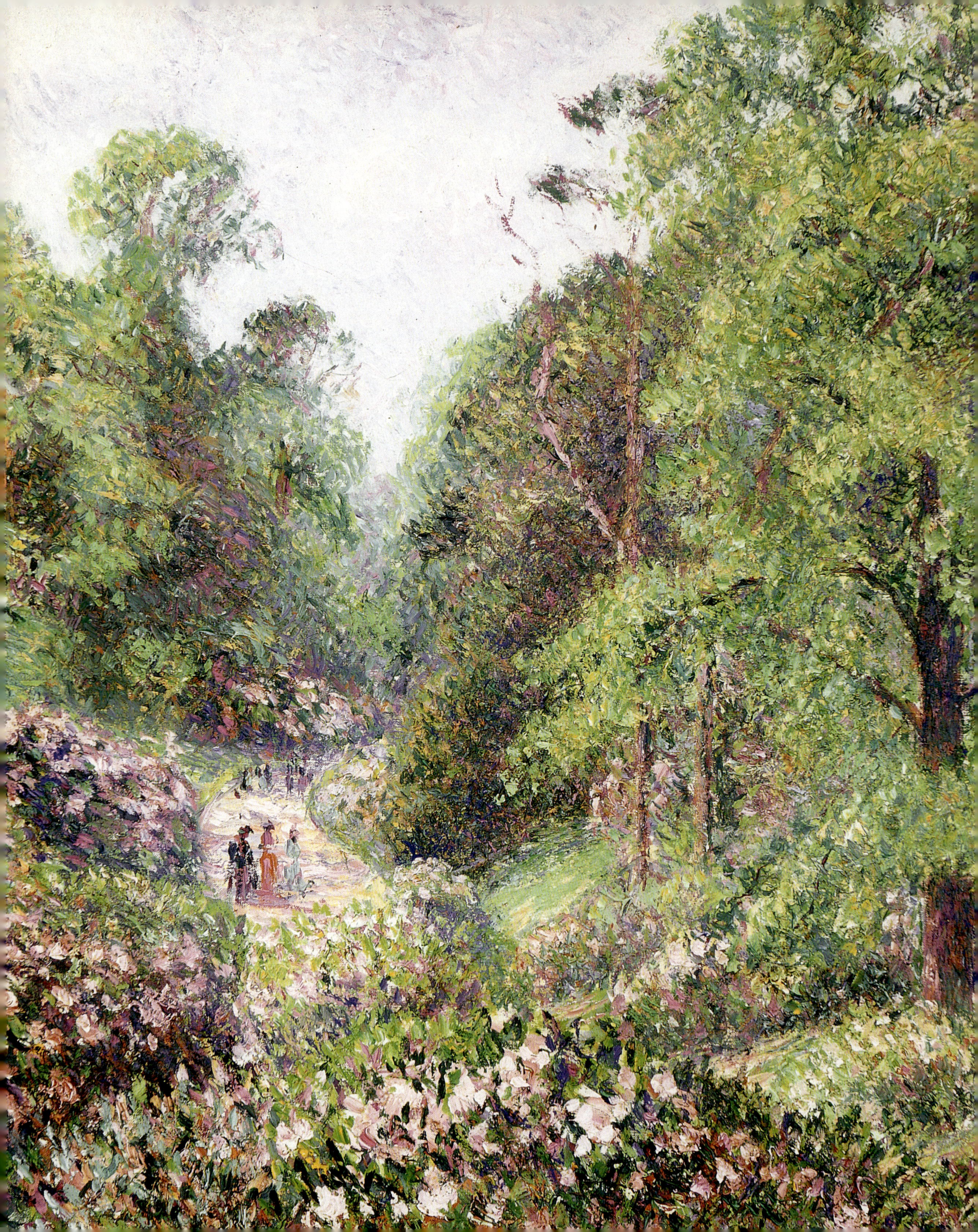

Carol Jacobi

Through French Eyes

French artists painted London with an outsider's eye. Their points of interest sometimes coincided with that of the tourist. The landmarks, parks and views that they depicted were familiar from guidebooks written by earlier exiles: the *Guides Joanne* series published *Londres illustré* by Elisée Reclus (p.192), with engraved plates and a fold-out map, and Alphonse Esquiros's *Guide Joanne de l'Angleterre* (1867).[1] They offered invaluable information for all pockets, on transport and the postal service, for example, essential for receiving news of fast-moving events in France, and on French restaurants, hotels and lodgings in London, but also on English society and habits.[2] Artists were working visitors, however, many of them refugees undergoing change or crisis in their careers and lives; their viewpoint was neither that of the tourist nor the native.

French enclaves and occupations

Artists exiled as a result of the Prussian conflict and the Commune were part of a wave of French refugees, most of them Communards who stayed on until the 1880 amnesty.[3] Since Huguenot days, French expatriates had gathered around three adjacent areas at the centre of the city.[4] In 1853 the writer Charles Dickens called the area 'the Patmos of London ... an island bounded by four squares; on the north by that of Soho, on the south by that of Leicester [Square], on the east by the quadrangle of Lincoln's Inn Fields ... and on the west by Golden Square'.[5] In that perimeter were a French church and the Société des Refugiés de la Commune, and the artist George Sala recalled French shops and hotels and trades on the upper floors, 'almost as French as the Rue Montmartre'.[6] Venues ranged from the fashionable Café Royal (established 1865) to the Communard patisserie, Maison Bertaux, still flourishing today.[7] In a city of three million, exiles were a minority, however, and while these fragments of familiarity may have been a consolation, poverty, cultural disorientation and the plight of France could lead to disheartenment.

Exiles had left behind their employment and all except the wealthiest had to improvise a living in a strange country with a strange language. Some trades where French expertise was especially respected, such as cooks and tailors, readily found work; others, such as Camille Monet, offered French lessons. At the other end of the scale, the dealer Durand-Ruel continued his business at the German Gallery at 168 New Bond Street and began annual exhibitions of the Society of French Artists. Writers and artists found employment in Britain's thriving print trade; articles by the exiled politician and future diplomat Camille Barrère, for example, appeared in *The Graphic*, and James Tissot was employed by Thomas Gibson Bowles to create cartoons for *Vanity Fair*.[8] Some taught: Alphonse Legros, who had relocated voluntarily in 1863, was employed at the South Kensington School of Art and appointed professor at the Slade School of Fine Art in 1876. Others had prior connections: the picture dealer Adolphe Goupil already had a London branch and the Barbizon painter Charles-François Daubigny had met collectors when he visited in 1866.

Camille Pissarro
Kew Gardens, Rhododendron Dell 1892
(detail, see p.205)

Well-established French artists and dealers settled in prosperous, leafy parts of West London, near the Kensington Museums, and integrated, to a certain extent, into British society. When Tissot arrived in 1871, he was taken in by Bowles at 88 St James Street.[9] This world is vividly reflected in the subject matter and the style of his paintings: his portraits of figures such as *Captain Frederick Burnaby* (pp.88–9), who supported *Vanity Fair*, and scenes of polite pastimes such as *Too Early* 1873 (p.94) and *Hush!* 1874 (pp.88–9). When Tissot moved north to his own property at 17 Grove End Road in the more liberal area of St John's Wood in early 1873 (p.96–7), he redecorated it in the aesthetic, eclectic manner of London artists' homes and entertained there. Many works were set in the studio and garden and painted with attention to beautiful accessories and effects of colour and light, for example *Holyday* (pp.202–3). Claude Monet, Camille and little Jean had less money and shared a lodging house in Kensington High Street.[10] *Meditation (Madame Monet on the Sofa)* shows Camille in the drawing room early in 1871 (pp.68–9). Her sad expression, the veiled window, closed book (resembling a red and gold Baedeker guide) and subdued light evoke *l'exilité*, the ennui described by the Communard Poncerot as 'this terrible exile, a malady which disturbs the sight and prevents it from going beyond a certain radius'.[11]

Camille Pissarro's mother had reached London a few months before he arrived in December, and gone to the Jewish community in Lower Norwood, one of the newer suburbs south of the river, recently connected by the railway. Pissarro and his family joined them, living first at Canham's Dairy on Westow Hill, next to a public house, and then 2 Chatham Terrace, Palace Road, Upper Norwood.[12] All but two of the fourteen canvases Pissarro made during his six-month residence depicted the environs of his home, a compromise between country and town with modest red brick buildings.

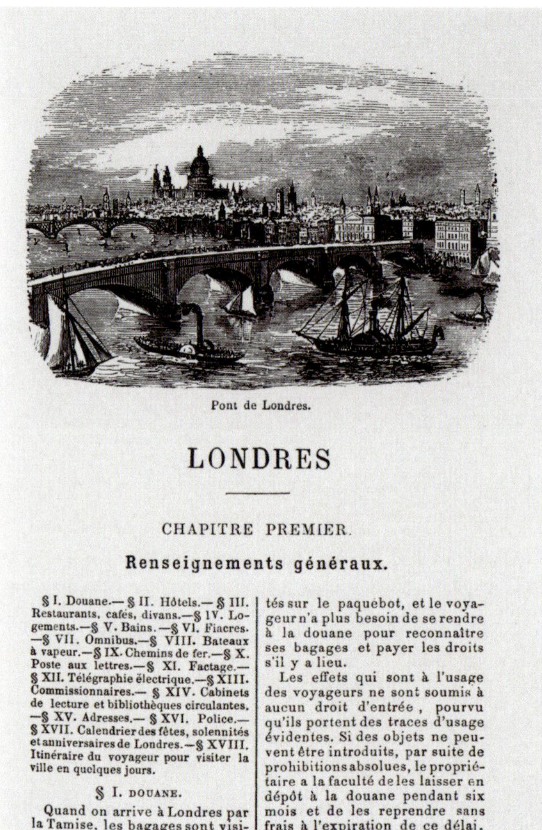

Pont de Londres.

LONDRES

CHAPITRE PREMIER.

Renseignements généraux.

§ I. Douane.— § II. Hôtels.— § III. Restaurants, cafés, divans.—§ IV. Logements.—§ V. Bains.—§ VI. Fiacres.—§ VII. Omnibus.—§ VIII. Bateaux à vapeur.—§ IX. Chemins de fer.—§ X. Poste aux lettres.—§ XI. Factage.—§ XII. Télégraphie électrique.—§ XIII. Commissionnaires.— § XIV. Cabinets de lecture et bibliothèques circulantes.—§ XV. Adresses.— § XVI. Police.—§ XVII. Calendrier des fêtes, solennités et anniversaires de Londres.—§ XVIII. Itinéraire du voyageur pour visiter la ville en quelques jours.

§ I. DOUANE.

Quand on arrive à Londres par la Tamise, les bagages sont visités sur le paquebot, et le voyageur n'a plus besoin de se rendre à la douane pour reconnaître ses bagages et payer les droits s'il y a lieu.

Les effets qui sont à l'usage des voyageurs ne sont soumis à aucun droit d'entrée, pourvu qu'ils portent des traces d'usage évidentes. Si des objets ne peuvent être introduits, par suite de prohibitions absolues, le propriétaire a la faculté de les laisser en dépôt à la douane pendant six mois et de les reprendre sans frais à l'expiration de ce délai.

'London Bridge'
Londres Illustré 1865

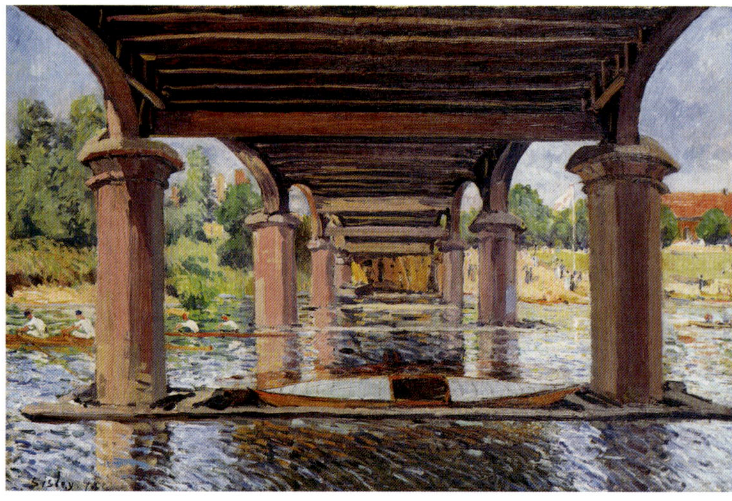

Alfred Sisley
Under the Bridge at Hampton Court
1874
Oil paint on canvas 50 × 76

Kunstmuseum Winterthur

Favoured locations for artists like Tissot, Pissarro and Monet

London was the largest city in the world, often described in guides and travel writing as a 'monster' that was impossible to completely explore or navigate, but French expatriates were drawn to certain locations. The global scope of the collection of the British Museum had no parallel in Paris, and the Reading Room became a favourite of exiles in the wet winter months, for its 'heating, lighting, pens and ink were free'.[13] Individual maps and guides for museums and galleries were provided in books such as *Londres illustré*. Tissot's *London Visitors* (p.108), set on the steps of the National Gallery in front of the church of St Martin-in-the-Fields, portrays a man consulting a well-thumbed manual while his companion catches our eye and points with her umbrella through the columns to Trafalgar Square. Monet and Pissarro visited Dulwich Picture Gallery, and Pissarro painted the brand new buildings of *Dulwich College* (built by Charles Barry Jr, 1870; p.72), inspired both by Gothic and Italian architecture, while Monet made his first picture of the Gothic towers and pinnacles of the new Palace of Westminster in *The Thames below Westminster* (pp.66–7). Daubigny and Monet painted together by the Thames and Daubigny began a view of the distinctive London skyline with the dome of St Paul's Cathedral in *St Paul's from the Surrey Side* 1871 (pp.64–5). Such recognisable motifs were, and still are, a staple of artists painting abroad in any location, enhancing the authenticity and the saleability of their pictures: in the mid-1870s Giuseppe de Nittis travelled from Paris to London to make a series of similar views, including *The National Gallery* 1877 (p.109) and *Westminster* 1878 (pp.208–11).

The Thames was an established subject for artists such as Turner and Constable, and in the 1870s its new embankment, bridges and traffic made it London's grandest spectacle. The opening image of *Londres illustré*, 'London Bridge', shows these in a view of the north bank similar to Daubigny's *St Paul's from the Surrey Side*. The river was a means of transport and guidebooks gave details of steamboats departing every ten minutes, which for a penny or halfpenny, transported passengers from quay to quay, providing artists with access to vantage points from the tranquil upstream villages to busy docks in the west.[14] Throughout the 1870s Tissot depicted pleasure seekers and travellers in the recommended locations and on the river itself.[15] Pissarro and, later, Monet painted Westminster seen beyond Charing Cross Bridge (also known as Hungerford Bridge; pp.222–3, 66–7) and, up the river, the more placid environs of Hampton Court, such as Sisley's *Molesey Weir, Hampton Court, Morning* 1874 (p.79). London was the most industrialised city in the world, with factories all along the Thames. In 1866 Daubigny sought out the wharves and warehouses of the then fashionable estuary resort of Erith (p.62); and four years later Daubigny and Monet followed the example of Whistler's etching series 'The Thames Set' 1871 and painted the less picturesque south bank and the docks, warehouses and tall ships downriver seen in Monet's *Pool of London* (National Museum of Wales, Cardiff) and *Boats in the Pool of London* 1871 (p.227).[16] Pissarro and Sisley's interest in the new iron lattice-work Hungerford Bridge (1864) and Hampton Court Bridge (1865), in Sisley's *Bridge at Hampton Court, Mitre Inn* 1874 (p.199) and his striking image of the four cast-iron columns *Under the Bridge at Hampton Court* 1874 (p.192), underlines the fascination the French felt for the new engineering structures spanning the Thames.

The artists brought their individual viewpoints to such subjects, however. Pissarro recorded that he and Monet were painting directly from nature, and their paintings of London were in keeping with the attention to everyday motifs and transient atmospheric effects that they had been pursuing in France. Norwood reminded Pissarro, perhaps, of his home in Louveciennes, also a modern suburb, and there is a noticeable continuity between the South London scenes and the modest plein-air representations that he and his associates had been painting the previous year. *Fox Hill, Upper Norwood* 1870 (p.70), painted in the cold winter, recalls *Road to Versailles at Louveciennes: Winter and Snow* 1869–70 (Thyssen-Bornemisza Museum), with the exception of the industrial red-brick building materials of the houses.[17] The enormous iron-and-glass Crystal Palace, designed by Charles Paxton for the first International Exhibition in 1851 and the subject of an entire chapter of *Londres Illustré*, had been moved to nearby Sydenham and was depicted by Pissarro in *Crystal Palace, Upper Norwood* 1871 (p.71).[18] The fabulous structure, half a kilometre long, is reduced to a shape on the horizon, however. Like *The Avenue, Sydenham* (pp.74–5) showing Lawrie Park Avenue and a village church, *Crystal Palace, Upper Norwood* looks at the suburb springing up around the landmark. Later impressionist paintings followed this pattern. In 1890 Pissarro returned and made six views of London. He went as far west up the river as Molesey, the site of Hampton Court Palace, but he painted the old stable buildings overlooking the green, then the Cardinal Wolsey Inn, rather than the palace itself (p.204).

Monet brought a similarly modern, realist eye to London sites. He worked in the parks in the spring of 1871, painting *Hyde Park* (p.200–1) and *Green Park* (Philadelphia Museum of Art).[19] He avoided the grand buildings, military parades and aristocratic riders and carriages that were discussed in the guidebooks and presented a Barbizon-style view reminiscent of Camille Corot, a green bank with a few small figures and a relatively anonymous Bayswater skyline, punctuated by London's characteristic church spires.[20] The famous royal parks may also have reminded French visitors of the outskirts of Paris. They had impressed Napoleon III when he sheltered in the city before coming to power in France in 1851, and the informal layout with meandering streams and lakes provided the model for two new green spaces, the Bois de Boulogne and Bois de Vincennes. Monet chose a curving carriageway, rather than one of the straight paths, for his foreground in *Hyde Park*. In 1890 Pissarro painted the main thoroughfare Rotten Row in *Hyde Park* 1890 (Tokyo Fuji Art Museum) and *The Round Pond, Kensington Gardens* (private collection), with Kensington Palace in the background and the round pond echoing its pair in the Parc Bagatelle, Bois de Boulogne.

In Paris, public gardens such as the Tuileries were laid out formally and the visitors were confined to geometric networks of paths. Monet's paintings of people scattered on the grass imaged the relative freedom of London parks. Hyde Park had deeper associations of liberty, renowned Europe-wide as an exemplar of Britain's tolerance of free association and speech. People gathered and spoke at the blackened stump of the Reformers' Tree, burned down during Reform League protests in 1866 and replaced by 117s' Corner in 1872.[21] French exiles enjoyed latitude to speak and publish, and Esquiros's essays on England published in *Revue des Deux Mondes* declared: 'The inhabitant of London … can purchase for a trifle newspapers, in which men dare to say everything.'[22]

The London royal parks had been open to the public since the 1851 Crown Lands Act and their mixing of the rich and other classes was represented in English literature, paintings and prints such as George Housman Thomas's widely reproduced *Rotten Row* 1855 (private collection).[23] The spectacle of the gentry riding along this famous thoroughfare was an attraction for tourists and locals alike. De Nittis's *Flirtation, Hyde Park* 1874 (p.195) showed a similar array of people watching gentlemen and ladies. He took the point of view of the crowd, however, closer in spirit to the attitude of Charles Baudelaire's essay 'The Painter of Modern Life' or paintings such as Manet's *Music in the Tuileries* 1862 (National Gallery, London).[24] The classes are less legible than Thomas's spectators; the chatting girls with parasols and the well-dressed woman courted by the top-hatted man could be the middle classes relaxing, or the working classes dressed in their best. Pissarro's *Hyde Park* also represented the riders and carriages but screened by a row of trees. Most of his park views were inhabited by ordinary-looking people, as in *Kew Green* 1892 (pp.206–7) and the milling throng of *Bank Holiday, Kew* 1892 (pp.212–13).

British traditions and social contrasts

French travellers took special interest in British habits and rituals. Pissarro developed a lifelong affection for the traditions of the 'unusual' English Christmas, especially the tree and the pudding.[25] Artists such as Tissot liked depicting uniforms, in *Portsmouth Dockyard* c.1877 (p.113), for example, and the blue and yellow garb of the Christ's Hospital schoolboys in *London Visitors*. Expatriates were also attracted to *les sports anglais*, as developed and formalised in mid-century by an expanding sector of private schools. French people had considered English sports as uncouth, but their value to nation and empire in promoting fitness and collective values was increasingly appreciated, especially after the military humiliation of the Prussian War. The games, kit and rituals became popular with the *haute bourgeoisie*. In Paris the Anglo-French Jockey Club de Paris already presided over horse racing and associated social events, and by 1883 the Racing Club de France was a centre for everything from rugby to golf.[26] Pissarro, who developed a passion for cricket, painted its formalities in *Hampton Court Green* and *Kew Green*. When he stayed with his son Lucien in Bedford Park, West London, in 1897, he recorded a match between Hammersmith and Shepherd's Bush Police and Tradesmen played on 22 June in honour of Queen Victoria's diamond jubilee.

Water sports and their inherent social codes particularly appealed to outsider artists. Sisley's *Bridge at Hampton Court, Mitre Inn* features two coxed pairs racing on the river. On the same visit, he caught the gaiety of the *Regatta at Hampton Court* (Foundation Bührle) and the *Regatta at Molesey* (p.198). In that year Tissot painted a royal dance scene at the large annual regatta at Cowes, on the Isle of Wight, *The Ball on Shipboard* (pp.196–7). The quintessentially English subject executed in a finely detailed manner expected by the Royal Academy audience was perceived by *The Times* as an 'appropriation of English styles and subjects' by a 'clever French painter'.[27] *Holyday* (pp.202–3), painted the following year, offered similar mixed messages, young men in cricket caps lounging with young ladies, as did *On the Thames* (p.220), portraying a man and two women setting off for a jaunt on a steam launch. Like de Nittis, Tissot dealt with the intrigue and illegibility of modern public life, *la vie extérieure*.

French artists in London observed the instability and flux of English society. French guides, travel writing and memoirs stressed the speed and freedom of circulation of England's industrialised society: 'The inhabitant of London has already at his orders more railways than exist in any capital of the world,' wrote Esquiros, 'and he commands a network of electric wires ever ready to transmit his messages and wishes from one place to another.'[28] London's swarming thoroughfares astonished visitors and the crowd was a common motif for conveying the size and movement of the city, busy roads and crossroads such as Trafalgar Square, seen in de Nittis's *National Gallery* and his *Piccadilly: Wintry Walk* (pp.208–9). De Nittis observed these scenes from a cab and enhanced the dynamic effect with diagonal directional brush strokes.[29] As Esquiros's passage suggests, to be in London was to be reminded constantly of the world beyond, the river being a conduit for goods arriving from and leaving for the British Empire, especially as represented by Whistler, Doré, Daubigny and Monet. The empire was equally present in the oriental accessories and textiles that decorate interior scenes such as *Meditation*. Tissot's *Captain Frederick Burnaby* reclines below a map of the Indian Ocean and Southeast Asia, governed over via the newly opened Suez Canal.

Some French visitors decried the contrast between the enormous wealth and the conditions of the working class that they observed in the city. These were vividly portrayed in the novels of Dickens and in Henry Mayhew's social survey *London Labour and the London Poor (1840–1851)*, which informed Alexandre Ledru-Rollin's *De la décadence de l'Angleterre* (1850). In 1872 Gustave Doré and Blanchard Jerrold published *London: A Pilgrimage*, in which 180 engravings represented the city from the genteel parks in the west to the abject poverty in the east, and in the following years leading Communard Jules Vallès published a critical series, 'La Rue à Londres'.[30] Ledru-Rollin's and Vallès's books contained engravings of London types illustrated in Mayhew and some of these appear in French paintings, for example the sandwich-board men and the flower seller, juxtaposed with the finely dressed ladies in de Nittis's *National Gallery*.[31] The sandwich-board man reappears in *Piccadilly* with other typical street inhabitants such as the cabby and the policeman. The presence of a turbanned street sweeper critiques the British Empire.[32]

Coldness of English temperament and climate

Alongside this sympathy for the poor was a convention of characterising English people as mercenary, calculating and lacking in feeling, their temperament equated to their weather.[33] An exile from the 1848 generation, Victor Schoelcher, called England 'the coldest country on Earth in all meanings', an opinion that came through again in the comparison of 'Frenchman and Englishmen' that concluded Hippolyte Taine's *Notes sur l'Angleterre* (1872).[34] This is apt for some of Tissot's paintings, his

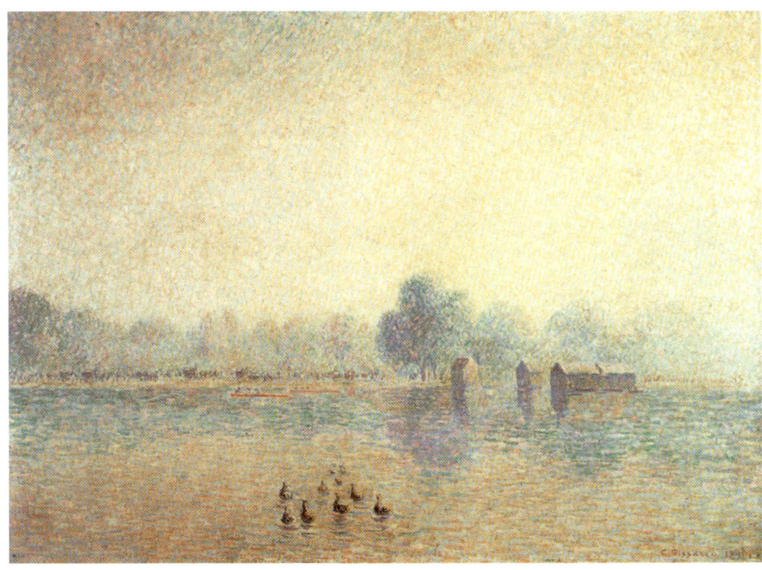

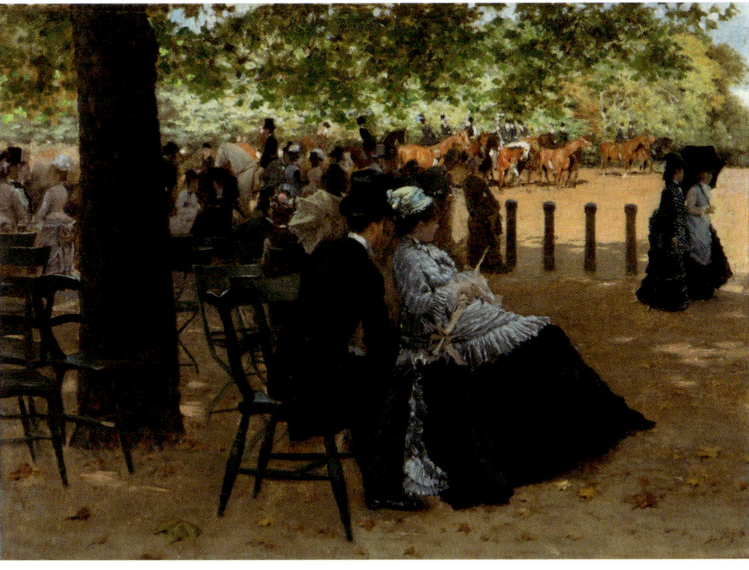

Camille Pissarro
Serpentine, Hyde Park, London, Fog Effect
Oil paint on canvas 54 × 73
Private collection

Giuseppe de Nittis
Flirtation, Hyde Park 1874
Oil paint on canvas 33 × 43
Private collection, Naples

cool tonality and characterisation of *London Visitors*, criticised at the time for its 'arctic frigidity', the figures 'curiously cold and antipathetic'.[35] In 1875 Charles Hugo condemned the 'immense city' as 'without grandeur ... Three million inhabitants who come, circulate, speculate, swarm and do not live ... Three million bewildered beings have but one aim: money.'[36] The Thames, its teeming wharves and factories, introduced many travel accounts and became a ubiquitous metaphor for Britain as a whole. Ledru-Rollin begins *De la décadence de l'Angleterre* with a paean to Britain's vast wealth and mastery 'greater than the Roman universe', only to experience 'vertigo': 'From one of those bold bridges flung across the Thames, the eye grows weary, and the head becomes dizzy in tracing, in the midst of a hallucinatory atmosphere of smoke and vapour, the hundreds of vessels that pass beneath your feet.'[37] The unstable angles of Tissot's *On the Thames* captures this actual and cultural disorientation.

Pissarro stated that he and Monet found most interest in the challenge of churning, changing atmospheric effects, which were perhaps the most ubiquitous feature of traveller accounts.[38] Monet's *Hyde Park* resonates with a description of a park by Hippolyte Taine: 'The bathed light, the air charged with vapour, the insensible and continuous changes of the vast exhalation which softens, imparts a bluish tint to, and dims the contours, the whole producing the impression of a great life, vague, diffused and melancholy, the life of a humid country.'[39] In 1890 Pissarro painted *Serpentine, Hyde Park, London, Fog Effect*, which dissolves the distant grass and trees between luminous sky and water. Monet returned to the Savoy Hotel, with its river views and superb French cuisine under the command of Auguste Escoffier, to paint his famous Thames Series. In 1901 he took time out to return to his first foothold, Leicester Square, and observe, and finally capture, the surging city crowds. Three extraordinary pictures of *Leicester Square* illuminated by new electric lights, viewed from an oblique angle, capture the excitement and bewilderment of London (pp.214–15).

'No Frenchman goes to England for pleasure, or resides there by choice', wrote Hector Malot in *La vie moderne en Angleterre* in 1862.[40] French visitors to Britain were inevitably influenced by the size and strangeness of the city and by the history of animosity and ambivalence between the two cultures, and it is possible to perceive the alienating vision of London expressed in expatriate literature and art. Monet recalled his first seven-month sojourn as a 'miserable time', which seems to be reflected in the subdued, distanced early pictures.[41] As Nancy Ireson has observed, however, anglophobia was not shared by everyone, and an informed, alternative attitude was one of the ways that the French avant-garde distinguished itself from the mainstream.[42] The hints at caricature, ambivalence and ennui in French representations of London are only some of many nuances of their eye for the modern: new urban and suburban landscapes and lifestyles, and uncertain human relationships.

James Tissot
1836–1902
The Ball on Shipboard c.1874
Oil paint on canvas 84.1 × 129.5

Tate. Presented by the Trustees of the Chantrey Bequest 1937

The Ball on Shipboard was Tissot's most ambitious modern-life drama, assembling over twenty figures into elegant groupings divided by the boat's deck. Each August, high society would flock to the Isle of Wight, off the south coast of Britain, to enjoy the sun, sailing races and parties. The ball provided Tissot with an opportunity to render an English occasion closer to those being created by his impressionist contemporaries in Paris, a festive modern-life scene in full sunlight, which, as one critic put it, looked 'as if it has fallen against a damp rainbow'.[1]

Krystyna Matyjaszkiewicz has recently linked the painting to an afternoon dance held on the royal naval frigate *HMS Ariadne* on 12 August 1873, at which the Prince and Princess of Wales, Albert and Alexandra, and Tsarevitch Alexander and his wife Maria (Alexandra's sister) were present.[2] Alexandra and Maria were in the habit of dressing identically and did so on this occasion.[3] Matyjaszkiewicz identifies them as the two women in white outfits, one glancing at the viewer. Beside them, Matyjaszkiewicz has recognised Thomas Egerton, 2nd Earl of Wilton and Commodore of the Royal Yacht Squadron, the subject of a Tissot caricature later that month.[4] Photographs and news reports of visitors, boats and events of the regatta circulated widely, and Tissot travelled to Cowes to observe subjects for his caricatures in *Vanity Fair*. His close friend, the magazine's editor Thomas Gibson Bowles, was a guest at the *Ariadne* dance and may have secured Tissot an invitation. The man leaning on the railing on the extreme left, with the boater has been identified as Bowles or Tissot himself.[5] Tissot relied on his own models and props for his highly finished style, however, and painted the work in his studio. He owned the flags, chairs and many of the dresses, which appeared in other paintings.

The ship is given over to style and pleasure. The only sails are those of nearby yachts and the *Ariadne*'s own rigging is decked in bunting. No lifeboats hang in the davits, seen beyond the group in blue and turquoise dresses. The sailors have become spectators, lined up watching the dancing at the back of the boat, and only two armed soldiers stand out in their red coats. Naval attire blends with the ball costume; the princesses wear white silk and naval braiding, and masculine and feminine become less distinct; both sexes, including the princesses, sport boater hats. The princesses' matching outfits have been adopted by other women in the picture and the paired figures showing the dresses from different angles recall the convention of fashion plates. This eye for the performance in modern life was characteristic of the paintings being shown in Paris by Tissot's friend Manet and impressionist painters, inspired by Charles Baudelaire, but it troubled some British critics. 'Unreality creeps into everything,' wrote one journalist: it was an 'age of shams'.[6] CJ

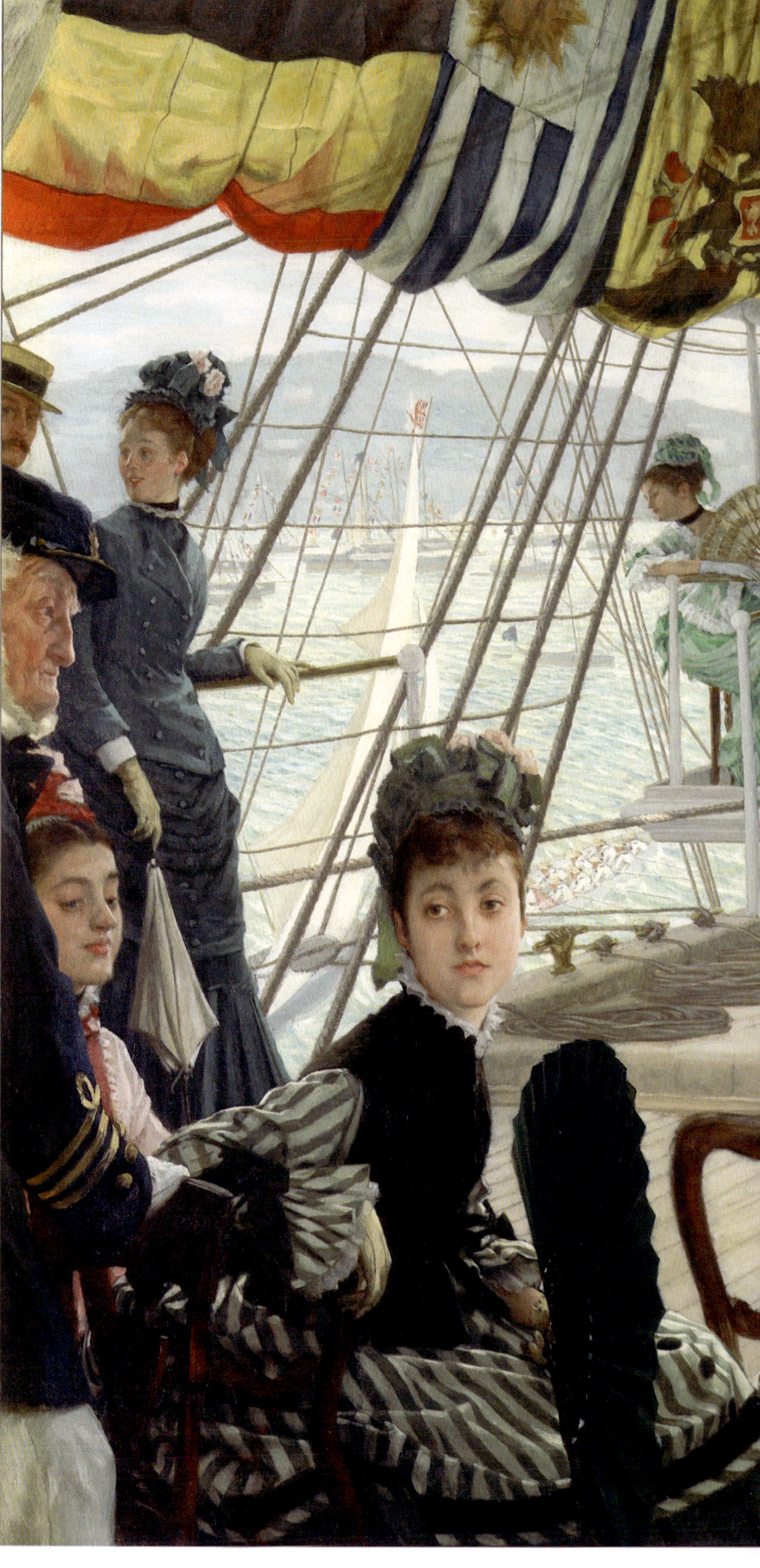

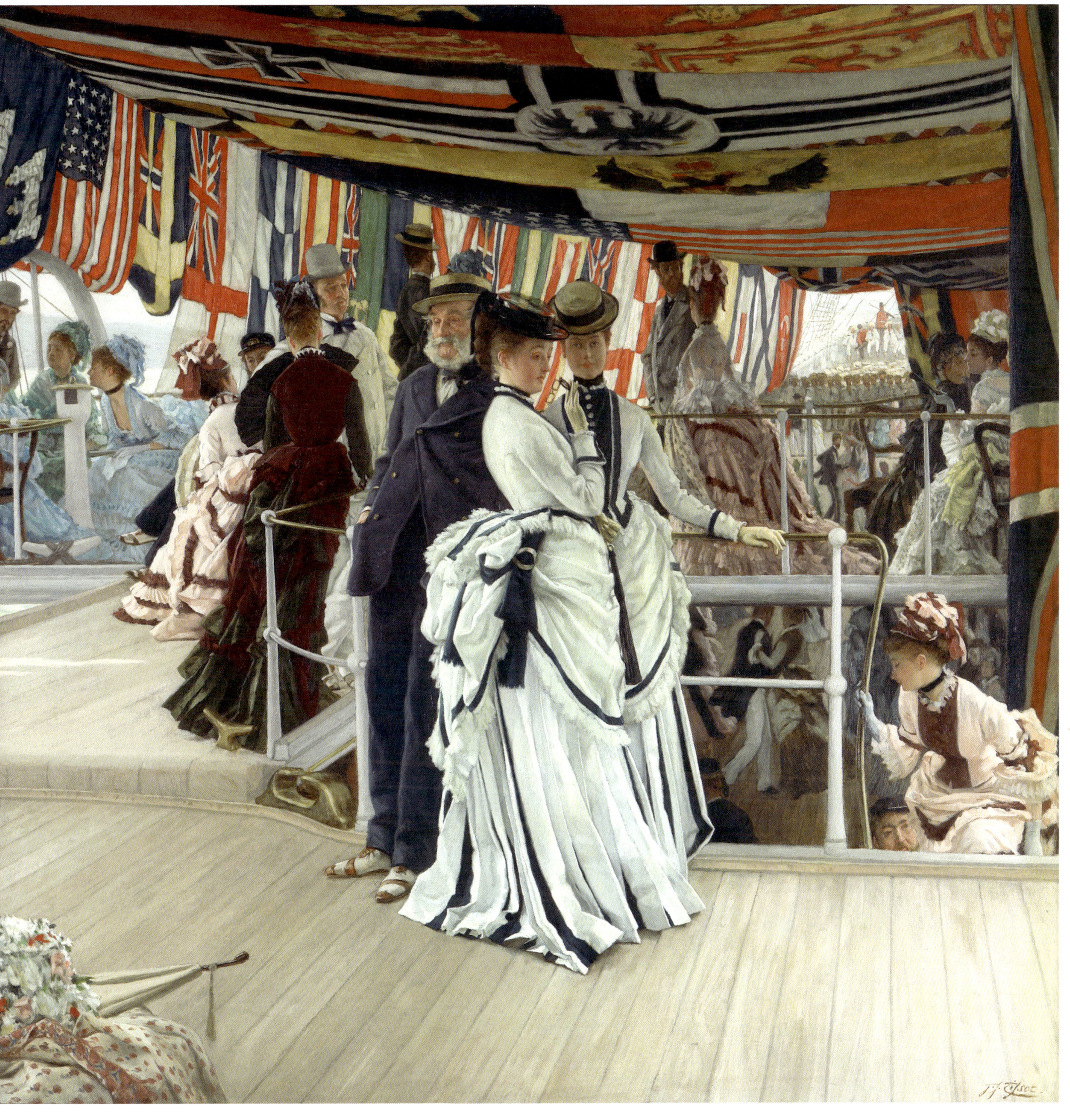

Alfred Sisley
1839–1899
The Regatta at Molesey 1874
Oil paint on canvas 66 × 91.5

Musée d'Orsay, Paris. Bequeathed by Gustave Caillebotte, 1894

The organisation of the first official regattas on the Thames dates back to the late eighteenth century. The practice of sculling developed in the very privileged context of the great English colleges and universities. The extension of railroads from 1840 made it possible for this sport to develop by facilitating access to new navigable sites. Situated on the London and South Western Railway line that had connected Vauxhall with Southampton since 1840, Hampton Court was able to host nautical competitions by 1867. The regattas at Molesey were inaugurated in 1873, not long before they inspired one of Sisley's most audacious compositions.

The painter has placed himself behind the finishing line to observe the approach of the boats going at top speed. The social and sporting codes that governed this encounter did not escape this informed anglophone's eye. He noted the presence of a few elegant members of the sculling club in white uniforms and blue caps grouped at the foot of the mast that holds the black and white flag of the Molesey Boat Club. The race is a large one. The teams face off in long, pointed eights with coxes, following the prestigious example of encounters between Oxford and Cambridge earlier in the season. The formal presence of the large flags of the Union Jack, the English Crown and the Royal Navy, which are stretched above the water to welcome the winners, is somewhat shaken by the wind. In painting these regattas, Sisley remains above all a landscape painter who is even more attentive to the caprices of light than to the vivacity of men.

Monet who, in this same period, had settled in Argenteuil, would also attempt to paint the elusive atmosphere of the banks of the Seine in broken brush strokes. His luminous *Regatta at Argenteuil* 1872 (Musée d'Orsay) was bought by Gustave Caillebotte in 1876. This companion of impressionist exhibitions, who was a great fan of rowing and nautical sports, would also acquire *The Regatta at Molesey.* Thanks to the Caillebotte legacy, Sisley's work entered the Musée du Luxembourg, Paris, in 1896. IC

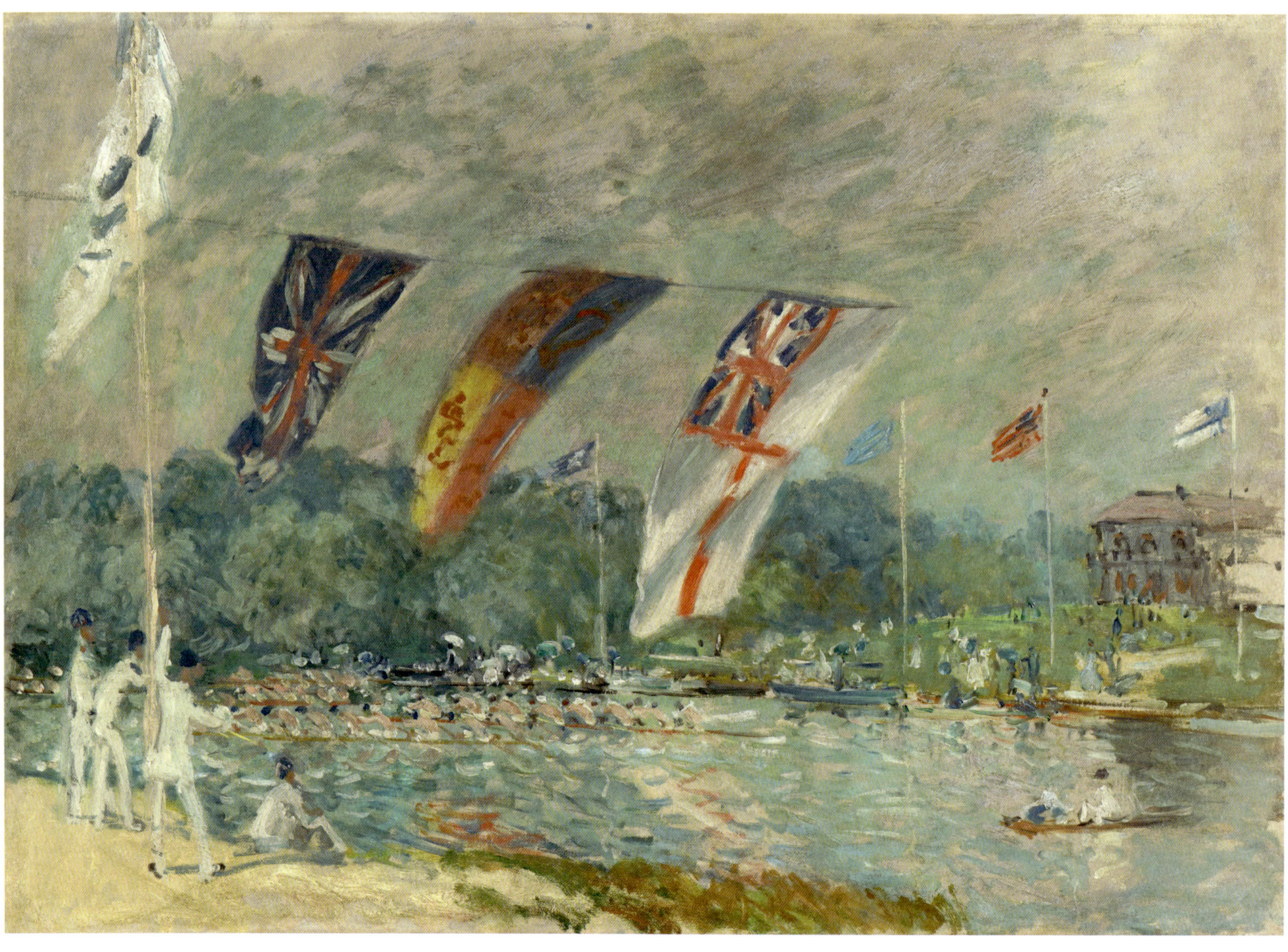

Alfred Sisley
1839–1899
The Bridge at Hampton Court, Mitre Inn 1874
Oil paint on canvas 46 × 61

Wallraf-Richartz-Museum & Foundation Corboud, Cologne

The months spent in England were all the more fertile as Sisley discovered an environment along the Hampton Court river banks that was comparable to what he had known in France. Working outside on site allowed him to reinvent space by releasing him from 'conventional layouts, whose landscapes painted in a studio had not been allowed to completely fall to pieces'.[1] This newly-found freedom gained new impetus beside the Thames. Built on a metal framework in 1865, the Hampton Court Bridge dominates the composition with its singular massiveness. The view of it from the shore recalls that of the *Bridge at Villeneuve-la-Garenne* painted in 1872 (Metropolitan Museum of Art, New York). Sisley positioned himself near the arches below the bridge on the southern bank, the Moseley side. At the end of the bridge, the Mitre Inn can be recognised by its red-brick walls and sloping roof standing out from the sky in beautiful weather. The air seems to circulate through the canvas, making the colours of the flag hoisted on the shore vibrate. In this geometrically defined space, the artist's brush does not linger to specify outlines. A few touches of colour suffice to suggest the movement of men rowing at top speed or to give presence to the women seated on the grass in the shade of their umbrellas.

At the risk of shocking the English public proud of its historic cultural heritage, and without considering the imposing presence of the castle that is very close, Sisley gives the impression that all the seasonal activity is oriented towards nautical sports. Even worse, he gives a magisterial position to the functional architecture of a modern bridge without paying the least attention to the remnants of Tudor grandeur.

The work, which was contrary to Victorian taste, was brought back to France and the collection of Théodore Duret, the rich heir to a brand of Cognac, who had undertaken the defence of impressionism early on, after making friends with Manet. In 1906 he wrote the history of the movement. Duret had also played an important role in the spread of japonisme, which he had discovered at the Universal Exhibition in London in 1862. Condemned for having defended the federates during the Commune, he left the country for the Far East with his friend Henri Cernuschi and stayed for a long period in Japan in 1871–2. Enriched by his discussions on painting with Manet, Pissarro and Monet, Duret analysed Ukiyo-e prints in terms of an impressionist vision. This enlightened art collector's decision to acquire *The Bridge at Hampton Court* could have been guided by his dual passion. IC

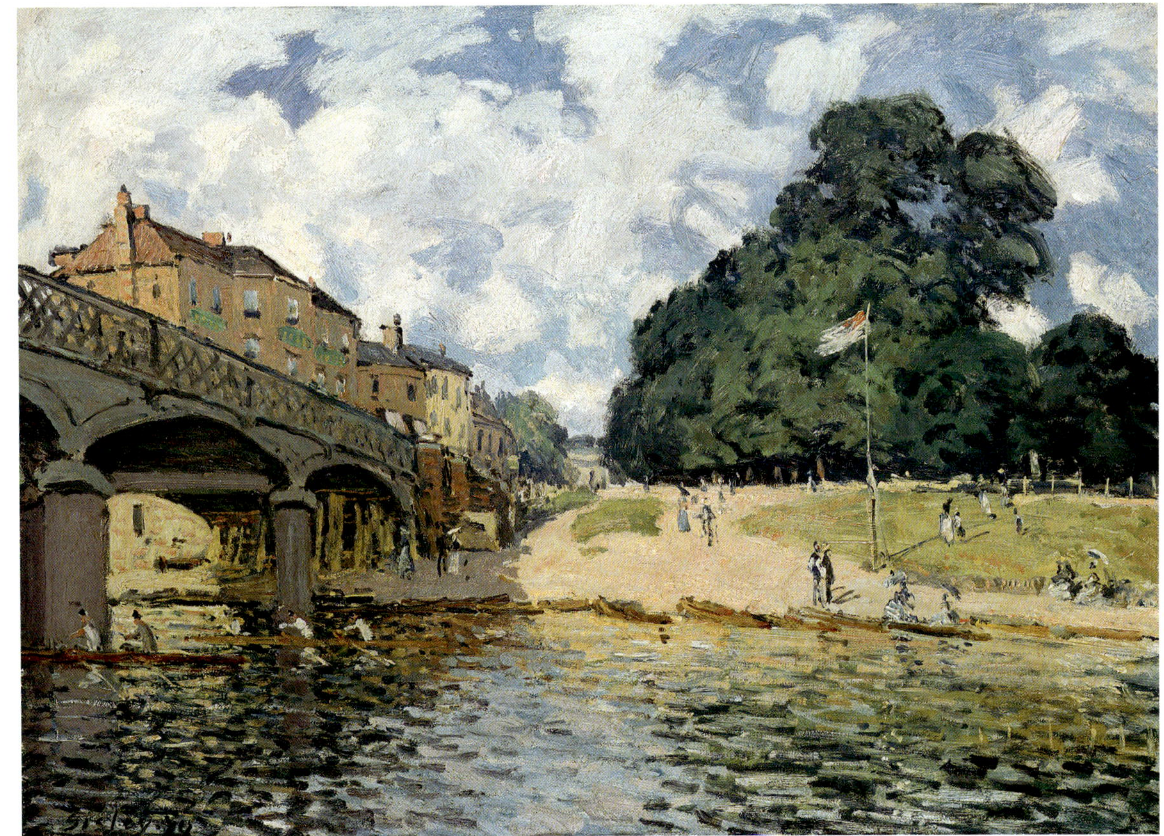

Claude Monet
1840–1926
Hyde Park 1871
Oil paint on canvas 40.5 × 74

Museum of Art, Rhode Island School of Design, Providence. Gift of Mrs Murray S.Danforth

During his exile in London, Monet's attention was divided between London parks and the Thames. He painted three views of the river, and two of parks: *Green Park* 1871 (Philadelphia) and the present view of *Hyde Park*.

In both paintings Monet adopted a panoramic format emphasising the vast expanses of nature at the heart of the city, and the sense of freedom that they must have generated. By contrast, parks and squares in Paris were smaller, highly landscaped, and in many of them it was forbidden to walk on the grass. Monet must have been struck by the scale of London parks, and the social interplay for which they provided a setting.

Monet swiftly brushed in most of the strollers' figures with black paint, as silhouettes, but they are characterised enough to identify that the artist recorded several social categories side by side in the park. A modest couple stands out closest to the viewer, the woman with her Venetian red hair loose, the man wearing a simple felt hat. The vivid colour of the woman's hair combined with the red of her skirt lift an otherwise muted palette. They are about to walk past two ladies sitting on the patchy lawn, and a gentleman with a top hat standing beside them, which suggests that he comes from a more privileged social background than the couple. Other top hats can be seen scattered through Hyde Park, and most figures are grouped, indicating social interaction. Very few of them are actually walking on the path that leads from the Serpentine to Bayswater Road. The houses on the horizon to the right are those lining that road. The church spire towards the centre is that of St James's Sussex Gardens, and the spire to the left belonged to Christ Church, Lancaster Gate.[1] CCP

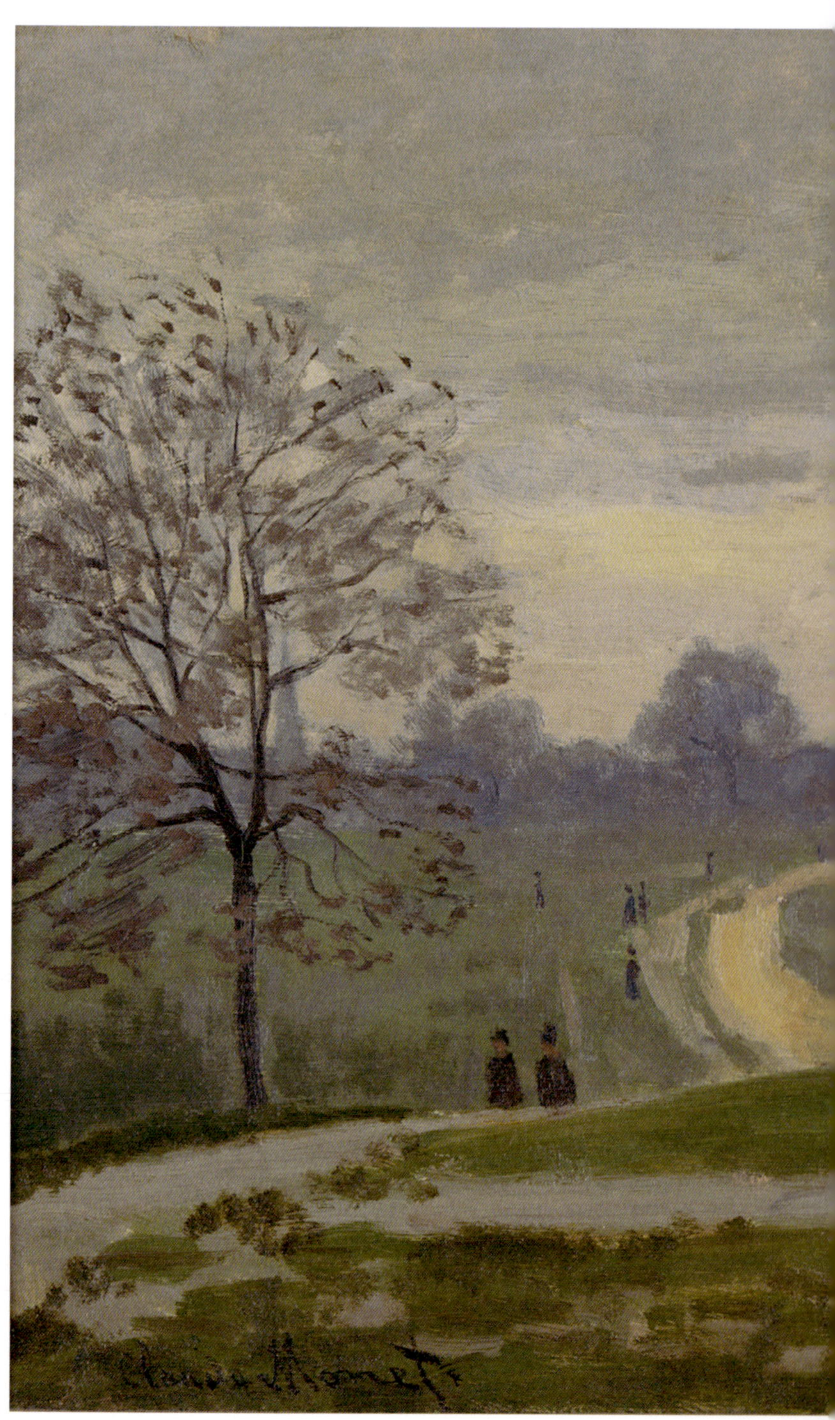

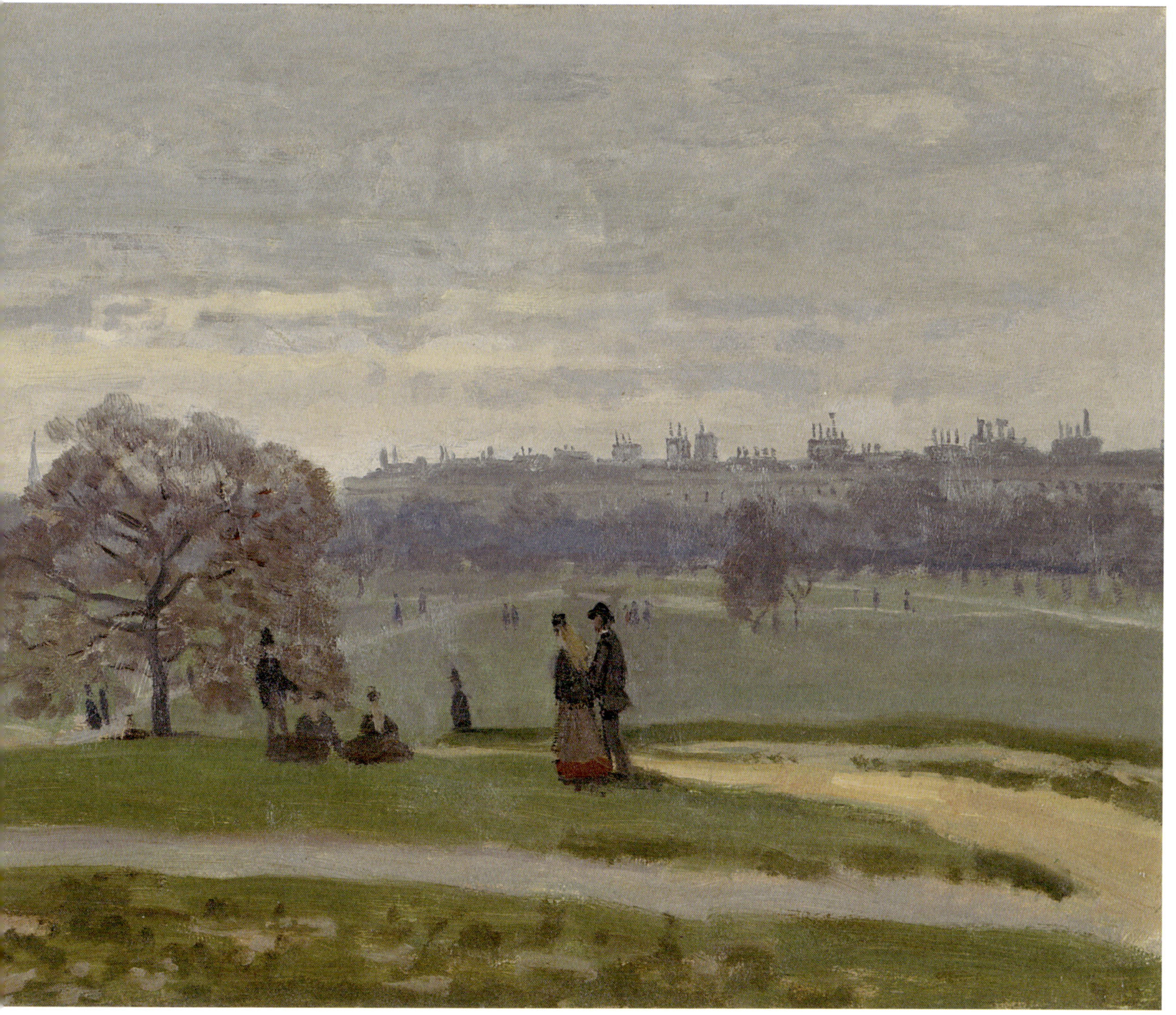

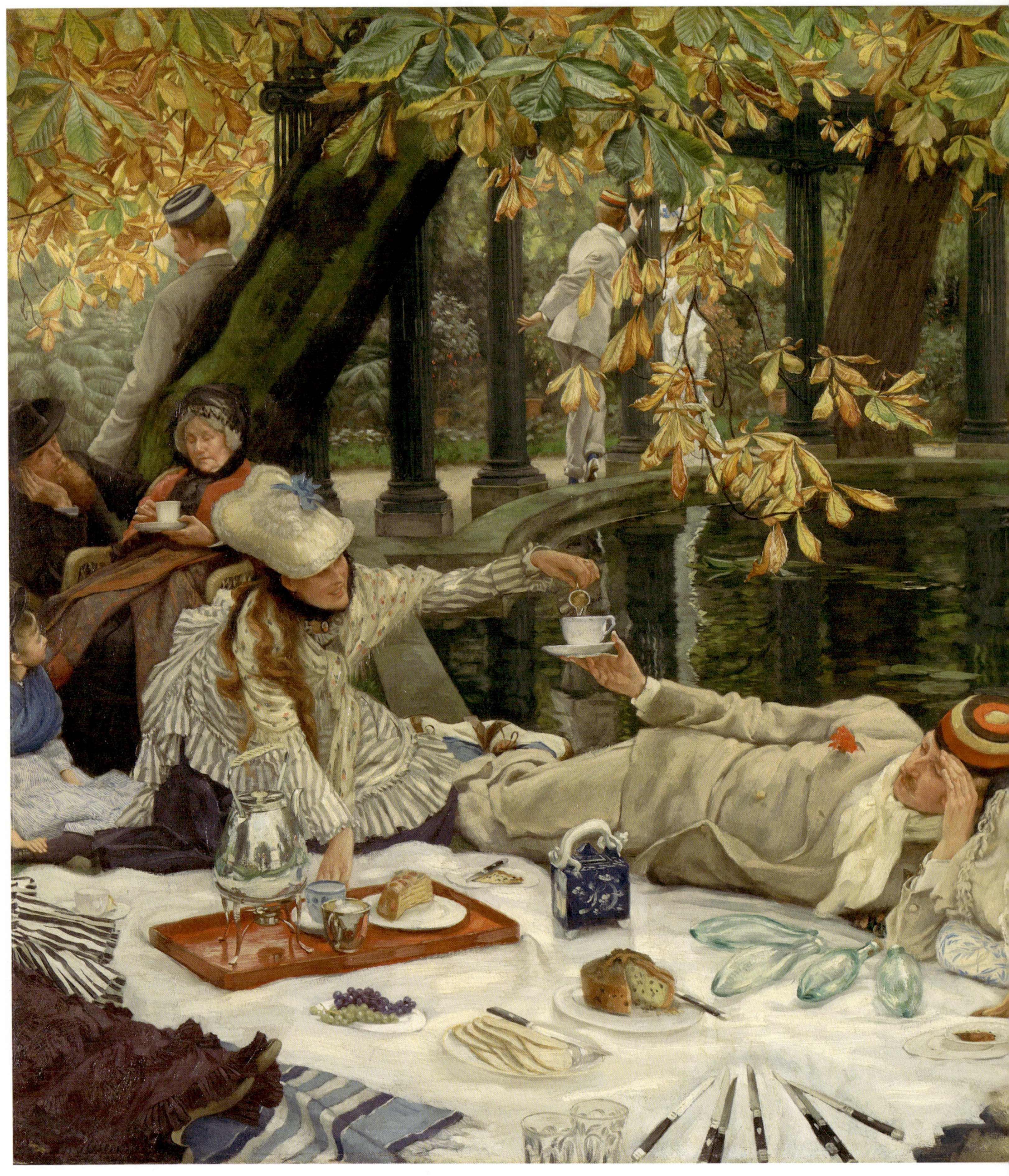

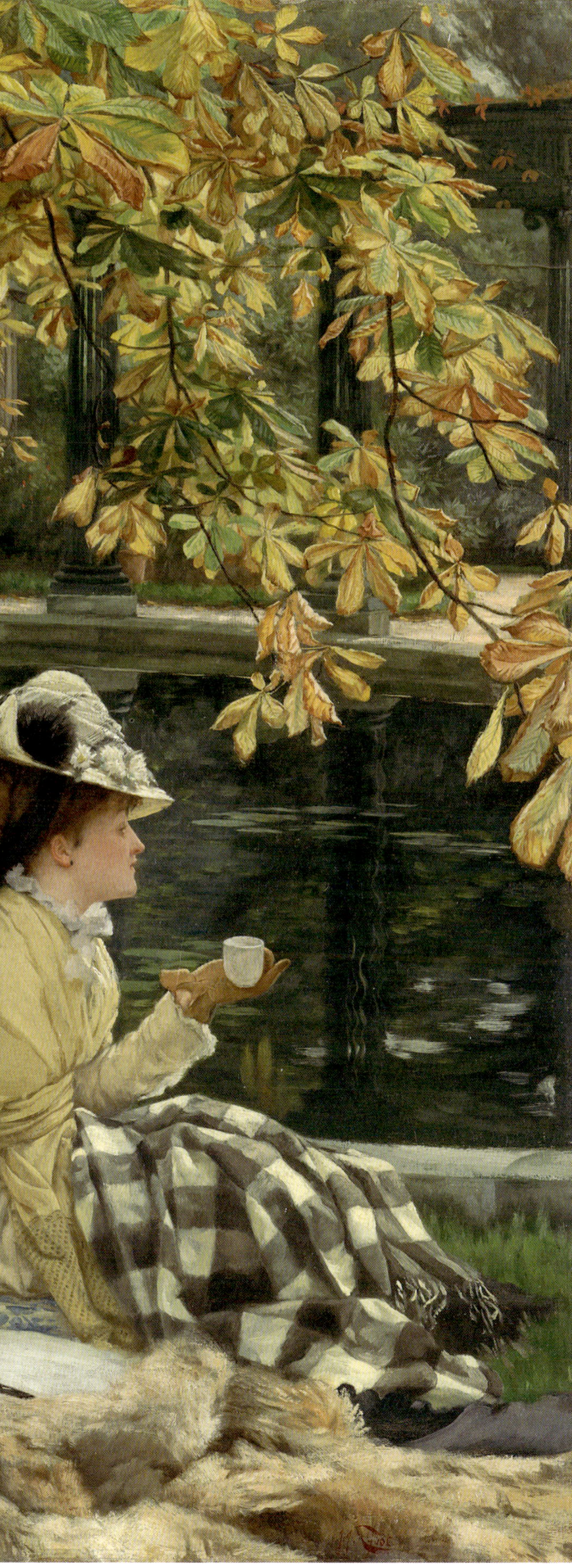

James Tissot
1836–1902
Holyday c.1876
Oil paint on canvas 76.2 × 99.4

Tate. Purchased 1928

Tissot's eighteenth-century house, 17 Grove End Road, became a setting for numerous paintings: *Holyday* is set around the pool, which Tissot had shaped to resemble ornamental ponds in French parks, under an ionic cast-iron colonnade like one in Parc Monceau, Paris.[1] The detailed finish accords with English taste for Pre-Raphaelite painting, and the subject of lovers in a garden was popular in Victorian art and literature, but Tissot's treatment recalls the plein-air picnics being executed by his friends across the channel. The absence of a horizon and the pattern of foliage, fabric and dappled shadow chime with similar scenes by Manet and Monet. The sunshine filtering intermittently through the chestnut leaves is a particularly beautiful light effect. The cutlery, china and food distributed on a white table cloth seen from above were also familiar from impressionist compositions. The knives fanned out at the picture's lower edge half-echo the four soda bottles above them and the splayed shape of the chestnut leaves.

The title alludes to the new leisure activities that were enjoyed by the middle classes, the mainstay of impressionist painters. Two of the three young men wear the distinctive red, black and yellow cricket cap of I Zingari (the Gypsies), the amateur cricket team of Old Harrovians ('old boys' of Harrow private school). Tissot's home was very close to Lord's Cricket Ground where they regularly played fixtures. Sports, promoted especially in schools, were an increasingly important element of British society and identity, believed to encourage British values, health, self-discipline, fairness and team spirit, so there is a mischievous irony in the lounging attitudes of their wearers in the picture. The lowered eyes of the chaperone alert the viewer to flirtation among the young people. The two couples in the mid-ground, behind the tree and in the distance, behind the colonnade, have drawn apart from the others. The eight knives on the tablecloth imply an unseen eighth person, whose foot can be glimpsed in the left-hand lower corner. The man in the foreground seems caught between two young women, a favourite theme of Tissot. He leans familiarly against the back of one and holds up his teacup lazily, unbalanced on its saucer, for the other. She is forced to stretch to pour the milk, her gesture echoed by the shape of the branch above. In 1877 Tissot exhibited *Holyday* at the newly opened Grosvenor Gallery, which favoured poetic, aesthetic subjects. There the picture found an audience more sympathetic to its decorative aspect and French flavour, although some critics continued to disparage the propriety of the figures.[2] Tissot did not exhibit at the Royal Academy again until 1881. CJ

Camille Pissarro
1830–1903
Hampton Court Green 1891
Oil paint on canvas 54.3 × 73

National Gallery of Art, Washington, Ailsa Mellon Bruce Collection

Twenty years after his first stay in London, Pissarro returned for a few weeks. The month of June 1890 was auspicious for outdoor painting. The artist began several canvases that would be finished in the Eragny studio in France. The excursion to Hampton Court was among the most appreciated by London tourists. Situated 15 miles from the capital on the left bank of the Thames, the site was accessible in less than an hour by the south-west railway line or by omnibus.[1]

Pissarro observed the surroundings of the venerable royal residence in resolutely modern terms. As opposed to the noble facades of Henry VIII's palace, he preferred the more modest ones of the former stables, the Royal Mews, which had been converted into the Cardinal Wolsey Inn. The roof line strictly parallel to the edge of the picture marks the horizon. The red ochre of the bricks heightens the vivid green lawn where a cricket match is taking place – the quintessential British sport that 'reigned as an absolute master from the month of April to the end of August' because 'love of this game is innate to the English'.[2] In fact, Pissarro would be completely won over by this sport, which he would play with his family in France.

The artist places the players at some distance away on his canvas, leaving its whole extent for the landscape. With the low horizon, the cloudy sky occupies more than half the picture. This stay in London was also the occasion for constant visits to museums. The memory of the vast skies in Dutch painting could have guided Pissarro in his composition. After a period of experimenting with pointillism in the wake of Georges Seurat, the artist, stimulated by these new landscapes, returned to a broader, more spontaneous approach. The range of particularly rich colours brilliantly recreates the damp luminosity of English springtime.

Not long before his departure for London, Pissarro advised his son Georges, whose artistic career he encouraged, that he could avoid routine if he looked to nature for the visual excitement necessary for renewal:

> How have I managed to find my subjects for years, and I am often at a loss, I let my imagination go without thinking too much ... At times it happens that I find just what I want by watching a movement, a group, a landscape, a sky is sometimes enough; once the idea is found, the rest comes through study, selection, composition, character, colour, etc.[3]

Hampton Court Green seems to have responded perfectly to his expectations. The picture was sold to Paul Durand-Ruel as early as 24 February 1892. IC

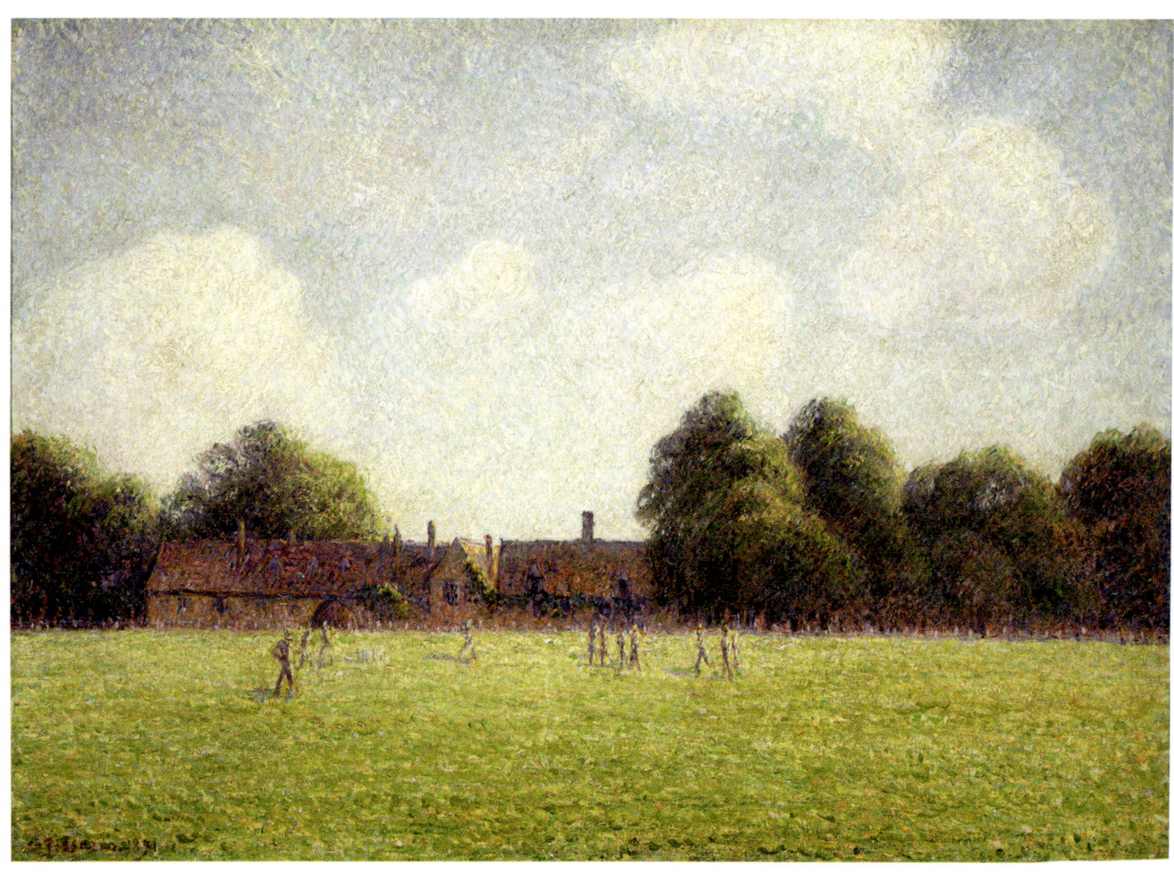

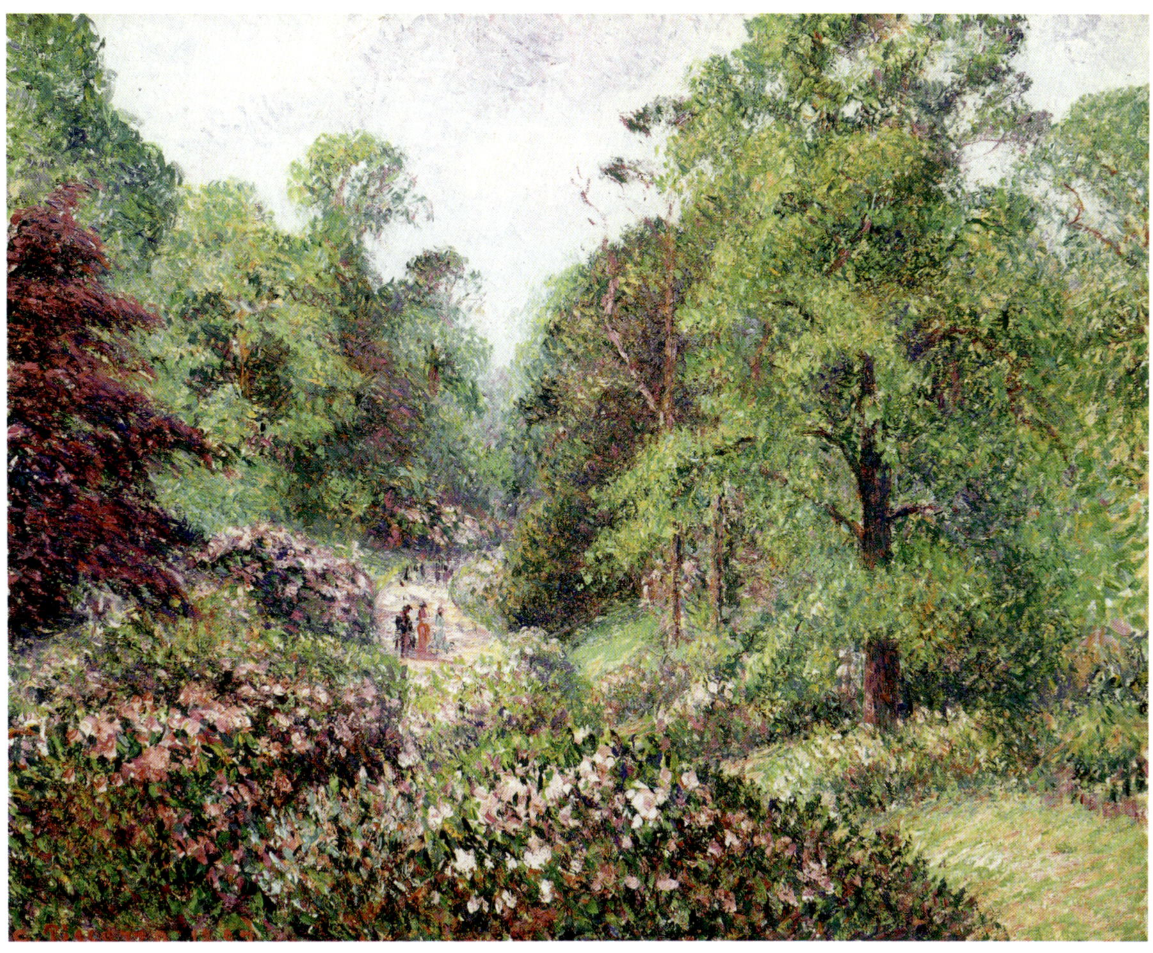

Camille Pissarro
1830–1903
Kew Gardens, Rhododendron Dell
1892
Oil paint on canvas 54 × 64.8

Private collection, USA

Kew Gardens were separated from the Royal Parks of Kew and Richmond in 1840. Situated 10 miles from the centre of London, this property, where access was then free, already attracted several million visitors every year. It covered an area of about 30 hectares, stretched along the south bank of the Thames and was open to the public every afternoon.[1] In search of new subjects, Pissarro went there as soon as he arrived in early June. The Rhododendron Dell offered, along with the azalea garden, one of the main attractions of Kew during the months of May and June.[2] Luckily for Pissarro, the British sky cooperated. In a letter addressed to his dealer and dated 10 June, he confided his enthusiasm, as well as his doubts, in facing this botanical magnificence: 'I am very busy at the moment in Kew Garden where I've found a series of magnificent themes, which I try to render as well as possible. The weather is very favourable, apparently even exceptional, but how difficult; more than ever "I feel my feebleness" in front of such an arduous task!'[3] The eleven canvases painted at Kew represent almost all the work he produced during his 1892 trip.

The discreet presence of people strolling in the centre of *Kew Gardens, Rhohodendron Dell* is a reminder of the domestic character of this abundant nature. Pissarro favoured the typically British aspects of Kew and paid no attention to either the greenhouses of exotic plants or to the picturesque buildings – pagodas, temples, mosques and ruins – which are among the site's curiosities. Satisfied with his picture, he planned to paint it again on a larger canvas when he was settled in his studio in Eragny. The project was abandoned after Durand-Ruel bought the original canvas six months after the artist's return to France. Edmond Cousturier, the critic, who saw the picture exhibited at the dealer's, wrote: 'I believe that in the series of Kew Gardens, one can't forget the picture of a certain *Rhododendron Dell* where the tufted domes of flowers are repeated in perspective, while in comparison with the pink path by which ramblers descend, trees with strong sap spread their foliage in blue and green arabesques like peacocks spreading their tails.'[4]
IC

Camille Pissarro
1830–1903
Kew Green 1892
Oil paint on canvas 46 × 55

Musée d'Orsay, deposited at the Musée des Beaux-Arts de Lyon. Bequeathed by Clément and Andrée Adès, 1979

St Anne's Church in Kew 1892
Oil paint on canvas 54.8 × 46

From the Collection of Professor Mark Kaufman

At the end of June, Pissarro rented a small apartment in Kew at 1 Gloucester Terrace, so as to be able to paint straight away in the morning without having to take the hour-long ride from London beforehand. 'Continuous variations in the weather' slowed progress on the work begun on several canvases at once.[1] His wife Julie, who had remained in France, actively went about buying a house in Eragny and took the initiative of requesting financial aid from Monet, who gave it willingly. Although the Pissarro family's material situation was henceforth less precarious, the determination both to reimburse Monet as quickly as possible and to continue helping his own children became a constant preoccupation for the sixty-two-year-old Pissarro.

The building where he moved in Kew was situated at the corner of two streets with windows opening towards the west and north. This situation made it possible for him to paint while sheltered from wind and rain, as well as benefit from an elevated consistent viewpoint and be able to continue to work when it became difficult to paint from nature.

In the distance to the west, the artist could glimpse St Anne's Church, whose bell tower and graduated rooftops he painted between two large trees with massive foliage. Though it is raining, the palette remains light. The road connecting Kew to Richmond provides a fleeting view of passers-by and horse-drawn carriages. With an infinite range of soft greens and red ochre, the urban landscape opens out in parallel planes in the style of the Japanese prints that had so interested Pissarro. The picture is painted in a standard format that Pissarro chose several times to achieve his purposes over the summer: 'I have a dozen things to do here; I don't want to miss my season.'[2]

Kew Green was painted in the Kew apartment in the same manner and identical format as *St Anne's Church*. Pissarro was positioned on the north side of the third floor, enjoying a more open view. With an outsider's perception of the London landscape, he decided to represent Kew Green as a varied zone that included as much green space as it did residential and industrial areas. The picture is dominated on the left by the Kew Bridge Pumping Station's high standpipe tower, which was not considered very picturesque by the Victorians. The common that stretches out in front of it is used for cricket, which enlivens the vista as at Hampton Court. Players' silhouettes are extended into coloured shadows by the late afternoon light. Pissarro's brush describes infinite chromatic variations in a strict composition organised along strong vertical and diagonal lines.

During his third stay in England, Pissarro abandoned his divisionist tendencies for more orthodox impressionism. This evolution was encouraged by Durand-Ruel who acquired the Kew pictures in December 1893. The urban scenes with high viewpoints painted from Gloucester Terrace prefigured those that Pissarro would elaborate in his later years in Le Havre, Rouen and Paris. IC

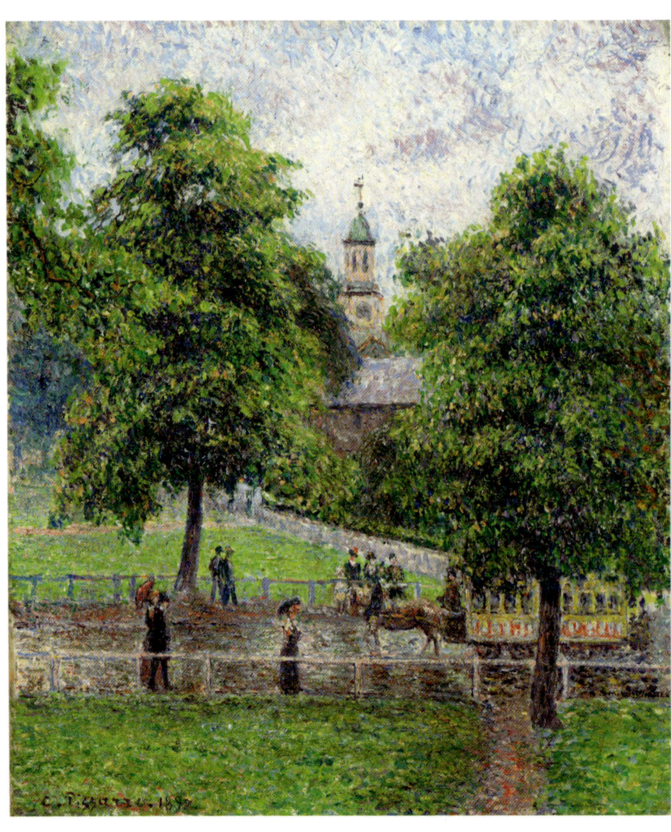

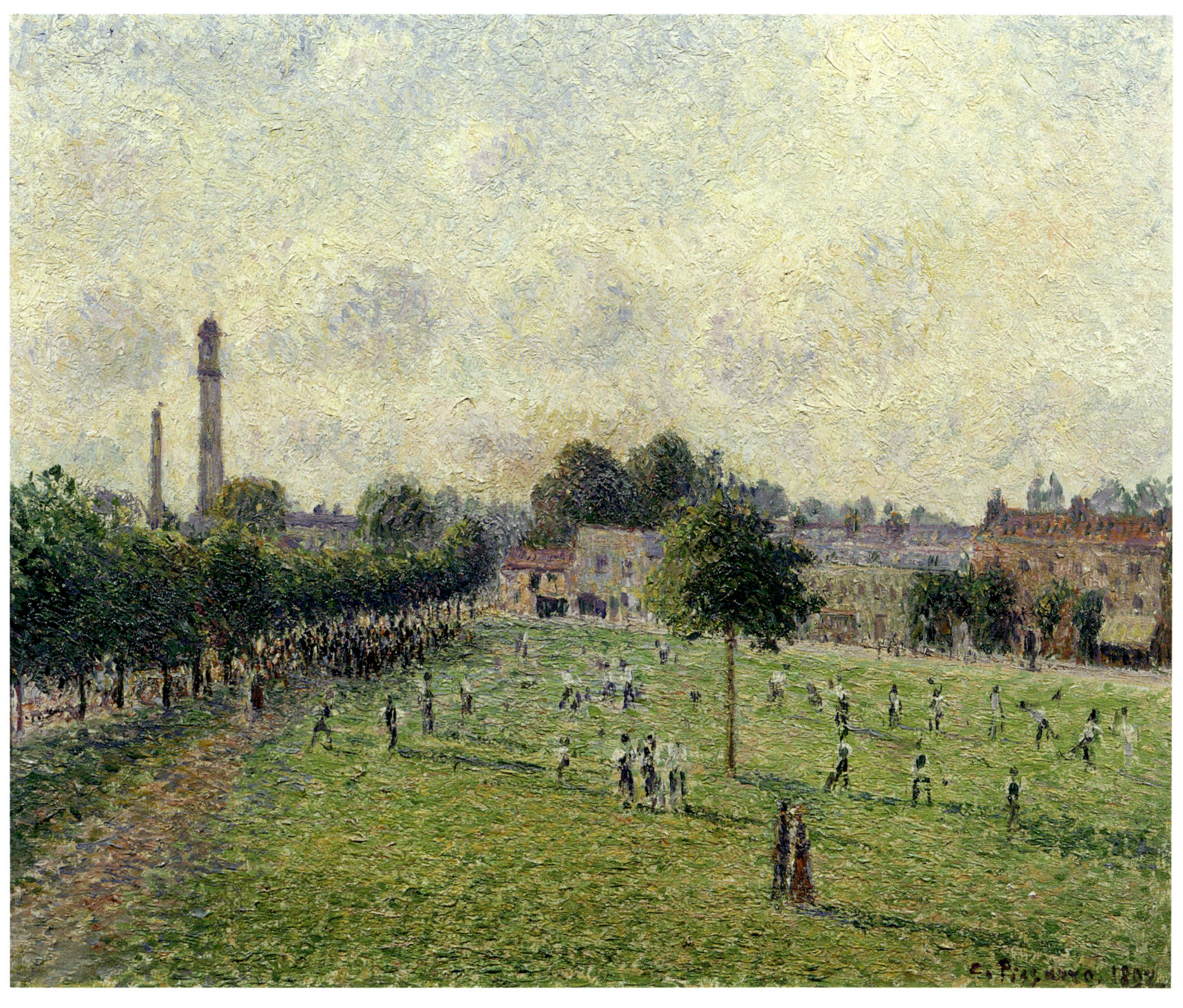
C. Pissarro.

Giuseppe de Nittis
1846–1884
Piccadilly: Wintry Walk in London
1875 (1)
Oil paint on canvas 68.5 × 104

Private collection

Westminster 1878 (2)
Oil paint on canvas 110 × 195

Private collection

These paintings by Giuseppe de Nittis were commissioned by Kaye Knowles (see p.109), a wealthy colliery proprietor from Lancashire who became the painter's main patron in England. As Tulliola Sparagni has noted, it is very likely that de Nittis and Knowles were attempting 'to update, according to the criteria of the 19th century, the legacy of the landscapes of Canaletto and his English followers'.[1] Knowles did not own two, but twelve views of London by de Nittis, eight of which were exhibited to great acclaim at the Universal Exhibition of 1878, creating what must have been a very striking panorama of London. De Nittis's ability to record the city's movement through unexpected crops and freeze-frame effects no doubt added to the immersive quality of the room. So did his 'tried and tested method ... of observing the outside world from inside a cab',[2] which introduces a moderate but noticeable plunging view in his compositions: this points to his artfulness, and the mediation of the cityscape by his eye and brush. Apart from the fact that he primarily depicted highlights of London, his outsider's perception of the capital is only increased by this type of distancing or alienation.

In the centre of *Piccadilly: Wintry Walk in London*, a lady and a little girl are caught on canvas in mid-air, hastening to cross

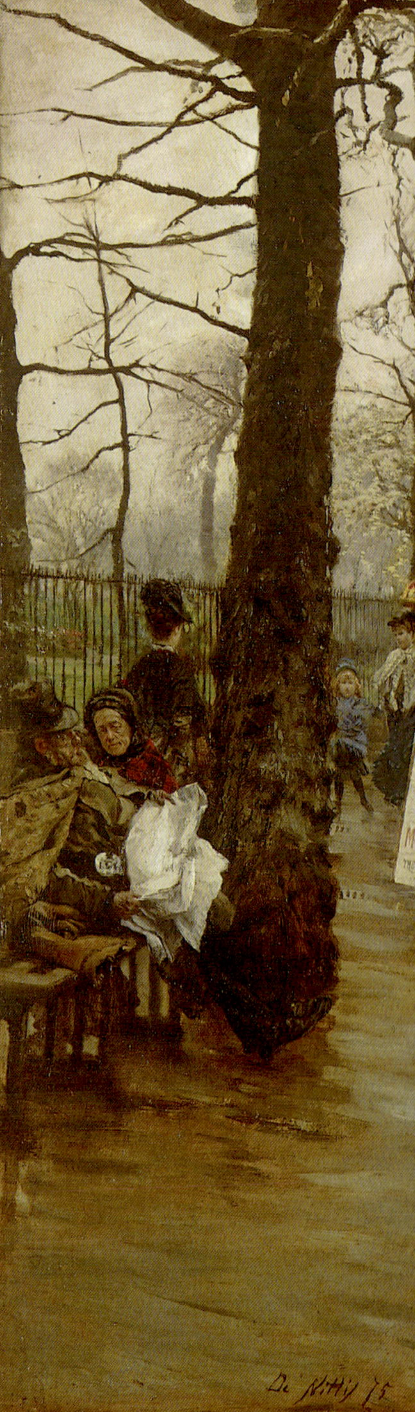

1

one of London's busiest streets. Towering above them, in the far distance, is the monumental equestrian sculpture of the 1st Duke of Wellington by Matthew Cotes Wyatt, symbol of national identity and British supremacy. In the foreground to the left, an elderly man wearing a red turban, standing by a policeman and nearby sandwich-board men, is another reminder of the extent of the British Empire of which London was the centre. He is sweeping the street. The winter rain has just stopped, and the sky is mirrored by the water on the muddy road as a few rays of sunshine pierce through the clouds with difficulty. Léonce Bénédite remarked: 'The same feeling for local conditions, so deeply accentuated still by his Italian eye, brought De Nittis under the London sky. Has one ever rendered with such sensitivity the somewhat funereal splendour of this woolly, stifled sky whose rusty mist creates a neutral background on which all hues sing more vividly?'[3]

The rusty mist described by Bénédite is nowhere more apparent than in *Westminster*, which by its sheer size, would have been a focal point of de Nittis's exhibits at the 1878 Universal Exhibition. In this instance, the symbol par excellence of Britain's power occupies the whole canvas, and appears as a forerunner of Monet's Houses of Parliament series, executed more than twenty years later. Here, however, the bridge and the Thames workers having a smoke in the foreground act as a *repoussoir*, and add a social component to the composition. CCP

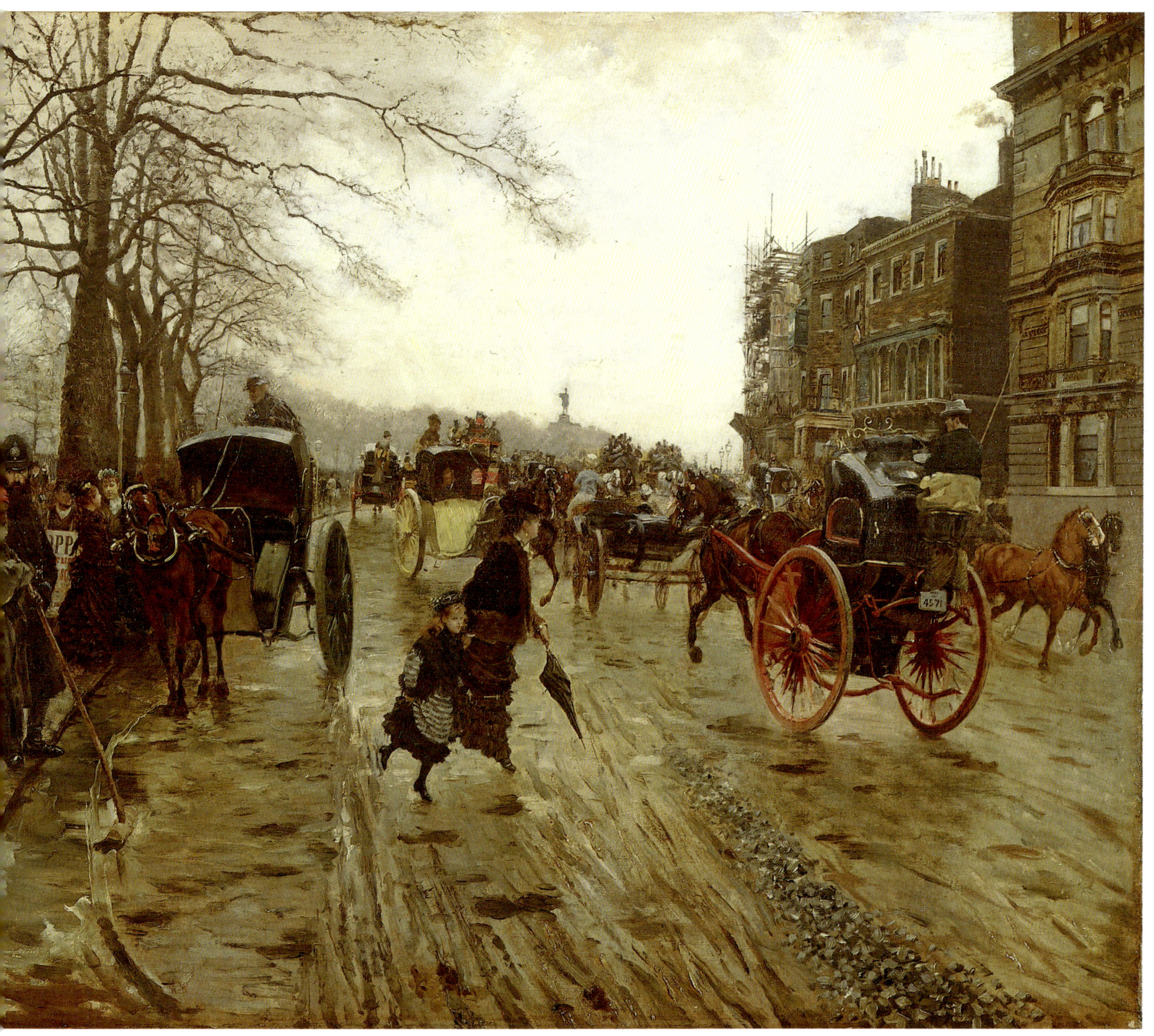

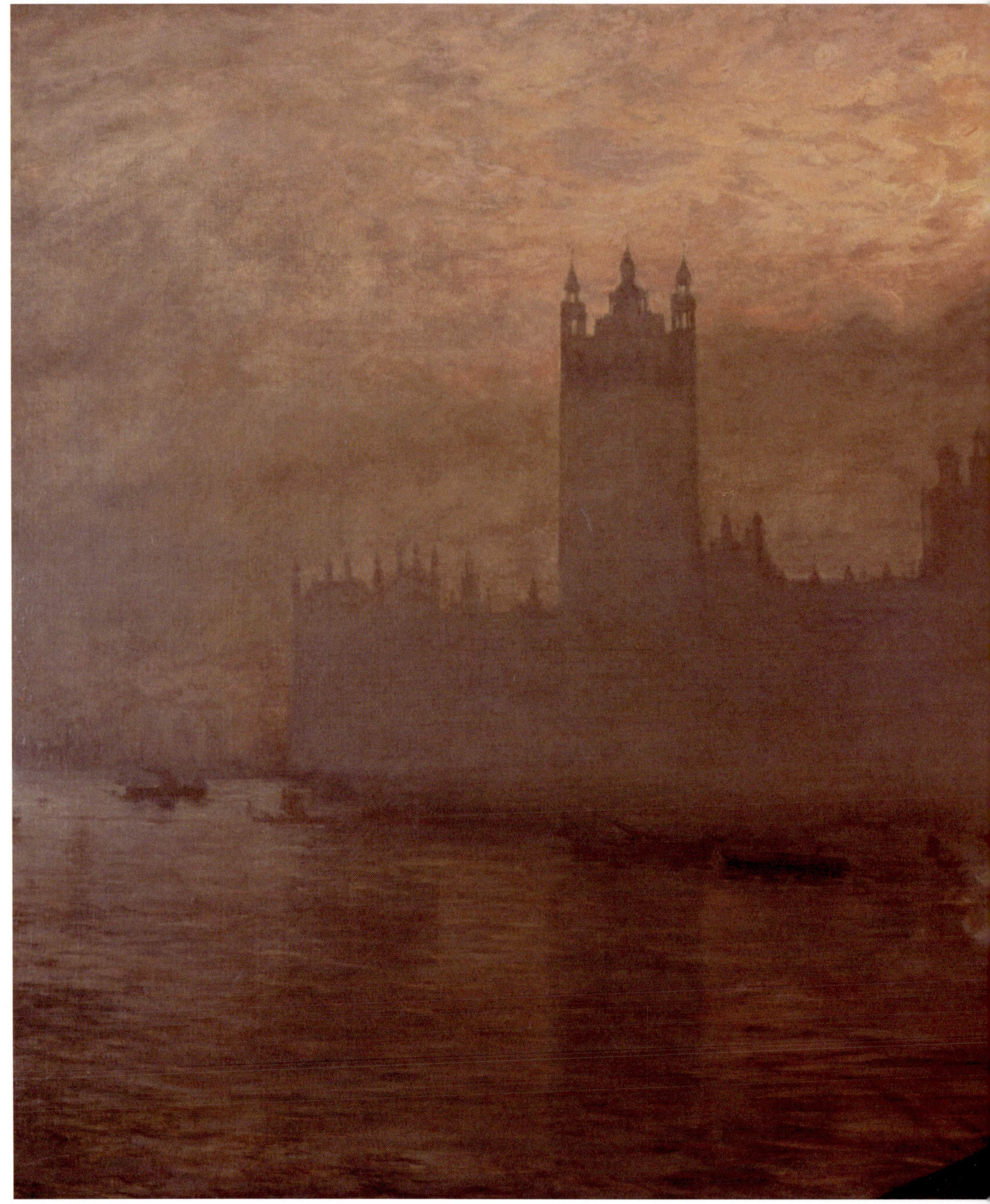

2

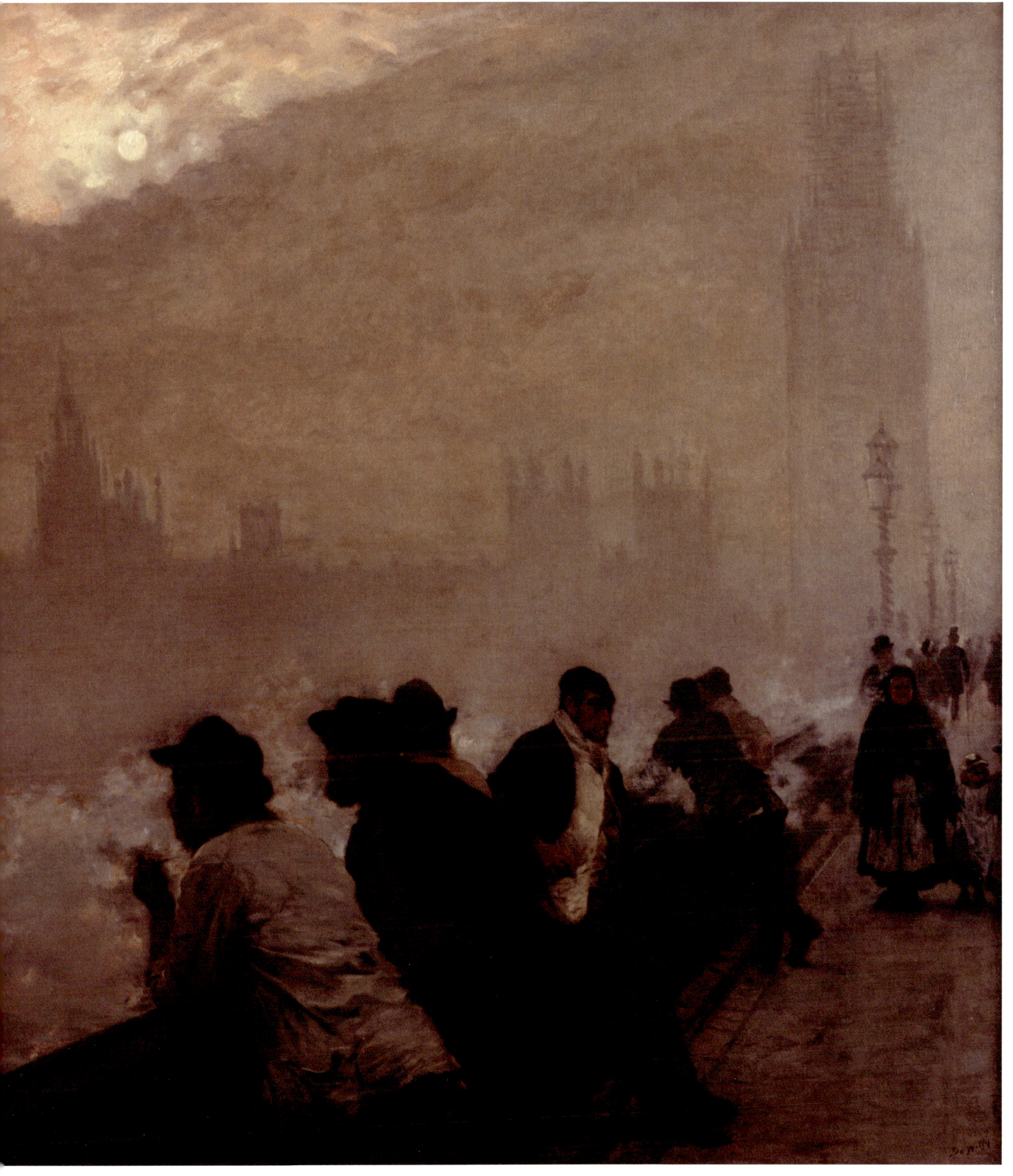

Camille Pissarro
1830–1903
Bank Holiday, Kew 1892
Oil paint on canvas 46 × 55

Private collection

This unusual painting of Kew is not dominated by the gardens, but by Pissarro's observation of social interaction. Painting from his lodgings at Kew, above a bakery, the artist adopted a plunging view to depict Kew Green on 6 June 1892, thronged with locals and day-trippers on the Whit Bank Holiday.

People of all ages, some coming from London in crammed buses, are shown crowding towards the popular gardens to make the most of a sunny day. They appear to be dressed in their best clothes. Bank holidays had only been introduced in 1871 for workers to benefit from some statutory time off. The figures populating the scene are not individualised and are broadly painted by Pissarro. Some, in the background, are only indicated by schematic dots or short vertical strokes, which reinforces the impression of an anonymous crowd. The animation of *Bank Holiday, Kew*, relies more on the rhythm of its broken brush strokes than in the movement imparted to Pissarro's somewhat stiff figures. The often stated influence of Camille Pissarro on the painter L.S. Lowry is particularly evident in this picture.

Bank Holiday, Kew reflects Pissarro's continued engagement with modern life in the suburbs, but it is unique among his London pictures in its depiction of a swarming space. It predates his crowded Parisian scenes of the late 1890s. The dense population of London (5.5 million in Greater London in the 1891 census, as opposed to 3.3 million for the Parisian agglomeration) was undoubtedly a striking trait of the London capital for an outsider, especially on a day when Londoners flocked to Kew in search of some fresh air and greenery. CCP

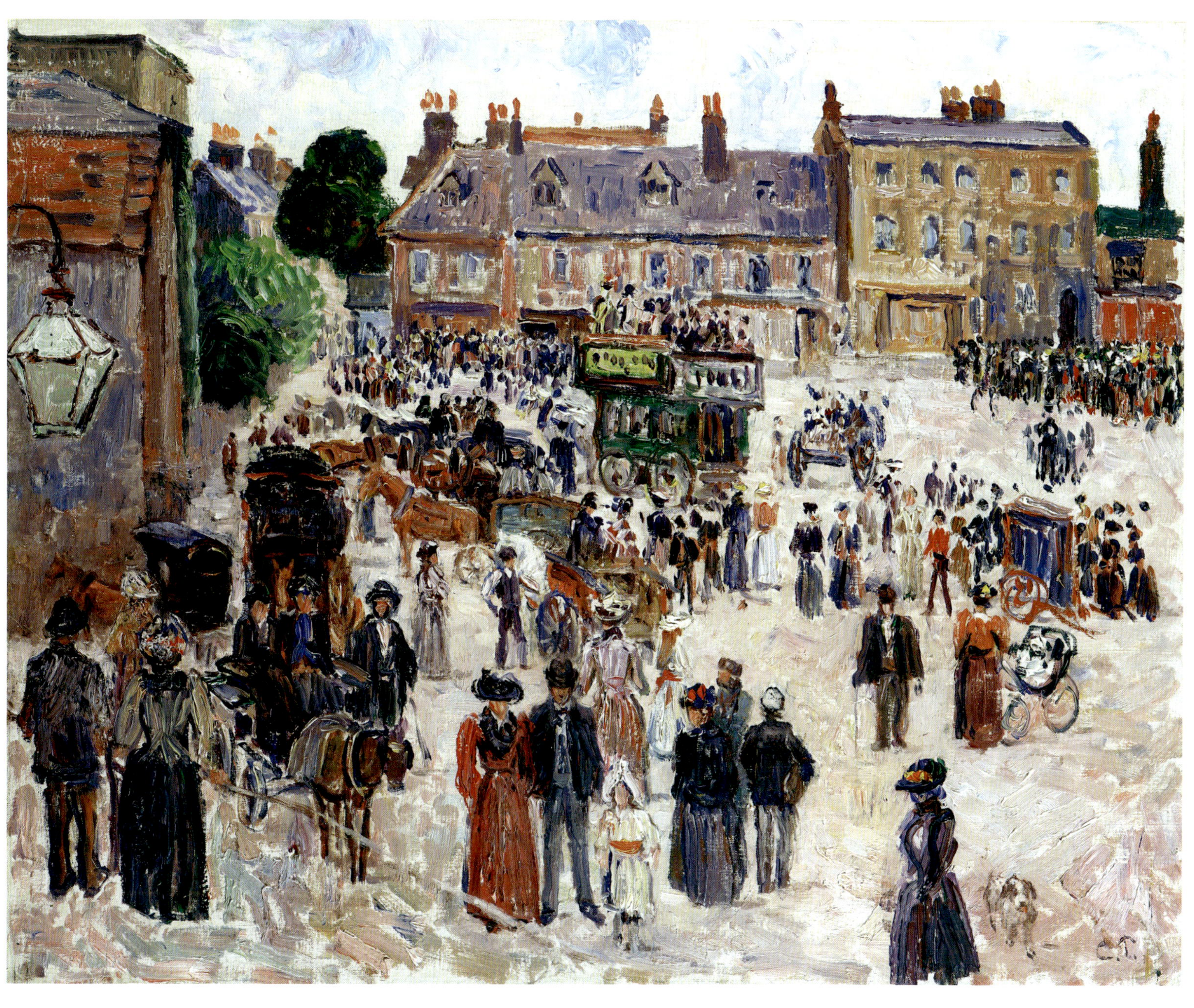

Claude Monet
1840–1926
Leicester Square at Night c.1901
Oil paint on canvas 80 × 64.8

Collection Fondation Jean et Suzanne Planque, deposited at the Musée Granet (Aix-en-Provence)

Leicester Square at Night is one of three sketches ('pochades') painted by Monet in early March 1901, during the painter's last working campaign in London for his Thames series. Its rhythmic brush strokes and bold colours form a surprising picture that captures the electrifying atmosphere of London by night. The lights of the Empire Theatre shine to the left, while in the lower part of the picture, passers-by on their way to or back from Leicester Square can be made out walking along what in all likelihood is Swiss Court.[1] Monet probably painted the scene from the Lyric Club, at the corner of Whitcomb Street and Coventry Street, rather than from the Green Room Club,[2] as previously thought, given that it did not move to its premises in St Martin's Street until 1903. The Lyric Club overlooked from a high vantage point the central axis of Swiss Court and Leicester Square, hence this plunging view.

Monet had already expressed his fascination for thronging London when witnessing the funeral of Queen Victoria from a window, a month earlier: 'What a crowd! ... I wish I could have made a sketch of it.'[3] This interest in the buzzing capital was also revealed in his admiration for Regent Street and Piccadilly Circus and their illuminations at night:

> As [Sargent and I] were discussing my passion for these admirable night effects, like those we frequently observed on leaving the Café Royal and that I still keep observing when I go that way, he offered to enquire as to whether I could have a small space at my disposal at a club in which there is a very beautiful view. If he succeeds and if I think it is possible, I will try and make a sketch for myself.[4]

Monet had hopes that via the director of the Savoy, he would gain access to a balcony in Regent Street itself,[5] but it seems that this trail went cold, and that it was indeed with the support of his friend the painter John Singer Sargent that Monet secured a window at 'the New Lyric Club ... supposedly very noisy, as its name suggests'.[6] Monet was not fully satisfied with his makeshift studio, in a minuscule room that was used as a cellar, but peace and a 'superb view' redeemed the disadvantages of the space.[7] Monet enjoyed working on this view of Leicester Square for himself and made a clear distinction between this undertaking and his all-consuming Thames paintings (pp.232–41).[8] It is unlikely that he ever envisaged his *Leicester Square* sketches as a series, even embryonic. Exhaustion and a bad cold prevented the artist from pursuing work on this motif. CCP

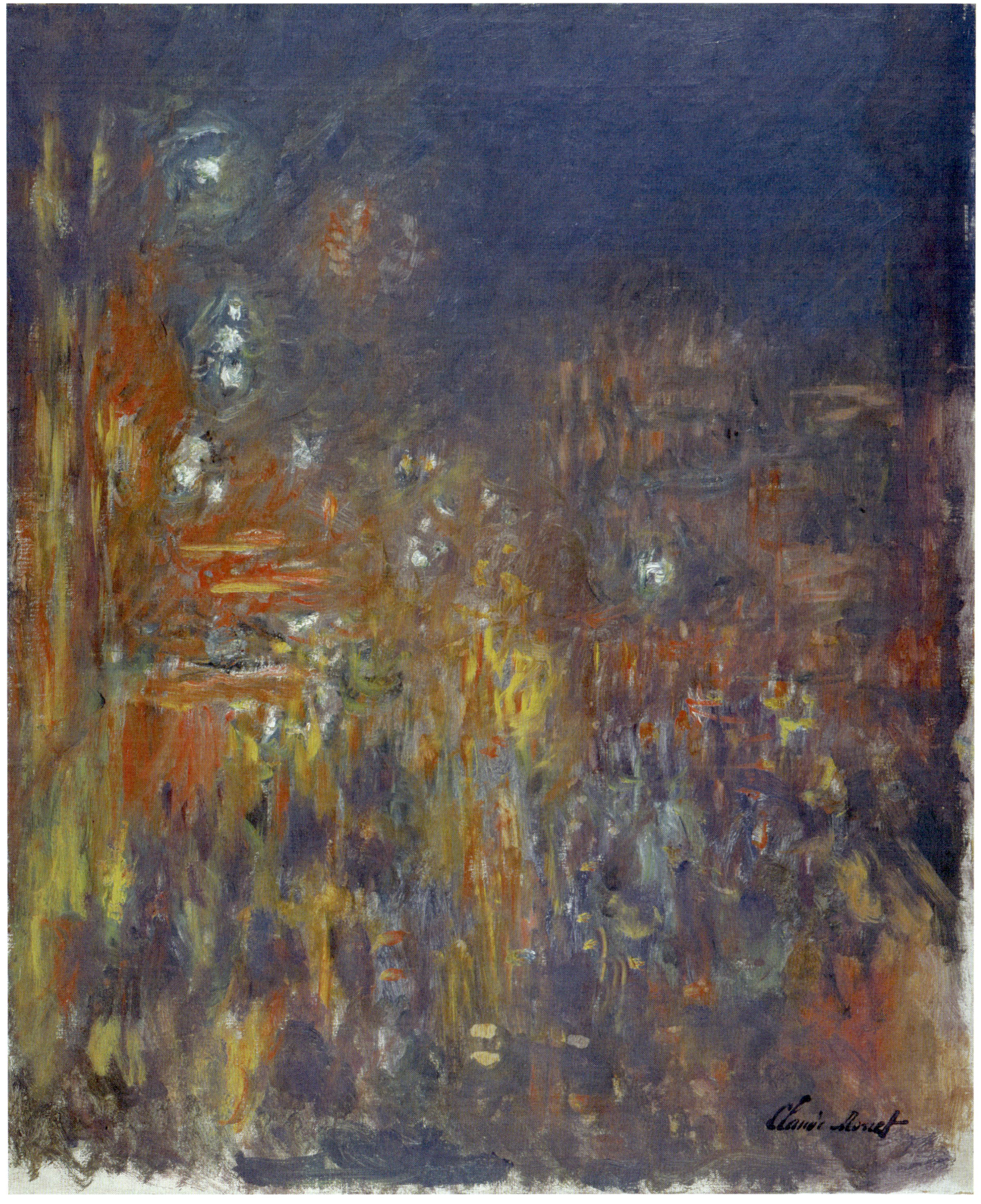

James Abbott McNeill Whistler
1834–1903
Nocturne: Blue and Gold – Old Battersea Bridge c.1872–5 (1)
Oil paint on canvas 68.3 × 51.2

Tate. Presented by the Art Fund 1905

Nocturne: Blue and Silver – Chelsea 1871 (2)
Oil paint on wood 50.2 × 60.8

Tate. Bequeathed by Miss Rachel and Miss Jean Alexander 1972

Nocturne: Blue and Silver – Cremorne Lights 1872 (3)
Oil paint on canvas 50.2 × 74.3

Tate. Bequeathed by Arthur Studd 1919

In 1859 the American-born artist James McNeill Whistler arrived in London. Although he had studied in Paris, where his close friends included the artists Henri Fantin-Latour and Alphonse Legros, he had also spent considerable time in London, staying with his half-sister, Deborah, and her husband, the physician and etcher Francis Seymour Haden. Whistler had published a warmly received issue of his first set of etchings, *Twelve Views from Nature*, which he referred to as the 'French Set', from the Hadens' Sloane Street address the previous year, and spoke positively of London, a city that he said 'welcomed young artists'.[1]

The river was a source of fascination for Whistler from his arrival and inspired his next series of etchings, 'The Thames Set'. In terms of his paintings, it is the stiller, night-time subjects of the 'Nocturnes', begun later, in the early 1870s, that have come to define Whistler's vision of the river. *Nocturne: Blue and Silver – Chelsea* was the first. This view across the Thames from Battersea towards Chelsea sees the river landscape reduced to the bare essentials, the high horizon line allowing the river to dominate the panel, with a sliver of shoreline and a single figure indicated with a few strokes in the foreground.

This and the other Thames Nocturnes presented a new and radically different interpretation of the river, with Whistler citing 'line, form and colour' as his primary concerns,[2] a shift away from the more naturalistic approach demonstrated within the Thames series. The Nocturnes received a mixed critical response when first exhibited in the 1870s. One reviewer, writing in 1872, referred to them as 'lunacies of art'.[3] In contrast, in 1875 a reviewer of the Dudley Gallery spoke of 'those wonderful lamplit, twilit, moonlit river scenes sent some seasons ago', which included *Nocturne, Blue and Silver – Chelsea*.[4]

Nocturne: Blue and Silver – Cremorne Lights shows the Cremorne Pleasure Gardens illuminated to the right of the canvas, the view seen through a haze. Whistler's fascination with London's fog dated back several years: he wrote of his concern with capturing 'an effect of fog' in a letter of 1864, for example.[5] In the Nocturnes of the 1870s, however, he brought his depiction of fog to full effect, embracing misty, atmospheric weather conditions as integral to his night-time views of the Thames, using thin, shimmering layers of paint to suggest the diffused glow of artificial light seen through mist. Although fog, smog and mist were nothing new to Victorian London, Whistler claimed the city's fogs for his own, writing in 1879: 'My own lovely London fogs! They are lovely those fogs – and I am their painter!'[6]

Nocturne: Blue and Gold – Old Battersea Bridge was one of Whistler's most controversial exhibits. When the painting was brought in as evidence at the Whistler-Ruskin trial of 1878, the accuracy of Whistler's depiction of Battersea Bridge was challenged. In his reply, in line with his overarching concern with form and colour, he disassociated the painting from exacting subject matter: 'I did not intend it to be a correct portrait of the bridge, but only a painting of a moonlight scene.'[7] Nonetheless, the subject is recognisable. The unusual viewpoint of the bridge itself dominates the composition, while, in the distance, Chelsea Church tower can be seen to the left and the Albert Bridge on the right. Whistler's other version of this subject, the painted screen *Blue and Silver: Screen, with Old Battersea Bridge* (The Hunterian, University of Glasgow), is thought to predate the Tate canvas. As MacDonald and de Montfort have argued, in this other version the Albert Bridge is dark, suggesting the picture was made before the bridge opened to the public, while in the presumed later painting, it is illuminated.[8] As such, the perceived reality of the night-time landscape – the Albert Bridge illuminated or not depending on when Whistler observed it – is important too; while the Nocturnes are concerned primarily with aesthetics, they are also representations of the river as Whistler saw it, his inspiration the landscape itself. He often observed the river during after-dark outings in a boat with his studio assistants Walter and Henry Greaves, taking his remembrances of watery views shrouded by darkness back to his studio.

The Thames Nocturnes, with their restricted colour palettes, decorative 'butterfly' signatures and distinctive compositions, also reveal the influence of Japanese aesthetics. Whistler's collection of Japanese art and artefacts included woodblock prints by Utagawa Hiroshige. Hiroshige's compositions have often been compared to *Nocturne: Blue and Gold – Old Battersea Bridge* and other Nocturnes. In Paris, along with Dante Gabriel Rossetti and James Tissot, Whistler frequented the shop La Porte Chinoise, a treasure-trove of oriental items. In this way some of the objects inspiring the Japanese-influenced aesthetic in paintings of the period crossed the channel as well as continents.[9] EJ

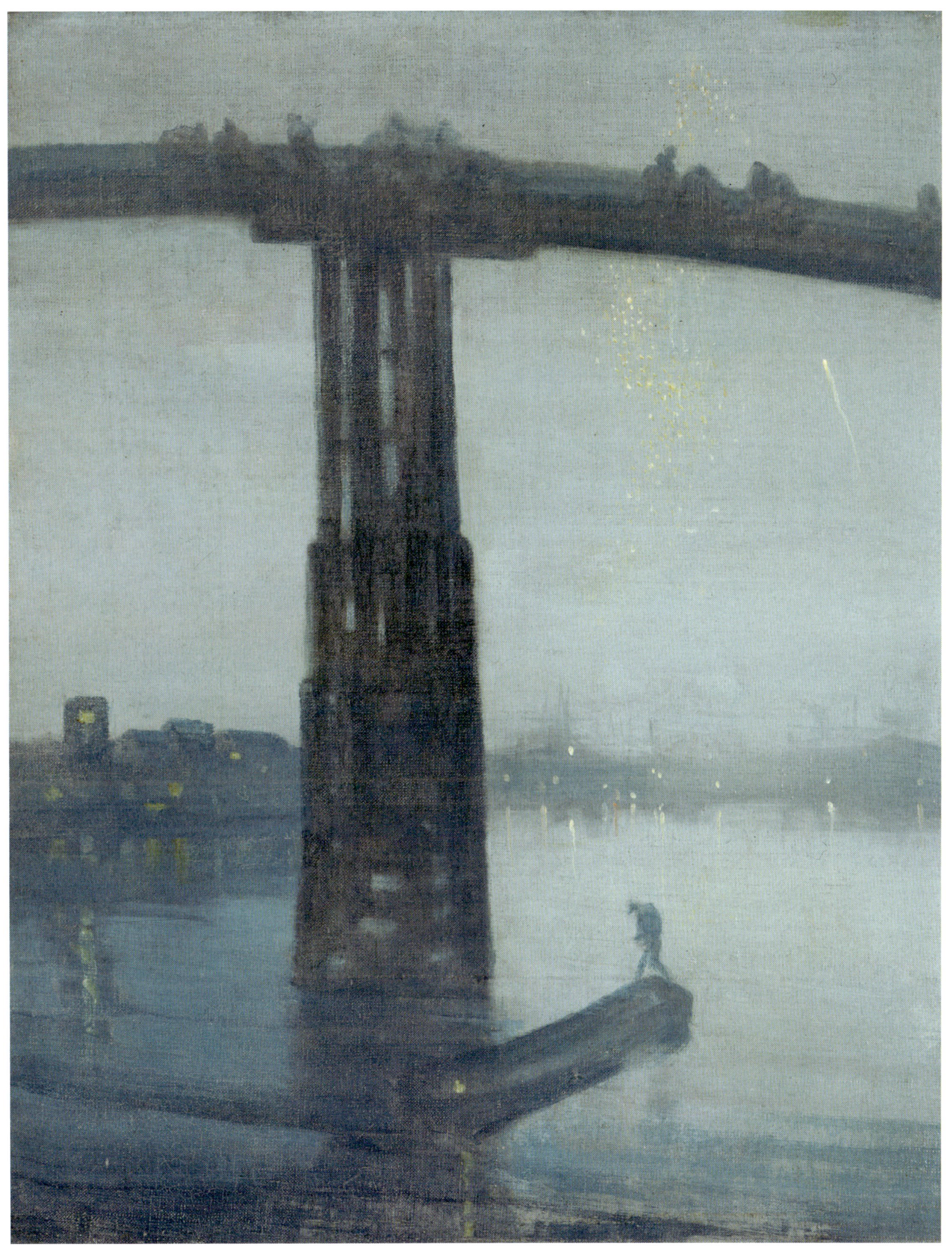

1

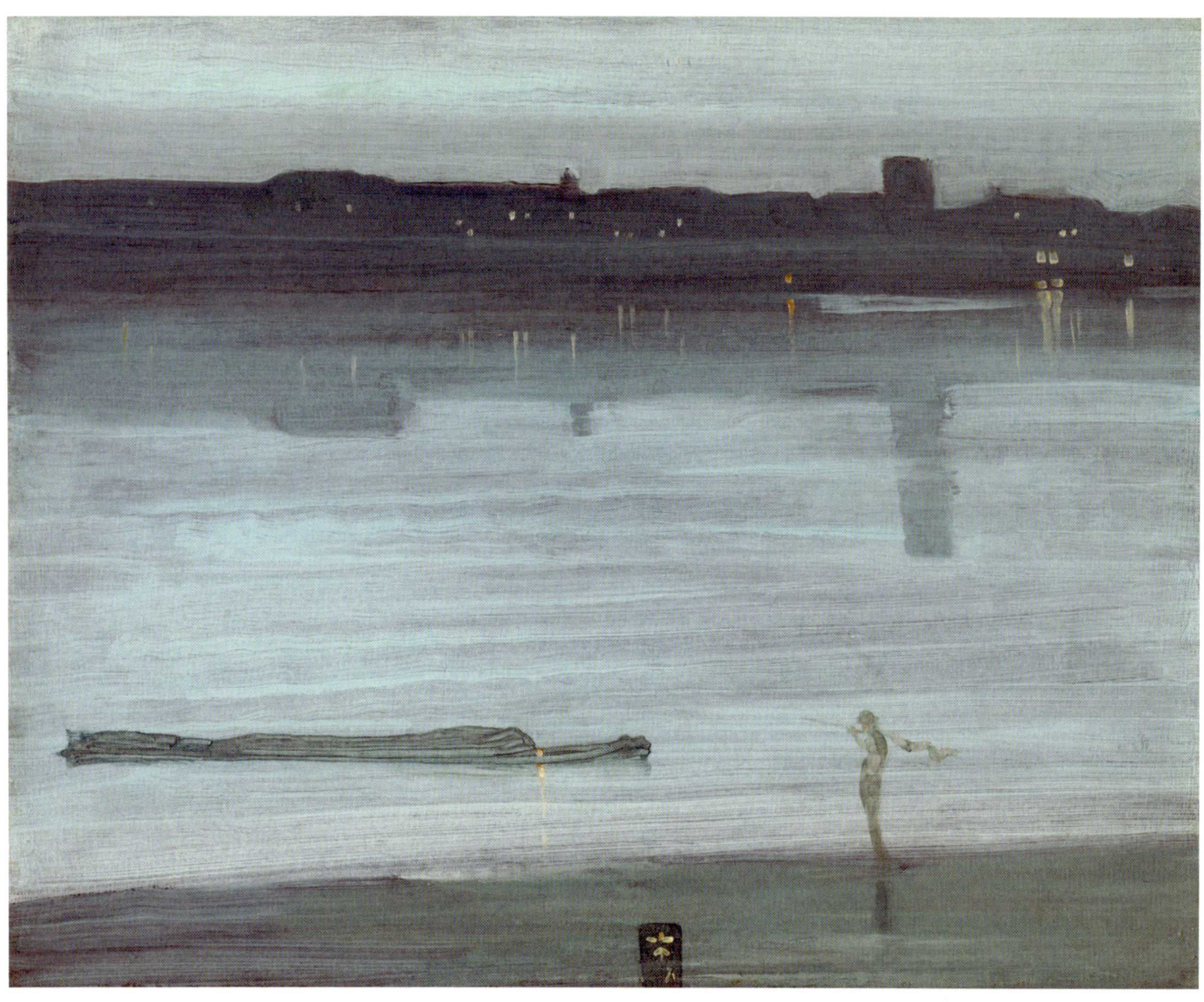

2

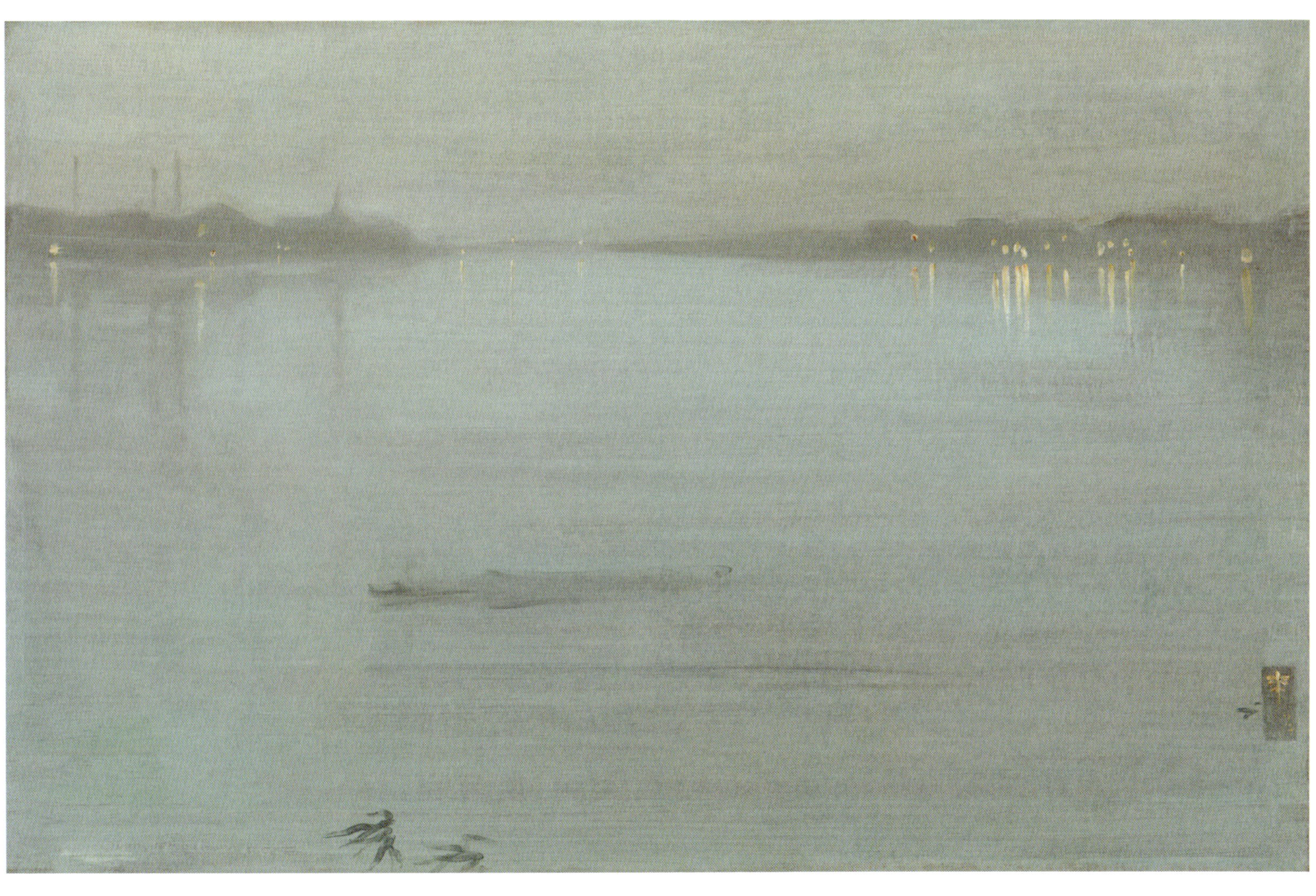

3

James Tissot
1836–1902
On the Thames c.1876
Oil paint on canvas 74.8 × 110

The Hepworth Wakefield (Wakefield Permanent Art Collection)

There was a long tradition of maritime subjects in British art. Tissot had been brought up in Nantes and was familiar with the traffic of a busy port. He was experienced in accurately depicting sails and rigging, and boats featured in many of his paintings. In 1876 Tissot sent this unconventional painting with a maritime theme to the Royal Academy.

On the Thames is set in the Pool of London, a stretch of river beyond London Bridge navigable by the large and tall-masted ships that traded around the world. In the right-hand background Tissot has taken immense trouble to depict the quays crowded with vessels, and the cranes, warehouses and factories. A steamer issuing black smoke tows a looming Blackwall frigate, while to the left is a barge with red sails. Behind it is another steamer and distant ships in full sail, silhouetted in the smoky air. In the foreground a man and two women are borne along in one of the small steam launches that had become common on the Thames. They were popular but uncomfortable conveyances; in an entry on them in his book *Our River Thames*, the painter George Dunlop Leslie wrote:

> I do not believe it is possible to really appreciate the river from on board a launch. In the bows the wind and spray render a steady gaze a-head very uncomfortable, and a smoke out of the question. All is gritty and black from the smoke stack. The odious smell of the rancid engine oil is anything but the attar of roses.'[2]

The women's umbrellas and the squinted, introspective eyes of their companion fit this description, as does the murky atmosphere. Leslie added:

> The motion of the boat causes the perspective, both in front and behind, to alter so rapidly in a converging and diverging manner, as to have on the eye quite a painful effect.

Tissot's disorientating viewpoint provides an equivalent. The far-seeing gaze of the ghostly female figurehead of the frigate above them, with her hand shading her eyes, offers a telling contrast with the travellers below.

The viewer feels equally disorientated by the relationship between the figures. The device of a choice between two lovers was familiar during this period in novels, paintings and popular prints, but Tissot's characters are difficult to read. The blue ensign fluttering behind was used, after 1864, by various royal yacht clubs as well as the Navy Reserve, and Tissot obscured the part of the flag that would identify the unseen owner and pilot of the boat. The two-tone 'spectator shoes' of the man were associated with cricket and yachting and are worn by men in *The Ball on Shipboard* (pp.196–7) and *Holyday* (pp.202–3). Critics were perturbed by the absence of narrative and moral closure in the picture and the *Graphic* declared that it was 'hardly nice in its suggestions. More French, shall we say, than English.' The *Times* reviewer eyed the champagne bottles in the picnic hamper and pronounced it 'questionable material'.[3] CJ

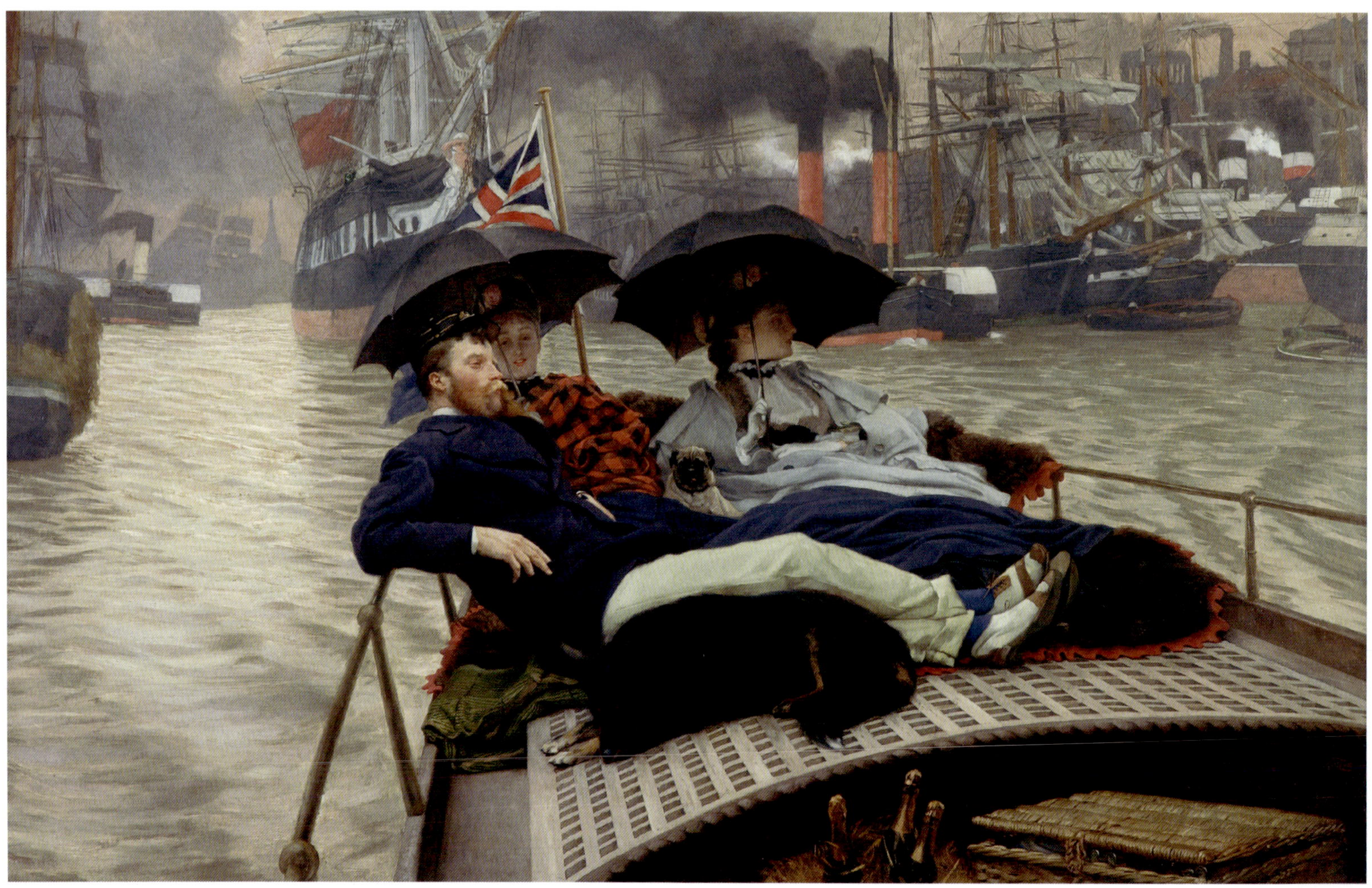

John Thomson
1837–1921
Workers on the 'Silent Highway'
1877
Woodburytype 11.5 × 9 (print), 27.2 × 21 (page)

Wilson Centre for Photography

This photograph by the Scottish geographer and traveller John Thomson is one of thirty-seven to form a photographic study of the working class in London. Accompanied by texts by the journalist Adolphe Smith, the survey was originally published in 1877–8 in serial form under the title *Street Life in London*. Categorised as types, the vigorous men in Thomson's photograph are meant to represent the 'rough and … poorly educated' but 'worthy men, who hold licences from the Watermen's Company, or from the Thames Conservancy'. The marbled sky and opaque waters of the Thames chime with Tissot's painting *On the Thames* (p.220), which is almost the exact contemporary of the photograph. Although wharves and a factory chimney can clearly be seen in the background, smoke is pervading the sky, giving a sense of the pollution that beset the centre of London.

The expression 'silent highway' had almost become a cliché by the 1870s in reference to the immense traffic gliding along the Thames. It was also the title of a famous *Punch* cartoon by John Leech in 1858,[1] in which the allegorical figure of death was represented rowing a boat on the polluted and foggy river, with dead animals floating by, a chimney factory in the background. CCP

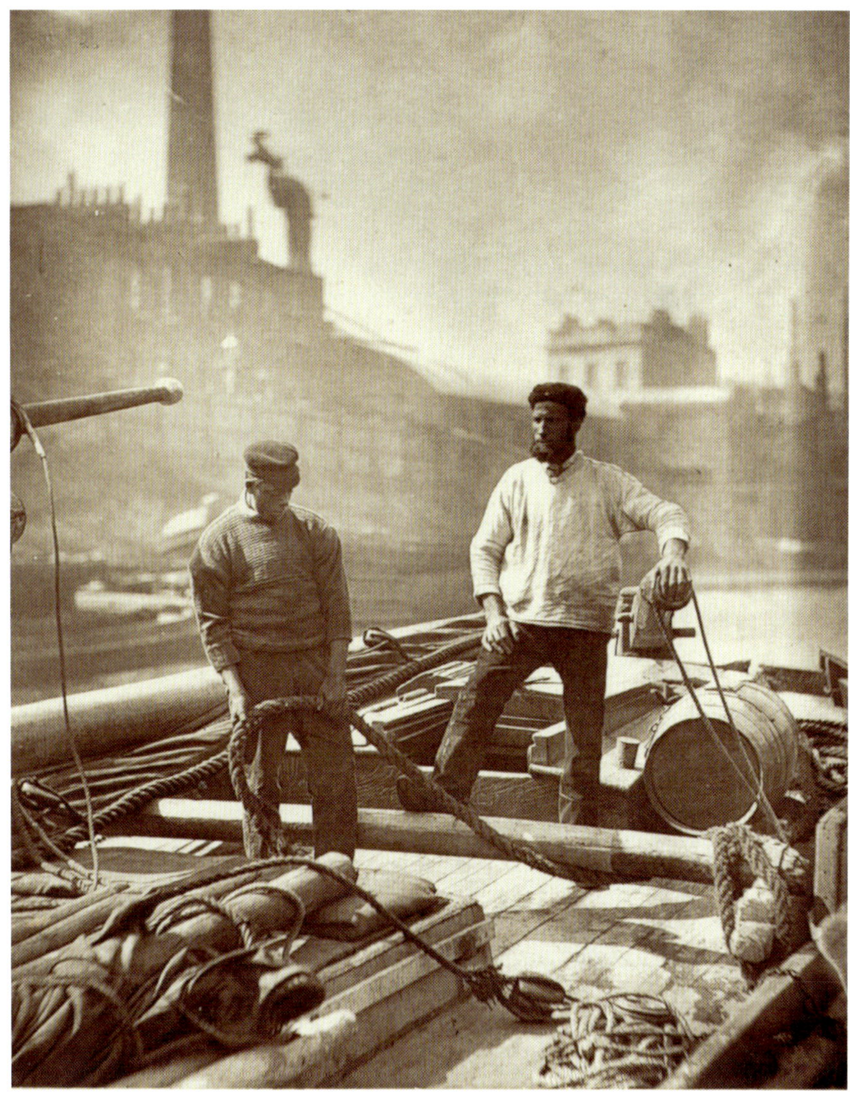

Camille Pissarro
1830–1903
Charing Cross Bridge, London 1890
Oil paint on canvas 60 × 90

National Gallery of Art, Washington, Collection of Mr. and Mrs. Paul Mellon

While in Britain in 1870–1, Pissarro spent time in Central London with his compatriots, visiting museums and the Café Royal, but he restricted his subjects to Norwood and its neighbourhood. He did not return to London until the end of May 1890, at a time when he had come to terms with the fact that strict divisionism, which he had adopted in the early 1880s, impeded his creativity – and also failed to sell. Pissarro had long wanted to return to London, and it is likely that one of the reasons why he eventually crossed the channel in 1890 was the favourable impression he had earlier that year, when rediscovering at Durand-Ruel's one of his own paintings from his exile, *The Avenue, Sydenham* (pp.74–5), in which he identified a freshness of approach. His ambition to do something new merged with his project to revisit London, as expressed in a letter full of hope to Theo van Gogh on 5 April: 'I am still planning on going to London around mid-May. This trip means a lot to me. I think I will come back with new things. It will be much more appealing to me to do some motifs of a different order; my sensations will be rekindled, and who knows, perhaps it will be a condition of success?'.[1]

This time, Pissarro stayed in Notting Hill and tackled views of central London. He painted subjects that Monet had treated in 1870–1, such as Hyde Park and the Thames, perhaps partly guided by the hope that easily recognisable London subjects would have more commercial appeal. Along the river, Pissarro set up his easel at Chelsea, Battersea, and Waterloo Bridge, from which he painted this panoramic view of the Thames looking upstream. Above the strong horizontal line of Charing Cross Bridge, plotting the vast width of the Thames, rise the familiar silhouettes of the Houses of Parliament, Westminster Abbey and Whitehall Court, in the hazy distance. Cleopatra's needle can be seen to the right. Pissarro used divisionism principles by combining small touches of complementary colours to render the projection of light on the steel bridge. But he rejected pointillism in favour of a looser impressionist brushwork, comma-like for the sky, and broken and horizontal for the river. The subtle modulations in both style and colour resulted in outstanding luminosity.

Pissarro had to return to Eragny before he could complete his canvas, and had to entrust his niece's help to ensure the general topography of his painting was correct. Above all, the paddle steamers in the right foreground troubled him, and he requested a drawing from her: 'if I were rich, I would take the train to Calais or any port, in the search for my boat, but… I will have to invent it.'[2] The evident parallels between his largest ship and the most prominent one represented by Gustave Doré in 'All London at Boat-Race' in *London: a Pilgrimage* (pp.52–3) would suggest that he referred to this engraving, rather than to Esther's drawing, if she did produce one. CCP

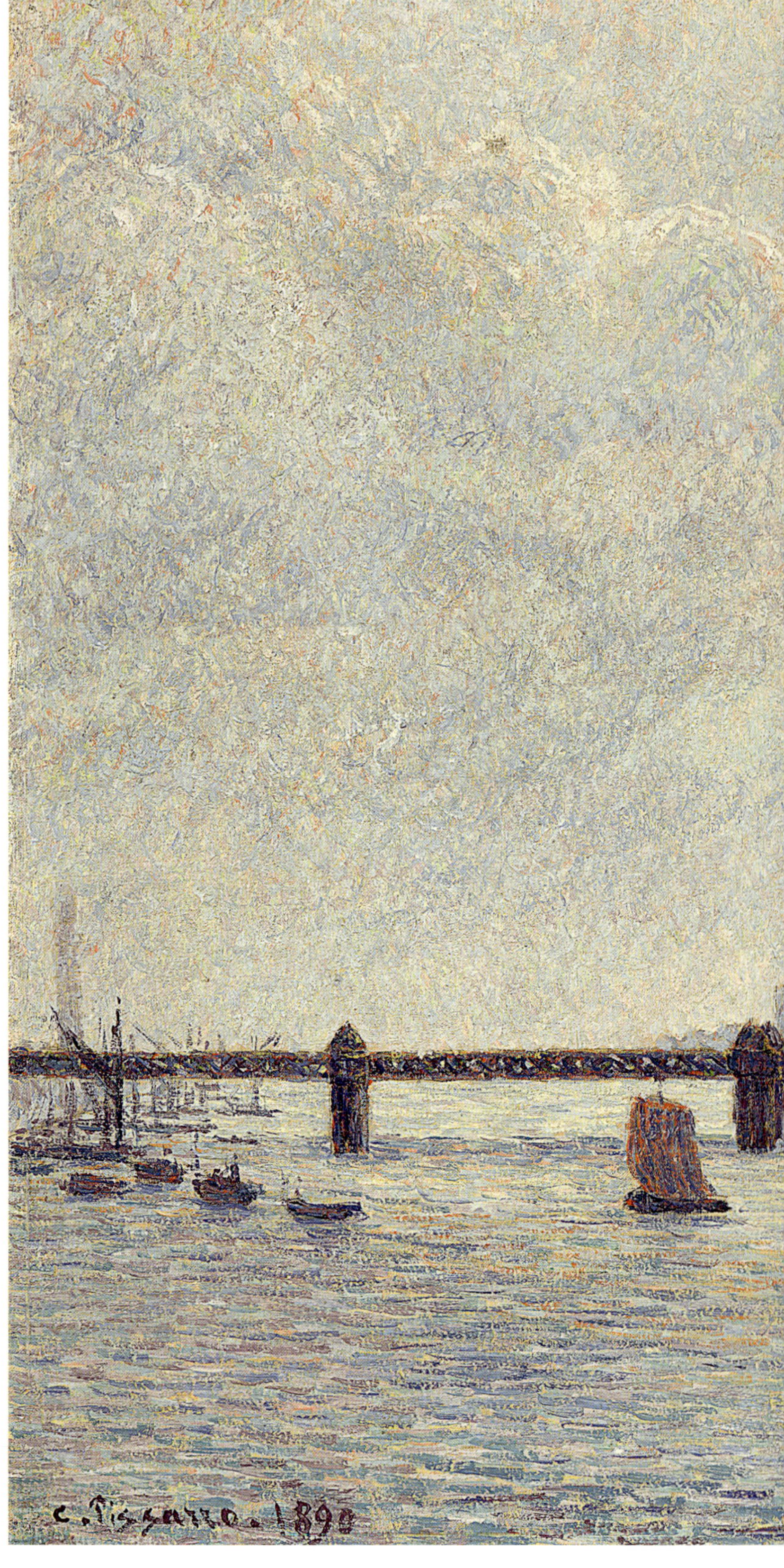

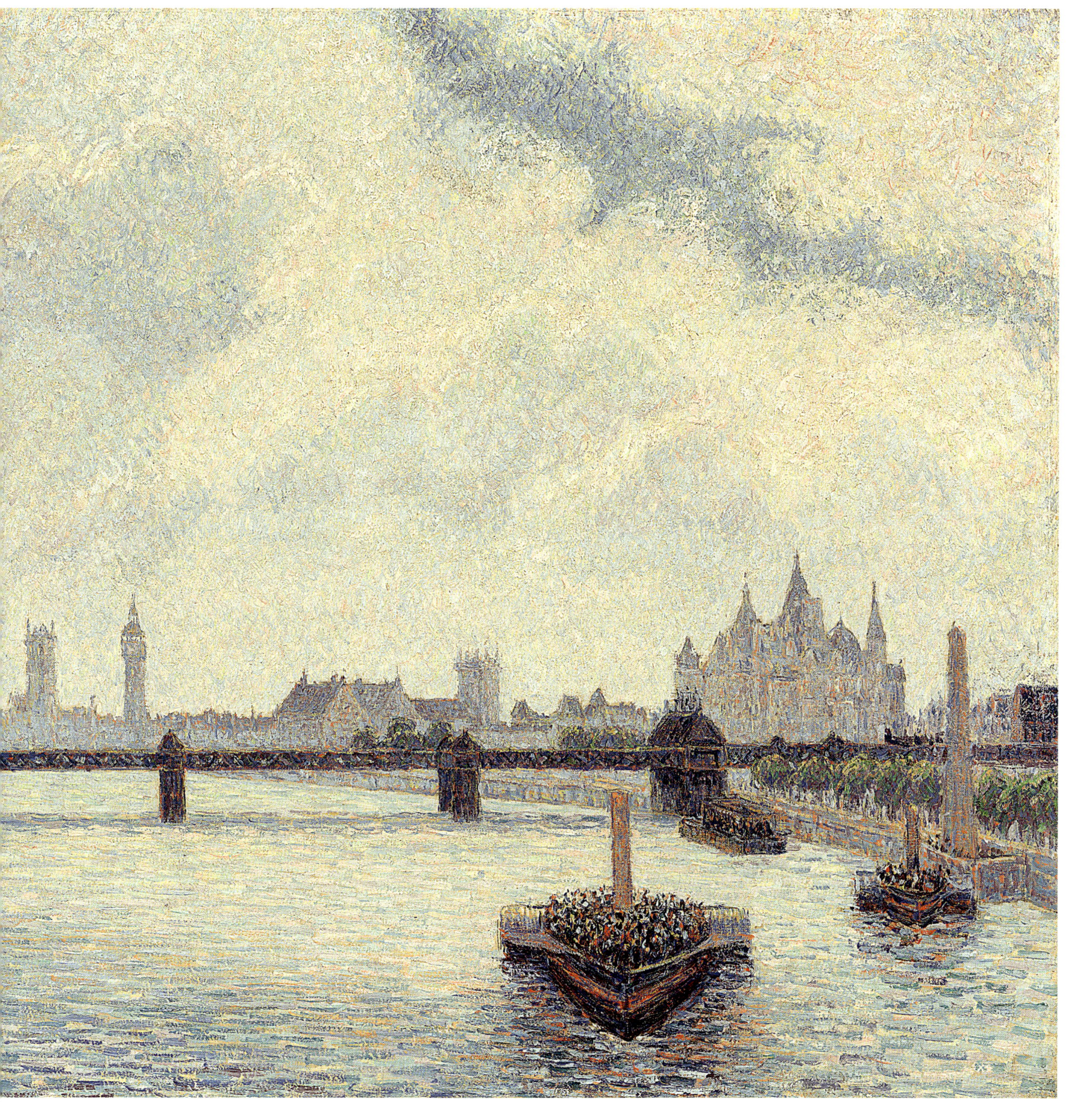

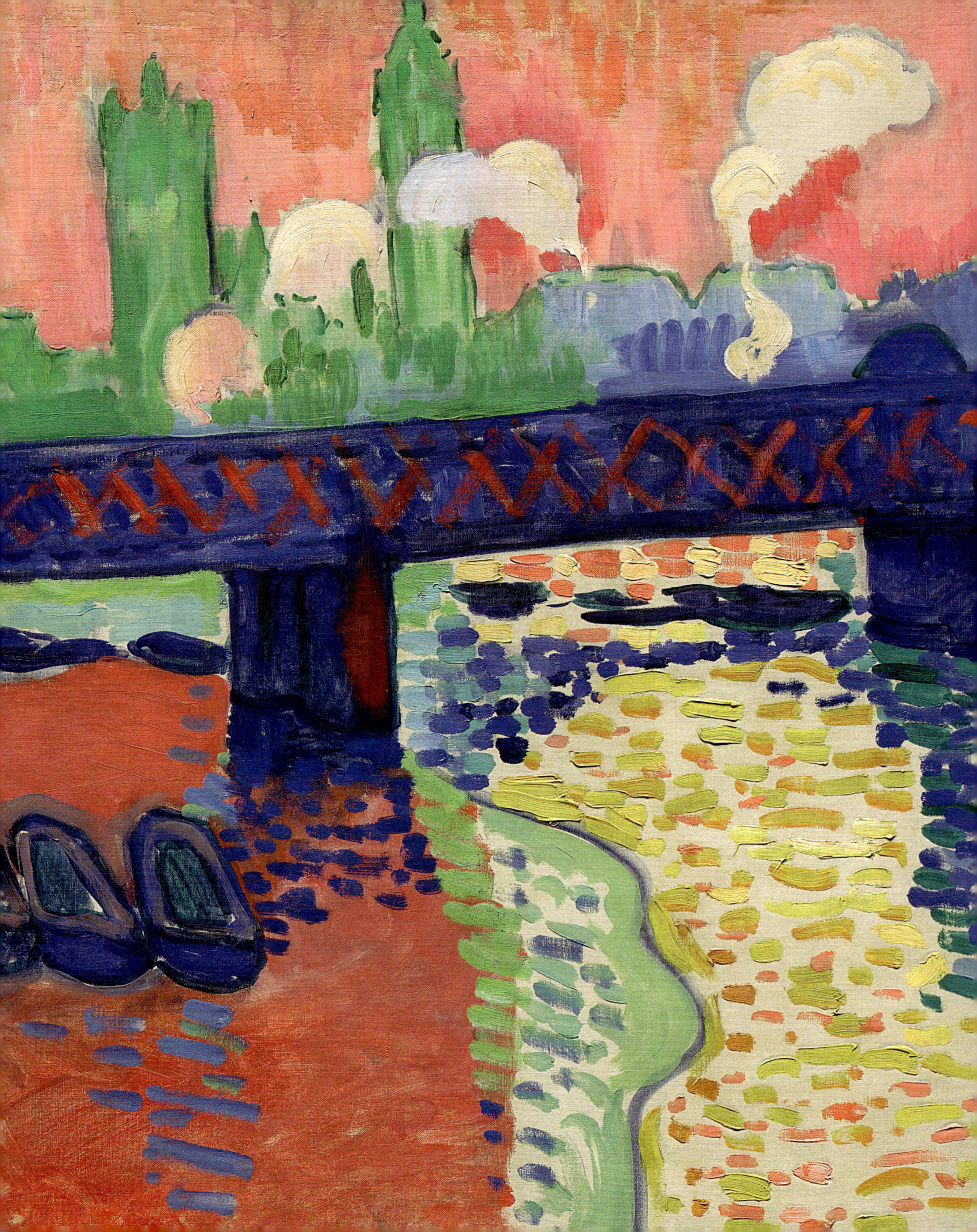

Caroline Corbeau-Parsons

The Thames and Westminster: From Motif to Leitmotif

André Derain
Charing Cross Bridge, London
1906–7
(detail, see pp.242–3)

What I like most of all in London is the fog. How could English painters of the 19th Century have painted its houses brick by brick? Those fellows painted bricks they didn't see, bricks they could not see. It's the fog that gives London its marvellous breadth. Its regular massive blocks become grandiose in this mysterious cloak.
Claude Monet, 1918 and 1920[1]

A naturalist approach

Monet painted five views of London during his self-enforced exile, of which three represent the Thames, focusing on two of its most celebrated sites: the Pool of London with the Custom House, and the Houses of Parliament. Both were highly symbolic, the former as the seat of Britain's trade, through which all goods transited, and the latter as the seat of government and power. Both were also top destinations in contemporary London guides. *The Pool of London* (National Museum Wales, Cardiff) does not depict the Custom House 'brick by brick' – the building and architecture receding in the distance are veiled in a blue mist blurring all details – but it shows that the artist was nevertheless topographically minded. The array of ships and boats represented in the painting are close to forming an orderly semi-circle around Custom House, as if to signify the attraction of its power. The picture's composition, if not its shorthand treatment, could have been adopted by a Victorian artist such as Henry Pether (p.226), whose detailed style contrasts with Monet's approach to naturalism, understood as the representation of his subject as he saw it, fog included. As highlighted in *The Book of the Thames*, 'There are few sights in the world more striking – certainly none more calculated [than the Pool from Tower Stairs] to make an Englishman proud of his country',[2] and it was a popular, patriotic subject among British artists (see, e.g., William Wyllie's *Toil, Litter, Grime and Wealth on a Flowing Tide*, 1883, Tate). A Frenchman could not have failed to have been impressed by the sheer scale of the Thames and its traffic, but the appeal of the scene to potential British clients may also have guided Monet's choice of subject. In his second version of the same view, *Boats in the Pool of London* (p.227), the landmarks of the Custom house and Billingsgate market, deep in fog, are merely indicated behind masts and riggings. Their bluish grey masses are relegated to the misty distance as the hustle and bustle of the port becomes the artist's primary focus. Factory chimneys exuding smoke, pulleys and cargo take centre stage. In the foreground an elegant couple in a green rowboat is about to reach the muddy bank and join other identical embarkations, chaotically moored. As if to assert that this hectic scene was the real London, Monet uniquely added the name of the capital by his signature.

In *The Thames below Westminster* (pp.66–7) dominated by a pale, muted palette, the viewer's eye is first drawn to a dark wooden jetty. It is being dismantled by workmen after the completion of the Victoria embankment, depicted to the right, with its freshly planted trees. Above the jetty rises the new Palace of Westminster, in the same blue-grey hue that Monet

Henry Pether
View of the Thames, Pool of London, from Billingsgate to London Bridge
c.1862
Oil paint on canvas 91 × 137
Saffron Walden Museum

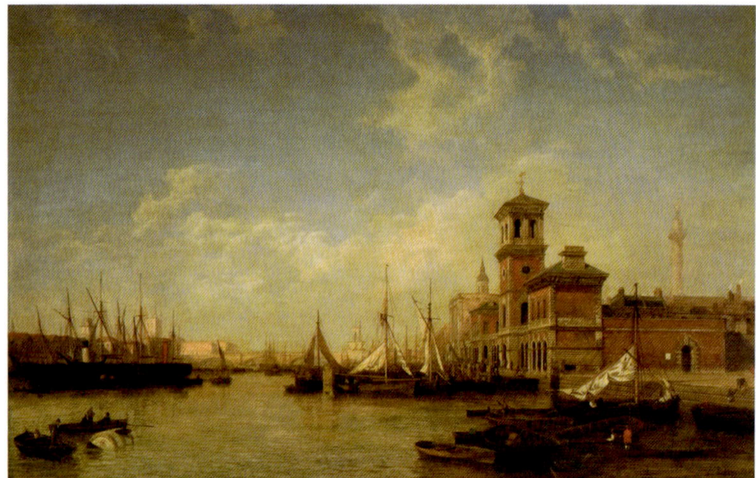

had already adopted to paint London landmarks in his paintings of the Pool of London. Of the three tall towers, only the clock tower, completed in 1859, presents a certain degree of detailing. Along Westminster Bridge, inaugurated in 1862, the artist punctuated the substantial width of the Thames at high tide with modern steamboats. It is difficult to the modern eye to perceive this, so well known is the site that Monet represented, but with *The Thames below Westminster*, he painted the resolutely new London and gave a sense of the soaring economy of Britain.

A painting made by Daubigny only five years earlier (p.229), prior to his own exile, shows the same stretch of the Thames, the embankment still far away from completion. It gives the measure of the way in which this structure transformed London, but beyond this obvious difference, Daubigny's representation of the new palace presents numerous parallels with *The Thames below Westminster*. According to the art historian Etienne Moreau-Nélaton, the two artists met while painting the Thames during the Franco-Prussian war, but Monet had been a fervent admirer of Daubigny's art since 1859.[3] Both shared the credo of plein-air painting as a source of naturalism. Neither of them concealed the men at work on the embankment, giving them almost equal importance to the Palace of Westminster. And both artists painted the Houses of Parliament in a shade of grey, only suggesting architectural details, hereby capturing the effect of fog on the palace in the middle distance. Daubigny was a master at painting agitated skies, and it is unlikely that his *Westminster*, which remained unsigned in his studio, was considered finished by his standards. Its sky is gesturally painted on panel with *frotté* brush strokes,[4] but not brought to completion to the same degree as the rendition of fog in *St Paul's from the Surrey Side* (pp.64–5). Monet also treated the sky of *The Thames below Westminster* with a scumbling technique consisting of building thin, broken layers of paint ranging from ivory to a subtle salmon pink top right, all softly modulated over a pale grey ground showing through. The similarity between Daubigny's and Monet's respective representations of Westminster, at the height of their naturalistic tendencies, suggests that it was direct observation that led them not to depict the palace 'brick by brick', and to adopt similar techniques to render what they saw.

A palace worthy of a rich and powerful nation

As to the appeal of the palace as a motif, Elisée Reclus, in his 1862 London guide, gave a clue to how the new palace would have been perceived by the French at the time. He stressed, in a whole chapter dedicated to the Houses of Parliament, that the old palace occupied only a quarter of the surface of the new one, the latter being built on the principle that it should be 'worthy by its grandeur and magnificence of a rich and powerful nation'. After a mention that the new edifice 'had already cost the British nation 55 millions of fcs [francs]',[5] a long description of the palace ensued, hinting at the hubris of the enterprise (the Victoria tower, 101 metres high, was then the tallest in Europe). Reclus's conclusion was abrupt: 'Such is the exterior of this enormous construction which the English dare compare with the magnificent Belgian town halls of Ypres, Ghent, Luven, and Brussels. In reality, the sole beauty of the Houses of Parliament lies in its mass.'[6] This was echoed in 1872 by Hippolyte Taine's *Notes on England*: 'Leaping and twisted lines, complicated mouldings, trefoils and rose-windows diversify the enormous mass which covers four acres, and produces on the mind the idea of a tangled forest.'[7]

The impression that the sheer scale of the building made on foreign painters is probably best expressed on canvas by Giuseppe de Nittis's *Westminster* 1878 (pp.208–11), almost 2 metres wide and by far the largest of the paintings of London that he executed for Kaye Knowles (see p.109). The palace is depicted shrouded in fog and smoke, and a striking *contre-jour* gives a ghost-like quality to it, as if so imposing a monument could only be a mirage. Monet would exploit this backlighting effect twenty years later in his Houses of Parliament series.[8] The Thames workers smoking on Westminster Bridge after a hard day of labour do not solely act as a *repoussoir* in the composition.[9] Their prominence suggests that they make up the British nation as much as the evanescent symbol above their heads. Despite his Italian nationality, de Nittis was a 'Parisian through and through',[10] and at a time when certain areas of Paris were still in ruins, or only in the process of being rebuilt following the events of 1871, the grandeur of the Palace of Westminster would inevitably have invited comparisons with France's slow reconstruction, both figuratively and literally. The Houses of Parliament had risen from the ashes of the old palace and in that sense were a model to follow, but in the eyes of a Parisian, there must have been something fascinating, but also overwhelming, in the massive monument, emblematic of Britain and its vast empire. At the 1878 Universal Exhibition, de Nittis showed no less than eight

Claude Monet
Boats in the Pool of London c.1871
Oil paint on canvas 47 × 73

Private collection

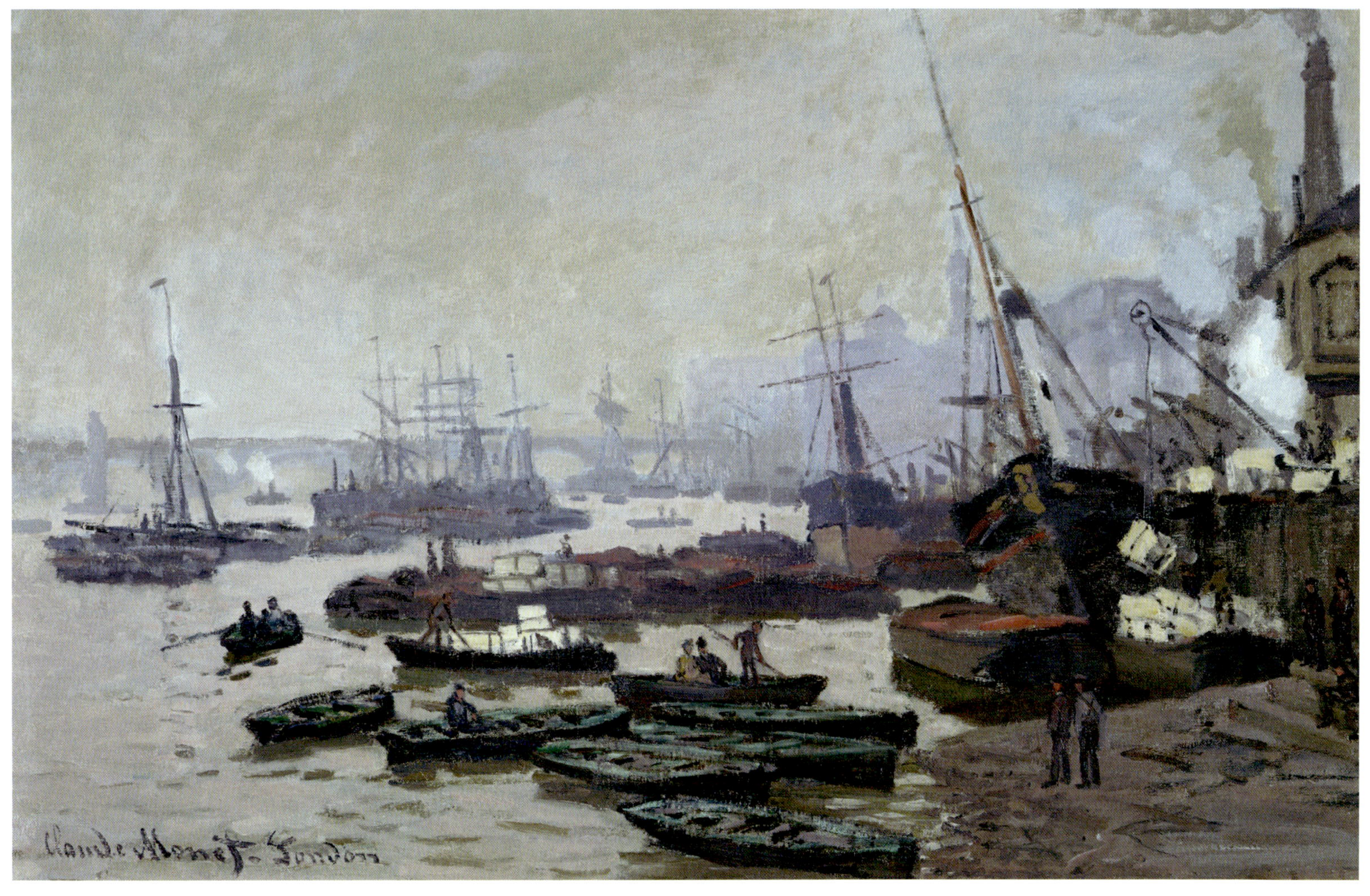

views of London, including *Westminster*, but also a contrasting *Place des Pyramides* 1875 (p.228), in which imposing scaffoldings dominate the Parisian scene.

The invention of fogs

Another foreigner in London who, on the other hand, *did* ignore the architecture of the Palace of Westminster, was the American James Abbott McNeill Whistler. This is not to say that he did not paint it. In *Nocturne in Grey and Gold* c.1874 (Corporation of Glasgow, Burrell Collection), which looks upstream from Westminster Bridge, the southern end of the palace's river front can be made out in the obscurity, but its well-known silhouette is not recognisable as such. As Robin Spencer has noted, the Houses of Parliament 'are lost to darkness, their profile nearly undistinguishable from other public buildings'.[11] Whistler's nocturnes changed the way in which the Thames and London were aesthetically perceived, and painted. Oscar Wilde explained this phenomenon in *The Decay of Lying*:

> Where, if not from the Impressionists, do we get these wonderful brown fogs that come creeping down our streets? To whom, if not to them and to their master, do we owe these lovely silver mists that brood over our river and turn to faint forms of fading grace, curved bridge and swaying barge. The extraordinary change that has taken place in the climate of London in the last ten years is entirely due to this particular school of art. One does not see anything until one sees its beauty. Then, and only then, does it come into existence. At present, people see fogs not because there are fogs but because poets and painters have taught them the mysterious loveliness of such effects. There may have been fogs for centuries in London – I daresay there were – but no one saw them, and so we don't know anything about them. They didn't exist until art had invented them.[12]

When referring to the impressionists and their master, Wilde misleadingly meant Whistler, who painted fogs for their transformative, sublimating effect on the Thames. The painter famously stated in his 'Ten o'Clock' lecture of 1885:

> And when the evening mist clothes the riverside with poetry, as with a veil, and the poor buildings lose themselves in the dim sky, and the tall chimneys become campanili, and the warehouses are palaces in the night, and the whole city hangs in the heavens and fairyland is before us ... Nature, who for once has sung in tune, sings her exquisite song to the artist alone.[13]

As the art historian John House underlined, this positive view of London fogs and their aestheticising power was pioneered as early as 1842 by the French writer Théophile Gautier, who praised the way in which 'this smoke ... blurs harsh angles, veils the meanness of buildings, enlarges view, gives mystery and vagueness to the most positive objects',[14] words that are strongly echoed by Whistler. As to why it was left to foreigners to 'invent fogs' in the artistic realm, the reason appears simple: the vaporousness of the London atmosphere was taken for granted by Londoners, who in their daily life certainly saw this heavy pollution as a hindrance to contend with, rather than celebrate. This shift of attention to fogs in art

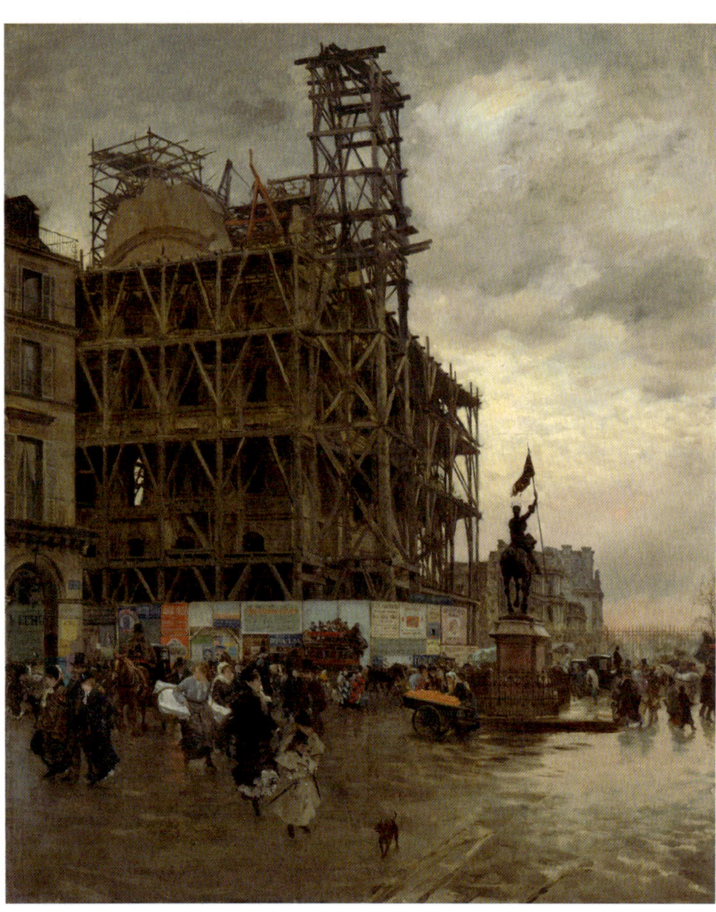

Giuseppe de Nittis
La Place des Pyramides 1875
Oil paint on canvas 92.3 × 75

Musée d'Orsay, Paris

from the 1870s onwards can be perceived in the way in which the title of Monet's *Thames below Westminster* evolved. Exhibited as *The Houses of Parliament* in 1873 at the seventh exhibition of the Society of French Artists, it was renamed *The Banks of the Thames and the Parliament. Fog Effect* by 1878, when it passed from Ernest Hoschedé's collection to that of Jean-Baptiste Faure.[15]

The return of the impressionists

In 1871 around 3.3 million people lived in inner London (more than in 2011), a figure that rose to 4.6 million in 1901. This overpopulation added to already substantial coal emissions along the Thames – the artery for trade, commerce and industry – whose banks were dotted with polluting factories. At the heart of the city, erected on this river via which all goods transited, were the Houses of Parliament, synecdochic of the power of Britain and its imperial expansion, then reaching its peak. By a process of association, fogs, the Thames and the Houses of Parliament got so entwined as to become symbols of Britain. The Thames, its atmospheric effects and the Palace of Westminster became primary motifs for French painters for aesthetic and symbolic reasons, but also because they nurtured the hope that these subjects would be highly marketable. The strength of the London art market had already been a decisive factor for French artists when establishing the destination of their exile during the Franco-Prussian war, and it remained so.

As early as 1880, Monet wrote to the critic Théodore Duret, who had links with London (see p.199): 'When you come through Paris, you can advise me on what the chances could be for me in coming to spend several weeks in London where I could paint some aspects of the Thames.'[16] This project would not come to fruition until the turn of the century, but Monet, throughout the 1880s, repeatedly expressed his wish to paint the Thames's atmospheric effects. According to the art historian Katharine Lochnan, one of the reasons why Monet kept postponing painting the Thames was to preserve his friendship with Whistler, whom he visited in London in 1887.[17] By then, they had become close, and indeed Monet did not start his Thames series until his notoriously sensitive friend had given up painting Nocturnes in the aftermath of his famous court case against the critic, John Ruskin. Camille Pissarro was aware of Monet's project, and a healthy sense of rivalry between the two old friends may have prompted Pissarro to tackle the Thames as a subject before Monet, and for the first time: his views of London during his exile had hitherto been restricted to the suburbs of Norwood and its surroundings. Unlike Monet, Pissarro and his family had longstanding ties with London (see p.15), and these were strengthened when Camille's son Lucien (1863–1944) settled in London in 1890. This was a decisive factor to paint London again for Pissarro, who himself contemplated moving to London at several points in his life.[18]

Prior to his return to London in 1890, Pissarro wrote to the dealer Theo van Gogh: 'This trip means a lot to me. I think I'll come back with new things. It will be much more appealing to me to do some motifs of a different order; my sensations will be rekindled, and who knows, perhaps it will be a condition of success?'[19] In 1890 he painted *Battersea Bridge* (private collection) at sunset and *Charing Cross Bridge* (pp.222–3), 'with Parliament' as he emphasised, adding that he 'would probably continue the series',[20] most certainly in the sense of a group, like Canaletto and Giuseppe de Nittis had done before him (see pp.208–9). In his *Charing Cross Bridge* Pissarro adopted a panoramic format, and his composition to the left stops just short of including the south bank of the river, giving the illusion that the river is even wider than it is. In the centre of the picture rises the Palace of Westminster, but of equal importance is the vast, vaporous sky. Pissarro painted London in its light summer mist,

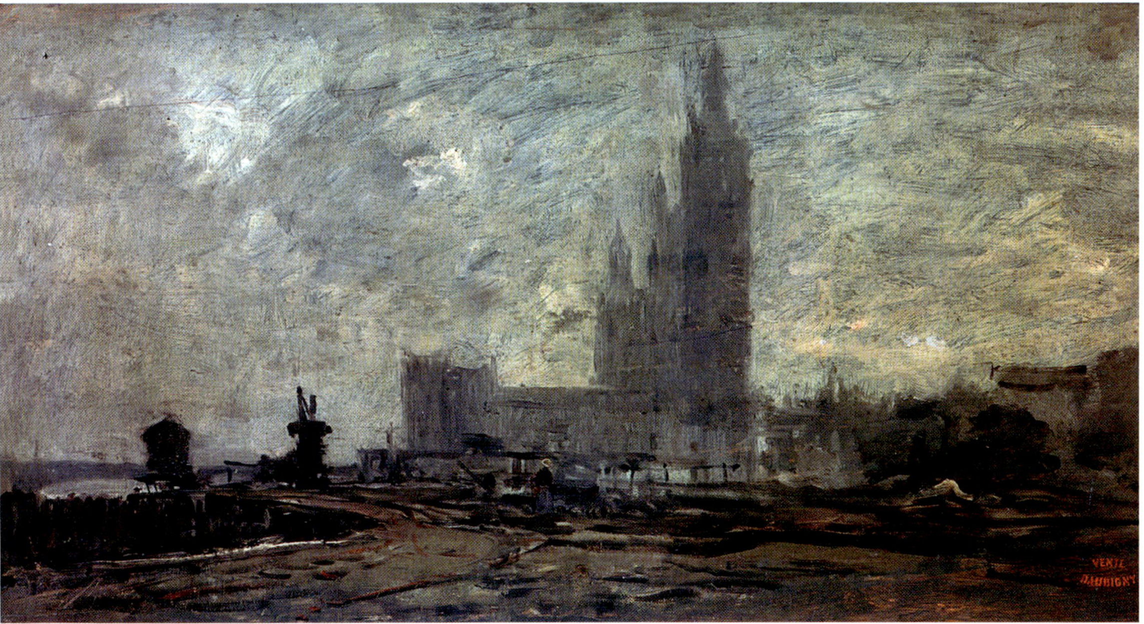

Charles-François Daubigny
Westminster 1866
Oil paint on panel 32 × 59

The Pushkin State Museum of Fine Arts, Moscow

refracting opal tones, the blue sky piercing through the clouds. Drawing on some of the principles of divisionism that he had embraced from the mid-1880s, but going beyond its constraints, he returned in *Charing Cross Bridge* to a more spontaneous technique and a variety of brush strokes, achieving prodigious luminosity. Maximilien Luce, who accompanied his close friend Pissarro to London in 1892, would paint a pointillist *Thames and Westminster* (see below) from the same point of view of Monet's *Thames below Westminster*.[21] The Palace of Westminster had already become a motif through which to take the measure of oneself against other artists.

A revenge on the 'miserable time'

Around the age of sixty, Monet expressed the wish to revisit important sites where he had painted, 'to take up each of the categories of motifs which have shared my attention in turn, to create a kind of synthesis where I would sum up, in one canvas, sometimes two, my impressions and sensations of the past'.[22] The Thames series fell within this project, but Monet's original plan to paint one or two canvases vastly expanded. Between 1899 and 1901 Monet started in the region of a hundred canvases of Charing Cross Bridge, Waterloo Bridge, and the Houses of Parliament (see pp.232–41), which he began last and, out of the three Thames subjects, rated the most. It presents greater uniformity in conception as a group than the other two: the bespoke canvases are all the same dimensions, and the scale of the palace in relation to the canvas does not vary either. Backlit, consistently painted late in the day or at sunset, the forms of the weighty architecture of the palace seem to evaporate through a process of diffusion and refraction of colour and sunlight through fog. Monet described to an interviewer the challenge he was facing:

> The fog in London assumes all sorts of colours; there are black, brown, yellow, green, purple fogs, and the interest in painting is to get the objects as seen through all these fogs. My practiced eye has found that objects change in appearance in a London fog more and quicker than in any other atmosphere, and the difficulty is to get every change down on canvas.[23]

In his series Monet was pursuing his quest for instantaneity (*l'instantanéité*[24]) by capturing the transience of the Thames's atmospheric effects. A few years earlier, he had expressed his concern with 'the *enveloppe*, the same light spread over everything',[25] and the motif of the Houses of Parliament, no matter how familiar, became a set with which to observe and record the performance of the Thames and its fogs, a theme for infinite chromatic variations. Monet was both conductor and interpreter for the series, which developed on a symphonic scale. He worked simultaneously on his canvases until 1904,[26] when he finally parted with them to exhibit thirty-seven *Views of the Thames* at Durand-Ruel's gallery in Paris, the year of the Entente Cordiale. This proved a great critical and financial success. Monet had not only revisited his past by painting the Thames

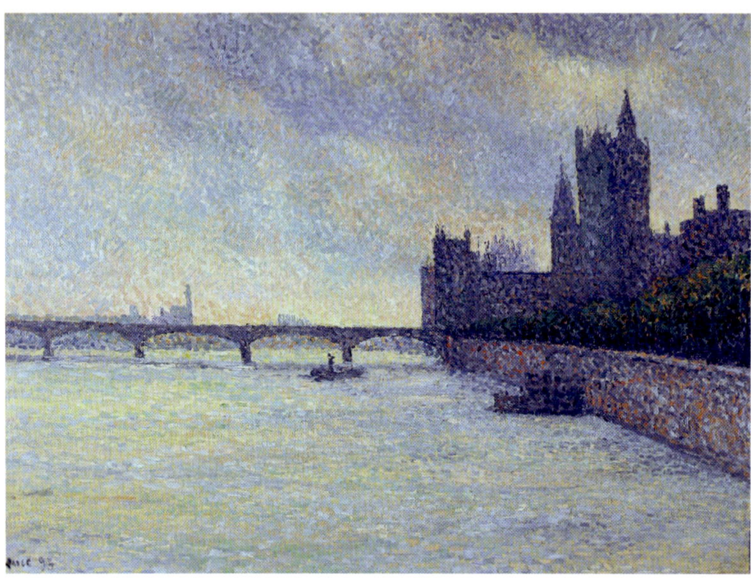

[above]
Maximilien Luce
The Thames and Westminster 1893
Oil paint on canvas 81.5 × 100

Private collection

[opposite]
André Derain
Westminster 1906
Oil paint on canvas 49.5 × 65.5

Musée de L'Annonciade, Saint-Tropez

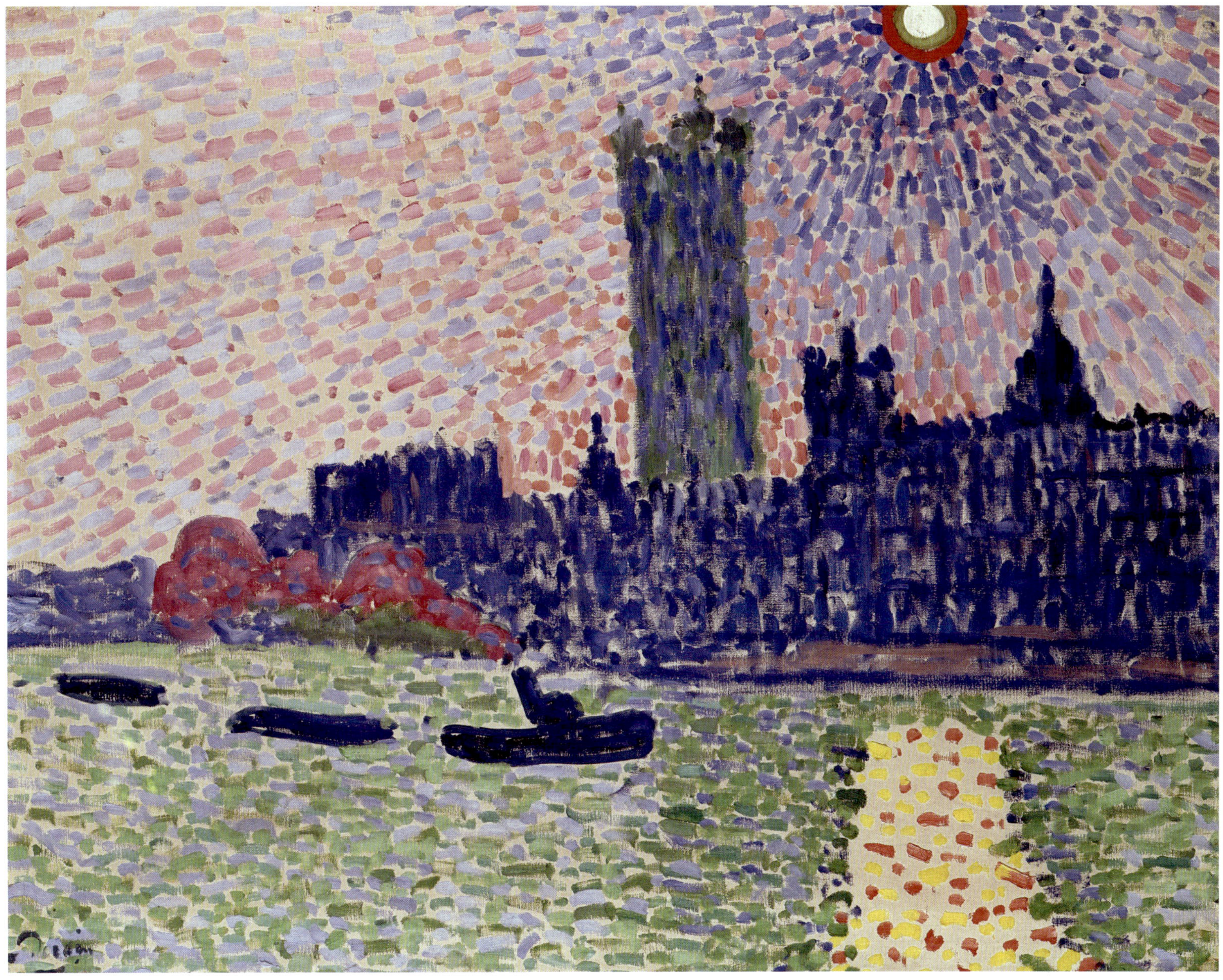

and Westminster. For all the ups and downs of their partnership, he admitted that Durand-Ruel had saved him from starving completely. Their joint success, more than thirty years after their meeting and 'a miserable time' in London,[27] was a revenge on his past for Monet. He had plans – never realised – to show his Thames series in London, at the Dowdeswell galleries: 'I have always had the desire to show my *London* here, for my own personal satisfaction'.[28]

The exhibition that may have offered Monet some sort of closure vis-à-vis his relationship to London marked the beginning of another chapter in the representation of the city, and the Palace of Westminster in particular. The young André Derain was among visitors to Monet's exhibition, and his art dealer, Ambroise Vollard, was another. Mindful of Durand-Ruel's success at a difficult time for the art market in France, Vollard sent Derain to London to paint views of the city. Derain would produce thirty of them, mostly of the Thames, some very consciously paying homage to Monet but also challenging him through the same motifs. Among these were Derain's *Charing Cross Bridge* pp.242–3), which looks back to Monet's paintings of the same subject, and, above all, *Westminster* (above), which uses the same viewpoint and quotes the same barges that often appear in Monet's *Houses of Parliament*. This resolutely signalled the appropriation of the motif of the Palace of Westminster as a palimpsest for artistic expression.

Claude Monet
1840–1926
Houses of Parliament, Sunlight Effect 1903 (1)
Oil paint on canvas 81.3 × 92.1

Brooklyn Museum. Bequest of Grace Underwood Barton

Houses of Parliament, Effect of Sunlight in the Fog 1904 (2)
Oil paint on canvas 81.5 × 92.5

Musée d'Orsay, Paris

Houses of Parliament c.1900–1 (3)
Oil paint on canvas 81.2 × 92.8

The Art Institute of Chicago. Mr and Mrs Martin A Ryerson Collection

Houses of Parliament, Fog Effect 1903 (4)
Oil paint on canvas 81 × 92

Le Havre, Musée d'art moderne Andre Malraux

Houses of Parliament, Sunset 1904 (5)
Oil paint on canvas 81 × 92

Kunstmuseen, Krefeld

Houses of Parliament, Fog Effect 1903 (6)
Oil paint on canvas 81 × 92

The Metropolitan Museum of Art, New York. Bequest of Julia W. Emmons, 1956

Charing Cross Bridge 1899–1902 (7)
Oil paint on canvas 65 × 100

Private collection

Charing Cross Bridge 1904 (8)
Oil paint on canvas 65 × 95

Private collection

Monet first painted the Palace of Westminster in 1871, in *The Thames below Westminster* (pp.66–7). In this early painting his focus was split between the treatment of London as a modern capital, and the effect of mist on the architectural landmark. Around his sixtieth birthday, in 1900, he formed the wish to explore anew earlier motifs, 'to sum up, in one canvas, sometimes two, [his] impressions and [his] sensations of the past' (see p.230). His Thames series fell within this project and was divided into three groups or subseries: Waterloo Bridge and Charing Cross Bridge, both painted from the Savoy,[1] and the Houses of Parliament.

The river and its ever-changing atmospheric effects was the overarching motif of the series, but the Palace of Westminster was central too. The landmark first reappeared in Monet's art in 1899 when working on his Charing Cross Bridge group. In these pictures, on which he continued to work during his next two London painting campaigns, the palace appears in the right background (see p.241), when not completely obscured by the fog (p.240). However, it was to take centre stage in his Houses of Parliament subseries, which Monet did not start until 13 February 1900, during his second London sojourn for the Thames series. Mrs Charles Hunter, one of John Singer Sargent's patrons, had made arrangements with her friend Dr Joseph Franck Payne for Monet to paint the Houses of Parliament from a covered terrace in St Thomas's Hospital. Monet enthusiastically reported to his wife Alice: 'What I have begun there is marvellous to paint and much more interesting than what I have been doing at the Savoy.'[2] Monet only worked there when the Houses of Parliament were backlit, from 4 pm until sunset, and as with his Waterloo Bridge and Charing Cross Bridge subseries, on which he usually focused in the morning and in the afternoon respectively, he painted them in the winter season, when fogs were the most spectacular.

Monet had initially tried to capture the changes in climatic and light effects by going over the same canvases to modify them, especially in 1899. However, his correspondence with Alice the following year records how he was now working simultaneously on an ever-increasing number of canvases:

> Today was a day of terrible struggle, and it will be the same until the day I leave. Only I needed more canvases, for the only way of achieving something is to start new ones for all kinds of weather, all kinds of harmonies, it is the real way, and, at the beginning, one always expects to find the same effects again and finish them, hence these unfortunate alterations which are useless.[3]

Monet persisted and refined his method further, indicating to Alice a few days later:

> I am making progress every day in understanding this very special climate, and have got to the point where I can work with big slashing strokes on canvases that had given me a lot of trouble, which were more or less finished, but were not London-like enough, and that is what I am trying to convey with this broad brushwork.[4]

Houses of Parliament c.1900–1 (p.236), gives a sense of this working process: long sweeping brush strokes, especially visible on the Victoria tower, were painted over densely worked areas of the canvas.[5] Nevertheless, despite the modification of his approach to the Thames paintings and all his intensive discipline, the artist warned his wife towards the end of his second sojourn that his efforts remained inconclusive: 'You need not expect to see anything in a finished state: they are only experiments, investigations, preparatory steps, and overall, crazy, useless research.'[6] He returned to Giverny with eight crates, containing eighty canvases.

On 25 January 1901 Monet arrived in London for his last campaign, painting until mid-March, when it became apparent that he was ill. The artist was back in Giverny in April. His correspondence with Alice during his last sojourn describes the same struggles encountered previously. Shortly before falling ill, he wrote to her: 'I went about it the wrong way, it's not a country where you can finish things on the spot: the effects are never repeated, and I should only have done quick sketches, real impressions.'[7] Monet made no secret that he finished the vast majority of his Thames series in his studio at Giverny.[8] He did not paint in London after 1901, but he was still hard at work in 1904, shortly before his seminal and highly successful exhibition of thirty-seven *Views of the Thames*, which took place at Paul Durand-Ruel's gallery in Paris between 9 May and 7 June 1904, the year of the Entente Cordiale.[9]

As Grace Seiberling has noted, with this being the last group Monet started on, there is some indication that he was more confident as to how to treat the Houses of Parliament.[10] As opposed to the Charing Cross and Waterloo Bridge subseries, no sketchier versions remain of this one. There are also fewer canvases, and they show greater unity in conception. Monet ordered non-standard canvases from Lechertier-Barbe of Jermyn Street,[11] all of the same dimensions, unlike those used for the other two groups, which vary in sizes. The scale of the Palace of Westminster in relation to the canvas is also relatively uniform, and compared to the Charing Cross and Waterloo Bridges subseries, the main variations in the Houses of Parliament are chromatic.

The proportion shown of the building, however, varies. In *Houses of Parliament, Sunlight Effect* (p.234), for instance, Monet represented a large part of the palace, with the central spire and adjacent small square tower visible, partly balancing Victoria Tower, the tallest and widest of the palace. It is worth noting that in none of his Houses of Parliament pictures does the clock tower (now popularly known as Big Ben) appear. Instead, the Victoria tower is the architectural element that dominates these paintings (see p.226), especially as he considerably elongated it. Paintings in which the tower is to the right of the composition (which, according to Daniel Wildenstein, were painted last) are reminiscent of *The Thames below Westminster* – not only because of the motif of the palace itself, but also compositionally. Although the early painting stretches out more to the left, if one compares it to *Houses of Parliament, Effect of Sunlight in the Fog* (p.235), the impression of the palace in relation to the canvas and the waterline is almost identical, and so is the 45°-angled line formed by the Victoria embankment in the earlier painting, replicated by the shadow of the palace on the Thames in the later one. The same can be said of some of the most elongated Charing Cross canvases, in which the Palace of Westminster appears to the right (p.241), in which the bridge structures the composition, as Waterloo Bridge did in *The Thames below Westminster*, albeit in the background, not the middle ground. In the work on p.240, however, it is apparent that Monet concerns himself primarily with rendering fog, smoke and light, and the 'envelope' that their combination produces.

In the Houses of Parliament subseries, and to a certain extent in the Charing Cross bridge paintings too, the strong backlighting makes a floating, ghostly apparition of the palace, which gives a sense that in the wider scheme of the series it is also a foil for atmospheric effects. In a number of the Houses of Parliament paintings Monet included, in some instances quite late in his working process, yawls (pp.237, 239). In the close-up compositions of the Houses of Parliament, just across the river, these give a measure of the scale of the architecture and of the depth of the fog, but also bring a certain mysterious Stygian quality to the paintings. As Grace Seiberling underlined, '[Monet's] wish for synthesis, of which he had spoken to Thiébault-Sisson, suggests that part of the work on the series was aimed at finding some essential quality, which was suggestive and emotional.'[12] CCP

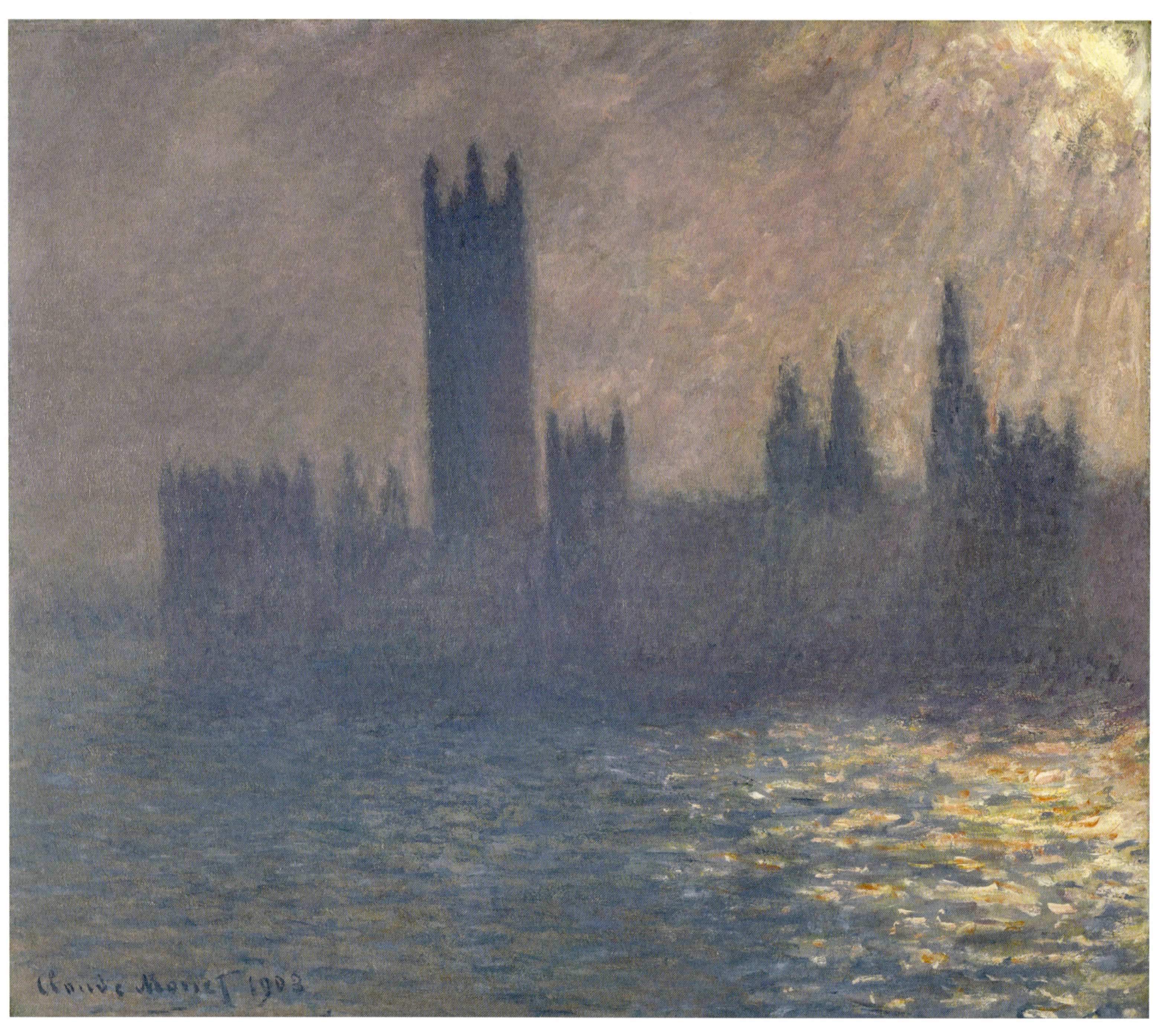

1

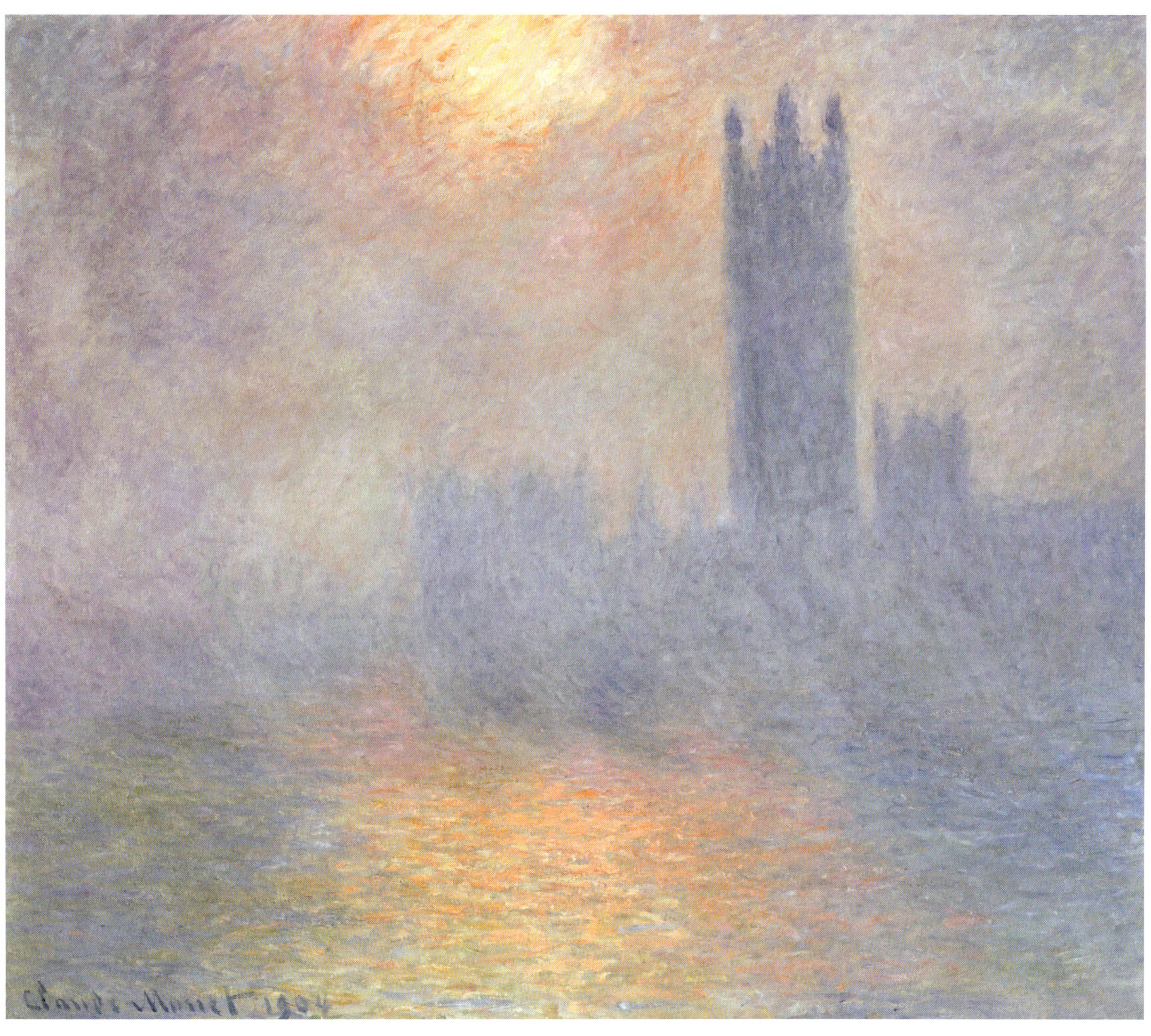

2

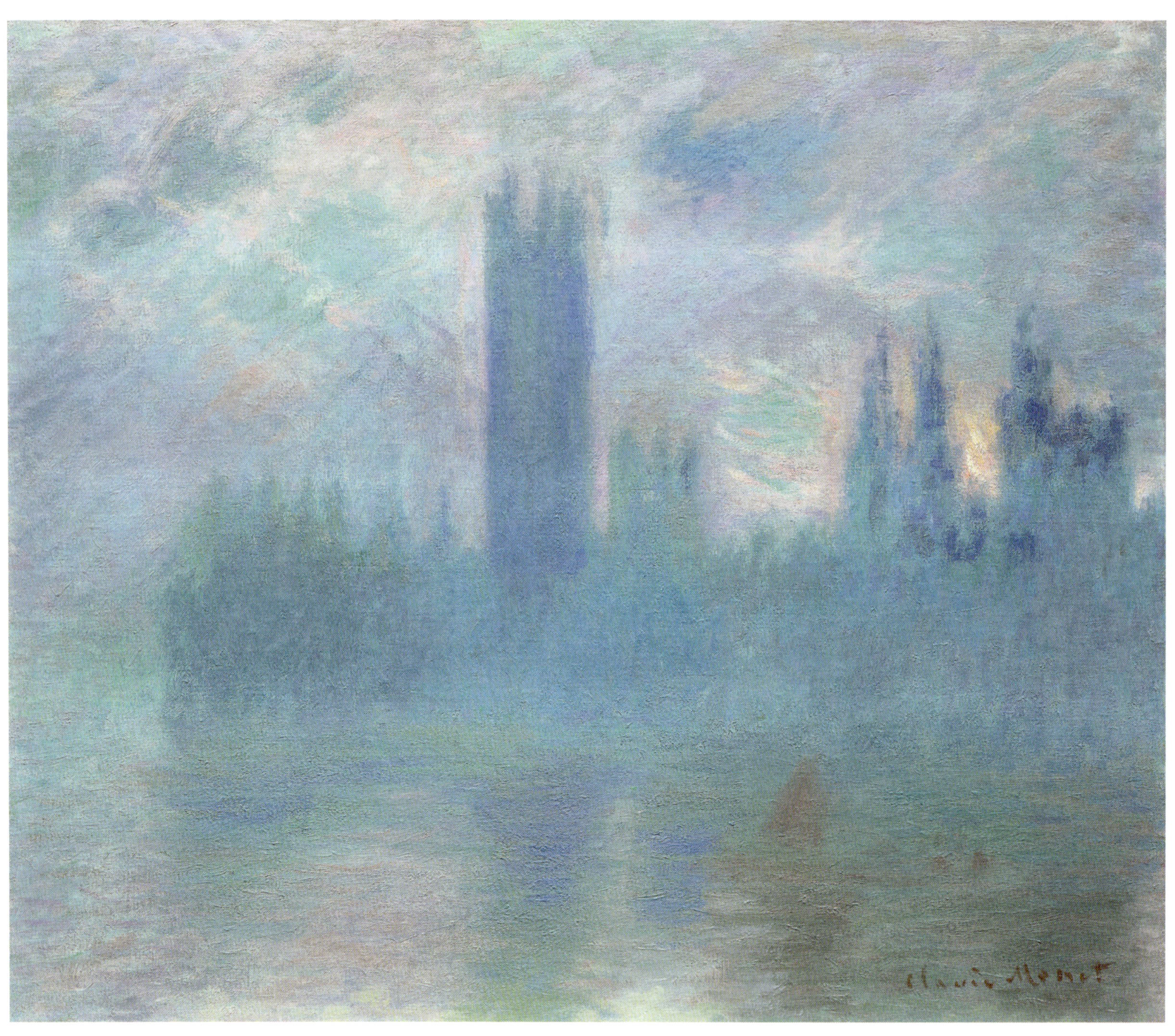

3

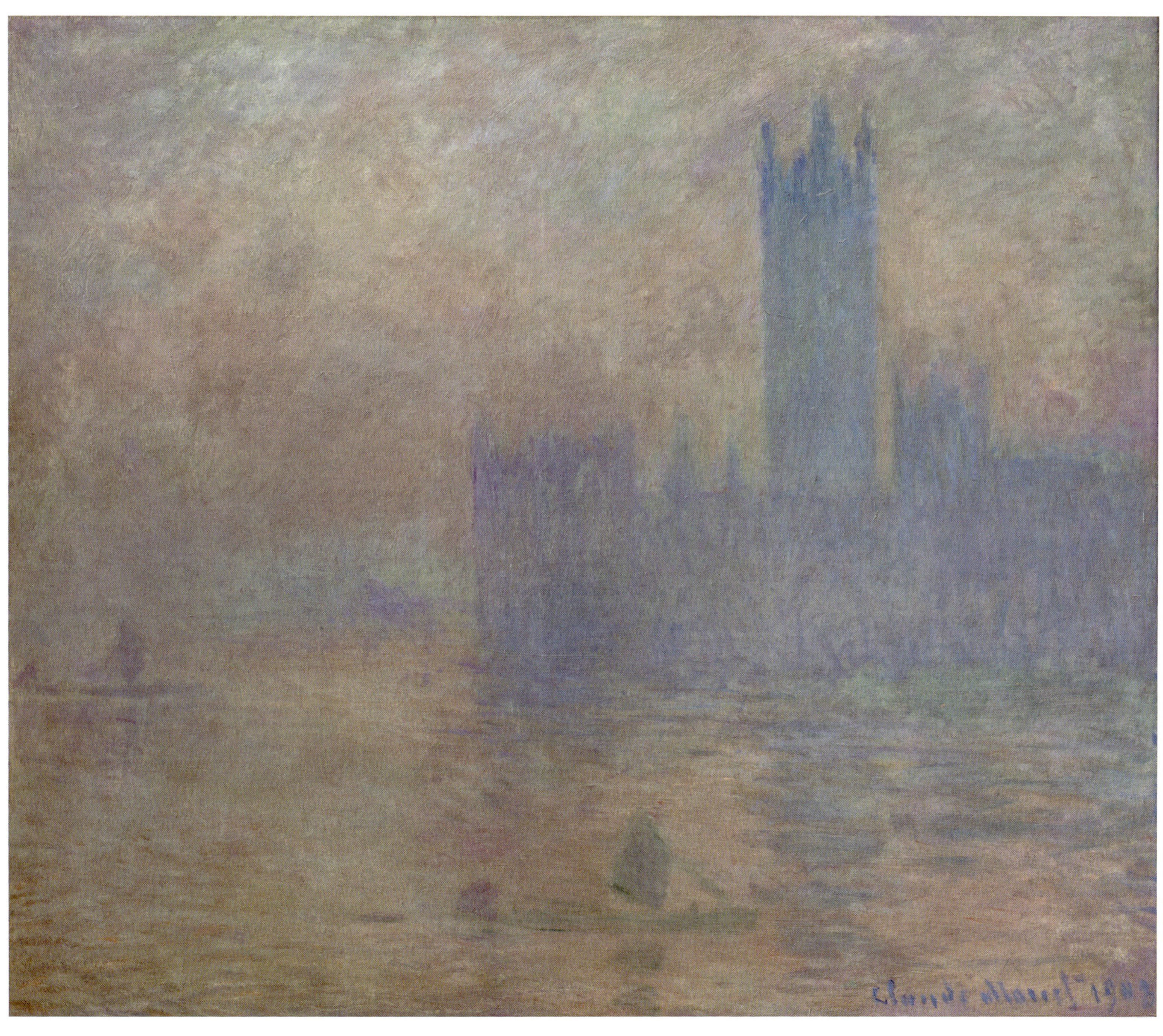

4

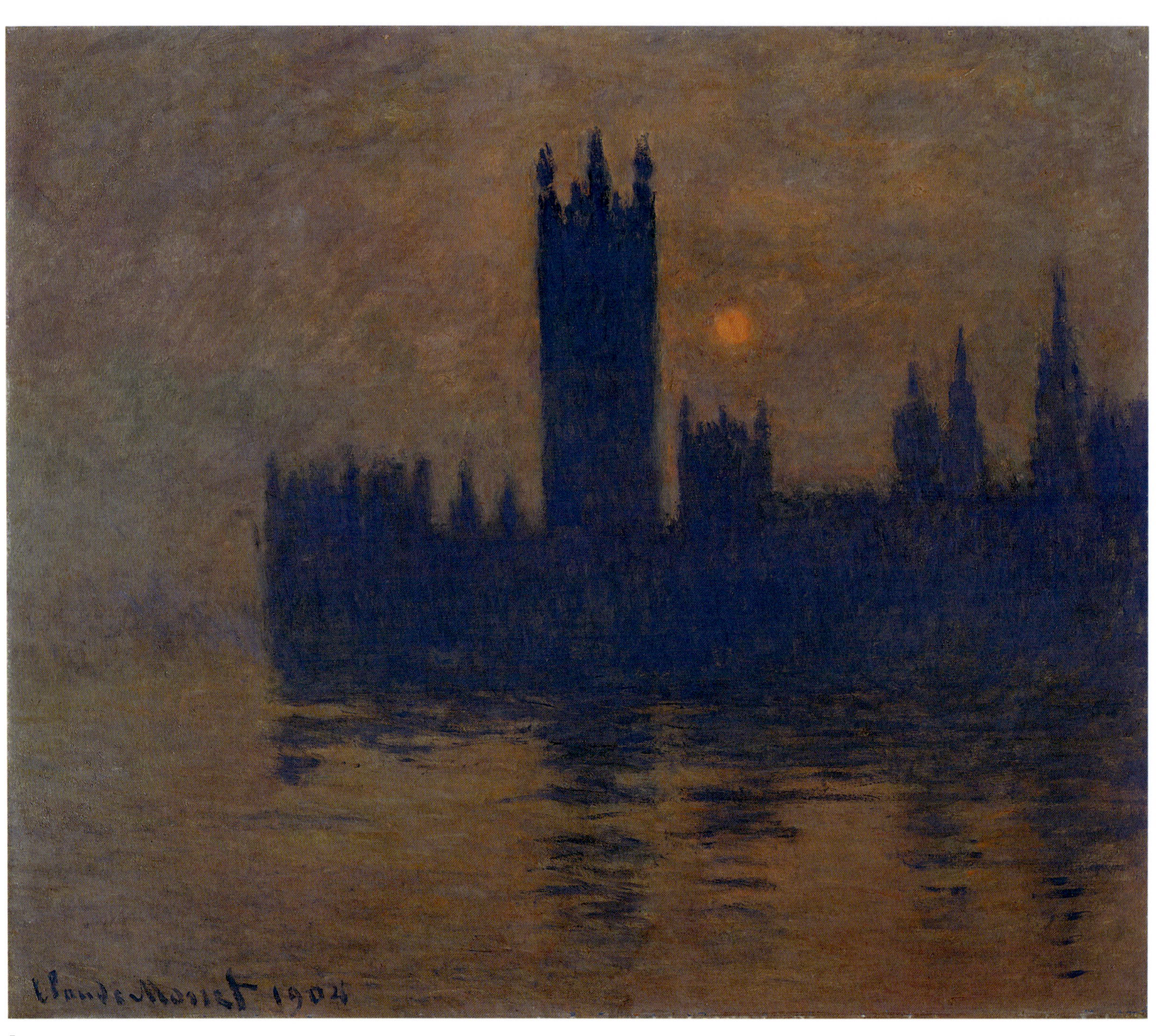

5

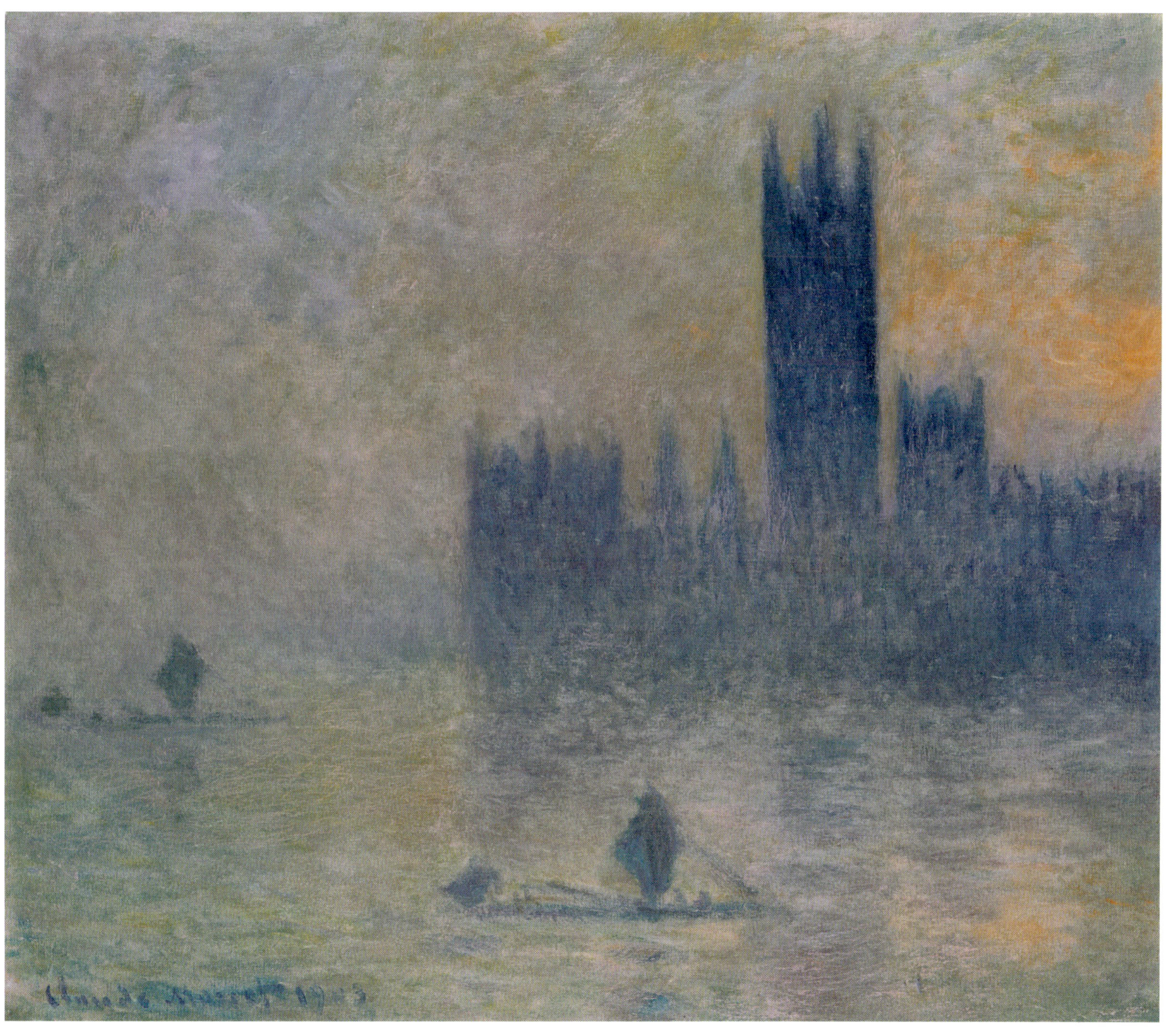

6

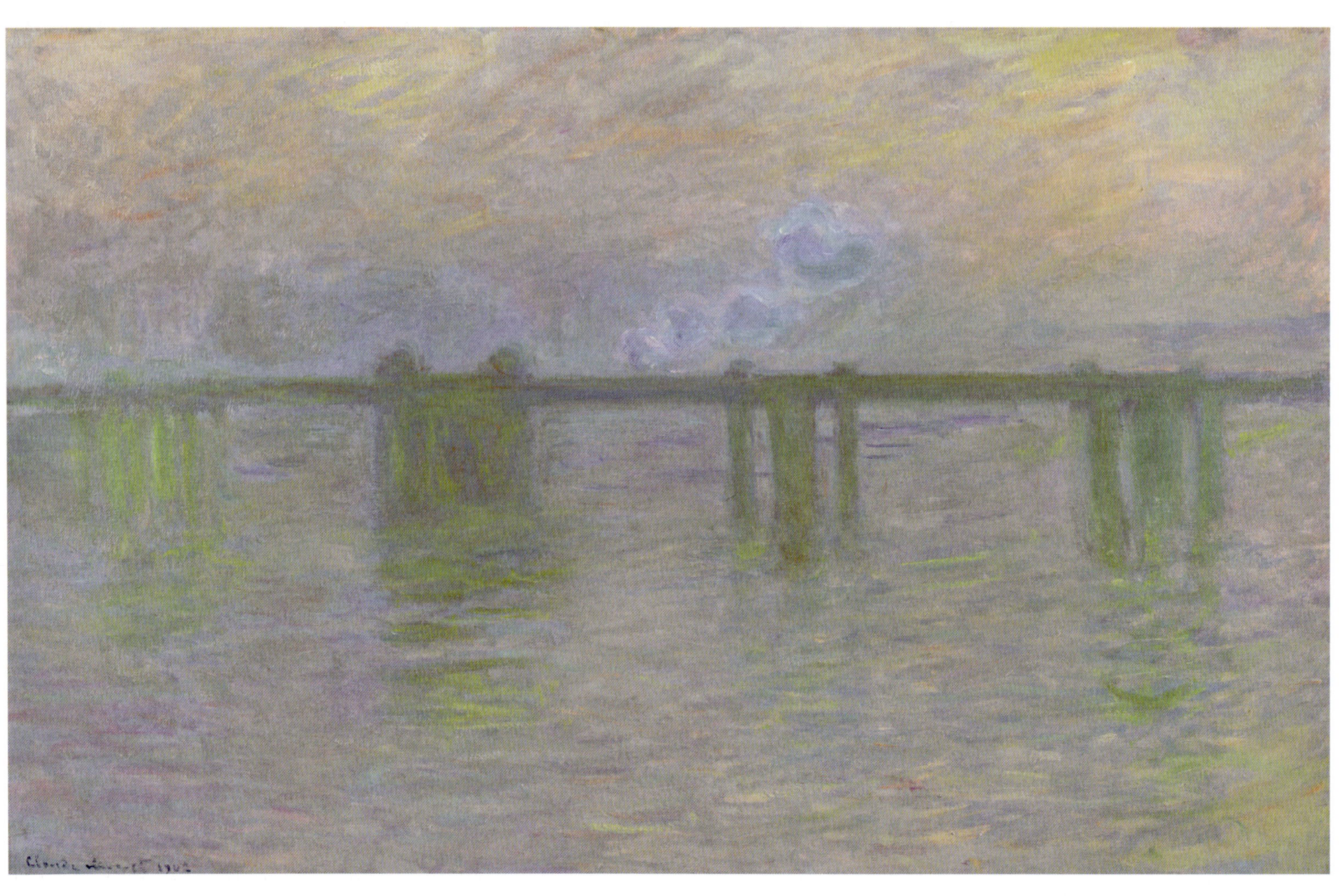

7

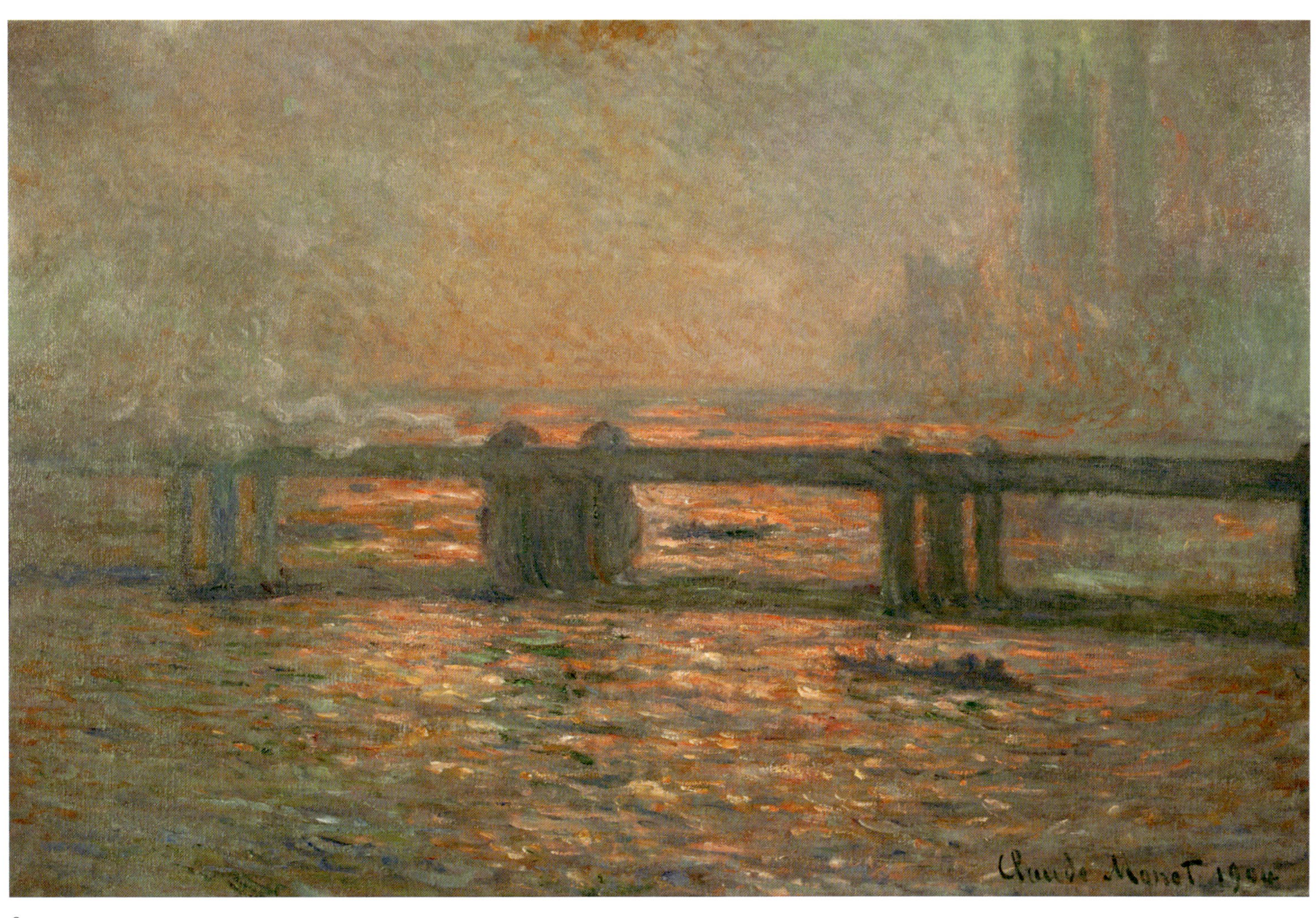

8

André Derain
1880–1954
Charing Cross Bridge, London 1906–7 (1)
Oil paint on canvas 80.3 × 100.3
National Gallery of Art, Washington, John Hay Whitney Collection

Big Ben 1906–7 (2)
Oil paint on canvas 79 × 98

Musée d'Art Moderne de Troyes. Gift of Pierre and Denise Lévy

The Pool of London 1906 (3)
Oil paint on canvas 65.7 × 99.1

Tate. Presented by the Trustees of the Chantrey Bequest 1951

Barges on the Thames 1906–7 (4)
Oil paint on canvas 81 3 × 99

Leeds Museums and Galleries (Leeds Art Gallery)

One of the visitors to Monet's exhibition *Views of the Thames* at Durand-Ruel's gallery in Paris in 1904 (9 May–7 June 1904) was the twenty-three-year-old André Derain, on leave from military service. As soon as he was discharged in September, he threw himself into painting, teaming up with Maurice Vlaminck and Henri Matisse, who, with others, were developing bright, expressive painting influenced by divisionism. In Collioure in southern France that summer, Derain and Matisse intensified their colours, selecting complementaries to achieve maximum power, and abandoned small marks in favour of vivid strokes and patches. When they exhibited their paintings at the Salon d'Automne, they were decried as *les Fauves*, 'the wild beasts', but others found their works exciting.[1] Derain was taken up by the dealer Ambroise Vollard, who, mindful of the continuing celebrity of Monet's Thames series, paid for Derain to go to London and commissioned him to paint fifty cityscapes. 'After a stay in London [he] was very enthusiastic and wanting paintings inspired by the London atmosphere,' Derain recalled. 'He sent me in the hope of a complete renewal of expression that Claude Monet had so strikingly achieved.'[2]

Derain arrived on 6 March 1906. After eleven days he popped back to Paris to help Matisse hang his one-man show at Gallery Druet and attend the opening of the Salon des Indépendants, but otherwise remained until April. Where the Mediterranean provided good weather for plein-air painting most of the year, the famous London fogs had become a destination for the colder months. Unfortunately, Derain was at first met with clear skies and, interestingly, he felt that London 'effects of sunlight' would not satisfy Vollard's needs.[3] He was not able to provide the agreed number of canvases and returned the following year, staying for five weeks between 7 January and 10 February 1907.

Derain lived in a lodging house, knew nobody and spoke little English. Matisse had visited in 1898, on the advice of Camille Pissarro, to study the paintings of J.M.W. Turner, and Derain followed in his footsteps, becoming an enthusiast for the museums and galleries. He was especially taken by the African and Oceanic collections in the British Museum. He sketched, bought art supplies, and walked widely through the city, observing the same sights that had caught the attention of his predecessors, the crowds and the parks (he painted Regent Street and Hyde Park), and of course the bridges and busy boats of the Thames, of which he made twenty-nine recorded pictures.

The Salon des Indépendants, the first time the Fauves all exhibited together, sparked debate. Matisse had turned to 'the dangerous prescriptions of M. Derain. He has abandoned points to end up with colouration in flat colours', Vauxcelles wrote.[4] Many thought the artists had gone too far, but François Crucy declared in the newspaper *L'Aurore* that, compared with Monet's views of the Thames, which had recently been re-exhibited, they had not gone far enough: 'No one else has made such paintings of the atmosphere, the air, a light, multi-coloured veil floating between earth and sky. The Indépendants do not seem to relish such patient research or such long periods of study.'[5]

These words must have been in Derain's mind when he returned to the smoky Thames a few days later. At twenty-five, he was forging his reputation, embarking on his first major commission and challenging the painter who had inspired his 'renewal of expression'. He wrote to Vlaminck:

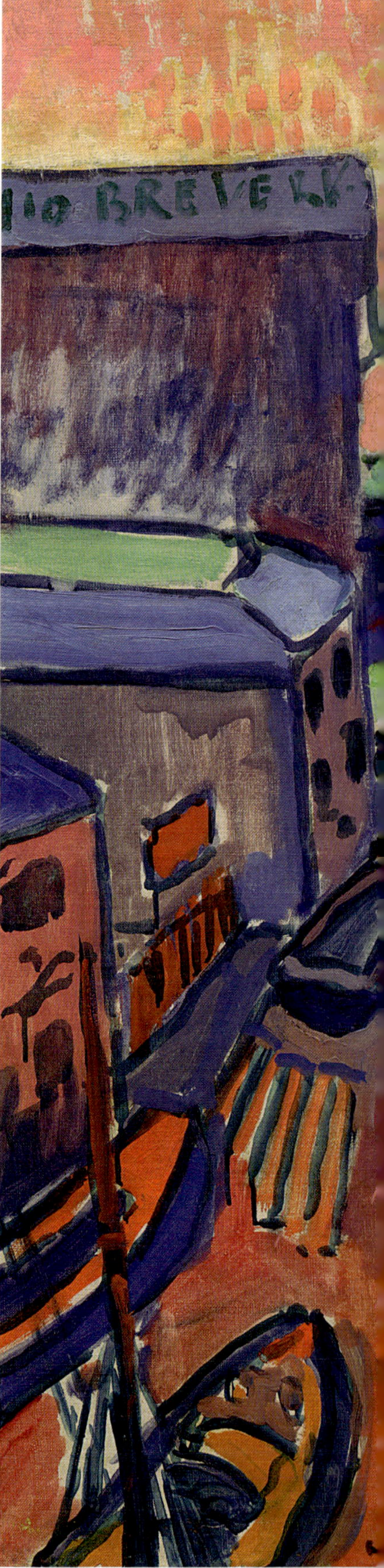

1

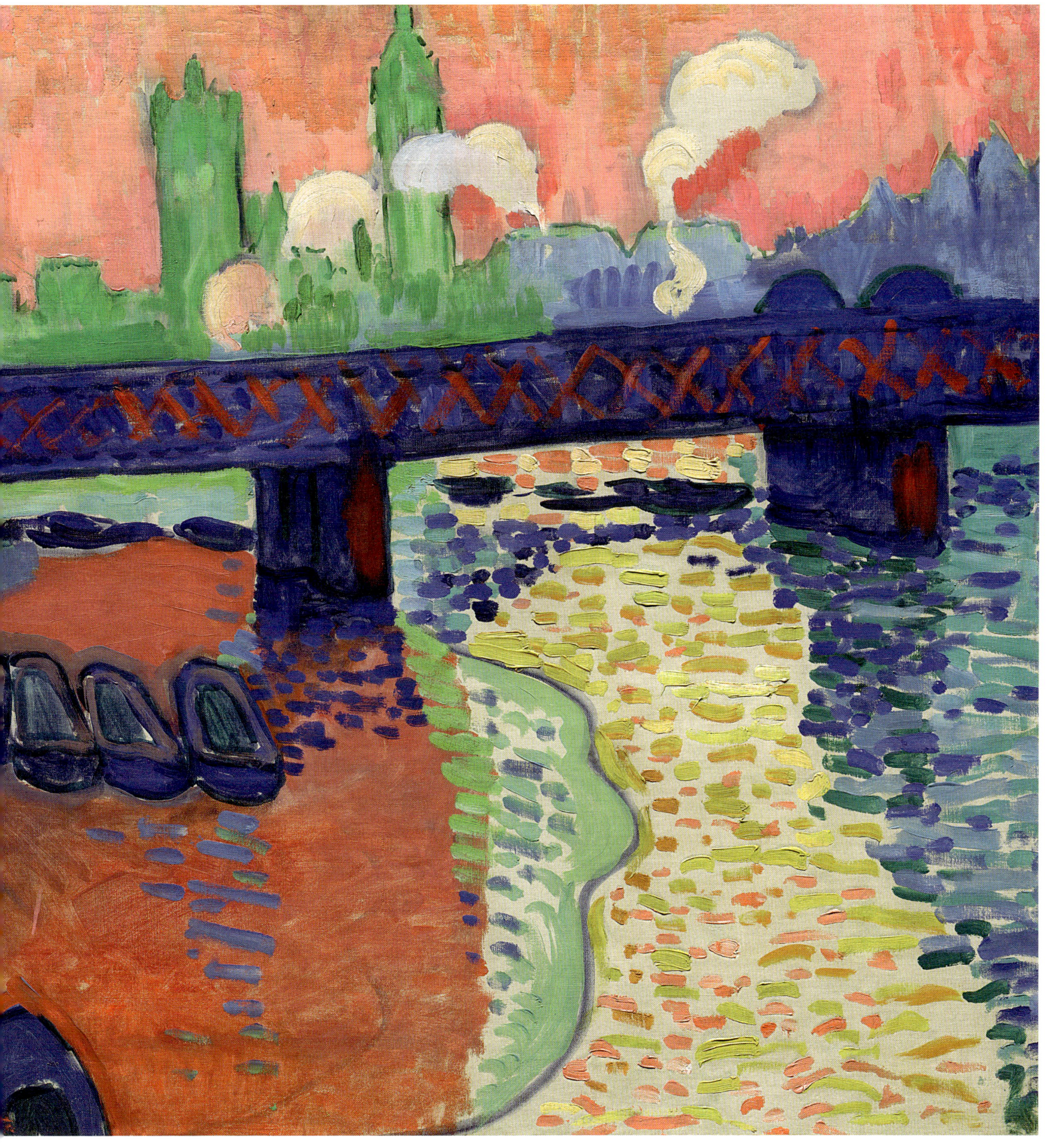

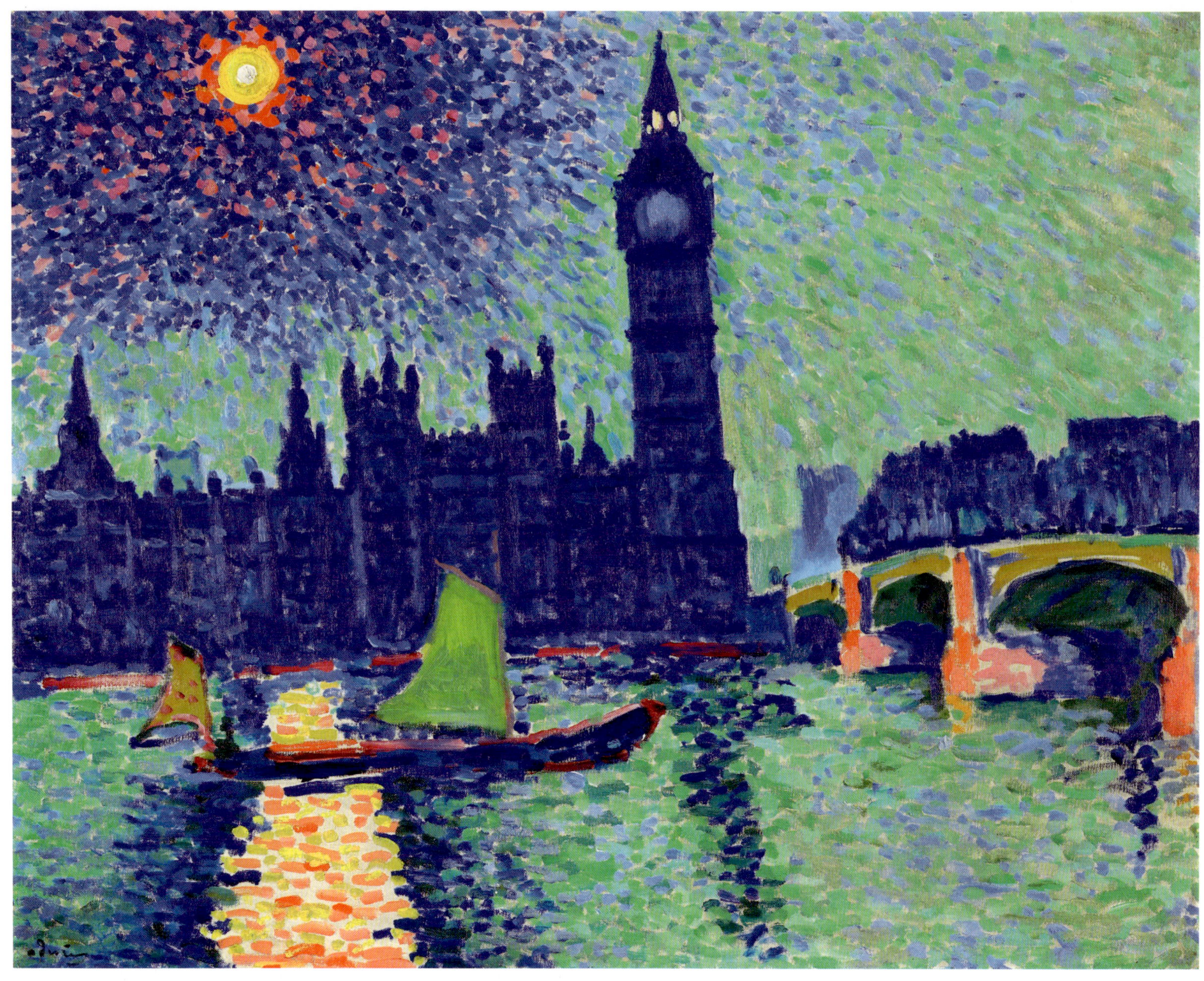

2

In spite of everything, I adore him [Monet]. Wasn't he right to render with his fugitive and durable colour, the natural impression which is no more than an impression, without lasting power, and did he not increase the character of this painting? As for myself, I'm looking for something different, something in nature which, on the contrary, is fixed, eternal, complex.[6]

Accordingly, he departed from Monet's technique and planned his subjects in his sketchbooks, labelling them with preconceived colour schemes. He worked on the canvases in the studio as well as outdoors, even after he returned to Paris.[7] As Remi Labrusse and Jacqueline Munck have noted in the book *André Derain: The London Paintings* (2005), the diversity of cultures he encountered in London drove a new philosophy distinct from Monet, divisionism and even Matisse.[8] His experiments with colour in Collioure, as well as his study of Turner and the, to his eyes, abstract forms of the oceanic artefacts in the British Museum, all convinced him that art should aspire to autonomous expression: 'With the primitives there is a complete difference between the spirit of the thing, elevated by its colour and line, and its seemingly objective position.'[9] In a strange echo of John Ruskin's condemnation of Tissot's Thames paintings as 'mere coloured photographs of vulgar society', Derain wrote to Matisse: 'I have seen some Hindu sculptures and Egypto-Roman embroideries of the greatest beauty that strongly encourage me to make of the Thames something other than coloured photographs.'[10] 'To define reality is to debase painting ... It is also to starve methods that have so much expression of their own.'[11]

Monet's mistakes, Derain said, 'teach me valuable lessons'.[12] He appears to have sketched *The Thames below Westminster* 1871 (pp.66–7) when it was exhibited at Durand-Ruel's gallery while he was in Paris at the end of March 1906.[13] One of his first paintings, *Westminster* 1906 (p.231), was from a nearly identical vantage point to that used in Monet's Westminster views. Derain's sketch of a similar scene divides it up into clear areas, each described by lines in a different direction and colour. The painting retains this clarity. The firm, discrete strokes build the forms systematically: radiating in the sky, vibrating vertically in the Palace of Westminster (evoking their Perpendicular Gothic style decorations) and flowing horizontally in the river. The sense of an 'impression' of light and atmosphere is retained by the divisionist dabs that break up and animate the atmosphere, but the even distribution of patches of pale canvas between the strokes provides a kind of unity across the picture. The colours, too, are distinct, blue and orange complementing each other in the sky, thinning and lightening towards the buildings so their heavy turquoise and blue stand out strongly. The yellow and orange of the target sun is picked up in dabs of yellow and orange paint in the path of light that interrupts the dark water. Red smoke billows out of a blue steam tugboat trailing two flat-bottomed barges.

Big Ben was observed from just a little further down the embankment than *Westminster*. It is more densely painted, suggesting it may have been worked on more in the studio. Only the path of light on the water reveals large areas of the canvas between the pink and yellow strokes, standing out more brightly from its surroundings. This enhanced drama of light and dark is echoed in the matching pinks of the piers of the bridge that blush against the shadows of the arches and buildings behind. Instead of a generally painted tugboat, Derain includes the characteristically shaped yawl, with its two lugsails, seen in Monet's views (pp.237, 239). Unlike Monet's *Houses of Parliament, Fog Effect*, it is a dark shape that stands out strongly against a bright reflection. Derain executed two more views of the Houses of Parliament, from the Albert Embankment, and three more from further away, from beyond Westminster and Charing Cross Bridges.

Derain spent the summer of 1906 in L'Estaque, near Marseilles, and developed more complex compositions comprising swinging contours and rich fields of colour. He was encouraged in his commitment to autonomous colour by Paul Gauguin's retrospective at the Salon d'Automne (6 October to 15 November 1906). *Charing Cross Bridge* reflects these developments. It is a more assured and complex composition than *Westminster* and *Big Ben*, and may have been altered after his first

London visit, or painted the following year. John House suggests that its viewpoint refers back to Camille Pissarro's *Charing Cross Bridge, London* 1890 (pp.222–3).[14] The picture is divided by the wrought iron Hungerford Bridge, with its blocky, brick buttresses, and the huddle of rectangular buildings on the bank, the largest being the Lion Brewery. Its cool, dark tones enhance the rosy glow above and below, picked up in the red strokes that notate the metal lattice-work of the bridge. The dark structure also introduces a rhythm of three across the canvas, signalling the rhythmic elements throughout the picture, the five lighters and the five steps. Four graceful plumes of smoke from steam trains passing across the bridge loosely echo the two smaller and two taller towers of the Palace of Westminster. The towers of Westminster Abbey, visible in Derain's initial sketches, are replaced by the more delicate blue silhouette of Whitehall. This is mirrored below in elongated form by the blue reflection, just as the area of green in the centre relates to the green palace above.

Unlike Monet, Derain rarely returned to the same viewpoint, preferring to address new problems of composition at the same time as new problems of light. He painted all along the river as far as east Greenwich, including six views of Tower Bridge erected only twelve years before, all from different perspectives. The bridge was one of London's most popular tourist attractions, but Derain reduced the landmark to its distinctive profile in the distance as a foil for the boats and commerce in the foreground. *Barges on the Thames* takes this the furthest. Tower Bridge is cropped top and bottom by London Bridge and Cannon Street Bridge and the entire scene takes on the geometrical quality of its industrial components. Like *Charing Cross Bridge*, the middle ground is bisected by the hefty shape of Cannon Street rail bridge (also designed by John Hawkshaw). A green train puffs off towards the left-hand side. However, everything in the composition is on opposing slants. The foreground is dominated by three angled barges, two lighters and a spritsail sailing barge. The latter's rigging, furled sails and masts slice up the forms of the bridges and the river. This, combined with the crane to the right, its hook strangely dropping just below the top edge, and the poles and cables along the bridge, further dissect and animate the scene. The broken brush strokes and delicate rose and turquoise of the river and sky are reminiscent of earlier views of the river such as *Charing Cross Bridge*, but they are dominated now by the strong, dark contours and areas of solid colour.

The Pool of London offers the most angled perspective with a large boat surging diagonally across the canvas. The Upper Pool was itself a tourist attraction, famous for its large steam-powered freighters that came in from all corners of the empire, and the radical cut-off view of the boat, dwarfing the little barges around it, communicates its impressive size. Sketches made of the scene focus on this diagonal, the strong vertical created by the smokestack meeting the upright of Tower Bridge behind and the gaping opening of the hold. The river is even more broken up by the boat's rigging and the barges and steamers angled this way and that. The effect is amplified by the slabs of bright colour, adding to the energy of the scene. The high key of *The Pool of London* reflects the brighter April days when it was painted, just before Derain concluded his first London stay. It was worked on further in France, and may also reflect the bright pictures Derain painted in the summer at L'Estaque. In both *Barges on the Thames* and *The Pool of London* the masts play a similar role to the trees in the paintings Derain made there, animating the horizontal landscape format with bold contours as well as colour.

Whistler, Monet, Pissarro and de Nittis had painted London through smoke and fog. Derain retraced their steps in the darkest seasons to experience the same effect, but he rendered his impression of the city with a new force, constructed in bold line and contrasts of colour. As the series progressed, the works became increasingly precise in their observation of the architecture and traffic, and original in the compositional means by which they caught the spirit of place. As John House has noted: 'Observed and immediately recognisable sights [are] treated in radically anti-natural ways, in combinations of coloured zones and marks that resolutely resist being viewed as records of momentary sensory experience.'[15] Derain returned to France an anglophile (a hallmark of the French avant-garde artist, alternative to the mainstream) and was admired for his 'English chic', as Fernande Olivier described his style.[16] Vollard bought all of Derain's London paintings, but did not exhibit them as a group, so the 'renewal of expression' was never seen, judged, or compared as a series. Vollard kept most of the London works until the end of his life.[17] CJ

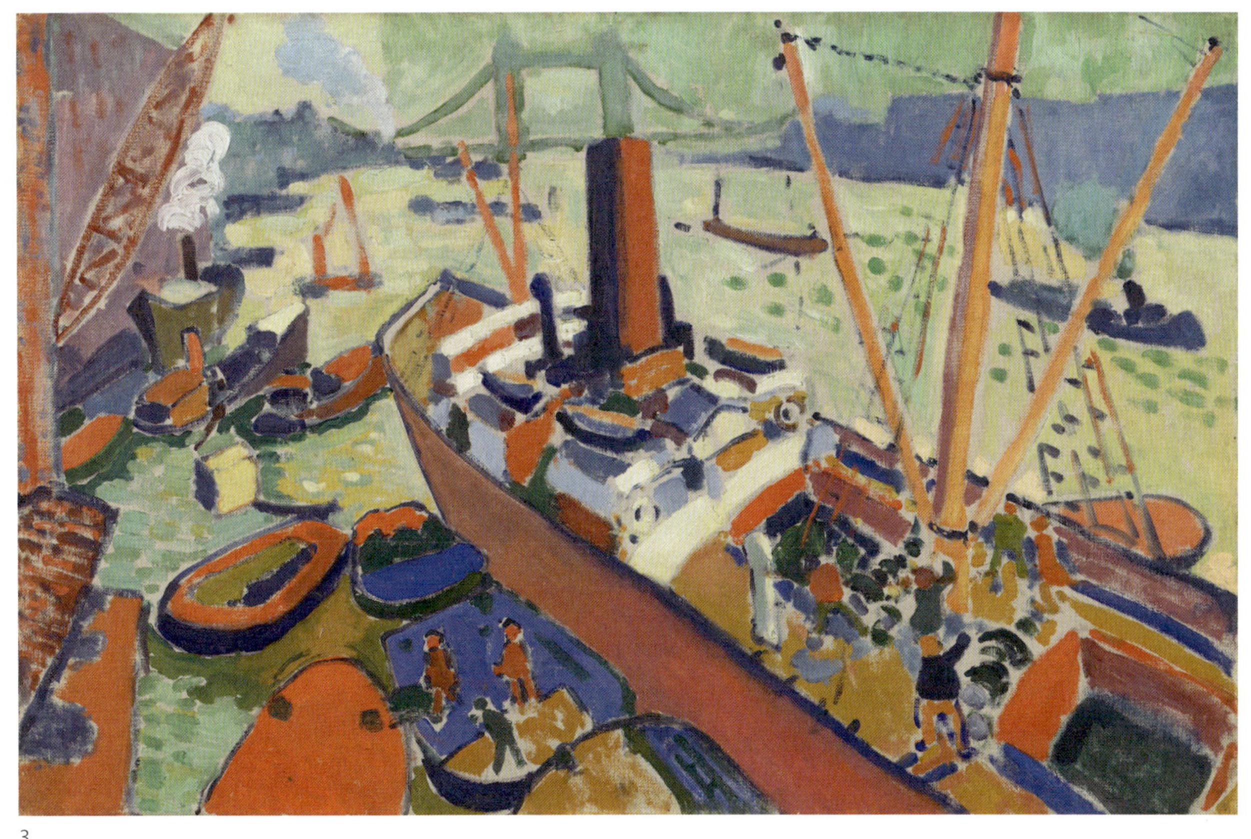

3

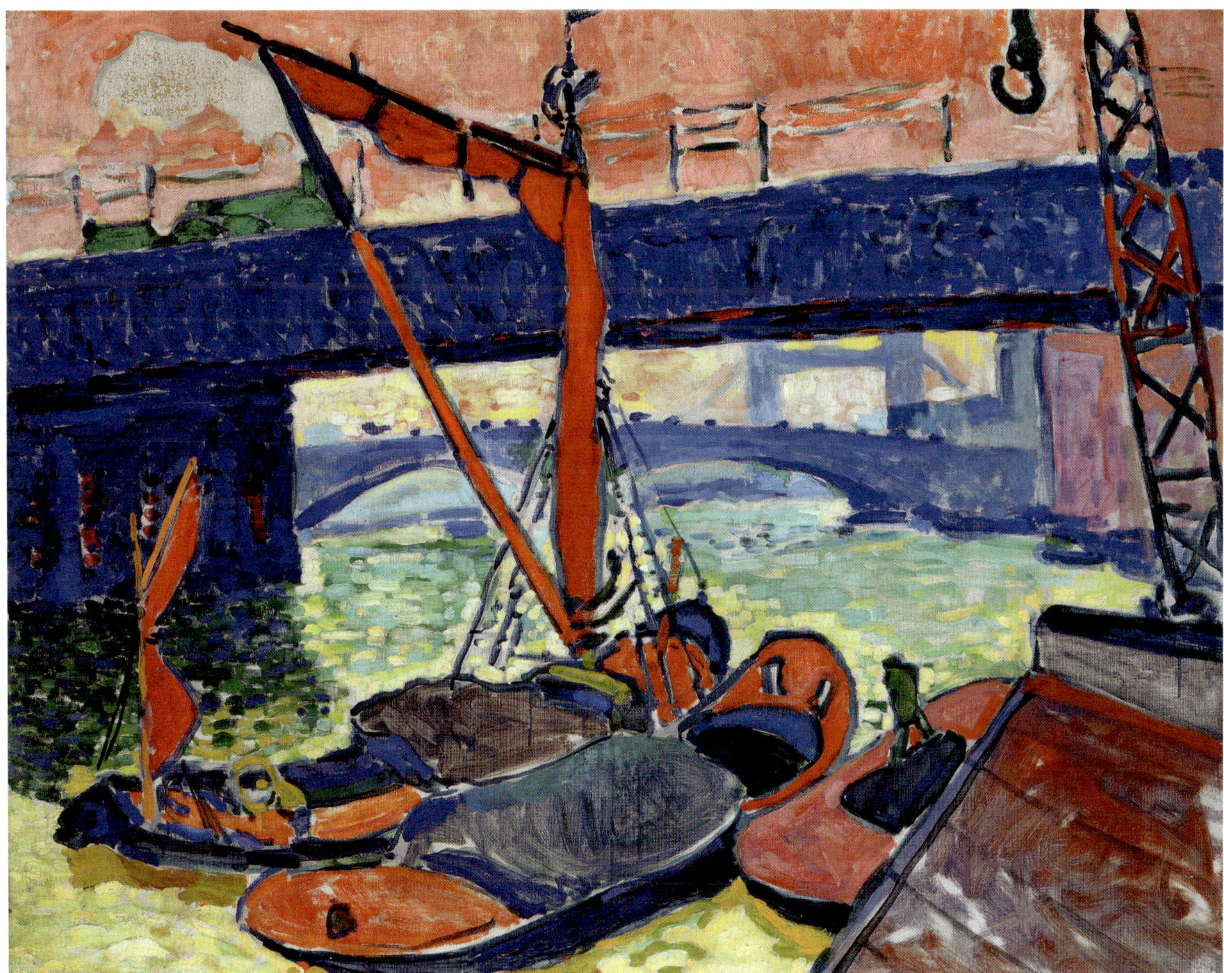

4

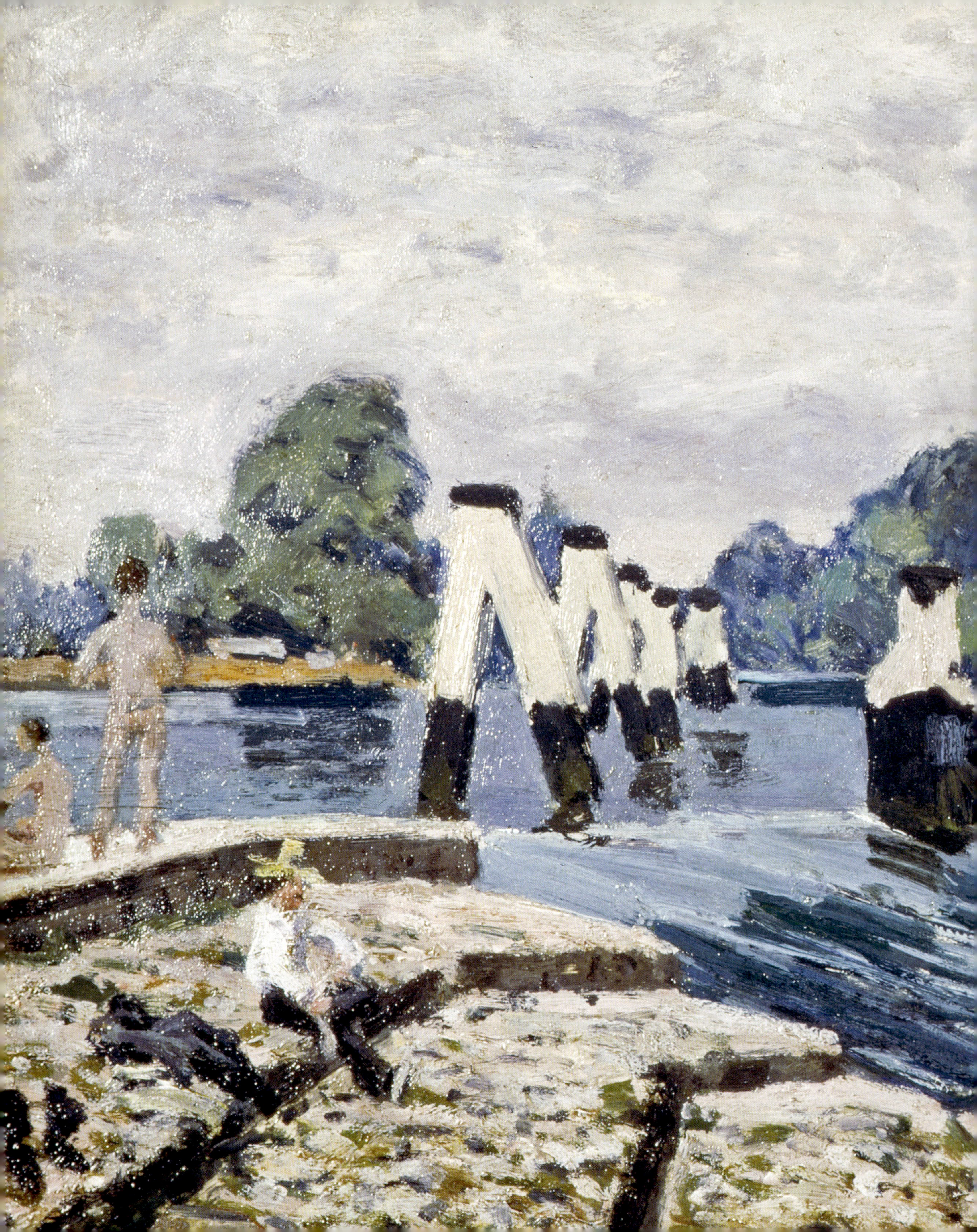

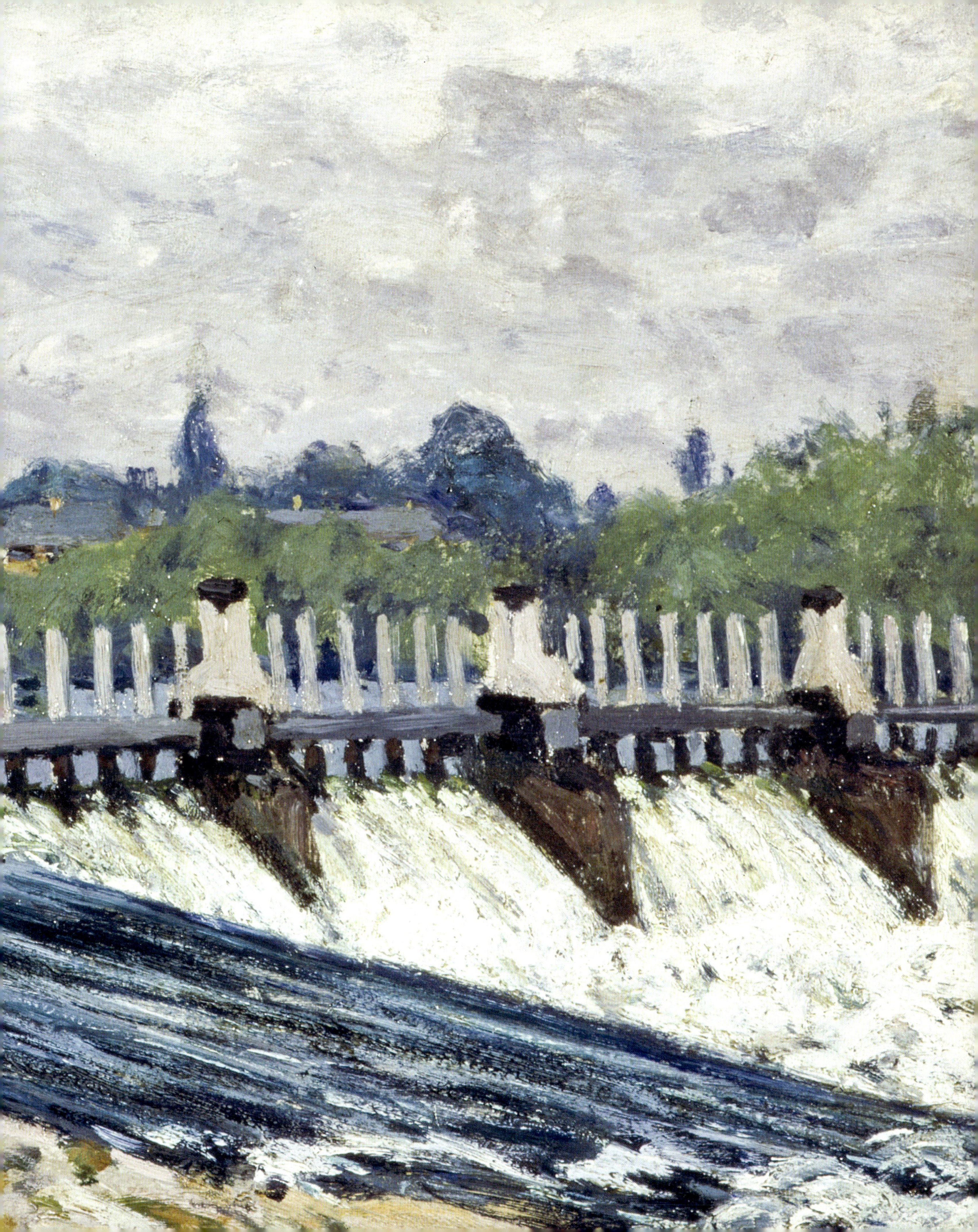

Chronology

Elizabeth Jacklin

1817
15 February: Charles-François Daubigny is born in Paris.

1827
11 May: Jean-Baptiste Carpeaux is born in Valenciennes.

1830
10 July: Camille Pissarro is born in St Thomas in the Danish West Indies (now the US Virgin Islands).

1836
15 October: James Tissot is born in Nantes.

1837
8 May: Alphonse Legros is born in Dijon.

1838
31 December: Jules Dalou is born in Paris.

1838
30 October: Alfred Sisley is born in Paris.

1840
14 November: Claude Monet is born in Paris.

1846
25: Giuseppe de Nittis is born in Barletta, Italy.

1848
1 November: Edouard Lantéri is born in Auxerre.

Early 1850s
Legros studies under Horace Lecoq de Boisbaudran at the 'Petite Ecole' in Paris alongside Henri Fantin-Latour, Guillaume Régamey and Auguste Rodin.

1856–9
James McNeill Whistler enters the Paris studio of Charles Gleyre; fellow students include George du Maurier and Edward Poynter.

1858
Autumn: Whistler, Fantin-Latour and Legros form the Société des Trois in Paris.

1862
Legros is a catalyst in the creation of the Société des Aquafortistes (Society of Etchers) in Paris.

1862–4
Monet enters the Paris studio of Charles Gleyre, where he studies sporadically; fellow students include Pierre-Auguste Renoir, Alfred Sisley and Frédéric Bazille.

1863
Encouraged by Whistler, Legros arrives in London. He finds great supporters in the artists George Frederic Watts and, above all, Dante Gabriel Rossetti.

1865
Daubigny makes his first visit to London with the printer and dealer Alfred Cadart.

16 November: Edward Burne-Jones introduces Legros to George Howard.

1866
Summer: war between Austria and Prussia. In the aftermath Prussia annexes numerous territories to form the North German Confederation; France becomes increasingly concerned.

Daubigny is invited to London by Frederic Leighton and other British artists. He exhibits at the Royal Academy.

1869
Tissot's first caricatures for the British society publication *Vanity Fair* include a depiction of Napoleon III.

1870
12 July: when the Spanish throne is offered to the House of Hohenzollern-Sigmaringen, a branch of the ruling House of Prussia, it is rejected following French protest. But King William I of Prussia refuses to give France further assurances.

14 July: Otto von Bismarck edits the 'Ems Dispatch', a report of William I's encounter with the French ambassador, to insinuate that each man had insulted the other and further antagonise the French government.

19 July: France, under the false impression that its army is superior, declares war on Prussia.

2 September: Napoleon III surrenders at Sedan and is subsequently imprisoned at Wilhelmshöhe.

4 September: fall of the Second Empire and proclamation of the Third Republic, with a government of national defence.

8 September: the French art dealer Paul Durand-Ruel departs for London, where he has already sent his stock and that of some of his clients, including the famous opera baritone Jean-Baptiste Faure. Durand-Ruel is joined by his wife Eva and four of his children.

19 September: the Siege of Paris begins. Tissot and Manet are among the artists who stay in Paris as members of the National Guard.

Mid–late September or early October: Monet flees to London to avoid military conscription. He is joined by his wife Camille and their three-year-old son Jean.

Autumn: Sisley's home in Bougival is destroyed by occupying Prussian forces, along with most of his work.

Early October: Daubigny flees to London with his family.

November: François Bonvin arrives in London.

25 November: Monet and Legros visit Dulwich Picture Gallery, along with Julien de La Rochenoire.

28 November: Frédéric Bazille, friend and contemporary of Monet, Sisley and Manet, is killed in action in France.

Early December: Camille Pissarro arrives in London with his partner Julie Vellay and their two children; after a brief spell in Lower Norwood they settle in Upper Norwood. Their house in Louveciennes has been invaded by the Prussian army. Most of his output to date was destroyed, as well as some of Monet's works left in Pissarro's studio for safekeeping.

10 December: Durand-Ruel opens his First Exhibition of the Society of French Artists at the German Gallery at 168 New Bond Street.

17 December: an exhibition opens in Pall Mall to raise awareness of, and funds for, the desolation caused by the Franco-Prussian War. Daubigny, Monet, Frederic Leighton and Lawrence Alma-Tadema contribute work.

1871
19 January: the celebrated young artist Henri Regnault is killed in action at Buzenval, outside Paris.

21 January: Durand-Ruel puts Pissarro in touch with Monet. They go on to visit galleries together, admiring works by Turner and Constable, and both dine at the home of Legros.

28 January: the French government of national defence agrees to an armistice for four weeks. Negotiations lead to the humiliating Treaty of Frankfurt.

February: Manet leaves Paris to join his family in south-west France; he returns to the city in June.

March: Carpeaux arrives in London with his wife Amélie and young son.

18 March: Proclamation of the Paris Commune, an uprising against the French government and its acquiescence to Prussia.

1 May: the London International Exhibition opens, but the French section, because of the war, does not open officially until 19 June. Daubigny, Monet and Pissarro exhibit work.

May: Monet leaves London for the Netherlands, returning to France in the autumn.

21 May: government forces enter Paris, commencing the Bloody Week.

28 May: government forces repress the Commune and the Bloody Week ends. Mass killings and imprisonments continue.

29 May: Tissot witnesses the execution of Communards at Porte Dauphine in Paris.

End of May: Daubigny leaves London.

June: Tissot arrives in London. He soon builds on earlier forays into exhibiting in the capital, showing at the Royal Academy and the London International Exhibition the following year.

Durand-Ruel records the first works bought from Monet and Pissarro.

14 June: Pissarro and Julie are married at Croydon Register Office. Shortly afterwards they return to France.

July: Dalou flees to England, having identified himself publicly with the Paris Commune. Together with his wife Irma and young daughter Georgette, he stays at first with Legros.

30 September: Durand-Ruel returns to Paris and sends paintings to London.

Autumn: Bonvin returns to France.

1872
Carpeaux returns to France. He visits London sporadically over the next two years, exhibiting regularly at the Royal Academy.

October: encouraged by Dalou, Lantéri arrives in London. He is immediately employed by the émigré sculptor Joseph Edgar Boehm, who had himself moved to England in 1862.

1873
9 January: death of Napoleon III.

April: Marshal MacMahon becomes President of France, beginning a 'moral order' regime.

1874
March: Carpeaux's last visit to England.

14 April: Giuseppe de Nittis leaves Paris for the first of his yearly trips to London, where he meets Kaye Knowles, a patron also of Tissot.

April–May: the *First Impressionist Exhibition* (then referred to as the first exhibition of the Société anonyme) takes place in Paris; exhibitors include the group that would become the core Impressionists – Cézanne, Degas, Monet, Morisot, Pissarro, Renoir and Sisley – as well as de Nittis, Félix Bracquemond and others.

June: Monet sells work to Jean-Baptiste Faure.

July: Sisley's second visit to London, this time in the company of Faure, who has commissioned six paintings. He stays until October.

1875
Durand-Ruel's London gallery closes.

Legros is appointed Professor of Etching at the National Art Training School in South Kensington.

1876
Legros replaces Edward Poynter as professor at the Slade School of Fine Art.

March–April: The *Second Impressionist Exhibition* takes place in Paris at Durand-Ruel's gallery; this time Legros is among the exhibitors.

1877
11 May: Dalou begins teaching modelling at the National Art Training School. In the same year he receives a commission from Queen Victoria.

1878
January: Jules Grévy becomes President of France following elections.

19 February: Daubigny dies in Paris.

1879
In France a bill gives amnesty to Communards, but is restricted to those not convicted of criminal acts.

20 May: Dalou receives official confirmation that he has been pardoned for his role in the Commune; he visits Paris.

1880
Legros becomes a British citizen.

April: Dalou returns to France. Lantéri succeeds him as Master of Modelling at the National Art Training School.

10 June: André Derain is born in Chatou, near Paris.

11 July: the French government grants a total amnesty for Communards.

31 July: first meeting of the Society of Painter-Etchers, presided over by Francis Seymour Haden. Tissot and Legros become committee members.

9 December: Monet writes that he wishes he could visit London to seek sales and to paint the Thames.

1882
November: following the death of his companion Kathleen Newton, Tissot returns to Paris. Lawrence Alma-Tadema purchases his London house.

1885
Founding of the New English Art Club, which embraces the influence of French art. Their first exhibition takes place the following year, in May.

1887
May: Monet returns to London for his first visit since 1871; Whistler urges him to exhibit with the Society of British Artists, and he contributes four works to the group's November exhibition.

1890
May: Pissarro arrives to spend a few weeks in London, painting views of the capital for the first time since 1871.

1891
Lantéri becomes a British citizen.

1892
June: Pissarro, in London for the summer, begins painting Kew Gardens, a subject that dominates the paintings made during this stay.

1893
Legros retires from the Slade.

1897
May: Pissarro arrives in the London suburb of Bedford Park, where his son Lucien is ill. He returns to Paris in July.

July: Sisley returns for a second painting campaign in Britain, staying initially in London and Cornwall before spending time on the Welsh coast. On 5 August he marries Eugénie Lescouezec at Cardiff Town Hall.

1898
April: Whistler organises an exhibition of the International Society in South Kensington. It includes works by Monet, Sisley and Renoir.

1899
29 January: Sisley dies in Moret-sur-Loing.

September–October: Monet stays at the Savoy Hotel in London, painting Charing Cross Bridge and Waterloo Bridge as viewed from his window.

1900
February: during a two-month spell in London, Monet begins a series of paintings of the Houses of Parliament. His vantage point is a terrace in St Thomas's Hospital. He continues his paintings of the bridges of Charing Cross and Waterloo.

1901
January–April: Back in London, Monet continues work on his Thames canvases, also making sketches of Leicester Square at night.

22 January: death of Queen Victoria. Monet watches the state funeral in February.

1901–4
Monet continues work on his Thames pictures from his studio in Giverny.

1902
15 April: Dalou dies in Paris.

8 August: Tissot dies in Doubs.

1903
17 July: Whistler dies in London.

13 November: Pissarro dies in Paris.

1904
8 April: the Entente Cordiale, a series of agreements between Britain and France, is signed, improving Anglo-French relations in the decade before the First World War.

9 May–4 June: thirty-seven of Monet's London pictures are exhibited at Durand-Ruel's gallery in Paris. It is the most successful exhibition of Monet's career to date and is extended to 7 June. Derain is among the visitors.

7–9 December: With plans to exhibit his London paintings in the city that inspired them, Monet makes his final trip to London. The exhibition does not materialise.

1905
January–February: Durand-Ruel holds a large impressionist exhibition at the Grafton Galleries, London.

November: Ambroise Vollard becomes Derain's dealer.

1906
March–April: Derain makes two visits to London to work on Vollard's commission for fifty cityscapes modelled on the London paintings Monet had exhibited in 1904.

1907
January–February: Derain's third visit to London. By July his London series numbers thirty canvases; he probably completes (or entirely paints) them in France, using his London sketchbooks. The paintings are never exhibited as a group.

Notes

Crossing the Channel (pp.13–19)

1 Letter from Claude Monet to Eugène Boudin, Le Havre, 9 Sept. 1870, Wildenstein I (1974), letter w.55 (p.427).
2 See Thomas C. Jones and Robert Tombs, 'The French left in exile: Quarante-huitards and Communards in London, 1848–80', in Debra Kelly and Martyn Cornick (eds.) *A History of the French in London: Liberty, Equality, Opportunity*, London 2013, pp.165–91, esp. p.169.
3 Etienne Moreau-Nélaton, *Bonvin raconté par lui-même*, Paris 1927, p.75 (entry for 4 Jan. 1871).
4 'Le Communards peints par eux-mêmes', *Le Figaro*, 17 Aug. 1873, p.1.
5 Jones and Tombs 2014, p.171.
6 Jones and Tombs 2014, p.170.
7 It comprised a succession of monographic rooms and was not specifically concerned with the traumatic circumstances that brought these artists together to Britain. More recently, the excellent *Pissarro in London* at the National Gallery in 2003, *Sisley in England and Wales* in 2008 at the same institution, and *Dalou in England: Portraits of Womanhood, 1871–1879* in 2009 at the Yale Centre for British Art also looked at this period through a monographic approach. *Inventing Impressionism* (National Gallery, 2015) examined the relationship of the impressionists and the art dealer Paul Durand-Ruel, whose network in 1870–1 represented a small part of the exhibition's argument.
8 The following year he made an additional group representing the 4-year-old Princess Marie of Hesse, Princess Alice's daughter, who died in 1878.
9 *Times*, 1 May 1871.
10 Katharine Lochnan, 'Whistler and Monet: Impressionism and Britain', in Lee Glazer et al. (eds.), *James McNeill Whistler in Context: Essays from the Whistler Centenary Symposium, University of Glasgow, 2003*, Washington, DC 2008, p.49.
11 Pissarro, Tissot and Lantéri, in due course, spoke excellent English, but Monet, Bonvin and Carpeaux struggled to make themselves understood. Legros, an extreme case, lived in England for almost forty years and never learnt how to speak English properly.
12 *L'Illustration*, vol.58, no.1488, 2 Sept. 1871, p.147. My thanks to Philip Ward-Jackson for bringing this quote to my attention.
13 He first arrived in London in August for a short spell, returned to Paris and fled to London again in September. See Edward Morris, *French Art in Nineteenth-Century Britain*, New Haven and London 2005, p.154.
14 *Diary of W. -M. Rossetti*, ed. O. Bornand, Oxford 1977, p.64.
15 Tate Archive, TGA 995/2/2/4, entries for 1 and 12 Feb. 1874. The diary casually mentions 'Mr Régamey stayed to dinner' in both instances, and as Guillaume and Frédéric lived in France, one can speculate that it was Félix.
16 One is at the Kunsthaus, Zurich, and the other, a smaller version, at the Musée d'Orsay, both dated c.1881.
17 Tate Archive, TGA 995/2/2/4, 24 Sept. 1874 entry. Jourde also had breakfast and dinner with Legros on 4 Oct.1874.
18 Moreau-Nélaton 1927, p.75.
19 See Anna Gruetzner Robins's essay here. Just after his departure from London, Monet asked Legros to either buy two frames Monet had used for the 1871 International exhibition, or suggest who might in his view be interested in purchasing them (letter from Monet to Pissarro, 2 June 1871, Daniel Wildenstein, *Claude Monet: Biographie et catalogue raisonné*, vol.3, Lausanne and Paris 1974, vol.3, no.58).
20 See Anne Robbins, 'Durand-Ruel's Conquest of London', in Sylvie Patry (ed.), *Inventing Impressionism: Paul Durand-Ruel and the Modern Art Market*, exh. cat., National Gallery, London 2015, pp.172–3.
21 'Mémoires de Paul Durand-Ruel', in L. Venturi, *Les Archives de l'impressionnisme. Lettres de Renoir, Monet, Pissarro, Sisley et autres. Mémoires de Paul Durand-Ruel. Documents*, 2 vols., Paris and New York 1939, vol.2, pp.143–220, esp. p.175.
22 Venturi 1939, p.176.
23 *Art Journal*, 1870, p.364.
24 M. Elder, *Chez Claude Monet à Giverny*, Paris 1924, p.24.
25 Moreau-Nélaton 1927, p.80.
26 Etienne Moreau-Nélaton, *Daubigny raconté par lui-même*, Paris 1925, p.104.
27 Letter from Pissarro to Wynford Dewhurst, 6 Nov. 1902, in Wynford Dewhurst, 'Impressionist painting: Its genesis and development, Second article', *The Studio*, no.29, 1903, p.94.
28 On further retractions and the question of the actual influence of these masters on Pissarro and Monet, see John House, 'Tinted Steam: Turner and Impressionism', in Katharine Lochnan (ed.), *Turner Whistler Monet*, exh. cat., Art Gallery of Ontario, Toronto, 2004, pp.109–140.
29 *The Studio*, no.29, 1903, p.94.
30 Janine Bailly-Herzberg (ed.), *Correspondance de Camille Pissarro*, vol.1, Paris 1980, p.64.
31 Moreau-Nélaton 1925, p.104.
32 Letters from Dalou to Cornaglia, 9 April and 5 May 1879, Musée d'Orsay, RF 2465. My thanks to Amélie Simier for the reference.
33 Marion H. Spielmann, *British Sculpture and Sculptors of Today*, London, Paris, New York and Melbourne 1901, p.1.
34 See Morris 2005, pp.35–6, and Timothy Wilcox, *Alphonse Legros, 1837–1911*, exh. cat., Musée des Beaux Arts, Dijon, pp.101–3.
35 See Wilcox 1987–8, p.102.
36 Isabel G. McAllister, 'Edward Lantéri: Sculptor and Professor', *The Studio*, vol.57, 1912–1913, pp.25–31, esp. p.28.
37 P. Jacomb-Hood, *With Brush and Pencil*, London 1925, p.11.

Painters Tested by the Terrible Year, 1870–1 (pp.23–7)

1 Cited by John Rewald, *Histoire de l'impressionnisme*, Paris 1986, p.171.
2 Alfred Sensier and Paul Mantz, *La vie et l'oeuvre de Jean-François Millet*, Paris 1881, p.111.
3 Jean-François Lecaillon, *Les peintres français et la guerre de 1870 (1870–1914)*, ed. Bernard Giovanangeli, Paris 2016.
4 Cf. Gonzalo J. Sánchez, *Organizing Independence: The Artists Federation of the Paris Commune and its Legacy, 1871–1889*, Lincoln, NE 1997.
5 Petra ten-Doesschate Chu (ed.), *Correspondance de Courbet*, Paris 1996.
6 *Journal officiel de la Commune* (15 April 1871), republished in 3 vols., Coeuvres-et-Valsery 1997, vol.2, p.273.
7 See Millet's reaction addressed to the director of the journal *La France*, which reproduced it on 25 April 1871.
8 This letter is reproduced by Alfred Darcel, in 'Les Musées, les arts et les artistes pendant la Commune', *Gazette des Beaux-Arts*, vol.5, 1872, p.51.
9 Bertrand Tillier, *La Commune de Paris, révolution sans images? Politique et représentations dans la France républicaine (1871–1914)*, Epoques series, Seyssel 2004, p.122.
10 Jules Castagnary, *Gustave Courbet et la colonne Vendôme*, ed. Bertrand Tillier, Tusson 2000.
11 He described the Commune as 'ignoble ridiculous folly, where vanity and chauvinism fooled the most capable': letter from Fantin-Latour to Otto Scholderer, 15 June 1871, cited in *Correspondance entre Henri Fantin-Latour et Otto Scholderer, 1858–1902*, ed. Mathilde Arnoux, Passages/Passagen series, Paris 2011.
12 Reported by Forain, cited in Henri Loyrette, *Degas*, Paris 1991, p.260.
13 Tillier 2004, p.213 et seq.
14 Letter from Auguste De Gas to Thérèse Morbilli (3 June 1871), cited in Loyrette 1991, pp.264–5.
15 Letter of 5 June 1871, cited in Eric Darragon, *Manet*, Pluriel series, Paris 1991, p.198.
16 Letter from Manet to Théodore Duret, Aug. 1871, in Darragon 1991, p.199.
17 Letter from Gustave Flaubert to his niece Caroline (Croisset, 22 Aug. 1872): http://flaubert.univ-rouen.fr/correspondance/conard/lettres/72c.html.
18 Edouard-Désiré Fromentin, 'Jean-Baptiste Carpeaux', *Valentiana, Revue d'histoire des pays du Hainaut français*, no.19, June 1997, p.167.
19 Laurence des Cars, 'Carpeaux témoin de son temps : "des œuvres de voyant"', in *Carpeaux peintre*, exh. cat., Musée du Luxembourg, Paris 1998, p.124.
20 François Robichon, *Alphonse de Neuville, 1835–1885*, Paris 2010.
21 François Robichon, *Edouard Detaille, Un siècle de gloire militaire*, Paris 2007.
22 See *Alphonse de Neuville, La bataille de l'image*, exh. cat., Musée de l'hôtel Sandelin, Saint-Omer 2014.
23 François Robichon, *La peinture militaire française de 1871 à 1914*, Paris 1998, pp.46–50.
24 Gustave Goetschy, *Les Jeunes peintres militaires*, Paris 1878, p.87.
25 Edmond and Jules de Goncourt, *Journal, Mémoires de la vie littéraire*, 3 vols., ed. Robert Ricatte, Bouquins series, Paris 1989, vol.2, p.451 (entry for 28 May 1871).
26 In Joris-Karl Huysmans, 'Fantaisie sur le Musée des arts décoratifs et sur l'architecture cuite', *Revue indépendante*, Nov. 1886, reprinted in *L'art moderne, Certains*, Paris 1975, p.399.
27 Théophile Gautier, *Tableaux de siège: Paris, 1870–1871*, Paris 1871, reprinted in *Paris et les Parisiens*, ed. Claudine Lacoste-Veysseyre, Paris 1996, p.622.
28 Daryl Lee, 'Uncanny City: Paris in Ruins', PhD thesis, Yale University, New Haven, CT 1999, pp.298–300. See also *La Commune photographiée*, exh. cat., Musée d'Orsay, Paris 2000, in which the main photographs are inventoried, pp.120–5.
29 Alfred Robaut and Etienne Moreau-Nélaton, *L'Oeuvre de Corot par Alfred Robaut, Catalogue raisonné et illustré*, 5 vols., Paris 1965, vol.1, p.249.
30 Robaut and Moreau-Nélaton 1965, vol.3, no.2352.

28 *The Dream: Paris Burning*

1 Alfred Robaut and Etienne Moreau-Nélaton, *L'Oeuvre de Corot, Catalogue raisonné et illustré*, 4 vols., Paris 1905, vol.1, p.360.
2 Bertrand Tillier, *La Commune de Paris, révolution sans images? Politique et représentations dans la France républicaine (1871–1914)*, Seyssel 2004, p.267.
3 Tillier 2004, p.267.

33 *Sketchbook on the Siege of Paris*

1 Inv.35722, recto.

34 *The Green Room of the Théâtre Français/The Wounded Soldier/ Grand'garde/La Cantinière/The Defence of Paris; Narrated as it Was Seen*

1 *New York Times*, 29 Jan. 1871, p.3.
2 Krystyna Matyjaszkiewicz (ed.), *James Tissot*, London 1984, p.105.
3 Nancy Rose Marshall and Malcolm Warner, *Victorian Life/Modern Love*, New Haven 1999, p.49.
4 Thomas Gibson Bowles, *The Defence of Paris; Narrated as it Was Seen*, London 1871, p.26.
5 Thomas Cardoza, *Intrepid Women: Cantinières and Vivandières of the French Army*, Bloomington, IN 2010, p.172.
6 Bowles 1871, p.32.

38 *The Exectution of Communards*

1 These notes written by Tissot are on a sheet that has been kept with the watercolour.
2 Our thanks to Krystyna Matyjaszkiewicz for bringing our attention to the existence of this watercolour.

39 *Suresnes Bridge/Châtillon/ Vendôme Column/ Marsan Pavilion/The Ministry of Finances in Ruins/Château d'Eau Fountain*

1 Jules Moinaux, 'Revue comique des tribunaux', *Le Charivari*, nos.2–3, p.24.
2 Théophile Gautier, *Tableaux de siège: Paris 1870–1871*, Paris 1871, p.327.
3 Ludovic Hans and J.J. Blanc, *Guide à travers les ruines: Paris et ses environs*, Paris 1871, pp.8–9, quoted and translated by Alisa Luxenberg, 'Creating Désastres: Andrieu's Photographs of Urban Ruins in the Paris of 1871', *Art Bulletin*, vol.80, no.1, March 1998, p.119.
4 This fountain was moved to the Place Félix-

Eboué in the late 1870s. It was designed by Gabriel Davioud, and the lions were the work of Henri-Alfred Jacquemart.

5 Luxenberg 1998, p.119.

49 *The Barricade/Civil War*

1 A. Tabarant (ed.), *Une correspondance inédite d'Edouard Manet: les lettres du siège de Paris (1870–1871)*, Paris 1935, p.33.

2 According to Manet's friend Antonin Proust, they both witnessed violent reprisals (Antonin Proust, 'Edouard Manet: Souvenirs', in *Revue Blanche*, Paris, 1897, p.176).

3 Théodore Duret, *Histoire d'Edouard Manet et de son oeuvre*, Paris 1902, p.127.

4 See Françoise Cachin et al., *Manet 1832–1883*, exh. cat., Musée d'Orsay, Paris 1983, pp.323–5, and Juliet Wilson-Bareau, *Manet and the Execution of Maximilian: Painting, Politics and Censorship*, London 1992, p.73.

5 Cachin et al. 1992, p.325.

6 Cachin et al. 1992, p.327.

52 *London Wharfs/The Docks of London/ Over London By Rail/ Westminster Stairs*

1 William Blanchard Jerrold, *Life of Gustave Doré*, London 1891, pp.153–4.

2 Jerrold 1891, p.156.

Monet, Pissarro and Fellow Painters (pp.57–61)

1 *Times*, 19 Dec. 1870, p.4, about Durand-Ruel's first exhibition held at the German Gallery, New Bond Street, London. See also K. Flint, *Impressionists in England: The Critical Reception*, London 1984.

2 Letter from Pissarro to Dewhurst, 6 Nov. 1902, in Wynford Dewhurst, 'Impressionist Painting: its Genesis and Development', *The Studio*, no.29 1903, p.94.

3 Etienne Moreau-Nélaton, *Bonvin raconté par lui-même*, Paris 1927.

4 Anisabelle Berès and Michel Arveiller, *François Bonvin: The Master of the 'Realist School' 1817–1887*, exh. cat., Galerie Berès, Paris 1998, cat.70.

5 Thomas C. Jones and Robert Tombs, 'The French left in exile: Quarante-huitards and Communards in London, 1848–80', in D. Kelly and Martyn Cornick (eds.), *A History of the French in London: Liberty, Equality, Opportunity*, London 2013, p.171.

6 Etienne Moreau-Nélaton, *Daubigny raconté par lui-même*, Paris 1925, p.101. His son Karl Daubigny, also a painter, had enrolled in the Mobile National Guard.

7 Daubigny's unpublished address list includes collectors and artists – George Howard, Henry Moore (seascapist), Legros, Monet, Whistler, William Michael Rossetti, Val Prinsep, Arthur Severn, George Price Boyce, Seymour Haden – in John House, 'New Material on Monet and Pissarro in London in 1870–71', *Burlington Magazine*, vol.120, no.907, Oct. 1978, p.641.

8 Advertised in *The Athenaeum*, no.2246, 12 Nov. 1870; review in *Art Journal*, 1871, vol.33, pp.50–1. This important exhibition, which was held at the Society of British Artists on Pall Mall, included major old master paintings from private collections (the Queen's and the Duke of Wellington's), as well as contemporary paintings for sale. A drawing by French painter Adolphe Yvon entitled *1870* is described as 'embodying in one very masterly allegory the dire calamities of Paris and France'.

9 The Monet work, no.85, was praised in *The Examiner*, 21 Jan. 1871, p.11: 'Some very exquisite landscapes and sea-pieces are to be found on the walls, among which are ... Claude Monet's Sea Shore at Trouville.'

10 House 1978, p.636. In fact, as a married man, Monet would not have been called up anyway.

11 Janine Bailly-Herzberg (ed.), *Correspondance de Camille Pissarro*, vol.1, Paris 1980, p.67.

12 Letters from Rachel Pissarro to Camille, 9 and 30 Sept. 1870, in J. Pissarro and Claire Durand-Ruel-Snollaerts, *Pissarro: Critical Catalogue of Paintings*, 3 vols., Milan and Paris 2005, vol.1, p.128.

13 Ibid.

14 Pissarro and Durand-Ruel-Snollaerts 2005, vol.1, p.129.

15 Lucien was mocked for wearing wooden clogs: Kathleen Adler, *Pissarro in London*, London 2003, p.5.

16 Bailly-Herzberg 1980, p.64.

17 Monet's father died on 17 Jan. 1871.

18 Communard Poncerot: Jones and Tombs 2013, p.180.

19 Etienne Moreau-Nélaton, *Bonvin raconté par lui-même*, Paris 1927, p.75 (4 Jan. 1871).

20 Letter from Daubigny to La Rochenoire, Lisle Street, Leicester Square, 15 Oct. 1870, in Moreau-Nélaton 1925, pp.102–3.

21 Robert Hellebranth, *C.F. Daubigny 1817–1878*, Morges 1976, p.187, no.565: 'Le Port de Bordeaux', 1864.

22 François Thiébault-Sisson, 'Claude Monet: les années d'épreuves', *Le Temps*, 26 Nov. 1900, quoted by M. Elder, *Chez Claude Monet à Giverny*, Paris 1924.

23 Daniel Wildenstein, *Claude Monet: Biographie et catalogue raisonné*, Lausanne and Paris 1974–91, nos.134, 135, 136 (1869); nos.151, 152, 153. See also Madeleine Fidell-Beaufort, 'Hasty Departures for London by French Artists in 1870. Daubigny, Monet, Pissarro and some compatriots', in *Le Départ à l'époque victorienne*, Metz 2002, p.76.

24 Wildenstein 1974: W77, Monet, *Port of Honfleur*, 1866; W77a, Monet, *Boats in the Port of Honfleur* 1866–7.

25 Wildenstein 1974, no.66, fig.6.

26 Letter from Pissarro to Dewhurst, 6 Nov. 1902, in Dewhurst 1903, p.94.

27 Built in Hyde Park for the 1851 Universal Exhibition and reassembled on this South London site, at Sydenham, between 1852 and 1854.

28 Pissarro first rented accommodation in Lower Norwood; his next address was Canham's Dairy, Westow Hill, Upper Norwood. By April 1871 he had moved to 2 Chatham Terrace, Palace Road, off Anerley Hill, also Upper Norwood.

29 Paul Verlaine, 'Londres', *Oeuvres poétiques complètes*, Paris 1992, p.636. Verlaine arrived in London in September 1872.

30 Jules Vallès, *La Rue à Londres*, Paris 1950, in Jones and Tombs 2013, p.174.

31 Bonvin moved into the Rathbone Hotel, 35 Rathbone Place, north of Oxford Street. Daubigny first checked into the Hôtel de l'Etoile on Great Windmill Street. By 15 Oct. 1870 he was living on Lisle Street, Leicester Square, then by 20 Oct. on 13 Canning Place, West Kensington: Moreau-Nélaton 1925, p.102.

32 Monet's first address in London was 11 Arundel Street, close to Piccadilly Circus, off Shaftesbury Avenue. By 21 Jan. 1871 the family was living in 1 Bath Place, Kensington (now 183 Kensington High Street), staying with Mrs Phoebe Theobald, a dressmaker who was keeping boarders: N. Reed, *Monet and the Thames*, London 1998, p.3.

33 Harry Kessler, *Journey to the Abyss: The Diaries of Count Harry Kessler*, ed. Laird McLeod Easton, New York 2011, p.311, 28 Nov. 1903; Sylvie Patry (ed.), *Inventing Impressionism: Paul Durand-Ruel and the Modern Art Market*, exh. cat., National Gallery, London 2015, p.175.

34 Paul Durand-Ruel, *Memoirs of the First Impressionist Art Dealer (1831–1922)*, ed. Paul-Louis Durand-Ruel and F. Durand-Ruel, Paris 2014, p.78.

35 Letter from Daubigny to La Rochenoire, Lisle Street, Leicester Square, 15 Oct. 1870, in Moreau-Nélaton 1925, pp.102–3.

36 The second hanging of Durand-Ruel's first Society of French Artists exhibition, from 6 March 1871, included one painting by Monet and two by Pissarro (Monet, *Entrance to the Port of Trouville*; Pissarro presumably *Fox Hill, Upper Norwood*): Patry 2015, p.180.

37 Letter from Durand-Ruel to Pissarro, 21 Jan. 1871, in Patry 2015, pp.175–6.

38 Letter from Durand-Ruel to Pissarro, 6 May 1871, from Society of French artists, Durand-Ruel Archives, Paris.

39 Durand-Ruel sent money to Millet who had remained at Cherbourg, to Dupré at Cayeux-sur-Mer, to Fromentin at La Rochelle, and to Diaz: Durand-Ruel 2014, p.79.

40 Letter from Bonvin, London, 4 Jan. 1871, Moreau-Nélaton 1927, p.75. Also in Berès and Arveiller 1998, cat.71.

41 Letter from Daubigny, London, 2 Nov. 1870, in Moreau-Nélaton 1925, p.104.

42 Moreau-Nélaton 1925, p.104.

43 Thiébault-Sisson 1924.

44 Frances Fowle, *Monet and French Landscape: Vétheuil and Normandy*, Edinburgh 2006, p.142.

45 Jules Berthel was introduced to Pissarro by Théodore Duret, collector and art critic, and the painter's friend. Described as a 'charming young man', Berthel worked for his [Duret's] father's business – a cognac sales company – managing its London branch. He lived at 26 Tavistock Street. Berthel and Duret (on a visit to London) went to see Pissarro in Norwood probably on Saturday, 17 June 1871. Berthel bought Pissarro's *Road in Upper Norwood* 1871 (Neue Pinakothek, Munich): C.F. Frankiss, 'Camille Pissarro, Théodore Duret and Jules Berthel in London in 1871', *Burlington Magazine*, vol.146, July 2004, pp.470–2, esp. p.470.

46 Letter from Pissarro to Duret, before 5 June 1871, in Bailly-Herzberg 1980, pp.63–4.

47 Letter from Pissarro to Duret, 17 Jan. 1881, in Bailly-Herzberg 1980, pp.144–5. Submissions to the Royal Academy had to be made on 27–8 March 1871; see House 1978, p.637.

48 Thiébault-Sisson 1924.

49 *Hamlet*, opera by Ambroise Thomas, 1870: Patry 2015, p.172.

50 Anne Distel, *Impressionism: The First Collectors*, New York 1990, p.75. In 1870, after every performance, Faure sang 'La Marseillaise' kneeling and wrapped in the tricolour.

51 Sylvie Patin, *Claude Monet en Grande-Bretagne*, Paris 1994, p.8. Also Madeleine Fidell-Beaufort, 'Hasty Departures for London by French Artists in 1870. Daubigny, Monet, Pissarro and some compatriots', in *Le Départ à l'époque victorienne*, Metz 2002, p.76.

52 Moreau-Nélaton 1925, p.105.

62 *The Thames at Erith*/ID25 *The Mouth of the Thames*

1 Letter from James McNeill Whistler to Henri Fantin-Latour, 16 Aug. [1865], Library of Congress, Washington, Manuscript Division, Pennell-Whistler Collection, PWC 1/33/1

2 Gary Tinterow and Henri Loyrette, *Origins of Impressionism*, exh. cat., Metropolitan Museum of Art, New York 1994, p.25.

65 *St Paul's from the Surrey Side*

1 Dulwich Gallery visitors' book, 25 Nov. 1870.

2 Etienne Moreau-Nélaton, *Daubigny raconté par lui-même*, Paris 1925, p.102.

3 Moreau-Nélaton 1925, p.103.

4 Durand-Ruel commissioned three paintings of Villerville from Daubigny by 2 Nov. 1870 (Moreau-Nélaton 1925, p.104).

5 See Christopher Riopelle and Ann Sumner, *Sisley in England and Wales*, exh. cat., National Gallery, London 2008, p.15.

66 *The Thames below Westminster*

1 John House, 'Visions of the Thames', in *Monet's London: Artists' Reflections on the Thames, 1859–1914*, exh. cat., Museum of Fine Arts, St Petersburg, FL 2005, p.27.

2 Anthea Callen, *Jean-Baptiste Faure, 1830–1914: A Study of a Patron and Collector of the Impressionists and their Contemporaries with a Catalogue of his Collection* (MA thesis, University of Leicester), Leicester 1971, p.331.

69 *Meditation (Madame Monet on the Sofa)*

1 John House, 'New Material on Monet and Pissarro in London in 1870–71', *Burlington Magazine*, vol.120, no.907, Oct. 1978, pp.636–41, esp. p.642.

70 *Fox Hill, Upper Norwood*

1 Sylvie Patry (ed.), *Inventing Impressionism: Paul Durand-Ruel and the Modern Art Market*, exh. cat., National Gallery, London 2015, p.260.

74 *The Avenue, Sydenham*

1 Letter from Camille Pissarro to Lucien Pissarro, Jan. 1883, in John Rewald (ed.), *Camille Pissarro: Letters to his Son Lucien*, New York 1943, p.21.

2 Janine Bailly-Herzberg (ed.), *Correspondance de Camille Pissarro*, vol.2, Paris 1986, no.583, p.345.

77 *Lordship Lane Station, Dulwich*

2 On 4 Sept. 1871, see Joachim Pissarro and Claire Durand-Ruel-Snollaerts, *Pissarro: Critical Catalogue of Paintings*, 3 vols., Milan and Paris 2005, vol.2, pp.159, 163.

3 Pissarro and Durand-Ruel-Snollaerts 2005, p.163.

78 *View of the Thames: Charing Cross Bridge*

1 In his *Histoire des Peintres impressionnistes* (p.122), which was published in Paris in 1906, Théodore

Duret thought it necessary to insist on this point: 'He was everything that is the most French in his habits, ideas, preferences, and he felt extremely out of place in England.'

2 Four pictures by Sisley were presented at the fourth exhibition of the Society of French Artists, at the German Gallery, 168 New Bond Street, in 1872; three pictures at the sixth and seventh exhibitions in 1872; and three pictures at the eighth exhibition in 1874.
3 The quoted passage is taken from Henry James, *English Hours*, Cambridge 1905, p.164, Hathi Trust Digital Library on-line version: https://catalog.hathitrust.org/Record/009574743.
4 James 1905, p.41.

79 *Molesey Weir, Hampton Court, Morning*

1 Jerome K. Jerome, *Three Men in a Boat (To Say Nothing of the Dog)*, London 1889, p.125.
2 MaryAnne Stevens (ed.), *Alfred Sisley, 1839–1899*, exh. cat., Royal Academy of Arts, London 1992, p.146, no.28.
3 Nicholas Reed, *Sisley on the Thames and the Welsh Coast*, Folkestone 2008.

James Tissot, The Englishman (pp.81–5)

1 Georges Bastard, 'Nos peintres. James Tissot. Note intimes', *Revue de Bretagne*, 1906, vol.36, p.276.
2 Bastard 1906, vol.36; Edmond and Jules de Goncourt, *Journal: Mémoires de la vie littéraire (1851–1896)*, Paris 1989.
3 His father had a fashion-wear shop near the castle of the Dukes of Brittany.
4 *Saint Marcel and Saint Oliver*, Salon of 1859, no.2871, and *Saint James the Major and Saint Bernard* (no.2870), or *The Meeting of Faust and Marguerite* 1860 (Musée d'Orsay, Paris).
5 Now Avenue Foch.
6 The friendship between Degas and Tissot was close before it began to disintegrate in the 1880s. On this friendship, see Cyrille Sciama, *James Tissot et ses Maîtres*, Paris 2005, pp.32–41.
7 Mme Desoye ran a shop selling Japanese objects in the rue de Rivoli, Paris.
8 Bastard 1906, pp.262–3. See Krystyna Matyjaszkiewicz, forthcoming online Tate Paper.
9 In his *Mémoires* Blanche fancifully narrates dining with Paul Helleu and Tissot in a small inn in Sydenham. His opinion about Tissot's involvement in the Commune is no longer accepted.
10 No.2748, 1870; Christie's sale, New York, 2 May 2001, lot 44.
11 P.A. Lesmoine, *Degas et son oeuvre*, Paris 1946–9, vol.1, p.67.
12 De Maigret sale, Paris, 17 March 2004, lot 102.
13 My thanks to Krystyna Matyjaskiewicz for this information. Bowles apparently did not move to Cleeve Lodge before the end of 1877.
14 Alison Smith, 'James Tissot et l'Angleterre', in Cyrille Sciama, *James Tissot et ses maîtres*, Rome 2015 (reworking and development of Sciama 2005).
15 Edmond and Jules de Goncourt, *Journal. Mémoires de la vie littéraire*, 3 vols., Paris 1989, vol.3, p.596 (3 Nov. 1874).
16 *Degas inédit*, p.358.
17 On this subject, see Paolo Serafini, 'Bought and sold: Tissot et la Arthur Tooth & Sons Gallery in Londra', in Sciama 2015, pp.44–9.
18 See Jane Abdy, 'Amici e ospiti londinesi di Tissot', in Emanuela Angiuli and Katy Spurrell (eds.), *De Nittis ed Tissot*, Milan 2006, pp.53–9.
19 P. Dini and G.L. Martini, *De Nittis*, Turin 1990, pp.305–6.
20 See Cyrille Sciama, 'Giuseppe de Nittis, tra James Tissot ed Edgar Degas', in Angiuli and Spurrell 2006, pp.81–5.
21 Jessica Rutherford, 'Les émaux cloisonnés de James Tissot,' *James Tissot, 1836–1902*, exh. cat., pp.94–9.
22 Michael Wentworth, *James Tissot*, Oxford 1984, p.58 n.51.
23 Through the publication of a small brochure by Charles Yriarte, *J.J. Tissot. Eaux-fortes, manière noire, pointes sèches*, Paris 1886.
24 W.E. Misfeldt, 'The Economics of James Tissot's printmaking', *J.J. Tissot: Prints from the Gotlieb Collection*, Alexandria, VA 1991, pp.19–21.
25 Goncourt 1989, vol.3.
26 See Nancy Rose Marshall, 'Transcripts of Modern Life?' The London Paintings of James Tissot 1871–1882', PhD thesis, Yale University, New Haven, CT 1998.
27 De Goncourt 1989, vol.2, pp.204–5.
28 Note that Alma-Tadema acquired his residence and modified it extensively.
29 Alfred de Lostalot, 'Le Musée des Arts Décoratifs. Exposition de MM. Le Comte Lepic et James Tissot. Le Salon des Arts Décoratifs', *Gazette des Beaux-arts*, 1883, vol.1, pp.452–4.
30 *Exposition J.J. Tissot – Quinze Tableaux sur La Femme à Paris*, Galerie Sedelmeyer, Paris, 19 April–15 June 1885.

86 *Napoleon III, Emperor of France ('Sovereigns No.1. "Le régime parlementaire."')*

1 Nancy Rose Marshall and Malcolm Warner, *Victorian Life/Modern Love*, New Haven 1999, p.11.
2 Krystyna Matyjaszkiewicz (ed.), *James Tissot*, London 1984, p.106.
3 Marshall and Warner 1999, p.11.
4 Nancy Rose Marshall, 'Transcripts of Modern Life: The London Paintings of James Tissot 1871–1882', PhD thesis, Yale University, New Haven, CT 1999, p.87.

87 *Portrait of Mrs B.*

1 Discussion with Krystyna Matyjaszkiewicz, 23 Aug. 2016.

89 *Captain Frederick Burnaby*

1 Jules Claretie, *Peintres et sculpteurs contemporains*, Paris 1873, p.374, quoted in Jan Marsh, entry on the portrait, in online NPG *Later Victorians Portraits Catalogue*.
2 Louise Jopling, *Twenty Years of my Life, 1867–1887*, London 1925, p.60.

90–1 *A Huguenot*/ID45 *Les Adieux* (The Farewells) 1871

1 Inscription on the drawing dated 19 June 1871 (Duke of Devonshire collection, Chatsworth).
2 According to Millais's son, J.G. Millais, during Lady Waldegrave's lifetime a small copy of Millais's picture hung next to the Reynolds at Strawberry Hill: J.G. Millais, *The Life and Letters of Sir John Everett Millais*, London 1899, vol.2, p.40.

94 *Too Early*

1 'The Royal Academy Summer Exhibition', *The Builder*, 3 May 1873, pp.339–40.
2 Ibid.
3 Charles Baudelaire, 'Le Peintre de la vie moderne', *Le Figaro*, Nov. 1863, translated in Charles Baudelaire, *The Painter of Modern Life, and Other Essays*, trans. Jonathan Mayne, London 1964, p.3.
4 Louise Jopling, *Twenty Years of my Life*, London 1925, p.60.

95 *Hush!*

1 James Laver, 'Vulgar Society', *The Romantic Career of James Tissot 1836–1902*, London 1936, pp.33–4.
2 Ibid.
3 See Krystyna Matyjaszkiewicz, forthcoming Tate paper.
4 *Illustrated London News*, 22 May 1875, p.10.

97 *View of the Garden at 17 Grove End Road*/ID56 *My Garden at St John's Wood*

1 Nancy Rose Marshall and Malcolm Warner, *Victorian Life/Modern Love*, New Haven 1999, p.13.
2 Krystyna Matyjaszkiewicz (ed.), *James Tissot*, London 1984, p.117.

98 *Woman in Outdoor Costume, Sleeping on a Couch*

1 It also features in *The Captain's Daughter* (Southampton City Art Gallery). Our thanks to Krystyna Matyjaszkiewicz for highlighting this.

100 *Kathleen Newton/In Full Sunlight/Kathleen Newton (Rêverie)/Reading in the Park*

1 Willard E. Misfeldt, *J.J. Tissot: Prints from the Gotlieb Collection*, Alexandria, VA 1991, p.15.
2 Marita Ross, 'The Truth about Tissot', *Everybody's Weekly*, 15 June 1946, p.7.
3 Nancy Rose Marshall and Malcolm Warner, *Victorian Life/Modern Love*, New Haven 1999, p.136.

104 *The Three Crows Inn*

1 My thanks to Krystyna Matyjaszkiewicz for the information. 'Daws' is short for 'jackdaws', which belong to the crow family.
2 See Krystyna Matyjaszkiewicz's forthcoming Tate paper.
3 Francis Seymour Haden, *About Etching: Part 1*, London 1879, p.27.
4 Martin Hardie, 'Goulding, Frederick (1842–1909)', rev. Paul Goldman, *Oxford Dictionary of National Biography*, Oxford University Press, 2004: http://www.oxforddnb.com/view/article/33495, accessed 31 Jan 2017.

105 *Emigrants*

1 Nancy Rose Marshall and Malcolm Warner, *Victorian Life/Modern Love*, New Haven 1999, p.90.

106 *Trafalgar Tavern in Greenwich*

1 Gustave Doré and William Blanchard Jerrold, *London: A Pilgrimage*, London 1872, p.ix.
2 Thomas Gibson Bowles, *Flotsam and Jetsam*, London 1882, p.33.

109 *The National Gallery*

1 Léontine de Nittis, *Notes et souvenirs du peintre Joseph De Nittis*, Paris 1895, p.225.
2 Tulliola Sparagni, 'De Nittis à Londres: impressions d'un "étranger de passage"', in *Giuseppe de Nittis: La modernité* élégante, exh. cat., Petit Palais, Paris 2010, p.41.
3 De Nittis 1895, p.144.

110 *Summer (A Portrait)*

1 Krystyna Matyjaszkiewicz, 'Royalty, Romance and Rivalry: Unlocking James Tissot's Ball on Shipboard and related works', forthcoming Tate paper, 2017.
2 Letter from Dante Gabriel Rossetti to Frances Rossetti, 12 Nov. 1864: Oswald Doughty and John Robert Wahl, *Letters of Dante Gabriel Rossetti*, 4 vols., Oxford, 1965–7, vol.2, p.527, no.563.
3 *J.J. Tissot: Eaux-fortes, Manière Noire, Pointes Sèches*, Paris 1886, no.17.

112 *The Gallery of HMS Calcutta (Portsmouth)*

1 Nancy Rose Marshall and Malcolm Warner, *Victorian Life/Modern Love*, New Haven 1999, p.85.
2 C. Hughes, *Henry James and the Art of Dress*, Basingstoke 2001, p.17.
3 Nancy Rose Marshall, 'Transcripts of Modern Life: The London Paintings of James Tissot 1871–1882', PhD thesis, Yale University, New Haven, CT 1999, p.116.
4 *The Graphic*, no.16, 18 Aug. 1877, supplement, p.150.
5 Marshall and Warner 1999, p.85.
6 Discussion with Krystyna Matyjaszkiewicz, who plans to publish new information on this piece.
7 Marshall and Warner 1999, p.124.

113 *Portsmouth Dockyard*

1 Michael Justin Wentworth, *James Tissot: Catalogue Raisonné of his Prints*, Minneapolis 1978, p.140.
2 Wentworth 1978, p.140.

Alphonse Legros (pp.115–19)

1 Henri Fantin-Latour to James MacNeill Whistler, 26 June 1859, in Margaret MacDonald, Patricia de Montfort and Nigel Thorp (eds.), *The Correspondence of James McNeill Whistler, 1855–1903*, online edition, University of Glasgow, GUW 01073 (accessed 2 Feb. 2017): http://www.whistler.arts.gla.ac.uk/correspondence.
2 Whistler to Henri Fantin-Latour, 12/17 July 1863, in MacDonald et al., *Correspondence of James McNeill Whistler*, GUW 08031 (accessed 2 Feb. 2017).
3 Daphne du Maurier (ed.), *The Young George du Maurier*, London 1951, p.216.
4 William Michael Rossetti, 'Art Exhibitions in London', *Fine Arts Quarterly Review*, Oct. 1864, p.30.
5 Edmond Duranty, 'Ceux qui seront les peintres', in Fernand Desnoyers (ed.), *Almanach parisien, 6e année, 1867*, cited in translation in Michael Fried, *Manet's Modernism or, The Face of Painting in the 1860s*, Chicago and London 1996, p.441.
6 Timothy Wilcox, *Alphonse Legros, 1837–1911*, exh. cat., Musée des Beaux Arts de Dijon 1987–8. Wilcox (p.78) states that Legros and Howard were introduced by Burne-Jones on 16 Nov.1865.
7 Edouard Manet to Edgar Degas, 29 July 1868, pm, cited in Henri Loyrette, *Degas*, Paris 1991, p.222. 'Cicerone', from the Italian,

is an archaism meaning 'a guide'.
8 I am grateful to Juliet Bareau for this information about Manet's trip to London.
9 The names of all three men appear in the Dulwich Gallery visitor book for Friday, 25 Nov. 1870: Visitor Book, vol.3 (21 June 1870–11 Sept. 1871).
10 Letter from Camille Pissarro to Lucien Pissarro, 22 July 1883, cited in John Rewald (ed.), *Camille Pissarro Letters to his Son Lucien*, Boston 2002, p.39.
11 Etienne Moreau-Nélaton, *Bonvin raconté par lui-même*, Paris 1927, p.75.
12 Andrew Watson, 'Constantine Ionides and his Collection of 19th-Century French Art', *Journal of the Scottish Society for Art History*, 1998, p.27.
13 The picture is listed in the catalogue as *A Study of a Head* (cat.8).
14 William Michael Rossetti, *The Diary of William Michael Rossetti, 1870–73*, Oxford 1977, p.48.
15 Legros's trip to Paris was reported in 'Fine Art Gossip', *The Athenaeum*, 26 March 1875, p.399.
16 William Michael Rossetti, 'The Society of French Artists', *Academy*, 22 May 1875, p.539.
17 The information about this unrecorded exhibition comes from 'The Society of French Artists, Bond Street', *Art Journal*, Aug. 1875, p.245.
18 Beth Jourde and Regamey visited Legros at home. I am grateful to Caroline Corbeau-Parsons for this information.
19 Wilcox 1987–8, pp.92–3.
20 Anon., 'Jules Vallès', *Manchester Guardian*, 16 Feb. 1885.
21 *The Tinker* was admired by Félix Régamey who made an etching after it (National Gallery of Art, Washington)
22 'Contemporary Portraits, new Series – No.26, M. Alphonse Legros', *University Magazine*, Feb. 1880, p.198.
23 'The School of Giorgione' was first published in the *Fortnightly Review* in 1877, and was republished in *The Renaissance* 1888. I am grateful to Liz Prettejohn for her help with the identification of the Legros etching.
24 Sidney Colvin, 'The Etchings of M. Alphonse Legros', *Portfolio*, Jan. 1870, pp.140–1. Colvin was ostensibly discussing Legros's etchings but he devoted most of the article to a discussion of his painting.
25 Louis Emile Edmond Duranty, 'The New Painting: Concerning the Group of Artists Exhibiting at the Durand-Ruel Galleries, 1876', cited in Charles Moffet (ed.), *The New Painting: Impressionism 1874–1886*, San Francisco 1986, pp.37–50, esp. p.41.
26 Letter from Edgar Degas to Alphonse Legros, Oct. 1871, cited in Theodore Reff, 'Some Unpublished Letters of Degas', *Art Bulletin*, March 1968, p.89.
27 Letter from Otto Scholderer to Henri Fantin-Latour, winter 1874, correspondence between Henri Fantin-Latour and Otto Scholderer (1858–1902), ed. Mathilde Arnoux et al., Centre allemand d'histoire de l'art, 2014, http://quellen-perspectivia.net/fantin-scholderer, 1874 07. Legros's address, 'Westall Villa/Brook Green/Hammmersmith/Londres', where he lived from 1874, is recorded in Theodore Reff, *The Notebooks of Edgar Degas: A Catalogue of the Thirty-Eight Notebooks in the Bibliothèque Nationale and Other Collections*, Oxford 1976, vol.1, notebook 26, p.98.
28 See Reff 1976, notebook 32, 1B, where 'Legros/University College/Gower Street/Londres' is recorded.
29 Alphose Legros, *Studies of Hands*, black chalk, 13 x 19cm, Musée du Louvre, Paris, Départment des Arts Graphiques (RF 15888), Collection Sale 1:216.
30 R.A.M. Stevenson, 'Preface', *The Dutch Gallery Exhibition of Pictures, Water-Colour Drawings, & Etchings by Mr. Alphonse Legros*, 1897, p.vi.
31 R.A.M. Stevenson, 'Professor Legros', *Pall Mall Gazette*, 6 April 1897, p.4.
32 St P. [W.R. Sickert], 'Alphonse Legros', *Speaker*, 10 April 1897, cited in Anna Gruetzner Robins (ed.), *Walter Sickert: The Complete Writings on Art*, Oxford 2000, p.155.

120 *Ex-Voto*

1 Maurice Dreyfous, 'Alphonse Legros, peintre, dessinateur, graveur', *L'Art et les artistes*, Sept. 1908, pp.262–9, esp. p.263.
2 William Michael Rossetti, *Fine Arts Quarterly Review*, Oct. 1864.

124 *The Drawing Room of Mr Edwin Edwards at Sunbury/Mr and Mrs Edwin Edwards*

1 Laure Dalon (ed.), *Fantin-Latour à fleur de peau*, exh. cat., Musée du Luxembourg, Paris 2016, p.152.
2 Letter from Fantin-Latour to Edwin Edwards, 26 Nov. 1874, Tate catalogue file N01952.
3 Adolphe Jullien, *Fantin-Latour: sa vie et ses amitiés*, Paris 1909, p.22.

126 *Edward Burne-Jones*

1 Daphne du Maurier, *The Young George du Maurier*, London 1951, p.249.
2 See Timothy Wilcox, 'Alphonse Legros (1837–1911): Aspects of his Life and Work', MPhil Thesis, University of London, 1981, p.43.

127 *The Tinker*

1 Oscar Wilde, 'Grosvenor Gallery', *Dublin University Magazine*, July 1877, http://www.gutenberg.org/files/14062/14062-h/14062-h.htm: 'M. Alphonse Legros sends nine pictures, and there is a natural curiosity to see the work of a gentleman who holds at Cambridge the same professorship as Mr. Ruskin does at Oxford. Four of these are studies of men's heads, done in two hours each for his pupils at the Slade Schools. There is a good deal of vigorous, rough execution about them, and they are marvels of rapid work. His portrait of Mr. Carlyle is unsatisfactory; and even in No.79, a picture of two scarlet-robed bishops, surrounded by Spanish monks, his colour is very thin and meagre. A good bit of painting is of some metal pots in a picture called *Le Chaudronnier*.'

129 *Hilly Landscape*

1 Champfleury, *Le Réalisme*, Paris 1857, p.8.
2 Timothy Wilcox, *Alphonse Legros, 1837–1911*, exh. cat., Musée des Beaux-Arts de Dijon, 1987, pp.106–7.
3 For example, Legros's *Rehearsing the Service* 1870 (Tate) based on Titian's *Concert* 1510 (Pitti Palace): Elizabeth Prettejohn, *After the Pre-Raphaelites: Art and Aestheticism in Victorian England*, Manchester 1999, pp.40–1.
4 Walter Pater, *The School of Giorgione*, 1877, reprinted in Walter Pater, *The Renaissance*, London 1888, pp.140–1.

130 *Frédéric Régamey*

1 A. Poulet-Malassis and A.-W. Thibaudeau, *Catalogue raisonné de l'oeuvre gravé et lithographié de M. Alphonse Legros*, Paris 1877.

131 *Death of the Vagabond*

1 'Multiple Arts and Popular Culture Items', *The Standard*, 26 June 1876, p.6: *British Library Newspapers*, tinyurl.galegroup.com/tinyurl/4V8DW8, accessed 7 March 2017.
2 Timothy Wilcox, *Alphonse Legros, 1837–1911*, exh. cat., Musée des Beaux-Arts de Dijon, 1987, p.98.
3 Wilcox 1987, p.98.
4 'EXHIBITION OF WORKS IN BLACK AND WHITE', *Pall Mall Gazette*, 20 June 1876: *British Library Newspapers*, tinyurl.galegroup.com/tinyurl/4V7p64, accessed 7 March 2017.
5 Timothy Wilcox, 'Legros, Alphonse (1837–1911)', *Oxford Dictionary of National Biography*, Oxford University Press, 2004; online edn, May 2008: http://www.oxforddnb.com/view/article/34480, accessed 7 March 2017.
6 See A.P. Malassis and A.W. Thibaudeau, *Catalogue raisonné de l'oeuvre gravé et lithographié de M. Alphonse Legros, Slade Professor of art au Collége de l'Université de Londres, Professeur de gravure à l'eau-forte à l'École de South Kensington*, Paris 1877, p.vi.

133 *The Gust of Wind/By the Riverside, Morning Effect*

1 Jane Munro and Paul Stirton, *The Society of Three: Alphonse Legros, Henri Fantin-Latour, James McNeill Whistler*, Cambridge 1998, p.5. Delâtre's studio in Paris was shelled by the Prussians in 1870, and he subsequently came as a refugee to London, where he practised until 1879.
2 Margaret Dunwoody, 'Alphonse Legros and the Etching Revival in Great Britain', MA thesis, Courtauld Institute of Art, London 1977, p.59.
3 'Multiple Arts and Popular Culture Items', *Morning Post*, 14 June 1875, p.2: *British Library Newspapers*, accessed 20 Sept. 2016.

134 *A Storm*

1 Antony Griffiths, *Prints and Printmaking: An Introduction to the History and Techniques*, London 1996, p.76.
2 Timothy Wilcox, *Alphonse Legros, 1837–1911*, exh. cat., Musée des Beaux-Arts de Dijon, 1987, pp.115–16, no.75.

135 *Portrait of Edward Poynter*

1 Timothy Wilcox, 'Legros, Alphonse (1837–1911)', *Oxford Dictionary of National Biography*, Oxford University Press, 2004; online edn, May 2008: http://www.oxforddnb.com/view/article/34480, accessed 7 March 2017.
2 Timothy Wilcox, *Alphonse Legros 1837–1911*, exh. cat., Musée des Beaux-Arts de Dijon, 1987, p.104.
3 Arthur M. Hind, *A History of Engraving & Etching from the 15th Century to the Year 1914*, New York 1923, p.319.

137 *Alphonse Legros/George Frederic Watts R.A.*

1 Mary Watts, *George Frederic Watts: The Annals of an Artist's Life*, 3 vols., London 1912, vol.1, p.246.
2 Watts 1912, vol.1, p.247.

139 *Head of Alphonse Legros/Portrait of Auguste Rodin*

1 Ruth Butler, *Rodin, La solitude du génie*, Paris 1998, p.99.
2 Tomoko Ando, 'Rodin's Reputation in Great Britain: The Neglected Role of Alphonse Legros', *Nineteenth-Century Art Worldwide*, Autumn 2016: http://www.19thc-artworldwide.org/index.php/autumn16/ando-on-rodin-reputation-in-great-britain-neglected-role-of-alphonse-legros
3 Catherine Lampert et al., *Rodin*, exh. cat., Royal Academy of Arts, London 2006.
4 Letter from Rodin to Maurice Haquette, in Alain Beausire and Florence Cadouot (eds.), *Correspondance de Rodin*, vol.1, Paris 1985, p.54, no.4; Frederick Lawton, *François-Auguste Rodin*, New York 1908, p.242.
5 Musée Rodin Archives.
6 Antoinette Le Normand-Romain, *The Bronzes of Rodin: Catalogue of Works in the Musée Rodin*, Paris 2007, p.480.
7 Manchester City Galleries, gift of the Legros heirs in 1912: 'A mon ami A. Legros.'
8 Timothy Wilcox, *Alphonse Legros 1837–1911*, exh. cat., Musée des Beaux-Arts de Dijon, 1987, p.131.

140 *Bust of Jules Dalou*

1 François Blanchetière, *L'Enfer selon Rodin*, exh. cat., Musée Rodin, Paris 2016.

143 *Portrait of the Artist*

1 Timothy Wilcox, *Alphonse Legros 1837–1911*, exh. cat., Musée des Beaux-Arts de Dijon, 1988, p.23.
2 Timothy Wilcox, 'Legros, Alphonse (1837–1911)', *Oxford Dictionary of National Biography*, Oxford University Press, 2004; online edn, May 2008: http://www.oxforddnb.com/view/article/34480, accessed 7 March 2017.

A French Demonstration (pp.145-9)

1 Marion H. Spielmann, *British Sculpture and Sculptors of Today*, London 1901, p.1.
2 Cited in G. McAllister, 'Edward Lantéri: sculptor and professor', *The Studio*, vol.57, 1912–13, p.25.
3 See detailed article by Melissa Hamnett: Melissa Hamnett, 'Edouard Lantéri. Sculptor, medallist and mentor', *The Medal*, no.63, 2013, pp.4–25.
4 Re-edited: Edouard Lantéri, *Modelling and Sculpting the Human Figure* and *Modelling and Sculpting Animals*, New York 1985.
5 For an overview, see Edward Morris, *French Art in Nineteenth-Century Britain*, New Haven and London 2005, ch.3.
6 F.T. Palgrave, *Essays*, cited by Benedict Read, *Victorian Sculpture*, New Haven and London 1982, p.20.
7 Morris 2005 p.34.
8 Mark Stocker, *Royalist and Realist: The Life and Work of Sir Joseph Edgar Boehm*, New York and London 1988, pp.25–32.
9 Susan Beattie, *The New Sculpture*, New Haven and London 1983, pp.23–4.
10 Stéphane Laurent, *Histoire de l'Ecole nationale supérieure des arts décoratifs de 1766 à nos jours*, Paris 2004.
11 Horace Lecoq de Boisbaudran, *L'Education de la Mémoire Pittoresque*, 1847, republished in *L'éducation de la mémoire*

pittoresque et la formation de l'artiste, Paris 1920.

12 Maurice Dreyfous, *Dalou, sa vie et son oeuvre*, Paris 1903, pp.6, 25.

13 Gonzalo J. Sánchez, *Organizing Independence: The Artists' Federation of the Paris Commune and its Legacy, 1871–1889*, Lincoln, NE 1997, p.66.

14 As named retrospectively by Edmund Gosse, critic at the *Art Journal*, in 1894.

15 Veronica Franklin Gould, *Mary Seton Watts (1849–1938): Unsung Heroine of the Art Nouveau*, exh. cat., Watts Gallery, Compton 1998, pp.22–3.

16 Diane Bilbey with Marjorie Trusted, *British Sculpture 1470–2000: A Concise Catalogue of the Collection in the Victoria and Albert Museum*, London 2002, p.228; Emilia, Mrs Pattison, Lady Dilke, 'Randolph Caldecott', *The Artist*, 1898, vol.22, pp.64–6, esp. p.65.

17 Beattie 1983, ch.2.

18 *Precis of the Board Minutes of the Science and Art Department, 23 December 1869 to 31 December 1877*, London 1878 (National Library of Art), p.113.

19 *Precis of the Board Minutes of the Science and Art Department, from 1 January 1878 to 31 December 1880*, London 1881 (National Library of Art), p.311.

20 Note that in 1877 Dalou was paid £7–10s. [shillings] per session, i.e. £300 a year for one session per week; Legros had been hired as an engraving teacher in 1875 for £4–4s. per session, once every two weeks; Lantéri, whose sculpted work is not comparable in importance to Dalou's, succeeded Dalou in 1880 at £200 a year, for two days a week.

21 Spielmann 1901.

22 Lantéri 1985.

23 Walter Armstrong, 'Mr. Harry Bates', *Portfolio*, 1888, pp.170–4, esp. p.171.

24 Spielmann 1901, pp.1, 115; Kineton Parkes, *Sculpture of Today, vol.1: America, Great-Britain, Japan*, London 1921, pp.94–5.

25 Spielmann 1901, pp.109–14; Alfred Lys Baldry, 'A notable sculptor: Alfred Drury, A.R.A.', *The Studio*, 1906, vol.36, p.10; Jolyon Drury, *Revelation to Revolution: The Legacy of Samuel Palmer: The Revival and Evolution of Pastoral Printmaking by Paul Drury and the Goldsmiths School in the 20th Century*, Ashford 2006, pp.228–9; Ben Thomas (ed.), *Alfred Drury and the New Sculpture*, exh. cat., University of Kent, Canterbury 2013–14.

26 Parkes 1921, pp.78–9.

27 Edouard Lantéri, 'Jules Dalou: Sculptor', *Magazine of Art*, 1902, p.376.

28 McAllister 1912–13, p.25.

29 Beattie 1983, ch.2, p.22.

30 Baldry 1906, pp.3–4.

31 See Jonathan Black, 'The New (British) Sculpture and the struggle for realism between the wars', *Sculpture Journal*, vol.21(2), 2012, pp.23–36.

32 As Rodin said of Antoine Bourdelle, that he was 'a trailblazer of the future'.

150 *Alphonse Legros/Portrait of M.J. Dalou, Sculptor/Portrait of Jules Dalou*

1 Maurice Dreyfous, *Dalou, sa vie et son oeuvre*, Paris 1903, p.46.

2 Dreyfous 1903, pp.46, 48–50, 69–70.

3 National Archives, Fontainebleau, Versement no.860352, ET-C-1575, 22 May 1903, post-mortem inventory; catalogue of post-mortem sale for J. Dalou, Paris Drouot, 24 Dec. 1906.

4 Timothy Wilcox, *Alphonse Legros 1837–1911*, exh. cat., Musée des Beaux-Arts de Dijon, 1987, cat.41.

5 A. Poulet-Malassis and A.-W. Thibaudeau, *Catalogue raisonné de l'oeuvre gravé et lithographié de Alphonse Legros*, Paris 1877, no.41, p.23; the engraving shown is an example of the fifth state, as it is described by Poulet-Malassis and Wyatt.

6 Philip Gilbert Hamerton, *Etching & Etchers*, London 1876, p.227.

7 Dreyfous 1903, p.66.

8 Diane Bilbey with Marjorie Trusted, *British Sculpture 1470–2000: A Concise Catalogue of the Collection in the Victoria and Albert Museum*, London 2002, cat.372, pp.245–6.

9 Louis Decamps, 'Exposition d'œuvres d'art exécutées en noir et blanc', *L'Art*, no.87, 27 Aug. 1876, pp.199–206.

10 Léonce Bénédite, 'Alphonse Legros', *La Revue de l'Art*, 1897, p.343.

152 *Palm Sunday in Boulogne*, or *Woman from Boulogne*

1 See *A May Service for Young Women* 1868 (Victoria and Albert Museum).

2 Howard Archives, Rosalind Howard Diary, J23/102: the date is thought to refer to this statuette. My warmest thanks to Christopher Ridgway for this information.

3 Maurice Dreyfous, *Dalou, sa vie et son oeuvre*, Paris 1903, p.79.

4 Boehm: post-mortem sale, London, 6 Feb. 1891, cat.110; Holman Hunt: Sotheby's sale, London, 16 March 1983, cat.170; Hutchinson: post-mortem sale, London, 25 Feb. 1892, cat.170.

153 *French Peasant Woman Nursing a Baby*

1 Maurice Dreyfous, *Dalou, sa vie et son oeuvre*, Paris 1903, pp.62, 51–2.

2 With appreciation and thanks to Alicia Robinson, Antonia Bostrom, Victor Borges, Sara Mittica and their colleagues at the Victoria and Albert Museum for having shared these observations made from an x-ray of the work.

3 See Diane Bilbey with Marjorie Trusted, *British Sculpture 1470–2000: A Concise Catalogue of the Collection in the Victoria and Albert Museum*, London 2002, cat.367.

4 '"*TIENS TOI DONC TRANQUILLE !*" (with Apologies to M. Dalon [sic])' (HOLD STILL!): *Punch, or the London Charivari*, 1 Feb. 1875, repr. p.38; my thanks to Leonee Ormond who alerted me to this engraving and to Shirley Nicholson who found it.

154 *Rosalind Howard*/ID71 *George Howard*

1 Birmingham Museums and Art Gallery.

2 Maurice Dreyfous, *Dalou, sa vie et son oeuvre*, Paris 1903, p.51.

3 Howard Archives, Rosalind Howard diary, J23/102.

4 Howard Archives, Rosalind Howard Account Book, J23/105/4.

5 Edward Morris, *French Art in Nineteenth-Century Britain*, New Haven and London 2005, p.85.

6 Howard Archives, Letter to George Howard, J22/96/404.

7 Talon Rouge, 'The Social Week', *Vanity Fair*, 7 April 1877. Talon Rouge (Red Heel) was the pseudonym of Lord Ronald Sutherland Leveson Gower. Sculptor, art critic and politician, he was trained in the studio of Carrier-Belleuse in Paris in 1875–7; brother-in-law of the Duke of Westminster, he was also close to George Howard.

8 Diane Bilbey with Marjorie Trusted, *British Sculpture 1470–2000: A Concise Catalogue of the Collection in the Victoria and Albert Museum*, London 2002, cat.381.

9 Charles Roberts, *The Radical Countess: The History of the Life of Rosalind Countess of Carlisle*, Carlisle 1962; Virginia Surtees, *The Artist and the Autocrat: George and Rosalind Howard, Earl and Countess of Carlisle*, Salisbury 1988.

165–7 *Bust of Laura Theresa Epps, Lady Alma-Tadema/Jules Dalou, his Wife and Daughter*

1 Letter from Lawrence Alma-Tadema to Léonce Bénédite, 15 Feb. 1907, file for the work RF 1977-23, Musée d'Orsay documentation.

2 File for the work RF 2307, Musée d'Orsay documentation.

3 Letter, 15 Feb. 1907 from Lawrence Alma-Tadema to Léonce Bénédite, 15 Feb. 1907, Musée d'Orsay (as n.1).

4 Ibid.

158–9 *Woman Reading in an Armchair (Mrs Dalou Reading)/English Sketchbook No.1/Woman Reading (Mrs Dalou Reading)/Woman Doing a Little Girl's Hair (Mrs Dalou and Georgette?)*

1 Signed and dated 1877 on the work, on loan from Manchester Art Galleries to the Victoria and Albert Museum, London.

2 Letter to Cornaglia, 3 Dec. 1879, Musée d'Orsay RF 2465.

3 Maurice Dreyfous, *Dalou, sa vie et son oeuvre*, Paris 1903, p.29: 'quand on est assez fort pour marcher tout seul, on ne se met pas dans les souliers de Carrier-Belleuse'; p.55.

4 Dreyfous 1903, p.29.

5 Ibid.d, p.59, repr.: 'A celle qui a inspiré cette statue. J. Dalou. 1875'.

160 *Hush-a-Bye, Baby*, or *The Rocking Chair*

1 Amélie Simier, *Jules Dalou, le sculpteur de la République*, Paris 2013, cat.289.

2 John Dubouloz, 'Lettres Anglaises – le Salon Anglais,' *Gazette des Beaux-Arts* 1874, vol.2, repr. p.178.

3 Letter to Cornaglia, 9 April 1879, Musée d'Orsay, RF 2465.

4 John Dubouloz, 'London Season', *L'Art*, vol.2, 1876, repr. p.39; *Illustrated London News*, 26 Aug. 1876, repr. p.197.

5 Edward Morris, 'The sculpture collections at Eaton Hall, Cheshire, 1820–1914,' *Sculpture Journal*, Jan. 2010, vol.19, no.1, pp.62–78, esp. p.62.

161 *Arthur St Clair Anstruther Thomson*

1 Colonel Anstruther Thomson, *Eighty Years' Reminiscences*, London 1904, 2 vols.

2 Mark Stocker, *Royalist and Realist: The Life and Work of Sir Joseph Edgar Boehm*, New York and London 1988, pp.14–16; Anstruther Thomson 1904, vol.1, pp.361–8.

3 Amélie Simier, '*Ni moulage sur nature ni photographie ne seront jamais de l'art*. Quelques réflexions autour de la découverte de photographies de *Cache-cache* d'Aimé Jules Dalou', *Mélanges Anne Pingeot*, Paris 2008, pp.188–91, repr. p.189.

4 Maurice Dreyfous *Dalou, sa vie et son oeuvre* Paris 1903, p.78

5 Christie's Sale, London, 20 March 1984, cat. 28. My thanks to Dr Godfrey Evans, Principal Curator of European Decorative Arts at the National Museums Scotland, who shared his knowledge.

6 A suggestion made by Gordon Balderston, whom I thank.

162 *Bust of a Young Man*

1 Reported by Jolyon Drury in the biography of his father, the engraver Paul Drury, son of Alfred Drury – Jolyon Drury, *Revelation to Revolution: The Legacy of Samuel Palmer: The Revival and Evolution of Pastoral Printmaking by Paul Drury and the Goldsmiths School in the 20th Century*, Ashford 2006, pp.228–9 – and in Ben Thomas (ed.), *Alfred Drury and the New Sculpture*, exh. cat., Studio 3 Gallery, University of Kent, Canterbury 2013, p.7.

2 Maurice Dreyfous, *Dalou, sa vie et son oeuvre*, Paris 1903, p.70.

3 Dreyfous 1903, p.70.

4 John Park, *Study from Model by J. Dalou*, British Museum, 1879-0510-477.

163 *Sketch for 'An Athlete Wrestling with a Python'*

1 Edmund Gosse, 'The New Sculpture: 1879–1894', *Art Journal*, vol.56, p.140.

2 Richard and Leonee Ormond (eds.), *Frederick Leighton, 1830–1896*, exh. cat., Royal Academy of Arts, London 1996, p.182.

3 David Getsy, *Body Doubles: Sculpture in Britain, 1877–1905*, New Haven and London 2004, p.191 n.11.

4 Emilie [Mrs Russell] Barrington, *The Life, Letters and Work of Frederick Leighton*, 2 vols., London 1906, pp.178, 200.

164 *Italian Peasant*

1 Amélie Simier, *Jules Dalou, le sculpteur de la République*, Paris 2013, cats.132–241.

165 *Alfred Lord Tennyson*

1 See Timothy Wilcox, *Alphonse Legros, 1837–1911*, exh. cat., Musée des Beaux-Arts de Dijon, 1987, p.139.

2 Wilcox 1987, p.140.

3 Quoted in the *Derby Daily Telegraph*, 16 Jan. 1882, p.4.

4 Philip Attwood, *Artistic Circles: The Medal in Britain, 1880–1918*, London 1992, p.7.

5 With my grateful thanks to Leonee Ormond for her help with this entry.

166–7 *Head of a Peasant/Proserpinae Cultor/Joseph Edgar Boehm/Modelling: A Guide for Teachers and Students*

1 Mark Stocker, *Royalist and Realist: The Life and Work of Joseph Edgar Boehm*, New York and London 1988, p.34.

2 It was known as the Royal College of Art from 1896. Lantéri had been Assistant Master of Modelling there since 1874 (see Melissa Hamnett below, n.7).

3 Stocker 1988, p.332 n.112.

4 Spielmann 1988, p.125.

5 Marion H. Spielmann, *British Sculpture and Sculptors of Today*, London 1901, p.127.

6 Edouard Lantéri, *Modelling: A Guide for Teachers and Students*, London 1904, vol.2, pp.72–88.

7 See Melissa Hamnett, 'Edouard Lantéri: Sculptor, medallist and mentor', *The Medal*, no.63, 2013, pp.4–23, esp. p.11, reproducing the medal and statuette of 'the fencing master'.

8 Edgcumbe Staley, 'Edward Lantéri, Artist and Teacher', in *Art Journal*, 1903, pp.241–5, esp. p.243.

9 F. Parkes Weber, 'Medals and Medallions of the Nineteenth Century, Relating to England, by Foreign Artists', *The Numismatic Chronicle and Journal of the Numismatic*

Society, Third Series, vol.14 (1894), pp.101–78, esp. p.163.

168 *Fraternity*

1 National Art Library, Victoria and Albert Museum, London, DALOU 86.WW.1 MSL/1975/5116/581.
2 Amélie Simier, *Jules Dalou, le sculpteur de la République*, Paris 2013, pp.84–5.
3 Edouard Lantéri, *Modelling and Sculpting the Human Figure* and *Modelling and Sculpting Animals*, New York 1985, figs.101, 106.
4 Musée d'Orsay, RF 2465.

169 *George Frederic Watts, O.M., R.A.*

1 A report in a newspaper in July, however, commented on 'the splendid piece of golden bronze, flashing with vitality and movement' (*Western Mail*, 1 July 1889). The original plaster is in the collection of the Royal Academy.
2 *Pall Mall Gazette*, April 1889, p.1.
3 Mary Watts, *George Frederic Watts: The Annals of an Artist's Life*, 3 vols., London 1912, vol.2, p.135.
4 Richard Dorment (ed.), *Alfred Gilbert: Sculptor and Goldsmith*, exh. cat., Royal Academy of Arts, London 1986, p.120.
5 Quoted in Melissa Hamnett, 'Edouard Lantéri: Sculptor, medallist and mentor', *The Medal*, no.63, 2013, pp.4–25, esp. p.7.
6 Quoted in Isabel McAllister, 'Edward Lantéri: Sculptor and Professor', *The Studio*, vol.57, 1912–13, pp.25–31, esp. p.25.

Jean-Baptiste Carpeaux In the Footsteps of his Idols (pp.171–5)

1 On 17 March 1874 Carpeaux wrote from London to his lawyer, Thomas Nicquevert, telling him that he was hoping to stay until the end of July: Valenciennes, Archives Municipales, Fonds Carpeaux, Dossier intime VI (1G), ph57–8, fol.16v. The Christie's sale was held in London on 11 March 1874.
2 Letter from Carpeaux addressed to Dalou c/o Mr. Buhm (J.E. Boehm), 14 May 1874: Fonds Becker.
3 E. and J. de Goncourt, *Portraits intimes du XVIIIe siècle*, 1st series, Paris 1857, pp.193–271.
4 E. and J. de Goncourt, *Journal*, 3 vols., ed. Robert Laffont, Paris 1989, vol.1, pp.1145–6 (entry for 16 March 1865).
5 Goncourt 1857, pp.245–8.
6 C. Clément, *Géricault* (reimpression of the third edition of 1879), Paris 1973, p.194.
7 E.-D. Fromentin, 'Jean-Baptiste Carpeaux', *Valentiana, Revue d'histoire des pays du Hainaut français*, no.19, June 1997, p.169.
8 Fromentin 1997, p.169.
9 Goncourt 1989, pp.892, 939.
10 See Véronique Belle, *D'ombre de bronze et de marbre: Sculptures en Val-de-Marne*, [Nantes] 1999, p.92. Also Tom Stammers, 'Scavenging Rococo; *trouvailles*, bibelots and counter-revolution', in M. Lee-Hyde and K. Scott (eds.), *Rococo Echo: Art History and Historiography from Cochin to Coppola*, Oxford 2014, p.71, and À nos grands hommes, 2 CD set, repertory of commemorative monuments in France, Musée d'Orsay and INHA, with Macromedia, 2004.
11 P. Rosenberg and L.-A. Prat, *Antoine Watteau 1684–1721. Catalogue raisonné des dessins*, 3 vols., Milan 1996, vol.2, pp.758–9, cat.445. The drawing is in the Musée Cognacq-Jay, Paris.
12 E. Morris, *French Art in Nineteenth-Century Britain*, New Haven and London 2005, p.247.
13 Louise Clément-Carpeaux, *La vérité sur l'oeuvre et la vie de J.-B. Carpeaux (1827–1875)*, 2 vols., Paris 1934–5, vol.1, p.332.
14 Fromentin 1997, pp.168, 198.
15 See P. Ramade and L. de Margerie (eds.), *Carpeaux peintre*, exh. cat., Musée des Beaux-Arts de Valenciennes, 1999.
16 *The Exhibition of the Royal Academy of Arts, 1873*, London 1873, p.58, no.1509, and sale catalogue, Christie, Manson & Woods, 2 April 1903, lot 136.
17 Letter from Carpeaux to Dumas, 19 Nov. 1874, in Fromentin 1997, p.198.
18 *Leeds Mercury*, 22 Dec. 1874.
19 Goncourt 1989, vol.1, p.1190 (entry for 3 Sept. 1865).
20 Letter of 26 July 1863 in Fromentin 1997, p.101; and Goncourt 1989, vol.1, p.190 (entry for 3 Sept. 1865).
21 Goncourt 1857, p.204.
22 *The Examiner*, 11 July 1874, p.747.
23 'Celebrities at Home, no.CCXXI, Mr J.G. [sic] Boehm A.R.A at The Avenue', *The World*, no.333, 17 Nov. 1880, pp.3–5.
24 *Art Journal*, Jan. 1876, p.12.
25 The plaster of Dalou's *Bacchanal*, exhibited at the Royal Academy in 1879, is now in the Victoria and Albert Museum, London (434-1896).

178–9 *Henry James Turner*/ID98 *Mrs Henry James Turner* 1871

1 Musée d'Orsay, inv. RF 8678.

182 *Daphnis and Chloe*

1 Letter from Jean-Baptiste Carpeaux to Alexander Dumas *fils*, 19 Nov. 1874, cited by Michel Poletti, *Jean-Baptiste Carpeaux, l'homme qui faisait danser les pierres*, Paris 2012, p.179.

183 *Jean-Léon Gérôme*

1 Letter from Gérôme to Fromentin, 25 Aug. 1878, cited in Édouard-Désiré Fromentin, 'Jean-Baptiste Carpeaux. Essai biographique : la vie, l'œuvre du statuaire valenciennois d'après sa correspondance' (MS loaned to the Bibliothèque nationale in 1922), *Valentiana, Revue d'histoire des pays du Hainaut français*, no.19, June 1997, pp.169–70.

184–5 *Bust of Charles Gounod*/Visitors' Book, Tavistock House, Tavistock Square, London

1 Letter from Gounod to Fromentin, 28 Oct. 1876, cited in Édouard-Désiré Fromentin, 'Jean-Baptiste Carpeaux. Essai biographique : la vie, l'œuvre du statuaire valenciennois d'après sa correspondance' (MS loaned to the Bibliothèque nationale in 1922), *Valentiana, Revue d'histoire des pays du Hainaut français*, no.19, June 1997, p.178.
2 My thanks to Philip Ward-Jackson for bringing my attention to both Georgina Weldon's visitors' book and her diary.

Through French Eyes (pp.191–5)

1 Elisée Reclus, *Londres illustré, guide spécial pour l'exposition de 1862*, Paris 1862; Alphonse Esquiros, *Guide Joanne de l'Angleterre*, in Richard Audin, *Itinéraire descriptif et historique de l'Écosse, l'Angleterre et l'Irlande*, Paris 1867; also Alphonse Esquiros, *L'Angleterre et la vie anglaise*, Paris 1859.
2 Reclus 1862, pp.32–6.
3 Thomas Jones and Robert Tombs, 'The French left in exile: Quarante-huitards and Communards in London, 1848–80', in Debra Kelly and Martyn Cornick (eds.), *A History of the French in London: Liberty, Equality, Opportunity*, London 2013, p.169.
4 Jones and Tombs 2013, p.172.
5 Charles Dickens, *Household Words*, 12 March 1853, p.26.
6 Notre Dame de France (church), Leicester Place, established 1861; George Sala, *Things I Have Seen and People I Have Known*, London 1894, vol.2, pp.243–4.
7 See Karl Baedeker, *Londres suivi d'excursions dans l'Angleterre du Sud*, Koblenz 1866, more detailed than the English edition *Great Britain Handbook for Travellers*, p.8.
8 Isabelle Janvrin and Catherine Rawlinson, *The French in London: From William the Conqueror to Charles de Gaulle*, London 2016, p.221.
9 Thanks to Krystyna Matyjaszkiewicz for clarifying Tissot's addresses in London.
10 According to the 1871 Census, Camille and Jean Monet shared a lodging house with nine others at 1 Bath Place (now Kensington High Street).
11 Poncerot's full name is not known, Cortepon (Poncerot): letter to Jules Vallès, 2 Feb. 1878, in Gerard Delfau, *Jules Vallès, L'Exil à Londres 1870–1880*, Paris 1971, p.167; see Paul Martinez, 'Paris Communard Refugees in Britain, 1871–1880', D.Phil thesis, University of Sussex 1981, p.206.
12 Rachel Pissarro lived at 100 Rosendale Road and Alfred Pissarro and his family on Knight's Hill.
13 Graham Robb, *Rimbaud*, New York 2000, pp.196–7.
14 Reclus 1862, p.42.
15 Nancy Rose Marshall and Malcolm Warner, *James Tissot: Modern Life/Modern Love*, New Haven and London 1999, p.64.
16 James Abbott McNeill Whistler, *A Series of Sixteen Etchings of Scenes on the Thames*, London 1871.
17 Letter from Lucian Pissarro to Camille Pissarro.
18 Reclus 1862, pp.438–69; see also three chapters in Alphonse Esquiros, *Religious Life in England*, London 1867, pp.190–238.
19 Letter from Camille Pissarro to Wynford Dewhurst, 6 Nov. 1902, quoted in Wynford Dewhurst, *Impressionist Painting: Its Genesis and Development*, London 1904, p.31.
20 Christ Church needle spire, still standing although the church is destroyed, and St James, Sussex Gardens: Nicholas Reid, *Monet and the Thames: Paintings and Modern Views of Monet's London*, London 1998, p.14.
21 Esquiros 1867b, p.185.
22 Alphonse Esquiros, *The English at Home: Essays from the 'Revue des Deux Mondes'* (1861), trans. Frederick Wraxall, London 1863, p.370.
23 For example, '"Rotten Row in the Season", a sketch of a portion of the painting by the late GH Thomas', *The Graphic*, 5 July 1873, double-page insert.
24 Charles Baudelaire, 'Le Peintre de la vie moderne', *Le Figaro*, 26 and 29 Nov., and 3 Dec. 1863.
25 Ralph E. Shikes and Paula Harper, *Pissarro: His Life and Work*, London 1980, p.90.
26 Isabelle Tombs and Robert Tombs, *That Sweet Enemy: The British and the French from the Sun King to the Present*, London 2010, pp.413–14.
27 Exhibition at the Royal Academy, *Times*, 2 May 1874, p.12.
28 Esquiros 1863, pp.369–70.
29 Dominique Morel et al., *Giuseppe de Nittis: La modernité élégante*, exh. cat., Petit Palais, Paris, 2010, cat.64, p.188.
30 Henry Mayhew, *London Labour and the London Poor; an Encyclopaedia of the condition of earnings of those that will, work, those that cannot work, and those that will not work*, London 1840–1851, 3 vols.; Alexandre Ledru-Rollin, *De la décadence de l'Angleterre*, Paris 1850; Jules Vallès, 'La Rue à Londres' series published in *L'Événement*, and 'La Rue à Londres' published in *Le Voltaire*, reprinted in Jules Vallès, *La Rue à Londres*, Paris 1884; Gustave Doré and Blanchard Jerrold, *London: A Pilgrimage*, London 1872.
31 Jules Vallès, series 'La Rue à Londres' published in *L'Événement* and 'La Rue à Londres' published in *Le Voltaire*, reprinted in Jules Vallès, *La Rue à Londres*, Paris 1884, pp.4, 14.
32 Vallès 1884, pp.2–20 (the first chapter 'La Rue', where the policeman and other types are surveyed).
33 Sabine Freitag (ed.), *Exiles from European Revolution: Refugees in Mid-Victorian England*, London and New York 2003, p.91.
34 Letter from Victor Schoelcher to Louis Blanc, 25 June 1863, in Nelly Schmidt (ed.), *La correspondance de Victor Schoelcher*, Paris 1995, p.255; Hippolyte Taine, *Notes sur l'Angleterre*, Paris 1872, translated by W. Rae, *Notes on England*, New York 1885, pp.376–7.
35 'Exhibition at the Royal Academy: Third Notice,' *Illustrated London News*, 16 May 1874, p.470.
36 Charles Hugo, *Les Hommes de l'exil*, Paris 1875, p.324.
37 Ledru-Rollin, Paris 1850, p.3.
38 Letter from Camille Pissarro to Wynford Dewhurst, 6 Nov. 1902, quoted in Dewhurst 1904, p.31.
39 Taine 1885, pp.25–6.
40 Hector Malot, *La vie moderne en Angleterre*, Paris 1862, quoted in Christine Geoffroy and Richard Sibley (eds.), *Going Abroad: Travel, Tourism, and Migration. Cross-Cultural Perspectives on Mobility*, Cambridge 2009, p.33.
41 Letter from Claude Monet to Alice Monet, 16 March 1900, in Daniel Wildenstein, *Claude Monet: Biographie et catalogue raisonné*, Lausanne and Paris 1974, vol.1, no.1530.
42 Nancy Ireson, 'André Derain's Wild London', in Rémi Labrusse, Ernst Vegelin van Claerbergen and Barnaby Wright, *André Derain: The London Paintings*, exh. cat., Courtauld Institute, London 2005, p.60.

196 *The Ball on Shipboard*

1 'Exhibition at the Royal academy', *Tablet*, 27 June 1874, p.810.

2 Krystyna Matyjaszkiewicz, 'Royalty, Romance and Rivalry: Unlocking James Tissot's Ball on Shipboard and related works', forthcoming paper, 2017.

3 'Entertaining on Board H.M.S. Ariadne at Cowes', *Morning Post*, 18 Aug. 1873, p.5.

4 James Tissot, '2nd Earl of Wilton', *Vanity Fair*, 23 Aug. 1873.

5 Dorothy Bailey, in communication with Willard Misfeldt, 'James Jaques Tissot: A Bio-Critical Study', PhD thesis, Washington University, 1971, p.151.

6 'Dress', *London Society*, 1867, p.286, quoted in Susan David Bernstein and Elsie Browning Michie, *Victorian Vulgarity: Taste in Verbal and Visual Culture*, Farnham 2009, p.211.

199 *The Bridge at Hampton Court, Mitre Inn*

1 Théodore Duret, *Histoire des Peintres impressionistes*, Paris 1906, p.38.

200–1 *Hyde Park*

1 The spire and tower of Christ Church still exist, but were converted into housing in the late 1970s. The block of flats is now known as Spire House.

202–3 *Holyday*

1 Willard Misfeldt, 'James Jaques Tissot: A Bio-Critical Study', PhD thesis, Washington University, 1971, p.127.

2 Oscar Wilde, 'The Grosvenor Gallery, 1877', *Dublin University Magazine*, 1877, pp.125–6.

204 *Hampton Court Green*

1 Élisée Reclus, *Londres illustré, guide spécial pour l'exposition de 1862*, Paris 1862, p.203.

2 F. de Bernhardt, *Londres et la vie à Londres*, Paris 1906, p.124.

3 Letter to Georges Pissarro, Paris 13 May 1890, no.589, in Janine Bailly-Herzberg (ed.), *Correspondance de Camille Pissarro*, 3 vols., Paris 1986, vol.2, p.352.

205 *Kew Gardens, Rhododendron Dell*

1 W.J. Bean, *The Royal Botanic Gardens, Kew: Historical and Descriptive*, London 1908.

2 William Jackson Hooker, *Kew Garden, or a Popular guide to the royal botanic gardens of Kew*, London 1857, p.104.

3 Letter to Durand-Ruel, London, 10 June 1892, no.791, in Janine Bailly-Herzberg (ed.), *Correspondance de Camille Pissarro*, 3 vols., Paris 1986, vol.2, p.238.

4 *Entretiens*, vol.6, no.40, 10 April 1893, p.332.

206 *St Anne's Church in Kew/Kew Green*

1 Letter to Durand-Ruel, Kew, 6 July 1892, no.801bis, in Janine Bailly-Herzberg (ed.), *Correspondance de Camille Pissarro*, 3 vols., Paris 1986, vol.2, p.246.

1 Letter to Julie Pissarro, Kew, 6 July 1892, no.801, in Bailly-Herzberg 1986, p.245.

208–9 *Westminster/Piccadilly: Wintry Walk in London*

1 Tulliola Sparagni, 'De Nittis à Londres: impressions d'un "étranger de passage"', in *Giuseppe de Nittis: La modernité élégante*, exh. cat., Petit Palais, Paris, 2010, p.42.

2 Sparagni 2010, cat.64, p.188.

3 Quoted in Sparagni 2010, cat.68, p.197.

214 *Leicester Square at Night*

1 Then New Coventry Street.

2 Daniel Wildenstein, *Monet: Catalogue Raisonné*, 4 vols., Köln 1996, vol.4, p.720.

3 Daniel Wildenstein, *Claude Monet: Biographie et catalogue raisonné*, Lausanne and Paris 1974, vol.4, no.1592, 2 Feb. 1901.

4 Wildenstein 1974, vol.4, no.1606a, 17 Feb. 1901.

5 See Wildenstein 1974, vol.4, no.1608c, 22 Feb. 1901.

6 Daniel Wildenstein, *Claude Monet: Biographie et catalogue raisonné: supplément aux peintures, dessins, pastels*, Lausanne and Paris 1991, vol.5, no.2999 (no.1609a), 25 Feb. 1901.

7 Wildenstein 1974, vol.4, no.1610, 26 Feb. 1901.

8 See Wildenstein 1991, vol.5, no.2999 (no.1609a).

216 *Nocturne: Blue and Silver – Chelsea/Nocturne: Blue and Silver – Cremorne Lights/Nocturne: Blue and Gold – Old Battersea Bridge*

1 Margaret MacDonald and Patricia de Montfort, *An American in London: Whistler and the Thames*, London 2013, p.14.

2 Richard Dorment and Margaret F. MacDonald, *James McNeill Whistler*, exh. cat., Tate Gallery, London 1994, p.122.

3 *The Era*, 27 Oct. 1872, issue 1779.

4 Review of the Dudley Gallery in *The Examiner*, 13 Nov. 1875, no.3537.

5 Letter from Whistler to Henri Fantin-Latour, 4 Jan.–3 Feb. 1864, Library of Congress PWC 1/33/15; Margaret F. McDonald, Patricia de Montfort and Nigel Thorp (eds.), *The Correspondence of James McNeill Whistler, 1855–1903*, online edition, University of Glasgow, GUW 08036: http://www.whistler.arts.gla.ac.uk/correspondence.

6 Letter from Whistler to Helen Euphrosyne Whistler, Oct./Nov. 1879, GUL MS Whistler W680; McDonald et al., *Correspondence of James McNeill Whistler*, GUW 06686.

7 Quoted in MacDonald and de Montfort 2013, p.145 n.127.

8 MacDonald and de Montfort 2013, p.145.

9 Letter from Whistler to Henri Fantin-Latour, [May 1864], Library of Congress PWC 1/33/19; McDonald et al., *Correspondence of James McNeill Whistler*, GUW 08039.

220 *On the Thames*

1 George Dunlop Leslie, *Our River Thames*, London 1881, p.257.

221 *Workers on the Silent Highway* 1877

1 *Punch*, 10 July 1858, no.35.

222 *Charing Cross Bridge, London* 1890

1 Janine Bailly-Herzberg, vol.II, no.584.

2 Letter to Esther Isaacson, Ibid., no.594.

The Thames and Westminster (pp.225–31)

1 René Gimpel, *Journal d'un collectionneur, marchand de tableaux*, Paris 1963, pp.88, 156: diary entries for 28 Nov. 1918 and 1 Feb. 1920.

2 Mr and Mrs S.C. Hall, *The Book of the Thames* (first published 1859), London [1877], p.418.

3 See Gary Tinterow and Henri Loyrette, *Origins of Impressionism*, exh. cat., Metropolitan Museum of Art, New York 1994, pp.24–5.

4 The *frotté* ('rubbed'), or *frottis*, technique relies on the vigorous application of a thin layer of oil to create depth, usually prior to subsequent layering.

5 Elisée Reclus, *Londres illustré, guide spécial pour l'exposition de 1862*, Paris 1862, p.159.

6 Reclus 1862, p.160.

7 Hippolyte Taine, *Notes on England*, trans. W.F. Rae, New York 1885, p.221.

8 Whether or not Monet knew de Nittis's painting remains speculative, but de Nittis bought four of Monet's pictures, including *Les Dindons* and *Vue de l'ancien port du Havre*, respectively acquired in 1877 and 1878, so it is likely that he did.

9 *Repoussoir* is the use, in the extreme foreground and to one side, of an object or figure(s) to direct the viewer's attention to the main subject of the painting.

10 Marius Vachon, *Les Peintres* étrangers *à l'exposition universelle de 1878*, Paris 1878, p.14.

11 Robin Spencer, 'The Aesthetics of Chance: London as seen by James McNeill Whistler', in Malcolm Warner, *The Image of London: Views by Travellers and Emigrés, 1550–1920*, exh. cat., Barbican Art Gallery, London 1987, p.52.

12 Oscar Wilde, 'The Decay of Lying', first published in *Nineteenth Century*, Jan. 1889, here quoted from revised version in *Intentions*, 1891, p.40.

13 *Mr Whistler's 'Ten o'Clock'*, first published 1888, reprinted in James McNeill Whistler, *The Gentle Art of Making Enemies*, London 1890, p.144.

14 Théophile Gautier, 'Une journée à Londres', *Revue des deux mondes*, 15 April 1842, p.282.

15 Anthea Callen, *Jean-Baptiste Faure, 1830–1914: A Study of a Patron and Collector of the Impressionists and their Contemporaries with a Catalogue of his Collection* (MA thesis, University of Leicester), Leicester 1971, p.331.

16 Quoted by Grace Seiberling, *Monet in London*, exh. cat., High Museum of Art, Atlanta, GA 1988, p.34.

17 Katharine Lochnan, 'Whistler and Monet: Impressionism and Britain', in Lee Glazer et al. (eds.), *James McNeill Whistler in Context: Essays from the Whistler Centenary Symposium, University of Glasgow, 2003*, Washington, DC 2008, pp.45–64, esp. p.56.

18 The purchase of a house at Eragny and his wife's attachment to it prevented this.

19 Janine Bailly-Herzberg (ed.), *Correspondance de Camille Pissarro*, Paris 1986, vol.2, no.584.

20 Bailly-Herzberg 1986, no.591.

21 He may have known the painting from the collection of Jean-Baptiste Faure or, more likely, from the 1889 *Monet Rodin* exhibition at the Galerie Georges Petit.

22 François Thiébault-Sisson, 'Un nouveau musée parisien: Les Nymphéas de Claude Monet: L'Orangerie des Tuileries', *Revue de l'art ancien et moderne*, no.52 (1927), p.48, quoted in Seiberling 1988, p.14.

23 E. Bullet, 'Macmonnies, the sculptor, working hard as a painter', *Brooklyn Eagle*, 8 Sept. 1901, quoted in John House, 'The Impressionist Vision of London', in Ira Bruce Nadel and F.S. Schwarzbach (eds.), *Victorian Artists and the City: A Collection of Critical Essays*, New York and Oxford 1980, p.88.

24 The term appeared in a letter to G. Geffroy at the beginning of the Grain Stacks series, 7 Oct. 1890: Daniel Wildenstein, *Claude Monet: Biographie et catalogue raisonné*, Lausanne and Paris 1974, vol.3, no.1076.

25 Ibid.

26 He did not return to London to paint after 1901, but spent his winters working on the Thames series at Giverny.

27 Letter from Claude to Alice Monet, 16 March 1900, in Wildenstein, *1974, vol.4*, no.1530.

28 Letter from Monet to Durand-Ruel, 8 Dec. 1904, in Wildenstein 1974, vol.4, no.1751.

232-3 *Houses of Parliament, Sunlight Effect/ Houses of Parliament/ Houses of Parliament, Sunset/Houses of Parliament, Fog Effect/Houses of Parliament (Effect of Fog)/Houses of Parliament, Effect of Sunlight in the Fog/Charing Cross Bridge/ Charing Cross Bridge*

1 In 1899 Monet stayed in room 641, and in 1900 in room 541, which he used as a studio, sleeping in room 542. These rooms have since been remodelled, but roughly correspond to room 508. See Nicholas Reed, *Monet and the Thames*, London 1998, pp.42–3.

2 Letter from Claude Monet to Alice Monet, 17 Feb., 4 pm, translated and reproduced in Sylvie Patin, *Monet in Great Britain*, Vanves 1994, p.90.

3 Letter to Alice Monet, 18 March 1900, 5 pm, reproduced in Patin 1994, p.93.

4 Letter to Alice Monet, 25 March 1900, reproduced in Patin 1994, p.95.

5 See conservation analysis in online catalogue, *Monet Paintings and Drawings at the Art Institute of Chicago*: http://www.artic.edu/research/digital-publications/online-scholarly-catalogues.

6 Letter to Alice Monet, 28 March 1900, 6.30 p.m., reproduced in Patin 1994, p.95.

7 Letter to Alice Monet, 10 March 1901, reproduced in Patin 1994, p.97.

8 See Grace Seiberling, *Monet in London*, Seattle and London 1988, pp.74–90; Patin 1994, pp.80–2; and Daniel Wildenstein, *Monet: Catalogue Raisonné*, 4 vols., Köln 1996, vol.1, p.364.

9 *Claude Monet: Vues de la Tamise à Londres* was due to finish on 4 June, but was extended.

10 Seiberling 1988, p.62.

11 Wildenstein 1996, vol.1, p.345. *Monet Paintings and Drawings at the Art Institute of Chicago*, online resource, https://publications.artic.edu/monet/reader/paintingsanddrawings/section/135618, cat.41, accessed 24 Nov 2016.

12 Seiberling 1988, p.54.

242 *Charing Cross Bridge, London/Big Ben/The Pool of London/Barges on the Thames*

1 Louis Vauxcelles, 'Le Salon d'Automne', *Gil Blas*, supplement, no.6, 17 Oct. 1905.

2 Letter from André Derain to Ronald Alley, 15 May 1953, in Ronald Alley, *Catalogue of the Tate Gallery's Collection of Modern Art Other than Works by British Artists*, London 1981, pp.167–8.

3 Letter from André Derain to Ambrose Vollard, in Ambrose Vollard, *Souvenirs d'un marchand de tableaux*, Paris 1957, p.256.

4 Louis Vauxcelles, 'Le Salon des

Indépendants', *Gil Blas*, 20 March 1906.
5 François Crucy, 'Le Salon des Indépendants', *L'Aurore*, 21 March 1906.
6 Letter from André Derain to Maurice Vlaminck, June 1904, in *André Derain, Lettres à Vlaminck*, Paris 1994.
7 Rémi Labrusse, Ernst Vegelin van Claerbergen and Barnaby Wright, *André Derain: The London Paintings*, exh. cat., Courtauld Institute of Art, London 2005, pp.13–14.
8 Rémi Labrusse and Jacqueline Munck, 'André Derain in London', in Labrusse et al. 2005, p.26.
9 Letter from André Derain to Henri Matisse, 25 March–5 April (?), reproduced in Labrusse et al. 2005, pp.136–7.
10 John Ruskin, Letter 79, July 1877, in E.T. Cook and Alexander Wedderburn (eds.), *The Works of John Ruskin*, vol.29, *Fors Clavigera*, London 1907, p.161; André Derain, letter to Henri Matisse, 25 March–5 April (?), reproduced in Labrusse et al. 2005, pp.136–7.
11 Letter from André Derain to Henri Matisse, 8 March 1906, quoted by Nancy Ireson, 'André Derain's Wild London', in Labrusse et al. 2005, p.58.
12 Ibid.
13 John House, 'The Thames Transfigured, André Derain's London', in Labrusse et al. 2005, p.39.
14 House 2005, pp.38–9.
15 House 2005, p.48.
16 Fernande Olivier, *Picasso et ses Amis*, Paris 1933, p.125.
17 Letter from André Derain to Ronald Alley, 15 May 1953, in Alley 1981, p.168.

Publications Cited

À nos grands hommes, 2 CD set, repertory of commemorative monuments in France, Musée d'Orsay and INHA, with Macromedia, 2004
Jane Abdy, 'Amici e ospiti londinesi di Tissot', in Angiuli and Spurrell 2006, pp.53–9
Kathleen Adler, *Pissarro in London*, London 2003
Ronald Alley, *Catalogue of the Tate Gallery's Collection of Modern Art Other than Works by British Artists*, London 1981
Tomoko Ando, 'Rodin's Reputation in Great Britain: The Neglected Role of Alphonse Legros', *Nineteenth-Century Art Worldwide*, Autumn 2016: http://www.19thc-artworldwide.org/index.php/autumn16/ando-on-rodin-reputation-in-great-britain-neglected-role-of-alphonse-legros
Emanuela Angiuli and Katy Spurrell (eds.), *De Nittis ed Tissot*, Milan 2006
Colonel Anstruther Thomson, *Eighty Years' Reminiscences*, London 1904, 2 vols.
Walter Armstrong, 'Mr. Harry Bates', *Portfolio*, 1888, pp.170–4
Art Journal, 1870, vol.9
Art Journal, 1871, vol.33
Art Journal, Jan. 1876
The Athenaeum, no.2246, 12 Nov. 1870
Philip Attwood, *Artistic Circles: The Medal in Britain, 1880–1918*, London 1992
Karl Baedeker, *Londres suivi d'excursions dans l'Angleterre du Sud*, Koblenz 1866
Janine Bailly-Herzberg (ed.), *Correspondance de Camille Pissarro*, vol.1, Paris 1980
Janine Bailly-Herzberg (ed.), *Correspondance de Camille Pissarro*, vol.2, Paris 1986
Alfred Lys Baldry, 'A notable sculptor: Alfred Drury, A.R.A.', *The Studio*, 1906, vol.36
Emilie [Mrs Russell] Barrington, *The Life, Letters and Work of Frederick Leighton*, 2 vols., London 1906
Georges Bastard, 'Nos peintres. James Tissot. Note intimes', *Revue de Bretagne*, 1906, vol.36, pp.253–78
Charles Baudelaire, 'Le Peintre de la vie moderne', *Le Figaro*, 26 and 29 Nov., and 3 Dec. 1863
W.J. Bean, *The Royal Botanic Gardens, Kew: Historical and Descriptive*, London 1908
Susan Beattie, *The New Sculpture*, New Haven and London 1983
Alain Beausire and Florence Cadouot (eds.), *Correspondance de Rodin*, vol.1, Paris 1985
Véronique Belle, *D'ombre de bronze et de marbre: Sculptures en Val-de-Marne*, [Nantes] 1999
Léonce Bénédite, 'Alphonse Legros', *La Revue de l'Art*, 1897
Anisabelle Berès and Michel Arveiller, *François Bonvin: The Master of the 'Realist School' 1817–1887*, exh. cat., Galerie Berès, Paris 1998
F. de Bernhardt, *Londres et la vie à Londres*, Paris 1906
Diane Bilbey with Marjorie Trusted, *British Sculpture 1470–2000: A Concise Catalogue of the Collection in the Victoria and Albert Museum*, London 2002
Jonathan Black, 'The New (British) Sculpture and the struggle for realism between the wars', *Sculpture Journal*, vol.21(2), 2012, pp.23–36
François Blanchetière, *L'Enfer selon Rodin*, exh. cat., Musée Rodin, Paris 2016
Thomas Gibson Bowles, *The Defence of Paris; Narrated as it Was Seen*, London 1871
Thomas Gibson Bowles, *Flotsam and Jetsam*, London 1882
E. Bullet, 'Macmonnies, the sculptor, working hard as a painter', *Brooklyn Eagle*, 8 Sept. 1901
Ruth Butler, *Rodin, La solitude du génie*, Paris 1998
Françoise Cachin et al., *Manet 1832–1883*, exh. cat., Musée d'Orsay, Paris 1983, pp.323–5
Anthea Callen, *Jean-Baptiste Faure, 1830–1914: A Study of a Patron and Collector of the Impressionists and their Contemporaries with a Catalogue of his Collection* (MA thesis, University of Leicester), Leicester 1971
Thomas Cardoza, *Intrepid Women: Cantinières and Vivandières of the French Army*. Bloomington, IN 2010
Laurence des Cars, 'Carpeaux témoin de son temps : "des œuvres de voyant"', in *Carpeaux peintre*, exh. cat., Musée du Luxembourg, Paris 1998, pp.117–29
Jules Castagnary, *Gustave Courbet et la colonne Vendôme*, ed. Bertrand Tillier, Tusson 2000
'Celebrities at Home, no.CCXXI, Mr J.G. [sic] Boehm A.R.A at The Avenue', *The World*, no.333, 17 Nov. 1880, pp.3–5
Champfleury, *Le Réalisme*, Paris 1857
Christie, Manson & Woods, sale catalogue, 2 April 1903, lot 136
Jules Claretie, *Peintres et sculpteurs contemporains*, Paris 1873
C. Clément, *Géricault* (reimpression of the third edition of 1879), Paris 1973
Louise Clément-Carpeaux, *La vérité sur l'œuvre et la vie de J.-B. Carpeaux (1827–1875)*, 2 vols., Paris 1934–5
Sidney Colvin, 'The Etchings of M. Alphonse Legros', *Portfolio*, Jan. 1870, pp.140–1
'Le Communards peints par eux-mêmes', *Le Figaro*, 17 Aug. 1873
La Commune photographiée, exh. cat., Musée d'Orsay, Paris 2000
'Contemporary Portraits, new Series – No.26, M. Alphonse Legros', *University Magazine*, Feb. 1880
Correspondance de Courbet, ed. Petra ten-Doesschate Chu, Paris 1996
Correspondance entre Henri Fantin-Latour et Otto Scholderer, 1858–1902, ed. Mathilde Arnoux, Passages/Passagen series, Paris 2011
Correspondence between Henri Fantin-Latour and Otto Scholderer (1858–1902), ed. Mathilde Arnoux et al., Centre allemand d'histoire de l'art, 2014, http://quellen-perspectivia.net/fantin-scholderer, 1874 07
François Crucy, 'Le Salon des Indépendants', *L'Aurore*, 21 March 1906
Laure Dalon (ed.), *Fantin-Latour à fleur de peau*, exh. cat., Musée du Luxembourg, Paris 2016
Alfred Darcel, 'Les Musées, les arts et les artistes pendant la Commune', *Gazette des Beaux-Arts*, vol.5, 1872
Eric Darragon, *Manet*, Pluriel series, Paris 1991
François Daulte, *Alfred Sisley: Catalogue Raisonné de l'oeuvre peint*, Lausanne 1959
Louis Decamps, 'Exposition d'œuvres d'art exécutées en noir et blanc', *L'Art*, no.87, 27 Aug. 1976, pp.199–206
Gerard Delfau, *Jules Vallès, L'Exil à Londres 1870–1880*, Paris 1971
André Derain, *Lettres à Vlaminck*, Paris 1994
Derby Daily Telegraph, 16 Jan. 1882
Wynford Dewhurst, 'Impressionist painting: Its genesis and development', *The Studio*, no.29, 1903
Wynford Dewhurst, *Impressionist Painting: Its Genesis and Development*, London 1904
Diary of W.M. Rossetti, ed. O. Bornand, Oxford 1977
Charles Dickens, *Household Words*, 12 March 1853
Emilia, Mrs Pattison, Lady Dilke, 'Randolph Caldecott', *The Artist*, 1898, vol.22, pp.64–6
P. Dini and G.L. Martini, *De Nittis*, Turin 1990
Anne Distel, *Impressionism: The First Collectors*, New York 1990
Gustave Doré and Blanchard Jerrold, *London: A Pilgrimage*, London 1872
Richard Dorment (ed.), *Alfred Gilbert: Sculptor and Goldsmith*, exh. cat., Royal Academy of Arts, London 1986
Richard Dorment and Margaret F. MacDonald, *James McNeill Whistler*, exh. cat., Tate Gallery, London 1994
Oswald Doughty and John Robert Wahl, *Letters of Dante Gabriel Rossetti*, 4 vols., Oxford, 1965–7
James David Draper and Edouard Papet (eds.), *The Passions of Jean-Baptiste Carpeaux*, exh.cat., Metropolitan Museum of Art, New York 2014
Maurice Dreyfous, *Dalou, sa vie et son œuvre*, Paris 1903
Maurice Dreyfous, 'Alphonse Legros, peintre, dessinateur, graveur', *L'Art et les artistes*, Sept. 1908, pp.262–9
Jolyon Drury, *Revelation to Revolution: The Legacy of Samuel Palmer: The Revival and Evolution of Pastoral Printmaking by Paul Drury and the Goldsmiths School in the 20th Century*, Ashford 2006
John Dubouloz, 'Lettres anglaises – le Salon anglais', *Gazette des Beaux-Arts* 1874, vol.2, repr. p.178
Dudley Gallery Review in *The Examiner*, 13 Nov. 1875, no.3537
Daphne du Maurier (ed.), *The Young George du Maurier*, London 1951
Margaret Dunwoody, 'Alphonse Legros and the Etching Revival in Great Britain', MA thesis, Courtauld Institute of Art, London 1977
P. Durand-Ruel, *Memoirs of the First Impressionist Art Dealer (1831–1922)*, ed. P.-L. Durand-Ruel and F. Durand-Ruel, Paris 2014
Louis- Edmond Duranty, 'The New Painting: Concerning the Group of Artists Exhibiting at the Durand-Ruel Galleries, 1876', cited in translation in Charles Moffet (ed.), *The New Painting: Impressionism 1874–1886*, San Francisco 1986
Louis-Edmond Duranty, 'Ceux qui seront les peintres', in Fernand Desnoyers (ed.), *Almanach parisien, 6e année, 1867*, cited in translation in Michael Fried, *Manet's Modernism or, The Face of Painting in the 1860s*, Chicago and London 1996
Théodore Duret, *Histoire d'Edouard Manet et de son oeuvre*, Paris 1902
Théodore Duret, *Histoire des Peintres impressionistes*, Paris 1906
Marc Elder, *Chez Claude Monet à Giverny*, Paris 1924
Entretiens, vol.6, no.40, 10 April 1893, p.332
The Era, 27 Oct. 1872, issue 1779
Alphonse Esquiros, *L'Angleterre et la vie anglaise*, Paris 1859
Alphonse Esquiros, *The English at Home: Essays from the 'Revue des Deux Mondes'* (1861), trans. Frederick Wraxall, London 1863
Alphonse Esquiros, *Guide Joanne de l'Angleterre*, in Richard Audin, *Itinéraire descriptif et historique de l'Écosse, l'Angleterre et l'Irlande*, Paris 1867a
Alphonse Esquiros, *Religious Life in England*, London 1867b
The Examiner, 21 Jan. 1871
The Examiner, 11 July 1874
The Exhibition of the Royal Academy of Arts, 1873, London 1873
'Exhibition at the Royal Academy', *Times*, 2 May 1874, p.12
'Exhibition at the Royal Academy: Third Notice', *Illustrated London News*, 16 May 1874, p.17
'Exhibition at the Royal Academy', *Times*, 29 May 1876, p.6
'EXHIBITION OF WORKS IN BLACK AND WHITE', *Pall Mall Gazette*, 20 June 1876, pp.10-1
M. Fidell-Beaufort, 'Hasty Departures for London by French Artists in 1870. Daubigny, Monet, Pissarro and some compatriots', in *Le Départ à l'époque victorienne*, Metz 2002
'Fine Art Gossip', *The Athenaeum*, 26 March 1875, p.399
K. Flint, *Impressionists in England: The Critical Reception*, London 1984
Frances Fowle, *Monet and French Landscape: Vétheuil and Normandy*, Edinburgh 2006
La France, 25 April 1871
Charles F. Frankiss, 'Camille Pissarro, Théodore Duret and Jules Berthel in London in 1871', *Burlington Magazine*, vol.146, July 2004, pp.470–2

Sabine Freitag (ed.), *Exiles from European Revolution: Refugees in Mid-Victorian England*, London and New York 2003
Edouard-Désiré Fromentin, 'Jean-Baptiste Carpeaux', *Valentiana, Revue d'histoire des pays du Hainaut français*, no.19, June 1997
Théophile Gautier, 'Une journée à Londres', *Revue des deux mondes*, 15 April 1842, p.282
Théophile Gautier, *Tableaux de siège, Paris, 1870–1871*, Paris 1871
David Getsy, *Body Doubles: Sculpture in Britain, 1877–1905*, New Haven and London 2004
René Gimpel, *Journal d'un collectionneur, marchand de tableaux*, Paris 1963
Gustave Goetschy, *Les Jeunes peintres militaires*, Paris 1878
Edmond and Jules de Goncourt, *Portraits intimes du XVIIIe siècle*, 1st series, Paris 1857
Edmond and Jules de Goncourt, *Journal, Mémoires de la vie littéraire*, 3 vols., ed. Robert Ricatte, Bouquins series, Paris 1989
Edmund Gosse, 'The New Sculpture: 1879–1894', *Art Journal*, vol.56
Veronica Franklin Gould, *Mary Seton Watts (1849–1938): Unsung Heroine of the Art Nouveau*, exh. cat., Watts Gallery, Compton 1998
The Graphic, no.16, 18 Aug. 1877, supplement
Antony Griffiths, *Prints and Printmaking: An Introduction to the History and Techniques*, London 1996
Francis Seymour Haden, *About Etching: Part 1*, London 1879
Mr and Mrs S.C. Hall, *The Book of the Thames* (first published 1859), London [1877]
Philip Gilbert Hamerton, *Etching & Etchers*, London 1876
Melissa Hamnett, 'Edouard Lantéri. Sculptor, medallist and mentor', *The Medal*, no.63, 2013, pp.4–25
Ludovic Hans and J.J. Blanc, *Guide à travers les ruines: Paris et ses environs*, Paris 1871
Martin Hardie, 'Goulding, Frederick (1842–1909)', rev. Paul Goldman, *Oxford Dictionary of National Biography*, Oxford University Press, 2004: http://www.oxforddnb.com/view/article/33495
Robert Hellebranth, *Charles-François Daubigny 1817–1878*, Morges 1976
Arthur M. Hind, *A History of Engraving & Etching from the 15th Century to the Year 1914*, New York 1923
William Jackson Hooker, *Kew Garden, or a Popular guide to the royal botanic gardens of Kew*, London 1857
John House, 'New Material on Monet and Pissarro in London in 1870–71', *Burlington Magazine*, vol.120, no.907, Oct. 1978, pp.636–41
John House, 'Tinted Steam: Turner and Impressionism', in Katharine Lochnan (ed.), *Turner Whistler Monet*, exh. cat., Art Gallery of Ontario, Toronto 2004, pp.109–40
John House, 'The Thames Transfigured, André Derain's London', in Vegelin van Claerbergen and Wright 2005, pp.31–52
John House, 'Visions of the Thames', in *Monet's London: Artists' Reflections on the Thames, 1859–1914*, exh. cat., Museum of Fine Arts, St Petersburg, FL 2005, pp.15–37
Clair Hughes, *Henry James and the Art of Dress*, Basingstoke 2001
Charles Hugo, *Les Hommes de l'exil*, Paris 1875
Joris-Karl Huysmans, 'Fantaisie sur le Musée des arts décoratifs et sur l'architecture cuite', *Revue indépendante*, Nov. 1886, reprinted in *L'art moderne, Certains*, Paris 1975
Illustrated London News, 22 May 1875
L'Illustration, vol.58, no.1488, 2 Sept. 1871
Nancy Ireson, 'André Derain's Wild London', in Vegelin van Claerbergen and Wright 2005, pp.53–70
P. Jacomb-Hood, *With Brush and Pencil*, London 1925
Henry James, *English Hours*, Cambridge 1905
Isabelle Janvrin and Catherine Rawlinson, *The French in London: From William the Conqueror to Charles de Gaulle*, London 2016
Jerome K. Jerome, *Three Men in a Boat (To Say Nothing of the Dog)*, London 1889
William Blanchard Jerrold, *Life of Gustave Doré*, London 1891
Thomas C. Jones and Robert Tombs, 'The French left in exile: Quarante-huitards and Communards in London, 1848–80', in Debra Kelly and Martyn Cornick (eds.), *A History of the French in London: Liberty, Equality, Opportunity*, London 2013, pp.165–91
Louise Jopling, *Twenty Years of my Life, 1867–1887*, London 1925
Journal officiel de la Commune (15 April 1871), republished in 3 vols., Cœuvres-et-Valsery 1997
Adolphe Jullien, *Fantin-Latour: sa vie et ses amitiés*, Paris 1909
H. Kessler, *Journey to the Abyss: The Diaries of Count Harry Kessler*, ed. L.M. Easton, New York 2011
Rémi Labrusse and Jacqueline Munck, 'André Derain in London', in Vegelin van Claerbergen and Wright 2005, pp.13–30
Catherine Lampert et al., *Rodin*, exh. cat., Royal Academy of Arts, London 2006
Edouard Lantéri, 'Jules Dalou: Sculptor', *Magazine of Art*, 1902
Edouard Lantéri, *Modelling: A Guide for Teachers and Students*, 3 vols, London 1902–11
Stéphane Laurent, *Histoire de l'Ecole nationale supérieure des arts décoratifs de 1766 à nos jours*, Paris 2004
James Laver, *Vulgar Society: The Romantic Career of James Tissot*, London 1936
Frederick Lawton, *François-Auguste Rodin*, New York 1908
Jean-François Lecaillon, *Les peintres français et la guerre de 1870 (1870–1914)*, ed. Bernard Giovanangeli, Paris 2016
Horace Lecoq de Boisbaudran, *L'Education de la Mémoire Pittoresque*, 1847, republished in *L'éducation de la mémoire pittoresque et la formation de l'artiste*, Paris 1920
Alexandre Ledru-Rollin, *De la décadence de l'Angleterre*, Paris 1850
Daryl Lee, 'Uncanny City: Paris in Ruins', PhD thesis, Yale University, New Haven, CT 1999
Leeds Mercury, 22 Dec. 1874
Antoinette Le Normand-Romain, *The Bronzes of Rodin: Catalogue of Works in the Musée Rodin*, Paris 2007
George Dunlop Leslie, *Our River Thames*, London 1881
Paul-André Lesmoine, *Degas et son œuvre*, Paris 1946–9
Katharine Lochnan, 'Whistler and Monet: Impressionism and Britain', in Lee Glazer et al. (eds.), *James McNeill Whistler in Context: Essays from the Whistler Centenary Symposium, University of Glasgow, 2003*, Washington, DC 2008, pp.45–64
Alfred de Lostalot, 'Le Musée des arts décoratifs. Exposition de MM. Le comte Lepic et James Tissot. Le salon des arts décoratifs', *Gazette des Beaux-arts*, 1883, vol.1, pp.452–4
Louis Blanc Lettres de l'Angleterre, Paris 1865–8
Henri Loyrette, *Degas inédit*, exh. Cat. Musée d'Orsay, Paris 1989
Henri Loyrette, *Degas*, Paris 1991
Alisa Luxenberg, 'Creating Désastres: Andrieu's Photographs of Urban Ruins in the Paris of 1871', *Art Bulletin*, vol.80, no.1, March 1998, pp.113–37
Isabel G. McAllister, 'Edward Lantéri: Sculptor and Professor', *The Studio*, vol.57, 1912–13, pp.25–31
Margaret MacDonald, Patricia de Montfort and Nigel Thorp (eds.), *The Correspondence of James McNeill Whistler, 1855–1903*, online edition, University of Glasgow, GUW 01073 (2017-02-17): http://www.whistler.arts.gla.ac.uk/correspondence
Margaret MacDonald and Patricia de Montfort, *An American in London: Whistler and the Thames*, London 2013
Hector Malot, *La vie moderne en Angleterre*, Paris 1862, quoted in Christine Geoffroy and Richard Sibley (eds.), *Going Abroad: Travel, Tourism, and Migration. Cross-Cultural Perspectives on Mobility*, Cambridge 2009, p.33
Nancy Rose Marshall, 'Transcripts of Modern Life: The London Pictures of James Tissot 1871–1882', PhD thesis, Yale University, New Haven, CT 1998
Nancy Rose Marshall and Malcolm Warner, *James Tissot: Modern Life/Modern Love*, New Haven and London 1999
Paul Martinez, 'Paris Communard Refugees in Britain, 1871–1880', D.Phil thesis, University of Sussex 1981
Krystyna Matyjaszkiewicz (ed.), *James Tissot*, London 1984
Krystyna Matyjaszkiewicz, 'Royalty and Rivalries: Unlocking James Tissot's B*all on Shipboard* and *Portrait of ex-Empress Eugenie*'; 'James Tissot's *A Portrait* Retitled and Personal Associations Revealed in *The Thames, Portsmouth Dockyard* and Gallery of HMS Calcutta, Tate Papers, 2017
Henry Mayhew, *London Labour and the London Poor; an Encyclopaedia of the condition of earnings of those that will work, those that cannot work, and those that will not work*, London 1840–1851, 3 vols.
J.G. Millais, *The Life and Letters of Sir John Everett Millais*, London 1899, vol.2
Willard E. Misfeldt, 'James Jaques Tissot: A Bio-Critical Study', PhD thesis, Washington University, 1971
Willard E. Misfeldt , 'The Economics of James Tissot's printmaking', *J.J. Tissot: Prints from the Gotlieb Collection*, Alexandria, VA 1991, pp.19–21
Jules Moinaux, 'Revue comique des tribunaux', *Le Charivari*, nos.2–3, p.24
Monet Paintings and Drawings at the Art Institute of Chicago: http://www.artic.edu/research/digital-publications/online-scholarly-catalogues
Etienne Moreau-Nélaton, *Daubigny raconté par lui-même*, Paris 1925
Etienne Moreau-Nélaton, *Bonvin raconté par lui-même*, Paris 1927
Dominique Morel et al., *Giuseppe de Nittis: La modernité élégante*, exh. cat., Petit Palais, Paris, 2010
Edward Morris, *French Art in Nineteenth-Century Britain*, New Haven and London 2005
Edward Morris, 'The sculpture collections at Eaton Hall, Cheshire, 1820–1914', *Sculpture Journal*, Jan. 2010, vol.19, no.1, pp.62–78
'Multiple Arts and Popular Culture Items', *Morning Post*, 14 June 1875, p.2
'Multiple Arts and Popular Culture Items', *The Standard*, 26 June 1876, p.6
Jane Munro and Paul Stirton, *The Society of Three: Alphonse Legros, Henri Fantin-Latour, James McNeill Whistler*, Cambridge 1998
Ira Bruce Nadel and F.S. Schwarzbach (eds.), *Victorian Artists and the City: A Collection of Critical Essays*, New York and Oxford 1980
Alphonse de Neuville, La bataille de l'image, exh. cat., Musée de l'hôtel Sandelin, Saint-Omer 2014
New York Times, 29 Jan. 1871, p.3
Léontine de Nittis, *Notes et Souvenirs du peintre Joseph De Nittis*, Paris 1895
Fernande Olivier, *Picasso et ses Amis*, Paris 1933
Richard and Léonée Ormond (eds.), *Frederic Leighton, 1830–1896*, exh. cat., Royal Academy of Arts, London 1996
F.T. Palgrave, *Essays on Art*, London and Cambridge 1866
Pall Mall Gazette, April 1889
Kineton Parkes, *Sculpture of Today, vol.1: America, Great-Britain, Japan*, London 1921
F. Parkes Weber, 'Medals and Medallions of the Nineteenth Century, Relating to England, by Foreign Artists', *The Numismatic Chronicle and Journal of the Numismatic Society*, Third Series, vol.14 (1894), pp.101–78
Walter Pater, 'The School of Giorgione', in *Fortnightly Review*, 1877, republished in *The Renaissance*, London 1888, pp.107–27
Sylvie Patin, *Monet in Great Britain*, Vanves 1994
Sylvie Patry (ed.), *Inventing Impressionism: Paul Durand-Ruel and the Modern Art Market*, exh. cat., National Gallery, London 2015
Joachim Pissarro and Claire Durand-Ruel-Snollaerts, *Pissarro: Critical Catalogue of Paintings*, 3 vols., Milan and Paris 2005
Michel Poletti, *Jean-Baptiste Carpeaux, l'homme qui faisait danser les pierres*, Paris 2012
A. Poulet-Malassis and A.-W. Thibaudeau, *Catalogue raisonné de l'oeuvre gravé et lithographié de M. Alphonse Legros*, Paris 1877
Précis of the Board Minutes of the Science and Art Department, 23 December 1869 to 31 December 1877, London 1878 (National Library of Art)
Precis of the Board Minutes of the Science and Art Department, from 1 January 1878 to 31 December 1880, London 1881 (National Library of Art)
Elizabeth Prettejohn, *After the Pre-Raphaelites: Art and Aestheticism in Victorian England*, Manchester 1999
Antonin Proust, 'Edouard Manet: Souvenirs', in *Revue Blanche*, Paris, 1897
Punch, 10 July 1858, no.35
Punch, or the London Charivari, 1 Feb. 1875
Patrick Ramade and Laure de Margerie (eds.), *Carpeaux peintre*, exh. cat., Musée des Beaux-Arts de Valenciennes, 1999
Elisée Reclus, *Londres illustré, guide spécial pour l'exposition de 1862*, Paris 1862
Benedict Read, *Victorian Sculpture*, New Haven and London 1982
Nicholas Reed, *Monet and the Thames*, London 1998
Nicholas Reed, *Sisley on the Thames and the Welsh Coast*, Folkestone 2008
Theodore Reff, 'Some Unpublished Letters of Degas', *Art Bulletin*, March 1968
Theodore Reff, *The Notebooks of Edgar Degas: A Catalogue of the Thirty-Eight Notebooks in the Bibliothèque Nationale and Other Collections*, Oxford 1976

John Rewald (ed.), *Camille Pissarro: Letters to his Son Lucien*, New York 1943 (republished Boston 2002)
John Rewald, *Histoire de l'impressionnisme*, Paris 1986
Christopher Riopelle and Ann Sumner, *Sisley in England and Wales*, exh. cat., National Gallery, London 2008
Alfred Robaut and Etienne Moreau-Nélaton, *L'Oeuvre de Corot, Catalogue raisonné et illustré*, 5 vols., Paris 1905
Graham Robb, *Rimbaud*, New York 2000
Charles Roberts, *The Radical Countess: The History of the Life of Rosalind Countess of Carlisle*, Carlisle 1962
François Robichon, *La peinture militaire française de 1871 à 1914*, Paris 1998
François Robichon, *Edouard Detaille, Un siècle de gloire militaire*, Paris 2007
François Robichon, *Alphonse de Neuville, 1835–1885*, Paris 2010
Anna Gruetzner Robins (ed.), *Walter Sickert: The Complete Writings on Art*, Oxford 2000
P. Rosenberg and L.-A. Prat, *Antoine Watteau 1684–1721. Catalogue raisonné des dessins*, 3 vols., Milan 1996
Marita Ross, 'The Truth about Tissot', *Everybody's Weekly*, 15 June 1946
William Michael Rossetti, 'Art Exhibitions in London', *Fine Arts Quarterly Review*, Oct. 1864, p.30
William Michael Rossetti, 'The Society of French Artists', *Academy*, 22 May 1875, p.539
William Michael Rossetti, *The Diary of William Michael Rossetti, 1870–73*, Oxford 1977
'"Rotten Row in the Season", a sketch of a portion of the painting by the late GH Thomas', *The Graphic*, 5 July 1873
Jessica Rutherford, 'Les émaux cloisonnés de James Tissot', *James Tissot, 1836–1902*, exh. cat., Barbican, London 1984, pp.78–85
George Sala, *Things I Have Seen and People I Have Known*, London 1894
Gonzalo J. Sánchez, *Organizing Independence: The Artists Federation of the Paris Commune and its Legacy, 1871–1889*, Lincoln, NE 1997
Cyrille Sciama, *James Tissot et ses Maîtres*, Paris 2005
Cyrille Sciama, 'Giuseppe de Nittis, tra James Tissot ed Edgar Degas', in Angiuli and Spurrell 2006, pp.81–5
Cyrille Sciama (ed.), *James Tissot*, Rome 2015
Grace Seiberling, *Monet in London*, exh. cat., High Museum of Art, Atlanta, GA 1988
Alfred Sensier and Paul Mantz, *La vie et l'œuvre de Jean-François Millet*, Paris 1881
Paolo Serafini, 'Bought and sold: Tissot e la Arthur Tooth & Sons Gallery in Londra', in Sciama 2015, pp.44–9
Eric Shanes, *Impressionist London*, London 1994
Amélie Simier, *'Ni moulage sur nature ni photographie ne seront jamais de l'art.* Quelques réflexions autour de la découverte de photographies de *Cache-cache* d'Aimé Jules Dalou', *Mélanges Anne Pingeot*, Paris 2008, pp.188–91
Amélie Simier, *Jules Dalou, le sculpteur de la République*, Paris 2013
Alison Smith, 'James Tissot et l'Angleterre', in Sciama 2005, pp.11–46
'The Society of French Artists, Bond Street', *Art Journal*, Aug. 1875, p.245
Tulliola Sparagni, 'De Nittis à Londres: impressions d'un "étranger de passage"', in *Giuseppe de Nittis: La modernité élégante*, exh. cat., Petit Palais, Paris 2010, pp.40–5
Robin Spencer, 'The Aesthetics of Chance: London as seen by James McNeill Whistler', in Malcolm Warner, *The Image of London: Views by Travellers and Emigrés, 1550–1920*, exh. cat., Barbican Art Gallery, London 1987, pp.49–72
Marion H. Spielmann, *British Sculpture and Sculptors of Today*, London, Paris, New York and Melbourne 1901
Edgcumbe Staley, 'Edward Lantéri, Artist and Teacher', in *Art Journal*, 1903, pp.241–5
Tom Stammers, 'Scavenging Rococo; *trouvailles*, bibelots and counter-revolution', in M. Lee-Hyde and K. Scott (eds.), *Rococo Echo: Art History and Historiography from Cochin to Coppola*, Oxford 2014, p.71
MaryAnne Stevens (ed.), *Alfred Sisley, 1839–1899*, exh. cat., Royal Academy of Arts, London 1992
R.A.M. Stevenson, 'Preface', *The Dutch Gallery Exhibition of Pictures, Water-Colour Drawings, & Etchings by Mr. Alphonse Legros*, 1897
R.A.M. Stevenson, 'Professor Legros', *Pall Mall Gazette*, 6 April 1897
Mark Stocker, *Royalist and Realist: The Life and Work of Sir Joseph Edgar Boehm*, New York and London 1988
The Studio, no.29, 1903
Virginia Surtees, *The Artist and the Autocrat: George and Rosalind Howard, Earl and Countess of Carlisle*, Salisbury 1988
A. Tabarant (ed.), *Une correspondance inédite d'Edouard Manet : les lettres du siège de Paris (1870–1871)*, Paris 1935
Hippolyte Taine, *Notes sur l'Angleterre*, Paris 1872, translated by W. Rae, *Notes on England*, New York 1885
Talon Rouge, 'The Social Week', *Vanity Fair*, 7 April 1877
François Thiébault-Sisson, 'Un nouveau musée parisien: Les Nymphéas de Claude Monet: L'Orangerie des Tuileries', *Revue de l'art ancien et moderne*, no.52 (1927)
Ben Thomas (ed.), *Alfred Drury and the New Sculpture*, exh. cat., Studio 3 Gallery, University of Kent, Canterbury 2013
Bertrand Tillier, *La Commune de Paris, révolution sans images ? Politique et représentations dans la France républicaine (1871–1914)*, Epoques series, Seyssel 2004
Times, 19 Dec. 1870
Times, 1 May 1871
Gary Tinterow and Henri Loyrette, *Origins of Impressionism*, exh. cat., Metropolitan Museum of Art, New York 1994
J.J. Tissot: Eaux-fortes, Manière Noire, Pointes Sèches, Paris 1886
Isabelle Tombs and Robert Tombs, *That Sweet Enemy: The British and the French from the Sun King to the Present*, London 2010
Marius Vachon, *Les Peintres étrangers à l'exposition universelle de 1878*, Paris 1878
Jules Vallès, *La Rue à Londres*, Paris 1884
Jules Vallès, *Manchester Guardian*, 16 Feb. 1885
Louis Vauxcelles, 'Le Salon d'Automne', *Gil Blas*, supplement, no.6, 17 Oct. 1905
Louis Vauxcelles, 'Le Salon des Indépendants', *Gil Blas*, 20 March 1906
Ernst Vegelin van Claerbergen and Barnaby Wright (eds), *André Derain: The London Paintings*, exh. cat., Courtauld Institute of Art, London 2005
Lionello Venturi, *Les Archives de l'impressionnisme. Lettres de Renoir, Monet, Pissarro, Sisley et autres. Mémoires de Paul Durand-Ruel. Documents*, 2 vols., Paris and New York 1939
Paul Verlaine, 'Londres', *Oeuvres poétiques complètes*, Paris 1992
Ambrose Vollard, *Souvenirs d'un marchand de tableaux*, Paris 1957
Andrew Watson, 'Constantine Ionides and his Collection of 19th-Century French Art', *Journal of the Scottish Society for Art History*, 1998, pp.24–31
Mary Watts, *George Frederic Watts: The Annals of an Artist's Life*, 3 vols., London 1912, vol.1
Michael Justin Wentworth, *James Tissot: Catalogue Raisonné of his Prints*, Minneapolis 1978
Michael Wentworth, *James Tissot*, Oxford 1984
James McNeill Whistler, *A Series of Sixteen Etchings of Scenes on the Thames*, London 1871
Mr Whistler's 'Ten o'Clock', first published 1888, reprinted in James McNeill Whistler, *The Gentle Art of Making Enemies*, London 1890
Timothy Wilcox, 'Alphonse Legros (1837–1911): Aspects of his Life and Work', MPhil Thesis, University of London, 1981
Timothy Wilcox, *Alphonse Legros, 1837–1911*, exh. cat., Musée des Beaux Arts de Dijon, 1987
Timothy Wilcox, 'Legros, Alphonse (1837–1911)', *Oxford Dictionary of National Biography*, Oxford University Press, 2004; online edn, May 2008: http://www.oxforddnb.com/view/article/34480
Oscar Wilde, 'The Grosvenor Gallery, 1877', *Dublin University Magazine*, July 1877, http://www.gutenberg.org/files/14062/14062-h/14062-h.htm
Oscar Wilde, 'The Decay of lying', first published in *Nineteenth Century*, Jan. 1889, quoted from revised version in *Intentions*, 1891
Daniel Wildenstein, *Claude Monet: Biographie et catalogue raisonné*, Lausanne and Paris 1974
Daniel Wildenstein, *Claude Monet: Biographie et catalogue raisonné: supplément aux peintures, dessins, pastels*, Lausanne and Paris 1991
Daniel Wildenstein, *Monet: Catalogue Raisonné*, 4 vols., Cologne 1996
Juliet Wilson-Bareau, *Manet and the Execution of Maximilian: Painting, Politics and Censorship*, London 1992
Charles Yriarte, *J.J. Tissot. Eaux-fortes, manière noire, pointes sèches*, Paris 1886

Exhibited Works

This list is organised chronologically by artist. Measurements are given in centimetres, height before width and depth.
Works exhibited only in London or in Paris are identified with [L] or [P] after the title.
Page references for illustrations are given in bold at the end of entries.

Lawrence Alma-Tadema 1836–1912
Jules Dalou, his Wife and Daughter 1876
Oil paint on canvas 61 × 30
Musée d'Orsay, Paris
RF 1977–18
157

Anonymous artist
Suresnes Bridge c.1870 [L]
Albumen paper print 30 × 22.2
Wilson Centre for Photography
39

Anonymous artist
Kathleen Newton (Rêverie) c.1880–1 [L]
Photograph (modern print) 21 × 14
Tate Archive
TGA 7916/3
102

Anonymous artist
Kathleen Newton c.1881
Albumen print, 21 × 14
Tate Archive
TGA 7916/3
100

Charles-Joseph Beauverie 1839–1924
Ruins of the Tuileries: View taken from the Vestibule of the Grand Stairway June 1871 [P]
Pen and ink wash and gouache highlights on paper 21 × 32.2
Musée Carnavalet – Histoire de Paris
D4458
47

Ruins of the Hôtel de Ville: Stairway to the Prefect's Apartments June 1871 [P]
Pen and ink wash and gouache highlights on paper 36.7 × 25
Musée Carnavalet – Histoire de Paris
D4456
46

Thomas Gibson Bowles 1842–1922
The Defence of Paris; Narrated as it was seen, pub. Sampson Low, Son and Marston, 1871
Tate Library and Archive
34

Jean-Baptiste Carpeaux 1827–75
Sketchbook on the Siege of Paris during the Franco-Prussian War 1870–1
Drawings in chalk, pastel, pen and ink, sanguine, 76 pages, hardcover binding 11.7 × 15.3
Petit Palais, Musée des Beaux-Arts de la Ville de Paris
PPD1783
33

Jean-Léon Gérôme 1871
Plaster 61 × 26 × 24
Petit Palais, Musée des Beaux-Arts de la Ville de Paris. Gift of the sculptor Hector Lemaire, 1907
PPS948
183

Mrs Henry James Turner 1871
Marble 86 × 60 × 37.5
Victoria and Albert Museum, London. Given by Miss Jessica Turner to the Tate Gallery and transferred to the V&A
A.19-1984
179

Brother and Sister, Two Orphans of the Siege 1871–2 [P]
Oil paint on canvas 170 × 100
Musée des Beaux-Arts Eugène Leroy, Tourcoing
894-3-1
177

Venus, with Mercury and Cupid, after Correggio 1871–3 [P]
Oil paint on canvas 145 × 90
Petit Palais, Musée des Beaux-Arts de la Ville de Paris
PPP2082
187

Bust of Charles Gounod 1873 [L]
Plaster 73 × 50 × 44
Kindly loaned by The Royal Society of Musicians of Great Britain
ART-45
185

Bust of Charles Gounod 1873 [P]
Plaster 70 × 48 × 44
Petit Palais, Musée des Beaux-Arts de la Ville de Paris
PPS1551

Daphnis and Chloe 1873 [P]
Plaster 72 × 35 × 21.5
Petit Palais, Musée des Beaux-Arts de la Ville de Paris. Gift of Louise Clément Carpeaux, 1938
PPS 1562
182

Flora 1873
Marble 97 × 65 × 60
Museu Calouste Gulbenkian – Founders Collection, Lisbon
Inv.562
180

The Emperor Napoleon III in his Coffin on 13 January 1873 in St Mary's Church in Chislehurst 1873 [L]
Chalk on paper 34.1 × 55
Musée d'Orsay, Paris, deposited at the Musée national du Château de Versailles
RF 1963
189

Funerary Service for Napoleon III at Chiselhurst: the Chapel of Rest 1873 [P]
Chalk on paper 24.3 × 29.9
Musée d'Orsay, Paris, deposited at the Musée national du Château de Versailles
RF 1964
189

Henry James Turner 1873
Marble 63 × 57 × 31.5
Victoria and Albert Museum, London. Given by Miss Jessica Turner to the Tate Gallery and transferred to the V&A
A.20-1984
178

Notes and sketches in Blackwood's Small Pocket Book and Diary, London, 1871
Mixed media, 90 pages, portfolio binding in Morocco leather 10.7 × 7.5
Petit Palais, Musée des Beaux-Arts de la Ville de Paris
PPD1781
186

Napoleon III 1874
Marble 60 × 36.5 × 27
Victoria and Albert Museum, London
A.43-1983
188

Self-portrait 1874
Oil paint on canvas 40 × 32.2
Petit Palais, Musée des Beaux-Arts de la Ville de Paris
PPP 2075
176

Siebe Johannes ten Cate 1858–1908
The Place du Carrousel and Ruins of the Tuileries 1883
Oil paint on canvas 83 × 165.5
Musée Carnavalet – Histoire de Paris
P0594
50–1

Jean-Baptiste-Camille Corot 1796–1875
The Dream: Paris Burning 1870
Oil paint on canvas 30.5 × 54.5
Musée Carnavalet – Histoire de Paris
P1628
28

Jules Dalou 1838–1902
Palm Sunday in Boulogne, or, *Woman from Boulogne* 1872
Terracotta 65.5 × 21 × 21
The Castle Howard Collection
152

French Peasant woman nursing a baby 1873
Terracotta 136.5 × 70 × 80
Victoria and Albert Museum, London
A.8-1993
153

Rosalind Howard 1872
Bronze 52 × 40 × 44
The Castle Howard Collection
154

Hush-a-Bye, Baby, or *The Rocking Chair* 1875 [L]
Marble 116 × 105 × 64
Private collection
160

Bust of Laura Theresa Epps, Lady Alma-Tadema 1875
Terracotta 69.1 × 49 × 26
Musée d'Orsay, Paris. Gift of Anna and Laurence Alma-Tadema, daughters of the painters, 1934
RF 2307
156

Alphonse Legros c.1876
Painted plaster 51 h.
Victoria and Albert Museum, London. Gift of Mrs Knowles
A.7-1993
151

Bust of a Young Man 1877
Plaster 70 × 44 × 32
Private collection
162

George Howard 1877
Terracotta 73 × 53 × 31
The Castle Howard Collection
155

English Sketchbook no.1 1874–7
Closed: 8 × 13 × 1
Private collection, Becker estate
159

Woman Reading (Mrs Dalou Reading) 1877
Pencil and pen and ink, on a diary page 17.5 × 19
Private collection, Becker estate
159

Woman Doing a Little Girl's Hair (Mrs Dalou and Georgette?) 1870s
Pen and ink on paper 18.9 × 19.5
Private collection, Becker estate
159

Woman Reading in an Armchair (Mrs Dalou Reading) 1870s
Pencil, pen and ink on paper 11.5 × 9
Private collection, Becker estate
158

Arthur St Clair Anstruther Thomson 1877 [P]
Marble, 114 h.
National Museum of Scotland, Edinburgh
A.1984.120
161

Fraternity c.1878–9 [P]
Terracotta 51 × 34 × 10
Petit Palais, Musée des Beaux-Arts de la Ville de Paris
PPS 341
168

Italian Peasant 1889–98 [P]
Patinated plaster 43 × 28 × 23
Petit Palais, Musée des Beaux-Arts de la Ville de Paris
PPS 103
164

Charles-François Daubigny 1817–1878
The Mouth of the Thames 1866
Oil paint on panel 27 × 45.5
Musée des Beaux-Arts de Lyon. Bequeathed by Wuillermoz, 1875
X 923 E (Hellebranth 751)
63

The Thames at Erith 1866 [P]
Oil paint on panel 38 × 67
Musée du Louvre. Bequeathed by Georges Thomy Thiéry, 1902
RF 1365 (Hellebranth 746)
62

St Paul's from the Surrey Side 1871–1873
Oil paint on canvas 44.5 × 81
The National Gallery, London. Presented by friends of Mr. J.C.J. Drucker, 1912
NG 2876 (Hellebranth 756)
64–5

André Derain 1880–1954
Barges on the Thames 1906
Oil paint on canvas 81.3 × 99
Leeds Museums and Galleries (Leeds Art Gallery)
LEEAG.PA.1937.0039 (K85)
247

Charing Cross Bridge, London 1906–7
Oil paint on canvas 80.3 × 100.3
National Gallery of Art, Washington, John Hay Whitney Collection
1982.76.3 (K88)
242–3

The Pool of London 1906
Oil paint on canvas 65.7 × 99.1
Tate. Presented by the Trustees of the Chantrey Bequest 1951
247

Big Ben 1906–7 [P]
Oil paint on canvas 79 × 98
Musée d'Art Moderne de Troyes. Gift of Pierre and Denise Lévy
MNPL 103 (K77)
244

Gustave Doré 1832–1883
Sister of Charity Saving a Child, Episode in the Siege of Paris 1870–1
Oil paint on canvas 97 × 130
Le Havre, Musée d'art moderne André Malraux
1972.3.1
29

The Docks of London [P]
Watercolour and gouache on paper 55.7 × 37.8
Musée d'art moderne et contemporain de Strasbourg
55.992.13.19
53

London Wharfs [P]
Wood engraving 30.7 × 18.6
Musée d'art moderne et contemporain de Strasbourg
XXI 161 (1)
52

Over London – By Rail [P]
Wood engraving 19.8 × 24.7
Musée d'art moderne et contemporain de Strasbourg
XXII 81 (1)
54

Gustave Doré 1832–1883 and William Blanchard Jerrold 1826–1884
London: A Pilgrimage, pub. Grant & Co., London 1872 [P]
44 h.
Bibliothèque des Musées de Strasbourg
LB.F-0054
55

All London at a Boat-Race in *London: A Pilgrimage*, pub. Grant & Co., London 1876 [P]
38 h.
Bibliothèque des Musées de Strasbourg
GD.F-0035

Henri Dupray 1841–1909 and René Gilbert 1858–1914
Training the National Guard – The Departure of the Armand Barbès Balloon, Place Saint-Pierre 1889 [P]
Sketch for the Prefect's Office in the Hôtel de Ville, Paris
Oil paint on canvas, 49 × 109
Petit Palais, Musée des Beaux-Arts de la Ville de Paris
PPP3975
32

Rationing the Population – Bombardment of Paris 1889 [P]
Sketch for the Prefect's Office in the Hôtel de Ville, Paris
Oil paint on canvas, 48.5 × 155
Petit Palais, Musée des Beaux-Arts de la Ville de Paris
PPP9376
32

Alfred Gilbert 1854–1934
George Frederic Watts, O.M., R.A.[P]
Bronze 58.4 × 58.4 × 36.8
Tate. Presented by Mrs Watts by the wish of the late George Frederic Watts 1904
169

Edouard Lantéri 1848–1917
Proserpinae Cultor c.1890
Bronze medal, diam. 9.5
The British Museum, London
2000,0821.1
166

Sir Edgar Boehm 1891
Bronze medal, diam. 11.8
The British Museum, London. Presented by Dr F. Parkes Weber
1906,1103.4763
166

Head of a Peasant c.1901
Bronze 53.3 × 49.5 × 34.2
Tate. Presented by the artist's pupils 1902
167

Modelling: a Guide for Teachers and Students, pub. Chapman & Hall, London, 1902
24.5 × 38 × 55
Private collection

Henri Fantin-Latour 1836–1904
Mr and Mrs Edwin Edwards 1875
Oil paint on canvas 130.8 × 98.1
Tate. Presented by Mrs E. Edwards 1904
125

Alphonse Legros 1837–1911
Ex-voto 1860
Oil paint on canvas 174 × 197
Musée des Beaux-Arts de Dijon
CA 379
120–1

The Drawing Room of Mr Edwin Edwards at Sunbury 1861
Drypoint on paper 16.3 × 23.8
Private collection
Bliss 130
124

A Lectern 1863-5 [P]
Oil paint on canvas 102 × 107
Petit Palais, Musée des Beaux-Arts de la Ville de Paris
PDUT 1719
123

Edward Burne-Jones 1868–9
Oil paint on panel 46 × 37.2
Aberdeen Art Gallery & Museums Collections. Presented in 1922 by Sir James Murray
ABDAG002505
126

Portrait de M. Frédéric Régamey 1870s, before 1877
Drypoint on paper 23 × 16.4
The British Museum, London
1871,0510.385 (Bliss 22, iii or iv/v)
130

The Tinker exh. 1874
Oil paint on canvas 115 × 132.5
Victoria and Albert Museum, London. Bequeathed by Constantine Alexander Ionides
CAI.24
127

Death of the Vagabond 1875? [P]
Etching, aquatint and drypoint on paper 55.2 × 40
Musée des Beaux-Arts de Dijon
2022-16-122 (Bliss 89)
131

The Gust of Wind exh. 1875 [L]
Etching on paper 56.9 × 46.6
The British Museum, London
1875,0612.426 (Bliss 110)
133

The Gust of Wind exh. 1875 [P]
Etching on paper 57.4 × 44.5
Musée des Beaux-Arts de Dijon
CA.902 (Bliss 110)

Portrait of M.J. Dalou, Sculptor 1876 [L]
Etching and drypoint on paper 25.2 × 16.5
Victoria and Albert Museum, London. Bequeathed by Constantine Alexander Ionides
CAI.36 (Bliss 41)
151

Portrait of M.J. Dalou, Sculptor 1876 [P]
Etching and drypoint on paper 25.2 × 16.5
Private collection, Paris (Bliss 41)
151

Portrait of Jules Dalou c.1876 [P]
Graphite on paper 25.6 × 17
Private collection, Becker estate
DES 001
151

Portrait of Edward Poynter 1876 [P]
Etching on paper 21.5 × 15.6
Musée des Beaux-Arts de Dijon
2484 (Bliss 42)
135

Hilly Landscape 1876–7
Oil paint on canvas 76.2 × 50.2
Victoria and Albert Museum, London. Given by the artist
818-1877
129

Le Repas des pauvres (*The Soup Kitchen*) 1877
Oil paint on canvas 113 × 142.9
Tate. Presented by Rosalind, Countess of Carlisle 1912
128

By the Riverside, Morning Effect 1877-84 [L]
Etching, aquatint and drypoint on paper 34.5 × 40.5
The British Museum, London
1884,0112.20 (Bliss 218)
133

Portrait of G. F. Watts R.A. c. 1879? [L]
Etching and drypoint on paper 18.6 × 13.5
The British Museum, London
1949,0411.2237 (Bliss 198.iv)
137

Alfred Lord Tennyson 1881
Bronze one sided portrait medal, diam. 12
Victoria and Albert Museum, London
A.23-2013
165

Maria Valvona 1881 [P]
Plaster medal
Petit Palais, Musée des Beaux-Arts de la Ville de Paris
PPM1097

Portrait of Auguste Rodin 1882
Oil paint on canvas 55 × 46
Musée Rodin, Paris
P.7316
139

A Storm 1887? [L]
Drypoint on paper 17.9 × 25
The British Museum, London
1949,0411.2182 (Bliss 288)
134

A Storm 1887? [P]
Drypoint on paper 17.9 × 24.5
Musée des Beaux-Arts de Dijon
2002-16-164 (Bliss 288)
Portrait of the Artist c.1890–1904 [P]
Etching and drypoint on paper 29.4 × 20.6
Musée des Beaux-Arts de Dijon
Bliss 412
143

Erasmus (date unknown) [P]
Plaster medal, diam. 14
Petit Palais, Musée des Beaux-Arts de la Ville de Paris
PPM1096

Sir Frederic Leighton 1830-1896
Sketch for 'An Athlete Wrestling with a Python' c.1874 [P]
Plaster 25.1 × 15.6 × 13
Tate. Presented by Prof. Alphonse Legros 1897
163

Alphonse Liébert 1826–1914
Châtillon, Redoubt on the Plateau, No.70 c.1871 [L]
Albumen paper print 17.5 × 25.4
Wilson Centre for Photography
40

Edouard Manet 1832–1883
The Barricade c.1871 [L]
Lithograph on paper 46.2 × 32.5
The British Museum, London
1949,0411.3337 (Guérin 76.II)
49

Civil War 1871–3 [L]
Lithograph on paper 42.5 × 50.7
The British Museum, London
1949,0411.3336 (Guérin 75.II)

Jean Louis Ernest Meissonier 1815–1891
The Siege of Paris 1870–4 [P]
Oil paint on canvas 53.5 × 70.5
Musée d'Orsay, Paris. Bequeathed by Elisabeth Meissonier, the artist's widow, 1898
RF 1249
30

John Everett Millais 1829–1896
A Huguenot, on St Bartholomew's Day, refusing to shield himself from danger by wearing the Roman Catholic badge 1851–2
Oil paint on canvas 92.7 × 62.2
The Makins Collection
90

Claude Monet 1840–1926
Meditation (Madame Monet on the Sofa) c.1871
Oil paint on canvas 48.2 × 74.5
Musée d'Orsay, Paris. Bequeathed by M. et Mme Raymond Koechlin, 1931
RF 3665 (W163)
68–9

The Thames Below Westminster 1871 [L]
Oil paint on canvas 47 × 73
The National Gallery, London. Bequeathed by Lord Astor of Hever, 1971
NG 6399 (W166)
66–7

Hyde Park 1871
Oil paint on canvas 40.5 × 74
Museum of Art, Rhode Island School of Design, Providence. Gift of Mrs. Murray S. Danforth
42.218 (W164)
200–1

Charing Cross Bridge 1899–1902
Oil paint on canvas 65 × 100
Private collection
W1547
240

Leicester Square at Night c.1901
Oil paint on canvas 80 × 64.8
Collection Fondation Jean et Suzanne Planque, deposited at the Musée Granet (Aix-en-Provence)
FJSP-998-116 (W1615)
215

Houses of Parliament c.1900–1
Oil paint on canvas 81.2 × 92.8
The Art Institute of Chicago. Mr and Mrs Martin A. Ryerson Collection
1933.1164 (W1600)
236

Houses of Parliament, Fog Effect 1903
Oil paint on canvas 81 × 92
Le Havre, Musée d'art moderne André Malraux
A 487 (W1608)
237

Houses of Parliament, Sunlight Effect 1903
Oil paint on canvas 81.3 × 92.1
Brooklyn Museum. Bequest of Grace Underwood Barton
68.41.1 (W1597) Durand-Ruel, 1904, no.30
234

Houses of Parliament (Fog Effect) 1903–4
Oil paint on canvas 81.3 × 92.4
The Metropolitan Museum of Art, New York. Bequest of Julia W. Emmons, 1956
56.135.6 (W1609) Durand-Ruel, 1904, no.32
239

Houses of Parliament. Sunset 1904 [L]
Oil paint on canvas 81 × 92
Kunstmuseen, Krefeld
87/1907 (W1602) Durand-Ruel, 1904, no.36
238

Houses of Parliament. Effect of Sunlight in the Fog 1904 [L]
Oil paint on canvas 81.5 × 92.5
Musée d'Orsay, Paris
RF 2007 (W1610) Durand-Ruel, 1904, no.35
235

Charing Cross Bridge 1904 [L]
Oil paint on canvas 65 × 95
Private collection (W1545)
241

Frans Moormans 1832–1893
The Hôtel de Ville after the Fire of 1871 1871
Oil paint on canvas 55 × 82
Musée Carnavalet – Histoire de Paris
P2506
48

Giuseppe de Nittis 1846–1884
Piccadilly: Wintry Walk in London 1875
Oil paint on canvas 68.5 × 104
Private collection
Dini & Marini 541
208–9

The National Gallery 1877
Oil paint on canvas 70 × 105
Petit Palais, Musée des Beaux-Arts de la Ville de Paris
PPP743 (Dini & Marini 171)
109

Westminster 1878
Oil paint on canvas 110 × 195
Private collection
Dini & Marini 717
210–11

William Orpen 1878–1931
Group associated with the New English Art Club c.1904
Pencil, chalk (or charcoal), pen, ink and watercolour on paper 22.5 × 41.5
National Portrait Gallery, London. Purchased, 1995
NPG 6345
142

Isidore Pils 1813–1875
The Vendôme Column Toppled, 29 May 1871 1871 [P]
Graphite, watercolour and gouache on paper 32 × 51
Musée Carnavalet – Histoire de Paris
D6027
44

Ruins of the Tuileries 7 July 1871 [P]
Watercolour and gouache on paper 49.2 × 37
Musée Carnavalet – Histoire de Paris
D4185
45

Ruins of the Salon de Mars, Palais de Saint-Cloud 1871 [P]
Graphite, watercolour and gouache on paper 37.9 × 26.5
Musée Carnavalet – Histoire de Paris
D7546
45

Camille Pissarro 1830–1903
Dulwich College c.1870 [P]
Oil paint on canvas 50 × 61
Fondation Bemberg
P43 (PDRS 191)
72

Fox Hill, Upper Norwood 1870
Oil paint on canvas 35.3 × 45.7
The National Gallery, London. Presented by Viscount and Viscountess Radcliffe, 1964
NG 6351 (PDRS 180)
70

All Saints' Church, Beulah Hill, Upper Norwood 1871 [L]
Gouache on paper 18.2 × 22.8
Private collection
PV 1321
73

The Avenue, Sydenham 1871
Oil paint on canvas 48 × 73
The National Gallery, London. Bought, 1984
NG 6493 (PDRS 188)
74–5

Lordship Lane Station, Dulwich 1871 [L]
Oil paint on canvas 44.5 × 72.5
The Samuel Courtauld Trust, The Courtauld Gallery, London
P.1948.SC.317 (PDRS 189)
76–7

Crystal Palace, Upper Norwood c.1871 [L]
Oil paint on canvas 40 × 50.8
Private collection
PDRS 184
71

Hampton Court Green 1891
Oil paint on canvas 54.3 × 73
National Gallery of Art, Washington, Ailsa Mellon Bruce Collection
1970.17.53 (PDRS887)
204

Charing Cross Bridge, London 1890
Oil paint on canvas 60 × 90
National Gallery of Art, Washington, Collection of Mr. and Mrs. Paul Mellon
1985.64.32 (PDRS884)
222–3

Bank Holiday, Kew 1892 [L]
Oil paint on canvas 46 × 55
Private collection
PDRS942
213

Kew Gardens, Rhododendron Dell 1892
Oil paint on canvas 54 × 64.8
Private collection, USA
PDRS949
205

Kew Green 1892
Oil paint on canvas 46 × 55
Musée d'Orsay, Paris, deposited at the musée des Beaux-Arts de Lyon. Bequeathed by Clément and Andrée Adès, 1979
RF 1979 8 (PDRS941)
207

Saint Anne's Church in Kew, London 1892
Oil paint on canvas 54.8 × 46
From the collection of Professor Mark Kaufman
PDRS940
206

Charles B. Praetorius 1818–1900
Portrait of Jules Dalou after 1871 [P]
Albumen print 10.5 × 6
Private collection
PH001
151

Auguste Rodin 1840–1917
Head of Alphonse Legros 1881–2
Bronze 41 × 27 × 25
Petit Palais, Musée des Beaux-Arts de la Ville de Paris
PPS 996
138

Bust of Jules Dalou 1883 [L]
Bronze 52 × 43 × 24
Musée Rodin, Paris
S.482
141

Bust of Jules Dalou 1883 [P]
Plaster 53 × 42.5 × 27
Musée Rodin, deposited at the Petit Palais
S1975

Alfred Sisley 1839–1899
The Bridge at Hampton Court, Mitre Inn 1874 [L]
Oil paint on canvas 46 × 61
Wallraf-Richartz-Museum & Foundation Corboud, Cologne
WRM2929 (Daulte 123)
199

Molesey Weir, Hampton Court, Morning 1874
Oil paint on canvas 51.1 × 68.8
Scottish National Gallery, Edinburgh
NG 2235 (Daulte 118)
79

The Regatta at Molesey 1874
Oil paint on canvas 66 × 91.5
Musée d'Orsay, Paris. Bequeathed by Gustave Caillebotte, 1894
RF 2787 (Daulte 126)
198

View of the Thames: Charing Cross Bridge 1874
Oil paint on canvas 33 × 46
The Andrew Brownsword Arts Foundation, on loan to the National Gallery, London
L.986 (Daulte 113)
78

Charles Soulier 1840–1875
Paris in Ruins, May 1871 [Château d'Eau Fountain] 1871 [L]
Albumen paper print 19.3 × 25.1
Wilson Centre for Photography
42–3

Paris in Ruins, May 1971 [The Ministry of Finance, Rue du Luxembourg] 1871 [L]
Albumen paper print 25.2 × 19.3
Wilson Centre for Photography
42

John Thomson 1837–1921
Workers on the 'Silent Highway' 1877 [L]
Woodburytype 11.5 × 9 (print), 27.2 × 21 (page)
Wilson Centre for Photography
221

James Tissot 1836–1902
Napoléon III, Emperor of France ('Sovereigns, No.1. "Le regime parlementaire."') 1869
Published in *Vanity Fair*, 4 Sept. 1869
Chromolithograph 34.2 × 21.4
National Portrait Gallery, London
NPG D43395
86

Captain Frederick Burnaby 1870
Oil paint on panel 50 × 61
National Portrait Gallery, London. Purchased 1933.
NPG 2642
88–9

The Wounded Soldier c.1870
Watercolour on paper 35.3 × 25.2
Tate. Purchased 2016
34

A Cantinière of the National Guard 1870–1871
Graphite on paper 19.9 × 12.2
Malingue S.A., Paris
34

The Execution of Communards by French Government Forces at Fortifications in the Bois de Boulogne 29 May 1871
Watercolour on paper 28.3 × 19
Private collection
38

Les Adieux (The Farewells) 1871
Oil paint on canvas 100.3 × 62.5
Bristol Museums & Art Gallery
K2432
91

London Visitors (originally *Country Cousins*) 1873
Oil paint on canvas 86.3 × 63.5
Layton Art Collection Inc. at the Milwaukee Art Museum. Gift of Frederick Layton
L1888.14
108

Too Early 1873
Oil paint on canvas 71 × 102
Guildhall Art Gallery, City of London
738
94

Woman in Outdoor Costume, Sleeping on a Couch c.1873 [L]
Chalk with watercolour and bodycolour on paper 22 × 28.8
The Ashmolean Museum, University of Oxford. Purchased 1951
WA1951.218
98

Hush! 1874
Oil paint on canvas 73.7 × 112.2
Manchester Art Gallery
1933.56
95

The Ball on Shipboard c.1874
Oil paint on canvas 84.1 × 129.5
Tate. Presented by the Trustees of the Chantrey Bequest 1937
196–7

Empress Eugénie and the Prince Imperial in the grounds of Camden Place, Chislehurst 1874–5
Oil paint on canvas 105 × 150
Musée national du Palais de Compiègne
C 38.2557
92–3

View of the Garden at 17 Grove End Road c.1874–82
Oil paint on canvas 27 × 21
The Geffrye, Museum of the Home, London
26/2006
96–7

Holyday c.1876
Oil paint on canvas 76.2 × 99.4
Tate. Purchased 1928
202–3

On the Thames c.1876
Oil paint on canvas, 74.8 × 110
The Hepworth Wakefield
(Wakefield Permanent Art Collection)
A1.323
220

Summer (a Portrait) 1876
Oil paint on canvas 91.4 × 50.8
Tate. Purchased 1927
111

Portrait of Mrs B. 1876
Etching on paper 27.5 × 19.2
Victoria and Albert Museum, London
E.274-1951 (Wentworth 21)
87

The Gallery of HMS Calcutta (Portsmouth) c.1876
Oil paint on canvas 68.6 × 91.8
Tate. Presented by Samuel Courtauld 1936
112

The Green Room of the Theatre Français 1877 [L]
Etching on paper 38 × 27.6
Musée Carnavalet – Histoire de Paris
G 24744 (Wentworth 27)
34

The Three Crows Inn 1877
Etching on paper 20.5 × 29.5
Arwas Archives
Wentworth 29.ii
104

Portsmouth Dockyard c.1877
Oil paint on canvas 38.1 × 54.6
Tate. Bequeathed by Sir Hugh Walpole 1941
113

Grand'garde 1878
Etching and drypoint on paper 45.5 × 29
Victoria and Albert Museum, London
E.272-1951 (Wentworth 42)
34

My Garden at St John's Wood 1878
Etching and drypoint on paper 18.7 × 11.5
Arwas Archives
Wentworth 39
97

Trafalgar Tavern in Greenwich 1878
Etching and drypoint on paper 34.5 × 16
Arwas Archives
Wentworth 36
107

Emigrants 1880
Etching and drypoint on paper 34.5 × 16
Arwas Archives
Wentworth 45
105

In Full Sunlight 1881
Etching and drypoint on paper 19 × 29.7
Arwas Archives
Wentworth 54
100–1

Reading in the Park 1881 [P]
Oil paint on canvas 92 × 73
Musée des Beaux-Arts de Dijon
2718
100–3

Charles Anthony Tune 1814–1887
Plate 176 [Marsan Pavilion, Louvre] c.1871 [L]
Albumen paper print 17.3 × 22.1
Wilson Centre for Photography
41

Plate 179 [Vendôme Column] c.1871 [L]
Albumen paper print 17.2 × 22.1
Wilson Centre for Photography
41

George Frederic Watts 1817–1904
Alphonse Legros c.1879
Etching on paper 12.8 × 9.9
National Portrait Gallery, London
D18060
136

James Abbott McNeill Whistler 1834–1903
Nocturne: Blue and Silver – Chelsea 1871
Oil paint on wood 50.2 × 60.8
Tate. Bequeathed by Miss Rachel and Miss Jean Alexander 1972
218

Nocturne: Blue and Silver – Cremorne Lights 1872
Oil paint on canvas 50.2 × 74.3
Tate. Bequeathed by Arthur Studd 1919
219

Nocturne: Blue and Gold – Old Battersea Bridge c.1872–5
Oil paint on canvas 68.3 × 51.2
Tate. Presented by the Art Fund 1905
217

Georgina Weldon and guests
Visitors' book originally used at Tavistock House, Tavistock Square, London, 1871–1913
1871–1913
Bound manuscript 28 × 21
Victoria and Albert Museum, London
38041800961013

Credits

Copyright
André Derain © ADAGP, Paris and DACS, London 2017 224, 231, 242-3, 244, 247

Photo credits
Aberdeen Art Gallery & Museums Collections 126
© The Andrew Brownsword Arts Foundation 56, 78
The Art Institute of Chicago, IL, USA / Gift of Mr. and Mrs. B. E. Bensinger / Bridgeman Images 60 bottom
© 2017. The Art Institute of Chicago / Art Resource, NY/ Scala, Florence front cover 236
Arwas Archives / Photography by Katerina Praskova 97, 101, 104, 105, 107
© Ashmolean Museum, University of Oxford 98
© Bayonne, musée Bonnat-Helleu / cliché A. Vaquero 60 top
© Bristol Culture 91
© Brooklyn Museum 234
The Bucharest Municipality Museum 175
© Calouste Gulbenkian Foundation, Lisbon. Calouste Gulbenkian Museum, photo: Carlos Azevedo 180
The Castle Howard Collection / Photography by Peter Smith 152, 154, 155
Photo © CCI / Bridgeman Images 170, 172
Conway Library, The Courtauld Institute of Art, London 173 bottom
© 2017. DeAgostini Picture Library/Scala, Florence 85 bottom
© Direction des Musées et du Patrimoine de Dijon/François Jay 135
Collection of Ben Doller, courtesy of Rafael Valls and Agnews 106
© Eric Emo / Petit Palais / Roger-Viollet 182, 183
© 2017. Photo Fine Art Images/Heritage Images/Scala, Florence 229
Fine Art Museums of San Francisco / Photograph by Randy Dodson 83 top
Fondation Jean et Suzanne Planque, on deposit at the Musée Granet, Aix-en-Provence (inv. FJSP-998-116) © photo Luc Chessex 215
Geffrye Museum, London / John Hammond 96
The Goldsmiths' Company 147
Photography by Erik Gould, courtesy of the Museum of Art, Rhode Island School of Design, Providence 8, 200-1
Guildhall Art Gallery, City of London 80, 94
© The Hepworth Wakefield (Wakefield Permanent Collection) 220
From the Collection of Professor Mark Kaufman 206
Kunstmuseen Krefeld, Photo: Volker Döhne 238
Kunstmuseum Winterthur, Donated by Dr Herbert und Charlotte Wolfer-de Armas, 1973 © Schweizerisches Institut für Kunstwissenschaft, Zürich, Lutz Hartmann 192 bottom
Layton Art Collection Inc., Gift of Frederick Layton, at the Milwaukee Art Museum. Photograph by P. Richard Eells 2, 108
Leeds Museums and Galleries (Leeds Art Gallery) U.K. / Bridgeman Images 247 bottom
Image © Lyon MBA – Photo Alain Basset 63
The Makins Collection / Bridgeman Images 90
Malingue S.A., Paris. Photo: Florent Chevrot, Paris 37 left
Manchester Art Gallery, UK / Bridgeman Images 95
© The Metropolitan Museum of Art, New York 239
© MuMa Le Havre / Florian Kleinefen 29; / David Fogel 237
© Musée Carnavalet / Roger-Viollet 20-1, 28, 35, 44, 45, 46, 47, 48, 50-1
© Musée des Beaux-Arts de Dijon/François Jay 103, 131, 132, 143; /Hugo Martens 120-1
Musée des Beaux-Arts Eugène Leroy, Tourcoing 177
Photo (C) Musée d'Orsay, Dist. RMN-Grand Palais / Patrice Schmidt 22, 26 bottom
© Musée Rodin 139; /photo Adam Rzepka 141
Museum of Fine Arts (Szepmuveszeti) Budapest, Hungary / Photo © Tarker / Bridgeman Images 59 bottom
Museum of Modern and Contemporary Art in Strasbourg. Photo Museums of Strasbourg, Mr Bertola 52, 53, 54, 55
© The National Gallery, London 10-11, 64-5, 66-7, 70, 74-5
National Gallery of Art, Washington 116, 204, 222-3, 224, 242-3
The National Museum of Art of Romania, Bucharest 59 top
© National Museums Scotland 161
© National Portrait Gallery, London 86, 88-9, 118 top, 136, 142
NY Carlsberg Glypthotek, Copenhagen / Photo: Ole Haupt 174
© Petit Palais / Roger-Viollet 32, 33, 123, 138, 168, 176, 186, 187
Private collection 195 top, 208-9, 213, 240-1; Maurice Aeschimann 230; / Bridgeman Images 71, 160; / Photo © Christie›s Images / Bridgeman Images 99; /Photography by Luca Di Giorgio 210-11; / Photo © Lefevre Fine Art Ltd., London / Bridgeman Images 227; /Photography by Edward Martin 184; / Naples 195 bottom; / photograph courtesy of Richard Green Gallery, London 73; / Rights Reserved 144, 151 top right, 151 bottom right, 158-9; /USA 117 bottom, 190, 205
Rheinisches Bildarchiv Köln / Wallfraf Richartz Museum & Fondation Corbound 199
Photo (C) RMN-Grand Palais / Gérard Blot 231, 85 top; / Hervé Lewandowski 26 top; / Stéphane Maréchalle 173 top; Mathieu Rabeau 72; / Jean Schormans 207; (domaine de Compiègne) / Thierry Le Mage 189; / Franck Raux 92-3; (musée d'Orsay) / Gérard Blot 68-9; / Christian Jean 156; / Hervé Lewandowski 25, 30-1, 83 bottom, 117 top, 157, 198, 228, 235; / Tony Querrec 62; / Michel Urtado 17
© The Royal Society of Musicians of Great Britain 185
Saffron Walden Museum 226
The Samuel Courtauld Trust, The Courtauld Gallery, London 76-7
© 2017. Photo Scala, Florence/bpk, Bildagentur fuer Kunst, Kultur und Geschichte, Berlin 61
Scottish National Gallery 79, 248-9
© Tate, 2017 118 bottom, 119, 148, 149 bottom, 163, 167, 169; /Lucy Dawkins 12, 36 left, 217; /Lucy Dawkins and Samuel Cole 112, 113, 128, 202-3, 247 top; /Joe Humphrys 111, 125, 219; /David Lambert 14, 37 right, 100, 102 (Tate Archive TGA 7916/3), 196-7, 218; /David Lambert and Rod Tidnam 16, 38, 124, 162; /Rod Tidnam 18, 149 top, 192 top (Tate Library and Archive)
Troyes, musée d'Art moderne © Laurent Lecat 244
© The Trustees of the British Museum 49, 130, 133, 134, 137, 166
© Victoria and Albert Museum, London 36 right, 87, 114, 127, 129, 151 bottom left, 151 top left, 153, 165, 178, 179, 188
© Julien Vidal / Petit Palais / Roger-Viollet 109, 164
© Wilson Centre for Photography 39, 40–1, 42–3, 221

Index

Page numbers in *italic* type refer to illustrations.

Supporting Tate

Tate relies on a large number of supporters – individuals, foundations, companies and public sector sources – to enable it to deliver its programme of activities, both on and off its gallery sites. This support is essential in order for Tate to acquire works of art for the Collection, run education, outreach and exhibition programmes, care for the Collection in storage and enable art to be displayed, both digitally and physically, inside and outside Tate. Please contact us at:

Development Office
Tate
Millbank
London SW1P 4RG
Tel: +44 (0)20 7887 4900
Fax: +44 (0)20 7887 8098

Tate Americas Foundation
520 West 27 Street Unit 404
New York, NY 10001
USA

Tel: 001 212 643 2818
Fax: 001 212 643 1001

Donations, no matter the size, are gratefully received, either to support particular areas of interest, or to contribute to general activity costs.

Legacies

A legacy to Tate may take the form of a residual share of an estate, a specific cash sum or item of property such as a work of art. Legacies to Tate are free of inheritance tax, and help to secure a strong future for the Collection and galleries. For further information please contact the Development Office.

Offers in lieu of tax

Inheritance Tax can be satisfied by transferring to the Government a work of art of outstanding importance. In this case the amount of tax is reduced, and it can be made a condition of the offer that the work of art is allocated to Tate. Please contact us for details.

Tate Members

Tate Members enjoy unlimited free admission throughout the year to all exhibitions at Tate, as well as a number of other benefits such as exclusive use of our Members' Rooms and a free annual subscription to *Tate Etc.* Whilst enjoying the exclusive privileges of membership, members also help secure Tate's position at the very heart of British and modern art. Members support actively contributes to new purchases of important art, ensuring that Tate's collection continues to be relevant and comprehensive, as well as funding projects in London, Liverpool and St Ives that increase access and understanding for everyone.

Tate Patrons

Tate Patrons share a passion for art and are committed to supporting Tate on an annual basis. The Patrons help enable the acquisition of works across Tate's broad collecting remit, support the staging of major exhibitions in the galleries, and also give their support to vital conservation, learning and research projects. The scheme provides a forum for Patrons to share their interest in art and meet curators, artists and one another in an enjoyable environment through a regular programme of events. These events take place both at Tate and beyond and encompass curator-led exhibition tours, visits to artists' studios and private collections, art trips both in the UK and abroad, and access to art fairs. The scheme welcomes supporters from outside the UK, giving the programme a truly international scope. For more information, please contact the Patrons Office on +44(0)20 7887 8740 or at patrons.office@tate.org.uk.

Corporate Membership

Corporate Membership at Tate Modern, Tate Britain and Tate Liverpool offers companies opportunities for corporate entertaining and the chance for a wide variety of employee benefits. These include special private views, special access to paying exhibitions, out-of-hours visits and tours, invitations to VIP events and talks at members' offices.

Corporate Investment

Tate has developed a range of imaginative partnerships with the corporate sector, ranging from international interpretation and exhibition programmes to local outreach and staff development programmes. We are particularly known for high-profile business to business marketing initiatives and employee benefit packages. Please contact the Corporate Partnerships team for further details.

Charity Details

The Tate Gallery is an exempt charity; the Museums & Galleries Act 1992 added the Tate Gallery to the list of exempt charities defined in the 1960 Charities Act. Tate Members is a registered charity (number 313021). Tate Foundation is a registered charity (number 1085314).

Tate Americas Foundation

Tate Americas Foundation is an independent charity based in New York that supports the work of Tate in the United Kingdom. It receives full tax exempt status from the IRS under section 501(c)(3) allowing United States taxpayers to receive tax deductions on gifts towards annual membership programmes, exhibitions, scholarship and capital projects. For more information please contact the Tate Americas Foundation office.

Tate Britain Donors to the Centenary Development Campaign
The Annenberg Foundation
The Asprey Family Charitable Foundation
Ron Beller and Jennifer Moses
Alex and Angela Bernstein
The Charlotte Bonham-Carter Charitable Trust
Lauren and Mark Booth
Ivor Braka
The CHK Charitable Trust
The Clore Duffield Foundation
Sadie Coles
Giles and Sonia Coode-Adams
Alan Cristea
Thomas Dane
The D'Oyly Carte Charitable Trust
Sir Harry and Lady Djanogly
The Dulverton Trust
Maurice and Janet Dwek
Friends of the Tate Gallery
Bob and Kate Gavron
Sir Paul Getty, KBE
Alan Gibbs
Mr and Mrs Edward Gilhuly
Helyn and Ralph Goldenberg
Nicholas and Judith Goodison
Richard and Odile Grogan
Pehr and Christina Gyllenhammar
Heritage Lottery Fund
Jay Jopling
Mr and Mrs Karpidas
Howard and Lynda Karshan
Peter and Maria Kellner
Madeleine Kleinwort
Brian and Lesley Knox
The Kresge Foundation
Catherine and Pierre Lagrange
Mr and Mrs Ulf G Linden
Ruth and Stuart Lipton
Anders and Ulla Ljungh
Lloyds TSB Foundation for England and Wales
David and Pauline Mann-Vogelpoel
Sir Edwin and Lady Manton
Nick and Annette Mason
Viviane and James Mayor
Anthony and Deirdre Montagu
Sir Peter and Lady Osborne
Maureen Paley
William A Palmer
Mr Frederik Paulsen
The Pet Shop Boys
The P F Charitable Trust
The Polizzi Charitable Trust
John and Jill Ritblat
Barrie and Emmanuel Roman
Lord and Lady Sainsbury of Preston Candover
Mrs Coral Samuel, CBE
David and Sophie Shalit
Mr and Mrs Sven Skarendahl
Pauline Denyer-Smith and Paul Smith
Mr and Mrs Nicholas Stanley
The Jack Steinberg Foundation
Charlotte Stevenson
Tate Gallery Centenary Gala
Carter and Mary Thacher
Mr and Mrs John L Thornton
The Trusthouse Charitable Foundation
David and Emma Verey
Dinah Verey
Clodagh and Leslie Waddington
Gordon D Watson
Mr and Mrs Anthony Weldon
The Duke of Westminster, OBE TD DL
Sam Whitbread
Mr and Mrs Stephen Wilberding
Michael S Wilson
The Wolfson Foundation
and those who wish to remain anonymous

Donors to The Tate Britain Millbank Project
Alan Cristea Gallery
The Deborah Loeb Brice Foundation
Clore Duffield Foundation
Sir Harry and Lady Djanogly
The Gatsby Charitable Foundation
J Paul Getty Jr Charitable Trust
Heritage Lottery Fund
The Hiscox Foundation
James and Clare Kirkman
The Linbury Trust and The Monument Trust
The Manton Foundation
The Mayor Gallery
Ronald and Rita McAulay
Midge and Simon Palley
PF Charitable Trust
The Porter Foundation
The Dr Mortimer and Theresa Sackler Foundation
Mrs Coral Samuel, CBE
Jake and Hélène Marie Shafran
Tate Members
The Taylor Family Foundation
Sir David and Lady Verey
Sir Siegmund Warburg's Voluntary Settlement
Garfield Weston Foundation
The Wolfson Foundation
and those who wish to remain anonymous

Tate Britain Benefactors and Major Donors
We would like to acknowledge and thank the following benefactors who have supported Tate Britain prior to June 2017.
Abrishamchi Family Collection
Raad Zeid Al-Hussein
Dilyara Allakhverdova and Elchin Safarov
Olga de Amaral
The Ampersand Foundation
Gregory Annenberg Weingarten and the Annenberg Foundation
The Fagus Anstruther Memorial Trust in memory of the late Hartley Ramsden and Margot Eates
Art Fund
Artangel
Arts and Humanities Research Council
Arts Council England
The Artworkers Retirement Society
Celia and Edward Atkin, CBE
Roger Ballen
Charles and Tetyana Banner
Lionel Barber
The Estate of Peter and Caroline Barker-Mill
Corrine Bellow Charity
Big Lottery Fund
Anton and Lisa Bilton
Nicola Blake
Blavatnik Family Foundation
Bloomberg Philanthropies
Oliver Bolitho
The Charlotte Bonham-Carter Charitable Trust
Estate of Louise Bourgeois
Frank Bowling, Rachel Scott, Benjamin and Sacha Bowling, Marcia and Iona Scott
Sir Alan Bowness
Pierre Brahm
Ivor Braka
The Estate of Dr Marcella Louis Brenner
Deborah Loeb Brice Foundation
Rory and Elizabeth Brooks Foundation
Beatrice Bulgari | In Between Art Film
The Estate of Mrs KM Bush
Piers Butler
Jamal Butt
Carl Freedman Gallery / Counter Editions, London
Mr and Mrs Nicolas Cattelain
The Estate of Marigold Ann Chamberlin
Priti Chandaria
Francise Hsin-Wen Chang
Trustees of the Chantrey Bequest
The Chaplaincy to the Arts and Recreation in North East England, Durham
Judy Chicago in honour of Frances Morris
David and Rose Cholmondeley
City of London Corporation's charity, City Bridge Trust
The Clore Duffield Foundation
The Clothworkers' Foundation
Denise Coates Foundation
R and S Cohen Foundation
Sadie Coles
Contemporary Art Society
The Ernest Cook Trust
Douglas S Cramer
The Cranford Collection
Alan Cristea
The Daniel Katz Gallery
Kate-Jane Davie
Tiqui Atencio Demirdjian and Ago Demirdjian
Department for Business, Innovation and Skills
Department for Digital, Media, Culture and Sport
Paul Dickens
The Estate of F.N. Dickins
Braco Dimitrijevic
James Diner
Anthony and Anne d'Offay
Joe and Marie Donnelly
Peter Dubens
The Easton Foundation
Lonti Ebers

Maryam and Edward Eisler
John Ellerman Foundation
Carla Emil and Richard Silverstein
Tracey Emin
European Union
Monir Shahroudy Farmanfarmaian
The Estate of Maurice Farquharson
The Estate of Mary Fedden and Julian Trevelyan
Mr Paul Findlay
The Finnis Scott Foundation
Wendy Fisher
Dr. Kira and Neil Flanzraich, in honor of Anthony D'Offay and ARTIST ROOMS
Eric and Louise Franck
Freelands Foundation
The Estate of Lucian Freud
Amanda and Glenn Fuhrman
The FLAG Art Foundation
Gagosian Gallery
Gaia Art Foundation, UK
Galeria Luisa Strina, São Paulo
Frank Gallipoli
Garcia Family Foundation
Georg Geyer
Adrian Ghenie
Glenstone Foundation
Estate of Kaveh Golestan
Sir Nicholas and Lady Goodison
Antony Gormley
Lydia and Manfred Gorvy
Noam Gottesman
The Granville-Grossman Bequest
Greene Naftali Gallery
Calouste Gulbenkian Foundation
The Estate of Mr John Haggart
The Hakuta Family
Paul Hamlyn Foundation
The Ray and Diana Harryhausen Foundation
Sandford Heller in Honour of Sir Nicholas Serota
Barbara Hepworth Estate
Heritage Lottery Fund
The Hintze Family Charitable Foundation
Damien Hirst
David Hockney
Hazlitt Holland-Hibbert
Trustees of Lord Howard of Henderskelfe's Will Trust
Sally Hudson
Michael and Ali Hue-Williams
The Estate of Malcolm Hughes
The J Isaacs Charitable Trust
Kikuji Kawada
Dr Martin Kenig
KÖNIG GALERIE
The Estate of Fay Elspeth Langford
The Leathersellers' Company Charitable Fund
The Leche Trust
Edward and Agnès Lee
Legacy Trust UK
The Leverhulme Trust
Ruben Levi
Lisson Gallery
London Art History Society
Luhring Augustine Gallery
LUMA Foundation
Lyndsey Ingram Ltd
Mace Foundation
Simon A Mackintosh
Francisca Mancini
Robert Manoukian
The Estate of Sir Edwin Manton
The Manton Foundation
Marian Goodman Gallery
Rebecca Marks
David Mayor
Lord McAlpine of West Green
Susan McDonald
The Estate of Kenneth McGowan
The Mead Family Foundation
The Andrew W. Mellon Foundation
The Paul Mellon Centre for Studies in British Art
Boris and Vita Mikhailov
Sir Geoffroy Millais
Henry Moore Foundation
Elisabeth Murdoch
National Heritage Memorial Fund
James O'Connell
Outset Contemporary Art Fund
Pace Gallery
Maureen Paley
The Pasmore Estate
Jan-Christoph Peters
Catherine Petitgas
Piano Nobile, Robert Travers (Works of Art) Ltd
Stanley Picker Trust
The Pivovarov Family
The Porter Foundation
David W Posnett, OBE
Gilberto Pozzi
Massimo Prelz Oltramonti
Andrey Prigov
Emilio Prini
Maya and Ramzy Rasamny
The Redfern Gallery
Barrie and Emmanuel Roman
The Estate of Eugene and Penelope Rosenberg
The Rothschild Foundation
Edward Ruscha
Keith and Katherine Sachs
The Estate of Simon Sainsbury
Doris Salcedo
Nadia and Rajeeb Samdani
Julião Sarmento
John Schaeffer
Gregor Schneider
Marc Selwyn
Jake and Hélène Marie Shafran
Dasha Shenkman
Taryn Simon
Andy Simpkin
Bob and Roberta Smith
Chris Steele-Perkins
Emile Stipp
The Estate of Michael Stoddart
Mercedes and Ian Stoutzker
Mrs Virginia Surtees
T293
Tamares Real Estate Holdings Inc. in collaboration with the Zabludowicz Collection
Aldo Tambellini
Tate 1897 Circle
Tate Africa Acquisitions Committee
Tate Americas Foundation
Tate Asia-Pacific Acquisitions Committee
Tate International Council
Tate Latin American Acquisitions Committee
Tate Members
Tate Middle East and North Africa Acquisitions Committee
Tate North American Acquisitions Committee
Tate Outreach Appeal
Tate Patrons
Tate Photography Acquisitions Committee
Tate Russia and Eastern Europe Acquisitions Committee
Tate South Asia Acquisitions Committee
Terra Foundation for American Art
The Estate of Mr Nicholas Themans
Tomasso Brothers Fine Art Ltd
Phillip Trevelyan
The Hon Robert H Tuttle and Mrs Maria Hummer-Tuttle
Luc Tuymans
Two Palms Press
Cy Twombly Foundation
V-A-C Foundation
Mercedes Vilardell
Marie-Louise von Motesiczky Charitable Trust
Alexa Waley-Cohen
Offer and Mika Waterman
The Estate of Kenneth Ernest Webster
Anthony Whishaw
David and Maria Wilkinson
Jane and Michael Wilson
WME | IMG
The Lord Leonard and Lady Estelle Wolfson Foundation
Mr Nelson Woo
Bill Woodrow
Erwin Wurm
The Estate of Mrs Monica Wynter
Yuz Foundation
The Estate of Mr Anthony Zambra
and those who wish to remain anonymous

Platinum Patrons
Ghazwa Mayassi Abu-Suud
Maria Adonyeva
Mr Shane Akeroyd
Basil Alkazzi
Celia and Edward Atkin, CBE
Alex Beard
Beecroft Charitable Trust
Jacques Boissonnas
Natalia Bondarenko
Rory and Elizabeth Brooks
The Lord Browne of Madingley, FRS, FREng
Karen Cawthorn Argenio
Caroline Cole
Mr Stephane Custot
Pascale Decaux
Sophie Diedrichs-Cox
Mira Dimitrova and Luigi Mazzoleni
Valentina Drouin
Mr David Fitzsimons
The Flow Foundation
Edwin Fox Foundation
Stephen Friedman
Mrs Lisa Garrison
Hugh Gibson
Alexis and Anne-Marie Habib
David Herro
Misha and Theresa Horne
Mr and Mrs Yan Huo
Mr Phillip Hylander
Ms Natascha Jakobs
Mrs Gabrielle Jungels-Winkler
Maria and Peter Kellner
Judith Licht
Mr and Mrs Eskandar Maleki
Lali Marganiya
Scott and Suling Mead
Pierre Tollis and Alexandra Mollof
Mr Donald Moore
Mary Moore
Ife Obdeijn
Idan and Batia Ofer
Anthony and Jacqueline Orsatelli
Hussam Otaibi
Simon and Midge Palley (Chair)
Jan-Christoph Peters
Mr and Mrs Paul Phillips
Mr Gilberto and Mrs Daniela Pozzi
Frances Reynolds
Ralph Segreti
Jake and Hélène Marie Shafran
Andrée Shore
Maria and Malek Sukkar
Annie Vartivarian
Michael and Jane Wilson
Lady Wolfson of Marylebone
Chizuko Yoshida
Poju Zabludowicz and Anita Zabludowicz, OBE
Meng Zhou
and those who wish to remain anonymous

Gold Patrons
Yasmine Abou Adal
Eric Abraham
Fahad Alrashid
Shoshana Bloch
Elena Bowes
Louise and Charlie Bracken
Nicolò Cardi
Angela Choon
Melanie Clore
Beth and Michele Colocci
Harry G David
Ms Miel de Botton
Mr Frank Destribats
Mrs Maryam Eisler
Tiina Lee
Fiona Mactaggart
Paul and Alison Myners
Mr Francis Outred
Mathew Prichard
Garance Primat
Valerie Rademacher
Debra Reuben
Luciana Rique
Mr and Mrs Richard Rose
Almine Ruiz-Picasso
Carol Sellars
Mr and Mrs Stanley S Tollman
Nicholas Wingfield Digby
Manuela and Iwan Wirth
Barbara Yerolemou
and those who wish to remain anonymous

Silver Patrons
Sharis Alexandrian
Ryan Allen and Caleb Kramer
Gregor Alpers
Mrs Malgosia Alterman
The Anson Charitable Trust
Toby and Kate Anstruther
Mr and Mrs Zeev Aram
Mrs Charlotte Artus
Aspect Charitable Trust
Mrs Liz Astaire
Peter Barham
Mrs Jane Barker
Oliver Barker
Mr Edward Barlow
Victoria Barnsley, OBE
Jim Bartos
Dr Amelie Beier
Mr Harold Berg
Ms Anne Berthoud
Madeleine Bessborough
Janice Blackburn
David Blood and Beth Bisso
Bruno Boesch
Mrs Sofia Bogolyubov
Laurel Bonnyman
Mr Brian Boylan
Viscountess Bridgeman
Mr Dan Brooke
Ben and Louisa Brown
Beverley Buckingham
Michael Burrell
Mrs Marlene Burston
Piers Butler
Mrs Aisha Cahn
Sarah Caplin
Timothy and Elizabeth Capon
Mr Francis Carnwath and Ms Caroline Wiseman
Sir Roger Carr
Countess Castle Stewart
Roger Cazalet
Lord and Lady Charles Cecil
Dr Peter Chocian
Cynthia Clarry
Frank Cohen
Mrs Jane Collins
Dr Judith Collins
Terrence Collis
Mr and Mrs Oliver Colman
Mayte Comin
Carole and Neville Conrad
Giles and Sonia Coode-Adams
Cynthia Corbett
Mark and Cathy Corbett
Pilar Corrias
Tommaso Corvi-Mora
Mr and Mrs Bertrand Coste
Kathleen Crook and James Penturn
James Curtis
Daniella Luxembourg Art
Fiona Davies
Sir Howard Davies
Sir Roger and Lady De Haan
Elisabeth De Kergorlay
Giles de la Mare
Mr Damon and The Hon Mrs de Laszlo
Alexander de Mont
Anne Chantal Defay Sheridan
Michael Donovan
Joan Edlis
Lord and Lady Egremont
John Erle-Drax
Dr Nigel Evans
Stuart and Margaret Evans
Eykyn Maclean LLC
Leonie Fallstrom
Mrs Heather Farrar
David Fawkes
Mrs Margy Fenwick
Mr Bryan Ferry, CBE
Laurie Fitch
The Sylvie Fleming Collection
Lt Commander Paul Fletcher
Katherine Francey Stables
Mr and Mrs Laurent Ganem
Mala Gaonkar
Geoffrey and Julian Charitable Trust
Mr Mark Glatman
Ms Emily Goldner and Mr Michael Humphries
Emma Goltz
Aphrodite Gonou
Kate Gordon
Dimitri Goulandris
Penelope Govett
Svitlana Granovska
Judith and Richard Greer
Martyn Gregory
Richard and Odile Grogan
John Howard Gruzelier
Mrs Helene Guerin-Llamas
Ms Nathalie Guiot
Jill Hackel Zarzycki
Louise Hallett
Diane Hamilton
Arthur Hanna
Mark Harris
Michael and Morven Heller
Christian Hernandez and Michelle Crowe Hernandez
Muriel Hoffner
James Holland-Hibbert
Lady Hollick, OBE
Holtermann Fine Art
Jeff Horne
John Huntingford
Helen Janecek
Sarah Jennings
Mr Haydn John
Mr Michael Johnson
Mike Jones
Jay Jopling
Mrs Brenda Josephs
Tracey Josephs
Mr Joseph Kaempfer
Andrew Kalman
Ghislaine Kane
Dr Martin Kenig
Mr David Ker
Mr and Mrs Simon Keswick
Sadru Kheraj
Mrs Mae Khouri
David Killick
Mr and Mrs James Kirkman
Brian and Lesley Knox
David P Korn
Kowitz Trust
Mr and Mrs Herbert Kretzmer
Linda Lakhdhir
Simon Lee
Mr Gerald Levin
Leonard Lewis
Sophia and Mark Lewisohn
Mr Gilbert Lloyd
George Loudon
Mrs Elizabeth Louis
Mark and Liza Loveday
Jeff Lowe
Alison Loyd
Mrs Ailsa Macalister
Kate MacGarry
Sir John Mactaggart
Marsh Christian Trust
Stephen and Sharon Mather
Daniele Mattogno
Ms Fiona Mellish
Mrs R W P Mellish
Professor Rob Melville
Dr Helen Metcalf
Dr Basil Ross Middleton
Victoria Miro
Jan Mol
Lulette Monbiot
Mrs Bona Montagu
Mrs William Morrison
Ms Terrina Narbett
Louise Nathanson
Ms Deborah Norton
Julian Opie
Pilar Ordovás
Sayumi Otake
Desmond Page
Maureen Paley
Dominic Palfreyman
Michael Palin
Mrs Kathrine Palmer
Mathieu Paris
Mrs Véronique Parke
Anna Pennink
Frans Pettinga
Trevor Pickett
Frederique Pierre-Pierre
Mariela Pissioti
Mr Alexander Platon
Penelope Powell
Susan Prevezer, QC
Mr and Mrs Ryan Prince
Ivetta Rabinovich
Patricia Ranken
Mrs Phyllis Rapp
The Reuben Foundation
Lady Ritblat
David Rocklin
Frankie Rossi
Mr David V Rouch
Mr James Roundell
Mr Charles Roxburgh
Hakon Runer and Ulrike Schwarz-Runer
Jackie Donnelly Russell
Naomi Russell
Mr Alex Sainsbury and Ms Elinor Jansz
Mr Richard Saltoun
Cherrill and Ian Scheer
Sylvia Scheuer
Mrs Cara Schulze
Ellen Shapiro
The Hon Richard Sharp
Neville Shulman, CBE
Ms Julia Simmonds
Simon C Dickinson Ltd
Louise Spence
Mr Nicos Steratzias
Marie-Claude Stobart
Mrs Patricia Swannell
Mr James Swartz
The Lady Juliet Tadgell
Isadora Tharin
Elaine Thomas
Anthony Thornton
Marita Thurnauer
Mr Henry Tinsley
Ian Tollett
Victoria Tollman O'Hana
Karen Townshend
Andrew Tseng
Melissa Ulfane
Mrs Jolana Vainio and Dr Petri Vainio
Nazy Vassegh
Mrs Cecilia Versteegh
Gisela von Sanden
Andreas Vourecas-Petalas
Audrey Wallrock
Stephen and Linda Waterhouse
Offer Waterman
Miss Cheyenne Westphal
Professor Sarah Whatmore
Mr David Wood
Mr Douglas Woolf
Alice Zhou
Sharon Zhu
and those who wish to remain anonymous

Young Patrons
Katrina Aleksa
Miss Noor Al-Rahim
HRH Princess Alia Al-Senussi
Miss Sharifa Alsudairi
Miss Katharine Arnold
Lucy Attwood
Miss Olivia Aubry
Daniel Axmer
Charles and Tetyana Banner
Katrina Beechey
Penny Johanna Beer
Francesca Bellini Joseph
Dr Maya Beyhan
Poppy Boadle
Roberto Boghossian
Georgina Borthwick
Chantal Bradford
Kit Brennan
Ms Blair Brooks
Verena Butt d'Espous
Jamie Byrom
Mr Tommaso Calabro
Alexander Carel
Federico Martin Castro Debernardi
Alexandra and Kabir Chhatwani
Yoojin Choi
Arthur Chow
Aidan Christofferson
Bianca Chu
Zuzanna Ciolek
Julia Clemente
Thamara Corm
Tara Wilson Craig
Eleonore Cukierman
Mr Joshua Davis
Countess Charlotte de la Rochefoucauld
Giacomo De Notariis
Agnes de Royere
Eleanor Dilloway
Indira Dyussebayeva
Alexandra Economou
Danae Filioti
Jane and Richard Found
Aude Fourcade
Sylvain Fresia
Laurie Frey
Mr Andreas Gegner
Lana Ghandour
Molly Grad
Alex Haidas
Jurg Haller
Shiori Hamada
Sara Harrison
Max Edouard Friedrich Hetzler
Louise Holten
Andrew Honan
Simona Houldsworth
Kamel Jaber
Karim Jalbout
Aled Jones
Sophie Kainradl
Miss Meruyert Kaliyeva
Mrs Vasilisa Kameneva
Miss Tamila Kerimova
Zena Aliya Khan
Marika Kielland
Ms Chloe Kinsman
Maria Korolevskaya
Zoe Kuipers
Nicholas M Lamotte
John Lellouche
Alexander Lewis
Claire Livingstone
Guy Loffler
Lucy Loveday
Thomas Luypaert
Yusuf Macun
Frederic Maillard
Ms Sonia Mak
Dr Christina Makris
Mr Jean-David Malat
Kamiar Maleki
Daria Manganelli
Zoe Marden
Ignacio Marinho
Magnus Mathisen
Charles-Henri McDermott
Fiona McGovern
Mary McNicholas
Chelsea Menzies
Miss Nina Moaddel
Mr Fernando Moncho Lobo
John-Christian Moquette
Joseph Nahmad
Vanita Nathwani
Natasha Norman
Ikenna Obiekwe
Aurore Ogden (Co-Chair, Young Patrons Ambassador Group)

Reine and Boris Okuliar
Berkay Oncel
Periklis Panagopoulos
Christine Chungwon Park
Alexander V Petalas, (Co-Chair, Young Patrons Ambassador Group)
Robert Phillips
Mr Mark Piolet
Megan Piper
Courtney Plummer
Maria-Theresia Pongracz
Nadim Rabaia
Mr Eugenio Re Rebaudengo
Sydney Rogers
Ms Nadja Romain
Tarka Russell
Nour Saleh
Umair Sami
Paola Saracino Fendi
Rachel Schaefer
Rebekka Schaefer
Franz Schwarz
Mr Richard Scott
Count Indoo Sella Di Monteluce
Nasiha Shaikh
Robert Sheffield
Eric Shen
Henrietta Shields
MinJoo Shin
Ms Marie-Anya Shiro
Amar Singh
Jag Singh
Tammy Smulders
Dominic Stolerman
Nayrouz Tatanaki
Vassan Thavaraja
Soren S K Tholstrup
Omer Tiroche
Simon Tovey
Mr Giancarlo Trinca
Mr Philippos Tsangrides
Ms Navann Ty
Celine Valligny
Mr Lawrence Van Hagen
Alexandra Warder
Ewa Wilczynski
Elizabeth Wilks
Kim Williams
Kate Wong
Alexandra Wood
Edward Woodcock
Tyler Woolcott
Vanessa Wurm
Jian Xu
Shelly Yang
Yuchen Yang
Miss Burcu Yuksel
Evgeny Zborovsky
Marcelo Osvaldo Zimmler
and those who wish to remain anonymous

International Council Members

Mr Segun Agbaje
Staffan Ahrenberg, Editions Cahiers d'Art
Mr Geoff Ainsworth, AM
Dilyara Allakherdova
Doris Ammann
Mrs Maria Baibakova and Mr Adrien Faure
Anne H Bass
Nicolas Berggruen
Mr Pontus Bonnier
Paloma Botín O'Shea
Frances Bowes
Ivor Braka
The Deborah Loeb Brice Foundation
The Broad Art Foundation
Andrew Cameron, AM
Nicolas and Celia Cattelain
Mrs Christina Chandris
Richard Chang (Vice Chair)
Pierre TM Chen, Yageo Foundation, Taiwan
Mr Kemal Has Cingillioglu
Mr and Mrs Attilio Codognato
Sir Ronald Cohen and Lady Sharon Harel-Cohen
Mr Douglas S Cramer and Mr Hubert S Bush III
Mr Dimitris Daskalopoulos
Mr and Mrs Michel David-Weill
Ms Miel de Botton
Tiqui Atencio Demirdjian and Ago Demirdjian
Joseph and Marie Donnelly
Mrs Olga Dreesmann
Barney A Ebsworth
Füsun and Faruk Eczacibaşi
Stefan Edlis and Gael Neeson
Mr and Mrs Edward Eisler
Carla Emil and Rich Silverstein
Fares and Tania Fares
HRH Princess Firyal of Jordan
Mrs Doris Fisher
Mrs Wendy Fisher
Dr Kira Flanzraich
Dr Corinne M Flick
Amanda and Glenn Fuhrman
Mrs Belma Gaudio and The Butters Foundation
Candida and Zak Gertler
Mrs Yassmin Ghandehari
Mr Giancarlo Giammetti
Alan Gibbs
Lydia and Manfred Gorvy
Mr Laurence Graff
Ms Esther Grether
Konstantin Grigorishin
Mr Xavier Guerrand-Hermès
Mimi and Peter Haas Fund
Margrit and Paul Hahnloser
Andy and Christine Hall
Mrs Susan Hayden
Marlene Hess and James D. Zirin
André and Rosalie Hoffmann
Ms Maja Hoffmann
Vicky Hughes
Dakis and Lietta Joannou
Sir Elton John and Mr David Furnish
Pamela J Joyner
Mr Chang-Il Kim
Jack Kirkland
C Richard and Pamela Kramlich
Mrs Grazyna Kulczyk
Andreas and Ulrike Kurtz
Catherine Lagrange
Mr Pierre Lagrange
Bernard Lambilliotte
The Lauder Foundation - Leonard and Judy Lauder Fund
Agnès and Edward Lee
Mme RaHee Hong Lee
Jacqueline and Marc Leland
Mrs Fatima Maleki
Panos and Sandra Marinopoulos
Mr and Mrs Donald B Marron
Mr Ronald and The Hon Mrs McAulay
Mark McCain and Caro MacDonald
Mr Leonid Mikhelson
Naomi Milgrom, AO
Mr Donald Moore
Simon and Catriona Mordant
Mrs Yoshiko Mori
Mr Guy and The Hon Mrs Naggar
Fayeeza Naqvi
Mrs Judith Neilson, AM
Dr Mark Nelson
Mr and Mrs Takeo Obayashi
Mr and Mrs Eyal Ofer
Andrea and José Olympio Pereira
Hideyuki Osawa
Irene Panagopoulos
Young-Ju Park
Yana and Stephen Peel
Daniel and Elizabeth Peltz
Catherine Petitgas (Chair)
Sydney Picasso
Jean Pigozzi
Lekha Poddar
Miss Dee Poon
Ms Miuccia Prada and Mr Patrizio Bertelli
Laura Rapp and Jay Smith
Maya and Ramzy Rasamny
Patrizia Sandretto Re Rebaudengo and Agostino Re Rebaudengo
Robert Rennie and Carey Fouks
Sir John Richardson
Michael Ringier
Lady Ritblat
Ms Hanneli M Rupert
Ms Güler Sabanci
Dame Theresa Sackler, DBE
Mrs Lily Safra
Muriel and Freddy Salem
Rajeeb and Nadia Samdani
Alejandro Santo Domingo
Dasha Shenkman, OBE
Dr Gene Sherman, AM
Poonam Bhagat Shroff
Uli and Rita Sigg
Norah and Norman Stone
Julia Stoschek
John J Studzinski, CBE
Maria and Malek Sukkar
Mr Christen Sveaas
Mr Robert Tomei
The Hon Robert H Tuttle and Mrs Maria Hummer-Tuttle
Mrs Ninetta Vafeia
Paulo A W Vieira
Mercedes Vilardell
Robert and Felicity Waley-Cohen
The Hon Hilary M Weston
Angela Westwater and David Meitus
Diana Widmaier Picasso
Christen and Derek Wilson
Mrs Sylvie Winckler
The Hon Dame Janet Wolfson de Botton, DBE
Poju Zabludowicz and Anita Zabludowicz, OBE
Michael Zilkha
and those who wish to remain anonymous

Africa Acquisitions Committee

Kathy Ackerman Robins
Anshu Bahanda
Adnan Bashir
Priti Chandaria Shah
Mrs Kavita Chellaram
Salim Currimjee
Harry G David
Mr and Mrs Michel David-Weill
Robert and Renee Drake
Mrs Wendy Fisher
Diane B. Frankel
Aita Ighodaro Menet
Andrea Kerzner
Samallie Kiyingi
Alexander Klimt
Matthias and Gervanne Leridon
Caro Macdonald
Dale Mathias
Professor Oba Nsugbe, QC
Ms Ndidi Okpaluba
Mr Hussam Otaibi
Pascale Revert Wheeler
Emile Stipp
Mr Varnavas A Varnava
Mercedes Vilardell (Chair)
Alexa Waley-Cohen
Peter Warwick
Ms Isabel Wilcox
Marwan G Zakhem
and those who wish to remain anonymous

Asia-Pacific Acquisitions Committee

Sara A Alireza
Matthias Arndt
Bonnie and R Derek Bandeen
Mrs Bambi Blumberg
Andrew Cameron, AM
Mr and Mrs John Carrafiell
Richard Chang
Jasmine Chen
Adrian Cheng
Lawrence Chu
Mr Yan d'Auriol
Katie de Tilly
Ms Kerry Gardner
Mrs Yassmin Ghandehari
Mr Reade and Mrs Elizabeth Griffith
Philippa Hornby
Mr Yongsoo Huh
Shareen Khattar Harrison
Mr Chang-Il Kim
Mr Jung Wan Kim
Ms Yung Hee Kim
Ms Ellie Lai
Alan Lau (Co-Chair)
Woong-Yeul Lee
Jasmine Li
Mr William Lim
Ms Dina Liu
Alan and Yenn Lo
Ms Kai-Yin Lo
Anne Louis-Dreyfus
Lu Xun
Elisabetta Marzetti Mallinson
Elaine Forsgate Marden
Marleen Molenaar
Mr John Porter
The Red Mansion Foundation
Dr Gene Sherman, AM (Co-Chair)
Leo Shih
Ed Tang
Chikako Tatsuuma
Dr Andreas Teoh
Dr Neil Wenman
Yang Bin
Fernando Zobel de Ayala
and those who wish to remain anonymous

Latin American Acquisitions Committee

Monica and Robert Aguirre
José Antonio Alcantara
Luis Benshimol
Celia Birbragher
Estrellita and Daniel Brodsky
Miguel Angel Capriles Cannizzaro
HSH the Prince Pierre d'Arenberg
Tiqui Atencio Demirdjian (Chair)
Marta Regina Fernandez Holman
Barbara Hemmerle-Gollust
Carola Hinojosa
Julian Iragorri
Anne Marie and Geoffrey Isaac
Nicole Junkermann
Aimee Labarrere de Servitje
José Luis Lorenzo
Fatima and Eskander Maleki
Francisca Mancini
Felipe and Denise Nahas Mattar
Susan McDonald
Veronica Nutting
Victoria and Isaac Oberfeld
Silvia Paz Illobre
Esther Perez Seinjet
Catherine Petitgas
Claudio Federico Porcel
Mr Thibault Poutrel
Frances Reynolds
Erica Roberts
Alin Ryan Lobo
Catalina Saieh Guzman
Lilly Scarpetta
Camila Sol de Pool
Juan Carlos Verme
Tania and Arnoldo Wald
Juan Yarur Torres
Teresita Soriano Zucker
and those who wish to remain anonymous

Middle East and North Africa Acquisitions Committee

Ahmad and Sirine Abu Ghazaleh
HRH Princess Alia Al-Senussi
Abdelmonem Bin Eisa Alserkal
Mr Abdullah Al-Turki
Mehves Ariburnu
Marwan T Assaf
Niloufar Bakhtiar Bakhtiari
Perihan Bassatne
Ms Isabelle de la Bruyère
Füsun Eczacibaşi
Maryam Eisler (Co-Chair)
Shirley Elghanian
Delfina Entrecanales, CBE
Noor Fares
Hossein and Dalia Fateh
Negin Fattahi-Dasmal
Raghida Ghandour Al Rahim
Mareva Grabowski
Aysegül Karadeniz
Mr Elie Khouri
Maha and Kasim Kutay
David Maupin
Tansa Mermerci Eksioglu
Basma Haout Monla
Falak Naqvi
Dina Nasser-Khadivi
Shulamit Nazarian
Ebru Özdemir
Mr Moshe Peterburg
Ramzy and Maya Rasamny (Co-Chair)
Thomas Rom
Mrs Madhu Ruia
Shihab Shobokshi
Maria and Malek Sukkar
Faisal Tamer
Berna Tuglular
Yesim Turanli
Sebnem Unlu
Madhi Yahya
Mr Zahid and Ms Binladin
Roxane Zand
and those who wish to remain anonymous

North American Acquisitions Committee

Carol and David Appel
Jacqueline Appel and Alexander Malmaeus
Abigail Baratta
Dorothy Berwin and Dominique Lévy
Dillon Cohen
Michael Corman and Kevin Fink
Theo Danjuma
Anne Dias
James E Diner
Wendy Fisher
Jill Garcia
Victoria Gelfand-Magalhaes
Amy Gold
Nina and Dan Gross
Pamela J Joyner
Monica Kalpakian
Elisabeth and Panos Karpidas
Christian Keesee
Naznin and Mahmood Khimji
Marjorie and Michael Levine
James Lindon
Rebecca Marks
Lillian and Billy Mauer
Nancy McCain
Jeff Menashe
Stavros Merjos
Gregory R Miller
Rachelli Mishori and Leon Koffler
Shabin and Nadir Mohamed
Jenny Mullen
Amy and John Phelan
Laura Rapp and Jay Smith
Kimberly Richter Shirley and Jon Shirley
Carolin Scharpff-Striebich
Komal Shah
Dasha Shenkman, OBE
Beth Swofford
Juan Carlos Verme
Christen and Derek Wilson
Leyli Zohrenejad
and those who wish to remain anonymous

Photography Acquisitions Committee

Ryan Allen
Artworkers Retirement Society
Nicholas Barker
Cynthia Lewis Beck
Carolin Becker
Pierre Brahm
Mrs William Shaw Broeksmit
Elizabeth (Co-Chair) and Rory Brooks
Marcel and Gabrielle Cassard
Nicolas (Co-Chair) and Celia Cattelain
Beth and Michele Colocci
Mr and Mrs Michel David-Weill
Mr Hyung-Teh Do
Nikki Fennell
David Fitzsimons
Lisa Garrison
Ms Emily Goldner and Mr Michael Humphries
Ann Hekmat
Alexandra Hess
Bernard Huppert
Jack Kirkland
David Knaus
Mr Scott Mead
Sebastien Montabonel
Mr Donald Moore
Tarek Nahas
Kristin Rey
David Solo
Saadi Soudavar
Nicholas Stanley
Maria and Malek Sukkar
Francois Trausch, in memory of Caroline Trausch
Michael and Jane Wilson
and those who wish to remain anonymous

Russia and Eastern Europe Acquisitions Committee

Dmitry Aksenov
Dilyara Allakhverdova
Maria Baibakova
David Birnbaum
Maria Rus Bojan
Maria Bukhtoyarova
Francise Hsin-Wen Chang
Mark Čuček
Dr Kira Flanzraich (Chair)
Lyuba Galkina
Dr Joana Grevers
Konstantin Grigorishin
Cees Hendrikse
Mr Vilius Kavaliauskas and Rita Navalinskaite
Carl Kostyál
Mrs Grażyna Kulczyk
Peter Kulloi
Krzysztof Madelski
Eduard Maták
Teresa Mavica
Luba Michailova
Maarja Oviir-Neivelt
Neil K Rector
Valeria Rodnyansky
Robert Runták
Ovidiu Şandor
Zsolt Somlói
Elena Sudakova
The Tretyakov Family Collection
Miroslav Trnka
Jo Vickery
Veronika Zonabend
Mr Janis Zuzans
and those who wish to remain anonymous

South Asia Acquisitions Committee

Shohidul Ahad-Choudhury
Mrs Sheetal Ansal
Maya Barolo-Rizvi
Krishna Bhupal
Dr Arani and Mrs Shumita Bose
Akshay Chudasama
Jai Danani
Zahida Habib
Shalini Hinduja
Aparajita Jain
Simran Kotak and Vir Kotak
Ms Aarti Lohia
Yamini Mehta
Mr Yogesh Mehta
Mohammad N. Miraly
Shalini Misra
Mr Rahul Munjal and Mrs Pooja Munjal
Mrs Chandrika Pathak
Puja and Uday Patnaik
Lekha Poddar (Co-Chair)
Nadia Samdani
Rajeeb Samdani (Co-Chair)
Mrs Tarana Sawhney
Osman Khalid Waheed
Manuela and Iwan Wirth
Ambreen Zaman
and those who wish to remain anonymous

The 1897 Circle

Marilyn Bild
David and Deborah Botten
Geoff Bradbury
Charles Brett
Sylvia Carter
Eloise and Francis Charlton
Mr and Mrs Cronk
Alex Davids
Jonathan Davis
Professor Martyn Davis
Sean Dissington
Ronnie Duncan
Joan Edlis
V Fabian
Lt Cdr Paul Fletcher
Mr and Mrs R.N. and M.C. Fry
Tom Glynn and Margaret Anne Glynn
Richard S Hamilton
LA Hynes
John Janssen
Dr Martin Kenig
Isa Levy
Jean Medlycott
Susan Novell and Graham Smith
Martin Owen
Simon Reynolds
Dr Claudia Rosanowski
Ann M Smith
Deborah Stern
Jennifer Toynbee-Holmes
Estate of Paule Vézelay
D Von Bethmann-Hollweg
Audrey Wallrock
Professor Brian Whitton
Kay and Dyson Wilkes
Simon Casimir Wilson
Andrew Woodd
Mr and Mrs Zilberberg
and those who wish to remain anonymous

Tate Britain Corporate Supporters

BMW
BP
Christie's
EY
Hyundai Card
Hyundai Motor
IHS Markit
Microsoft
Qantas
RSM
Sotheby's
and those who wish to remain anonymous

Tate Britain Corporate Members

Bank of America Merrill Lynch
BCS Consulting
Bloomberg
Christie's
Clifford Chance LLP
The Cultivist
Deutsche Bank AG London
Dow Jones
EY
Finsbury
Floreat Group
Holdingham Group
HSBC
Hyundai Card
Imperial College Healthcare Charity
JATO Dynamics
JCA Group
Linklaters
The Moody's Foundation
Morgan Stanley
Oliver Wyman
Siegel + Gale
Tishman Speyer
and those who wish to remain anonymous